Lotus 1-2-3 Release 2.2 for Business

Lotus 1-2-3 RELEASE 2.2 For Business

Integrating Lotus 1-2-3 across the business curriculum

Roy Ageloff
University of Rhode Island

Course Technology, Inc. One Main Street, Cambridge, MA 02142

Lotus 1-2-3 for Business is published by Course Technology, Inc.

Product Management	Susan Solomon Communications
Product Design	Josh Bernoff
Desktop Publishing	Kim Munsell
	Debbie Crane
	Julie Uhler
Artwork	Stacey Alickman
Text Design	Glenna Collett
	Andy Giammarco
Cover Design	Caryl Hull Design Group
Copy Editing	Nancy Wirtes
Proofreading	Linda Adler
Quality Assurance	Mark Valentine
	Tim McNerney
	Eric Cimon
	Jamie Brache
	Jonathan Karp
Manufacturing	Mark Dec

Trademarks

Course Technology and the open book logo are trademarks of Course Technology, Inc.
Lotus and 1-2-3 are registered trademarks of Lotus Development Corporation.
Some of the product names used in this book have been used for identification purposes only and may be
  trademarks or registered trademarks of their respective manufacturers and sellers.

Disclaimer

Course Technology, Inc. reserves the right to revise this publication and make changes from time to time in its
  content without notice.

ISBN 1-878748-27-0 (includes software, 5¼-inch disks)   ISBN 1-878748-38-6 (book plus 5¼-inch Data Disk)
ISBN 1-878748-28-9 (includes software, 3½-inch disks)   ISBN 1-878748-39-4 (book plus 3½-inch Data Disk)

10 9 8 7 6 5 4

A Foreword from IBM Corporation

Today, business students and business professionals face two common personal productivity issues: the business problems they must solve are increasingly complex and less time is available to solve these problems. In addition, professional educators and educational policy makers face the issue of "instructional productivity" — how can they put more instructional content into the same number of curriculum hours? IBM's information technology can meet the challenges posed by all of these issues.

Course Technology, Inc.'s (CTI) instructional material provides a tool for a student to master the appropriate professional problem solving technique using application software and IBM information technology. By integrating text curriculum materials, software, and the skill-building use of information technology, CTI enhances the student's educational experience. This pedagogical approach aids the instructor as well, because it spans the gap between theory and practice. It weds quality curriculum content with state-of-the-art technology. It leverages classroom time and makes the instructional experience more meaningful and productive for the student. The time required to master the problem solving techniques, application software, and computer proficiency is compressed, because they are concurrent activities.

A student who is proficient in the use of professional problem solving techniques, application software, and IBM's technology will be more confident and productive as he or she assumes the responsibilities of professional life.

IBM's Academic Information Systems (ACIS) supports the efforts of Course Technology, Inc. to bring information technology teaching tools to college classrooms.

IBM
Academic Information Systems
472 Wheelers Farms Road
Milford, CT 06460

A Note from Lotus Development Corporation

To Professors

Abraham Lincoln once wrote: "Upon the subject of education … I can only say that I view it as the most important subject which we, as a people, can be engaged in. … "

Much has changed in the more than 100 years since Lincoln uttered this aphorism, but considering the implications of global markets and shifting balances of economic power, that statement has even greater meaning today.

One obvious change since Lincoln's time is the advent of the personal computer, which has fundamentally changed the way people do business. Today's global businesses require a work force that knows how to use personal computers and other information technology for analysis and decision making. Today's business professional must be adept in using software tools like 1-2-3 to understand, analyze, and solve complex problems.

Lotus recognizes that our institutions of higher education are under pressure to produce students with greater skills so that U.S. companies in all industries can compete globally. We also recognize that you, as an instructor, need new tools to accomplish this goal. Lotus can help. Working together with Course Technology, we have produced *Lotus 1-2-3 for Business* to help prepare your students to use personal computers for business applications.

This modern text and software combination introduces students to information technology and its application in solving business problems. We hope you find it helpful as you prepare your students for challenging careers in the business world.

To Students

To succeed in business today, you must know how to use the personal computer and other information technology tools to solve business problems. *Lotus 1-2-3 for Business* will help you learn 1-2-3 — the language of business — within the context of problem-solving and decision making.

Good luck with your careers!

Preface

Lotus 1-2-3 for Business represents a new approach to microcomputer applications education by combining a carefully developed text with fully functional software. It is designed for any first course on how spreadsheets are used in business and assumes only that students have an introductory knowledge of DOS.

The Textbook

This textbook presents a unique approach to teaching how to use Lotus 1-2-3. Students learn to plan before they press keys. They learn to analyze the business problem and design the worksheet. Then they solve the problem by following a distinctive step-by-step methodology, frequently referring back to their original plan. From this process students learn that a spreadsheet is not meant just to record data and perform calculations, but that it is a valuable tool to help them make informed business decisions.

Organization

The textbook consist of four parts:

Part I	Getting Started
Part II	The Tutorials
Part III	Additional Cases
Part IV	Reference

Part I — Getting Started   This part contains three chapters that acclimate students to how spreadsheets are used in business and to the capabilities of Lotus 1-2-3. Chapter 1, *Using Spreadsheets in Business,* presents an overview of business, explains how spreadsheets are used in four areas of business, and gives real examples of how recent business graduates use spreadsheets as a decision-making tool. Chapter 2, *Preparing to Use Lotus 1-2-3 for Business,* gives instructions on how to install and initialize the 1-2-3 software. Finally, Chapter 3, *A Tour of Lotus 1-2-3,* takes students on a brief tour of the worksheet, database, graphics, and macro capabilities of 1-2-3.

Part II — The Tutorials   This part contains seven hands-on tutorials with step-by-step instructions on how to use 1-2-3 to solve business problems.

Part III — Additional Cases   This part provides five completely new cases that allow students to apply what they have learned about 1-2-3 to solve comprehensive business problems.

Part IV — Reference   This part contains complete documentation of 1-2-3. Along with the Glossary and detailed Index, the Reference can be a valuable resource for students during and after their Lotus 1-2-3 course.

Approach

The *Lotus 1-2-3-for Business* textbook employs a problem-solving approach to teach students how to use 1-2-3. This approach is achieved by including the following features in each tutorial:

Objectives   A list of objectives orients students to the goals of each tutorial.

Tutorial Case   This case presents the business problem that the student will solve in the tutorial. The business problem is geared to what the typical student taking this course is likely to know or is able to intuit about business. Thus, the process of solving the problem using 1-2-3 will be meaningful to the student. All of the key business areas — accounting, finance, marketing, production, and management — are represented.

Planning the Worksheet   Each tutorial's case also includes discussion about planning the worksheet. Students learn to analyze the business problem and then set clear goals for the solution before they press keys. Planning sheets and worksheet sketches are introduced as basic tools.

Step-by-Step Methodology   This unique methodology integrates concepts and keystrokes. Students are asked to press keys always within the context of solving the problem. The text constantly guides students, letting them know where they are in the problem-solving process and referring them back to the planning sheet and sketch.

Page Design   Each page is designed to help students easily differentiate between what they are to *do* and what they are to *read*. In addition, the numerous screen shots include labels that direct students' attention to what they should look at on the screen.

Exercises   Each tutorial concludes with meaningful, conceptual questions that test students' understanding of what they learned in the tutorial.

Tutorial Assignments   These assignments provide students with additional practice on the individual 1-2-3 skills that they learned in the tutorial. Students practice by modifying the business problem that they solved in the tutorial. Also included is at least one assignment that requires students to use the Reference section (Part IV).

Case Problems   Each tutorial concludes with several additional business problems that have approximately the same scope as the Tutorial Case. Students are asked to use the 1-2-3 skills they learned in the tutorial to solve the case.

Additional Cases   The progression from Exercises to Tutorial Assignments to Case Problems culminates in five completely new cases in Part III. These Additional Cases range from relatively simple to challenging. They require students to *integrate* their business problem-solving skills with the 1-2-3 skills they learned in the tutorials. A list of the 1-2-3 skills required to solve the case appears at the beginning of each Additional Case.

The Lotus 1-2-3 Software

Lotus 1-2-3 for Business is available with a full-sized (256 columns by 8192 rows) and fully functional version of the Lotus 1-2-3 spreadsheet software. All the 1-2-3 features are included, with the exception of Allways.

Coupon

Students who do not buy this textbook packaged with Lotus 1-2-3 software can purchase their own copy of the software for a nominal price. Look for the special offer coupon included with this textbook.

Disks

The Lotus 1-2-3 software is available in 3½-inch and 5¼-inch formats and includes the following diskettes:

3½-inch Disk Name	Contents	Function
System Disk with PrintGraph and Help	1-2-3 Program	Runs the spreadsheet software
	INIT Program	Identifies authorized user
	On-line Help	Assists with information about 1-2-3 topics
	Access system	Starts 1-2-3, PrintGraph, or Install from a menu
	PrintGraph	Prints graphs created in 1-2-3
	Macro Library Manager	Stores macros created with 1-2-3
Utilities Disk	Install program	Records information about the computer system used with 1-2-3
	Driver library	Runs 1-2-3 with the computer system used

5¼-inch Disk Name	Contents	Function
System Disk	1-2-3 Program	Runs the spreadsheet software
	Initialization	Identifies authorized user
	Access system	Starts 1-2-3, PrintGraph, or Install from a menu
Help Disk	On-line Help	Assists with information about 1-2-3 topics
PrintGraph Disk	PrintGraph	Prints graphs created in 1-2-3
Utilities Disk	Install program	Records information about the computer system used with 1-2-3
	Macro Library Manager	Stores macros created with 1-2-3
Install Library Disk	Driver library	Runs 1-2-3 with the computer system used

The Supplements

Data Disk

The Data Disk includes all of the worksheets needed to complete all of the Tutorial Cases, Tutorial Assignments, Case Problems, and Additional Cases.

Instructor's Manual

This supplement includes:

- Answers and solutions to the all of the text's Exercises, Tutorial Assignments, Case Problems, and Additional Cases
- A diskette (3½-inch or 5¼-inch) containing solutions to all of the text's Tutorial Assignments, Case Problems, and Additional Cases
- A trouble-shooting guide
- Hardware driver information
- Tips on customizing installation

Test Bank

This supplement contains fifty questions per tutorial in multiple choice, fill-in-the-blank, and matching formats. Each question has been quality assurance tested by students for accuracy and clarity. The Test Bank is also available in a computerized package that is MS DOS compatible.

Certificate of Accomplishment

Upon adoption, schools can participate in the Certificate of Accomplishment Program. Course Technology Inc. will provide certificates to schools for students who successfully complete a course using *Lotus 1-2-3 for Business*. Contact CTI for more details.

Acknowledgments

Many people provided their special contributions to the successful completion of this book. While "thank you" never seems enough, this is my thanks to each of them.

I want to thank the many reviewers of this text, in particular: Jon E. Juarez, New Mexico State University – Dona Ana Branch Community College; Mel Martin, ETON Technical Institute; June A. Parsons, Northern Michigan University; and David Stephan, Baruch College – CUNY.

Thanks to my colleagues and friends, Marco Urbano and Hilda Allred, for their case suggestions. Thanks also to Lo-Ping Esther Ling for her thorough reading of the entire manuscript and her sound suggestions for improvement.

My appreciation goes to the Course Technology staff for working tirelessly under tight deadlines to produce a quality, professional product. I especially thank Josh Bernoff, for managing production; Andy Giammarco, for managing the desktop publishing; Mark Valentine and Tim McNerney, for their energetic quality assurance; and Ann Montgomery, for her marketing savvy.

Thanks to Lotus Development Corporation, in particular, Alan Minard, and to IBM Corporation's ACIS Division for their support and encouragement.

To John Connolly goes my admiration and thanks for creating an exciting, innovative company that will have a significant impact on education of college students for years to come.

Last, but certainly not least, I give special thanks to editor Susan Solomon for her advice, counsel, and suggestions that have significantly shaped and improved this text. I can only hope that we have other opportunities to continue this partnership again very soon.

To my wife, Hilda, and daughter, Shana, a special thanks for their encouragement and support during this project. Without their efforts I'd never have completed this project "on-time."

Roy Ageloff

Brief Contents

Table of Contents

Part Two
The Tutorials

My Goal(s):

Develop a worksheet that calculates the Krier Marine Services payroll.

What results do I want to see?

Weekly Payroll Report

What information do I need?

Employee name

Number of hours each employee worked during the week

Employee's rate of pay per hour

What calculations will I perform?

Gross pay for each employee

Total gross pay of all employees

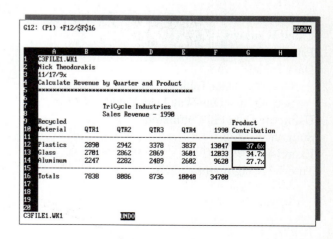

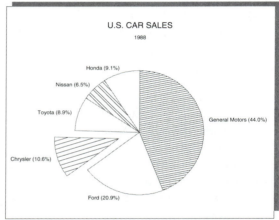

```
J29: '/f~s~r                                              READY

        I        J         K       L       M       N       O
21  MACRO AREA
22
23  Name       Macro              Description
24  ---------------------------------------------------------
25  \P         /pp                print the payroll worksheet
26             ra8.d28~           specifies print range
27             agpq               align, go, page, quit
28
29  SAVEPAY    /f~s~r             saves a worksheet file
30
31  NAMEARANGE /rnc{?}~{?}~        assign range name to a range of cells
32
33  CURRENCY2  /rfc~{END}{D}~      format range of cells to currency
34
35
36
37
38
39
40
    S7FILE1.WK1            UNDO
```

Part Three
Additional Cases

Part 4
Reference

Part One . . .

Getting Started

Chapter 1

Using Spreadsheets in Business

Generations of frustrated people who worked with numbers using only pencils and erasers would envy you. They added long columns of numbers, and if a figure changed, they had to erase and recalculate. Or they multiplied to determine percentages and erased and multiplied again if a mistake crept in. The arrival of the calculator saved time, but until computers became available, people remained subject to the tyranny of pencil and eraser.

With Lotus 1-2-3, the computer automatically erases and re-calculates for you, saving countless hours. Projects whose complexity could eat up pencils and erasers can now be accomplished in minutes. When you learn how to use 1-2-3, imagine how much easier it will be to create a budget, prepare an invoice, or calculate interest on a loan. Instead of one option, you can evaluate several, for example, "What if advertising costs average $2,000 instead of $1,500 per month?" "What if this year's bonus is four percent, six percent, or eight percent?"

Not surprisingly, businesses are enthusiastic users of spreadsheet software. That's because in almost any department of a company, spreadsheets can help people do their jobs more quickly and more effectively.

What Is a Business?

Your local drugstore is a business, as are the neighborhood cleaner, florist, market, and restaurants. So are Sears, General Motors, and Kodak. All of these businesses provide products and services people need; in return, they earn money to compensate employees and owners for their hard work and money invested. Thus, we can say that a *business* is an organization that seeks profit by providing goods or services.

You may be planning a business career, for example, as a storeowner, stockbroker, accountant, or manager. Even if you are not a business major, you engage in business activities. If you earn money, you have to decide how to spend it, how to save it, and what taxes to pay. If you become a lawyer or a doctor, you will have to pay rent for your office and compensate your employees; you may have to market your skills to prospective clients or patients. If you become an artist, you will have to acquire materials and sell your works. So even if you don't decide on a traditional business career, you can still use a spreadsheet program to help you make wise business decisions.

Computers in Business

People — employees — are an important resource in any business. To be effective employees, people need information. Information is sometimes described as a company's most valuable resource. It enables employees to review past business decisions and activities, and learn from their mistakes. It provides an accurate picture of the company's present position and a basis for forecasting the future. Decisions made throughout a company reflect the quality of information available to its employees.

In every department of a company, data accumulate — on sales volume and promotion costs for example, on customers, and on expenses for furniture, supplies, and entertainment. The challenge faced by all businesspeople is to transform data into meaningful information, to process data by creating structured reports. When this is done well, employees can rely on accurate information and thus provide better products and services for customers.

Pencils and erasers, even calculators and filing cabinets, are of little help in managing and organizing large quantities of data. Fortunately, computers have dramatically improved companies' ability to process data, to pull information together, and to provide reports on all aspects of their operations.

Spreadsheets are one of the most valuable computer tools for producing usable information. The availability of spreadsheet software made businesses recognize the speed and flexibility of the microcomputer. With 1-2-3 on microcomputers throughout a company, decision makers at every level can analyze past experience, forecast the future, and, even more importantly, test assumptions by posing "What if?" questions and studying the results. Let's define spreadsheets and then see how they can be used in various business settings.

What Is a Spreadsheet?

To understand a what a spreadsheet is, we must first look at the language of accounting. If you have ever seen a budget, listing months across the top of a page and income and expense items vertically along the left, you have seen a type of accounting worksheet, or ledger (Figure 1-1). A **worksheet** is a grid of intersecting vertical **columns** and horizontal **rows** that organizes data in an easily understandable way. With this grid organization, data are

columns

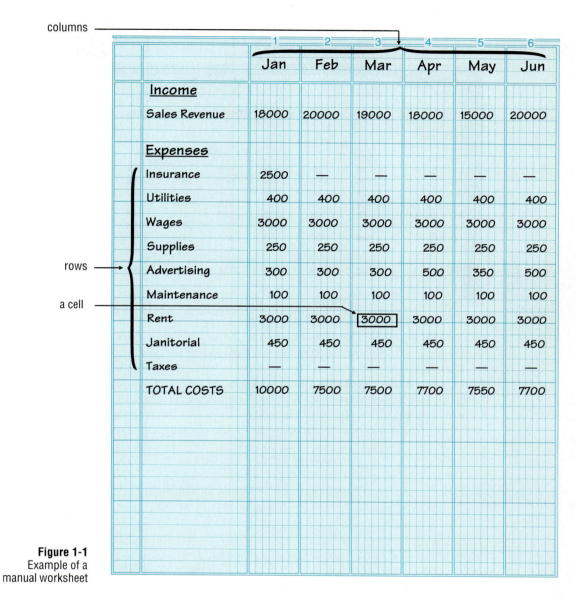

	Jan	Feb	Mar	Apr	May	Jun
Income						
Sales Revenue	18000	20000	19000	18000	15000	20000
Expenses						
Insurance	2500	—	—	—	—	—
Utilities	400	400	400	400	400	400
Wages	3000	3000	3000	3000	3000	3000
Supplies	250	250	250	250	250	250
Advertising	300	300	300	500	350	500
Maintenance	100	100	100	100	100	100
Rent	3000	3000	3000	3000	3000	3000
Janitorial	450	450	450	450	450	450
Taxes	—	—	—	—	—	—
TOTAL COSTS	10000	7500	7500	7700	7550	7700

rows

a cell

Figure 1-1
Example of a
manual worksheet

entered into the appropriate **cells**, the intersections of rows and columns. Until recently, you would have to use a calculator and a pencil to calculate totals and place them in the proper cells.

With the advent of the microcomputer came the *electronic* worksheet. This computer software, called a **spreadsheet**, creates a similar grid or worksheet on your computer screen (Figure 1-2) and instructs the computer to perform the calculations for you.

You don't have to be a computer expert to use a spreadsheet. You simply tell the software what result you want in certain cells, and the software adds the numbers in rows or columns, multiplies the contents of one cell by another, or applies formulas.

What if you want to see what happens if sales, salaries, or supplies vary? What if you simply change your mind or make a mistake? To consider another option or to correct an error, you enter the appropriate numbers and instructions. The computer recalculates and changes all relevant cells for you. You can print various versions of a worksheet, store them,

```
A1: [W13]                                                               READY

         A            B       C       D       E       F       G
 1                   Jan     Feb     Mar     Apr     May     Jun
 2   Income
 3   ------------
 4   Sales Revenue  15000   20000   19000   18000   15000   20000
 5
 6   Expenses
 7   ------------
 8   Insurance       2500
 9   Utilities        400     400     400     400     400     400
10   Wages           3000    3000    3000    3000    3000    3000
11   Supplies         250     250     250     250     250     250
12   Advertising      300     300     300     500     350     500
13   Maintenance      100     100     100     100     100     100
14   Rent            3000    3000    3000    3000    3000    3000
15   Janitorial       450     450     450     450     450     450
16   Taxes
17                  _____
18   Total Costs    10000    7500    7500    7700    7550    7700
19
20
LEDGER.WK1                       UNDO
```

Figure 1-2
Example of an
electronic
worksheet

and study their meanings at your convenience before you make a decision. You can even display the results in graphic form, for example, as a pie chart or a bar graph (Figure 1-3).

You can use 1-2-3 not only to produce a visual aid to clarify information, but also to produce reports that search for and extract specific data. With its data management function, for example, you can instruct 1-2-3 to list all employees at a certain salary level or to prepare a report showing all invoices that are 30 days overdue. The graphing and data management functions of 1-2-3 provide additional tools for interpreting, displaying, and reporting data.

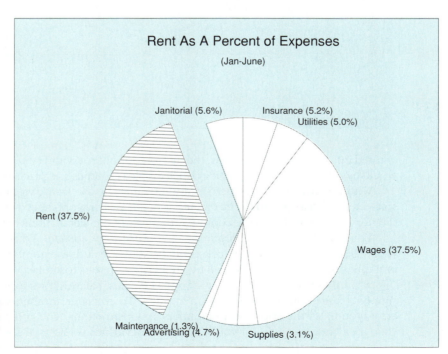

Figure 1-3
Example of a pie
chart generated by
Lotus 1-2-3

How Are Spreadsheets Used in Business?

Although businesses depend on spreadsheets to summarize numerical data and to keep records, spreadsheets are most powerful as a decision-making tool. The spreadsheet's ability to answer the question "What if?" helps businesspeople make sound decisions. For example, suppose you are planning to start your own business. The "what if" feature of 1-2-3 enables you to measure the effects on profit of paying one employee or two, of renting a more or a less expensive space, and of obtaining loans at different interest rates. What if sales the first six months are 100 units? 250 units? What if you pay employees a straight salary? Salary plus commission? 1-2-3 helps you see the whole picture and eliminates much of the guesswork.

This "what if" ability makes spreadsheets essential throughout an organization — in accounting, marketing, finance, and human resources management. Let's first define these basic business functions and then use a real example to demonstrate the use of spreadsheets in each. The people who contributed examples to this book are enthusiastic about their spreadsheet projects. Spreadsheets have enabled them to organize and display information and to make instant calculations. For entry-level employees all the way to top management, spreadsheets are an invaluable tool.

Using Spreadsheets in Accounting

Called "the language of business," accounting communicates information about the financial well-being of a company. Accountants classify transactions — for example, as purchases, sales, or entertainment costs — then record and summarize the financial data and help interpret the data for decision makers. They help managers find answers to questions like, "Will the company have enough cash to pay the bills next quarter?" "Which product that we make is least profitable?" People outside the firm, such as potential investors or bankers, look to the financial statements prepared by accountants to learn about a company's debt or cash surplus.

As organizations expand and grow more complex, the practice of accounting becomes more sophisticated. Thus, accounting is becoming increasingly dependent on computers to measure, analyze, and report information that is so essential in business today. For example, Veronica Villarreal's project at Mesilla Valley Mall illustrates the power of spreadsheets to record accounting information and produce reports. After Veronica earned an associate's degree in Business, she began working in the business office of the mall. When she arrived, gift certificates good for merchandise in mall stores were recorded and totaled by hand (Figure 1-4). This was a time-consuming job because it was done twice — once when a

Figure 1-4
A sample gift
certificate

certificate was issued and again when it was redeemed.

Veronica's manager asked her to use 1-2-3 to design a worksheet for tracking gift certificates, which were sold to customers, issued as special promotions, and presented as employee-of-the-month awards. The manager wanted to keep track of how many certificates in each category were issued each month. Furthermore, he wanted his staff to have a reliable way of recording which certificates were redeemed and which were still outstanding.

Veronica designed a worksheet that made keeping track of the gift certificates quicker and easier. A simplified version of her worksheet appears in Figure 1-5.

A1: [W2]   **READY**

Mesilla Valley Mall Gift Certificate

Cert #	Amt	Customer Sale	Promo	EOM	Cert Cleared	Cert Not Cleared
668	50			50	50	
669	10	10				10
670	25	25			25	
671	25	25				25
672	50		50			50
673	50		50		50	
674	15	15			15	
675	50	50				50
Subtotal	275	125	100	50	140	135

CERTIF.WK1   **UNDO**

Figure 1-5
A simplified version of Veronica Villarreal's worksheet

By eliminating tedious repetitive calculations, spreadsheets provide time for creative problem solving. They are essential for recording, summarizing, and analyzing data and producing accounting information such as monthly income statements, cash flow reports, budgets, and, as we've seen, even gift certificates.

Using Spreadsheets in Marketing

Building a better mousetrap won't earn profits for a company unless people need and want a better mousetrap. *Marketing* involves ensuring that a company's products or services satisfy customers' needs. When people find what they want and need, they will pay the company for its products or services, thus generating profits for that company.

To provide this important link between the company and its customers, market research identifies target customers by their age, income, lifestyle, and so on; it then attempts to determine the wants and needs of these target customers. Through advertising, the company strives to inform consumers about what it has to offer them. A systematic marketing effort depends on accurate information for planning a successful strategy and measuring sales results.

At Rauh Good Darlo & Barnes Advertising Agency, Kelly Seelig uses a spreadsheet for planning and scheduling advertising campaigns for her clients. She develops a budget for ads in newspapers and magazines, and for radio and television commercials. Then she

```
                              Media Schedule

    Publication        Jan      Feb      Mar     Apr     May     Jun    Subtotal

    HOTEL & TRAV                $6,094                          $6,094          $12,188
    Calif Sect.                 Spr Is                          Sum Is
    Circ:    63,795             4-color                         4-color

    CALIF MAG                   $3,600   $3,330                                 $6,930
    Trav. Planner               1/4 pg   1/4 pg
    Circ:   356,438

    LOS ANGELES                                                 $6,525          $6,525
    Issued annually                                             1/2 pg
    Circ:   222,629                                             4-color

    SUNSET             $2,695                                   $1,348          $4,043
    Entire circ.       1/4 pg                                   1/4 pg
    Circ:1,400,000     w/copy                                   w/copy
                       ------   ------   ------   ------   ------   ------ -------
    SUBTOTALS          $2,695   $9,694   $3,330      $0   $13,967      $0  $29,686
```

Figure 1-6
A portion of the printout for Kelly Seelig's media schedule worksheet

schedules these ads over a period of months for maximum effectiveness. Kelly finds a spreadsheet ideal for creating her media plan.

A portion of her media schedule worksheet for magazine advertising shows expenditures for each publication by month and calculates totals by month and by publication (Figure 1-6). The printed worksheet helps Kelly and her client, in this case a hotel, to see when and where the dollars will be spent. What if they schedule more or fewer ads? The impact on the budget is immediately clear.

Spreadsheets have many applications in marketing, not only in advertising but also in market research, product management, and sales. Marketing personnel rely on spreadsheets to analyze past experience, forecast future results, and test various assumptions. Spreadsheets help marketing personnel collect and interpret data about customers and measure the company's effectiveness in communicating with its customers. 1-2-3 can be the vital ingredient in a successful marketing effort.

Using Spreadsheets in Finance

In any business, you must consider not only your customers and what products they need and want, but also where to obtain funds for materials, manufacturing, and employee compensation. Sales of your product can vary from month to month, so you must be certain that you have cash on hand to pay the bills, including taxes, and that you can control expenses.

Finance is the business function of planning how to obtain funds and how to use them to achieve the company's goals. In addition to sales dollars, companies can obtain funds by selling shares in ownership (stocks and bonds), attracting venture capital, and borrowing money. Accountants collect, organize, and present data that the specialists in finance interpret to ensure the financial health of the company. Since forecasting, budgeting, and tax management are among their duties, finance specialists process volumes of numerical data. They rely on computers to transform these data quickly into useful information.

Spreadsheets enable people with a finance background to find creative solutions to problems. At Ungermann-Bass, a computer communications company, Wendy Ray studied this high-tech company's method of paying its bills. She knew that many of the company's suppliers offered discounts for prompt payment of their invoices, but the accounting department at Ungermann-Bass wasn't paying early enough to take advantage of these savings. Wendy decided to use a 1-2-3 worksheet to determine how many discounts were taken and how many were lost. With the data on 1-2-3, Wendy presented well-documented information to a company vice president and recommended a change in payment policy.

Figure 1-7 is a summary worksheet showing discounts taken for two quarters, the first before Wendy's recommendations were adopted and the second after. Notice that her worksheet analysis enabled the company to increase the number of discounts taken in those quarters from 91.14 percent to 97.95 percent. In a year, the company saved over $100,000, thanks to Wendy's recommendations.

A1: [W14]   READY

	A	B	C	D	E	F
1			Discounts Taken Summary			
2						
3	Date	Discounts	Discounts	% Taken	Discounts	% Lost
4		Available	Taken		Lost	
5						
6	October	23,576	19,052	80.81%	4,524	19.19%
7	November	32,149	28,911	89.93%	3,238	10.07%
8	December	36,647	36,225	98.85%	422	1.15%
9	Quarter Total	92,372	84,188	91.14%	8,184	8.86%
10						
11						
12	January	34,607	33,964	98.14%	643	1.86%
13	February	23,577	23,326	98.94%	251	1.06%
14	March	20,238	19,525	96.48%	713	3.52%
15	Quarter Total	78,422	76,815	97.95%	1,607	2.05%
16						
17						
18						
19						
20						

DISCOUNT.WK1   UNDO

Figure 1-7
A portion of Wendy Ray's summary worksheet

Besides helping to control expenses, finance specialists respond to requests for information coming from different departments of the company. The manufacturing department may ask for monthly reports of actual spending compared to its expense budget. Marketing may want to keep abreast of how its sales results to date compare with forecasts. 1-2-3 can generate these reports and provide comparisons with last year's results.

Without spreadsheets, these analyses and projections would require laborious calculations, subject at every step to errors. The spreadsheet user's ability to ask, "What if" and have 1-2-3 recalculate all the numbers has significantly improved financial planning and control.

Using Spreadsheets in Human Resource Management

A marketable product and the funds to manufacture it aren't enough. Businesses need people to get the job done. *Human resources management* is the process of determining a company's needs for employees and finding, training, and motivating those employees.

Each unit of a company must concern itself with managing the human resource; many companies also have a human resources or personnel department. Among such a department's tasks is providing job enrichment and compensation incentives to promote employee satisfaction and productivity and to reduce turnover. Human resource specialists are often charged with administering payroll and benefits, keeping salary records, and evaluating various forms of compensation such as profit sharing and bonuses. By facilitating the record-keeping functions, computers free human resource specialists to invest more time in training and motivating employees.

For example, human resource administrator Thalia Ohara of *PC World* magazine uses 1-2-3 to track profit sharing earned by employees. Profit sharing is a system that rewards employees for their role in producing profits by paying them a percentage of those profits.

At *PC World*, the amount of profit-sharing funds each employee earns is a percentage of the employee's gross salary. The profit-sharing worksheet that Thalia created shows each employee's profit sharing earned for the year, which is deposited in the employee's account (Figure 1-8). When an employee earns a raise in salary, Thalia enters the new salary, and 1-2-3 recalculates the amount of profit sharing and revises the totals. Profit sharing encourages employees to stay with the company for at least seven years. If they leave before seven years, they can withdraw only a percentage of the contribution, called the vesting percentage, based on their years of service.

Figure 1-8
A portion of Thalia Ohara's profit sharing worksheet

```
A1: [W1]                                                          READY

      A       B        C        D       E       F       G       H
1
2                            Profit Sharing Plan
3
4      Participant  Vesting     Date   Contrib  Annual   Amount  Pay out
5                      %        Hired     %      Salary   Contrib  Amount
6
7      V. Barnerd     10%    4/10/89     12%  $50,000   $6,000    $600
8      D. Bridges      0%    6/18/90     12%   28,000    3,360       0
9      W. Callaway    20%    8/24/88     12%   35,000    4,200     840
10     G. Chico      100%   11/26/82     12%   42,000    5,040   5,040
11     T. Elia        40%    1/05/87     12%   38,000    4,560   1,824
12     J. Hull         0%    4/02/90     12%   24,000    2,880       0
13     G. Liu         10%    5/22/89     12%   40,000    4,800     480
14
15
16
17
18
19
20
PROFSHAR.WK1                UNDO
```

As shown in this example, Thalia has streamlined and simplified salary and benefits administration, thanks to her worksheet. From tracking parking passes to calculating salaries, profit sharing, and bonuses, 1-2-3 makes human resources management more flexible and efficient.

What You Will Learn About Spreadsheets in Business

Spreadsheets have transformed the business of business by giving people quick access to information vital for doing their jobs. *Lotus 1-2-3 for Business* places this essential software tool in your hands right from the beginning. Through step-by-step tutorials, you will have the opportunity to apply spreadsheet principles to real business problems. As you learn about spreadsheets in business, you will develop business problem-solving skills that you can use in other courses and that you can take with you to whatever career you choose.

Lotus 1-2-3 is recognized as the spreadsheet standard. If you can list 1-2-3 skills on your resume, it will catch an employer's eye. Employers know that 1-2-3 enables employees to perform their jobs more efficiently and effectively. Because 1-2-3 improves your productivity, it increases your chances to get a job, to advance in your job, and to be successful.

In the tutorials and the cases that follow, you will look at 1-2-3 in a business context. *Lotus 1-2-3 for Business* will help you see that business problem solving is more than just collecting and recording data and that learning to use spreadsheets is more than simply pressing the right keys on your computer. *Lotus 1-2-3 for Business* emphasizes taking data and transforming them into information useful for understanding business relationships and for making sound business decisions.

Chapter 2

Preparing to Use *Lotus 1-2-3 for Business*

Before you can begin the tour of Lotus 1-2-3 in Chapter 3 and before you can start the tutorials, you must do three things:

- Collect information about your computer system.
- Initialize your 1-2-3 diskettes.
- Install 1-2-3 on your computer.

Thus, in this chapter you will first learn about the computer system on which you will use 1-2-3. You will do this by filling out a table of information. Once you have this information, you will initialize your 1-2-3 diskettes. Initializing is a process that you must complete before you can use 1-2-3. Finally, you will learn how to install 1-2-3 on your computer so you can use it to complete the tutorials and then to create useful, professional worksheets.

If you are using 1-2-3 in a lab where it is already installed on a computer, you should still read this chapter since you must copy your Data Disk. Also this chapter will help familiarize you with the process of installation should you later decide to install the diskettes package on your own computer.

Topics

This chapter covers the following topics:

- Your Computer and *Lotus 1-2-3 for Business*
- Initializing 1-2-3
- Copying the Diskettes in *Lotus 1-2-3 for Business*
- Installing 1-2-3

Your Computer and *Lotus 1-2-3 for Business*

Your computer must meet certain requirements to use your copy of Lotus 1-2-3. In the following sections, you will collect information about your computer system's hardware, memory, and operating system. This will help verify that your computer meets these requirements. If you are using 1-2-3 in a lab where it is already installed on a computer, you can skip this section and move to the next section, "Initializing 1-2-3."

Hardware Requirements

To use your copy of Lotus 1-2-3, you must have the following hardware:

- an IBM, COMPAQ, Toshiba, or Lotus-certified compatible personal computer
- two diskette drives, or a hard disk and a diskette drive
- a monochrome (one-color) or color monitor
- a keyboard
- a graphics card, if you want to display graphics

Memory Requirements

To use 1-2-3 your computer must have a minimum of 320 kilobytes (320K) of conventional or main memory.

If you have at least 512K of conventional memory, you will be less likely to run out of memory while working through the tutorials and the assignments. 1-2-3 supports up to 640K of conventional memory.

1-2-3 also supports up to 4 megabytes of additional memory that conforms to the L/I/M Expanded Memory Specification.

Operating System Requirements

To use 1-2-3, your computer must have version 2.0 or higher of the Disk Operating System (DOS) installed.

Collecting Information about Your Computer

Now that you know the hardware requirements to use your copy of 1-2-3, you should collect information about your computer system to ensure that it meets these requirements. We've provided the chart on the next page to help you record this information. Be sure to fill it out completely. If you need assistance in completing this chart, check with your instructor or technical support person.

Information about Your Computer

	Manufacturer	Model
Computer	_____	_____
Screen monitor	_____	_____
Text display adapter	_____	_____
Graphics display adapter	_____	_____
Text Printer	_____	_____
Graphics Printer	_____	_____
Plotter	_____	_____
Conventional memory	_____ KB	
Expanded memory	_____ MB	_____
Hard-disk capacity	_____ MB	(manufacturer)
Operating system		
DOS version	MS DOS _____ PC DOS _____	
Math co-processor	Yes ( ) No ( )	_____
Diskette drive size (check all that apply)		(manufacturer)
3½-inch high density (1.44 MB)	( )	
3½-inch low density (720K)	( )	
5¼-inch high density (1.2 MB)	( )	
5¼-inch low density (360K)	( )	
Memory-resident programs	_____	
Type of printer interface	_____	
Type of plotter interface	_____	

Initializing 1-2-3

Even if you use a computer with 1-2-3 installed on it already, you should still initialize the System Disk in *your copy* of 1-2-3.

When you initialize 1-2-3, you record your name and your school's name on your copy of the 1-2-3 System Disk. This identifies you as an authorized user of 1-2-3. Before you can install or use 1-2-3, you *must* initialize your diskette.

Follow the steps below to initialize 1-2-3. Start at your DOS prompt. If you make a typing mistake, use [Backspace] to erase characters to the left of the cursor.

To initialize 1-2-3:

❶   Be sure your DOS prompt is on the screen.

❷   Insert the 1-2-3 System Disk in drive A.

❸   Type **a:** and press **[Enter]**.

❹ Type **init** and press **[Enter]**. The copyright screen appears. After you read this screen, press **[Enter]** again to view the next screen, which describes the initialization process.

❺ Press **[Enter]** to start the initialization process. Your screen should look like Figure 2-1.

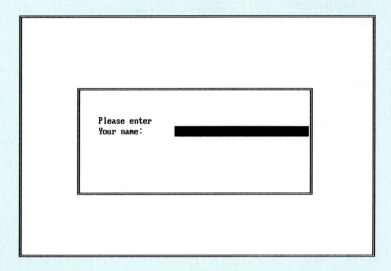

```
Please enter
Your name:       ███████████████
```

Figure 2-1
The initialization
name entry screen

❻ Type your first and last name and then press **[Enter]**. The screen should look similar to Figure 2-2.

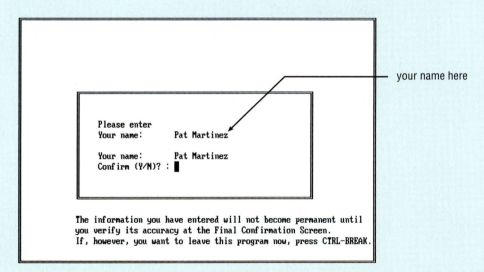

your name here

```
Please enter
Your name:        Pat Martinez

Your name:        Pat Martinez
Confirm (Y/N)? : █
```

```
The information you have entered will not become permanent until
you verify its accuracy at the Final Confirmation Screen.
If, however, you want to leave this program now, press CTRL-BREAK.
```

Figure 2-2
An initialization
confirmation screen

❼ If the information you typed is correct on your screen, type **y** to confirm and press **[Enter]**.

If the information is *not* correct, type **n** and press **[Enter]** so you can enter a new name. Then enter the correct name.

⑧ Type your school's name and press **[Enter]**. If you make a mistake, type **n** and press **[Enter]** to correct it. When you have typed the correct school name, type **y** and press **[Enter]** to confirm. Your screen should look similar to Figure 2-3.

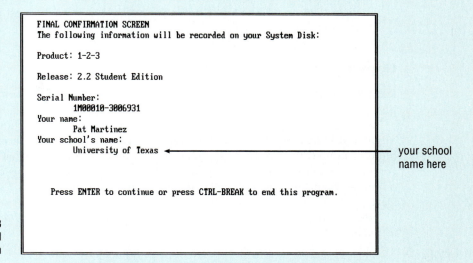

```
FINAL CONFIRMATION SCREEN
The following information will be recorded on your System Disk:

Product: 1-2-3

Release: 2.2 Student Edition

Serial Number:
      1M00010-3006931
Your name:
      Pat Martinez
Your school's name:
      University of Texas  ◄─────────────────────────     your school
                                                          name here


      Press ENTER to continue or press CTRL-BREAK to end this program.
```

Figure 2-3
The final
confirmation screen

Your screen should now show the name and the school you have entered. This information will be permanently recorded on the System Disk. *You will not be able to change these names once you complete Step 9.*

⑨ If you are sure that you have typed the correct information, press **[Enter]**.

If you are not certain that this is the information you want to record on the System Disk, press **[Ctrl][Break]**. Hold down **[Ctrl]** and while holding it down press **[Break]**. [Break] is on the same key as [Pause] or [Scroll Lock]. Check you computer keyboard. Pressing [Ctrl][Break] interrupts the installation process without recording any information. You can then begin the initialization again from Step 4.

⑩ When you see a message indicating that the initialization is complete, press **[Enter]** to return to the DOS prompt. Remove the System Disk from the diskette drive and write-protect it.

You have now initialialized your System Disk.

Copying the Diskettes in *Lotus 1-2-3 for Business*

Whenever you purchase software, one of the first things you should do is copy the original diskettes (onto other diskettes or onto your hard drive) and then store them in a safe place. In this section, you will copy your *Lotus 1-2-3 for Business* diskettes. Find the description of your computer system below and follow the appropriate instructions.

• If you are using 1-2-3 in a lab where it has already been installed: You will make copies of the Data Disk. Turn to the section "Copying the Data Disk" on the next page and follow the instructions.

- If your computer has two floppy diskette drives and no hard disk: You will make working copies of all of the diskettes. Turn to the section "Copying for a System with Two Diskette Drives" on the next page and follow the instructions.

- If your computer has a hard disk: You will copy all of the diskettes onto the hard disk. Turn to the section "Copying to a Hard Disk" on the next page and follow the instructions.

Copying the Data Disk

Read this section *only* if you will be using 1-2-3 on a computer where it has already been installed.

Whenever you purchase software, one of the first things you should do is to copy the original diskettes and then store the originals in a safe place. You should use the copies — often called working copies — whenever you use the software. That way, if the working copies are ever lost or damaged, you can always make new working copies from the stored originals. In this section, you will make a working copy of the *Lotus 1-2-3 for Business* Data Disk.

Before you begin, make sure you have your *Lotus 1-2-3 for Business* Data Disk and one formatted 5¼-inch or 3½-inch diskette.

To make a working copy of the Data Disk:

❶ Write-protect the original *Lotus 1-2-3 for Business* Data Disk.

❷ Insert the Data Disk in drive A. If you have two diskette drives, insert a formatted, blank diskette in drive B.

❸ Type **a:** and press **[Enter]**.

❹ Type **copy *.* b:** and press **[Enter]** to copy the contents of the 1-2-3 Data Disk in drive A to the blank diskette in drive B.

The drive lights go on, and DOS lists the filenames on your screen one by one as they are copied to the blank diskette.

If you have only one disk drive, the computer will eventually prompt you to insert the disk for drive B. Remove the Data Disk from drive A and insert your blank, formatted disk in drive A. Your computer continues copying files to the blank disk. When your computer again prompts you to insert the disk for drive A, replace the blank disk with the original Data Disk.

When all the files are copied, you will see a message telling you the number of files copied.

❺ Remove the Data Disk from drive A and put it aside. If you have a two-drive system, remove the working copy from drive B. Label the working copy "1-2-3 Release 2.2 Data Disk 1".

❻ Store the original Data Disk in a safe place. From now on, use your working copy.

Turn to Chapter 3 and begin *A Tour of 1-2-3.*

Copying for a System with Two Diskette Drives

Whenever you purchase software, one of the first things you should do is to copy the original diskettes and store the originals in a safe place. You should then use the copies — often called working copies — whenever you use the software. That way, if the working copies are ever lost or damaged, you can always make new working copies from the stored originals. In this section you will make working copies of all of the *Lotus 1-2-3 for Business* diskettes.

Before you begin, be sure you have either six original 5¼-inch diskettes and six blank formatted 5¼-inch diskettes or three original 3½-inch diskettes and three blank formatted 3½-inch diskettes.

To make copies of your original *Lotus 1-2-3 for Business* diskettes:

❶ Write-protect each of the original *Lotus 1-2-3 for Business* diskettes.

❷ Insert the 1-2-3 System Disk in drive A.

❸ Insert a formatted, blank diskette in drive B.

❹ Type **a:** and press **[Enter]**.

❺ Type **copy *.* b:** and press **[Enter]** to copy the contents of the 1-2-3 System Disk in drive A to the blank diskette in drive B.

   The drive lights go on, and DOS lists the filenames on your screen one by one as they are copied to the blank diskette. When all the files are copied, you will see a message telling you the number of files copied.

❻ Remove the 1-2-3 System Disk from drive A and put it aside. Remove the new working copy from drive B and label it "1-2-3 Release 2.2 System Disk."

❼ Put the second 1-2-3 diskette in drive A, and put a new blank diskette in drive B. Repeat Steps 4 through 6 to copy the second diskette. Repeat these steps for all of the original 1-2-3 diskettes and label each one appropriately.

❽ Store the original 1-2-3 diskettes in a safe place. From now on, use your working copies.

Now turn to "Installing 1-2-3" on page 21 and follow the instructions.

Copying to a Hard Disk

If you have a hard-disk system, you can copy the 1-2-3 diskettes to the hard disk. To do this, you first make a directory for the 1-2-3 program files.

The following steps assume you have installed DOS on your hard disk and that your hard disk is drive C. If your hard disk is not drive C, substitute the correct drive letter in the instructions. Also these steps assume that you do not have an earlier version of 1-2-3 already installed on your hard-disk. If you do, you must remove it before proceeding. See your instructor or technical support person for assistance.

Before you begin, make sure you have all of the *Lotus 1-2-3 for Business* diskettes. You should have either six original 5¼-inch diskettes or three original 3 ½-inch diskettes.

To create a 1-2-3 program directory:

❶ If you are not certain that C is the current drive, type **c:** and press **[Enter]**. Then type **cd ** and press **[Enter]**.

❷ At the C prompt, type **md \123** and press **[Enter]**. This creates a directory called "123" for your 1-2-3 program files.

If you want to give your directory a name other than "123," substitute any legal DOS name of your choice in Step 2. Be sure to use the name you chose in the steps that follow.

❸ Type **cd \123** and press **[Enter]** to make 123 the current directory.

Now you are ready to copy the program files to this directory.

❹ Write-protect each of the original diskettes.

❺ Insert the 1-2-3 System Disk in drive A.

❻ Be sure that C:\123 is the current directory. Then type **copy a:*.*** and press **[Enter]**.

The drive lights go on, and DOS lists the filenames on your screen one by one as they are copied to the hard disk. When all the files are copied, you will see a message telling you the number of files copied.

❼ Remove the 1-2-3 System Disk from drive A and put it aside. Replace it with the second 1-2-3 diskette. Repeat Step 6 for each of the other original diskettes *except* the Data Disk.

❽ Store the original 1-2-3 diskettes in a safe place.

Next you will create a subdirectory under the 1-2-3 directory. Then you will copy the Data Disk into this newly created subdirectory.

To create a subdirectory for the Data Disk:

❶ At the C:\123 prompt, type **md data** and press **[Enter]** to create a subdirectory.

❷ Type **cd data** and press **[Enter]** to make \123\DATA the current subdirectory.

Now you are ready to copy the Data Disk to the hard disk.

❸ Write-protect the Data Disk.

❹ Insert the Data Disk in drive A.

❺ Be sure C:\123\DATA is the current directory. Then type **copy a:*.*** and press **[Enter]** to copy the Data Disk to your hard disk.

❻ Remove the Data Disk from drive A.

❼ Store the original 1-2-3 Data Disk with your 1-2-3 program diskettes in a safe place.

Now you are ready to install 1-2-3.

Installing 1-2-3

When you install 1-2-3, you identify what types of monitors and printers you have so that 1-2-3 can work with them. Unless you install 1-2-3, you will not be able to see graphs on your screen or print your work.

The Install Program

A *program* is a set of instructions that tell your computer to perform certain actions. The Install program asks you questions about your computer and its monitor and printer. 1-2-3 includes a driver file for each type of monitor and printer. The driver file contains instructions that help 1-2-3 to communicate with your monitor and printer. The Install program *installs* the drivers appropriate for your monitor and printer, according to the information you give it. Once the drivers are installed, 1-2-3 can show and print graphs and reports, using the unique features of your monitor and printer.

Starting the Install Program

Be sure you have completed the instructions earlier in this chapter for initializing and copying your 1-2-3 diskettes before you begin.

To start the Install program:

❶ If you have a two-diskette system, insert the working copy of the Utilities Disk in drive A. Then type **a:** and press **[Enter]**.

If you have a hard-disk system, type **c:** and press **[Enter]** to make C the current drive. Then type **cd\123** and press **[Enter]** to make 123 the current directory.

❷ Type **install** and press **[Enter]** to run the Install program. The Install program will start in approximately 30 seconds.

❸ Study the introductory screen, as shown in Figure 2-4. This screen provides important information on using the Install program.

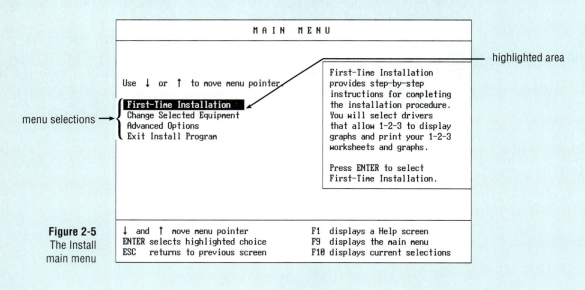

```
                        1-2-3 Install Program

                        Copyright 1986, 1989
                     Lotus Development Corporation
                        All Rights Reserved
                           Release 2.2

Note: Before you use Install, follow the instructions in the Getting
Started section of the User's Manual.

The Install program lets you tell 1-2-3 what equipment you have.  You
choose your equipment from a list of options by moving a highlighted
rectangle (the menu pointer) to your choice and pressing ENTER.  You
can start 1-2-3 without using the Install program first, but you will
not be able to display graphs or use a printer.

If you need more information to make a particular choice, press HELP (F1)
to see a Help screen.  You will also find it helpful to complete the
Hardware Chart in your student manual and have it available for
reference while you are using Install.
                   Press ENTER to begin the Install program.
```

this refers to Chapter 2 of your textbook

Figure 2-4
The Install program's introductory screen

❹ If you have a two-diskette drive system, the Install program may prompt you to change disks. Always use the working copies you made earlier, not the original disks. Change disks when the Install program prompts you to do so.

❺ Press **[Enter]** to display the Install main menu screen. See Figure 2-5.

```
                          M A I N   M E N U


                                           ┌──────────────────────────
                                           │ First-Time Installation
   Use ↓ or ↑ to move menu pointer.        │ provides step-by-step
                                           │ instructions for completing
                                           │ the installation procedure.
   ┌──────────────────────┐                │ You will select drivers
   │ First-Time Installation │             │ that allow 1-2-3 to display
   Change Selected Equipment               │ graphs and print your 1-2-3
   Advanced Options                        │ worksheets and graphs.
   Exit Install Program
                                           │ Press ENTER to select
                                           │ First-Time Installation.
                                           └──────────────────────────


   ↓ and ↑ move menu pointer          F1  displays a Help screen
   ENTER selects highlighted choice   F9  displays the main menu
   ESC   returns to previous screen   F10 displays current selections
```

highlighted area

menu selections

Figure 2-5
The Install main menu

The four lines at the left of the screen are *menu selections.* The highlighted area shows the current selection. You can move among the selections with the [↑] and [↓] arrow keys, and make selections with the [Enter] key.

You can also press [Esc] at any time to return to the previous screen, press [F1] to see a screen of helpful instructions, or press [F9] to return to the main menu.

You should now select "First-Time Installation" to tell the Install program what type of monitor and printer you have.

To select First-Time Installation:

❶ With the highlight on First-Time Installation, press the **[Enter]** key.

❷ Read the screen that describes drivers and how the Install program uses them.

❸ Press **[Enter]** to continue to the next screen.

Selecting a Screen Driver

In this part of the Install program, you describe your monitor(s) and adapter(s), and the Install program selects the appropriate screen driver.

To select a screen driver:

❶ The Install program asks if your computer can display graphs. If you have an IBM PS/2 or other computer with a built-in graphics adapter, or if your computer has a graphics adapter card, use the arrow keys to move the highlight to Yes and then press **[Enter]**.

If you have an IBM monochrome text card or some other display card that cannot display graphics, move the highlight to No and press **[Enter]**.

If you select Yes, Install then asks you how many monitors you have.

❷ If you have only one monitor connected to your computer system, move the highlight to One Monitor and press **[Enter]**.

If you have two monitors connected to your computer system, move the highlight to Two Monitors and press **[Enter]**.

Next a list of available screen drivers appears, as shown in Figure 2-6. For some displays, you can choose not only the type of display, but also the number of lines and the number of character per line shown on the screen. For example, "80 x 25" means 25 lines of text with 80 characters on each line. You should select the "80 x 25" drivers, since the resulting 1-2-3 screen displays are easier to read and better match the illustrations in this book.

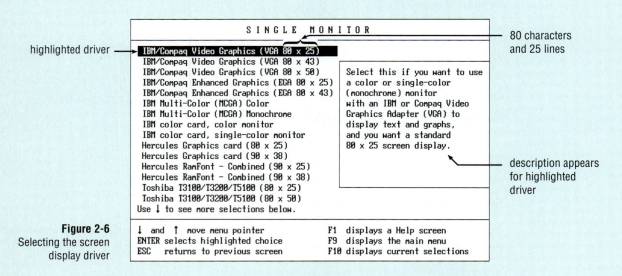

highlighted driver

80 characters
and 25 lines

description appears
for highlighted
driver

Figure 2-6
Selecting the screen
display driver

❸ Use the [↑] and [↓] to highlight the appropriate screen driver. Consult the chart on page 15.

As you highlight each driver, a description appears in the box at the right of the screen. If you don't see the driver for your screen and display card, press [↓] until new choices appear. Press [↑] to return to the original choices.

When you are sure you have highlighted the correct choice, press **[Enter]** to make the selection.

Selecting Printer Drivers

Now that you've told the Install program what type of screen and graphics adapter you have, the Install program asks if you have a text printer. In this section, you'll select a printer driver for text and a printer driver for graphics.

To select a text printer driver:

❶ Press **[Enter]** to select Yes, indicating that you have a printer connected.

You can use this selection if your printer is connected directly to your computer, or if it is on a local area network. The Install program next reveals a menu with the names of various printer manufacturers (Figure 2-7).

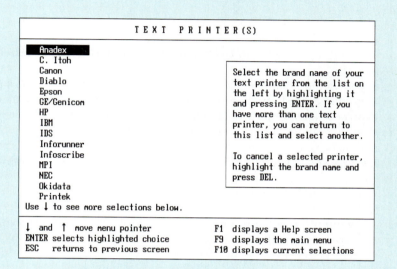

```
                    T E X T   P R I N T E R ( S )

    Anadex
    C. Itoh
    Canon                          Select the brand name of your
    Diablo                         text printer from the list on
    Epson                          the left by highlighting it
    GE/Genicom                     and pressing ENTER. If you
    HP                             have more than one text
    IBM                            printer, you can return to
    IDS                            this list and select another.
    Inforunner
    Infoscribe                     To cancel a selected printer,
    MPI                            highlight the brand name and
    NEC                            press DEL.
    Okidata
    Printek
    Use ↓ to see more selections below.

    ↓  and  ↑  move menu pointer        F1   displays a Help screen
    ENTER selects highlighted choice    F9   displays the main menu
    ESC   returns to previous screen    F10  displays current selections
```

Figure 2-7
Selecting the printer
manufacturer

❷ Move the highlight to the name of the manufacturer of your printer and press **[Enter]**. If you don't see the name of the your printer manufacturer, press **[↓]** to move the highlight past the bottom of the screen. New choices appear as you continue to press **[↓]**. Press **[↑]** again to return to the original choices. If you still do not see your printer on the list, follow the suggestions in Figure 2-8 on the next page.

Once you select a printer manufacturer, the Install program shows a list of individual printer models or model series.

❸ Move the highlight to your printer model or model series and press **[Enter]**. If you don't see the name of your printer model, press **[↓]** until new choices appear. Press **[↑]** to return to the original choices.

Once you select a printer model, the Install program asks if you have another text printer.

❹ Select No if you do not have an additional printer.

If you do have an additional printer, select Yes and choose the printer manufacturer and model as you did in Steps 2 and 3.

The Install program now asks you to select a graphics printer.

❺ Select Yes if your printer can print graphics. (Most dot-matrix, ink-jet, and laser printers can print graphics.) Most users use the same printer to print both text and graphics.

Select No if your printer cannot print graphs.

❻ Move the highlight to the name of the manufacturer of your printer and press **[Enter]**.

❼ Move the highlight to your printer model or model series and press **[Enter]**.

The Install program next asks if you have another graphics printer.

❽ Select No if you do not have an additional graphics printer.

If you do have an additional printer, select Yes and choose the graphics printer manufacturer and model as you did in Steps 6 and 7.

What to Do If Your Printer Driver Is Not Listed

If your printer manufacturer or model is not listed among 1-2-3's printer drivers, you may still be able to print from 1-2-3. Many printers from less popular manufacturers are designed to *emulate,* or work like, other popular printers. Check your printer manual to see if your printer emulates one of the printers on the list.

If you're still not sure about your printer, you might select the following choices:

- *Unlisted* for the text printer.

- *Epson FX* or *IBM Proprinter* for the graphics printer. If your printer is a dot-matrix or ink-jet printer, this choice might work. Many dot-matrix and ink-jet printers emulate these printers.

- *HP LaserJet* for the graphics printer. If your printer is a laser, this choice might work. Many laser printers emulate this printer.

Figure 2-8

Naming and Saving Your Driver Set

After you finish making equipment selections, the Install program reveals the "Naming Your Driver Set" screen. The *driver set* is the collection of drivers (screen, text printer, and graphics printer) that you just selected.

The Install program collects the drivers you selected and stores them in a disk file. Then, each time you start 1-2-3, the program finds this driver set and uses it to communicate with your screen and printer(s).

The Install program asks if you want to name the driver set. If you select Yes, you can select your own name; if you say No, the Install program will automatically name the file 123.SET.

To use 123.SET as the driver set name:

❶ Select No and press **[Enter]**.

The Install program next shows a screen about saving changes.

❷ Press **[Enter]** to go on to the next screen.

❸ If you have a two-diskette system, Install prompts you to switch diskettes so the program can copy the driver set to each of the 1-2-3 program diskettes. Be sure to use the working copies that you made, not the original diskettes. Be sure, also, that the diskettes are not write-protected.

Completing the Installation

Now that you've selected the appropriate drivers and saved them in a driver set, you can leave the Install program. But first, you should check the driver set you just created.

To check the driver set:

❶ If you're using a two-diskette system, be sure the System Disk is in drive A. If you're using a hard-disk system, go to Step 2.

❷ Press **[F10]** to display a list of the drivers in the driver set you just created.

Install displays a list of the selections you made. Install may also add some drivers to your driver set automatically. Figure 2-9 shows an example of a list of drivers.

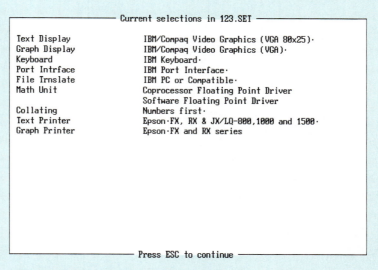

```
───────────── Current selections in 123.SET ─────────────

Text Display       IBM/Compaq Video Graphics (VGA 80x25)·
Graph Display      IBM/Compaq Video Graphics (VGA)·
Keyboard           IBM Keyboard·
Port Intrface      IBM Port Interface·
File Trnslate      IBM PC or Compatible·
Math Unit          Coprocessor Floating Point Driver
                   Software Floating Point Driver
Collating          Numbers first·
Text Printer       Epson·FX, RX & JX/LQ-800,1000 and 1500·
Graph Printer      Epson·FX and RX series




───────────────── Press ESC to continue ─────────────────
```

Figure 2-9
Sample list of
installed drivers

❸ Press **[Esc]** to leave the list and continue.

❹ Select Yes and press **[Enter]** to leave the Install program.

You've now successfully installed 1-2-3.

If Installation Is Not Successful

If you have trouble starting 1-2-3 in Chapter 3 or if you have trouble printing in Tutorial 1, you may have made incorrect choices in your installation. Check your hardware or get help from your instructor or technical support person. Then run through the Install program again. When you restart the Install program, select Change Selected Equipment from the Install main menu and change the screen display or printer selections as appropriate. You should once again save the new driver set as 123.SET.

Chapter 3

A Tour of 1-2-3

You are about to embark on a tour of 1-2-3 and see some of its worksheet, graphics, database, and macro capabilities.

Before you begin, be sure you have initialized 1-2-3 and installed it on your computer, as described in Chapter 2.

Topics

This chapter covers the following topics:

- How to Follow the Numbered Steps in *Lotus 1-2-3 for Business*

- Starting 1-2-3

- The Worksheet

- Moving the Cell Pointer

- Selecting Commands

- Entering Data in a Worksheet

- 1-2-3 Graphics

- Using a 1-2-3 Database

- Running a 1-2-3 Macro

- Using Help

- Quitting 1-2-3

How to Follow the Numbered Steps in
Lotus 1-2-3 for Business

In the *Lotus 1-2-3 for Business* tutorials, you will follow step-by-step instructions. These instructions are displayed as numbered lists on a shaded background, as shown in Figure 3-1. Notice in this figure:

- Boldface indicates keys that you should press.
- Function keys such as **[F2]** are followed by the 1-2-3 key name in parentheses.
- Key combinations, such as **[Alt][F4]**, mean that you press and hold down the first key, and then while holding the first key, you press the second key. You then release both keys.

To use the UNDO command:

❶   Press **[F2]** (Edit).

❷   Press **[Backspace]** three times to erase PAY, the incorrect label.

❸   Type **SALARY**, the correct label, and then press **[Enter]**. The new correct label is now in cell C7. See Figure 1-30.

❹   Press **[Alt][F4]** (Undo) to view the incorrect label once more. Press **[Alt][F4]** (Undo) again to restore the correct label.

❺   Select / File Save (**/FS**) to save the worksheet.

Figure 3-1

Starting 1-2-3

Start your computer. Be certain that the DOS prompt appears. If you are using 1-2-3 in a lab, you might need to ask your instructor or technical support person for instructions.

To start 1-2-3:

❶   If you have a *two-diskette* system, insert the System Disk in drive A. Also insert your working copy of the Data Disk in drive B. Then type **a:** and press **[Enter]**.

If you have a *hard-disk* system, type **cd\123** and press **[Enter]**.

This makes the directory that contains the 1-2-3 program files the current directory.

❷   At the DOS prompt, type **123** and press **[Enter]**.

An introductory screen appears, followed by a blank 1-2-3 worksheet. If the blank worksheet does not appear, your copy of 1-2-3 may not be installed correctly. See the instructions in Chapter 2 or check with your instructor or technical support person.

The Worksheet

The **worksheet** is the basic structure for storing and organizing data in 1-2-3. It is a grid made up of columns and rows (Figure 3-2).

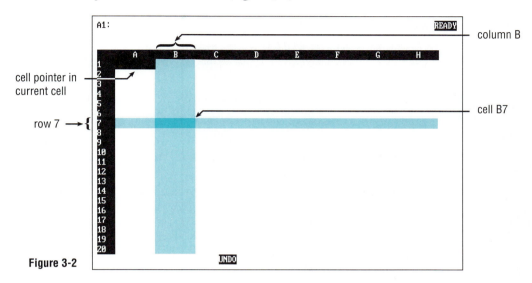

Figure 3-2

A **column** is a vertical section of the grid. Each column is identified by a letter. A **row** is a horizontal section of the grid and is identified by a number. 1-2-3 has 256 columns and 8192 rows. The intersection of a row and a column is called a **cell**. Each cell is named by its column and row. Thus, for example, the intersection of column B and row 7 is cell B7. B7 is called the **cell address**; whenever you specify a cell address, be sure to first name the column letter and then the row number.

Notice the highlighted rectangle in cell A1 in Figure 3-2; this is called the **cell pointer**. The cell pointer indicates the **current cell**, that is, the cell into which you can enter data.

The area at the top of the screen, the **control panel**, gives you information about the worksheet (Figure 3-3). It consists of the status line, the input line, and the menu line. The **status line** shows the location of the cell pointer, that is, the current cell address and what data are in the current cell. It also indicates what mode 1-2-3 is in; for example, when

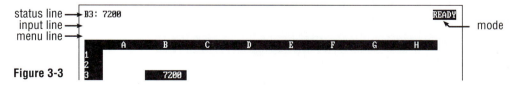

Figure 3-3

1-2-3 is ready for you to type data or enter a command, the mode indicator displays **READY**. The **input line** is immediately below the status line, and it shows you the characters you type in a cell, the command menu, or messages to guide you, also known as **prompts**. Finally, the **menu line**, just below the input line, gives you information about the menu item highlighted whenever 1-2-3 is in MENU mode. The significance of the control panel will become clearer to you as learn more about 1-2-3. For now, remember that understanding the worksheet — its parts and its layout — will help you to use 1-2-3 more efficiently.

Moving the Cell Pointer

You move the cell pointer up, down, left, and right with the pointer-movement keys on your keyboard. Let's try moving the cell pointer one cell at a time and several cells at a time. As you move it within the worksheet, notice how the location of the cell pointer changes in the status line of the control panel.

To move the cell pointer in the worksheet:

❶ Press **[Home]** once to move the cell pointer to A1, if it is not currently in A1.

❷ Press **[→]** once to move the cell pointer to B1.

❸ Press **[↓]** once to move the cell pointer to B2.

❹ Press **[PgDn]** once and then **[PgUp]** once to move the cell pointer down one screen and then up one screen in the worksheet.

❺ Press **[Tab]** once to move the cell pointer right one screen. Press **[Shift][Tab]** to move left one screen. Remember that to use key combinations, such as [Shift][Tab], you press and hold the first key. Then while holding the first key, you press the second key. Then release both.

❻ Press **[End]** once and then press **[↓]** once to move to the last row of the worksheet. The cell pointer should be in cell A8192.

❼ Press **[End]** and then press **[→]** to move to the last column of the worksheet. The cell pointer should be in cell IV8192.

❽ Press **[Home]** to return to cell A1.

Figure 3-4 lists the most commonly used pointer-movement keys.

Key	Moves cell pointer
[→]	Right one cell
[←]	Left one cell
[↓]	Down one cell
[↑]	Up one cell
[Tab]	Right one screen
[Shift] [Tab]	Left one screen
[Ctrl] [→]	Right one screen
[Ctrl] [←]	Left one screen
[Home]	To A1
[PgDn]	Down one screen
[PgUp]	Up one screen

Figure 3-4
Commonly used pointer-movement keys

Selecting Commands

A **command** is an instruction you give 1-2-3 to accomplish a specific task. In 1-2-3 you always press the slash key (/) first when you issue a command. Take a second now to locate the slash key in the lower right corner of your keyboard. Whenever you press the slash key, the command menu appears in the control panel. Then you select a command from the menu.

There are two ways to select a command. You can type the first letter or character of the command, or you can press [→], [←], [Home], or [End] to move the **menu pointer**, the rectangular highlight, to the command and then press [Enter] to select it. Selecting commands by highlighting takes a little more time, but it allows you to view more information about each highlighted command in the menu line. This is especially useful if you are unfamiliar with 1-2-3.

Let's practice using each of these two methods for selecting commands by issuing a very common command in 1-2-3 — the command to retrieve a file. To retrieve a data file, you first specify which drive or directory contains the file. As you work through these next steps, remember that you can press [Esc] to back up one step if you make a mistake.

To specify the current data directory:

❶ Press **[/]** (Slash) to display the main menu. See Figure 3-5.

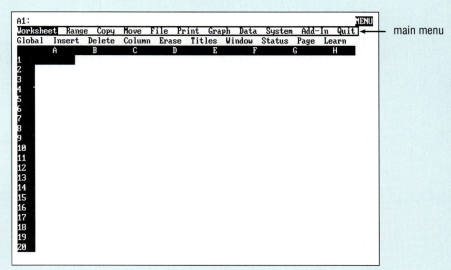

main menu

Figure 3-5
The 1-2-3 main menu

❷ Press **[→]** four times to highlight File. As you do, notice how the menu line in the control panel changes.

❸ Press **[Enter]** to select File and display the File menu. See Figure 3-6.

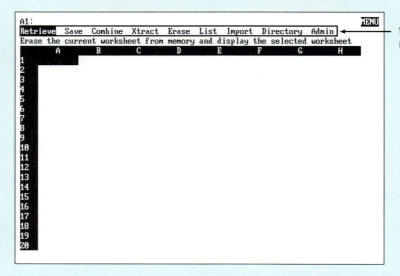

file commands on
menu line

Figure 3-6
The File command
menu

❹ Notice on the menu that the next to last command is Directory. Type **d**, the first letter of Directory, to select it. A prompt then appears on the input line of the control panel.

❺ If you are using a *two-diskette* system, type **b**:. If you are using a different drive for the Data Disk, type the letter for the drive you are using. Then press **[Enter]**.

If you are using a *hard-disk* system, type **c:\123\data** or the drive letter and directory name where you copied your *Lotus 1-2-3 for Business* Data Disk in Chapter 2. Then press **[Enter]**.

The prompt and the menu disappear, and the READY mode indicator appears in the upper right corner of your screen.

You are now ready to issue the File Retrieve command. This command lets you bring onto the screen worksheet files that are stored on the Data Disk or on your hard disk so you can view and work with them.

To retrieve a file:

❶ Press **[/]** to display the main menu.

❷ Select File (**F**) either by using the pointer-movement keys to highlight File and then pressing **[Enter]**, or by pressing **F**.

❸ Select Retrieve (**R**).

A menu of worksheet filenames from the drive or directory you specified appears on the menu line of the control panel.

❹ The highlight is on the first file, ATOUR-1.WK1. To select it, press **[Enter]**.

The worksheet file ATOUR-1.WK1 appears on the screen. This worksheet contains a company's quarterly and year-to-date sales in five international cities. Let's now take a tour of this worksheet and view its data.

To view data in the worksheet:

❶ Press [→] and [↓] as needed to move the cell pointer to B6. Notice that the control panel displays the value contained in B6.

❷ Press [↓] until the cell pointer is in B12.

Notice that the control panel shows @SUM(B6..B10) as the contents of the current cell. @SUM is a special 1-2-3 function, or built-in formula, that performs calculations. In this case, @SUM adds the contents of cells B6 through B10 and displays the total in cell B12.

❸ Press **[End]** and then **[Home]** to move the cell pointer to the end of the data area.

This very useful key combination moves the cell pointer to the lower right corner of the worksheet area that contains data.

❹ Press **[Home]** to return to cell A1.

Entering Data in a Worksheet

You enter data in a worksheet by moving the cell pointer to a cell, typing the data, and pressing [Enter]. As you type, the mode indicator changes to LABEL or VALUE, depending on how 1-2-3 interprets what you type. In 1-2-3, text or words are called **labels**. Numbers and formulas are called **values**.

Let's practice entering some data. You will change the data of cell C10 from $400,000 to $350,000. You will then see how 1-2-3 updates the totals automatically. If you make any typing errors and have not yet pressed [Enter], use [Backspace] to erase characters to the left of the cursor. If you have already pressed [Enter], move the cell pointer to the cell with the error. Then retype the entry and press [Enter].

To enter data:

❶ Before you enter any new data, notice that the value in cell C12 is $1,470,000 and that the year-to-date total in cell F12 is $6,450,000.

❷ Move the cell pointer to cell C10.

❸ Type **350000** (four zeros but no comma).

Notice that 1-2-3 displays what you type in the control panel.

④ Press **[Enter]** and watch how 1-2-3 recalculates all totals that depend on the new value, as shown in Figure 3-7.

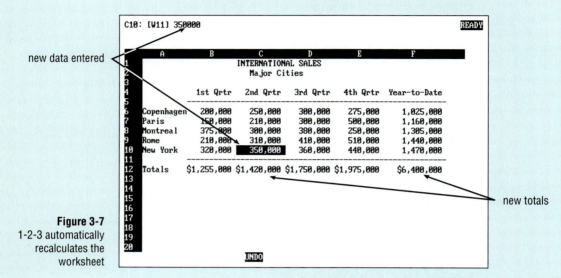

new data entered

Figure 3-7
1-2-3 automatically
recalculates the
worksheet

new totals

1-2-3 adjusts the first-quarter total in C12 to $1,420,000 and the year-to-date total in F12 to $6,400,000. If 1-2-3 does not adjust the totals on your worksheet, try pressing [F9] (Calc) to recalculate the totals.

1-2-3 Graphics

Whenever you use graphs or charts to present information, you are using **graphics**. Graphing or charting data in the worksheet helps you understand the relationships among the data and helps you analyze your results. Let's tour a few of the types of 1-2-3 graphics that you will learn how to create in the tutorials. Remember that for you to view these graphics, your computer system must have a graphics adapter.

To view a graph of this worksheet's data:

❶ Select /Graph (**/G**) to view the Graph menu and a form called the **graph settings sheet**. See Figure 3-8.

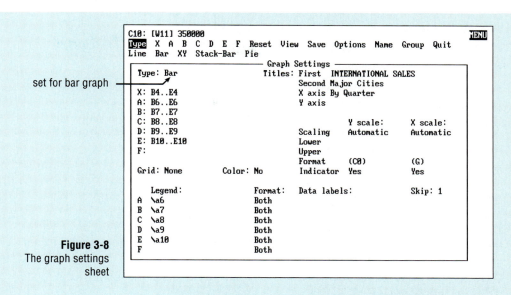

set for bar graph →

Figure 3-8
The graph settings
sheet

Notice on the sheet that the current graph settings are for a bar graph.

❷ Select View (**V**) to display the graph. See Figure 3-9.

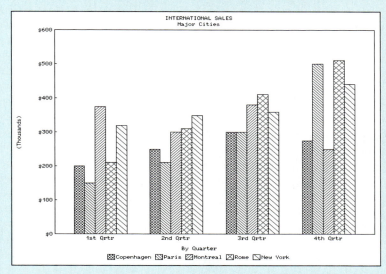

Figure 3-9
A bar graph of the
worksheet data

❸ Press [**Esc**] to return to the Graph menu and the graph settings sheet.

With 1-2-3, you can create several types of graphs, including bar graphs, pie charts, stacked bar graphs, and line graphs. You can add titles and legends to enhance the appearance and readability of your graphs.

Now let's see how easy it is to create a different type of graphic using the same worksheet data.

To view a stacked bar graph of this worksheet's data:

❶   Select Type and then select Stack-Bar (**TS**).

❷   Select View (**V**) to display the new graph.

❸   When you are ready, press **[Esc]** to return to the Graph menu.

With 1-2-3, you can name different graphs of the same worksheet's data so that you can later view or print these graphs.

To view a list of graphs created for this worksheet's data:

❶   Select Name Use (**NU**) to display a list of other graphs of this worksheet's data.

❷   Select PIE1 if you have a monochrome monitor or PIE2 if you have a color monitor. See Figure 3-10.

This pie chart compares the first-quarter totals of each city, presenting each total as a percent of the pie.

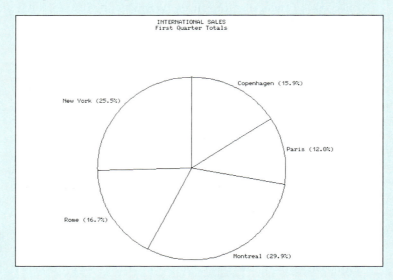

Figure 3-10
A pie chart of the
worksheet data

❸   When you are ready, press **[Esc]** to return to the Graph menu and select Quit (**Q**) to quit this menu and return to the worksheet.

Using a 1-2-3 Database

A **database** is an organized collection of data. Examples of business databases are a list of customers and the status of their accounts; employee information, such as social security number, salary, and job title; and inventory information, such as stock numbers, quantity in stock, color, and so on. In a list of customers, for example, all of the data about each customer is called a **record**, and each individual fact about each customer — name, paid status, invoice number, and so on — is called a **field**. In 1-2-3 the columns correspond to the fields and the rows correspond to the records.

Suppose you wanted to create a list of customers owing money and you wanted to arrange them in order from those owing the most to those owing the least. 1-2-3 can perform several database tasks, such as sorting, to help you organize your data.

To sort a database:

❶   Select /File Retrieve (**/FR**).

❷   Highlight the file, ATOUR-2.WK1, and press **[Enter]**. Notice that this file contains a database of accounts receivable with paid and unpaid invoice amounts. See Figure 3-11.

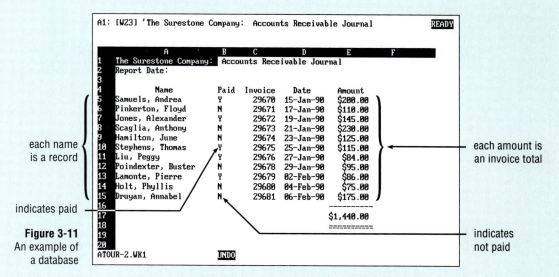

each name is a record

indicates paid

Figure 3-11
An example of a database

each amount is an invoice total

indicates not paid

Each record in this database (from row 5 through row 15) has a number in the Amount field (column E) that represents an invoice total. 1-2-3 can sort these amounts to determine who owes the most money.

❸   Select /Data Sort (**/DS**).

1-2-3 displays a settings sheet into which you can enter the sort instructions. In the Sort settings sheet, Primary-Key indicates which field 1-2-3 should use to sort the database. In our example, we want the Primary-Key field to be the Amount field in column E and the Sort-Order setting to be Descending, which instructs 1-2-3 to sort all of the amounts from the largest to the smallest value. See Figure 3-12 on the next page.

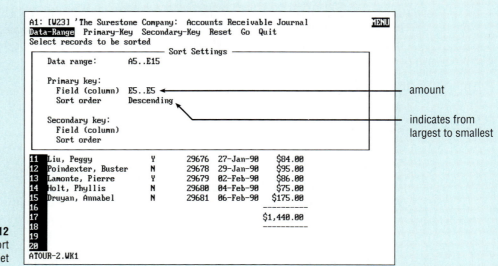

```
A1: [W23] 'The Surestone Company:  Accounts Receivable Journal      MENU
Data-Range  Primary-Key  Secondary-Key  Reset  Go  Quit
Select records to be sorted
                            ┌──── Sort Settings ─────
    Data range:       A5..E15

    Primary key:
      Field (column)  E5..E5  ◄─────────────────────────────   amount
      Sort order      Descending

    Secondary key:                                             indicates from
      Field (column)                                           largest to smallest
      Sort order
```

```
11  Liu, Peggy          Y      29676  27-Jan-90    $84.00
12  Poindexter, Buster  N      29678  29-Jan-90    $95.00
13  Lamonte, Pierre     Y      29679  02-Feb-90    $86.00
14  Holt, Phyllis       N      29680  04-Feb-90    $75.00
15  Druyan, Annabel     N      29681  06-Feb-90   $175.00
16                                               ──────────
17                                               $1,440.00
18                                               ──────────
19
20
ATOUR-2.WK1
```

Figure 3-12
The Data Sort
settings sheet

❹ Select Go (**G**).

Watch how quickly 1-2-3 sorts the database according to the invoice amounts in
descending order, from largest to smallest. It saves you time and energy and can
be a valuable decision-making tool.

Running a 1-2-3 Macro

With 1-2-3 you can create and store *sets* of commands and key strokes called **macro
instructions** or **macros**. Macros automate repetitive 1-2-3 tasks, such as entering a date in
your worksheet. Suppose, for example, that you must create a weekly report of all customers
who have not paid invoices over $100. Once you have created a macro for this task, you can
generate the report automatically each week by running the macro.

To run a macro:

1 Press **[Alt][F3]** (Run) to begin.

The names of several macros in this worksheet appear. See Figure 3-13.

names of macros →

Figure 3-13

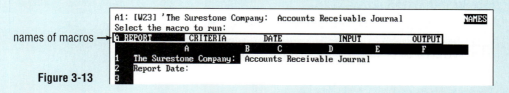

```
A1: [W23] 'The Surestone Company:  Accounts Receivable Journal      NAMES
Select the macro to run:
A_REPORT        CRITERIA        DATE            INPUT           OUTPUT
            A               B     C         D               E       F
1    The Surestone Company: Accounts Receivable Journal
2    Report Date:
3
```

2 Press **[→]** twice to move the menu pointer to DATE, then press **[Enter]**.

The DATE macro runs, automatically entering the date in cell D2 of your worksheet. Next let's generate the report.

3 Press **[Alt][F3]** (Run).

4 Since A_REPORT is already highlighted, press **[Enter]** to run this macro.

The A_REPORT macro compares the amount of each invoice to a specified amount, in this case, $100. 1-2-3 then creates a list of the customers who owe more than $100. See Figure 3-14.

Figure 3-14
Records with a
value of more than
$100 in the
amount field

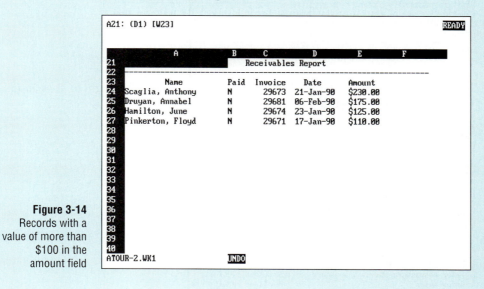

```
A21: (D1) [W23]                                                   READY

                A           B    C        D          E       F
21                              Receivables Report
22    ---------------------------------------------------------------
23              Name       Paid Invoice   Date      Amount
24    Scaglia, Anthony     N    29673   21-Jan-90   $230.00
25    Druyan, Annabel      N    29681   06-Feb-90   $175.00
26    Hamilton, June       N    29674   23-Jan-90   $125.00
27    Pinkerton, Floyd     N    29671   17-Jan-90   $110.00
28
29
30
31
32
33
34
35
36
37
38
39
40
ATOUR-2.WK1              UNDO
```

Using Help

You can press [F1] (Help) at any time while you are using 1-2-3 to get helpful information on a variety of topics. When a Help screen appears, the worksheet on which you are working temporarily disappears.

To use Help:

❶ If you are using a 5¼-inch *two-diskette* system, insert the Help Disk in drive A. If you are using a hard-disk system, go to Step 2.

❷ Press **[F1]** (Help).

1-2-3 displays the Help Index. See Figure 3-15.

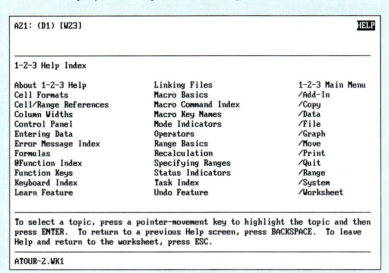

```
A21: (D1) [W23]                                                      HELP
 ───────────────────────────────────────────────────────────────────────
 1-2-3 Help Index

 About 1-2-3 Help         Linking Files              1-2-3 Main Menu
 Cell Formats             Macro Basics               /Add-In
 Cell/Range References    Macro Command Index        /Copy
 Column Widths            Macro Key Names            /Data
 Control Panel            Mode Indicators            /File
 Entering Data            Operators                  /Graph
 Error Message Index      Range Basics               /Move
 Formulas                 Recalculation              /Print
 @Function Index          Specifying Ranges          /Quit
 Function Keys            Status Indicators          /Range
 Keyboard Index           Task Index                 /System
 Learn Feature            Undo Feature               /Worksheet
 ───────────────────────────────────────────────────────────────────────
 To select a topic, press a pointer-movement key to highlight the topic and then
 press ENTER.  To return to a previous Help screen, press BACKSPACE.  To leave
 Help and return to the worksheet, press ESC.
 ───────────────────────────────────────────────────────────────────────
 ATOUR-2.WK1
```

Figure 3-15
The Help Index

❸ Use the pointer-movement keys to move the rectangular highlight to Task Index and press **[Enter]**. See Figure 3-16.

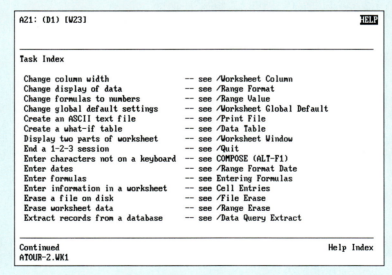

```
A21: (D1) [W23]                                                      HELP
 ───────────────────────────────────────────────────────────────────────
 Task Index

 Change column width              -- see /Worksheet Column
 Change display of data           -- see /Range Format
 Change formulas to numbers       -- see /Range Value
 Change global default settings   -- see /Worksheet Global Default
 Create an ASCII text file        -- see /Print File
 Create a what-if table           -- see /Data Table
 Display two parts of worksheet   -- see /Worksheet Window
 End a 1-2-3 session              -- see /Quit
 Enter characters not on a keyboard -- see COMPOSE (ALT-F1)
 Enter dates                      -- see /Range Format Date
 Enter formulas                   -- see Entering Formulas
 Enter information in a worksheet  -- see Cell Entries
 Erase a file on disk             -- see /File Erase
 Erase worksheet data             -- see /Range Erase
 Extract records from a database  -- see /Data Query Extract
 ───────────────────────────────────────────────────────────────────────
 Continued                                              Help Index
 ATOUR-2.WK1
```

Figure 3-16
Help Screen for
Task Index

1-2-3 displays a Help screen. On the left is a list of tasks you might want to do and on the right are the corresponding 1-2-3 commands. This Task Index is very useful when you are first learning 1-2-3.

④ Move the highlight to one of the commands and press **[Enter]** to display additional help.

⑤ When you are ready, press **[Esc]** to return to the worksheet.

1-2-3 Help is *context sensitive*. This means that if you press [F1] (Help) while you are performing a particular task, you will get Help on that task.

To see how Help is context-sensitive:

❶ Select /File Retrieve (**/FR**) and then press **[F1]** (Help).

1-2-3 displays a Help screen with detailed information about the File Retrieve command. You can use the pointer-movement keys to move to any of the highlighted words and press [Enter] to learn more.

❷ When you are ready, press **[Esc]** to quit Help.

❸ Because you won't be completing the File Retrieve command, press **[Esc]** until READY appears in the upper right corner of the screen.

Quitting 1-2-3

You have completed the tour of 1-2-3. Now it's time to learn how to end, or quit, a 1-2-3 session.

To quit 1-2-3:

❶ Select /Quit Yes (**/QY**).

If you have entered data into the worksheet or changed the data, a prompt appears asking if you want to quit without saving your changes. If this happens, select Yes (**Y**) again to quit without saving.

Part Two . . .

Tutorials

Tutorial 1

Creating a Worksheet

Preparing a Simple Payroll

Case: Krier Marine Services

Vince Diorio is an Information Systems major at the University of Rhode Island. To help pay for his tuition, he works part-time three days a week at a nearby marina, Krier Marine Services. Vince works in the Krier business office, and his responsibilities range from making coffee to keeping the company's books.

Objectives

In this tutorial you will learn to:

- Retrieve and save files

- Enter numbers, labels, and formulas

- Correct mistakes and erase entries

- Edit entries and use the UNDO key

- Define a range

- Print a worksheet

- Erase a worksheet

Recently, Jim and Marcia Krier, the owners of the marina, asked Vince if he could help them computerize the payroll for their four part-time employees. They explained to Vince that the employees work a different number of hours each week for different rates of pay. Marcia does the payroll manually and finds it time consuming. Moreover, whenever she makes errors, she is embarrassed and is annoyed at having to take additional time to correct them. Jim and Marcia hope that Vince can help them.

Vince immediately agrees to help. He tells the Kriers that he knows how to use Lotus 1-2-3 and that he can build a spreadsheet that will save Marcia time and reduce errors.

Vince does not begin working with the 1-2-3 software immediately. He knows that effective worksheets are well planned and carefully designed. So, he sits down and follows a process he learned in his courses at school.

Planning the Worksheet

Planning the worksheet first is a good habit to establish. If you plan first, your worksheet will be clear, accurate, and useful. Your plan will guide you as you try to solve business problems using 1-2-3.

You can divide your planning into four phases:

- Defining the problem
- Designing the worksheet
- Building the worksheet
- Testing the worksheet

Defining the Problem

Begin by outlining what you want to accomplish. Take a piece of paper and pencil and do the following:

1. List your goal(s).

2. Identify and list the results you want to see in the worksheet. This information is often called *output*.

3. Identify and write down the information you want to put into the worksheet. This information is often called *input*.

4. Determine and list the calculations that will produce the results you desire. These calculations become the *formulas* you will use in the worksheet.

When you finish, you will have completed the first phase of planning. You will have defined the problem and be ready to design the worksheet. Figure 1-1a shows how Vince defined the Krier payroll problem.

Figure 1-1a
Vince's planning sheet

My Goal(s):
   Develop a worksheet that calculates the
   Krier Marine Services payroll.

What results do I want to see?
   Weekly Payroll Report

What information do I need?
   Employee name
   Number of hours each employee worked
   during the week
   Employee's rate of pay per hour

What calculations will I perform?
   Gross pay for each employee

Designing the Worksheet

Next, on a piece of paper, sketch what you think the worksheet should look like. Include titles, row and column headings, totals, and other items of the worksheet. Figure 1-1b shows Vince's sketch.

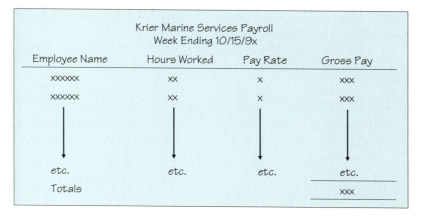

Figure 1-1b
Vince's sketch

Building the Worksheet

After defining the problem and sketching the worksheet, you are ready to type your worksheet design into 1-2-3. You enter titles, labels, formulas, input, and other items you listed and sketched when you defined your goal(s) and designed the worksheet.

Testing the Worksheet

After you have built a new worksheet, you should test it before you start to use it. If possible, develop some sample data, also known as test data, and manually calculate the results. Then put the same test data into your 1-2-3 worksheet. Are the results the same? If you discover any differences, you should find the reason(s) and correct any errors in the worksheet.

After completing this fourth phase, you are ready to begin using the worksheet.

■   ■   ■

In Tutorial 1, you will use Vince's problem definition and sketch (Figures 1-1a and 1-1b) as a guide when you build the worksheet for the Krier Marine Services payroll. You will create the worksheet that Vince developed for the Kriers. First you will retrieve a partially completed worksheet, which will serve as your starting point. Next you will enter the payroll data, employee names, hours worked, and rates of pay. Then you will enter formulas to calculate total gross pay for each employee. Finally you will calculate the gross pay for all employees. When the worksheet is complete, you will learn how to print and save it.

Retrieving the Worksheet

Before you begin, be sure you have completed the activities in Part 1, Chapter 2, "Preparing to Use 1-2-3." You will retrieve a file from your working copy of the *Lotus 1-2-3 for Business* Data Disk. The file from which you work will be on either a diskette copy of Data Disk or a copy of the files that you copied onto your hard disk. If you want to start over for any reason, such as to recover from a mistake, retrieve C1FILE1.WK1 again and repeat the steps. You will learn how to correct mistakes as you work through this tutorial.

To retrieve a 1-2-3 worksheet file:

❶   If your data are on a diskette, insert the diskette into the drive you specified in Part 1, Chapter 2, "Preparing to Use 1-2-3." If your data are on the hard disk, go to Step 2.

❷   Start 1-2-3 as you learned in Chapter 3.

❸   Press **/** (Slash) to activate the 1-2-3 main menu, which shows a list of commands you may choose. See Figure 1-2.

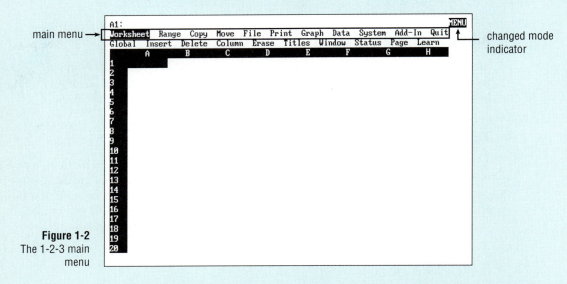

main menu →

changed mode indicator

Figure 1-2
The 1-2-3 main menu

The mode indicator in the upper right corner has changed from READY to MENU and a command menu appears on the second and third lines of the control panel. The second line lists the main actions or commands from which you may select. The third line, or submenu, lists the commands available if you select the command currently highlighted in the second line.

There are two ways to select a command from the command line:

• You can highlight a menu choice by pressing [→] or [←] to move the highlight to the command you want and press [Enter].

- You can type the first character of the command you wish to select. For example, to select File you type F.

❹ Select File (**F**). The choices available from the File Menu now appear on the second line of the control panel. See Figure 1-3.

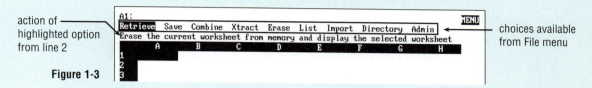

action of highlighted option from line 2

choices available from File menu

Figure 1-3

❺ Select Retrieve (**R**) to display the names of some of the worksheet files in the control panel. The top of your screen should look similar to Figure 1-4.

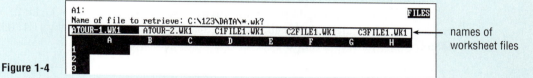

names of worksheet files

Figure 1-4

If the filenames do not appear press [Esc] to rearturn to READY mode and see page 78 for assistance. Also if you accidentally press the wrong key and select the wrong command from the menu, you can return to the previous step by pressing the [Esc] key. If you continue to press [Esc], you back up a step at a time until you return to READY mode.

❻ Using the [→] or [←] key, highlight the worksheet file C1FILE1.WK1. Then press **[Enter]**. 1-2-3 retrieves the file you selected. See Figure 1-5.

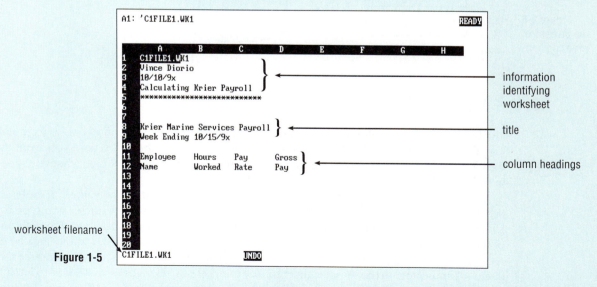

information identifying worksheet

title

column headings

worksheet filename

Figure 1-5

If the filename does not appear in the lower left corner of the screen, see page 78 for assistance.

The worksheet file you retrieved contains the beginning of the worksheet that Vince plans to use in developing the payroll worksheet. Currently, the worksheet consists of a title and descriptive column headings. These headings represent the data he will enter or calculate.

You no doubt have noticed that beginning in cell A1 there are four lines of identifying information:

- the name of the worksheet file
- the name of the person who developed the worksheet
- the date the worksheet was created or last modified
- a description of the worksheet.

You should include such a section of identifying information in *every* worksheet you develop, to remind you about what the worksheet contains.

To help you understand what occurs when you retrieve a worksheet file, look at Figure 1-6. When you select File Retrieve and then select the worksheet file C1FILE1.WK1, 1-2-3 copies the worksheet file from the disk to the computer's memory. C1FILE1.WK1 is, therefore, in both the computer memory and disk storage.

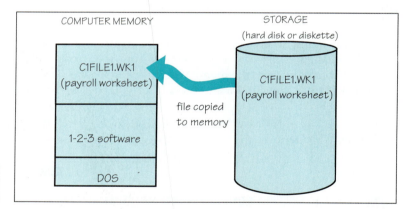

Figure 1-6
The process of
retrieving a file

Entering Labels

Most of the data you enter into a worksheet will be descriptive text, numbers, or formulas. To enter data into a worksheet, you move the cell pointer to the cell where you want the data to appear. You then type the data and press the [Enter] key. 1-2-3 stores what you typed in the cell.

1-2-3 categorizes all entries you type in a cell as either labels or values. **Labels** are descriptive text such as column headings or textual data. If the first character you type is a letter, 1-2-3 assumes you are entering a label in that cell. Also, if you begin typing with one of the four special characters ' " ^ \, 1-2-3 will store any characters that follow as a label. As soon as you begin entering a letter or one of these special characters, you'll notice that the mode indicator, in the upper right corner of your screen, changes from READY to LABEL.

The next step in developing Vince's worksheet is to enter the names of the Krier part-time employees. These entries are labels.

To enter an employee name:

❶   Press [↓] to move the cell pointer to cell A14.

❷   Type **Bramble**. Before you press [Enter], look at the top left of the screen. See Figure 1-7.

Bramble appears in control panel but not yet in cell A14

mode indicator

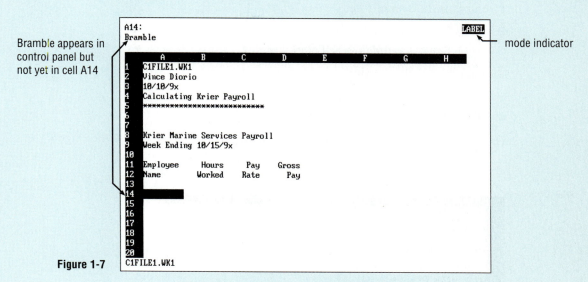

Figure 1-7

Notice that Bramble appears in the control panel but not in cell A14. Also notice that the mode indicator in the upper right corner of your screen has changed from READY to LABEL mode. This is because when you typed the letter B, 1-2-3 recognized that the entry was a label.

❸   Press **[Enter]**. Bramble now appears in cell A14. See Figure 1-8.

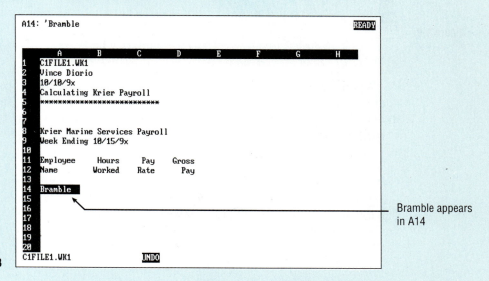

Bramble appears in A14

Figure 1-8

When you press the [Enter] key, the cell pointer remains in cell A14.

To enter the name of the second employee:

❹ Press [↓] once to move the cell pointer to cell A15.

❺ Type **Juarez** and then press **[Enter]**.

To enter the third employee:

❻ Press [↓] once to move the cell pointer to cell A16.

❼ Type **Smith** and then press **[Enter]**.

To enter the fourth employee:

❽ Press [↓] once to move the cell pointer to cell A17.

❾ Type **Diorio** and then press **[Enter]**.

The names of the four employees should now appear on your worksheet. See Figure 1-9.

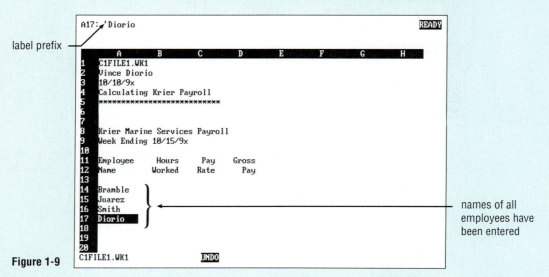

label prefix

names of all employees have been entered

Figure 1-9

When the cell pointer is in a cell that contains a label, the control panel displays the cell address, an apostrophe, and the label you entered. See Figure 1-9. The apostrophe before the label is called a **label prefix**. 1-2-3 automatically enters a label prefix whenever you enter labels in a worksheet.

Correcting Errors

The following steps show you two of the many ways to correct errors you make when you are entering text or numbers.

To correct errors as you are typing:

❶ Move the cell pointer to A16 and type **Smiht** but do not press [Enter]. Clearly this label is misspelled. Since you haven't pressed [Enter], you can use [Backspace] to correct the error. On most keyboards, this key is above the [Enter] key.

❷ Press **[Backspace]** twice to erase the last two characters you typed.

❸ Type the correct text — **th** — and press **[Enter]**.

If you notice an error any time *after* the text or value appears in the cell, you can correct the error by retyping the entry.

To correct errors in a cell:

❶ Be sure the cell pointer is in cell A16 and type **Smiht.** Press **[Enter]**. Smiht appears in cell A16. See Figure 1-10.

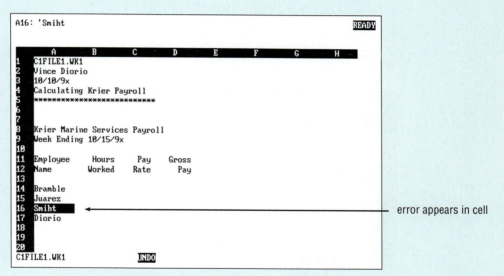

error appears in cell

Figure 1-10

❷ Type **Smith** in cell A16 and press **[Enter]**. As you can see, 1-2-3 enters the new text over the old. This is commonly called *typing over*.

Entering Values

A value in 1-2-3 can be a number or a formula. 1-2-3 interprets an entry in a cell as a **value** if the first character you type is a number (0 through 9) or one of the special characters + − @ . (# $. As soon as you begin entering a number or one of these special characters, you'll notice that the mode indicator changes from READY to VALUE.

Next, enter the hours worked by each employee at Krier Marine Services.

To enter the hours worked:

❶ Move the cell pointer to cell B14, the location of Bramble's hours worked.

Bramble worked 15 hours.

❷ Type **15** and press **[Enter]**. Do not include any symbols or punctuation, such as a dollar sign or a comma, when entering values.

❸ Press **[↓]** once to move the cell pointer to cell B15, the location of Juarez's hours worked. Juarez worked 28 hours.

❹ Type **28** and press **[Enter]**.

Smith worked 40 hours.

❺ Press **[↓]** once to move the cell pointer to cell B16, the location of Smith's hours worked.

❻ Type **40** and press **[Enter]**.

Diorio worked 22 hours.

❼ Press **[↓]** to move the cell pointer to cell B17, the location of Diorio's hours worked.

❽ Type **22** and press **[Enter]**. Your screen should look like Figure 1-11.

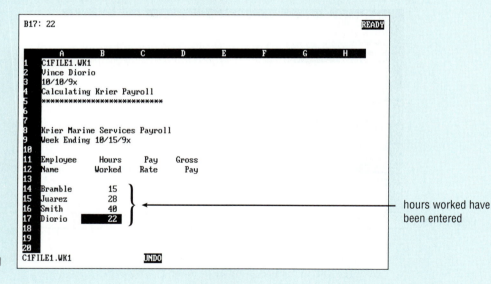

Figure 1-11

hours worked have been entered

There is another, faster way to enter data. You can enter data in a cell and move the cell pointer to a cell on any side of that cell in one step by pressing a pointer-movement key instead of [Enter]. The **pointer-movement keys** are the directional keys, such as [→], [←], [↑], [↓], [PgDn], and [PgUp] which you press to move the pointer in the worksheet. To learn how to do this, let's enter the hourly pay rates for each employee.

To enter hourly pay rates using pointer-movement keys:

❶ Move the cell pointer to C14, the location of Bramble's pay rate.

Bramble earns $7 an hour.

❷ Type **7** and press **[↓]** instead of the [Enter] key. Notice that you entered the value in cell C14 and moved the cell pointer to cell C15, the cell immediately below C14. C15 is the location of Juarez's pay rate.

Juarez earns $5 an hour.

❸ With the cell pointer in C15, type **5** and press **[↓]**.

Smith earns $7 an hour.

❹ In cell C16 type **7** and press **[↓]**.

Diorio earns $5 an hour.

❺ In cell C17 type **5** and press **[Enter]**. You have now entered all the data. Your worksheet should be similar to Figure 1-12.

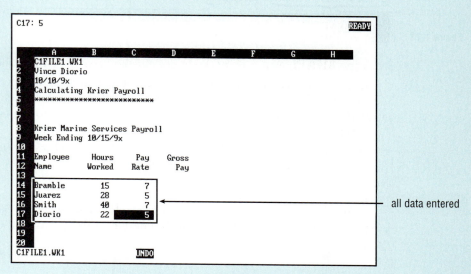

Figure 1-12

Saving a Worksheet

When you create or modify a worksheet, it is only temporarily stored in the computer's memory. To store your work permanently, you must save the worksheet to your hard disk or data diskette. It is always a good idea to save frequently as you work, rather than waiting until you've finished. Suppose the power goes out or you step away from your computer and someone starts working with another file. Unless you have been saving as you go along, all of your work could be lost.

Next we'll save all the entries you have made so far to a new file named, S1FILE1.WK1. Before you save the file you should change cell A1 to S1FILE1.WK1 so the identifying information in the worksheet will be consistent with the new filename.

To change the filename in cell A1 and the save the file:

❶ Press **[Home]** to move the cell pointer to cell A1.

❷ Type **S1FILE1.WK1** and press **[Enter]**.

❸ Select /File Save (**/FS**). Notice that the mode indicator in the upper right corner changes to EDIT. See Figure 1-13.

   1-2-3 prompts you for a filename in the control panel. It also shows the current filename, and the drive from which you retrieved the file.

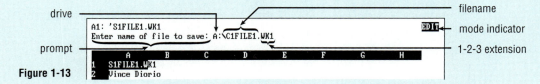

drive ──── filename ──── mode indicator ──── 1-2-3 extension

prompt

Figure 1-13

❹ Type **S1FILE1**. Notice that you do not have to erase the current filename.

   In 1-2-3, all filenames must consist of not more than eight characters. You can use uppercase or lowercase letters, numbers, and the special characters $ & % ( ) { } – _ to create a filename. 1-2-3 converts any lowercase letters to uppercase letters once you press [Enter]. You cannot use spaces in a filename.

❺ Press **[Enter]** to save the file in the drive and directory you specified. 1-2-3 will automatically add the file extension .WK1 to the filename.

Figure 1-14 shows the process that occurs when you select File Save and type S1FILE1. 1-2-3 copies the worksheet file from the computer's memory to your disk storage.

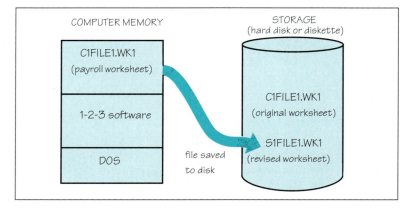

Figure 1-14
The process of saving a file

You have now saved your worksheet, including all the employee data you entered. If you previously saved this file with the name S1FILE1 and now see the prompt "Cancel Replace Backup," select Replace (R) to replace the previous version of this file.

Worksheet Filenames in *Lotus 1-2-3 for Business*

Besides saving frequently, another good habit to follow is to use descriptive names that will help you identify the contents of your files. Worksheet filenames can contain up to eight characters. These characters can be letters, numbers, and all symbols except for spaces, commas, colons, and asterisks. Although eight characters do not often allow you to create complete names, you can create meaningful abbreviations. For example, the Data Disk for *Lotus 1-2-3 for Business* contains over 50 files. To name these files so that you can recognize their contents, we categorized them as follows:

File Category	Description
Tutorial Case	The files you use to work through each tutorial
Tutorial Assignment	The files that contain the worksheets you need to complete the Tutorial Assignments at the end of each tutorial
Case Problem	The files that contain the worksheets you need to complete the Case Problems at the end of each tutorial or the Additional Cases in Part 3
Saved Worksheet	Any worksheet that you have saved

We used these categories to help name the worksheet files on your Data Disk. Let's take the filename C1FILE1, for example. This name may appear to have no meaning, but it does contain meaningful abbreviations. The first character of every worksheet filename on your Data Disk identifies the file as one of the four file categories discussed above. Thus,

If the first character is:	the file category is:
C	Tutorial **C**ase
T	**T**utorial Assignment
P	Case **P**roblem
S	**S**aved Worksheet

Based on these categories, we know that the file C1FILE1 is a Tutorial Case file.

The second character of every worksheet file identifies the tutorial from which the file comes. Thus, C1FILE1 is a Tutorial Case from Tutorial 1. The remaining six characters of the filename identify the specific file. All worksheets in tutorials are named FILE, and the number that follows the name FILE indicates a version number. Thus, C1FILE1 is the first Tutorial Case worksheet from Tutorial 1. T1FILE1 is the first worksheet found in the Tutorial Assignments from Tutorial 1, while T1FILE2 is a second version of this worksheet. As another example, P1TOYS is the filename of the Case Problem "Sales in Toyland" from Tutorial 1. Remember also that when you save a file, 1-2-3 automatically adds a three-character extension to the filename. In *Lotus 1-2-3 for Business* the extension for your saved files will always be WK1.

Entering Formulas

Next you will calculate the gross pay for each employee. To calculate gross pay, you use a formula. A formula is an entry in a worksheet that performs a calculation. Formulas normally refer to data stored in other cells. To use the cell-referencing capability of 1-2-3, you include in the formula the addresses of the cells holding the values you want to calculate. For example, if you enter the formula +B14+B15 in cell B19, 1-2-3 adds the value in cell B14 to the value in cell B15 and places the result in cell B19.

Using formulas is one way to tap into the power of a spreadsheet like 1-2-3. Once you have entered a formula, you can make changes to your data and get the new results immediately.

Now let's calculate the gross pay for each employee. Gross pay is the number of hours worked multiplied by the rate of pay (hours worked × rate of pay). You do not need to do the multiplication yourself; you enter a formula, such as +B14*C14, that tells 1-2-3 which cells to multiply. The [*] (Asterisk) represents multiplication. 1-2-3 performs the calculations immediately and displays the results in the cell containing the formula. The following steps show you one way to enter a formula:

To enter a formula to compute Bramble's gross pay:

❶ Move the cell pointer to cell D14, the location of Bramble's gross pay.

❷ Type **+B14*C14**. The plus sign is one symbol you can use to indicate to 1-2-3 that you are entering a formula and not a label.

Notice that the formula appears in the control panel as you type and that 1-2-3 is now in VALUE mode. See Figure 1-15. Remember, if you make a mistake, you can use [Backspace] if you are still entering the formula, or you can retype the formula if you have pressed [Enter].

formula to calculate Bramble's gross pay

mode has changed

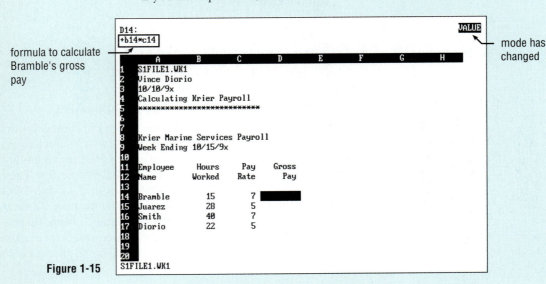

Figure 1-15

❸ Press **[Enter]**. 1-2-3 calculates the formula's value, 105, and the result appears in cell D14. If you get a different result, check the formula or the data values in B14 and C14. Retype, if you find any errors. See Figure 1-16.

formula appears in control panel

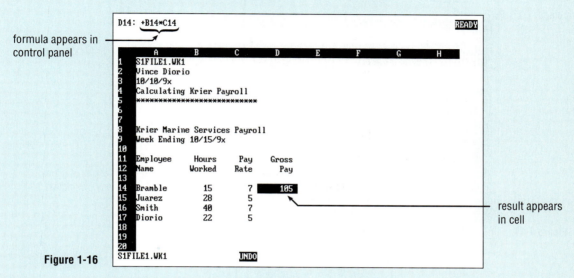

result appears in cell

Figure 1-16

Now enter the formula in cell D15 to calculate Juarez's gross pay.

❹ Move the cell pointer to cell D15. Type **+B15*C15** and press **[Enter]**. The result, 140, appears in cell D15.

Now enter the formula in cell D16 to calculate Smith's gross pay.

❺ Move the cell pointer to cell D16, type **+B16*C16**, and press **[Enter]**. The gross pay for Smith is 280, which appears in cell D16.

Finally, enter the formula in cell D17 to calculate Diorio's gross pay.

❻ Move the cell pointer to cell D17, type **+B17*C17**, and press **[Enter]**. Diorio's pay is 110, which appears in cell D17.

Figure 1-17 shows the gross pay calculated for all the employees.

formula for D17

results of gross pay calculation

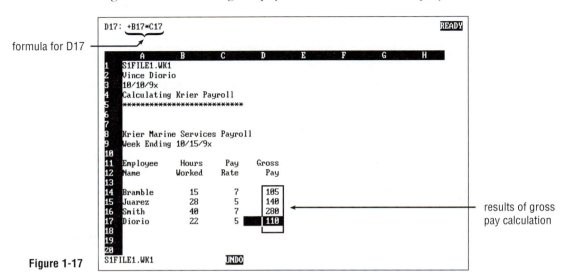

Figure 1-17

Calculating a Sum

Now let's calculate the total gross pay for all employees by adding the gross pay of Bramble, Juarez, Smith, and Diorio, that is, adding the values of cells D14, D15, D16, and D17.

To calculate a sum:

❶ Move the cell pointer to cell A19. Type the label **Totals** and press **[Enter]**.

❷ Move the cell pointer to D19. This is the cell in which we want to put the total gross pay.

The correct formula to calculate gross pay is +D14+D15+D16+D17. But for now, let's intentionally enter an incorrect formula.

❸ Type **+D14+D15+C17+D17** and press **[Enter]**. 1-2-3 calculates a total using this formula, and 360 appears in cell D19. See Figure 1-18.

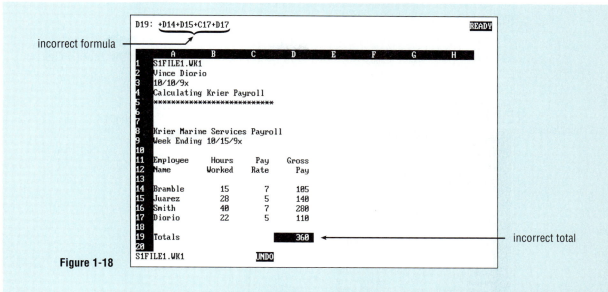

incorrect formula

incorrect total

Figure 1-18

Is the sum correct? If you add the gross pay of each employee (105 + 140 + 280 + 110), you get 635. Why does 360 appear in cell D19?   Look at the formula in the control panel. The correct formula is +D14+D15+D16+D17, but your panel shows +D14+D15+C17+D17.

We made this error intentionally to demonstrate that you always run the risk of making errors when you create a worksheet. Be sure to check your entries and formulas. In this case, you would add the results manually and compare them to the value in the worksheet.

Editing Entries in a Cell

If you notice an error in your worksheet, you have already learned that you can move the pointer to the cell with the error and retype the entry that contains the error. You can also use EDIT mode to correct the problem. EDIT mode is sometimes faster and easier to use, because you change only the incorrect characters and leave the rest of the entry intact. In 1-2-3, you use [F2] (EDIT) to edit an entry. In the following steps, you'll edit cell D19, which contains the incorrect formula for total gross pay.

To edit the contents of a cell:

❶ Be sure the cell pointer is in cell D19.

❷ Press **[F2]** (EDIT). The formula +D14+D15+C17+D17 appears in the second line of the control panel. See Figure 1-19.

formula to be edited ⟶

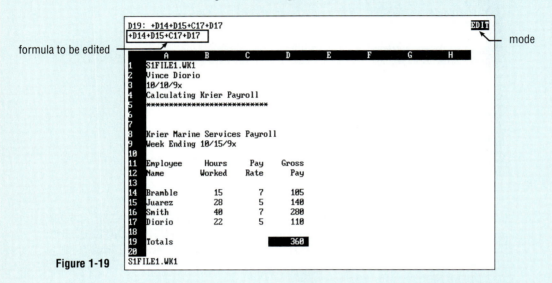

⟵ mode

Figure 1-19

❸ Press **[←]** to position the cursor under the letter C in the formula. Press **[Del]** three times to erase C17, the incorrect portion of the formula.

❹ Type **D16**. Press **[Enter]** and, as you do, notice that the value in D19 changes to 635, the correct total gross pay. Notice also that the correct formula, +D14+D15+D16+D17, appears in the control panel. See Figure 1-20.

correct formula ⟶

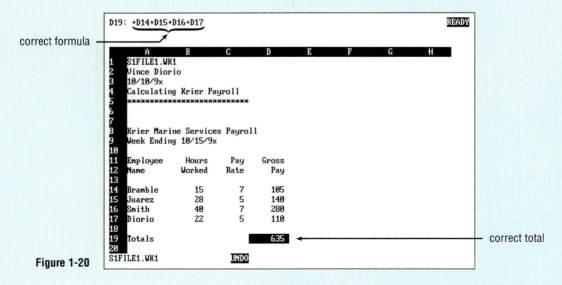

⟵ correct total

Figure 1-20

Be sure to take advantage of the [F2] (EDIT) key. It is often easier and more efficient to correct mistakes by typing only what needs to be changed.

Entering Lines

Worksheets often contain a row of lines below column headings and above and below subtotals to make the worksheet more readable. In addition, double lines are often used to indicate final totals. You could enter as many minus signs (–) or equal signs (=) as you need to create lines, but 1-2-3 provides a more convenient way. You first type \ (Backslash, not the slash symbol, /) and then type the character you want to use to draw the line. The backslash is a special label prefix that instructs 1-2-3 to repeat the character that follows it until the cell is filled.

To fill a cell with characters:

❶ Move the cell pointer to cell A13. This is a blank cell under a column heading.

❷ Type \ (Backslash) followed by a – (Minus Sign) to fill the cell with minus signs.

❸ Press **[Enter]**. See Figure 1-21. Notice how minus signs fill cell A13, producing a line in this cell.

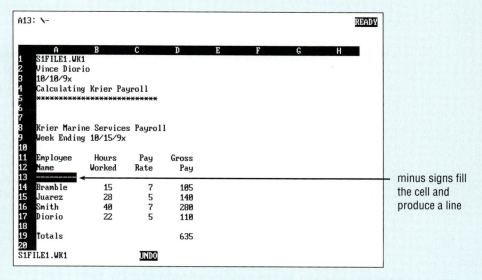

Figure 1-21

❹ Move the cell pointer to cell B13 and type \–, then press **[Enter]**.

❺ Move the cell pointer to cell C13, type \–, then press **[Enter]**.

❻ Move the cell pointer to cell D13, type \–, then press **[Enter]**. You have now entered a line across row 13.

❼ Move the cell pointer to cell D18, type \–, then press **[Enter]**. This enters a line in the gross pay column.

Your screen should be similar to Figure 1-22.

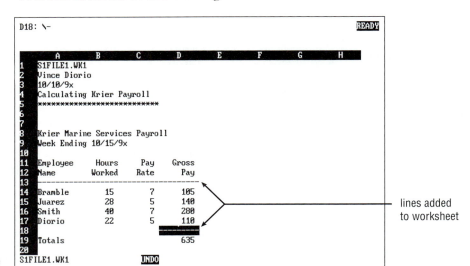

Figure 1-22

lines added to worksheet

Using UNDO to Correct Mistakes

What would you do if you accidentally typed over or erased a complicated formula? It would probably be a lot of work to figure out the formula again and reenter it. The UNDO feature can help. You can use it to cancel the *most recent* operation you performed on your worksheet.

To use UNDO, two indicators must appear on the screen. The word UNDO must appear in the status indicator at the bottom of your screen. Also, the word READY must appear in the mode indicator in the upper right corner of the screen. This means that your worksheet is in READY mode and can accept a keystroke.

Let's make an intentional mistake and use UNDO to correct it. Instead of typing the label ========= in cell D20, where it belongs, you will type it in cell D19, where it will erase the formula for total gross pay. Then you'll restore the original formula by using the UNDO feature.

To intentionally make a mistake:

❶ Move the cell pointer to cell D19, the cell that contains the formula for total gross pay.

❷ Type \ = and press **[Enter]**. See Figure 1-23.

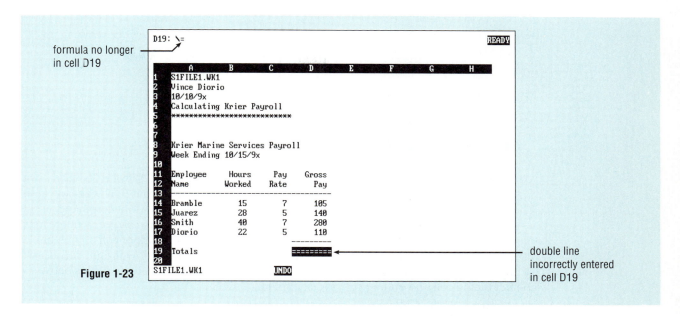

formula no longer in cell D19

double line incorrectly entered in cell D19

Figure 1-23

You have erased the entire formula and replaced it with =========, but don't worry. You can undo the mistake.

To use UNDO to cancel your *most recent* operation:

❶ Press the **[Alt]** key and, while holding it down, press the **[F4]** key ([Alt][F4]). Then release both keys. [Alt][F4] (UNDO) undoes your intentional mistake and restores the formula in D19. The value in D19 should again be 635.

❷ Now move the cell pointer to D20, the cell in which you should enter the double line. Type **\ =** and press **[Enter]**. See Figure 1-24.

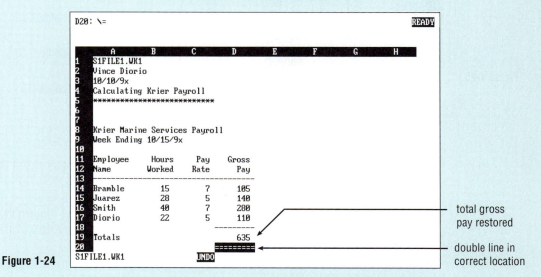

total gross pay restored

double line in correct location

Figure 1-24

❸   Select /File Save (**/FS**) and press **[Enter]**. Select Replace (**R**) to save your work again as S1FILE1.

Understanding Ranges

Vince has completed the payroll worksheet for Krier Marine Services. Now he wants to print it. The Print command requires you to identify the range of cells that you want to print. Therefore, you need to understand the term "range" before using the Print command.

A **range** in 1-2-3 consists of one or more cells forming a rectangular shape. A range may be a single cell, a row of cells, a column of cells, or a rectangular block of cells. To define a range, you indicate the upper left corner cell of the rectangle and the lower right corner cell of the rectangle. Two periods [..] separate these entries and represent all the values between the beginning cell and ending cell, for example C14..C17.

Figure 1-25 illustrates several examples of ranges that you can define in a worksheet.

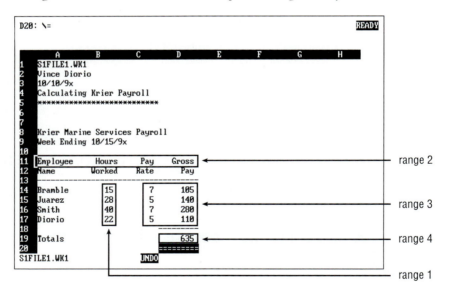

Figure 1-25

- The first example, labeled range 1, is identified as B14..B17. This forms a column of cells located in column B, beginning in row 14 and ending in row 17.

- The second example, range 2, represents a row of cells. The range is defined as A11..D11, which means the range of cells beginning at cell A11 and ending at D11.

- The third example, range 3, represents the rectangular block of cells C14..D17. A block of cells is identified in a worksheet by specifying a pair of diagonally opposite corner cells. C14, the upper left corner, and D17, the bottom right corner, define a block of eight cells.

- The fourth example, range 4, represents the single cell D19..D19. A single cell defined as a range has the same starting and ending cell.

Using the Print Command

You have entered the data, calculated gross pay and totals, saved your worksheet, and learned about ranges. You are now ready to print the Krier payroll worksheet and learn the basics of using the Print command. In 1-2-3, you print by first specifying a range to print and then printing the worksheet. You can print all or part of your worksheet by first defining a rectangular range of cells that you want to print. Vince wants to print the payroll report using the range A8 through D20.

To specify the print range A8..D20:

❶ Select /Print Printer (**/PP**). 1-2-3 displays a print settings sheet. See Figure 1-26.

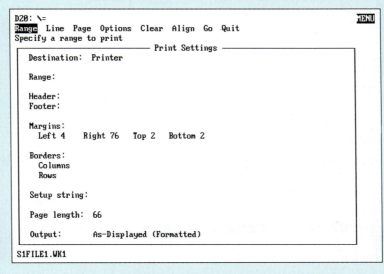

```
D20: \=                                               MENU
Range Line Page Options Clear Align Go Quit
Specify a range to print
                         ┌─── Print Settings ───┐
     Destination:  Printer

     Range:

     Header:
     Footer:

     Margins:
        Left 4    Right 76    Top 2    Bottom 2

     Borders:
        Columns
        Rows

     Setup string:

     Page length:  66

     Output:       As-Displayed (Formatted)

S1FILE1.WK1
```

Figure 1-26
The print
settings sheet

Anytime you print, the printed output will be formatted according to the specifications on this sheet. If you want to see the worksheet instead of the print settings sheet, you can press the function key [F6]. Press [F6] again and the print settings sheet reappears.

❷ Select Range (**R**). The worksheet reappears.

To define the print range, you must specify two cell addresses that are diagonally across from one another. Usually, the upper left corner and the lower right corner cells define the range.

❸ Move the cell pointer to A8, the upper left corner cell in the print range. See Figure 1-27.

beginning of
print range

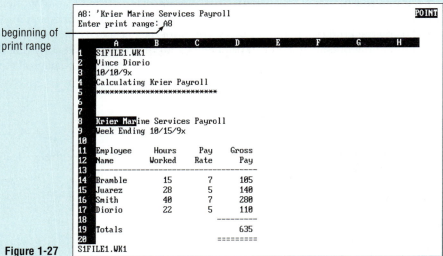

Figure 1-27

❹ Type **.** (Period). This fixes, or **anchors**, the cell. Whenever you want to specify range, you should move the cell pointer to the top left corner cell of a range and anchor this position by pressing **.** (Period). See Figure 1-28 and compare it to Figure 1-27. Notice how 1-2-3 now indicates that cell A8 is anchored.

.. indicates range is
now anchored

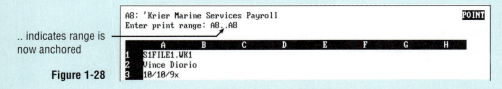

Figure 1-28

Once the range is anchored, you can expand it by using the cursor-movement keys. Pressing these keys highlights the range.

⑤   Press **[↓]** and **[→],** as needed, to highlight the range A8..D20. The highlighted range appears in the control panel. See Figure 1-29.

print range defined

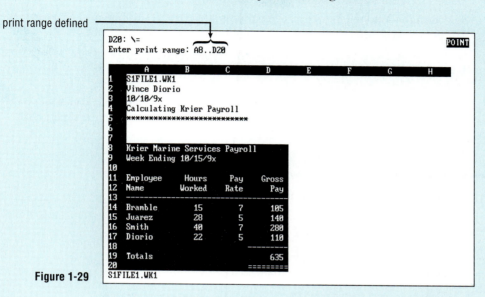

Figure 1-29

⑥   Press **[Enter]**. This completes the definition of the range, which now appears in the print settings sheet. See Figure 1-30.

range that will be printed

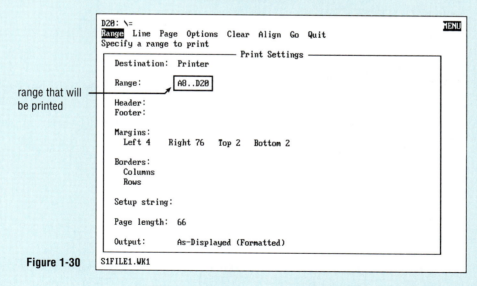

Figure 1-30

Now that you've instructed 1-2-3 what cells you want to print, you are ready to print the worksheet.

To print a specified range:

❶ Make sure your paper is positioned properly in your printer and the printer is on-line.

❷ Select Align (**A**) to tell 1-2-3 that the paper is correctly positioned and ready for printing. You should always choose Align before beginning to print.

❸ Select Go (**G**) to print the specified range. If the range does not print, your copy of 1-2-3 may not be installed correctly. See Chapter 2 for instructions on how to install 1-2-3 for use with a printer.

❹ Select Page (**P**). You need not wait for the printing to finish before you select Page. The Page command tells 1-2-3 to advance the paper to the top of the next page when it is finished printing. See Figure 1-31.

```
Lotus 1-2-3 Student Business Series          Vince Diorio


Krier Marine Services Payroll
Week Ending 10/15/9x

Employee    Hours    Pay      Gross
Name        Worked   Rate     Pay
-------------------------------------
Bramble       15       7       105
Juarez        28       5       140
Smith         40       7       280
Diorio        22       5       110
                              ---------
Totals                         635
                              =========
```

Figure 1-31
Printout of Krier
Marine Services
payroll worksheet

❺ Select Quit (**Q**) to leave the Print menu and return to READY mode with your worksheet displayed on your screen.

❻ Save your worksheet as S1FILE1 one last time (**/FS**). Press **[Enter]** and select Replace (**R**). This saves the print setting with the worksheet.

Erasing the Entire Worksheet

Once you have completed a worksheet, you may wish to start a new one. You can do this easily, but always remember to save your current worksheet. Then you can clear the worksheet from memory by using the Worksheet Erase command. You can also use this command if you begin a worksheet but decide you don't want it and have to start over. Let's erase the Krier payroll worksheet.

To erase a worksheet:

❶   Select /Worksheet Erase (**/WE**).

❷   Type **Y** (Yes) if you are sure you want to erase the worksheet. After you type Y, the worksheet disappears from the screen. See Figure 1-32. 1-2-3 *does not* erase the worksheet from your Data Disk, only from the computer's memory.

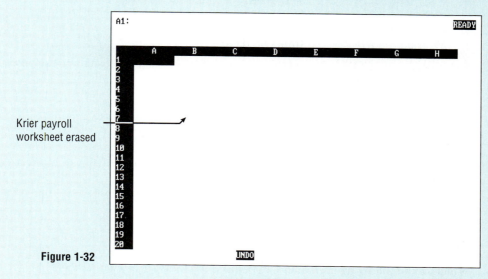

Krier payroll worksheet erased

Figure 1-32

Quitting 1-2-3

When you are ready quit 1-2-3, you choose the Quit command. You will be returned to the operating system prompt.

To quit a 1-2-3 session:

❶   Select /Quit Yes (**/QY**).

Summary

In this tutorial, you learned the basics of entering labels, values, and formulas in 1-2-3. You learned how to correct entry errors and other mistakes by using a variety of techniques, including retyping, backspacing, editing, and undoing. You also retrieved files, as well as saved and replaced them. Finally, you learned to print a worksheet.

Exercises

1. Would you enter the following data items as labels or values?
    a. 227-3541   (phone number)
    b. 6.45   (pay rate)
    c. 02384   (zip code)
    d. 46 Main Street   (address)
    e. 25   (units on hand)

2. The contents of cell B5 is 20 and the contents of B6 is 15. What result appears in cell B7 if the following formula is entered in B7?
    a. +B5-B6
    b. +B5*B6
    c. +B6*B5
    d. +B6/B5

3. Which of the following ranges defines a row of cells? Which range defines a block of cells?
    a. B1..B7
    b. B1..D7
    c. B1..E1
    d. B1..B1

4. How can you display series of plus signs, +++++++++, in a cell?

5. Which of the following filenames can be used to name a 1-2-3 worksheet?
    a. Q1.WK1
    b. 1991.WK1
    c. ACCTREC.WK1
    d. ACCT REC.WK1
    e. ACCT_REC.WK1
    f. ACCT.REC.WK1

6. What key(s) would you press to accomplish the following tasks?
    a. get to the Command menu
    b. back up one step in the 1-2-3 menu system
    c. move to cell A1
    d. edit a formula in a cell

Tutorial Assignments

1. Retrieve file T1FILE1, find the error, and correct it. (When 1-2-3 displays the list of work-sheet files, press [PgDn] several times to find the worksheet file T1FILE1.) What do you think the person who created the worksheet did when entering the gross pay formula for Bramble? Print the worksheet.

2. Retrieve file T1FILE2. Why isn't total gross pay adding correctly? Correct the worksheet and print it.

3. Retrieve file T1FILE3. Why is Bramble's gross pay zero? Hint: Think about how labels and values are stored in 1-2-3. Correct the error and print the worksheet.

Retrieve the file T1FILE4 and do the following:

4. Juarez worked 30 hours for the week, not the 28 hours that was entered. Correct this.

5. Smith's name is actually Smythe. Change the name.

6. In cell B19, write a formula to calculate total hours worked.

7. Add a single line in cell B18 and a double line in cell B20.

Continue using file T1FILE4 to complete the following problems on federal withholding tax (FWT). FWT is the amount of money that an employer withholds from an employee's paycheck to pay for federal taxes.

8. Assume that the amount withheld from an employee's pay check is 15 percent (.15) of gross pay. Use column E in your worksheet to display FWT. Include the column heading FWT in cell E12. Enter the formula for withholding tax for each employee (gross pay × .15) in cells E14, E15, E16, and E17.

9. Net pay is the gross pay less deductions (gross pay – FWT). Use column F to display the net pay for each employee. Enter the column label Net in cell F11 and the column label Pay in cell F12. Enter the net pay formula for each employee in cells F14, F15, F16, and F17.

10. Calculate the total FWT and the total net pay for all employees. Display these totals in cells E19 and F19, respectively.

11. Add single and double lines where appropriate.

12. Print the entire worksheet, including the identifying data at the top of the worksheet. Your print range is A1..F20.

13. Change cell A1 to S1FILE4.WK1. Now save your worksheet as S1FILE4.WK1.

Use the Reference section of *Lotus 1-2-3 for Business* to do the following:

14. Look at the column headings in file T1FILE4.WK1. Notice that the headings FWT and Net Pay are not aligned over the values in these columns. Read the section on label prefixes in the Reference. Then format the column headings for FWT and Net Pay so they align over the values in the columns. Print your worksheet. Save your worksheet at S1FILE5.

Case Problems

1. Sales in Toyland

An article in the *Wall Street Journal* focusing on sales in the toy industry for 1990 presented the following data:

Toy Companies Nine-month Sales
1990
(in millions)

Company	1990	1989
Galoob	105	169
Hasbro	1027	993
Matchbox	140	156
Mattel	1042	878
Tonka	541	625
Tyco	334	269

Retrieve the worksheet P1TOYS and do the following:

1. Calculate total sales for the toy industry for 1989 and 1990.

2. Calculate the change in sales from 1989 to 1990. Place this result in column D. Label the column heading Change and use the following formula:

    Change = 1990 sales – 1989 sales

3. Print the worksheet.

4. Save the worksheet as S1TOYS.

2. Travel Agency Survey

A travel industry association conducted a study of U.S. travel habits. The following table shows the amount of passenger miles traveled in the U.S. by various modes of transportation.

U.S. Travel Habits

Mode of Transportation	Passenger Miles (billions)
Cars	1586.3
Airlines	346.5
Buses	45.2
Railroad	18.7

Retrieve the worksheet P1TRVL and do the following:

1. Enter the formula to compute total U.S. passenger miles.

2. Enter the formula to compute the percent that each mode of transportation represents of the total U.S. passenger miles. (Divide the passenger miles for each mode of transportation by total passenger miles and then multiply by 100).

3. Print your worksheet.

4. Save your worksheet as S1TRVL.

3. A Trend Toward More Bankruptcies

Ms. Ganni is a lawyer who administers bankruptcy filings. In the last few years, she has seen a rapid increase in the number of bankruptcy cases. She states, "I know the number of bankruptcy cases I've handled has increased enormously. I don't have time for lunch anymore, much less time to analyze all the cases. We need more staff; our system is overloaded!"

As her assistant, you must help Ms. Ganni make a case to her bosses for additional resources.

Retrieve the worksheet file P1BNKRPT and do the following:

1. Calculate the total number of bankruptcies in 1989 and 1990.

2. Calculate the percent change in bankruptcies this year compared to last year for each type of bankruptcy as well as the overall percent change. The formula to calculate percent change in bankruptcies for each bankruptcy type in 1990 is:

$$\left(\frac{Bankruptcies\ in\ 1990 - Bankruptcies\ in\ 1989}{Bankruptcies\ in\ 1989} \right) \times 100$$

3. Print the worksheet.

4. Save the worksheet as S1BNKRPT.

Setting up Your Copy of 1-2-3

To use your copy of 1-2-3 with these tutorials, you must set up your copy so that your Data Disk filenames appear whenever you select /File Retrieve and so that the current filename appears in the lower left corner of your screen. To set up 1-2-3 correctly you must change two *global settings*, that is, two conditions that effect your copy of 1-2-3 every time you use it.

To change these settings:

❶ If you are using a *two-diskette* system, put the System Disk in drive A and the Data Disk in drive B. If you are using a *hard-disk system*, go to Step 2.

❷ Select Worksheet Global Default (**/WGD**). The global default settings sheet appears. See Figure 1-33.

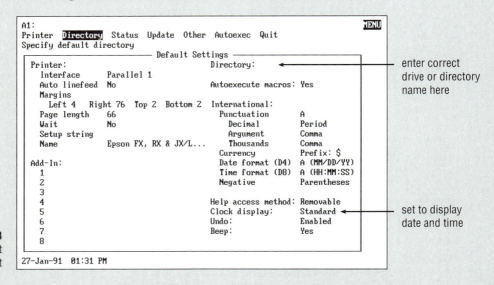

enter correct drive or directory name here

set to display date and time

Figure 1-33
1-2-3's global default settings sheet

This settings sheet shows the settings that 1-2-3 uses each time you start 1-2-3.

❸ Select Directory (**D**).

1-2-3 prompts you to enter the letter of the drive from which you will load your Data Disk files.

❹ Press **[Backspace]** to erase the current directory setting.

If you are using a *two-diskette* system, type **b:** (or the correct letter for the drive in which you have your Data Disk) and press **[Enter]**.

If you are using a *hard-disk* system, type **c:\123\data** and press **[Enter]**. (If you copied your Data Disk to a directory other than c:\123\data, enter the name of that directory instead.)

❺ Next select Other Clock Filename (**OCF**) to change the setting to display the filename instead of the date and time.

❻ To save these settings, select Update (**U**).

❼ To return to the worksheet, select Quit (**Q**).

Tutorial 2

Modifying a Worksheet

Pricing a Mutual Fund

Case: Allegiance Incorporated

Pauline Wu graduated last June with a degree in Finance. Today she is beginning her new job as a portfolio accountant with Allegiance Incorporated, an investment company. Pauline is very excited about getting this job, not only because Allegiance is reputed to be one of the best mutual fund companies in the US, but also because Allegiance is known for the superior training it provides its new employees.

People who have money to invest but who do not want to manage the investment themselves invest their money with Allegiance. Allegiance employs trained professionals to manage the money in what are called mutual funds. In these funds, the money is invested in stocks, bonds, and other publicly traded securities and managed by Allegiance employees, often called portfolio managers.

For example, a portfolio manager might manage a $10 million fund that was started by selling one million shares at $10 a share to people who then become the shareholders of the fund. The manager of this fund then invests the $10 million by buying shares in companies such as IBM, AT&T, and Coca-Cola. The goal of the portfolio manager and the shareholders is that the shares purchased will increase in value so the shareholders will make money.

As a portfolio accountant, Pauline will be responsible for reporting correct information to portfolio managers so they will be able to track how well a fund is performing. One of Pauline's responsibilities in her new job is each day to calculate the

---

O b j e c t i v e s

In this tutorial, you will learn how to:

- Use the @SUM function

- Change the way numbers are displayed

- Change column widths

- Adjust text alignments

- Insert rows

- Move a group of rows or columns to another worksheet area

- Erase a group of cells

value of the Balboa Equity Fund and to report this information to the national newspapers so shareholders can know the value of a share in this fund. Pauline knows that is an important responsibility. Even a minor error in her calculations could cause Allegiance to lose substantial amounts of money. She is eager to begin the new employee training program because it will help her to perform these important calculations accurately.

Pauline first meets the other new portfolio accountants and her training supervisor, Rochelle Osterhaut. Rochelle begins the training by discussing their daily responsibility to calculate the value of a mutual fund share. She hands out a fact sheet (Figure 2-1) that lists details about the Balboa Equity Fund. Rochelle explains that their first assignment is to use this information to calculate the value of a share of the Balboa Fund. She also reminds them that in college they probably learned that the value per share of a fund is usually called *net asset value*, or *NAV*.

```
Balboa Equity Fund    -    Fact Sheet

Mutual Fund Shares         2000

Net Asset Value              ?


Company Name      Shares Purchased       Current Price

IBM                    100                125
Coca-Cola               50                42 1/4
AT&T                   100                33 3/8
Boeing                 150                48 1/2
```

Figure 2-1
Balboa Equity Fund
fact sheet

Rochelle explains that to calculate the NAV they must first determine the market value of each investment owned by the fund. To do this, they multiply the current price of each company share owned by the fund by the total number of shares of this company that the fund purchased. For example, Balboa Equity Fund owns 100 shares of IBM, whose current price is $125 per share. Thus, the market value of these shares in the Balboa Fund is $12,500. After the market value of each security is determined, the accountants add together the market value of each investment and other assets owned by the fund, such as cash on hand. After calculating this total they divide it by the number of shares owned by the fund's shareholders. The result is the net asset value. In other words,

$$NAV = \frac{(current\ price \times shares\ of\ company\ A\ owned\ by\ fund\ ) + (current\ price \times shares\ of\ company\ B\ owned\ by\ fund\ ) + \ldots}{number\ of\ shares\ of\ the\ mutual\ fund\ owned\ by\ fund's\ shareholders}$$

Pauline is eager to begin the assignment. She decides to use Lotus 1-2-3 to help make the calculations and to produce a professional-looking report. First, however, she thinks about the project; she outlines her thoughts on a planning sheet and sketches the worksheet (Figures 2-2a and 2-2b).

Figure 2-2a
Pauline's planning
sheet

My Goal
    Calculate Net Asset Value for Balboa Equity Fund each day

What results do I want to see?
    Net Asset Value (Price/Share) of Balboa Equity Fund
    Breakdown of companies that make up the fund along with the market
    value of companies' stock

What information do I need?
    For each company stock owned by the fund
        Name of the company
        Number of shares of the company's stock owned by fund
        Current price company's stock is selling for

What calculations will I perform?
    Calculate market value of each stock in the fund
    Calculate total value for all stock in the fund
    Calculate Net Asset Value

Figure 2-2b
Pauline's
worksheet sketch

Mutual Fund Shares
Price per share (NAV)

Company Name	# of Shares	Current Price	Market Value
xxxx	xx	xx.xxx	xxxx.xx
xxxx	xx	xx.xxx	xxxx.xx
.			
.			
.			
Totals			xxxx.xx

In this tutorial, you will create the same worksheet that Pauline creates. You will experience the power of the specialized @functions, which speed and simplify the use of formulas, learn more about entering and editing data quickly, and learn how to make changes in the appearance of the worksheet.

Retrieving the Worksheet

To retrieve the worksheet:

❶ Select /File Retrieve (**/FR**) and highlight C2FILE1.WK1. Press **[Enter]**. See Figure 2-3.

This worksheet contains the Balboa Equity Fund Portfolio data. It includes the company names and the number of shares of each company's stock that the fund purchased. It also shows the current day's stock market price of each company that is part of the Balboa Fund Portfolio. In addition, the worksheet shows the number of mutual fund shares owned by people who have invested in the Balboa Fund.

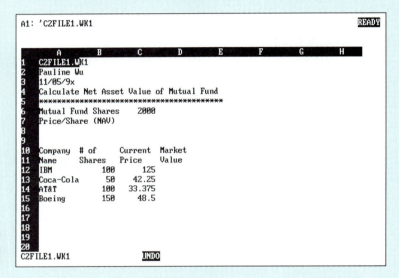

Figure 2-3
Data on Balboa
Equity Fund

Entering Formulas

Now that you have the basic data entered in the worksheet, your first step in pricing the mutual fund is to calculate the market value of each company's stock in the fund. The market value is calculated by multiplying the number of shares owned of each company's stock times the current market price of that company's stock, that is,

$$market\ value = number\ of\ shares \times current\ market\ price$$

To calculate the market value for each company:

First calculate the market value for IBM.

❶ Move the cell pointer to D12. Type **+B12*C12** and press **[↓]**.

To calculate the market value for Coca-Cola:

❷   In cell D13, type **+B13*C13** and press [↓].

To calculate the market value for AT&T:

❸   In cell D14, type **+B14*C14** and press [↓].

To calculate the market value for Boeing:

❹   In cell D15, type **+B15*C15** and press [**Enter**]. See Figure 2-4.

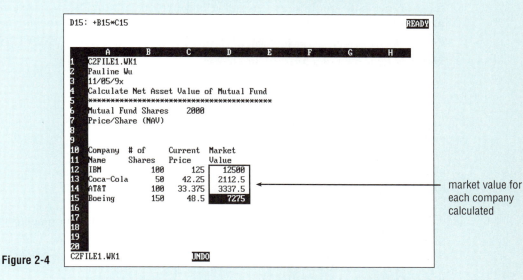

market value for each company calculated

Figure 2-4

Using the @SUM Function

Now that you have calculated the market value of each company's stock in this fund, you need to calculate the total market value of the fund. The total market value of the fund is the sum of market values of all the companies in the fund, that is,

total market value = market value of IBM + market value of Coca-Cola + ...

Remember that in Tutorial 1 you summed the total gross pay by specifying the cell location of each employee's gross pay. Similarly, you could calculate the total market value by entering the formula +D12+D13+D14+D15, but this would be tedious. It would be especially tedious if the fund had perhaps seventy-five different companies instead of just four. To make the process much easier, you'll use 1-2-3's @SUM (pronounced "at sum") function. This function allows you to total the values in a range of cells.

What is an @Function?

A **function** is a predefined routine that performs a series of operations or calculations and then gives you a result. It can be thought of as a *predefined formula* that is built into 1-2-3.

Functions save you the trouble of creating your own formulas to perform various arithmetic tasks.

Many functions are available in 1-2-3. They are divided into eight categories: mathematical, statistical, database, financial, logical, string, date/time, and special.

Each function begins with the @ (at) symbol followed by the name of the function. The name of the function is a three-character abbreviation that suggests the purpose of the function. In parentheses following the function name, you will put any information the function needs to perform its tasks. The information in parentheses is referred to as the **arguments** of the function. Depending on the @function, the arguments may be values, references to cells or ranges, range names, formulas, and even other @functions.

The general format of a function in 1-2-3 is:

@FUNCTION(arguments)

where:

    @ is the symbol that indicates that a function follows.

    FUNCTION is the name of the function.

    arguments represents the required information that the function needs to do its tasks.

Pauline is ready to calculate the total market value of the Balboa Equity Fund. To do this, she will use the @SUM function. Remember, the @SUM function adds a column of numbers. You specify the addresses of the first and the last cell of the column you want to add. In other words, @SUM(D12..D15) is equivalent to +D12+D13+D14+D15. The expression in parentheses, D12..D15, is the argument, representing the range of cells that will be added.

To use the @SUM function to calculate total market value:

❶ Move the cell pointer to A16 to enter the label. Type **[Space] [Space] Totals**. Press **[Enter]**.

❷ Now move the cell pointer to D16, where you will enter the formula to total the company market values.

❸ Type **@SUM(** to begin the formula. You may use either uppercase or lowercase when typing the function name SUM.

❹ Press **[↑]** to move the cell pointer to D12, the starting point for adding the market values of all companies in this fund. See Figure 2-5.

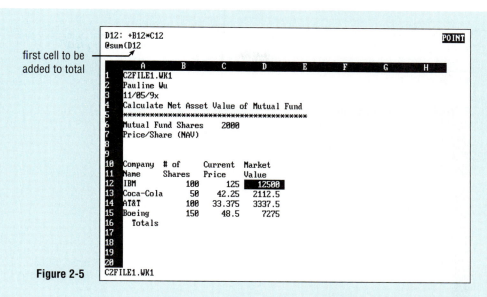

first cell to be added to total

Figure 2-5

⑤ Type **[.]** (Period) to anchor the cell. Two periods appear in the control panel to indicate that the cell is now anchored.

⑥ Press **[↓]** to highlight the range D12..D15. See Figure 2-6.

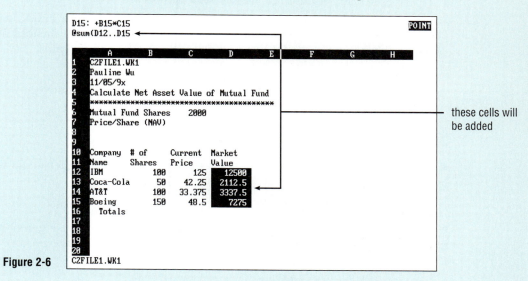

these cells will be added

Figure 2-6

❼ Type **[)]** (Right Parenthesis) and press **[Enter]**. The calculated result, 25225, appears in cell D16. See Figure 2-7.

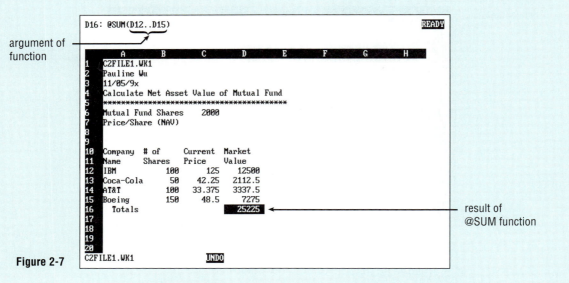

argument of function

result of @SUM function

Figure 2-7

You have now calculated the market value for the Balboa Equity Fund.

The final calculation to determine the net asset value is to divide the total market value of the fund by the number of shares invested in the fund. In other words,

$$NAV = \frac{total\ market\ value\ of\ mutual\ fund}{number\ of\ shares\ of\ fund\ owned\ by\ investors}$$

To calculate net asset value:

❶ Move the cell pointer to C7, where the net asset value will be calculated.

❷ Type **+D16/C6** and then press **[Enter]**.

The / (Slash) symbol represents division when used in a formula.

You've now completed the calculations of the net asset value (NAV). Figure 2-8 on the next page shows the worksheet with the NAV calculated. Each share is worth $12.6125.

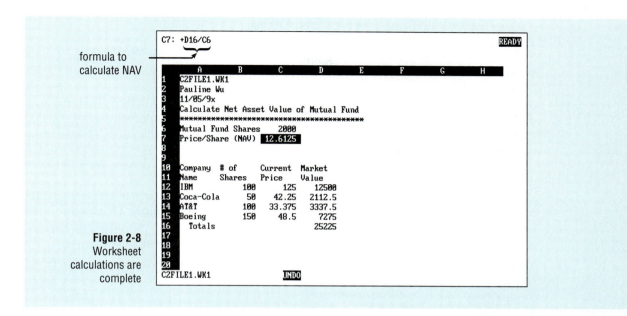

formula to
calculate NAV

Figure 2-8
Worksheet
calculations are
complete

Improving the Appearance of the Worksheet

Although Pauline has completed the calculations for pricing the mutual fund, she is not pleased with the appearance of the worksheet. For instance, the numbers in the current price and market value columns are not aligned at the decimal point. In addition, the monetary values do not show dollar signs, and the column headings are not aligned over the numbers in a column. Some improvements are needed to make the worksheet easier to read and use.

In the next several sections of this tutorial, you will learn to improve your worksheet's appearance. Figure 2-9 shows how the worksheet will look when you are finished.

Figure 2-9
Final version of
worksheet

Formatting Numbers

You probably found the numeric values in your worksheet difficult to read, because the list of current prices and market values are not aligned at the decimal point. Unless you instruct otherwise, a decimal point appears in a number only if the number has digits to the right of the decimal point. This is called the **general** format, and it is 1-2-3's default format. *Default* means that 1-2-3 automatically uses a format or setting unless you change it. Trailing zeros after the decimal are not displayed. Fortunately, you can change this by using the Format command. 1-2-3 provides several alternative formats that you can use to change the way numbers appear in your worksheet.

Figure 2-10 shows some types of numeric formatting available in 1-2-3. These formats allow you to alter the number of decimal places displayed with a number. They may include dollar signs and commas with numbers; they can place parentheses around negative numbers; and they can add percent signs to numbers representing percentages.

Format Type	Description	Examples
General	This is the default format; 1-2-3 stores numbers in this format when they are first entered.	0.5 −125
Fixed	This displays numbers to a fixed number of decimal places specified by the user.	0.50 1200.57
Currency	Numbers are preceded by dollar signs and commas are inserted after the thousands and millions places.	$1,200.57 ($125.00)
, (Comma)	Commas are inserted after the thousands and millions places. Negative numbers appear in parentheses.	1,200.57 (125.00)
Percent	This multiplies the value by 100 and inserts the percent sign to the right of the value.	50% 14.1%

Figure 2-10
Numeric formats

You can format all the cells in your worksheet using the Global Format command, which treats all the cells similarly. Or you can format a block of cells, a column, a row, or a single cell using the Range Format command. In the next steps, you will change the format of the current price and market value columns. To do this, you use the Range Format command.

To format the current prices to Currency format with three decimal places:

❶ Move the cell pointer to C12, the first cell of the Current Price column.

❷ Select /Range Format (**/RF**). The second line of the control panel lists all the formats available in 1-2-3. See Figure 2-11.

Format
commands
in 1-2-3

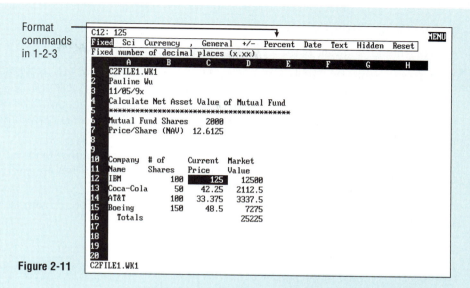

Figure 2-11

❸   Select Currency (**C**).

At this point, 1-2-3 asks you to enter the number of decimal places.

❹   Type **3** and press **[Enter]**. You chose three decimal places because stocks are bought and sold to the eighth of a dollar.

❺   At the range prompt, highlight the range C12..C15. Press **[Enter]**. See Figure 2-12.

Notice that 1-2-3 displays (C3) in the control panel, which means this cell is formatted using the currency format with three decimal places.

indicates cell is
formatted using
Currency format
with 3 decimal
places

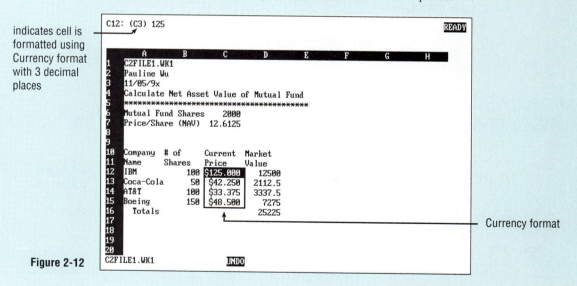

Currency format

Figure 2-12

Formatting Considerations

You should be aware of the following when formatting numbers:

- If you reduce the number of decimal places of a number, 1-2-3 rounds the number that appears in the cell. For example, if you type the value 25.6273 into a cell, but decide to display the number with only two decimal places, the rounded number, 25.63, appears in the cell. If you decide to display three decimal places, the number 25.627 appears in the cell.

- For all calculations, 1-2-3 uses the value stored in the cell, rather than the value that appears in the cell. Thus, for an entry stored as 25.6273, but appearing as 25.63, 1-2-3 uses 25.6273 for all calculations.

Now let's format the market value column using Currency format with two decimal places.

To change the format of the market value column:

❶ Move the cell pointer to D12, the first cell under Market Value.

❷ Select /Range Format Currency (**/RFC**).

❸ At the prompt for the number of decimal places, press **[Enter]**. Since two decimal places is the default, it is not necessary to type 2. If you wanted zero decimal places, you would type 0 before pressing [Enter].

❹ At the range prompt, press **[↓]** to highlight the range D12..D16. Press **[Enter]**. See Figure 2-13.

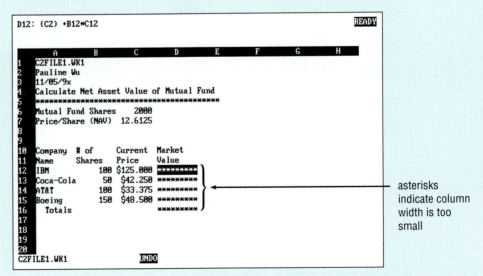

Figure 2-13

asterisks indicate column width is too small

Changing Column Widths

What happened to the values in the Market Value column? Why do asterisks appear in cells D12..D16? The asterisks indicate that the column width is not wide enough to display the values. 1-2-3 has a default width of nine characters in a cell. In this case, the asterisks indicate that the formatted market values require more than a nine-character-wide column. You must, therefore, widen the width of the Market Value column.

You can change the widths of all the columns in a worksheet at one time. We use the term **global** to describe a change that involves *all* similar items in a worksheet. You can also make a single column wider or narrower. In the next steps, you will widen a single column.

To change the width of column D:

❶ Make sure the cell pointer is in any cell in column D.

❷ Select /Worksheet Column Set-width (**/WCS**). See Figure 2-14.

preparing to change column width →

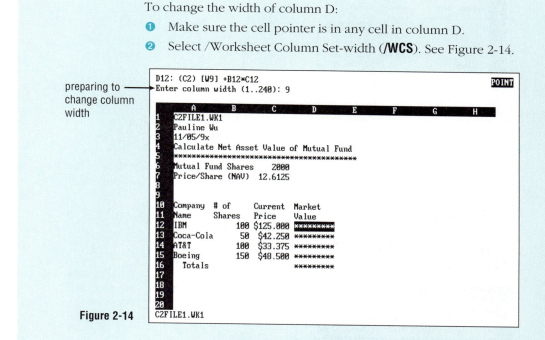

```
D12: (C2) [W9] +B12*C12                                    POINT
Enter column width (1..240): 9

     A        B        C        D        E     F     G     H
1  C2FILE1.WK1
2  Pauline Wu
3  11/05/9x
4  Calculate Net Asset Value of Mutual Fund
5  *******************************************
6  Mutual Fund Shares     2000
7  Price/Share (NAV)   12.6125
8
9
10 Company  # of      Current  Market
11 Name     Shares    Price    Value
12 IBM         100   $125.000  *********
13 Coca-Cola    50    $42.250  *********
14 AT&T        100    $33.375  *********
15 Boeing      150    $48.500  *********
16    Totals                   *********
17
18
19
20
   C2FILE1.WK1
```

Figure 2-14

You can use two methods to enter a new column width: using the pointer-movement keys or typing a number. First, let's use the pointer-movement keys.

③ Press [→] until the column is wide enough to display all the values.

Notice how the column width increases by one character each time you press the key. See Figure 2-15.

column width is 11

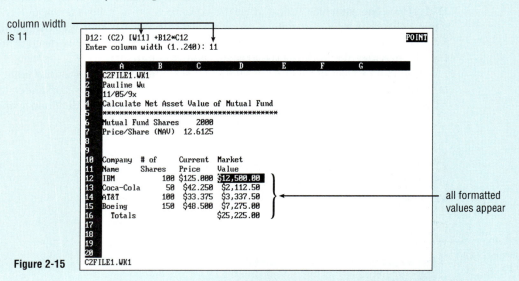

Figure 2-15

all formatted values appear

④ Press **[Enter]**.

Now let's try the second method to widen a column: typing a number. Let's widen the column to 15 characters so that it can accommodate an even larger number.

⑤ Select /Worksheet Column Set-width (**/WCS**).

⑥ Type **15** and press **[Enter]**. See Figure 2-16.

indicates cell formatted using Currency format with 2 decimal places

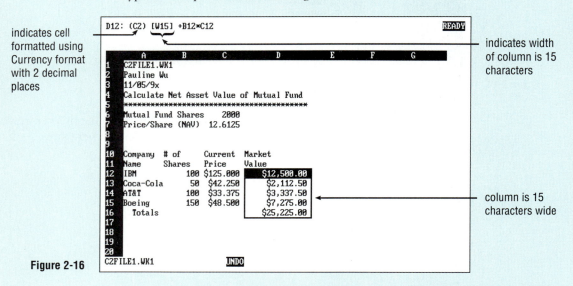

Figure 2-16

indicates width of column is 15 characters

column is 15 characters wide

Notice that [W15] appears in the control panel, indicating the current width of the column is 15 characters.

Remember that all columns have a default width of nine characters. You can change the column width to accommodate labels and numbers that are longer than the column's width. Sometimes you might find nine characters too large. In such cases, you can reduce the width of a column by following the same steps you did to widen it. Just remember to choose a number less than 9.

Long Labels

Another reason to change the width of a column is to accommodate labels that are longer than nine characters. Often text entered into a cell is longer than the column's width. For example, the company name Hewlett-Packard requires more than nine characters. These text items are called **long labels.** If the cell to the right of the cell containing a long label is blank, the long label appears in the blank cell. However, if the cell to the right is not blank, then only the characters that fit into the column's current width will appear. Remember that the default column width is nine characters; thus, only the first nine characters will appear in the cell.

Let's suppose that Pauline does not want to abbreviate the names of the companies in the fund. Let's enter the full name for IBM, International Business Machines, and observe the result.

To enter a long label:

❶ Move the cell pointer to A12.

❷ Type **International Business Machines** and press **[Enter]**. Since the default column width is 9, only the first nine characters appear — Internati. Look at the control panel; notice that the entire label appears there. This indicates that 1-2-3 has stored the entire label in the cell memory, but since the width of the column is 9, only the first nine characters appear on your screen. See Figure 2-17.

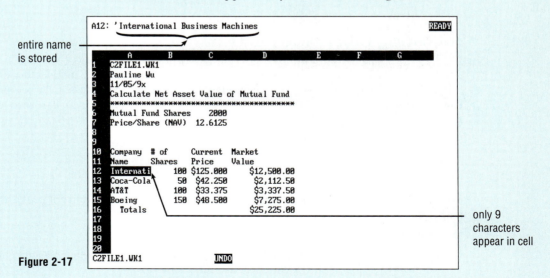

entire name is stored

only 9 characters appear in cell

Figure 2-17

Pauline wants the entire name of the company to appear, so we must increase the column width.

To increase the column width:

❶   Select /Worksheet Column Set-width (**/WCS**).

❷   Type **32** to allow enough characters for the entire name to appear on the screen.

❸   Press **[Enter]**. See Figure 2-18.

width of cell is
32 characters

entire name
appears in cell

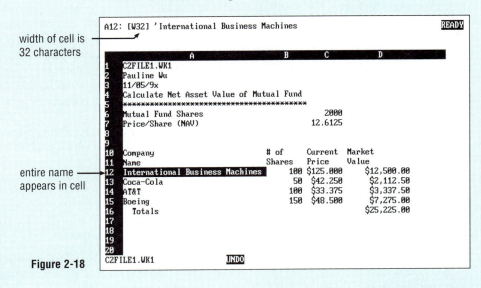

Figure 2-18

Adjusting Labels within a Cell

As you have seen, when you enter a label, 1-2-3 places it, by default, against the left edge of the cell. Such a label is said to be **left-justified** and has an apostrophe (') label prefix. You can easily change the alignment of labels to suit your needs. You can also center or right-justify labels.

Let's learn how to right-justify the labels in Pauline's worksheet.

To right-justify the column headings for the number of shares, the current price, and the market value:

❶   Move the cell pointer to B10.

❷   Select /Range Label Right (**/RLR**). See Figure 2-19. Notice that 1-2-3 automatically anchors the range at the location of the cell pointer, B10.

cell
automatically
anchored

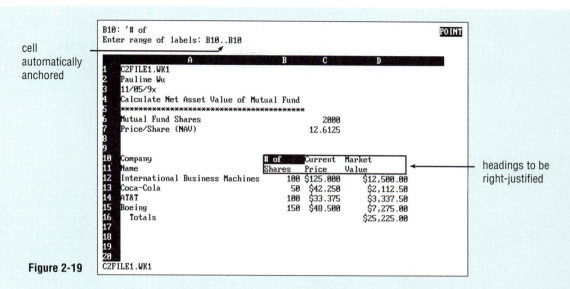

headings to be
right-justified

Figure 2-19

❸ Move the [→] and [↓] keys until the cell range B10..D11 is highlighted. Press **[Enter]**.
See Figure 2-20.

" label prefix
means
right-justified

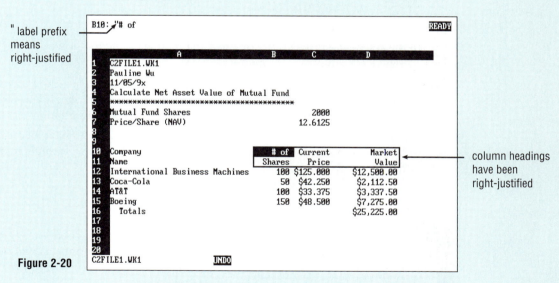

column headings
have been
right-justified

Figure 2-20

The headings in columns B, C, and D are now right-justified.

Notice in the control panel that a " (Quote) character now precedes the label. The "
character is the label prefix 1-2-3 uses to indicate a right-justified label.

To center the labels, you would select Range Label Center in Step 2.

You can also control label alignment as you type labels. For example, to center a label,
type the ∧ (Caret) character (found on the [6] key) in front of any label. To right-justify
a label, type a "(Quote) character in front of the label.

❹ Press **[Home]** to move the cell pointer to cell A1. Type **S2FILE1** and press **[Enter]**. This changes this identifying information in cell A1 so it will be consistent with the new filename.

❺ Save your worksheet (**/FS**), using the name S2FILE1.

Inserting Rows

You could improve the worksheet appearance by inserting a line between the column heading and the first company name. In addition, it would look better with a line between the last company name and the Totals row. But there isn't any room. Running out of room often happens when you are in the process of creating a worksheet. Fortunately, with 1-2-3 you can insert or delete one or more rows between two adjacent rows. You can also insert one or more columns between two adjacent columns. You use the Insert command to insert new rows or columns into your worksheet.

To insert a blank row between A11 and A12 in the worksheet:

❶ Move the cell pointer to A12, the first row that you want moved down.

❷ Select /Worksheet Insert Row (**/WIR**).

The prompt message "Enter row insert range: A12..A12" appears on the control panel. Since you are adding only one row, do not change the range. If you wanted to insert more rows, you would press **[↓]** for every row you wanted to insert.

❸ Press **[Enter]**. 1-2-3 has inserted one blank row. All the other rows have been pushed down below the blank row. Notice also that 1-2-3 has adjusted all formula relationships. See Figure 2-21.

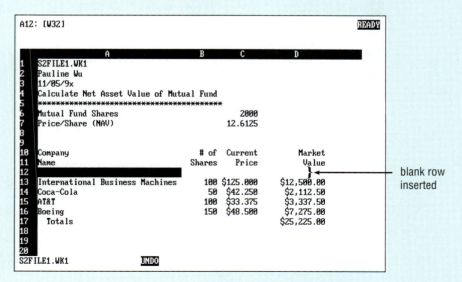

Figure 2-21

To insert a blank row after Boeing and before the Total Value row:

4 Move the cell pointer to A17.

5 Select /Worksheet Insert Row (**/WIR**).

6 Press **[Enter]**. A blank row is inserted between Boeing and the label Totals.

Now let's add some lines to improve the worksheet's appearance.

To underline the column headings:

1 Move the cell pointer to A12. Type \ – and press **[Enter]**.

2 Repeat Step 1 for cells B12, C12, and D12.

To add a row of lines to row 17:

3 Move the cell pointer to A17. Type \ – and press **[Enter]**.

4 Repeat Step 3 for cells B17, C17, and D17. See Figure 2-22.

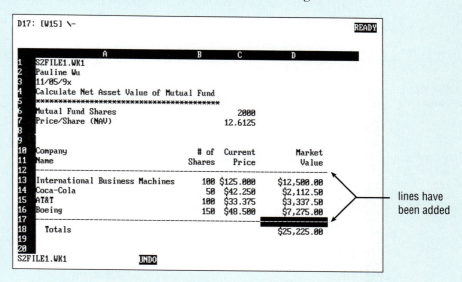

Figure 2-22

Moving Data

Pauline has made several changes that have improved the appearance of her worksheet. However, after reviewing the current worksheet, Pauline decides that she wants to make additional changes to improve it even further. First, she wants the summary data on mutual fund shares and net asset value to follow the company data. She feels the companies that make up the fund should be placed before the summary information on the NAV. (Report layout often is a matter of personal preference.) In addition, she realizes the report is actually incomplete because the company sells many different mutual funds. The worksheet does not indicate that these data are only for the Balboa Equity Fund. Also, she prices the fund at the end of each day, but the worksheet doesn't indicate the date of this report. Thus, Pauline decides to add the following two lines to the worksheet:

Balboa Equity Fund
Net Asset Value for November 5, 1990

She wants to place this title above the column headings, exactly where the Mutual Fund Shares label is now. How can she rearrange the worksheet without starting over?

Fortunately, Lotus 1-2-3 has a Move command. Its function is to move data from one part of the worksheet to another part of the same worksheet. This command is a powerful tool for creating and designing worksheets. Let's move the information on the number of shares owned and the NAV to begin in cell A19, so this information appears after the individual companies in the fund.

To move the range A6..C7 to a new location:

❶   Move the cell pointer to A6, the upper left corner of the range you want to move.

❷   Select /Move (**/M**). A6..A6 appears on the control panel as the move FROM range. The two periods mean the cell is anchored in A6. See Figure 2-23.

first cell in range
to be moved

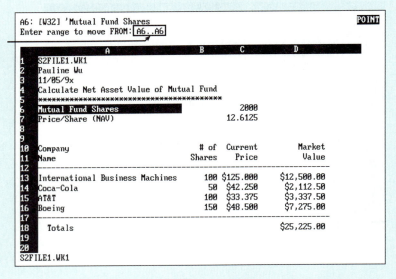

Figure 2-23

You next identify the entire range you want to move (A6 to C7):

❸   Highlight A6..C7. The highlighted area will be moved. See Figure 2-24.

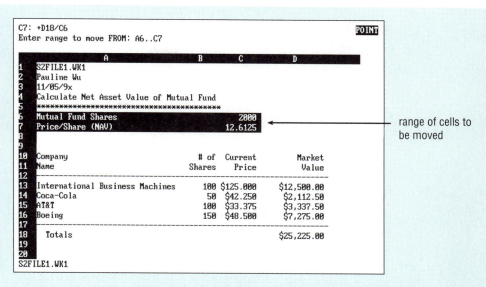

```
C7: +D18/C6                                                    POINT
Enter range to move FROM: A6..C7

                     A               B        C        D
1  S2FILE1.WK1
2  Pauline Wu
3  11/05/9x
4  Calculate Net Asset Value of Mutual Fund
5  ********************************************
6  Mutual Fund Shares                        2000
7  Price/Share (NAV)                      12.6125
8
9
10 Company                          # of  Current    Market
11 Name                           Shares    Price     Value
12 ------------------------------------------------------
13 International Business Machines    100 $125.000  $12,500.00
14 Coca-Cola                          50  $42.250   $2,112.50
15 AT&T                              100  $33.375   $3,337.50
16 Boeing                            150  $48.500   $7,275.00
17
18    Totals                                       $25,225.00
19
20
   S2FILE1.WK1
```

Figure 2-24

range of cells to be moved

④   Press **[Enter]**.

Now you identify the upper left corner of the new location for this block of cells:

⑤   Move the cell pointer to A19, the first cell of the move TO range. This is the cell where you want the label "Mutual Fund Shares" to begin.

⑥   Press **[Enter]**. The block of cells moves to its new location. See Figure 2-25. Notice that A6..C7 is empty.

Even if you move all or part of your worksheet, the worksheet retains all the functional relationships. 1-2-3 automatically adjusts all the formulas in the move FROM range.

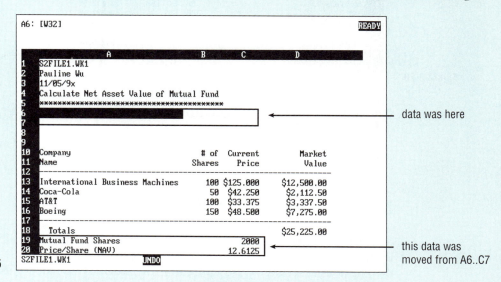

```
A6: [W32]                                                     READY

                     A               B        C        D
1  S2FILE1.WK1
2  Pauline Wu
3  11/05/9x
4  Calculate Net Asset Value of Mutual Fund
5  ********************************************
6
7
8
9
10 Company                          # of  Current    Market
11 Name                           Shares    Price     Value
12 ------------------------------------------------------
13 International Business Machines    100 $125.000  $12,500.00
14 Coca-Cola                          50  $42.250   $2,112.50
15 AT&T                              100  $33.375   $3,337.50
16 Boeing                            150  $48.500   $7,275.00
17 ------------------------------------------------------
18    Totals                                       $25,225.00
19 Mutual Fund Shares                        2000
20 Price/Share (NAV)                      12.6125
   S2FILE1.WK1                     UNDO
```

Figure 2-25

data was here

this data was moved from A6..C7

When you have completed moving the data, the cell pointer returns to the cell where you started the command.

● Move the cell pointer to the cell that contains the NAV, C20, and examine the formula in the control panel. The formula is now +D18/C19. When the formula was in cell C7, the formula was +D18/C6. The formula was automatically adjusted by 1-2-3.

Now you are ready to enter the two-line title: Balboa Equity Fund and Net Asset Value for November 5, 1990.

To enter the title:

● Move the cell pointer to cell A6.

● Type **Balboa Equity Fund** and press [↓].

● In cell A7, type **Net Asset Value for** and press [→].

● In cell B7, type **November 5, 1990** and press **[Enter]**. See Figure 2-26.

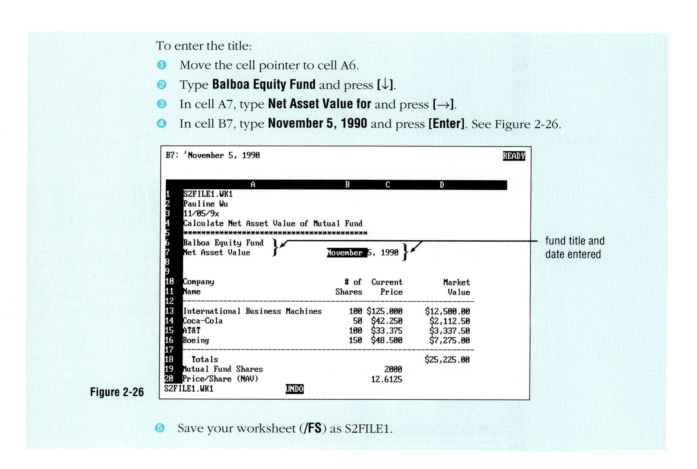

```
B7: 'November 5, 1990                                              READY

                    A                B       C           D
1  S2FILE1.WK1
2  Pauline Wu
3  11/05/9x
4  Calculate Net Asset Value of Mutual Fund
5  **************************************************                fund title and
6  Balboa Equity Fund                                                date entered
7  Net Asset Value              November 5, 1990
8
9
10 Company                        # of  Current      Market
11 Name                           Shares Price        Value
12 --------------------------------------------------------
13 International Business Machines  100 $125.000    $12,500.00
14 Coca-Cola                        50  $42.250     $2,112.50
15 AT&T                            100  $33.375     $3,337.50
16 Boeing                          150  $48.500     $7,275.00
17 --------------------------------------------------------
18    Totals                                       $25,225.00
19 Mutual Fund Shares                    2000
20 Price/Share (NAV)                   12.6125
S2FILE1.WK1                    UNDO
```

Figure 2-26

● Save your worksheet (**/FS**) as S2FILE1.

Erasing a Range of Cells

Now that the worksheet is complete, Pauline thinks about how she will use it on a daily basis. Each day, Pauline will enter the current day's prices for each company's stock. To make sure that she doesn't accidently use a price from the previous day, she wants to erase all the prices in the current price column before she enters the prices for the current day. To erase the prices, she will use the Range Erase command.

To erase the current prices in column C:

❶ Move the cell pointer to C13, the first cell to be erased.

❷ Select /Range Erase (**/RE**). The control panel reveals the address of the current cell and prompts you to specify the range you want to erase.

❸ Press [↓] to highlight the range C13..C16. See Figure 2-27.

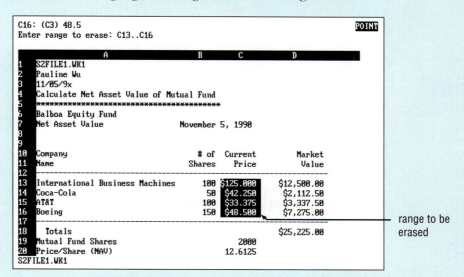

Figure 2-27

range to be erased

❹ Press **[Enter]**. 1-2-3 erases the entries in C13 to C16. The cell pointer returns to C13, the first cell in the range. See Figure 2-28.

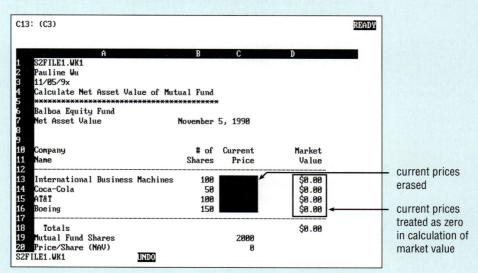

Figure 2-28

current prices erased

current prices treated as zero in calculation of market value

Notice that the market values are now zero. That is because their values are based on the daily prices, which are blank. 1-2-3 treats the blank cells as zero for any calculations that reference these cells.

The worksheet is now ready for Pauline to enter the prices for the next day.

❺   Save your worksheet (**/FS**) as S2FILE2.

Summary

In Tutorial 2, you learned how to move data and how to right-justify text in a cell. In using @SUM, you began learning how to use @functions.

You substantially increased your skills in modifying many aspects of a 1-2-3 worksheet. For example, you moved a range of cell to another part of a worksheet, inserted rows between adjacent rows and adjusted the width of a column. You also changed the format of numbers. Finally, you learned how to erase a range of cells in your worksheet.

Exercises

1. Suppose that you have a worksheet and cells F6, F7, F8, and F9 have values stored in them. Write two different formulas to calculate the total of these four cells.

2. Which formula adds six entries in row 3?
    a.   +A3+A4+A5+A6+A7+A8
    b.   @SUM(B3..E3)
    c.   @SUM(D3..I3)
    d.   +M3+N3+O3+P3

3. Suppose you type the value 1005.254 in cell A5. What format type would you select in each case to have the following values appear in the cell?
    a. $1,005.25
    b.   1,005.3
    c.   1005

4. Figure 2-29 shows a worksheet you started typing. The company name, Allied Freight, was typed in cell A3, and the address, 227 Mill St Canton Ohio 13456 was typed in B3. Why does the complete address appear in cell B3 but only Allied Fr in A3?

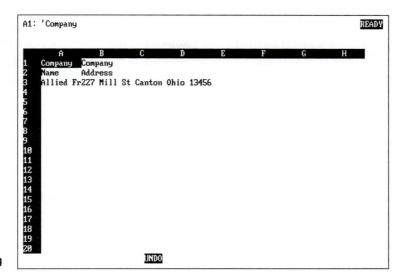

Figure 2-29

5. Figure 2-30 shows part of a worksheet. How would you improve the appearance of this worksheet?   What command(s) would you use?

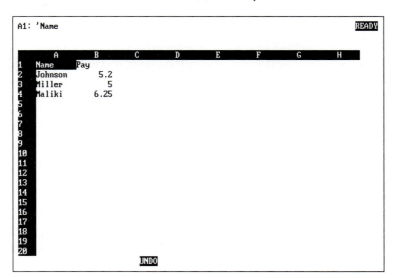

Figure 2-30

Tutorial Assignments

1. Retrieve the worksheet file T2FILE1.WK1. The formula in cell C20 is not correct. Price/Share (NAV) shows "ERR" when the worksheet is retrieved.
   a. Explain why ERR is displayed as the value for NAV.
   b. Correct the error.
   c. Print the corrected worksheet.
   d. Save the corrected worksheet as S2FILE3.

Retrieve the worksheet file T2FILE2.WK1 and do the following:

2. Adjust the labels, Mutual Fund Shares and Price/Share (NAV), so they are right-justified in their cells, A19 and A20, respectively.

3. Move the values associated with the labels in Tutorial Assignment 2 from cells C19 and C20 to B19 and B20.

4. Format NAV to two decimal places using the Currency format.

5. Print the revised worksheet. Use the print range A1..D20.

6. The worksheet is too cluttered. Move all the information in the range A6..D20 to a separate screen beginning at cell A21.

7. In cell A10 type **Press [PgDn] to view Net Asset Value Report.**

8. Save this worksheet as S2FILE4.

9. Erase the entire worksheet.

10. Retrieve the worksheet file S2FILE4.WK1.

11. Erase the current prices in the worksheet and then enter the following prices for November 6, 1990: 120.50, 43, 34.125, and 48.25. Remember to change the date in the worksheet. Print the worksheet. Save as S2FILE5.

The following exercises involve the worksheet developed in Tutorial 1. Retrieve the file T1FILE5.WK1 and do the following:

12. In cell B19, calculate total hours for all employees using the @SUM function.

13. Format the pay rate and gross pay columns to two decimal places using the Currency format.

14. A new employee, Jalecki, has been hired. Insert this name between the names Bramble and Juarez.

15. Print the revised worksheet.

16. Save the revised worksheet as S1FILE6.

Use the Reference section of *Lotus 1-2-3 for Business* to answer the following question:

17. Pauline doesn't like the fact that market values and NAV are recalculated every time she enters a stock price. Is there a way to turn off the automatic recalculation, so Pauline can control when recalculations are performed? Retrieve T2FILE2 and redo Tutorial Assignment 11 by turning off automatic recalculation. Save your revised worksheet as S2FILE6.

Case Problems

1. Z & Z Electronics Performance Report

Craig Keifer is the general manager of the manufacturing division of Z & Z Electronics. Each year Craig prepares estimated costs for manufacturing cabinets for computers and other electronic equipment. Manufacturing costs include wages/salaries, raw materials, utilities, supplies, and other costs. Craig prepares a performance report to measure his division's performance compared to his estimate. This monthly report compares the estimated costs with the actual costs for the month just ended and the year-to-date (YTD) cumulative costs. Craig also calculates the difference between estimated and actual costs, called the *variance*, for both the monthly and cumulative periods. He does this by subtracting estimated costs from the actual costs, in other words,

$$variance \ = \ actual \ cost \ - \ estimated \ cost$$

Retrieve the P2PERFRM.WK1 worksheet. This worksheet contains the cost data for the month of March 1990, as well as cumulative costs since the beginning of the year.

1. Calculate the total costs for both the estimated and the actual cost columns (columns B, C, E, and F).

2. Calculate the variances for each cost for both monthly and year-to-date periods (columns D and G).

3. Improve the appearance of the worksheet. Add titles, lines under headings, format values, and any other changes that will make the report more readable.

4. Print your worksheet.

5. Save your worksheet as S2PERFRM.

2. Ford Motor Company Car Sales

A Ford executive is preparing a presentation for a local Chamber of Commerce. The executive asks his assistant, Steve Duncan, to prepare a 1-2-3 worksheet with Ford's sales history (units sold) from 1985 to 1988. Steve starts to summarize the data for Ford's three divisions; Ford, Mercury, and Lincoln, but he becomes ill and cannot finish the assignment. His worksheet file, P2FORD.WK1, is incomplete:

*   He has not entered data for the Mercury division, which is shown in Figure 2-31 on the next page. The data for the Mercury division should be placed between the Ford and the Lincoln divisions.

*   Each division's sales need to be subtotaled, and then all three divisions' sales should be added to provide total sales for Ford Motor Company for each year. Only the labels for subtotals appear in the worksheet.

*   Finally, the worksheet must be more professional in appearance before the executive distributes it to the Chamber of Commerce.

	Units Sold—Mercury Division			
Mercury Division	**1985**	**1986**	**1987**	**1988**
Topaz	73554	65498	63217	85936
Sable	879	91314	103399	118117
Cougar	118554	112812	110112	102415
Grand Marquis	134139	118364	119015	115141

Figure 2-31

Complete Steve's worksheet by doing the following:

1. Retrieve the worksheet file P2FORD.WK1.

2. Add the data for the Mercury division between the Ford and the Lincoln divisions.

3. Calculate the subtotal for each division.

4. Calculate total sales for all the divisions.

5. Improve the appearance of the worksheet. Include a title, date, and lines under the column headings, align the column headings, and make any other changes you feel are appropriate.

6. Print the worksheet.

7. Save your worksheet as S2FORD.

3. Calculating the Dow Jones Industrial Average

The Dow Jones Industrial Average (DJIA) is the best-known indicator of how stock prices fluctuate on the New York Stock Exchange (NYSE). The DJIA represents the average price of thirty large, well-known industrial corporations considered leaders in their industry. All the companies are listed on the NYSE.

Each day the DJIA is calculated by summing the closing price of each of the thirty companies and dividing by a divisor. The formula for calculating the DJIA is:

$$DJIA = \frac{\textit{sum of daily closing prices for 30 companies}}{\textit{divisor}}$$

On September 5, 1990, the DJIA was 2613.14. The divisor was 0.5049.

Retrieve the file P2DOW.WK1 and do the following:

1. Finish the calculation of the DJIA (cell B43).

2. Experts suggest that changes in higher-priced stock have a greater impact on the DJIA than changes on lower-priced stock. For example, if IBM, a high-priced stock, were to increase by 10% (assume no other stock prices change), the new DJIA would change more than if Navistar, a low-priced stock, were to increase by 10%.
    a. In column C, labelled IBM Adjmt, increase IBM's price by 10% (1.10 × current price) and calculate the new DJIA (cell C43).

b. In column D, the Navistar column, increase Navistar's price by 10% and calculate the DJIA (cell D43).

c. Compare the new averages against the original average by calculating the percent change. Use the following formulas:

For the percent change in column C:

$$percent\ change = \frac{(IBM\ adjusted\ DJIA\ -\ original\ DJIA)}{original\ DJIA} \times 100$$

For the percent change in column D:

$$percent\ change = \frac{(Navistar\ adjusted\ DJIA\ -\ original\ DJIA)}{original\ DJIA} \times 100$$

Note that the original DJIA is in cell B43. How do these new averages compare to the original average?

3. Format your worksheet so it is more readable. Consider formatting values, centering or right-justifying column headings, adding descriptive labels, and making any other changes you think will improve the appearance of your worksheet.

4. Save your worksheet as S2DOW.

5. Print your final worksheet.

Tutorial 3

Working with Larger Worksheets

Preparing a Revenue Report

Case: TriCycle Industries

Nick Theodorakis is the assistant sales manager for TriCycle Industries, a recycling center serving the tri-state area of Kentucky, Indiana, and Illinois. For the last two years, TriCycle's sales were not high enough to generate a profit. This year, however, TriCycle was profitable and came very close to achieving its sales goals.

As assistant sales manager, Nick services fifteen customer accounts, scouts for new accounts, and provides administrative assistance to the TriCycle sales manager, Kay Schilling. At the end of each quarter, Nick assists Kay in preparing a quarterly sales report. Kay then formally presents the report to top management at TriCycle's quarterly meeting.

Objectives

In this tutorial you will learn how to:

- Copy contents of cells to other locations in the worksheet

- Copy relative cell references

- Copy absolute cell references

- Assign names to cell ranges

- Print using compressed type

Kay meets with Nick to discuss this quarter's report. She shows him the data she has compiled:

TriCycle Industries 1990 Revenue
(000 Omitted)

Recycled Material	First Quarter	Second Quarter	Third Quarter	Fourth Quarter
Plastics	2890	2942	3378	3837
Glass	2701	2862	2869	3601
Aluminum	2247	2282	2489	2602

Kay points out that these data represent the revenue for all four quarters of 1990. She wants to include totals and some additional information to help the top executives compare 1990 revenues to previous years. She asks Nick to create a worksheet using the data she's collected thus far and also showing the following:

- total revenue by quarter
- total revenue for the year 1990 by recycled material
- total 1990 revenue
- contribution of revenue from each material as a percentage of total 1990 revenue

Nick agrees and offers to give special attention to the appearance of the worksheet, because he knows how important this report will be. Nick spends time thinking about the project and develops a planning sheet and a sketch to assist him in completing the worksheet (Figures 3-1a and 3-1b).

My Goal
    Prepare the Sales Report for TriCycle management

What results do I want to see?
    Sales Revenue Report including totals by quarter and recycled material
    Contribution of each recycled material to total revenue

What information do I need?
    Quarterly sales revenue for each recycled material

What calculations will I perform?
    Calculate total revenue for each quarter
    Calculate total revenue for each recycled material for the year
    Calculate total revenue for year
    Calculate percent contribution of each recycled material to total
      revenue

Figure 3-1a
Nick's planning sheet

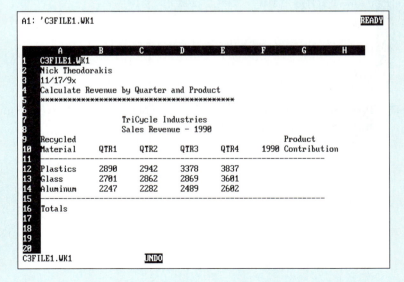

Figure 3-1b
Nick's worksheet
sketch

In this tutorial, you will use Kay's data to create Nick's report. You will learn how to copy formulas, a process that saves a great deal of time in creating a worksheet. You will also put to use several valuable 1-2-3 features, such as how to name ranges. You will also learn more about printing with 1-2-3, specifically how to use compressed type to print more data on one line.

Retrieving the Worksheet

Your first step in this tutorial is to retrieve the worksheet that Nick has started based on Kay's data.

To retrieve the worksheet:

❶ Retrieve the file C3FILE1.WK1. See Figure 3-2.

Figure 3-2
The retrieved
TriCycle worksheet
— quarterly
revenues by
recycled
material

```
A1: 'C3FILE1.WK1                                                        READY

        A        B        C        D        E        F        G        H
 1  C3FILE1.WK1
 2  Nick Theodorakis
 3  11/17/9x
 4  Calculate Revenue by Quarter and Product
 5  *************************************************
 6
 7                TriCycle Industries
 8                Sales Revenue - 1990
 9  Recycled                                    Product
10  Material    QTR1     QTR2     QTR3     QTR4    1990 Contribution
11  ------------------------------------------------------------------
12  Plastics    2890     2942     3378     3837
13  Glass       2701     2862     2869     3601
14  Aluminum    2247     2282     2489     2602
15
16  Totals
17  ------------------------------------------------------------------
18
19
20
C3FILE1.WK1                   UNDO
```

This file contains the quarterly revenues of TriCycle Industries categorized by the material they recycle. Titles have been entered; so have revenue amounts for each material for each quarter.

How did TriCycle perform in each quarter? Let's calculate total revenues for each quarter to summarize TriCycle's revenue picture. In Tutorial 2, you used the @SUM function to calculate total market value of a mutual fund. Now you will use the @SUM function to calculate total revenue for each quarter.

To calculate total revenue for the first quarter:

❶ Move the cell pointer to B16.

❷ Type **@SUM(**

❸ Move the cell pointer to B12 and then type **[.]** (Period) to anchor the cell pointer.

❹ Press **[↓]** to highlight the range B12..B14. See Figure 3-3.

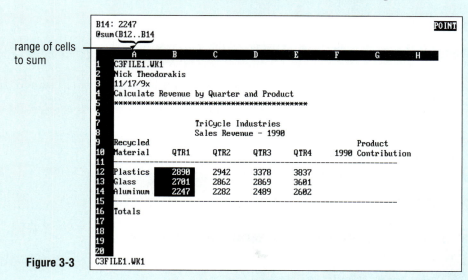

range of cells to sum

Figure 3-3

❺ Type **[)]** (Right Parenthesis) and press **[Enter]**. The total revenue in quarter 1, 7838, appears in cell B16. See Figure 3-4.

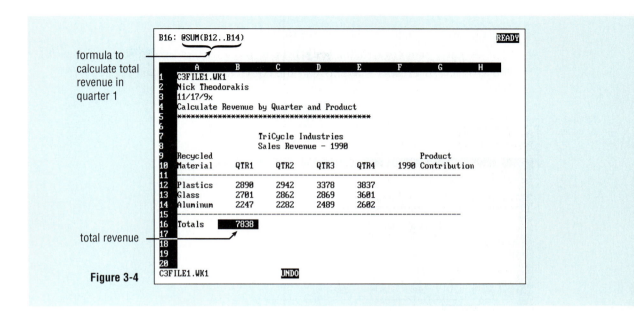

formula to calculate total revenue in quarter 1

total revenue

Figure 3-4

You might find it easier to type in the actual letters and numbers of the range, that is, B12..B14, instead of pointing to the cell range. If you had used this approach, Step 2 would have been

❷　Type **@SUM(B12..B14**

You would then skip Steps 3 and 4 and conclude with Step 5.

Copying Formulas

You can continue to use the @SUM function to calculate total revenue for the remaining quarters. A faster approach, however, is to use the Copy command. Experienced 1-2-3 users rely on the Copy command because it saves time and decreases the likelihood of errors. Let's calculate total revenues for quarters 2, 3, and 4 by copying the formula in cell B16 to cells C16, D16, and E16.

To copy a formula to cells C16, D16, and E16:

❶ With the cell pointer in B16, the cell whose formula will be copied, select /Copy **(/C)**.

The control panel displays B16..B16 as the copy FROM range, meaning cell B16 is to be copied to other cells. See Figure 3-5.

formula to be copied

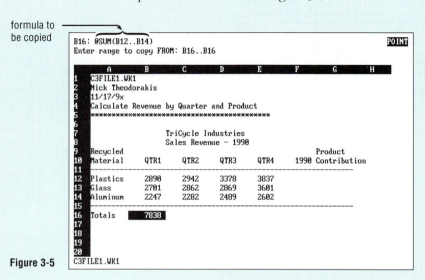

Figure 3-5

❷ Press **[Enter]**, because B16 is the only cell formula you want to copy. Notice that the panel text changes and requests the range of cells to copy this formula TO. See Figure 3-6.

formula to be copied

cell not anchored

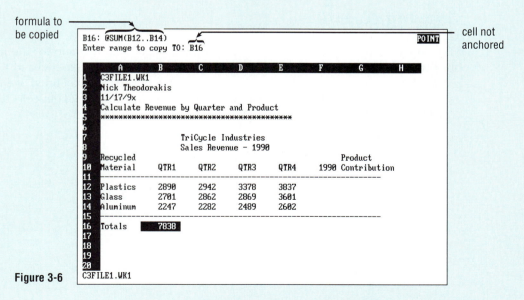

Figure 3-6

❸ Move the cell pointer to C16, the first cell in the range you are copying TO.

Now anchor this cell.

④   Press **[.]** (Period) to anchor the cell pointer. This designates C16 as the first cell in the copy TO range. See Figure 3-7.

cell anchored →

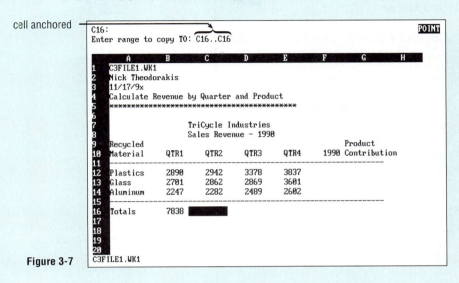

Figure 3-7

⑤   Press **[→]** as needed to highlight the range C16 to E16. This is the entire copy TO range. See Figure 3-8.

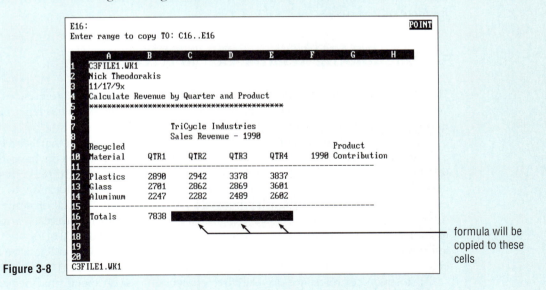

formula will be copied to these cells

Figure 3-8

❻   Press **[Enter]** to complete the command. See Figure 3-9.

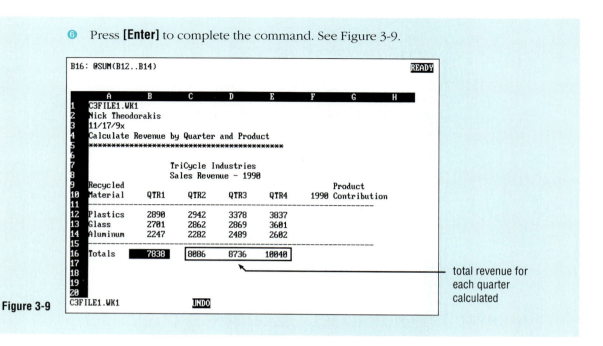

Figure 3-9

total revenue for
each quarter
calculated

Total revenue for each quarter has now been calculated. You entered the formula for the first quarter and then used the Copy command to copy this formula to the cell locations for quarters 2, 3, and 4.

Understanding Relative Cell References

How 1-2-3 copies a formula depends on whether you use relative cell references or absolute cell references in a formula. The concept of relative and absolute cell references is extremely important to your work with 1-2-3.

A **relative cell reference** is a cell or range of cells in a formula that 1-2-3 interprets as a location relative to the current cell. For example, in cell B16 you have the formula @SUM(B12..B14). 1-2-3 interprets this formula as "add the contents of three cells starting four cells above the formula cell." When you copy this formula to a new location, to cell C16, for example, you copy the relationship between the formula and the cell or range to which it refers. 1-2-3 automatically adjusts the addresses in the copied formulas to maintain the relationship. For example, if you copied the formula @SUM(B12..B14) to cell C16, 1-2-3 interprets the formula as "add the contents of three cells starting four cells above the formula cell"; then 1-2-3 adjusts the formula automatically to @SUM(C12..C14).

1-2-3 treats cell references as relative references unless you specify that they are absolute. You will learn about absolute cell references later in this tutorial.

Naming Ranges

Kay also wants to know how much revenue TriCycle earned from recycling each material during 1990. To calculate yearly revenue, you will continue to use the @SUM function. Instead of using cell addresses inside the @SUM function, however, you will use range names in the formulas. Whenever you are working with a large worksheet, you should use descriptive words instead of cell addresses for ranges in the formula. Descriptive words are more meaningful in a formula, since they remind you of the purpose of the calculation. 1-2-3 lets you assign descriptive names to individual cells or cell ranges. You can then use these names in place of cell references when building formulas. For example, the formula @SUM(PLASTICS) is easier to understand than @SUM(B12..E12).

Let's assign range names to the range of cells representing quarterly sales for each recycled material: plastics, glass, and aluminum. Let's also assign a range name to the range of cells representing the four quarterly totals (B16..E16).

To create a range name for revenue from plastics:

❶ Move the cell pointer to B12, the revenue from recycled plastics in the first quarter.

❷ Select /Range Name Create (**/RNC**).

❸ Type **PLASTICS** and press **[Enter]**. See Figure 3-10.

range name →

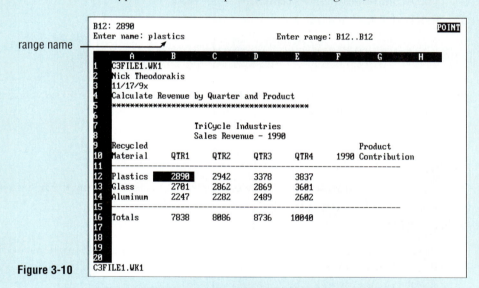

Figure 3-10

You can use lowercase or uppercase letters. 1-2-3 automatically converts lowercase to uppercase.

❹ Press **[→]** to highlight the range B12..E12. You don't need to anchor this range, because it is automatically anchored when you use the Range Name command.

❺ Press **[Enter]**. You have just named the range (B12..E12) PLASTICS.

Next, assign the range name GLASS to the revenue earned from recycling glass during the four quarters.

To assign the range name:

❶ Move the pointer to B13, the revenue from glass during the first quarter.

❷ Select /Range Name Create (**/RNC**).

❸ Type **GLASS** and press **[Enter]**.

❹ Press **[→]** to highlight the range B13..E13.

❺ Press **[Enter]**. You have just named the range (B13 .. E13) GLASS.

Now, assign the range name ALUMINUM to the revenue received from recycling aluminum materials during the four quarters.

To assign the range name:

❶ Move the cell pointer to B14, the revenue from aluminum in the first quarter.

❷ Select /Range Name Create (**/RNC**).

❸ Type **ALUMINUM** and press **[Enter]**.

❹ Press **[→]** to highlight the range B14..E14.

❺ Press **[Enter]**. You have just named the range (B14 .. E14) ALUMINUM.

Finally, assign the range name QTR_SALES to the revenue received from recycling all materials during the four quarters.

To assign the range name:

❶ Move the cell pointer to B16, the revenue from all products during the first quarter.

❷ Select /Range Name Create (**/RNC**).

❸ Type **QTR_SALES** and press **[Enter]**.

Notice the use of the [_] (Underscore) to connect words; spaces and hyphens are not permitted in range names.

❹ Press **[→]** to highlight the range B16..E16.

❺ Press **[Enter]**. You have just named the range (B16..E16) QTR_SALES.

If you select the Range Name Create command and then realize you want to highlight a range that starts in another location, press [Esc] to unanchor the cell pointer. Then move the cell pointer to the appropriate starting cell and press [.] (Period) to reanchor the cell pointer.

Range names can be up to 15 characters long, but they cannot include spaces or the characters + * − / & { @ and # . The underscore character is often used to connect words together. Do not use range names such as Q1, because 1-2-3 will interpret Q1 as a cell location instead of a range name.

Using Named Ranges in Formulas

Now you are ready to calculate total revenue earned by TriCycle Industries during 1990. In the previous steps, you created the range names PLASTIC, GLASS, ALUMINUM, and QTR_SALES. Assigning names to a range of cells will make formulas easier to create and interpret. You can use range names in formulas two ways: by choosing the one you want from a list of the previously named ranges or by typing the name of the range directly into the formula.

To obtain a list of range names while you are entering a formula, press [F3] (NAME) to display a list of range names created in this worksheet. Highlight the range name you want, and press [Enter]. The range name is entered in the formula.

To use a range name in an @SUM formula using the [F3] key:

❶ Move the cell pointer to F12; this is the cell in which you want total revenues from plastics for 1990 to appear.

❷ Type **@SUM(**.

❸ Press **[F3]** (NAME). This function key displays a list of all range names you have created for this worksheet. See Figure 3-11.

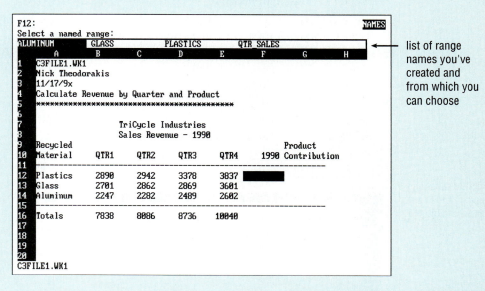

list of range names you've created and from which you can choose

Figure 3-11

❹ Move the cursor to the range name you want, PLASTICS, and press **[Enter]** to select it. Your entry should now look like that in Figure 3-12.

range name you selected for sum function

Figure 3-12

❺ Continue entering the formula by typing **[)]** (Right Parenthesis).

❻ Press **[Enter]**. 1-2-3 calculates the result, 13047, in cell F12. This is the sum of revenues earned from recycling plastics during 1990.

Alternatively, you could have typed in the range name, PLASTICS, directly after the left
parenthesis in Step 2.

❷   @SUM(PLASTICS.

You would then skip Steps 3 and 4, and conclude with Step 5.
Now let's enter the formula for glass.

To use a range name in an @SUM formula using the [F3] key:

❶ Move the cell pointer to F13; this is the cell in which you want total revenues from
glass for 1990 to appear.

❷ Type **@SUM(**.

❸ Press **[F3]** (NAME). This function key displays a list of all range names you have created for this worksheet.

❹ Move the cursor to the range name you want, GLASS, and press **[Enter]** to select it.

❺ Type **[)]** (Right Parenthesis).

❻ Press **[Enter]**. 1-2-3 calculates the result, 12033, in cell F13. This is the sum of revenues earned from recycling glass during 1990.

❼ Move the cell pointer to F14. Repeat Steps 2 through 5 to enter an @SUM formula
using the range name ALUMINUM to total revenue from aluminum in 1990. The
result in F14 should be 9620.

❽ Move the cell pointer to F16. Repeat Steps 2 through 5 to enter an @SUM formula
using the range name QTR_SALES to total revenue from all products in 1990. The
result in F16 should be 34700. See Figure 3-13.

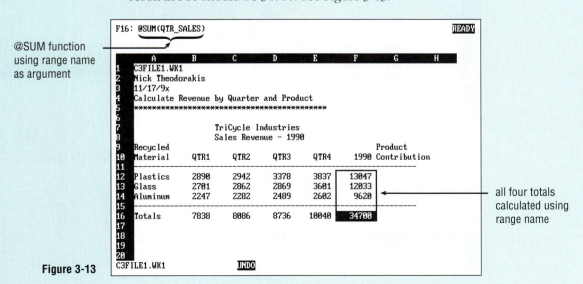

@SUM function
using range name
as argument

all four totals
calculated using
range name

Figure 3-13

If you accidently press [Enter] before typing the right parenthesis, 1-2-3 automatically beeps and moves to EDIT mode, in which you should type [ )] (Right Parenthesis) and press [Enter].

Deleting Range Names

If you create a range name and want to delete the range, select /Range Name Delete (/RND) and press the function key [F3]. Move the menu pointer to the name you want to delete from the list and press [Enter].

Copying Formulas with Absolute References

Nick has now calculated total revenue earned by TriCycle Industries during 1990, as well as individual revenues from plastics, glass, and aluminum. Next, Nick plans to calculate each material's percentage of total 1990 revenue. To calculate each material's contribution to total revenue, you divide the 1990 revenue for each material by total company revenue for 1990.

For example,

$$percent\ contribution\ of\ plastics\ to\ total\ revenue = \frac{1990\ revenue\ for\ plastics}{total\ TriCycle\ 1990\ revenue}$$

To calculate the percent contribution of plastics:

❶ Move the cell pointer to G12.

❷ Type the formula **+F12/F16**.

❸ Press **[Enter]**. The result, 0.375994, appears in cell G12. See Figure 3-14.

symbol for
division

formula to
calculate
contribution to
total revenue for
plastics

```
G12: +F12/F16                                                          READY

         A         B        C         D        E        F        G        H
1  C3FILE1.WK1
2  Nick Theodorakis
3  11/17/9x
4  Calculate Revenue by Quarter and Product
5  ****************************************************
6
7                     TriCycle Industries
8                     Sales Revenue - 1990
9  Recycled                                           Product
10 Material   QTR1      QTR2     QTR3      QTR4     1990 Contribution
11 ----------------------------------------------------------------
12 Plastics   2890      2942     3378      3837     13047 0.375994
13 Glass      2701      2862     2869      3601     12033
14 Aluminum   2247      2282     2489      2602      9620
15 ----------------------------------------------------------------
16 Totals     7838      8086     8736     10040     34700
17
18
19
20
   C3FILE1.WK1                   UNDO
```

Figure 3-14

Now that you have entered the formula +F12/F16 in cell G12, you can use the Copy command to copy this formula to other cells.

The steps that follow illustrate an approach that leads to incorrect results. We show these steps to demonstrate a common mistake made by many beginning students of 1-2-3, in the hopes of helping you avoid it.

To demonstrate a common mistake:

❶ Be sure the cell pointer is in G12, the cell that contains the formula to be copied. Select /Copy (**/C**). The control panel shows G12..G12 as the copy FROM range.

❷ Press **[Enter]**, since G12 is the only cell you want to copy.

❸ Move the cell pointer to G13, the first cell in the range you are copying to.

❹ Press **[.]** (Period) to anchor the cell pointer. G13 is now the first cell in the copy TO range.

❺ Highlight the range G13..G14. This is the copy TO range.

❻ Press **[Enter]** to complete the command, and notice that ERR appears in cells G13 and G14. See Figure 3-15.

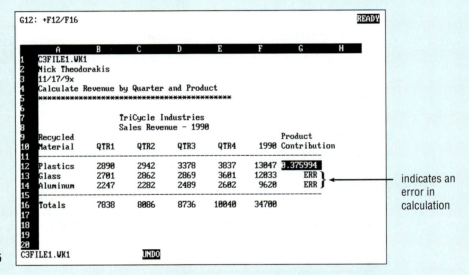

indicates an error in calculation

Figure 3-15

Move the cell pointer sequentially to each cell containing ERR and examine the formula in the control panel. Do you see what happened? The formula in cell G13 is +F13/F17, but what you want in G13 is the formula +F13/F16. You also have an incorrect formula in G14, +F14/F18 instead of +F14/F16. All the copied formulas have resulted in ERR appearing in the respective cells.

Why does ERR appear in these cells? When you copied the formula (+F12/F16) in cell G12, 1-2-3 assumed relative addressing and *adjusted* the cell references in the copied formula.

The following formulas resulted:

Cell	Formula
G13	+F13/F17
G14	+F14/F18

When 1-2-3 calculated the glass and aluminum contributions using the formulas in G13 and G14, it tried to divide by zero (the values below cell F16, F17 and F18, are both zero). Since division by zero is undefined, the message ERR appears in cells G13 and G14.

To calculate percent contribution of each material, you need to use the following formulas:

Recycled Material	Formula	Description
Plastic	+F12/F16	$\dfrac{1990\ revenue\ for\ plastic}{total\ TriCycle\ 1990\ revenue}$
Glass	+F13/F16	$\dfrac{1990\ revenue\ for\ glass}{total\ TriCycle\ 1990\ revenue}$
Aluminum	+F14/F16	$\dfrac{1990\ revenue\ for\ aluminum}{total\ TriCycle\ 1990\ revenue}$

Notice that the cells in the numerators vary (F12, F13, F14), while the cells in the denominators are always the same, F16. When you copy the formula for percent contribution to other cell locations, the cell addresses of the numerator should change relative to the cell formula. On the other hand, when you copy the cell address of the denominator to other cell locations, the cell address should remain unchanged. Thus, using relative referencing for the entire formula doesn't work. This is an example of a situation that requires absolute cell references.

Absolute Cell References

When you copy a formula, you sometimes want 1-2-3 to keep the original cell addresses in the copied formula. You do *not* want 1-2-3 to adjust the cell references for you. To keep the original cell or range reference constant, no matter where in the worksheet the formula is copied, you use an absolute reference. An **absolute reference** is a cell address or range name that *always* refers to the same cell, even if you copy the formula to a new location. To designate an absolute cell reference, you use [$] (Dollar Sign) to precede both the column letter and the row number or range name of the cell you want to remain unchanged. Thus, $F$16 is an absolute cell reference, whereas F16 is a relative reference. Initially, both reference the same cell location; however, if you copy the cell location $F$16 to another cell, the cell address in the new location remains unchanged, whereas if you copy the cell location F16 to another cell, the cell address in the new location is automatically adjusted to reflect its position relative to the original cell location.

To specify absolute cell references, you can either type the $ character before the column letter and row number when you enter (or edit) a formula, or you can use another of the 1-2-3 function keys, [F4] (ABS), the Absolute key. When you press the [F4] key while in EDIT mode, 1-2-3 inserts a $ character at the cursor location in the cell address in the control panel. You could also retype the formula using the $ symbol in the appropriate places, but using the [F4] key is usually faster and helps avoid entry errors.

Before you try using the absolute reference in your formula, let's erase the incorrect formulas in cells G13 and G14 that cause ERR to be displayed.

When you type or copy an entry into the wrong cell, you can erase the contents of the cell or cells with the Range Erase command.

To erase a range of cells:

❶ Move the cell pointer to G13, the first cell to be erased.

❷ Select /Range Erase (**/RE**). The control panel reveals the address of the current cell and prompts you to specify the range you want to erase.

❸ Press [↓] to highlight the range G13 to G14.

❹ Press **[Enter]**. 1-2-3 erases the entries in G13 and G14. The cell pointer returns to G13, the first cell in the range. The formulas have been erased from cells G13 and G14. See Figure 3-16.

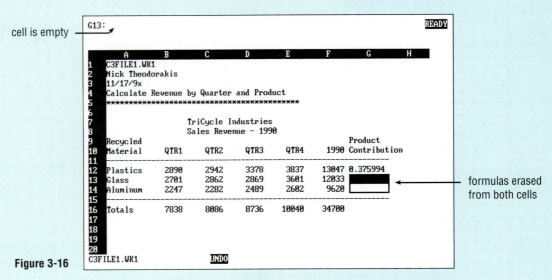

cell is empty →

formulas erased from both cells ←

Figure 3-16

Now let's correctly calculate the contribution to total revenue from glass and aluminum.

To use [F4] (ABS) to insert absolute cell references:

❶ Move the cell pointer to G12 and press **[F2]** (EDIT) to display the formula in the control panel. Notice that +F12/F16 appears in the second line of the control panel. See Figure 3-17.

line to be edited

mode

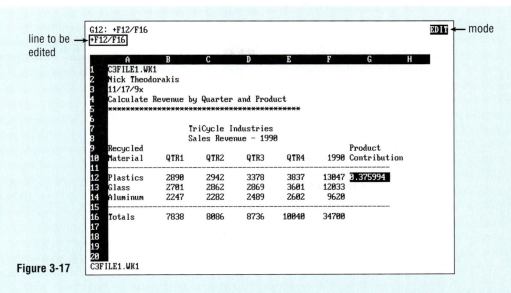

Figure 3-17

❷ Press [←] until the cursor is under the F in F16. Press **[F4]** (ABS) to make the cell reference absolute. Notice that $F$16 appears in the control panel. See Figure 3-18.

absolute cell reference

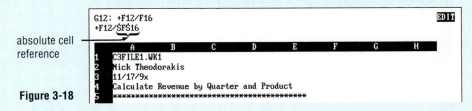

Figure 3-18

❸ Press **[Enter];** notice that the value in G12 does not change. However, a change does occur in the formula in the control panel. F16 becomes $F$16, an absolute reference. See Figure 3-19.

relative reference

formula with absolute cell reference

result is unchanged

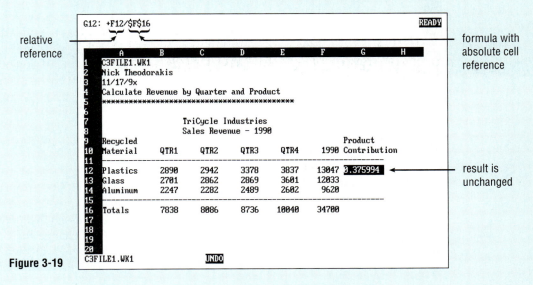

Figure 3-19

Now the formula in G12 contains absolute cell references to reference total 1990 revenues and uses relative references for each material's revenue. No matter what cell you copy the formula in G12 to, the cell reference $F$16 will not change. To demonstrate this process, let's copy the formula in G12 again to see what happens.

To copy G12 to G13..G14:

❶ Make sure the cell pointer is at G12 and select /Copy (**/C**).

❷ Press **[Enter]**, because G12 is the only cell you want to copy.

❸ Move the cell pointer to G13, the first cell in the range to which you are copying.

❹ Press **[.]** (Period) to anchor the cell pointer. G13 is now the first cell in the copy TO range.

❺ Highlight the range G13..G14. This is the copy TO range.

❻ Press **[Enter]** to complete the command. The percent contribution appears in cells G13 and G14. See Figure 3-20.

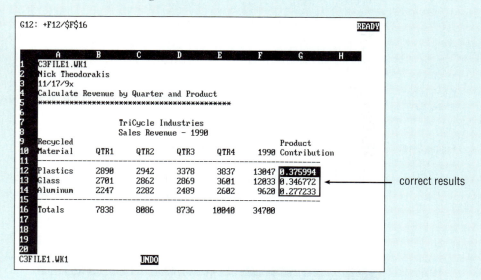

Figure 3-20

As a result of the Copy command, the following formulas appear in the control panel when you highlight cells G13 and G14:

Cell	Formula
G13	+F13/$F$16
G14	+F14/$F$16

Normally, each material's contribution to total revenue is expressed as a percent. In the worksheet, however, these values now appear as decimals. Let's change the contribution column so that all values will appear in Percent format. Numbers will then appear as percentages, that is, whole numbers followed by percent signs (%), for example, 15%. 1-2-3 multiplies the decimal number currently in the cell by 100 so that the number becomes a whole number. For example, .05 becomes 5%.

To format a range of cells to Percent format with one decimal:

❶ Make sure the cell pointer is in G12 and select /Range Format (**/RF**).

❷ Select Percent (**P**).

❸ Type **1** for the number of decimal places and press **[Enter]**.

❹ Highlight the cells G12..G14 and press **[Enter]**. See Figure 3-21.

indicates Percent format with 1 decimal place

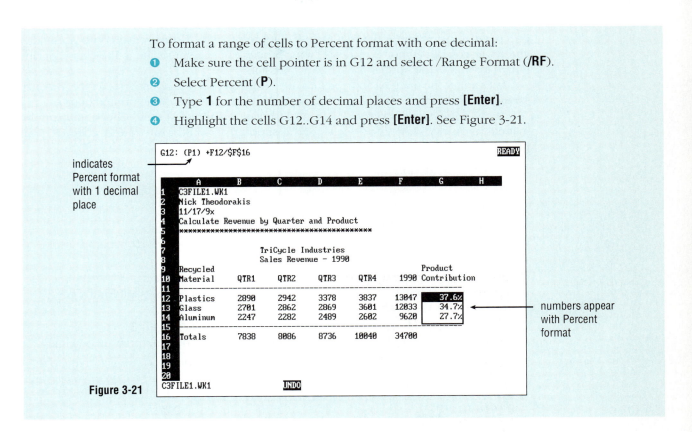

numbers appear with Percent format

Figure 3-21

The calculations are complete. All that remains is for Nick to save the worksheet and print the report.

To change the filename in cell A1 and to save the file:

❶ Press **[Home]** to move the cell pointer to cell A1.

❷ Type **S3FILE1.WK1**.

❸ Select /File Save (**FS**). Save the worksheet as S3FILE1.WK1.

Printing with Compressed Type

Larger worksheets are often too wide to fit on one printed page. What do you do if you want to show the entire worksheet on one page for easier interpretation? You can print more data on a page by instructing your printer to use compressed type. **Compressed type** is a smaller and more compact type. As a result, your printer can accommodate a 132-character line length instead of the normal 76 characters per line.

Let's adjust the margins and enter a setup string to print with compressed type. **A setup string** is a code sent to the printer to control the characteristics of the printed output.

Many printers use the code \015 to designate compressed type. Check your printer manual, or ask your instructor or technical support person for the correct code for your printer.

To set up for compressed type:

❶ Select /Print Printer (**/PP**).

❷ Select Options Setup (**OS**) to choose the option to enter the code for compressed type.

❸ Type **** (Backslash) **015** and press **[Enter]** to enter the setup string. \015 may not work for your printer. If it doesn't, ask your instructor or lab assistant for the correct code for your printer.

❹ Select Margins (**M**) from the Options menu and then select Right (**R**). The right margin options sets the maximum number of characters that can print on one line.

❺ Type **132** and press **[Enter]**. Your printer setting sheet should look similar to the one in Figure 3-22.

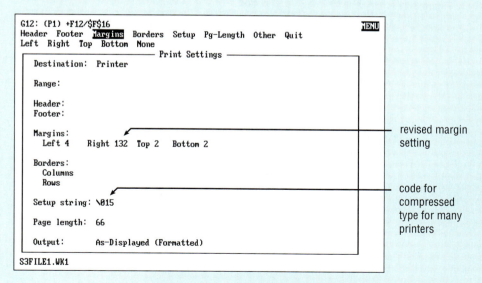

Figure 3-22

❻ Select Quit (**Q**) to leave the Options menu, then select Quit (**Q**) again to leave the Print menu.

Now let's print the TriCycle revenue report. Be sure your printer is ready before you begin.

To print the TriCycle report:

❶ Select /Print Printer (**/PP**).

❷ Select Range (**R**).

❸ Move the cell pointer to A7. Press **[.]** (Period) to anchor the cell.

❹ Highlight A7..H16, the cells that contain the report, then press **[Enter]**.

❺ Select Align Go Page (**AGP**) to print the report. See Figure 3-23.

```
    Lotus 1-2-3 Student Business Series          Nick Theodorakis


                           TriCycle Industries
                           Sales Revenue - 1990
    Recycled                                              Product
    Material      QTR1      QTR2      QTR3      QTR4    1990 Contribution
    -----------------------------------------------------------------
    Plastics      2890      2942      3378      3837   13047    37.6%
    Glass         2701      2862      2869      3601   12033    34.7%
    Aluminum      2247      2282      2489      2602    9620    27.7%
    -----------------------------------------------------------------
    Totals        7838      8086      8736     10040   34700
```

Figure 3-23
The final TriCycle revenue report in compressed type

❻ Select Quit (**Q**) to return to READY mode.

❼ Save the worksheet again as S3FILE1 (**/FS**).

Printing Checklist

Look at your printed output and check the following:

- **Headings** Does each listing contain a heading at the top that answers the questions who, what, and where?

- **Columns** Are all column widths correct? Do any cells contain asterisks, meaning that the values are too wide to appear in the column?

- **Margins** Are the margins adjusted evenly?

- **Accuracy** Is all the information correct? Are the numbers accurate? Are all words spelled correctly?

- **Lines** Do any blank lines appear in unintended places?

- **Appearance** Is the print legible? Do you need to install a new ribbon or make any adjustment?

Very often you will not be satisfied with your first printing of the worksheet. Fortunately, computers simplify the task of making changes. If necessary, edit your worksheet, save the changes, and print again. Do not handwrite corrections.

Summary

In this tutorial, you learned a number of techniques for managing larger worksheets. For example, with range names you can write clearer formulas. By using the Copy command, you can be more productive in developing worksheets. Finally, you can better present your worksheet by using compressed type.

Exercises

1. Cell D13 contains the formula:

    +D10+D11+D12

    After copying this formula to cells E13 and F13, what will the formulas be in cells E13 and F13?

2. Suppose cell D5 contains the formula:

    +A5*$B$5+C5

    What are the absolute and relative references in this formula?

3. Suppose you copy the formula in Excercise 2 to cells D6 and D7.
    a.   What will the formula be in cell D6?
    b.   What will the formula be in cell D7?

4. Suppose cell B10 has been assigned the range name SALES and cell B11 the range name COSTS.
    a.   What formula would you enter in cell B12 to calculate profits using cell addresses?
    b.   What formula would you enter in cell B12 to calculate profits using range names?

5. Figure 3-24 shows a worksheet to calculate new salaries for employees based on a percent increase applied to all employees. The percent increase is stored in cell C3.
    Cell C8 shows the formula currently used to calculate the salary increase for Harrod.

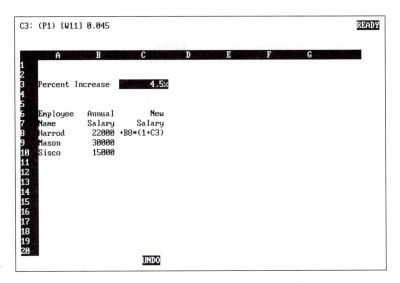

C3: (P1) [W11] 0.045   READY

	A	B	C	D	E	F	G
1							
2							
3	Percent Increase		4.5%				
4							
5							
6	Employee	Annual	New				
7	Name	Salary	Salary				
8	Harrod	22000	+B8*(1+C3)				
9	Mason	30000					
10	Sisco	15000					
11							

                                      UNDO

Figure 3-24

a.   Write the formulas needed in cells C9 and C10 to calculate new salaries for Mason and Sisco.

b.   If you were to copy the formula in C8 to C9 and C10, what would you do? List your steps.

Tutorial Assignments

Retrieve the worksheet T3FILE1 and do the following:

1.   You want to reduce column G, Product Contribution, to a width of 6. Make this change.

2.   Suppose TriCycle introduced paper recycling in the third quarter of 1990. Revenue for paper recycling was 300 in the third quarter and 400 in the fourth quarter. Include these data on the worksheet after aluminum. Be sure to adjust all formulas so the results are correct and to adjust all formats so the appearance of the worksheet is consistent.

3.   Print the revised worksheet.

4.   Save the worksheet as S3FILE2.

Retrieve the worksheet T1FILE6, a version of the final worksheet from Tutorial 1, and do the following:

5.   Use the Copy command to copy the gross pay formula in D11 to the cells of the other employees.

6.   Use the Copy command to copy the federal withholding formula (cell E11) to the cells of all other employees.

7.   Use the Copy command to copy the net pay formula (cell F11) to the cells of the other employees.

8. Assign the following range names:
   a. GROSS_PAY to cells D11..D14
   b. TAXES to cells E11..E14
   c. NET_PAY to cells F11..F14

9. Calculate total gross pay, total taxes withheld, and total net pay using the @SUM function and the range names you assigned in Assignment 8.

10. Print the worksheet.

11. Save the worksheet as S1FILE7.

Retrieve the Allegiance worksheet, T2FILE3, and do the following:

12. Assign the range name FUND_SHARES to cell C19, Mutual Fund Shares, and assign the range name TOTAL_VALUE to cell D17, the total value of the mutual fund.

13. Calculate net asset value (NAV) (cell C20) using the range names in the formula instead of the cell locations.
$$NAV = \frac{TOTAL\_VALUE}{FUND\_SHARES}$$

14. Print the results using compressed type. Save your worksheet as S2FILE7.

Use the Reference section of *Lotus 1-2-3 for Business* to answer the following question:

15. Nick Theodorakis would like to print a summary report that excludes quarterly details. Figure 3-25 is a design of the report Nick wants to print. Review the Print Borders option of the Print command or the Hide option of the Worksheet Column command. Retrieve worksheet T3FILE1, and select one of these options. Print the report that Nick wants. Save your worksheet as S3FILE4.

Recycled Material	1990	Product Contribution
Plastics	13047	37.6%
Glass	12033	34.7%
Aluminum	9620	27.7%
Totals	34700	

Figure 3-25

Case Problems

1. Employee Turnover Report

Each month, the director of human resources for the public accounting firm of Armstrong, Black & Calzone turns in a report summarizing the number of employees who have left the firm. The data in this employee turnover report is valuable information to the senior partners of the firm, because they want to compare their turnover rates with previous periods and industry averages. If their rates are particularly high, they might decide to investigate the cause of the high turnover. Turnover can result from a variety of reasons, such as noncompetitive salaries, poor managers, lack of training, or poor hiring practices.

Do the following:

1. Retrieve the worksheet file P3TRNOVR.
2. Calculate the number of employees in the company.
3. Calculate the total number of employees who have left the company (number of terminations).
4. Calculate the rate of turnover in each department as a percent of the number of employees in the department. Rate of turnover is calculated by using the following formula:

$$rate\ of\ turnover = \left(\frac{number\ of\ employees\ who\ left\ each\ department}{number\ of\ employees\ in\ each\ department} \right) \times 100$$

5. Calculate the rate of turnover in each department as a percent of the number of employees in the company. Rate of turnover is calculated by using the following formula:

$$rate\ of\ turnover = \left(\frac{number\ of\ employees\ who\ left\ each\ department}{number\ of\ employees\ in\ company} \right) \times 100$$

6. Include headings, formatting, and any other changes you think will improve the appearance of the final report.
7. Print the worksheet.
8. Save the worksheet as S3TRNOVR.

2. Leading Restaurant Chains

The managing editor of *Restaurant Happenings*, a weekly magazine, has asked his top writer, Gene Marchand, to research and write a lead article on the sales of U.S. restaurant chains. In researching the story, Gene first determines the U.S. sales for 1988 and 1989 (in millions of dollars) and then totals the number of individual stores in 1989 for each restaurant chain. As the publishing deadline approaches, Gene asks you — the office Lotus 1-2-3 whiz — to help him with this article. Gene wants you to use 1-2-3 to calculate the following four facts:

- industry totals for sales and number of stores
- percent change in sales between 1988 and 1989 for each restaurant chain
- each restaurant's share of total industry sales in 1989
- average sales per store for each chain in 1989

Do the following for Gene:

1. Retrieve the worksheet file P3RSTAUR.WK1.

2. Calculate the four facts listed above.
   a. Calculate totals for sales in 1988, sales in 1989, and number of stores.
   b. Calculate percent change in sales for each restaurant chain by using the following formula:

   $$percent\ change\ in\ sales = \left(\frac{(chain's\ 1989\ sales - chain's\ 1988\ sales)}{chain's\ 1988\ sales} \right) \times 100$$

   c. Calculate each chain's share of total industry sales in 1989 by using the following formula:

   $$chain's\ share\ of\ total\ industry\ sales\ in\ 1989 = \left(\frac{chain's\ sales\ in\ 1989}{total\ industry\ sales\ in\ 1989} \right) \times 100$$

   d. Calculate the average sales per store in 1989 by using the following formula:

   $$average\ sales\ per\ store\ in\ 1989 = \frac{chain's\ sales\ in\ 1989}{number\ of\ stores\ in\ chain}$$

3. Add titles and ruled lines and format the numeric values to make the worksheet easier to read.

4. Print the results.

5. Save the worksheet as S3RSTAUR.

3. Exchange Rates and Foreign Operations

As the world becomes "smaller", more and more companies operate in more than one country. A particular challenge for multinational companies is coping with doing business in different currencies. One interesting finance problem involves how to interpret financial results when different currencies are used. Typically, each country reports results in its local currency (dollar, mark, yen, franc, etc.). The challenge is to prepare a report that allows management to compare these results and accurately interpret them. Let's assume that a U.S. publishing company wants all the results of its different divisions converted to U.S. dollars.

Smithson Publishing International has divisions in England, France, Germany, and Italy. Quarterly, each division reports data on sales revenue to corporate headquarters in the U.S. where the data are combined. Each division reports its sales in its local currency (Figure 3-26).

Sales Revenue (Local Currency)				
Period	England (pound)	France (franc)	Germany (mark)	Italy (lira)
QTR1	270197	1943779	1282234	159887439
QTR2	272814	2218784	1385572	213441654
QTR3	346404	2760962	1372975	232303732
QTR4	375395	2711160	1458096	239693192

Figure 3-26

Since the data are reported in the currency of the local country, Smithson's top executives cannot accurately interpret these numbers. They cannot tell, for example, which division has the highest revenue or which division has the lowest. Thus, a staff assistant, Jim Newman, converts these foreign currencies to U.S. dollars. He collects data on exchange rates, which represent the price of one country's currency in terms of another. For example, if the exchange rate between the U.S. dollar and the British pound is 1:1.8505, for every British pound you would receive 1.8505 U.S. dollars.

Jim keeps track of the exchange rates between the U.S. and each of the four countries in which Smithson has divisions. At the end of each quarter, he enters the exchange rates into a second table (Figure 3-27).

Exchange Rates				
Period	England (pound)	France (franc)	Germany (mark)	Italy (lira)
QTR1	1.8505	0.1672	0.5773	0.0007818
QTR2	1.7445	0.1613	0.5486	0.0007447
QTR3	1.5740	0.1413	0.5062	0.0006993
QTR4	1.6119	0.1568	0.5316	0.0007301

Figure 3-27

Using these two tables, Jim can generate a third table, which shows the sales revenue for Smithson's four divisions converted to U.S. dollars.

To convert the sales data to U.S. dollars, each quarter's sales revenue for a country is multiplied by the corresponding exchange rate. For example, in Britain, sales in the first quarter were 270,197 pounds. At the end of the first quarter, the exchange rate between the U.S. dollar and the British pound was 1:1.8505. Therefore, first-quarter sales in Britain expressed in U.S. dollars would be:

revenues × exchange rate = converted amount

or in this case,

$$270,197 \times 1.8505 = \$500,000$$

Do the following:

1. Retrieve the worksheet named P3EXCHNG.WK1. This file contains the data shown in Figure 3-26 and Figure 3-27.

2. Create a third table that shows sales revenue expressed in U.S. dollars categorized by country and by quarter. Use the formula given above for converting currencies.

3. Also include in this table the calculation of total revenue by country.

4. Include in this table the calculation of total revenue by quarter.

5. Add titles and ruled lines, format the values, and make any other changes that will improve the appearance of the worksheet.

6. Print the three tables.

7. Save your worksheet as S3EXCHNG.

4. Salary Planning at Olmstead Corporation

The controller of Olmstead Corporation, a sports equipment manufacturer, gives each department head a worksheet containing a list of the employees in his or her department. For each employee on the worksheet, the worksheet shows name, department, performance rating for the year (1 = poor, 2 = fair, 3= good, 4 = outstanding), and annual salary as of January 1, 1990.

Five additional column headings appear in the worksheet but show no data. These five headings are:

- *Across-the-Board Increase*: a percent increase in salary that is applied equally to each employee's current salary regardless of how they perform

- *Merit Increase*: a percent increase in salary that is awarded to an employee according to how well the employee has performed on the job

- *Total Dollar Increase*: the sum of across-the-board and merit increases

- *Total Percent Increase*: the total salary increase an employee receives expressed as a percent of current salary, in other words,

$$\left(\frac{\textit{dollar amount of increase}}{\textit{dollar amount of current salary}\,(1/1/90)}\right) \times 100 = \textit{total percent increase}$$

- New Salary (1/1/91): sum of current salary (1/1/90) plus total dollar increase

With this worksheet, the controller also distributed the following human resources department's guidelines concerning salary increases:

> ### Guidelines for Salary Increases
>
> - Each employee will receive a 2% across-the-board increase.
> - Only employees with performance ratings of 3 and 4 will receive merit increases. In other words, employees who were rated 1 or 2 will not receive merit increases. Last year, the merit increases ranged from $500 to $4,000; the average was $1,800.
> - An employee cannot receive a total increase greater than 20% of his/her current salary.
> - Total percentage salary increase for each department can be *no more than 5%* of the total current salary for the department. For example, if current salaries in a department total $1,000,000, then $50,000 is the total amount of money available for both across-the-board and merit increases.

Assume that you are the head of a department. Do the following:

1. Retrieve the worksheet P3SALPLN.WK1.

2. Complete the worksheet by entering the formulas you need to calculate for each employee the across-the-board increase (column E), the total salary increase in dollars (column G), the total salary increase as a percent (column H), and the new salary (column I).

3. Assign merit pay to each of your employees, at your discretion. Keep in mind that:
   - Only employees with rating of 3 or 4 can receive merit increases (column C).
   - Each employee can receive a maximum 20% increase.
   - The total salary increase to your department cannot be greater than 5% of the total salaries in 1990.

   Hint: Include a section in your worksheet that will immediately show you how well you are doing toward meeting the total salary increase for your department of no more than 5 percent. You may have to adjust the merit pay you assign to certain employees several times before you meet all the requirements in the human resources guidelines.

4. Calculate department totals for the following:
   a. salaries in 1990
   b. across-the-board increases
   c. merit increases
   d. total dollar increase
   e. salaries in 1991.

5. Print your final worksheet using compressed type.

6. Save your worksheet as S3SALPLN.

Tutorial 4

Designing Professional Worksheets

Projecting Income

Case: Trek Limited

Hillary Clarke is an accountant at Trek Limited, a manufacturer of fine luggage that has been in business for 55 years. Hillary works in the controller's office and reports to the controller, Stephan Akrawi. Stephan was so impressed with Hillary's work over the 14 months she has worked for him, he selected her to attend Trek's employee development workshop series.

Objectives

In this tutorial you will learn how to:

- Freeze titles

- Use the @IF function

- Protect cells

- Use windows

- Document a worksheet

- Print cell formulas

- Use a one-way data table

- Use the Data Fill command

Today is Hillary's first day back at her regular job after attending the workshop series. She is excited about the many skills she has learned, and she tells Stephan that she'd like to use some of them immediately. She is particularly excited about the workshop called "Financial Planning Using Lotus 1-2-3," because she thinks she can use what she learned to help Stephan with some of his projects. Last year, Hillary assisted Stephan in updating Trek's Five-Year Plan, a collection of financial projections that help Trek's department managers make decisions about how to run the company. By making certain assumptions, such as that sales will increase 10% next year, the managers can plan, budget, and set goals accordingly. The plan includes the company's forecasts, or "best guesses," on what sales, expenses, and net income will be over the coming years.

In the past, Stephan prepared the plan manually, but this year Hillary wants Stephan to use Lotus 1-2-3. She points out how much more helpful the plan would be if the department managers could perform what-if analyses. Department managers could make different assumptions about the financial data to see what results those assumptions would have on the company's finances. For example, what if sales went down 10% next year instead of up? What would the results be on profits or on expenses? What if the price of cowhide increased 5% over the next two years? How would that affect the cost of manufacturing? How would it affect profits? What if analysis using Lotus 1-2-3 could help managers make better decisions. They would not have to face the drudgery of numerous recalculations; they could easily, quickly, and accurately consider different alternatives by changing the data and then having Lotus 1-2-3 recalculate the formulas and totals. Thus, managers would spend more time and creative energy on decision making because they would not have to recalculate formulas and totals every time they asked what if?.

Stephan agrees with Hillary about using Lotus. He gives her the latest data that the accounting department prepared for 1990 (Figure 4-1). They agree that Hillary should design a Lotus worksheet that reflects the Trek planning process. Then together they will perform some what-if analysis and show the department managers how they can use what-if analysis with 1-2-3.

Trek Limited Income Statement

	1990	Percent of Sales
Sales	$150,000	
Variable Costs:		
Manufacturing	75,000	50%
Selling	15,000	10%
Administrative	6,000	4%
Total Variable Cost	96,000	
Fixed Costs:		
Manufacturing	10,000	
Selling	20,000	
Administrative	5,000	
Total Fixed Cost	35,000	
Net income before taxes	19,000	
Income taxes	4,750	
Net income after taxes	$14,250	

Figure 4-1
Trek's accounting
department data

Hillary spends time studying the accounting department's data and begins to create her planning sheet (Figure 4-2a). After writing down her goal and her desired results, she considers what information she needs. She knows that, generally, the sales estimate is used as the starting point for projecting income. Why? Because production and selling are geared to the rate of sales activity.

My Goal:
   Develop a worksheet that easily tests alternative scenarios to help develop
   a five-year plan for Trek Limited

What results do I want to see?
   Projected income statements for 1991 to 1995

What information do I need?
   Information that can be changed:
      Sales estimate for 1991
   Information that remains unchanged:
      Annual growth rate in sales   (10%)
      Ratio of manufacturing costs to sales   (50%)
      Ratio of selling costs to sales   (10%)
      Ratio of administrative costs to sales   (4%)
      Fixed manufacturing costs   ($10)
      Fixed selling costs   ($20)
      Fixed administrative costs   ($5)

What calculations will I perform?
   1. sales first year = sales estimate for 1991
   2. sales subsequent years = previous year's sales × 110%
   3. variable manufacturing costs = 50% × sales estimate
   4. variable selling costs = 10% × sales estimate
   5. variable administrative costs = 4% × sales estimate
   6. total variable costs = variable manufacturing costs +
                               variable selling costs +
                               variable administrative costs
   7. total fixed costs =   fixed manufacturing costs ($10) +
                               fixed selling costs ($20) +
                               fixed administrative costs ($5)
   8. net income before taxes = sales - total variable costs - total fixed costs
   9. taxes = 25% × net income before taxes
   10. net income after taxes = net income before taxes - taxes

Figure 4-2a
Hillary's planning
sheet

Hillary decides to start her projections for 1991 sales at the same level as 1990, although she knows the managers will change this during their what-if analysis. Stephan suggests she build in a 10% increase per year in sales for 1992 to 1995. He believes sales will go up 10% annually as a result of a new line of luggage Trek Limited plans to introduce in 1991.

After looking at the sales side, Hillary turns her attention to costs. She must look at both variable and fixed costs. Variable costs are those that change in direct proportion to related volume. For instance, as sales volume goes up, variable costs such as materials, assembly labor, and sales commissions also go up. Fixed costs are costs that remain unchanged despite changes in related volume. For example, rent, property taxes, executive salaries, and insurance remain the same even when sales go up.

Once again, Hillary refers to the accounting department data in Figure 4-1. She decides to use the variable-cost percentages as the basis for calculating variable costs. For example, if sales were $200,000, the variable manufacturing costs would be calculated at 50% of sales, or $100,000. She also decides to use the fixed costs shown in the accounting data.

Next, Hillary considers the final group of calculations, net income. To calculate net income before taxes, Hillary takes the difference between sales and the total of variable and fixed costs. She assumes taxes will be 25% of net income before taxes. Finally, she calculates net income after taxes, that is, net income before taxes minus income taxes.

Figure 4-2a is Hillary's completed planning sheet. Figure 4-2b is a sketch of how she wants her worksheet to look. In this tutorial, you will use Hillary's plan and sketch to learn how to freeze titles, protect specified data, split screens, design and document your worksheet, and make use of data tables to ask what-if questions.

Figure 4-2b
Hillary's worksheet
sketch

Retrieving the Worksheet

Before you follow through on Hillary's plan, you will retrieve the worksheet she built based on her planning sheet and worksheet sketch, and you will practice using the what-if capability of 1-2-3.

To retrieve the worksheet:

❶ Select /File Retrieve (**/FR**).

❷ Highlight the file C4FILE1.WK1. Press **[Enter]**.

❸ Press **[PgDn]** to view the Projected Income Statements.

This worksheet contains projected income statements for Trek Limited for the years 1991 to 1995 (Figure 4-3). All values are shown in thousands. For example, sales in 1991 are shown as 150, which represents $150,000. Also note that to simplify the numbers in this worksheet, the cells were formatted to display zero decimal places. As a result, some totals do not appear to be correct. This is because the data are rounded whenever they appear on the screen.

```
                          Trek Limited
                    Projected Income Statement
                        For Year Ending

                      1991    1992    1993    1994    1995
                      ----------------------------------------
Sales                  150     165     182     200     220
Variable Costs:
    Manufacturing       75      83      91     100     110
    Selling             15      17      18      20      22
    Administrative       6       7       7       8       9
                      ----------------------------------------
    Total Variable Costs 96     106     116     128     141

Fixed Costs:
    Manufacturing       10      10      10      10      10
    Selling             20      20      20      20      20
    Administrative       5       5       5       5       5
                      ----------------------------------------
    Total Fixed Costs   35      35      35      35      35

Net Income Before Taxes 19      24      30      37      44
Income Taxes             5       6       8       9      11
                      ----------------------------------------
Net Income After Taxes  14      18      23      28      33
                      ========================================
```

Figure 4-3
Contents of the entire worksheet

Demonstrating the What-If Feature

To demonstrate 1-2-3's what-if capability using Hillary's worksheet, let's suppose that you increase the sales estimate for 1991 from $150,000 (entered as 150) to $175,000 (entered as 175).

To use the what-if capability:

❶ Move the cell pointer to cell B28, sales for 1991.

❷ Type **175** and press **[Enter]**. Watch how the sales, costs, and net incomes change as a result of the change to 1991 sales. See Figure 4-4.

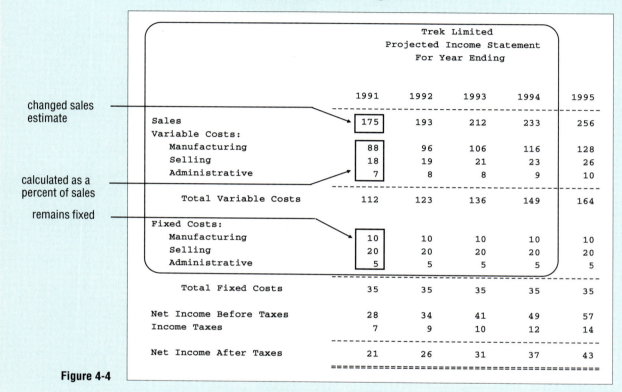

changed sales estimate

calculated as a percent of sales

remains fixed

Figure 4-4

Since the sales estimate for 1991 increased from 150 to 175, the variable costs, which are calculated as a percent of sales, also increased. Net income also changed, since both sales and variable costs changed. The fixed costs, however, did not change.

The sales estimates for 1992 to 1995 also increased. Because sales are estimated to grow at 10% each year, changing the starting sales estimate for 1991 changes the sales for 1992 to 1995.

Scrolling on Large Worksheets

Notice that the entire income statement does not fit on the screen — you cannot see the information for 1995. Also, the rows that follow "Administrative" in Hillary's worksheet sketch do not appear on the screen, even though she has typed them into her worksheet. To view this information, you use the cursor-movement keys to scroll down the screen. *Scrolling* is a way to view all parts of a large worksheet that cannot fit on one screen. For example, when you scroll down, a row previously unseen appears at the bottom of the screen and a row at the top disappears.

To scroll Hillary's worksheet:

❶ Press **[PgDn]** until Net Income After Taxes appears on the screen. Note that the column headings no longer appear on the screen. See Figure 4-5.

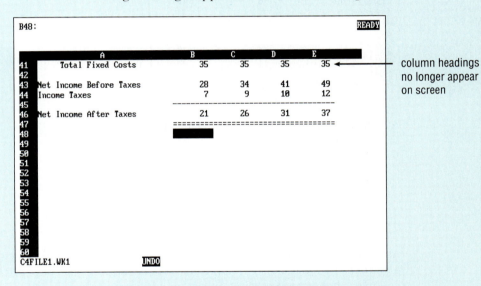

column headings no longer appear on screen

Figure 4-5

❷ Now move the cell pointer to cell A21.

The planning period for the company is 1991 to 1995, but 1995 does not appear on the screen. Let's scroll to the right to view the 1995 projections.

To scroll to the right:

❶   Press [→] until the 1995 column appears. Notice that the descriptive labels no longer appear on the left of the screen. This makes the worksheet data difficult to interpret. See Figure 4-6.

after scrolling to the right, column A no longer appears on screen

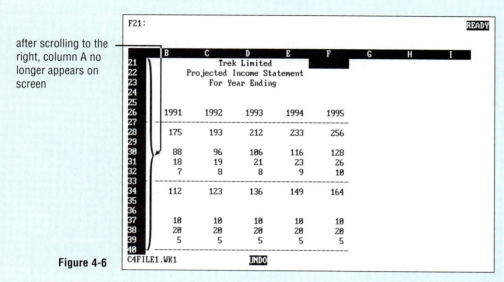

Figure 4-6

❷   Now move the cell pointer to cell A21.

Freezing Titles

As you move the cell pointer around a worksheet that is larger than the screen, you may find it difficult to remember row and column labels that may have disappeared. The Title command helps you keep your place on a large worksheet by "freezing" row and column titles on the screen; the titles remain on the screen as you move within the worksheet. The Titles command allows you to freeze rows, columns, or both. If you choose *Horizontal*, you freeze all rows above the cell pointer on the screen. If you choose *Vertical*, you freeze all columns to the left of the cell pointer. If you choose *Both*, you freeze all rows above and all columns to the left of the cell pointer. In the next steps, you freeze both the worksheet column headings and the account titles.

To freeze titles:

❶   Move the cell pointer to cell B28, the location below and to the right of the cells you want to remain on the screen.

❷   Select /Worksheet Titles (**/WT**). Your control panel should look like Figure 4-7.

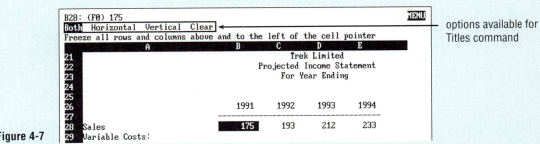

Figure 4-7

options available for
Titles command

❸ Select Both (**B**) from the options available.

❹ Press [↓] to move the cell pointer to cell B47 and then [→] to move the cell pointer to cell F47. The column and row titles remain in view. See Figure 4-8.

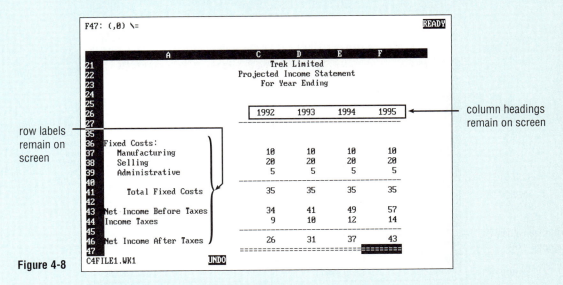

Figure 4-8

row labels
remain on
screen

column headings
remain on screen

❺ Press [**Home**].

Notice that the cell pointer returns to cell B28 rather than cell A1. Cell B28, the first unfrozen cell, becomes the upper left corner of the worksheet.

Unfreezing Titles

Once you freeze an area of the worksheet, you cannot move the cell pointer into that area. To make any changes to the headings or row labels, you must "unfreeze" the area before you can make those changes.

If you need to unfreeze titles, you would select the command /Worksheet Title Clear (/WTC). You would then be able to move the cell pointer into the area of the worksheet that was frozen and make the changes.

@IF Function

Now you are ready to follow Hillary's plan. The first thing Hillary wants to do is to see the effect of a poor sales year on net income. She assumes sales will be $75,000 (entered as 75) instead of $150,000 (entered as 150).

To consider the relationship between poor sales and income:

❶   Be certain the cell pointer is in cell B28.

❷   Type **75**. Press **[Enter]**.

❸   Move the cell pointer to cell B47 and look at the values in the rows for income taxes and net income after taxes. See Figure 4-9.

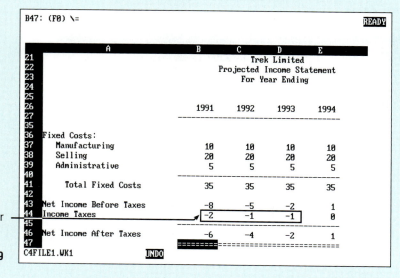

negative values for
income taxes

Figure 4-9

Notice that income taxes appear as negative values for 1991, 1992, and 1993. This is not correct. Taxes should be zero whenever the net income before taxes is less than zero. How can we correct this?

❹   Move the cell pointer to cell B44. Look at the control panel and observe that the formula for calculating income taxes is +B43*0.25 (25% of net income before taxes). This formula is correct, as long as net income before taxes is a positive number. If net income before taxes is a negative number, the worksheet should set income taxes equal to zero, not a negative value. What went wrong? Hillary represented the relationship between net income before taxes and income taxes incorrectly when she built her worksheet.

There are many situations where the value you store in a cell depends on certain conditions, for instance:

- An employee's gross pay may depend on whether that employee worked overtime.
- A taxpayer's tax rate depends on his or her taxable income.

- A customer's charge depends on whether the size of the order entitles that customer to a discount.

In 1-2-3, the @IF function allows you to make comparisons to determine which actions 1-2-3 should take. The @IF function has the following format:

> @IF(condition, true expression, false expression)

The parenthetic expression can be interpreted to mean that if the condition is true, then execute the "true expression"; otherwise, execute the "false expression."

The @IF function has three components:

- a *condition* is a logical expression that represents a comparison between quantities. This comparison results in a value that is either true, indicated by a value of 1, or false, indicated by a value of 0.
- a *true expression* is a value or label stored in a cell if the condition is true.
- a *false expression* is a value or label stored in a cell if the condition is false.

An example may help to illustrate the format of an @IF function. Suppose you need to determine whether an employee earned overtime pay, that is, whether he or she worked more than 40 hours in a week. This can be expressed as:

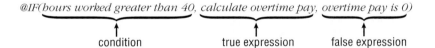

In this example, the condition is the comparison between the hours an employee works and 40 hours. The true expression is executed if an employee works more than 40 hours; then the condition is true and overtime pay is calculated. The false expression is executed if an employee works 40 hours or less, then the condition is false and overtime pay is 0.

The most common condition, a simple condition, is a comparison between two expressions. An **expression** may be a cell or range reference, a number, a label, a formula, or another @function. Besides the expressions, a condition contains a comparison operator. A **comparison operator** indicates a mathematical comparison, such as less than or greater than. Figure 4-10 shows the comparison operators allowed in 1-2-3.

Type of Comparison	1-2-3 Symbol
Less than	<
Greater than	>
Less than or equal to	< =
Greater than or equal to	> =
Equal to	=
Not equal to	< >

Figure 4-10
Comparison operators in 1-2-3

The comparison operator is combined with expressions to form a condition. For example, if we assume the hours worked is stored in cell D10, the condition *the number of hours worked is greater than 40* is expressed in 1-2-3 as @IF(D10>40...). Figure 4-11 illustrates several examples of conditional situations and how they can be expressed in 1-2-3.

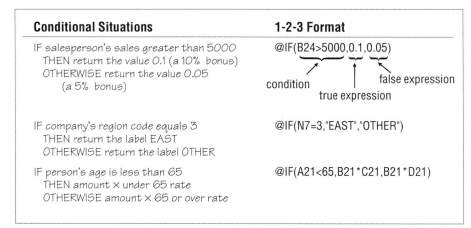

Figure 4-11
Examples of
conditional
situations

Let's now use the @IF function to correct Hillary's worksheet.

To use the @IF function to determine taxes:

❶   Make sure the cell pointer is in cell B44.

❷   Type **@IF(B43>0,0.25*B43,0)** and press **[Enter]**. See Figure 4-12.

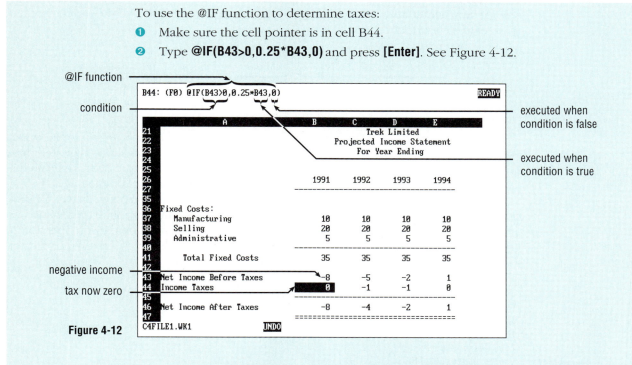

Figure 4-12

Do not include any spaces when you type this @function and be sure to separate each component with a comma. You can interpret this function as:

IF the value in cell B43 is greater than 0
THEN return the value .25*B43 to cell B44
OTHERWISE return the value 0 to cell B44

Now let's copy this function to the cells C44 to F44 so the correct formulas to calculate income taxes for the years 1992 to 1995 can be included in the worksheet.

To copy the function to cells C44..F44:

❶ Make sure the cell pointer is in cell B44.

❷ Select /Copy (**/C**). Press **[Enter]** since you are only copying the function in cell B44.

❸ Move the cell pointer to C44 and press **[.]** to anchor the cell pointer.

❹ Highlight the range C44..F44. Press **[Enter]**.

Notice that taxes are now zero. See Figure 4-13.

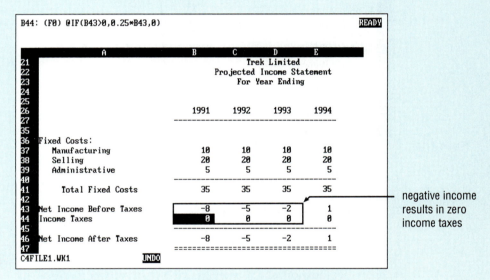

Figure 4-13

In addition to making changes to sales estimates, Hillary decides she wants to see how changes in the ratio of variable manufacturing costs to sales affects net income. To make this change, Hillary must change the formula for each cell that references variable manufacturing costs (B30, C30, D30, E30, F30). For example, she wants to change variable manufacturing costs from 50% to 52% of sales.

To change constants in a formula:

❶ Move the cell pointer to cell B30.

❷ Press **[F2]** (EDIT) to invoke the EDIT mode.

❸ Change 0.5 to 0.52 and press **[Enter]**. The formula appears in the control panel as 0.52*B28, and the variable manufacturing costs in 1991 are 39.

Now copy the formula to C30 .. F30, where the formulas for variable manufacturing costs for the years 1992 to 1995 are located.

To copy the formula to C30 .. F30:

❶   With the cell pointer in B30, select /Copy (**/C**). Press **[Enter]**.

❷   Move the cell pointer to C30. Press **[.]** to anchor the cell pointer.

❸   Highlight C30..F30. Press **[Enter]**. See Figure 4-14.

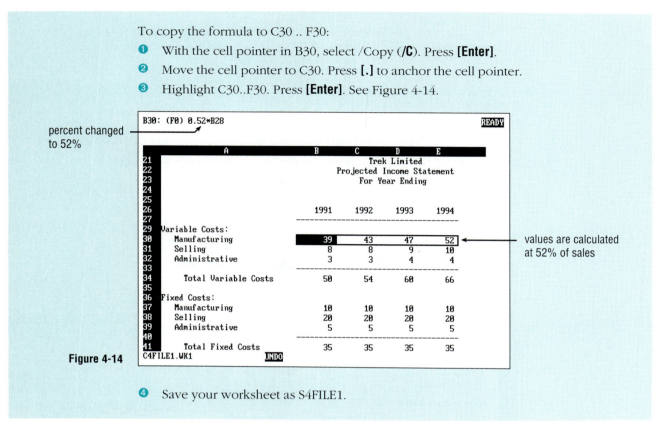

percent changed to 52%

values are calculated at 52% of sales

Figure 4-14

❹   Save your worksheet as S4FILE1.

To change variable selling costs from 10% to 11% requires a similar process. But is there a way to change the variable costs that takes less time and avoids the possibility of errors that can occur with so many changes? Hillary thinks about how to revise the worksheet. She realizes that the more she uses numeric constants in her formulas, the less flexibility she has if she wants to change those values. Thus, she decides to completely revise her worksheet. She prepares a new plan and worksheet sketch. Figure 4-15 shows her revised plan. Some of the major changes in this worksheet include:

- providing managers with five variables on which they can perform what-if analysis instead of one variable.

- replacing constants in formulas with range names, such as GROWTH, which reference cells in the input area.

Now you can retrieve the new worksheet that Hillary built.

My Goal:

    Develop a worksheet that easily tests alternative scenarios to help
    develop a five-year plan for Trek Limited

What results do I want to see?

    Projected income statements for 1991 to 1995

What information do I need?

    Information that can be changed:

        Sales estimate for 1991

    Information that remains unchanged:

        Annual growth rate in sales   (10%)

        Ratio of manufacturing costs to sales   (50%)

        Ratio of selling costs to sales   (10%)

        Ratio of administrative costs to sales   (4%)

        Fixed manufacturing costs   ($10)

        Fixed selling costs   ($20)

        Fixed administrative costs   ($5)

Hillary now wants to change this information → [handwritten annotation, circling the four ratio items above]

What calculations will I perform?

1. sales first year = sales estimate for 1991

2. sales subsequent years = previous year's sales × 110%   *[handwritten: Sales growth rate, pointing to 110%]*

3. variable manufacturing costs = 50% × sales estimate   *[handwritten: ratio of manufacturing costs to sales]*

4. variable selling costs = 10% × sales estimate   *[handwritten: ratio of selling costs to sales]*

5. variable administrative costs = 4% × sales estimate   *[handwritten: ratio of administrative costs to sales]*

6. total variable costs = variable manufacturing costs +
                          variable selling costs +
                          variable administrative costs

7. total fixed costs =   fixed manufacturing costs ($10) +
                       fixed selling costs ($20) +
                       fixed administrative costs ($5)

8. net income before taxes = sales - total variable costs - total fixed costs

9. taxes = 25% × net income before taxes   *[handwritten: If net income before taxes > 0 then ... Otherwise taxes = 0]*

Hillary will make this a conditional statement → [handwritten annotation pointing to item 9]

10. net income after taxes = net income before taxes - taxes

Figure 4-15
Hillary's revised
planning sheet

To retrieve a file:

❶ Select /File Retrieve (**/FR**).

❷ Highlight C4FILE2.WK1 and press **[Enter]**.

Notice in Figure 4-16 that Hillary has divided her new worksheet into four sections. An *identification section* on the first screen consists of the filename, the person who developed the worksheet, the date the worksheet was created or last modified, and a brief description.

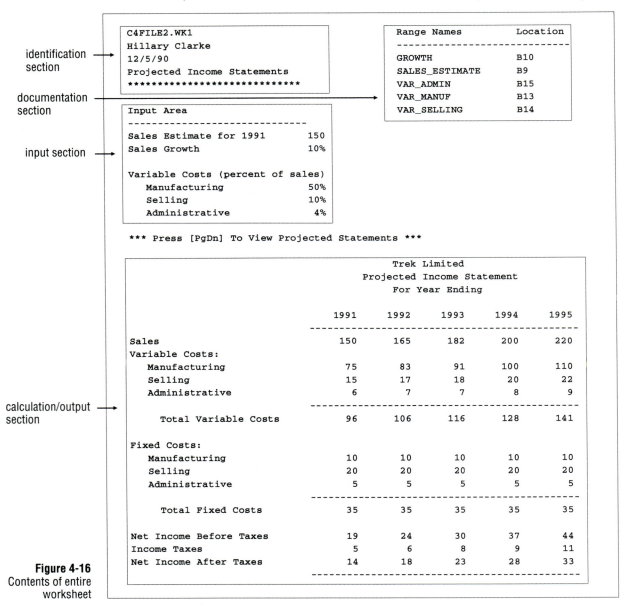

Figure 4-16
Contents of entire worksheet

Following the identification section is an *input section*, which lists the variables a manager at Trek can control and change in the worksheet. The manager can ask what-if questions by changing the values in the input section and then transferring these values to the output section.

The third section is the *calculation/output section*, which contains the projected income statements. Press [PgDn] to view this entire section. Press [Home] to return to A1.

The fourth section of the worksheet, a *documentation section*, contains a table of the named ranges used in this worksheet. Press [Tab] to see the table of named ranges. After you have examined the table, press [Home] to return to A1.

A Worksheet Map

A worksheet "map," similar to the one in Figure 4-17, can often accompany the worksheet to inform the user about the organization of the worksheet. Such a map is especially helpful in a large worksheet that consists of many sections. The map identifies each section and the cell range of each section. With the worksheet map, a user can quickly find different sections of a worksheet.

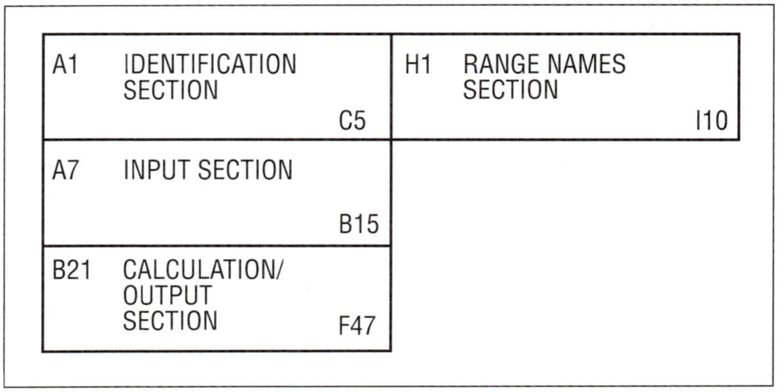

Figure 4-17
A map of Hillary's
worksheet

Demonstrating What-If with the Revised Worksheet

Remember that Hillary developed this new worksheet because the previous worksheet was difficult to use for what-if questions. Let's try this new worksheet and see if it is any easier to use for this purpose.

To use the revised worksheet to change the variable manufacturing cost percent from 50% to 52% of sales:

❶ Use the cursor keys to move the cell pointer to cell B13.

❷   Type **52%**. Press **[Enter]**. See Figure 4-18. You could also enter the value as .52.

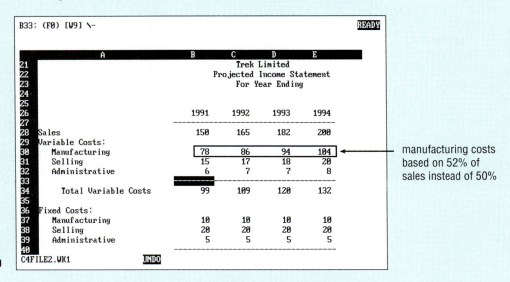

```
B13: (P0) [W9] 0.52                                              READY

                    A              B        C        D        E
1  C4FILE2.WK1
2  Hillary Clarke
3  12/5/90
4  Projected Income Statements
5  **************************************************
6
7  Input Area
8  --------------------------------
9  Sales Estimate for 1991          150
10 Sales Growth                     10%
11
12 Variable Costs (percent of sales)            changed value
13    Manufacturing                 52%         in input area
14    Selling                       10%
15    Administrative                 4%
16
17
18
19
20 *** Press [PgDn] To View Projected Statements ***
   C4FILE2.WK1                   UNDO
```

Figure 4-18

❸   Press **[PgDn]** and observe the projected income statement. See Figure 4-19. The variable manufacturing costs change from 75, 83, 91, 100, and 110 to 78, 86, 94, 104, and 114. Notice that we did not have to change formulas when we used this worksheet. When Hillary used the previous worksheet, she had to make changes to the formula every time a variable-cost percent changed. The new worksheet is designed to transfer the input percent to the output section, where the calculations are performed.

```
B33: (F0) [W9] \-                                               READY

                    A              B        C        D        E
21                                      Trek Limited
22                                 Projected Income Statement
23                                     For Year Ending
24
25
26                                1991     1992     1993     1994
27                               ----------------------------------
28 Sales                          150      165      182      200
29 Variable Costs:
30    Manufacturing               78       86       94      104      manufacturing costs
31    Selling                     15       17       18       20      based on 52% of
32    Administrative               6        7        7        8      sales instead of 50%
33                               =========================
34       Total Variable Costs     99      109      120      132
35
36 Fixed Costs:
37    Manufacturing               10       10       10       10
38    Selling                     20       20       20       20
39    Administrative               5        5        5        5
40                               ----------------------------------
   C4FILE2.WK1                   UNDO
```

Figure 4-19

④ Move the cell pointer to cell B30. See Figure 4-20.

no constant
in formula

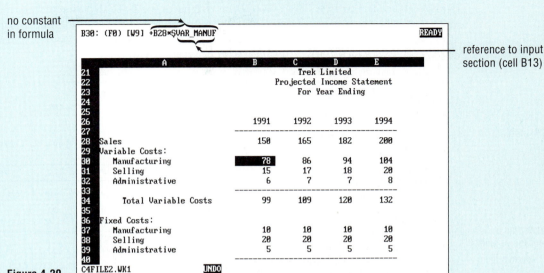

reference to input
section (cell B13)

Figure 4-20

Notice that in cell B30 the formula to calculate variable manufacturing costs uses a range name, VAR_MANUF, to reference the variable manufacturing cost percent (cell B13). The variable manufacturing cost formula in cell B30 is (+B28*$VAR_MANUF) instead of (.5*B28), which was the formula used in the previous worksheet. Cell B28 contains the sales estimate for 1991. Now all a user has to do is change the variable manufacturing to sales percent in the input area, and the formula in cell B30 will automatically recalculate.

Hillary thinks the revisions she has made to the worksheet will help managers more easily ask what-if questions. For example, suppose a manager wants to see what would happen if the growth rate increased from 10% to 15%.

To ask what if the growth rate for sales increased to 15%:

① Move the cell pointer to cell B10, the input area for the sales growth rate.

② Type **15%**. Press **[Enter]**. You can also enter the value as .15.

③ Press **[PgDn]**.

Observe the results in the output section. See Figure 4-21. Notice how sales in 1992 changed from 165 to 173. The revised sales estimates for 1992 also affected all the variable costs. The fixed costs, on the other hand, haven't changed. Net income before and after taxes have also changed. The increased growth rate also affects sales, variable costs, and income for 1993, 1994, and 1995.

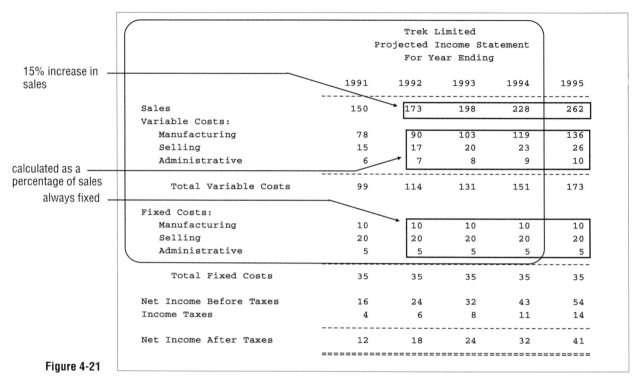

15% increase in sales

calculated as a percentage of sales

always fixed

```
                              Trek Limited
                      Projected Income Statement
                            For Year Ending

                      1991      1992      1993      1994      1995
                     ---------------------------------------------------
Sales                  150      173        198       228       262
Variable Costs:
    Manufacturing       78       90        103       119       136
    Selling             15       17         20        23        26
    Administrative       6        7          8         9        10
                     ---------------------------------------------------
    Total Variable Costs 99     114        131       151       173

Fixed Costs:
    Manufacturing       10       10         10        10        10
    Selling             20       20         20        20        20
    Administrative       5        5          5         5         5
                     ---------------------------------------------------
    Total Fixed Costs   35       35         35        35        35

Net Income Before Taxes 16       24         32        43        54
Income Taxes             4        6          8        11        14
                     ---------------------------------------------------
Net Income After Taxes  12       18         24        32        41
                     ===================================================
```

Figure 4-21

Hillary is pleased with her work and decides to ask Stephan to try the revised worksheet. But Stephan wants to ask different what-if questions. He moves the cell pointer to cell C28 in the output section and changes the sales in 1992 to 200.

Hillary explains to Stephan that all changes to the worksheet must be made in the input section, not the output section. She thinks to herself that she must prevent Stephan or other managers from inadvertently making the same mistake. She remembers from her workshop that she can protect cells. She decides first to correct the error Stephan made and then to protect the formulas in cell C28 and any other appropriate cells from being changed. Let's make the same mistake Stephan made.

To make Stephan's mistake:

❶ Move the cell pointer to cell C28. Notice the formula (1+$GROWTH)*B28 in the control panel.

❷ Type **200**. Press **[Enter]**. See Figure 4-22.

formula erased

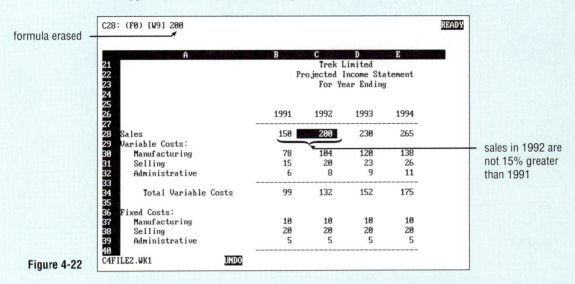

sales in 1992 are not 15% greater than 1991

Figure 4-22

Originally, cell C28 contained the formula (1+$GROWTH)*B28. When Stephan typed 200 in C28, he erased the formula and replaced it with the constant 200. The formula that was originally in this cell instructed 1-2-3 to increase sales for 1992 by the growth rate, currently 15%. Now that the formula is no longer in the cell, sales for 1992 do not reflect the anticipated 15% sales growth. Sales for 1992 are 200 and will remain 200 unless the formula is reentered in this cell.

Fortunately, Hillary is able to use the Undo feature and restore the worksheet to its previous state.

❸ Press **[Alt][F4]** (UNDO). Cell C28 now shows 173, and the formula (1+$GROWTH)*B28 appears in the control panel. If the Undo feature has not worked, type the formula (1+$GROWTH)*B28 into cell C28.

Protecting and Unprotecting Ranges

Hillary learned in her workshop that what Stephan did is a common mistake. Accidentally erasing worksheet formulas occurs often, so she learned it is a good idea to protect certain areas of a worksheet from accidental changes. She learned a combination of commands with which she can first protect an entire worksheet and then unprotect the range or ranges in which she or other users need to enter or edit data. In the steps that follow, you begin the process of protecting specific ranges in Hillary's worksheet by first protecting the entire worksheet.

To protect an entire worksheet:

❶ Select /Worksheet Global (**/WG**) to display the Global Settings sheet, as shown in Figure 4-23. Notice that the global protection default setting is "Disabled".

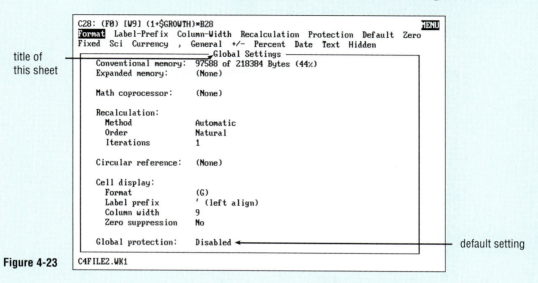

title of this sheet

default setting

Figure 4-23

❷ Select Protection Enable (**PE**) to turn on global protection. 1-2-3 then returns to the worksheet automatically.

❸ With the cell pointer in cell C28, type **200** and press **[Enter]**. You are now prevented from making a change to that cell.

A warning beep, the ERROR indicator in the upper right corner, and the message "Protected cell" in the status line all remind you that the cell is protected. Notice the control panel. The letters PR (protected) appear in the control panel whenever the cell pointer is on a protected cell. See Figure 4-24.

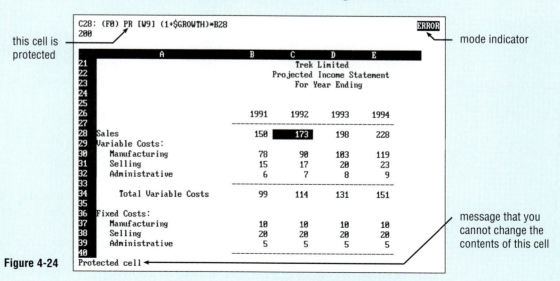

this cell is protected

mode indicator

message that you cannot change the contents of this cell

Figure 4-24

❹ Press **[Esc]** to return to READY mode.

Move the cell pointer to any other cell in the worksheet and try to enter data or make a change. You'll find that you cannot make a change.

Currently every cell in the worksheet is protected. So what do you do if you need to enter values in some cell? In Hillary's worksheet, for example, we know that managers might want to ask what if about data in cells B9 through B15. In the next steps, you will learn how to lift the protection, or unprotect, the range of cells that represents the input section of the worksheet.

To unprotect cells in a protected worksheet:

❶ Press **[Home]**. Then move the cell pointer to cell B9, the first cell to be unprotected.

❷ Select /Range Unprot (**/RU**).

❸ Press **[↓]** to highlight the range B9..B15, the range of the input section.

❹ Press **[Enter]**. The input area is now unprotected. See Figure 4-25.

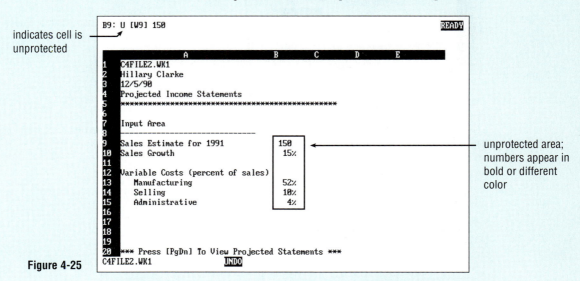

indicates cell is unprotected

unprotected area; numbers appear in bold or different color

Figure 4-25

You have now lifted protection from cells B9 to B15. The only area in the worksheet where you can make entries is the input area. Notice that the control panel's first line displays U (unprotected) whenever the cell pointer is in an unprotected cell. Another indication that protection is not in effect for these cells is that the values in these cells appear in boldface or in a different color.

To see if you can enter data in the input section, let's change the variable administrative costs to 5% in cell B15.

To make a change in cell B15:

❶   Move the cell pointer to B15, the cell for variable administrative cost percent.

❷   Type **5%** and press **[Enter]**. You can also enter this value as .05. Notice that data can now be entered in unprotected cells.

❸   Press **[PgDn]** to see the results. Variable administrative costs are now 8, 9, 10, 11, and 13 for the years 1991 to 1995. See Figure 4-26.

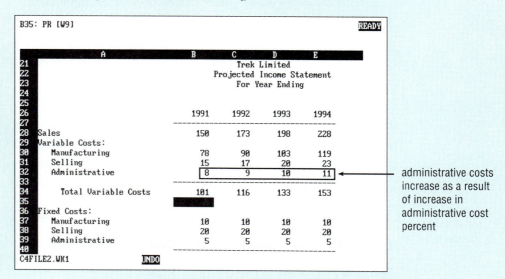

administrative costs increase as a result of increase in administrative cost percent

Figure 4-26

If you decide to modify formulas or labels in the worksheet, remember that you will have to turn protection off. Let's try that.

To turn protection off:

❶   Select /Worksheet Global Protection (**/WGP**).

❷   Select Disable (**D**).

When you have completed the changes, you can turn protection on again by selecting /Worksheet Global Protection Enable (/WGPE). Let's keep the protection feature off for now.

Although adding protection to the worksheet is certainly an improvement, Hillary still is not satisfied. When changes are made in the input section, she has to press [PgDn] to see the results. She must then move the cell pointer back to the input section or press [PgUp] if she wants to make another change. Is there a way to have both the input and output sections appear on the screen at the same time?

Using Windows

To keep separate parts of the worksheet in view at the same time, you can use the Worksheet Window command. This command lets you view two parts of a large worksheet simultaneously. You can observe the results from one part of a worksheet while you make changes to another. You use [F6] (WINDOW) to move the cell pointer between the two windows.

In the next steps, you will split the worksheet into two windows — one for the input section and the other for the Projected Income Statement.

To split the screen into two windows:

❶ Press **[Home]**. Then move the cell pointer anywhere in row 8, the point where you decide to split the worksheet.

❷ Select /Worksheet Window Horizontal (**/WWH**). This command instructs 1-2-3 to split the screen horizontally into two windows, one above and one below the cell pointer. See Figure 4-27.

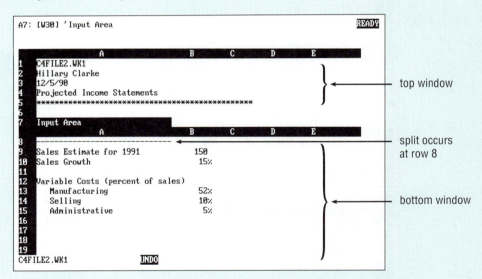

Figure 4-27

❸ Press **[F6]** (WINDOW) once to move the cell pointer to the bottom window. Press the key **[F6]** (WINDOW) again to switch back to the top window.

The Window key switches the cell pointer back and forth between the two windows.

❹ If necessary, adjust your view of the worksheet so the cells A9 to B15 are visible in the top window. Press [↓] until A9 to B15 appear in the top window. See Figure 4-28.

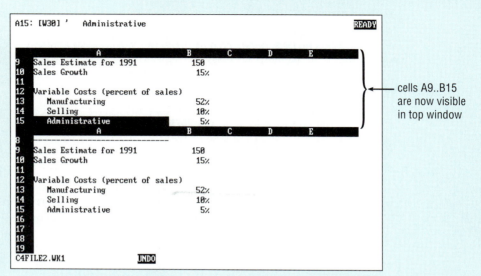

cells A9..B15 are now visible in top window

Figure 4-28

❺ Press **[F6]** (WINDOW) again to switch the cell pointer to the bottom window. Then press [↓] until row 47 is visible. Your screen should be similar to Figure 4-29.

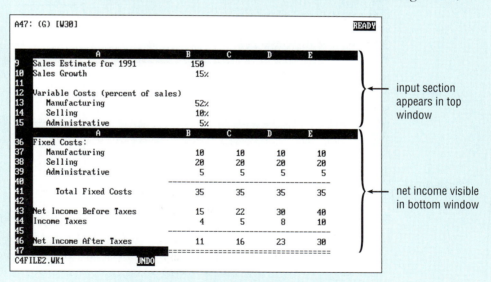

input section appears in top window

net income visible in bottom window

Figure 4-29

Now you can view, at the same time, part of the worksheet in the top window and part of the Projected Income Statement in the bottom window. Let's change the 1991 sales estimate to 225.

To make a change and immediately view the results:

❶ Press **[F6]** (WINDOW) to switch to the top window.

❷ Move the cell pointer to cell B9, the location for the sales estimate.

❸ Type **225** in cell B9. Press **[Enter]** and watch as the results of the change appear immediately. See Figure 4-30.

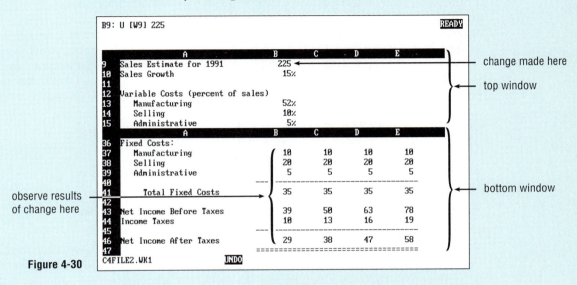

Figure 4-30

It will be easier to perform other tasks in this tutorial if you first clear the windows.

To clear the windows:

❶ Select /Worksheet Window Clear (**/WWC**).

Hillary now thinks that this worksheet is getting closer to her ideal, but she still is not completely satisfied. Each time she tries new input values, she finds herself writing down the results on a sheet of paper. She wonders if there is a way to make more than one change at a time and see the results. Hillary decides to ask an experienced 1-2-3 user at her company. She explains the problem and is told to try the Data Table command.

Before using this command, Hillary decides to set her worksheet aside. She wants to develop and experiment on a new worksheet so she does not accidentally lose or destroy her current worksheet.

To save the worksheet:

❶ Select /File Save (**/FS**). Type **S4FILE2** and press **[Enter]**.

Printing Cell Formulas

So that she will be able to come back and review the formulas in her current worksheet, Hillary prints the cell formulas that make up the current worksheet.

Printing the cell formulas is an option of the Print command. Using this option to create a printout of the cell formulas provides you with a record of the worksheet. It also allows you to see several formulas at once, thereby letting you see how formulas relate to one another. This is especailly helpful if you are trying to find a problem in your worksheet. Instead of moving from cell to cell and viewing the formula in the control panel, you have a printout of all the formulas. By attaching this printout to the usual output from your worksheet, you add valuable backup documentation for the worksheet. Let's now use the print-cell-formula option of the Print command to print the worksheet's formulas.

To print the cell formulas:

❶   Select /Print Printer Range (**/PPR**).

❷   Move the cell pointer to A28, the first cell of the print range.

❸   Press **[.]** to anchor the cell. Then highlight A28..F46 and press **[Enter]**.

The print range consists of the cells in the calculation/output area.

❹   Select Options Other Cell-Formulas (**OOC**) to cause the range to print as cell formulas rather than as values. Notice the change in the last setting, Output, in the lower left corner of the settings sheet. The setting sheet now specifies that cell formulas will be output. See Figure 4-31.

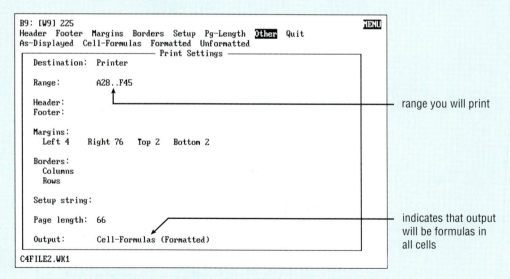

Figure 4-31

❺   Select Quit (**Q**) to leave the Options menu and return to the Print menu. Make sure the printer is ready.

❻   Print the cell formulas. Select Align Go Page (**AGP**). 1-2-3 prints a list of the cell formulas for each cell within the specified range. See Figure 4-32.

```
Lotus 1-2-3 Student Business Series                    Hillary Clarke

A28: (G) [W30] 'Sales
B28: (F0) [W9] +SALES_ESTIMATE
C28: (F0) [W9] (1+$GROWTH)*B28
D28: (F0) [W9] (1+$GROWTH)*C28
E28: (F0) [W9] (1+$GROWTH)*D28
F28: (F0) [W9] (1+$GROWTH)*E28
A29: (G) [W30] 'Variable Costs:
A30: (G) [W30] '   Manufacturing
B30: (F0) [W9] +B28*$VAR_MANUF
C30: (F0) [W9] +C28*$VAR_MANUF
D30: (F0) [W9] +D28*$VAR_MANUF
E30: (F0) [W9] +E28*$VAR_MANUF
F30: (F0) [W9] +F28*$VAR_MANUF
A31: (G) [W30] '   Selling
B31: (F0) [W9] +B28*$VAR_SELLING
C31: (F0) [W9] +C28*$VAR_SELLING
D31: (F0) [W9] +D28*$VAR_SELLING
E31: (F0) [W9] +E28*$VAR_SELLING
F31: (F0) [W9] +F28*$VAR_SELLING
A32: (G) [W30] '   Administrative
B32: (F0) [W9] +B28*$VAR_ADMIN
C32: (F0) [W9] +C28*$VAR_ADMIN
D32: (F0) [W9] +D28*$VAR_ADMIN
E32: (F0) [W9] +E28*$VAR_ADMIN
F32: (F0) [W9] +F28*$VAR_ADMIN
B33: (F0) [W9] \-
C33: (F0) [W9] \-
D33: (F0) [W9] \-
E33: (F0) [W9] \-
F33: (F0) [W9] \-
A34: (G) [W30] '      Total Variable Costs
B34: (F0) [W9] +B30+B31+B32
C34: (F0) [W9] +C30+C31+C32
D34: (F0) [W9] +D30+D31+D32
E34: (F0) [W9] +E30+E31+E32
F34: (F0) [W9] +F30+F31+F32
A36: (G) [W30] 'Fixed Costs:
A37: (G) [W30] '   Manufacturing
B37: (F0) [W9] 10
C37: (F0) [W9] 10
D37: (F0) [W9] 10
E37: (F0) [W9] 10
F37: (F0) [W9] 10
A38: (G) [W30] '   Selling
B38: (F0) [W9] 20
C38: (F0) [W9] 20
D38: (F0) [W9] 20
E38: (F0) [W9] 20
F38: (F0) [W9] 20
A39: (G) [W30] '   Administrative
B39: (F0) [W9] 5
C39: (F0) [W9] 5
D39: (F0) [W9] 5
E39: (F0) [W9] 5
F39: (F0) [W9] 5
```

Figure 4-32
Printout of cell
formulas
(continued on next
page)

```
Lotus 1-2-3 Student Business Series                      Hillary Clarke

B40: (F0) [W9] \-
C40: (F0) [W9] \-
D40: (F0) [W9] \-
E40: (F0) [W9] \-
F40: (F0) [W9] \-
A41: (G) [W30] '        Total Fixed Costs
B41: (F0) [W9] +B37+B38+B39
C41: (F0) [W9] +C37+C38+C39
D41: (F0) [W9] +D37+D38+D39
E41: (F0) [W9] +E37+E38+E39
F41: (F0) [W9] +F37+F38+F39
A43: (G) [W30] 'Net Income Before Taxes
B43: (F0) [W9] +B28-B34-B41
C43: (F0) [W9] +C28-C34-C41
D43: (F0) [W9] +D28-D34-D41
E43: (F0) [W9] +E28-E34-E41
F43: (F0) [W9] +F28-F34-F41
A44: (G) [W30] 'Income Taxes
B44: (F0) [W9] @IF(B43>0,B43*0.25,0)
C44: (F0) [W9] @IF(C43>0,C43*0.25,0)
D44: (F0) [W9] @IF(D43>0,D43*0.25,0)
E44: (F0) [W9] @IF(E43>0,E43*0.25,0)
F44: (F0) [W9] @IF(F43>0,F43*0.25,0)
B45: [W9] \-
C45: [W9] \-
D45: [W9] \-
E45: [W9] \-
F45: [W9] \-
A46: (G) [W30] 'Net Income After Taxes
B46: (F0) [W9] +B43-B44
C46: (F0) [W9] +C43-C44
D46: (F0) [W9] +D43-D44
E46: (F0) [W9] +E43-E44
F46: (F0) [W9] +F43-F44
```

Figure 4-32
(continued from
previous page)

Data Tables

Now let's see how Hillary can use a data table to make more than one change at a time and see the results. She decides she wants to make several changes to estimated 1991 sales and observe how those changes will affect net income before taxes.

A data table is an area of the worksheet set up to show the results a formula generates each time you change a value in that formula.

Let's illustrate this concept using a bank loan as an example. Suppose you are considering borrowing $100,000 to buy a home. The bank requires monthly payments over 25 years. What if you wanted to know how much your monthly payments would be at various interest rates, such as 9%, 10%, 11%, 12%, and 13%? To show the relationship between the monthly payments and the various interest rates, you could use a data table such as Figure 4-33.

Interest Rate	Monthly Payment
9%	839.20
10%	908.70
11%	980.11
12%	1053.22
13%	1127.84

Figure 4-33
Monthly loan payments at different interest rates

This figure shows how monthly payments increase as interest rates increase. The data table is a valuable tool because it allows you to try out several what-if questions at one time and observe their results. In the case of the monthly payments for the loan, you are saying:

What is the monthly payment *if* the interest rate is 9%?

What is the monthly payment *if* the interest rate is 10%?

What is the monthly payment *if* the interest rate is 11%?

What is the monthly payment *if* the interest rate is 12%?

What is the monthly payment *if* the interest rate is 13%?

Using a data table, you need only one formula to produce a table that shows the different results generated each time a new interest rate is substituted in the formula. When the value of only one variable in a formula is varied, the data table is referred to as a **one-way data table**.

One-Way Data Tables

The components and the layout of a one-way data table are shown in Figure 4-34. As you can see from the figure, a one-way data table includes an **input cell** and a **table range.** The table range consists of four components: a **blank cell**, a **formula**, **input values**, and a **results area.** The data table must contain these four components and be laid out as shown in this figure.

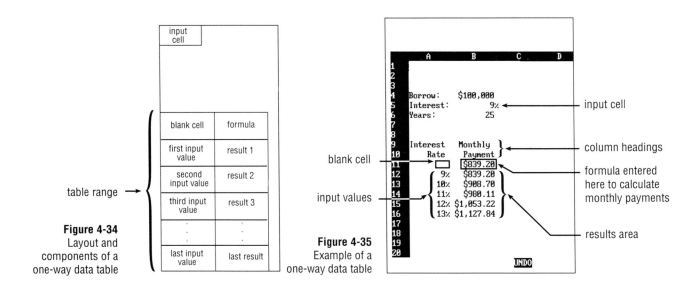

Figure 4-34
Layout and components of a one-way data table

Figure 4-35
Example of a one-way data table

Figure 4-35 illustrates the components of the data table using a bank loan example. (You do not have a worksheet file for this example.) The components are defined as follows:

- The *input cell* is an unprotected cell that can be anywhere in the worksheet. It can be blank or can contain one of the input values. In the bank loan example, cell B5 is the input cell.

- The *blank cell* is a cell that does not contain data and is located at the intersection of the first row and the first column of the table range. In the bank loan example, cell A11 is considered the blank cell.

- The *formula* (or formulas) must be in the first row of the table range, starting at the second cell from the left. The formula contains a **variable**. A variable is a part of the formula for which different values can be substituted. In the bank loan example, the formula to calculate the monthly payments is in B11.

- The *input values* must be in the first column of the table range, starting immediately below the empty cell. The input values are the values that 1-2-3 substitutes for a variable whenever it performs the calculations specified in the formula. In the bank loan example, the interest rates in cells A12 to A16 are the input values that are substituted in the formula to calculate the monthly payments.

- The *results area* is the unprotected area below the formula and to the right of the input values. 1-2-3 enters the results of each calculation next to the input value it used. The results area should be blank when you first set up the data table because 1-2-3 writes over any data in this area when it calculates results. In the the bank loan example, the results area appears in cells B12 to B16.

Setting up a One-Way Data Table

Hillary now has her list of formulas and she has read how to use the Data Table command in her 1-2-3 reference manual. She draws a sketch that will help her visualize the planned changes in estimated 1991 sales and how these changes affect net income before taxes. Figure

4-36 is her handwritten sketch of how she wants her data table to look. Notice that she has followed the correct layout for a data table and has included all the required components.

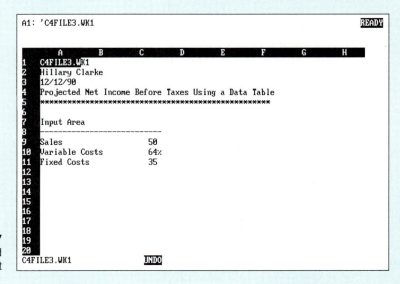

		Sales	NIBT
Sales	xxx	blank cell	sales - (variable cost ratio x sales) - fixed costs
Variable cost percent	xx%	50	
Fixed cost	xx	75	
		100	
		125	
		150	Results here
		175	
		200	
		225	
		250	
		275	
		300	

Figure 4-36
Hillary's sketch for her data table

Now let's construct Hillary's data table. Begin by retrieving the file C4FILE3.WK1.

To retrieve a file:

❶ Select /File Retrieve (**/FR**). Highlight C4FILE3.WK1, and press **[Enter]**.

Your screen should now look like Figure 4-37. Notice that this file contains the input values that Hillary will use. Sales start at $50,000 (remember, the worksheets indicate the number of thousands), and variable costs are 64% of sales. Variable costs are the sum of variable manufacturing (50%), variable selling (10%), and variable administrative (4%) costs. Fixed costs are $35,000, the sum of fixed manufacturing ($10,000), fixed selling ($20,000), and fixed administrative ($5,000) costs.

```
A1: 'C4FILE3.WK1                                                    READY

           A        B        C        D        E        F        G        H
1    C4FILE3.WK1
2    Hillary Clarke
3    12/12/90
4    Projected Net Income Before Taxes Using a Data Table
5    ********************************************************
6
7    Input Area
8    ------------------------------
9    Sales               50
10   Variable Costs      64%
11   Fixed Costs         35
12
13
14
15
16
17
18
19
20
C4FILE3.WK1                        UNDO
```

Figure 4-37
Hillary's retrieved worksheet

Your first step is to select a location in the worksheet to place the data table. The location of a data table can be any blank area of your worksheet. Let's use the cell range E8..F19.

Next, you must enter descriptive headings for the columns in the data table. Headings are *not* part of a data table, but you should enter them because they help you read the values in the data table. Hillary's sketch of the data table contains the headings you will now enter.

To enter headings for the data table:

❶ Move the cell pointer to cell **E7**. Type **"Sales** and press **[Enter]**. Notice that the label, Sales, is right-justified in the cell. That is because you typed the label prefix " (Quotation Mark) before you typed Sales.

❷ Move the cell pointer to F7 and type **"NIBT**, an abbreviation for net income before taxes. Press **[Enter]**.

Using the Data Fill Command

Now that you have entered the headings, let's enter the values in the input value section of the data table. Remember from the worksheet sketch that Hillary wants to see what will happen to NIBT as sales estimates increase in intervals of 25,000, starting at 50,000, and ending at 300,000 (remember, you type only the number of thousands, i.e., 50 for 50,000, 75 for 75,000, and so on).

You could enter each number — 50, 75, 100, and so on up to 300 — in each appropriate cell, but that would be rather time consuming. Instead you can use a new command, the Data Fill command, to enter all the sales estimates at one time into the input value section of the data table. The Data Fill command lets you enter a sequence of equally spaced values into a range of cells, either in one column or in one row. To use the Data Fill command, you first need to understand four new terms:

- **Fill range** is the range you want to fill with a series of sequential values. In Hillary's case, the fill range is E9..E19.

- **Start value** is the first value you want to enter in the fill range. In Hillary's case, 50 is the start value.

- **Step value** is the increment between the values in the sequence. Hillary wants to increase sales estimates in increments of 25.

- **Stop value** is the value you want to use as a limit for the sequence. Hillary wants her data table to stop at 300. The default limit is 8191.

To use the Data Fill command:

❶ Move the cell pointer to E9. Notice that cell E8, the first cell in the data table, is empty.

❷ Select /Data Fill (**/DF**).

Now let's enter the fill range.

③ At cell E9, press **[.]** to anchor the range.

④ Highlight the cells E9..E19 and press **[Enter]**.

⑤ Type **50** to enter the start value and press **[Enter]**.

⑥ Type **25** to enter the step value and press **[Enter]**.

⑦ Type **300** to enter the stop value. Take a look at the control panel. See Figure 4-38.

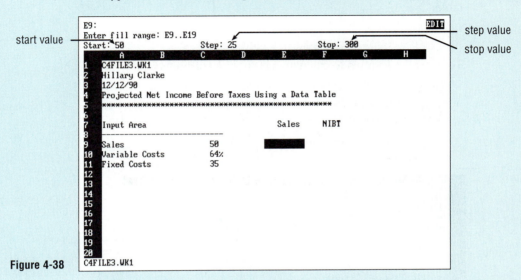

Figure 4-38

⑧ Press **[Enter]**. As you do, notice that the input values appear in column E of the data table. See Figure 4-39.

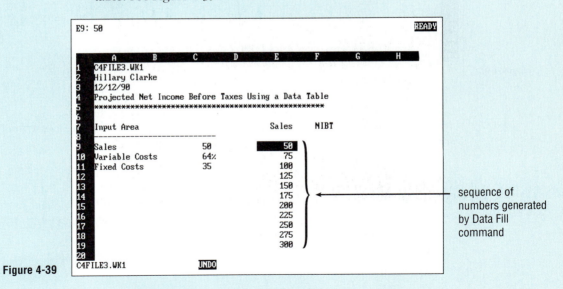

Figure 4-39

Now you should enter the formula to calculate net income before taxes (NIBT) into the formula section of the data table. Checking Hillary's sketch for her data table (Figure 4-36) you can see the formula is:

$$sales - (variable\ cost\ ratio \times sales) - fixed\ costs$$

Be sure to enter this formula in cell F8, that is, to the right of the empty cell of the data table.

To enter the formula to calculate net income before taxes:

❶ Move the cell pointer to F8, the first row of the data table.

❷ Type **+C9–(C10*C9)–C11**. Press **[Enter]** and as you do, notice that −17, the result of the calculation of this formula, appears in F8. See Figure 4-40.

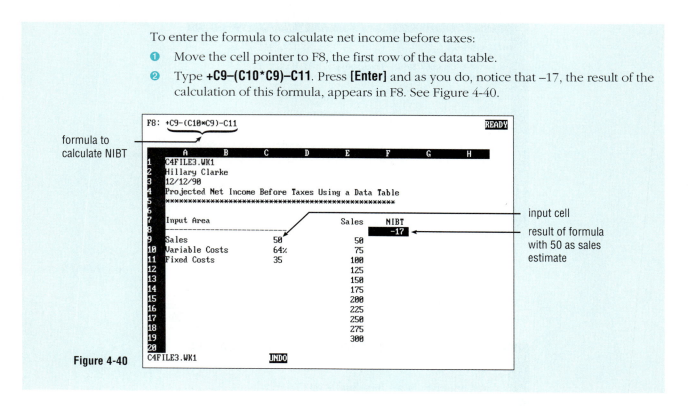

formula to calculate NIBT

input cell

result of formula with 50 as sales estimate

Figure 4-40

The components of the data table have been set up; now it's time to use the Data Table command.

To identify the cells that make up the table range of the data table:

❶ Select the command /Data Table 1 (**/DT1**) to set up a one-way data table. 1-2-3 prompts you to specify the data table range.

❷ Move the cell pointer to E8, the upper left corner of the table range.

❸ Anchor the cell by pressing **[.]**.

❹ Highlight the range E8..F19. See Figure 4-41.

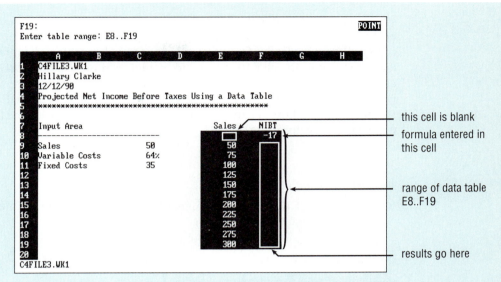

Figure 4-41

You have now defined the table range of the data table. Notice that the empty cell, E8, must be included in the range, but we have not included the column headings, which are in E7..F7.

⑤ Press **[Enter]**.

Next, 1-2-3 prompts you to specify which cell will be the input cell. The input cell will contain the values from the input value section of the data table.

⑥ Type **C9**. Press **[Enter]**. See Figure 4-42.

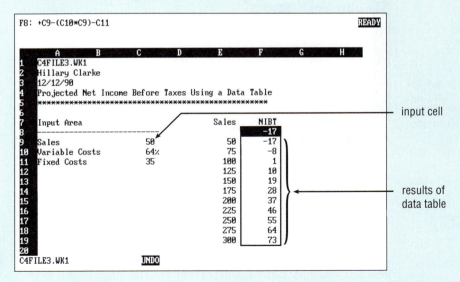

Figure 4-42

1-2-3 substitutes each value from the input section of the data table (E9..E19) into the input cell (C9), one at a time. Then using the formula in cell F8, 1-2-3 recalculates the formula using these input values and immediately displays the results in the results section of the data table (F9..F19). The data table is now complete.

⑦ Save the worksheet as S4FILE3.

Data tables can provide you even greater flexibility, because you can test the sensitivity of the results to various assumptions. Suppose, for example, that you believe the variable costs will increase from 64% to 66% of sales. With data tables, all you have to do is change the variable cost in cell C10 from 64 to 66 and then press [F8] (TABLE), to recalculate the entire table. Pressing [F8] repeats the last Data Table command you selected, in this case, Data Table 1. 1-2-3 uses the previous setting for the table range and the input cell.

Now let's see how Hillary can quickly change one value using the [F8] (TABLE) key and generate 11 new forecasts of NIBT.

To use [F8] for what if analysis:

❶ Move to cell C10, type **66%**, a revised variable cost and press **[Enter]**. You can also enter the value as 66.

No changes appear in the results area.

❷ Press **[F8]** (TABLE) to recalculate the table. See Figure 4-43.

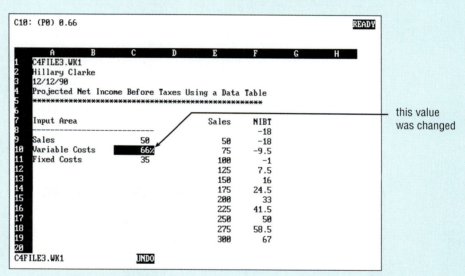

this value was changed

Figure 4-43
Results of data table using [F8] to recalculate results

Summary

In this tutorial, you learned some of the more advanced commands in 1-2-3. The @IF function provided you with conditional capabilities. The Titles command helped keep your place in a large worksheet by freezing rows and/or columns. The Windows command provided a way to split a screen so you could view different parts of a large worksheet simultaneously. Protecting parts of a worksheet prevents users from making entries into cells you don't want inadvertently deleted or changed.

Other commands in the tutorial gave you powerful calculation capability. The Data Table command allowed you to explore many what-if questions at the same time. You also learned more about spreadsheet design and documentation.

Exercises

1. Which of the following @IF functions would work in a 1-2-3 worksheet?
   a. IF(D-40>0,3,7)
   b. @IF(D4-40>0 , 3, 7)
   c. @IFD4-40>0,3,7
   d. @IF(D4-40>0,3,7)

2. Write an English statement that explains what this @IF function says.
   @IF(C15<0,"LOSS","PROFIT")

3. Use Figure 4-44 to write an @IF function that you could type in cell C4. This function should determine a salesperson's commission rate based on weekly sales. If weekly sales are above 10000, the commission rate is 12%; otherwise, commissions are 7.5%.

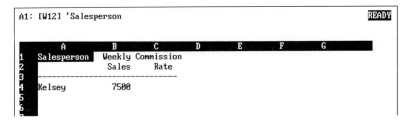

Figure 4-44

4. Use Figure 4-45 to do the following:
   a. Write an @IF function that you could enter in cell D3 that checks the value in column B and places in column D the word MALE or FEMALE, depending on whether the code in column B is M (male) or F (female).
   b. Write an @IF function that you could enter in cell E3 that places the phrase UNDER 21 or the phrase 21 AND OVER in the cell E3, depending on the age in column C.

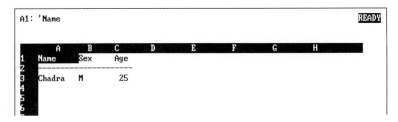

Figure 4-45

5. Identify the command you would use in the following situations:
   a. You have a list of 100 customer names, addresses, and phone numbers. As you scroll down the worksheet, the column headings disappear from the screen.
   b. Users of the worksheet keep erasing formulas accidently.
   c. You want an efficient way to do what-if analysis.
   d. You want to see two different parts of a large worksheet at the same time.
   e. You want to number cells in column A of your worksheet 1 to 500 without typing each number.

Tutorial Assignments

Before you begin these Tutorial Assignments, check your working copy of the Data Disk. Be sure you have space to save the additional worksheet files you'll create in these assignments (at least 40,000 bytes). If not, save your files as appropriate to another formatted diskette.

Retrieve the worksheet file T4FILE1 and do the following:

1. Split the screen so you can observe sales and all variable costs in the top window and net income before taxes, income taxes, and net income after taxes in the bottom window.

2. Change sales for 1991 to 160.

3. Save the worksheet as S4FILE4.

4. Clear the split screen.

5. Change the formula for variable administrative costs to 5% of sales for all five years.

6. Save the worksheet as S4FILE5.

Retrieve the worksheet T4FILE2 and do the following:

7. Scroll the worksheet to find the net income after taxes for 1991 to 1995.

8. Unfreeze the worksheet so you can move to the Input section of the worksheet.

9. Change the variable administrative costs from 4% to 5% (enter as either .05 or 5%).

10. Print the projected income statement using compressed type.

11. Save the worksheet as S4FILE6.

Retrieve the worksheet file T4FILE3 and do the following:

12. Change the fixed costs from 35 to 45 and recalculate the data table. Print your results.

13. Reduce the variable costs from 64% to 60% and recalculate the data table. Print the results.

14. Save the worksheet as S4FILE7.

Retrieve the worksheet file from Tutorial 2, T2FILE4, and do the following:

15. Protect the worksheet so the only cells that can be changed are the daily stock prices, cells C12..C15.

16. Attempt to type 125 in cell B12 (you should not be able to). Enter the following prices in cells C12 to C15: 130, 40, 30, and 50, respectively. Save your worksheet as S2FILE8.

Use the Reference section of *Lotus 1-2-3 for Business* to do the following:

17. Hillary recalls reading about a two-way data table as she was in the process of building her data table worksheet. Now, she wants to vary both sales and variable costs at the same time and observe the changes that occur in net income before taxes. Figure 4-46 is a sketch of her new data table.
    a. Read about two-way data tables in the Reference section (/Data Table 2).

b. Develop a two-way data table using sales and variable costs provided in Hillary's sketch.
c. Print your results.
d. Save your worksheet as S4FILE8.

Net Income Before Taxes						
Sales	Variable Cost Percent					
formula goes here	60%	61%	62%	63%	64%	65%
50	XXX	XXX	XXX	XXX	XXX	XXX
75	XXX	XXX	XXX	XXX	XXX	XXX
100	.	.	.	.	.	.
125	.	.	.	.	.	.
150	.	.	.	.	.	.
175						
200						
225						
250						
275						
300						

Figure 4-46

Case Problems

1. Price Breaks at PC Outlet

PC Outlet, a personal computer mail order company, wants to increase commercial orders by offering attractive discounts to customers who purchase in large quantities. One machine, a 386-MHz PC, is being sold at $1,630 per machine for purchases of 25 or fewer machines. If the customer orders 26 or more machines, each machine costs $1,480.

PC Outlet gives price quotes over the phone. Each customer service/sales operator has a 1-2-3 worksheet at his or her desk. Whenever a customer calls with a large order, the operator enters the order size into the worksheet and 1-2-3 calculates the total price (price per unit × order size), taking into account whether the discount applies.

Do the following:

1. Develop a worksheet based on the above information.

2. Enter a customer who orders 5 PCs. Print your results. Then enter a second customer who orders 30 PCs. Print your results.

3. What if PC Outlet decides to lower the price for orders above the break point? Now, if orders are 26 or more, the price per unit is $1,430. The design of your worksheet

should easily accommodate this type of change. Print your results using the data in Step 2 above.

4. What if PC Outlet lowers the break point for the quantity discount from 26 to 21 units? If orders are 21 or more, the price per unit is $1,430. The design of your worksheet should easily accommodate this type of change. Print your results using the data in Step 2 above.

5. Save your worksheet as S4PRICE.

6. Print the cell formulas of your worksheet.

2. Loan Repayment Schedule

Occasionally, businesses need to borrow money for new buildings, equipment, or other large purchases. If a business takes out a term loan, it must pay back the loan in installments over a specified period of time.

For example, assume Lockwood Enterprises borrows $10,000, payable over five years, at an interest rate of 16% per year on the unpaid balance. Each month Lockwood pays $243.18 to cover principal and interest. The principal is the amount of the loan still unpaid, and the interest is the amount paid for the use of the money.

Figure 4-47 is a partial repayment schedule that shows the monthly payments broken out into principal repaid (amount borrowed) and interest paid. If this table were carried out for 60 months (5 years × 12 months per year, or the life of the loan), it would show a remaining balance of 0 at the conclusion of the 60-month period.

Payment Number	Monthly Payment	Interest[1]	Principal[2] Repayment	Remaining Balance
0	0.00	0.00	0.00	10000.00
1	243.18	133.33	109.85	9890.15
2	243.18	131.87	111.31	9778.84
...				
60	243.18	3.20	239.98	0[3]

[1] Interest is equal to the monthly interest rate, .013333 (16% divided by 12 months), times the remaining balance from the previous period. For example, in month 1, interest equals $133.33 (.013333 × 10000). In month 2, interest equals $131.87 (.013333 × 9890.15).

[2] Principal repayment for each period is equal to the monthly payment ($243.18) minus the interest for the period. For example, in month 2, the monthly payment ($243.18) minus the interest ($131.87) equals the principal repaid ($111.31).

[3] Because of rounding, the result will not be exactly zero.

Figure 4-47

Do the following:

1. Develop a worksheet that prepares a complete loan payment schedule for this loan. At the bottom of the payment schedule, calculate the total payments and the total interest.

2. Print the repayment schedule.

3. Save your worksheet as S4LOAN.

4. What if the interest rate is 16.5%? The monthly payment is $245.85. Print a new repayment schedule.

3. Predicting Demand for Mars Automobiles

Lynette Spiller, an economist working at HN Motor Company headquarters, has developed the following formula to estimate demand for HN's new line of Mars automobiles:

$$D = 100{,}000 - 100P + 2{,}000N + 50I - 1{,}000G + 0.2A$$

where

D	=	demand for Mars automobiles (in units)
P	=	price of Mars automobile (in dollars)
N	=	population in United States (in millions)
I	=	disposable income per person (in dollars)
G	=	price of gasoline (cents per gallon)
A	=	advertising expenses by HN for Mars (in dollars)

The senior managers at HN are considering raising the price of Mars, but before they do, they want to determine how increasing the price will affect demand for this car. They ask Lynette to show how increasing the price in $100 increments from $10,000 to $11,000 will affect demand for the Mars.

Assume the following values when estimating demand:

N	=	250
I	=	$14,000
G	=	140 cents
A	=	$1,000,000

Do the following:

1. Design a worksheet using the Data Table command to solve this problem. The data table should include a column for possible car prices beginning at $10,000, increasing in $100 increments to $11,000. The second column should show the demand for cars at each price.

2. Print your results.

3. Save your worksheet as S4MARS.

4. What if gasoline prices are $1.75 (enter as 175 cents) per gallon? Rerun the worksheet using the new price of gasoline. Print your results.

5. What if gasoline prices are $1.75 a gallon and the advertising budget is increased to $1,500,000? Print your results.

6. Save the worksheet as S4MARS1.

4. Production Planning at QuikNails

QuikNails Manufacturing, makers of artificial fashion fingernails, anticipates selling 42,000 units of QuikNails in May. Currently, the company has 22,000 units ready in inventory. The QuikNails plant will produce the additional product (20,000 units) during April to have enough product to meet the sales forecast for May. In addition to meeting May's sales forecast, the plant manager wants to have 24,000 units of QuikNails in inventory at the end of May for anticipated sales at the beginning of June. Thus, the QuickNails production requirement for April is the sum of the QuikNails units necessary to meet May sales estimates (20,000) plus the units needed to meet the desired ending inventory level (24,000).

The major ingredient needed to produce QuikNails is a chemical called Zinex. Assume the production department needs three gallons of Zinex to make one unit of QuikNails. Currently, the company has an inventory of 100,000 gallons of Zinex. The plant will use all of this raw material to meet its production requirement for April. It also needs 110,000 gallons of Zinex on hand at the end of April for production in May.

Sally Dolling is in charge of inventory control for both raw materials and finished products. She needs to inform senior management and the purchasing manager how much Zinex is required for the current and future materials production. As Sally's assistant, you will develop a spreadsheet to help calculate the number of gallons of Zinex that she should tell the purchasing manager to buy in April for QuikNails to meet the production requirements. You decide to adapt the form that Sally has been using to develop her estimate for production and material requirements (Figure 4-48).

QuikNails Production:	Units
Monthly sales estimate for QuikNails	xxxx
Less QuikNails currently in inventory	.
Production needed to meet sales forecast	.
Plus QuikNails needed at end of month	.
Total QuikNails production requirement	xxxx
Zinex Purchases:	Gallons
Zinex needed to meet QuikNails production requirement	xxxx
Less Zinex currently in Inventory	.
Purchases of Zinex required to meet QuikNails production	.
Plus desired level of Zinex at end of month	.
Total Purchases of Zinex	xxxx

Figure 4-48

Design your spreadsheet so you can easily test alternative plans, such as different sales estimates and different inventory levels for QuikNails and Zinex.

Do the following:

1. Design a worksheet to calculate the production requirements of QuikNails and the amount of Zinex to purchase for the QuikNails manufacturing division. Use the form in Figure 4-48 as a guide in developing your worksheet.

2. Print the results.

3. Print the cell formulas.

4. Save your worksheet as S4NAILS.

5. What if the sales estimates of QuikNails for May is revised to 50,000 units? Print your revised results. What if the sales estimate for May is 30,000 units? Print your revised results.

Tutorial 5

Creating and Printing Graphs

Automobile Industry Sales: A Four-year Summary

Case: McAuliffe & Burns

Carl Martinez majored in human resources in college and was particularly interested in labor relations. Thus, he was delighted when he landed a job as a staff assistant with McAuliffe & Burns (M&B), a leading consulting firm in Washington, D.C. M&B specializes in consulting to unions on labor relations issues.

Objectives

In this tutorial you will learn to:

- Start 1-2-3 and PrintGraph from the Access menu

- Create pie, line, bar, and stacked bar graphs

- Add titles, legends, and axis formatting

- Name and save graph settings

- Save graphs for printing

- Customize and use PrintGraph to print saved graphs

When Carl began at M&B, his computer skills were not as polished as those of the other staff assistants. He knew how to use a word processor, but his spreadsheet skills were limited. But after M&B sent him to a two-day workshop on Lotus 1-2-3, Carl used Lotus 1-2-3 daily to prepare analyses for M&B's senior consultants. Over time, Carl's skills with Lotus 1-2-3 improved dramatically, and he was promoted to a staff associate.

In his new job, Carl is working for three senior consultants on a project for the United Auto Workers (UAW) union. Leaders of the UAW hired M&B to help them prepare testimony for upcoming Congressional committee hearings that will investigate whether the U.S. should establish import quotas for foreign cars.

Carl's first task is to research all automobile sales in the U.S. and gather data on unit sales by year and by company. After he gathers the data and creates a worksheet, Carl decides that he could present the data more effectively if he used the graphics function of Lotus 1-2-3. Carl is convinced that the data will make more of an impact on the Congressional subcommittee members if the UAW leaders show graphic representations of trends and markets. Carl plans to use a bar graph to show trends and a pie chart to show market shares. Figure 5-1a shows Carl's planning sheet for preparing his graphs. Figure 5-1b shows his sketches of the graphs he wants to create with 1-2-3.

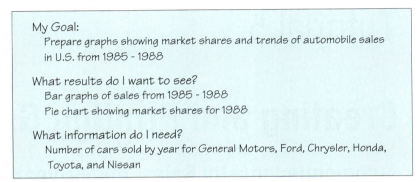

My Goal:
 Prepare graphs showing market shares and trends of automobile sales in U.S. from 1985 - 1988

What results do I want to see?
 Bar graphs of sales from 1985 - 1988
 Pie chart showing market shares for 1988

What information do I need?
 Number of cars sold by year for General Motors, Ford, Chrysler, Honda, Toyota, and Nissan

Figure 5-1a
Carl's planning
sheet

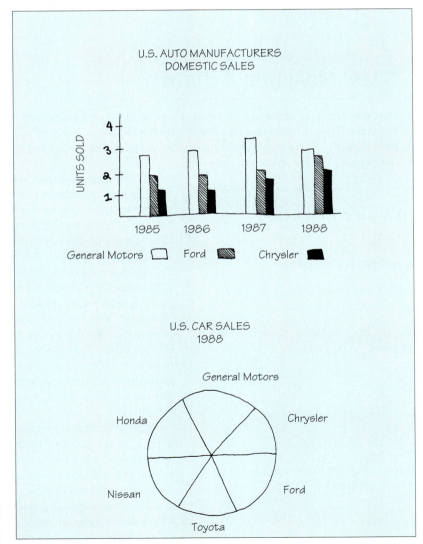

Figure 5-1b
Carl's sketches of
the graphs

This tutorial leads you through Carl's process of using graphs to analyze auto sales in the U.S. After starting 1-2-3 from the Access menu, you will create a series of graphs to learn which type of graph is best suited to your data. Finally, you will print the graphs.

Introduction to Graphics

In business, graphics are used to represent one or more data series in a more visually appealing and easily understood format. A **data series** is a single set of data represented by a line, a bar, or a pie. For example, a data series may include:

- Sales of a product by quarter (one data series)
- Sales of three products by quarter (three data series)
- Daily stock prices of a company over the past month (one data series)
- Daily stock prices of two companies over the past month (two data series)

With your computer and 1-2-3, you can create graphs that will help you communicate your ideas quickly and easily. Lotus 1-2-3 includes a variety of graphs: bar graphs, line graphs, stacked bar graphs, pie charts, and XY graphs.

A **bar graph** consists of a series of vertical or horizontal bars. Each bar in the chart represents a single value from a set of values. The length or height of each bar is determined by the size of each value relative to all the other values. A bar graph is used to compare related data items during one time period or over a few time periods, such as four quarters. Bar graphs use the x axis, or horizontal axis, to classify data over regions, over time, over products, and so on. The vertical, or y axis, shows the quantity you are measuring, such as dollars, units sold, weight, or number of employees. For example, revenue at TriCycle Industries (Tutorial 3) could be represented by a bar graph that shows the relationship of sales of recycled materials by quarter (Figure 5-2a).

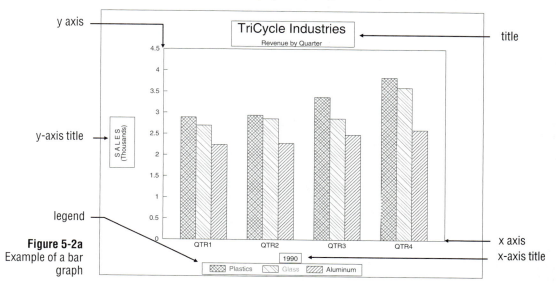

Figure 5-2a
Example of a bar graph

A **line graph** represents data with points and connects these points with a straight line. Line graphs are effective at showing trends in data over time. Each line represents one set of data, such as the daily stock prices of IBM. A line graph is a better choice than a bar graph to present a large number of data points over time. Figure 5-2b uses a line graph to show quarterly revenue for each recycled material at Tricycle Industries.

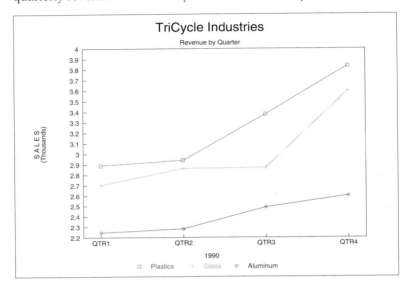

Figure 5-2b
Example of a line
graph

Stacked bar graphs show related data values on top of one another. These graphs show the components of several wholes. They are used to emphasize several totals and a breakdown of their components. For example, sales of each recycled material at TriCycle for the first quarter would appear on one bar, one on top of the other (Figure 5-2c). A second bar would represent the same data for the second quarter. A third and fourth bar would show the sales of the last two quarters. This graph can compare total sales over several quarters, while also identifying the components that make up each quarterly total.

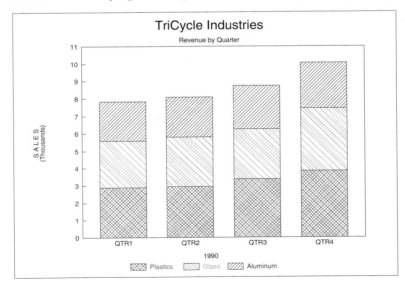

Figure 5-2c
Example of a
stacked bar graph

Pie charts are useful for showing how each value contributes to the whole. For example, the total 1990 sales at TriCycle are divided among plastic, glass, and aluminum (Figure 5-2d), each represented by a slice of the whole. The size of a slice depends on its component's value relative to the whole. When you want to express your data as percentages, consider using pie charts. You can emphasize one or more slices by using a cut, or "exploded," slice to draw the viewer's attention.

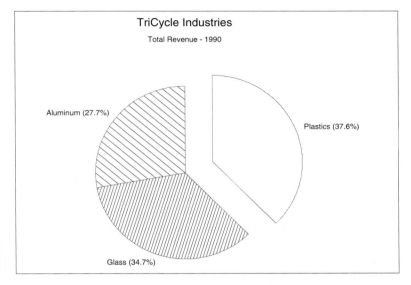

Figure 5-2d
Example of a pie chart

XY graphs, also called scatter graphs, show relationships between two variables. This graph shows how a change in one variable relates to another variable. For example, sales management at TriCycle graphed the relationship between the amount of waste in tons and sales revenue at TriCycle (Figure 5-2e). We will not cover XY graphs in this tutorial, but Lotus 1-2-3 can produce XY graphs.

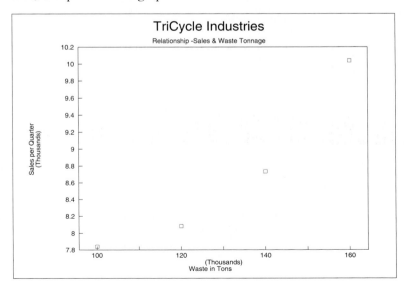

Figure 5-2e
Example of an XY graph

Starting 1-2-3 from the Access Menu

Whenever you plan to print graphs, you should start 1-2-3 differently from how you've started it in Tutorials 1 through 4. In this tutorial, you will print graphs, so you have to learn how to start 1-2-3 from the Access menu. By starting from the Access menu, you can move directly to PrintGraph once you are ready to print your graphs.

To start 1-2-3 from the Access menu:

❶ If you are using 1-2-3 on a hard-disk system, be sure the directory that contains the 1-2-3 program files is the current directory. Type **cd\123** and press **[Enter]**. If 123 is not the name of your directory, type the correct name instead. Then proceed to Step 2.

If you are running 1-2-3 on a two-disk system, insert the 1-2-3 System Disk in drive A and your Data Disk in drive B. Type **a:** and press **[Enter]**. If you are not using drive A for the System Disk, type the correct drive letter instead.

❷ Type **lotus** and press **[Enter]**. The Access system menu appears. See Figure 5-3.

use to print graphs

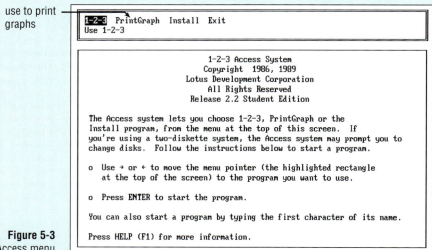

Figure 5-3
Access menu

From this menu, you can choose 1-2-3, PrintGraph, Install, or Exit.

❸ Highlight 1-2-3 and press **[Enter]**. A blank worksheet appears on your screen. If you start from the Access system, you are returned to the Access system menu when you quit 1-2-3. From now on in the tutorials, start 1-2-3 from either the operating system prompt or the Access system.

Creating a Bar Graph

Now let's retrieve one of Carl's worksheets that contains the number of cars sold in the U.S. from 1985 to 1988.

To retrieve this file:

❶ Retrieve the file C5FILE1.WK1. See Figure 5-4.

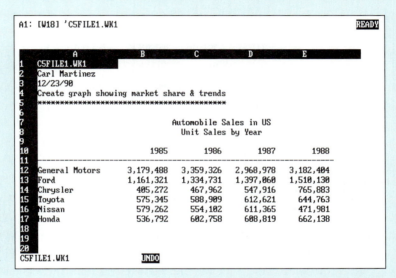

Figure 5-4
Carl's worksheet showing total car sales by manufacturer by year

Notice that the data in this worksheet contain the number of cars sold annually in the US from 1985 through 1988, broken down by manufacturer.

According to Carl's sketch, one of the graphs he wants to create is a bar graph showing car sales by manufacturer. Before creating the bar graph, you first need to learn about the Graph menu and the graph settings sheet.

To create any graph in 1-2-3, you must use the **Graph command**. This command reveals the **graph settings sheet,** in which you specify what data you want to graph and how you want to graph them. As you use the menu options available from the Graph command, 1-2-3 updates the graph settings sheet.

To create a graph, you must specify the following:

- The type of graph you want
- The range of cells that represent the labels for the x axis
- The data series you plan to use in the graph

Carl plans first to compare graphically total units sold by U.S. manufacturers (General Motors, Ford, Chrysler) over a four-year period (1985 to 1988) and then to compare these total U.S. units to units sold in the U.S. by Japanese manufacturers. Let's start by creating a bar graph of General Motors' data that shows unit sales over a four-year period.

To create a bar graph of cars sold by General Motors:

➊ Select /Graph (**/G**). 1-2-3 displays the graph settings sheet.

➋ Select Type (**T**) and then select Bar (**B**) to indicate the type of graph you want to create — a bar graph. See Figure 5-5.

type of chart

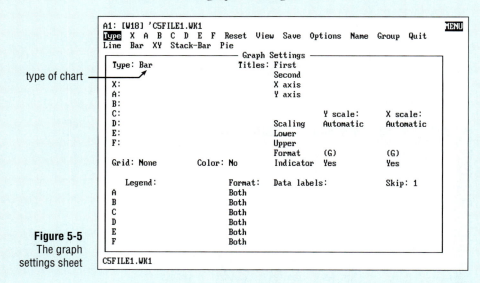

Figure 5-5
The graph
settings sheet

Next, specify the X data range, the worksheet range that contains the *labels* you want to place along the *x axis* (horizontal axis). Recall from Carl's sketch (Figure 5-1b) that you are using the years 1985, 1986, 1987, and 1988 as the x-axis labels.

➌ Select X to specify the X data range. 1-2-3 reveals Carl's worksheet.

➍ Move the cell pointer to cell B10, the first label to appear on the x axis. Press **[.]** (Period) to anchor the cell. Then highlight the range B10..E10 and press **[Enter]** to specify the X data range.

Now use the same method to specify the first data series, sales of General Motors cars from 1985 to 1988, to appear in the graph. The first data series is assigned to the A data range of your 1-2-3 graph menu.

➎ Select A to specify the A data range from the Graph menu. Move the cell pointer to B12, the cell containing General Motors sales data for l985. Press **[.]** to anchor the cell. Highlight B12..E12. See Figure 5-6a.

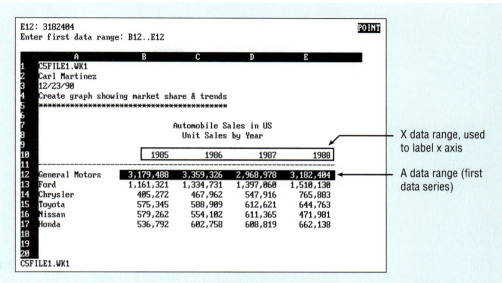

Figure 5-6a

⑥ Press **[Enter]**.

The graph settings sheet now indicates the graph type and the X and A ranges you specified. See Figure 5-6b. You can graph up to six data series at one time. 1-2-3 uses the letters A through F to represent these data series.

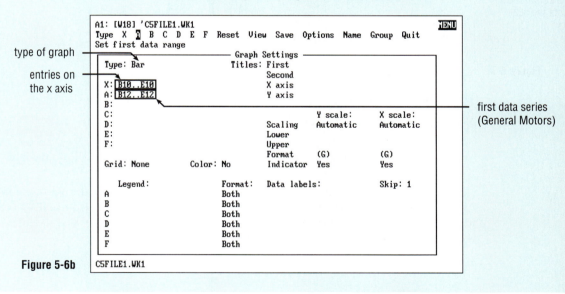

Figure 5-6b

Viewing the Current Graph

After you have chosen your graph type and specified the data ranges, you can view the graph on the screen.

To view the graph while in the Graph menu:

❶ Select View (**V**). The graph appears on the screen. See Figure 5-7.

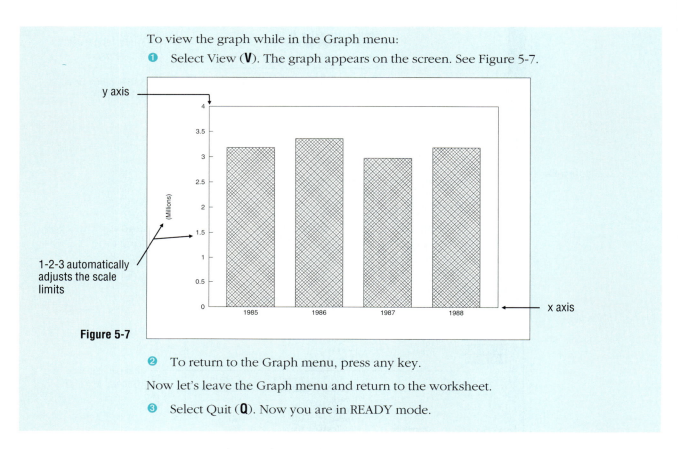

Figure 5-7

❷ To return to the Graph menu, press any key.

Now let's leave the Graph menu and return to the worksheet.

❸ Select Quit (**Q**). Now you are in READY mode.

In 1-2-3, the graph that appears on the screen when you enter the View command is called the **current graph**. When 1-2-3 is in READY mode, you can also use [F10] (GRAPH) to display the current graph directly from the worksheet. This feature allows you to change data in your worksheet and quickly see the results graphically.

To view the current graph by using the function key [F10]:

❶ Make sure 1-2-3 is in READY mode. Check the upper right corner of your screen.

❷ Press **[F10]** (GRAPH). The current graph appears.

❸ Press any key to return to the worksheet.

If you press [F10] (GRAPH) when there is no graph type, A data range, or X data range specified in the settings sheet, your screen will become blank. If that happens, press any key to return to the worksheet.

Adding Multiple Variables

Following Carl's plan, let's continue developing the graph by returning to the Graph menu and then adding the unit sales for Ford and Chrysler, that is, the B and C data ranges, to the bar graph.

To add the B and C data ranges to the bar graph:

❶ Select /Graph (**/G**) to return to the Graph menu. The second data series, cars sold by Ford, will be assigned to the second, or B, data range.

❷ Select B to specify the B data range from the Graph menu.

❸ Move the cell pointer to B13, the cell containing Ford sales data for 1985. Press **[.]** (Period) to anchor the cell. Highlight B13..E13. Press **[Enter]**.

The graph settings sheet now indicates the graph type and the X, A, and B ranges you have specified.

Now specify the third, or C, data range, sales of Chrysler cars from 1985 to 1988.

❹ Select C, for the C data range, from the Graph menu. You will assign the data for Chrysler to this range.

Move the cell pointer to B14, the cell containing Chrysler sales data for 1985. Press **[.]** (Period) to anchor the cell. Highlight B14..E14 and press **[Enter]**.

The graph settings sheet now indicates the graph type and the X, A, B, and C ranges you have specified. See Figure 5-8.

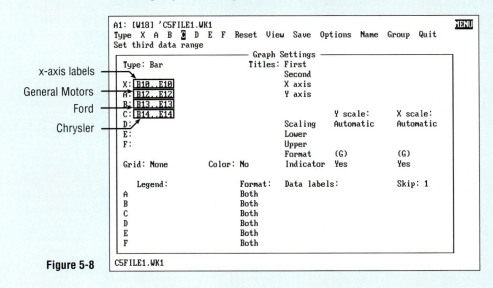

Figure 5-8

⑤ To view the current appearance of the graph, select View (**V**) from the Graph menu. See Figure 5-9.

A data range

B data range

C data range

Figure 5-9
View of bar graph
with three
companies' data
entered

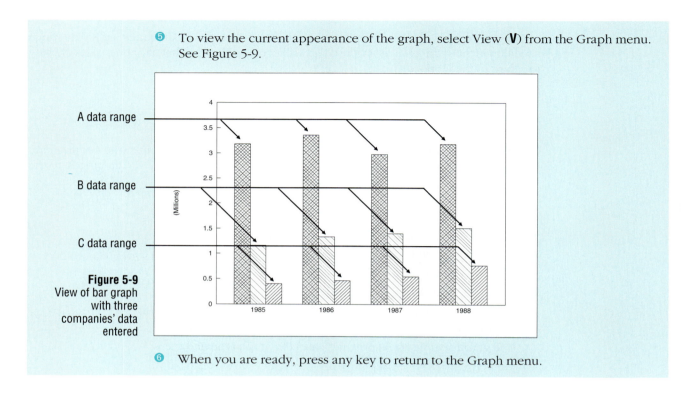

⑥ When you are ready, press any key to return to the Graph menu.

Experimenting with Different Graph Types

Some types of graphs may be more appropriate for your data than others. You can experiment with different types of graphs by simply selecting another graph type from the Graph menu. You can display the same data in different forms and see which form best presents the information. Let's illustrate this by changing the graph you just created to a line graph and then to a stacked bar graph.

To change graph type to a line graph:

❶ Select Type Line (**TL**) and then select View (**V**). The data appear as a line graph. See Figure 5-10.

 1-2-3 automatically scales the values along the y axis based on the values from the three data series (A, B, and C data ranges). For example, in 1985 General Motors sold 3,179,488 cars. On the y axis, this is shown as 3.2 million. 1-2-3 has automatically scaled this data and added the label "Millions" to the y axis. This automatic scaling occurs for bar and stacked bar graphs as well.

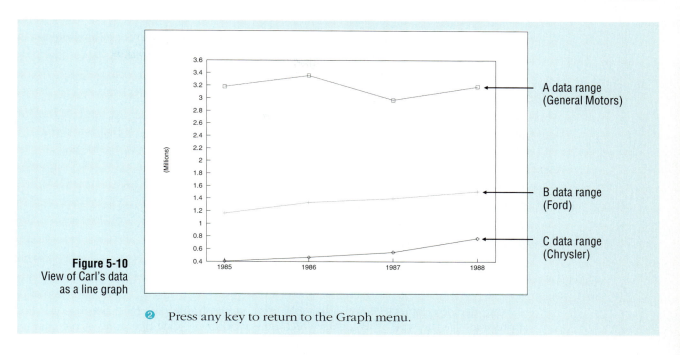

Figure 5-10
View of Carl's data
as a line graph

❷   Press any key to return to the Graph menu.

Now let's see how a stacked bar graph displays the data.

To display a stacked bar graph:
❶   Select Type and Stack-Bar (**TS**).
❷   Select View (**V**). See Figure 5-11.

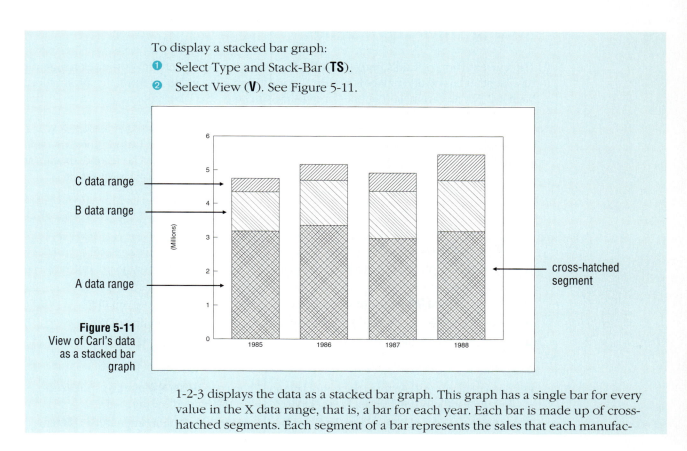

Figure 5-11
View of Carl's data
as a stacked bar
graph

1-2-3 displays the data as a stacked bar graph. This graph has a single bar for every value in the X data range, that is, a bar for each year. Each bar is made up of cross-hatched segments. Each segment of a bar represents the sales that each manufacturer contributed to total domestic sales in that year. Each bar viewed as a whole shows the total domestic sales in each year.

❸ Press any key to return to the Graph menu.

Carl decides that the relationship between the different companies over the small number of time periods can best be shown by a bar graph. Let's return the graph settings to a bar graph.

To return the graph settings sheet to a bar graph:

❶ Select Type Bar (**TB**).

❷ Select View (**V**). The bar graph appears on your screen.

❸ When you are ready, press any key to return to the Graph menu.

Carl decides not to try another popular type of graph, the pie chart, because it is not appropriate for the type of data with which he is working — data over time. A pie chart is more appropriate to show the relationship of the sales of each automobile company to total sales for a single year. You will create pie charts later in this tutorial.

Adding Titles and Legends

The current form of Carl's graph is difficult to interpret. What information does his graph represent? It has no title or labels to help anyone viewing the graph interpret the information. With 1-2-3, you can include a one- or two-line title and also label your x and y axes. Titles can be up to 39 characters.

Which bar in the graph represents General Motors sales? Ford sales? Chrysler sales? When you graph multiple data series, you should add a legend to identify the various lines on a line graph, the bars on a bar graph, or the segments on a stacked bar graph. The legend appears at the bottom of a graph. You can add a legend of up to 19 characters for each data series.

Now you will add titles and legends to the bar graph you've created.

To add titles and legends:

❶ From the Graph menu, select Options Titles First (**OTF**) to indicate you are entering the *first* line of the title.

❷ Type **U.S. Auto Manufacturers**, the title of Carl's graph, and then press **[Enter]**.

❸ Select Titles Second (**TS**) to indicate you are entering the second line of the title.

❹ Type **Domestic Sales** for the second line of the graph, then press **[Enter]**.

Now enter the legend for each car company.

❺ Select Legend A (**LA**) from the Graph menu. Then type **General Motors** to specify the legend for the A data range. Press **[Enter]** to enter the legend setting.

❻ Select Legend B (**LB**) and type **Ford** for the legend for the B data range. Press **[Enter]**.

➐ Select Legend C (**LC**) and type **Chrysler** for the legend for the C data range. Press [**Enter**]. See Figure 5-12.

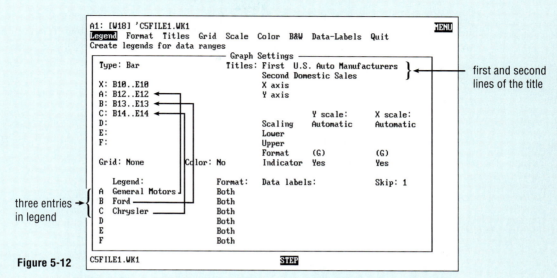

Figure 5-12

first and second lines of the title

three entries in legend

➑ Select Quit (**Q**) to leave the Options menu.

➒ Select View (**V**) to display the graph with the title and the legend. See Figure 5-13.

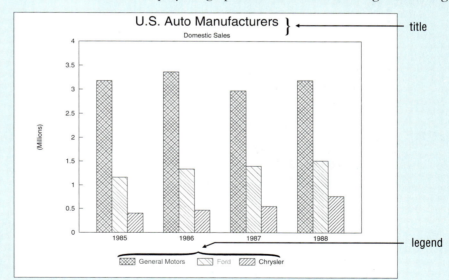

Figure 5-13
View of Carl's bar graph with title and legend

title

legend

➓ Press any key to return to the Graph menu.

Adding Axis Titles

You can add titles for both the horizontal (x) and the vertical (y) axes. Currently 1-2-3 indicates that the values on the y axis are in the millions. Millions of what? You can also add an axis title to improve the description of the y axis. The next step shows you how.

To add a y-axis title:

❶ From the Graph menu, choose Options Titles Y axis (**OTY**).

❷ Type **U N I T S   S O L D,** being sure to leave a space between each letter. Press **[Enter]**.

❸ Select Quit (**Q**) to return to the Graph menu.

❹ Select View (**V**) to see the revised graph. See Figure 5-14.

title added to y axis →

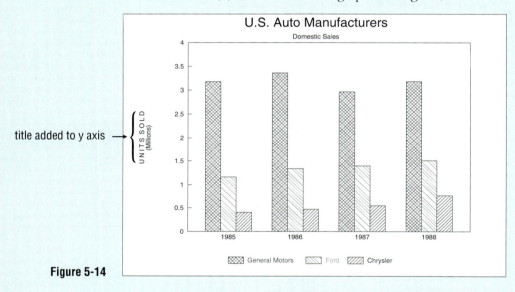

Figure 5-14

❺ Press any key when you want to return to the settings sheet.

❻ Select Quit (**Q**) to leave the Graph menu.

Naming the Current Graph

Carl plans to create several graphs within his worksheet. To have more than one graph available within your worksheet, you must assign a name to each graph. If you name this bar graph now, 1-2-3 stores all the settings needed to create this graph. Then whenever you want, you can view the graph without having to specify all the settings again.

Let's learn how to create named graphs in 1-2-3 by naming this bar graph BAR_BIG3. Note that the bar graph is the current graph, because it is the one you have most recently entered.

To name the current graph:

❶ Select /Graph Name Create (**/GNC**). The graph settings sheet appears on the screen showing the settings that will be assigned to the named graph.

Figure 5-15a illustrates the current worksheet in the computer's memory.

You can enter a name of up to 15 characters. As with range names, spaces within a name and certain characters are not allowed. It's often a helpful reminder to include the type of graph in the name you choose.

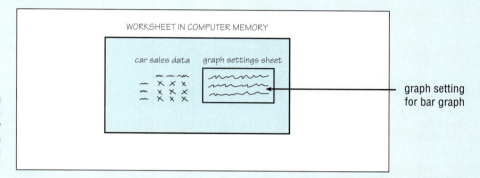

Figure 5-15a
Worksheet in memory immediately before /Graph Name Create command executed

❷ Type **BAR_BIG3** as the name of the graph and press **[Enter]**. You won't see any change in the settings sheet; this name does not appear on the setting sheet, but it does store the information found on the graph settings sheet as part of the worksheet. Figure 5-15b shows that the current graph settings are now named BAR_BIG3 and stand as part of the worksheet within the computer's memory.

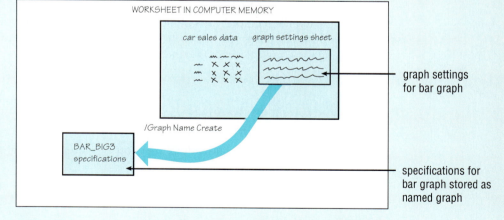

Figure 5-15b
Worksheet in memory after /Graph Name Create command executed

❸ Select Quit (**Q**) to leave the Graph menu and return to Ready mode. It is important to realize that when you name a graph you have not saved the graph specification to disk. You have only modified the worksheet in the computer memory. To include a named graph as part of a worksheet file on disk, you must use the File Save command.

❹ Save the worksheet file, which includes the named graph BAR_BIG3, as S5FILE1.WK1.

Now when you save your worksheet, each graph setting for the named graphs is saved as part of the worksheet. If you haven't named a graph, the settings for that graph will not be saved as part of the worksheet file. For example, earlier in the tutorial you created a line graph and a stacked bar graph. You did not, however, create a named graph for either of these graphs. Therefore, they were not saved as part of S5FILE1.WK1. See Figure 5-15c.

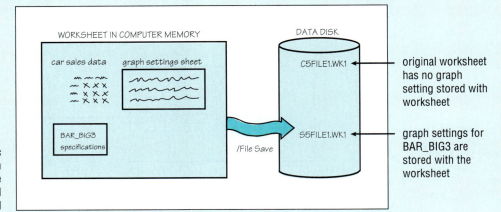

Figure 5-15c
Worksheet stored on Data Disk after /File Save command executed

Resetting Graph Settings

Once you have named a graph, you can define another graph. First, you may need to erase some or all of the current graph settings. You can erase the graph settings for the current graph by using the Graph Reset command.

To erase *all* the current graph settings:
❶   Select /Graph Reset (**/GR**). See Figure 5-16.
You can reset each setting individually, or you can reset the entire graph.

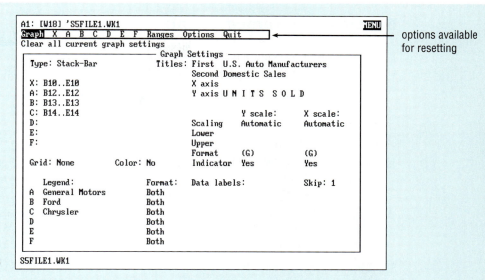

options available
for resetting

Figure 5-16

❷   Select Graph (**G**) to erase all the graph settings.

The current settings disappear from the graph settings sheet. See Figure 5-17.

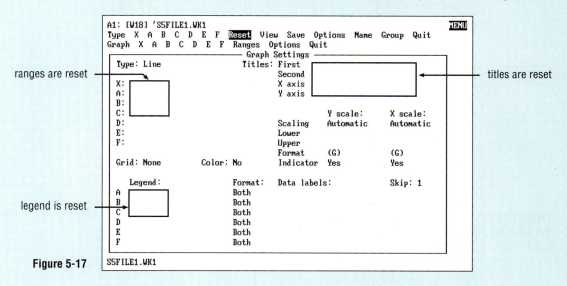

ranges are reset

titles are reset

legend is reset

Figure 5-17

❸   Select View (**V**). No graph appears because there are no current graph settings.

❹   Press any key to return to the graph settings sheet.

Even though the graph settings are cleared from the screen, the settings for BAR_BIG3 are still stored in memory as part of the worksheet. These settings are available by retrieving the named graph BAR_BIG3.

Retrieving a Named Graph

You were not able to view the bar graph after you erased the graph settings. However, since you have named your graph, the settings are still part of the worksheet. You can display the bar graph by selecting it from a list of named graph settings.

To view a named graph:

❶ Select Name Use (**NU**). 1-2-3 displays the names of all the different graph settings that are part of this worksheet. In this case, only one graph name appears because you have named only one so far in this tutorial.

❷ Highlight BAR_BIG3. Press **[Enter]** to view the graph. The bar graph appears on the screen. 1-2-3 has retrieved the graph settings for BAR_BIG3 that were stored as part of the worksheet and entered them as the current graph settings.

❸ Press any key. The graph settings sheet now contains the settings for the bar graph. See Figure 5-18.

❹ Select Quit (**Q**) to return to the worksheet.

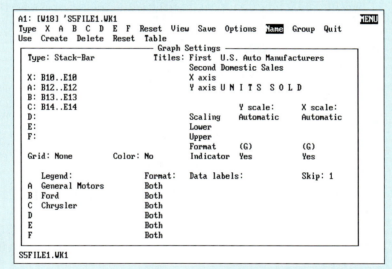

Figure 5-18
Current settings
for bar graph

Creating a Pie Chart

Now that Carl has looked at automobile sales over time, he decides to focus on sales in a single year — 1988, the last year for which he has complete data. A pie chart is a useful way to visualize data for an entire year, because pie charts typically represent the relative contribution of each part to the whole. The larger the slice, the greater that part's percentage of the whole. When you create a pie chart, you need:

- The set of values that represent the slices of the pie
- The set of labels that identify each slice of the pie chart

Before you can enter the settings for the pie chart, you must erase the bar graph settings.

To erase the current graph settings:

❶ Select /Graph (**/G**). Notice that the settings for the bar graph are the current settings.

❷ Select Reset Graph (**RG**). This erases the settings for the bar graph. See Figure 5-19.

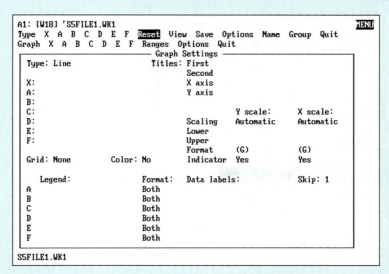

```
A1: [W18] 'S5FILE1.WK1                                              MENU
Type  X  A  B  C  D  E  F  Reset  View  Save  Options  Name  Group  Quit
Graph X  A  B  C  D  E  F  Ranges  Options  Quit
                            ┌──── Graph Settings ────
  Type: Line                     Titles: First
                                         Second
  X:                                     X axis
  A:                                     Y axis
  B:
  C:                                               Y scale:     X scale:
  D:                                     Scaling   Automatic    Automatic
  E:                                     Lower
  F:                                     Upper
                                         Format    (G)          (G)
  Grid: None          Color: No          Indicator Yes          Yes

    Legend:                    Format:  Data labels:          Skip: 1
  A                            Both
  B                            Both
  C                            Both
  D                            Both
  E                            Both
  F                            Both

S5FILE1.WK1
```

Figure 5-19
Graph settings
erased

Selecting the A Range

Now Carl can begin to enter the settings for the pie chart.

To create a pie chart for the number of cars sold in 1988:

❶ Select Type Pie (**TP**). The pie chart becomes the current graph type. The A data range is used to indicate the set of values that represent the slices of the pie.

❷ Select A, the range representing the set of values in the pie chart.

❸ Move the cell pointer to E12, number of cars sold by General Motors for 1988, and press **[.]** to anchor the cell. Highlight E12..E17 and press **[Enter]**. See Figure 5-20.

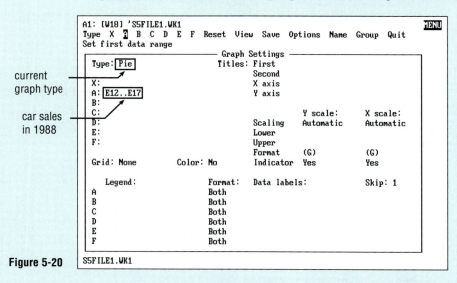

current graph type

car sales in 1988

Figure 5-20

❹ Select View (**V**) to view the status of your graph. See Figure 5-21.

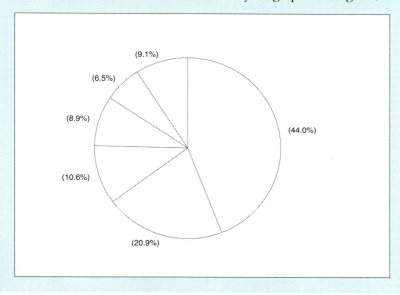

Figure 5-21
A view of Carl's unlabelled pie chart

Selecting the X range

As you view the graph, you cannot tell which car manufacturer is represented by which slice. Thus, you need to specify in the X range the labels that describe each slice. Use the names of the car manufacturers in column A of the worksheet as the labels for the slices of the pie chart.

To label each pie slice:

❶   Press any key to return to Graph menu.

❷   Select X.

❸   Move the cell pointer to A12, the cell holding the label General Motors. Press **[.]** to anchor the cell. Highlight A12..A17. Press **[Enter]**. Note that the labels in the X range correspond to the elements in the A range, that is, the first label in the X range will be the label of the first slice in the A range, and so on.

❹   Press View (**V**) to view the pie chart. See Figure 5-22. Now you can identify each slice in the pie chart with a manufacturer.

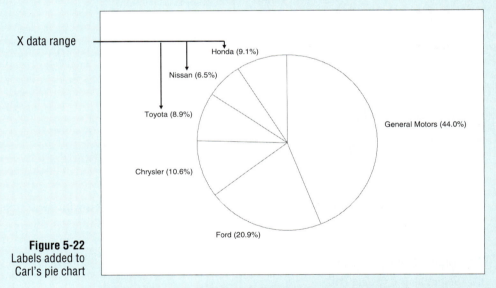

Figure 5-22
Labels added to
Carl's pie chart

❺   When you are ready, press any key to return to the Graph menu.

To help readers interpret your pie chart, you should add titles describing the pie chart. 1-2-3 allows you to include two title lines to the pie chart. Recall that Carl's sketch of the pie chart had a two-line title:

U.S. CAR SALES
1988

To add titles to the pie chart:

① Select Options Titles First (**OTF**) to add the first line of the title.

② Type **U.S. CAR SALES**, then press **[Enter]**.

③ Select Titles Second (**TS**) to add the second line of the title.

④ Type **1988** and press **[Enter]**.

⑤ Select Quit (**Q**) to leave the Options menu.

⑥ Select View (**V**) to see the title you have added to the graph. See Figure 5-23.

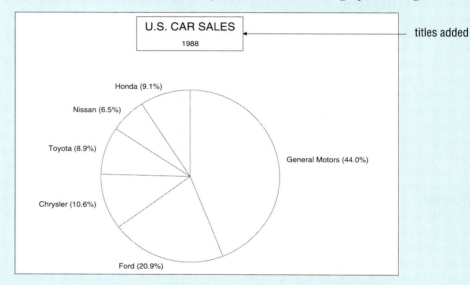

titles added

Figure 5-23

⑦ When you are ready, press any key to return to the Graph menu.

Let's now assign a name to the pie chart so its settings will be stored with the worksheet.

To assign a name to the pie chart:

① Select Name Create (**NC**).

② Type **PIE_88**, a descriptive name for this chart. Press **[Enter]**. Figure 5-24 shows that the current graph settings are now nameed PIE_88 and stored as part of the worksheet in the computer's memory.

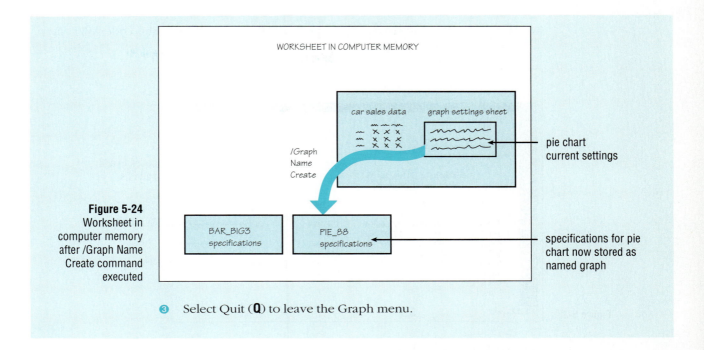

Figure 5-24
Worksheet in
computer memory
after /Graph Name
Create command
executed

❸ Select Quit (**Q**) to leave the Graph menu.

Selecting the B Range

To make the pie chart easier to read, shading (cross-hatched patterns) can be added to each slice of the pie chart. You use the B data range to add shading to your pie chart. The B data range is set up in your worksheet to correspond to the elements in the A data range. Each cell in the B range is associated with one cell in the A range. In each cell of the B range, you can enter a number between 1 and 7. 1-2-3 associates these numbers, when used in the B range of the graph settings for a pie chart, with different cross-hatched patterns. A value of 0, 8, or blank assigned to cells in the B range indicates you do not want shading in the associated slice.

Let's use cells F12 to F17 to enter the shading codes. The first cell, F12, will identify General Motors. The second cell, F13, will identify Ford. The final cell, F17, will identify Honda. In this graph you will assign shading to the slices for General Motors, Chrysler, and Nissan.

To assign cross-hatched pattern codes for slices of the pie chart:

❶ Move the cell pointer to cell F12, type **1,** and then press **[Enter]**. This code will assign a pattern to the General Motors' slice.

❷ Move the cell pointer to cell F14, type **2,** and then press **[Enter]**. This code will assign a pattern to Chyrsler's slice.

❸   Move the cell pointer to cell F16, type **3**, and then press **[Enter]**. This code will assign a pattern to Nissan's slice. See Figure 5-25.

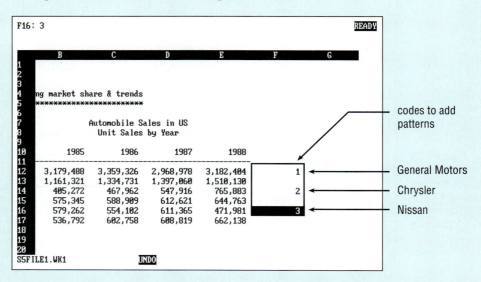

Figure 5-25

Notice that the cells identifying Ford (cell F13), Toyota (cell F15), and Honda (cell F17) are blank. 1-2-3 interprets these blank cells as zero, and no cross-hatched pattern will fill these slices of the pie chart. We have intentionally left these cells blank, because too many cross-hatched patterns make it difficult to distinguish slices.

For the shading to be included in the pie chart, the B range must be included in the graph settings.

To define the B range in the graph settings:

❶   Select /Graph B (**/GB**).

❷   Move the cell pointer to cell F12, the cell that corresponds to the first cell of the A data range. Press **[.]** to anchor the cell. Then highlight the range F12..F17 and press **[Enter]**. The B range is now included in the graph settings. See Figure 5-26.

codes for
cross-hatched
patterns

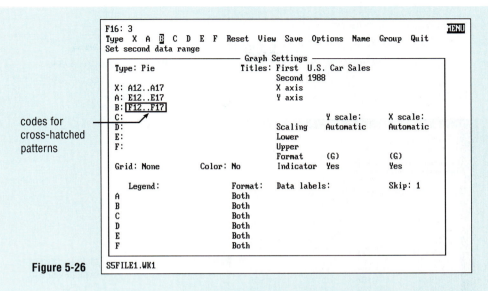

Figure 5-26

Be sure to highlight all cells in this range even though some may be blank. The B data range *must* contain the same number of cells as the pie chart's A data range.

❸ Select View (**V**) to display the new pie chart. See Figure 5-27.

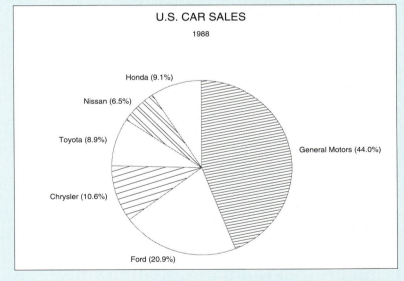

Figure 5-27
Pie chart with
shading

❹ When you are ready, press any key to return to the Graph menu.

You can call even more attention to a slice of the pie chart by "exploding" it, that is, separating it from the rest of the pie. In 1-2-3, you indicate that a slice is to be exploded by adding 100 to whatever the value is in the B range. For example, if the value is 2, you would enter 102 in the B range.

The next steps show you how to set up and use the B data range for exploding pie slices. Let's explode the slice representing Chrysler.

First, leave the graph menu:

❶ Select Quit (**Q**) to return to the worksheet.

❷ Move the cell pointer to F14, type **102,** and press **[Enter]**. See Figure 5-28.

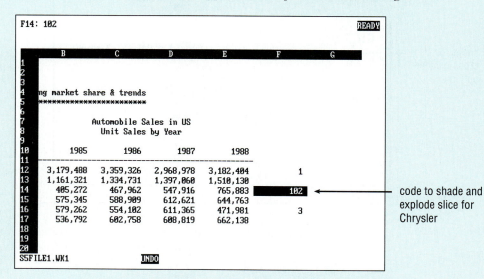

Figure 5-28

code to shade and explode slice for Chrysler

❸ Press **[F10]** (GRAPH) to view the pie chart. See Figure 5-29.

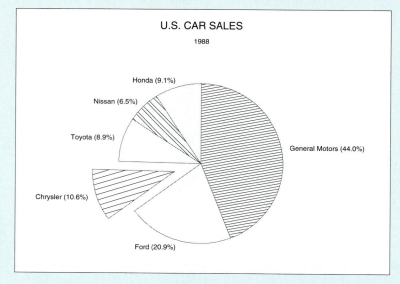

Figure 5-29
Pie chart with shading and "exploded" slice

❹ When you are ready, press any key to return to READY mode.

Let's now assign a name to the pie chart so its settings will be stored with the worksheet.

To assign a name to the pie chart:

❶   Select /Graph Name Create (**/GNC**).

❷   Type **PIE_88S**. Press **[Enter]**. Figure 5-30 shows that the current graph settings are now named PIE_88S and are stored as part of the worksheet in the computer's memory.

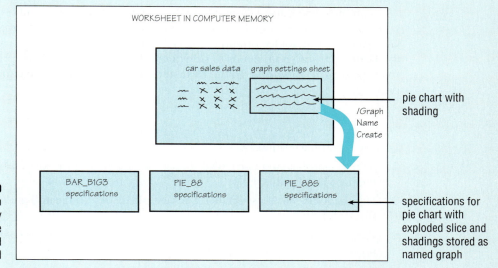

Figure 5-30
Worksheet in computer memory after /Graph Name Create command executed

❸   Select Quit (**Q**) to leave the Graph menu.

❹   Select /File Save (**/FS**), press **[Enter],** and select Replace (**R**). The current worksheet replaces the previous version of S5FILE1.WK1. This saved worksheet now includes three named graphs: BAR_BIG3, PIE_88, and PIE_88S. See Figure 5-31.

The use of the B range for shading and exploding slices applies to pie charts only. For other graph types, the B range is used for data. Except for this special use of the B range, pie charts use only the X and A ranges.

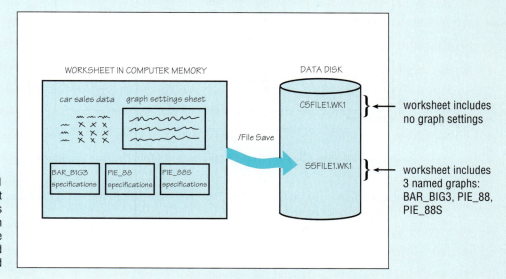

Figure 5-31
Current worksheet replaces S5FILE1.WK1 on Data Disk after /File Save command executed

Saving Graphs for Printing

In the previous section, you learned how to transform Carl's data into graphs. In this section, you will print two of the graphs you created and named. To print a graph, you must take two steps: (1) save the graphs for printing with the Graph Save command and (2) print the graph with the Lotus PrintGraph program.

You must use a special command — the Graph Save command — to save a graph that you want to print. Saving the worksheet by using /File Save only saves *named* graphs for later *viewing*, but not for printing. The /File Save command does *not* create the type of files the PrintGraph program needs to print a graph. To save a graph for printing, you *must use the Graph Save command*. In the next steps, you learn how to save graphs specifically for printing.

To save a graph for printing:

❶ Select /Graph Name Use (**/GNU**) to list the named graphs. Next, retrieve PIE_88, the chart you will print.

❷ Highlight **PIE_88**. Press **[Enter]**. The first pie chart you created and named appears on the screen.

❸ Press any key to return to the Graph menu. The graph settings for the pie chart appear in the graph settings sheet. See Figure 5-32.

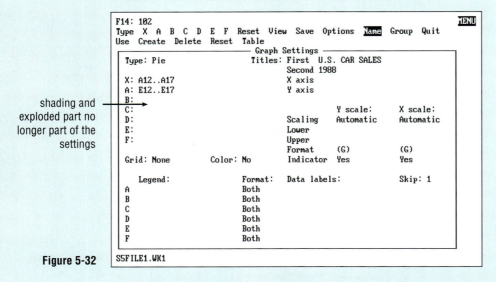

shading and exploded part no longer part of the settings

Figure 5-32

❹ Select Save (**S**) from the Graph menu. Only the current graph can be saved for printing.

Enter a name for the graph file. DOS limits the filename to eight characters, as it does for worksheet names.

❺ Type **PIE_US88** and press **[Enter]**.

1-2-3 saves the graph in a file named PIE_US88.PIC; it automatically adds the extension .PIC. Each graph that you want to print must be saved as a separate .PIC file. See Figure 5-33.

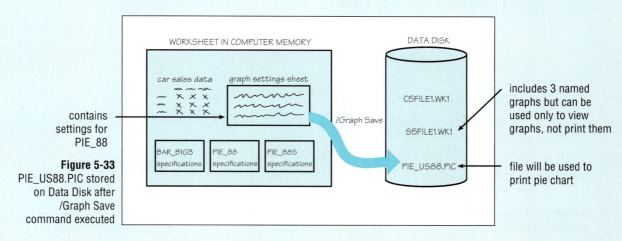

contains
settings for
PIE_88

Figure 5-33
PIE_US88.PIC stored
on Data Disk after
/Graph Save
command executed

Now let's save the bar graph so you can also print it.

To save the bar graph for printing:

❶ Select Name Use (**NU**) from the Graph menu. Next, retrieve BAR_BIG3, the bar graph you will print.

❷ Highlight BAR_BIG3. Press **[Enter]**. The bar graph appears on your screen, and the graph settings for the bar graph are now the current graph settings.

❸ Press any key to return to the Graph menu.

❹ Select Save (**S**).

❺ Type the graph filename **BAR_US**. See Figure 5-34. 1-2-3 saves the graph in a file named BAR_US.PIC.

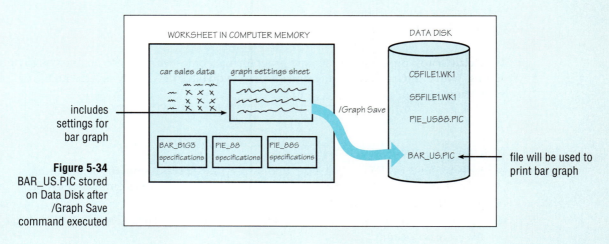

includes
settings for
bar graph

Figure 5-34
BAR_US.PIC stored
on Data Disk after
/Graph Save
command executed

6 Select Quit (**Q**) to return to READY mode.

Finding Your PIC Files

To check what graph (.PIC) files are on your disk or in your data directory, you can use the File List commands.

To display a list of the .PIC files:

1 Select /File List Graph (**/FLG**). See Figure 5-35. A list of the files that have the extension .PIC extension appears.

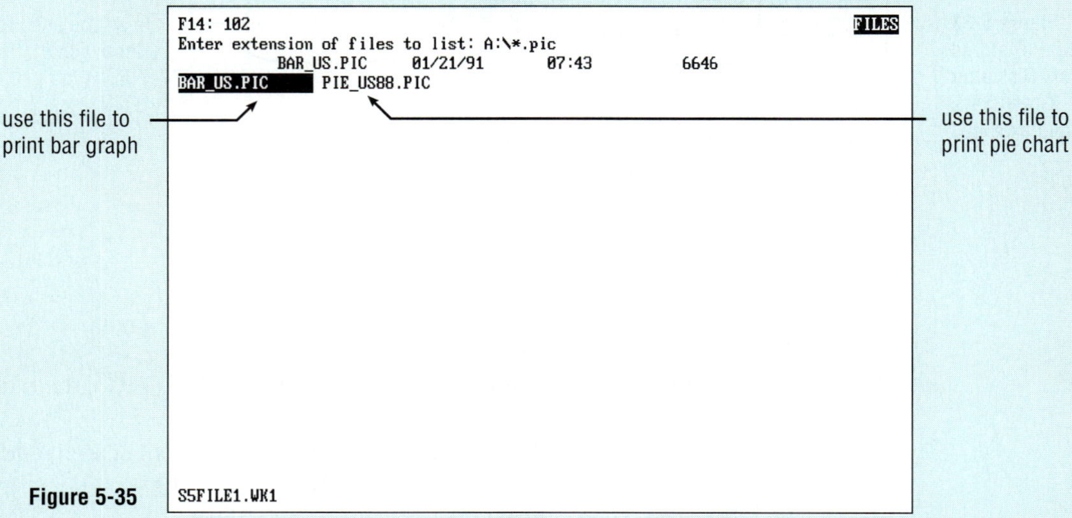

```
F14: 102                                                      FILES
Enter extension of files to list: A:\*.pic
           BAR_US.PIC      01/21/91        07:43          6646
BAR_US.PIC       PIE_US88.PIC
```

use this file to print bar graph

use this file to print pie chart

Figure 5-35   S5FILE1.WK1

2 Press [**Enter**] to return to the worksheet.

Using PrintGraph

The **PrintGraph** program is a separate program that comes with 1-2-3 to enable you to print graphs. With PrintGraph, you can print any graph you have previously saved with the Graph Save command.

To start PrintGraph:

1 Select /Quit Yes (**QY**) to quit 1-2-3 and display the Access menu. If you are using a hard-disk system, skip to Step 4. If you are using a two-disk system, you must first leave the Access system before you start PrintGraph.

2 For two-disk users *only*: insert your DOS disk in drive A. Then select Exit (**E**) to leave the Access system.

❸ For two-disk system users *only*: insert the PrintGraph disk in drive A and type **lotus**.

❹ Select PrintGraph (**P**) from the Access menu. The menu of PrintGraph commands appears at the top of the screen, and the current settings of PrintGraph appear below. Your screen should look similar to Figure 5-36.

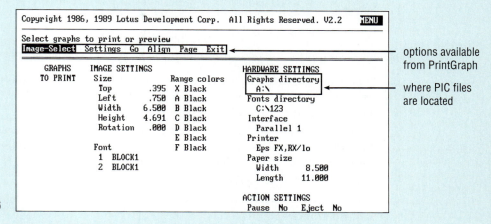

Figure 5-36

```
Copyright 1986, 1989 Lotus Development Corp.  All Rights Reserved. V2.2   MENU

Select graphs to print or preview
Image-Select  Settings  Go  Align  Page  Exit           ←——  options available
                                                               from PrintGraph
    GRAPHS    IMAGE SETTINGS                 HARDWARE SETTINGS
    TO PRINT  Size              Range colors Graphs directory  ←——  where PIC files
              Top       .395    X Black        A:\                   are located
              Left      .750    A Black      Fonts directory
              Width    6.500    B Black        C:\123
              Height   4.691    C Black      Interface
              Rotation  .000    D Black        Parallel 1
                                E Black      Printer
              Font              F Black        Eps FX,RX/lo
              1  BLOCK1                       Paper size
              2  BLOCK1                         Width     8.500
                                               Length   11.000

                                             ACTION SETTINGS
                                               Pause  No   Eject  No
```

If this is the first time you have ever started PrintGraph, the program assumes that your graph (.PIC) files and font (.FNT) files are located either on a PrintGraph Disk in drive A or, if you are using a hard-disk system, in your 1-2-3 directory. **Fonts** are the typefaces used to print the graph text.

Look at the rightmost column of the PrintGraph settings sheet at the entries under Graphs directory and Fonts directory. You might need to adjust the disk/directory information for your Graph and Font directories and be sure your printer is specified properly. If necessary, ask your instructor or technical support person for assistance. The next steps show you how to change the PrintGraph settings in case the current settings are not correct for your system. Once you make and save these changes, you will not need to go through these steps again unless you make a change in your system.

To adjust the default PrintGraph settings, you first must specify the directory that contains the graph (.PIC) files so PrintGraph knows where to find your graphs:

❶ Select Settings Hardware Graphs-Directory (**SHG**).

❷ Enter the name of the directory or drive where you saved your graph files.

If you are using a *two-disk* system, type **b:** (or the name of the drive that contains your data) and press **[Enter]**.

If you are using a *hard-disk* system, type **c:\123\data** if you keep the data files on the hard disk or **a:** (or the name of the directory or drive that contains your data) if you keep the files on a diskette in drive A. Then press **[Enter]**.

Next, specify the directory that contains the font (.FNT) files. PrintGraph needs to access these files to print your graphs.

❸ Select Fonts-Directory (**F**).

❹ Enter the name of the directory or drive where the fonts are stored.

If you are using a *two-disk* system, type **a:** or the letter for the drive with the Print-Graph disk. Press **[Enter]**.

If you are using a *hard-disk* system, type **c:\123** or the name of the directory that contains the 1-2-3 and PrintGraph programs. Press **[Enter]**.

Finally, select a graphics printer to print your graphs.

⑤ Select Printer (**P**) to display a list of installed printers.

If no printer names appear, rerun the Install program, as described in Chapter 2.

⑥ Follow the on-screen instructions. Press **[↓]** or **[↑]** to highlight the printer you want to use. Press **[Space]** to mark your selection. Then press **[Enter]**. The # sign indicates the printer that you have selected for printing your graphs.

If you have a choice of low and high density, choose low density so your graphs will print more quickly. If you select high density, the quality of the graph will improve, but the graph will take longer to print.

⑦ Select Quit (**Q**) to leave the Hardware menu and return to the PrintGraph menu.

⑧ Select Save (**S**) to save these settings so they will appear automatically the next time you run PrintGraph.

These settings will remain as the current PrintGraph settings if you decide to print your graphs now.

Now you are ready to print the two graphs you saved as PIC files.

To print a single graph:

① Select Image-Select (**I**) from the PrintGraph menu to display an alphabetized list of all the graphs that have been saved for printing. See Figure 5-37.

PIC files →

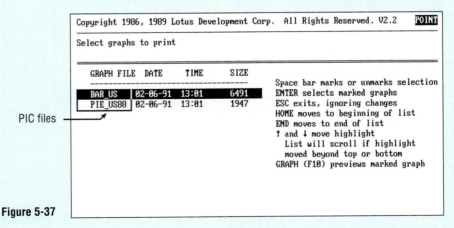

Figure 5-37

These are the files that you created with the Graph Save command and that 1-2-3 stored with a .PIC extension. Each file stores the description of one graph.

② Highlight BAR_US. Then press **[Space]** to mark your selection. The # sign indicates that a graph has been selected for printing. See Figure 5-38.

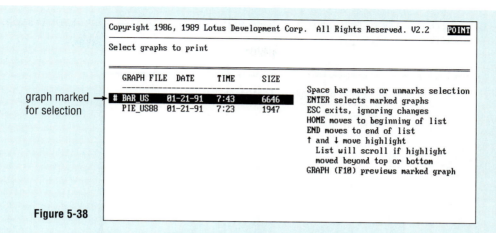

graph marked
for selection

Figure 5-38

If you change your mind about which graph to select, you can press [Space] to unmark the selection.

❸ Press **[F10]** (GRAPH) to preview the graph. The bar graph appears on your screen. You should always preview a graph before you print it to make sure you have selected the graph you want to print. Press any key to leave the preview and return to the Select Graph to Print screen.

❹ Press **[Enter]** to complete the selection process and return to the PrintGraph menu. Notice that a filename appears under the "Graphs to Print" section of the settings sheet. See Figure 5-39.

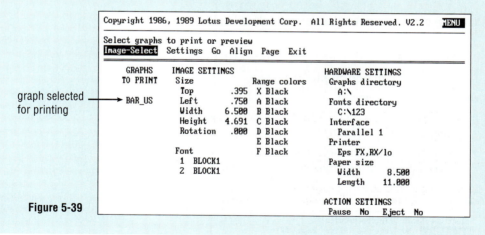

graph selected
for printing

Figure 5-39

⑤ Check that your printer is ready. Then select Align Go (**AG**) to print the first graph. See Figure 5-40.

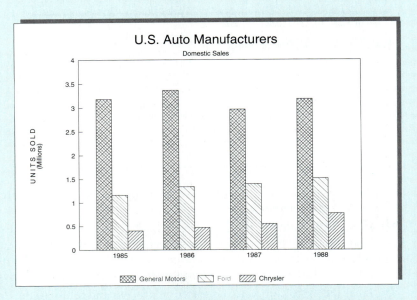

Figure 5-40

⑥ Select Page (**P**) to advance the printer to the top of the next page.

You can also print more than one graph on a page at a time.

To print more than one graph on a page:

❶ Select Image-select (**I**).

❷ Highlight the graph file PIE_US88. Press **[Space]** to mark the file PIE_US88 with a # sign. Then press **[Enter]**.

Now two graphs are selected for printing. See Figure 5-41.
If your printer uses single sheets, go to Step 5.

two graphs selected for printing →

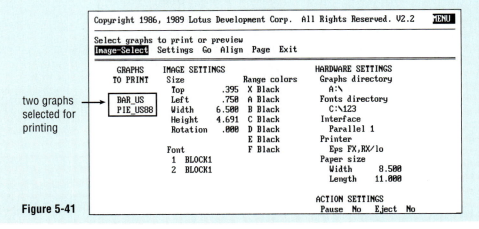

Figure 5-41

❸ Select Settings Image Size Half (**SISH**) to print each of these images on half a page.

❹ Select Quit (**Q**) three times to return to the PrintGraph menu.

❺ Select Align Go and Page (**AGP**) to print the two graphs. See Figure 5-42.

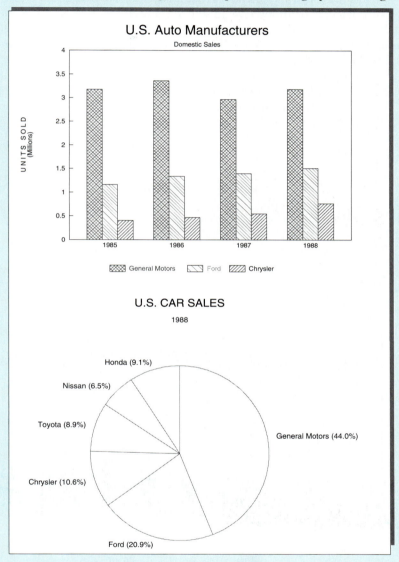

Figure 5-42

❻ Select Exit Yes (**EY**) to leave PrintGraph. You are now at the Access menu.

❼ Select Exit (**E**) to leave the Access menu and return to DOS.

Summary

In Tutorial 5, you learned how to use many 1-2-3 commands for creating and printing graphs. You began by learning how to start 1-2-3 from the Access system menu. Then you created bar, line, and stacked bar graphs, and pie charts using multiple data ranges. By adding titles and legends and labeling the axes, you learned some of the ways you can improve the appearance of graphs.

After creating, naming, and saving several graphs, you learned how to print them using the PrintGraph program. If you were using PrintGraph for the first time, you also learned how to specify PrintGraph's hardware settings to work with your computer system.

Exercises

1. Use Figure 5-43 to identify the following components of a graph:
    a. type of graph
    b. x-axis labels
    c. y-axis titles
    d. legend
    e. title
    f. x-axis title
    g. data series for projected sales

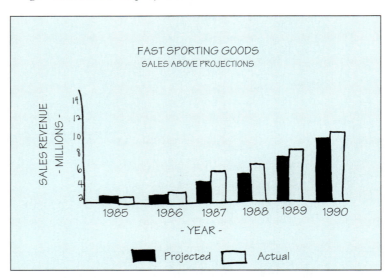

Figure 5-43

Retrieve the worksheet T5GRDEMO and do or answer the following:

2. Save this worksheet as S5GRDEMO.

3. Make the named graph PIE1 the current graph.

4. Change the value for first-quarter revenue of plastics from 2890 to 4890.

5. View the pie chart again. Did the appearance of the graph change? If yes, how did it change?

6. Make the named graph BAR the current graph. Is this graph based on the original data from the worksheet or the new data you entered in Exercise 4?

7. Save this worksheet as S5GRDEMO.

8. Erase the worksheet from the screen.

9. On your Data Disk is the file T5PIE.PIC, which contains the pie chart that you viewed in Exercise 3. If you were to print T5PIE.PIC, would the graph reflect the original data in the worksheet or the data after the change you made to the worksheet data in Exercise 4?

10. If you were to retrieve the worksheet S5GRDEMO.WK1 and view the graph named PIE1, would the pie chart be based on the original data or the revised data from Exercise 4?

Tutorial Assignments

Before you begin these Tutorial Assignments, check your working copy of the Data Disk. Be sure you have space to save the additional worksheet files you'll create in these assignments (at least 30,000 bytes). If not, save your files as appropriate to another formatted diskette.

Retrieve worksheet T5FILE1.WK1 and do the following:

1. Create a pie chart that illustrates the market share of each of the six auto manufacturers for 1987.

2. Include a title on the pie chart.

3. Explode the slice that represents Honda.

4. Name this graph PIE_87.

5. Save this graph as a .PIC file. Use the name PPIE_87.

6. Reset all the graph settings in this worksheet.

7. Prepare a bar graph showing the three Japanese companies' sales from 1985 to 1988.

8. Add a title and a legend to this graph.

9. Name this graph BAR_JPN.

10. Save this graph as a .PIC file. Use the name PBAR_JPN.

11. Change the graph to a stacked bar graph.

12. Name this graph STK_JPN.

13. Save this graph as a .PIC file. Use the name PSTK_JPN.

14. Save your worksheet as S5FILE2.

15. Print the graph file PPIE_87 on a separate page.

16. Print the graph files PBAR_JPN and PSTK_JPN on the same page.

Use the Reference section of *Lotus 1-2-3 for Business* to do the following:

17. Retrieve the graph named BAR_BIG3 from T5FILE1.
    a. Label the bars of the bar graph with the actual values, that is, the data labels.
    b. View the bar graph.
    c. Save your worksheet as S5FILE3.
    d. Save the bar graph as a PIC file. Use the name PBARBIG3.
    e. Print the bar graph.

Case Problems

1. Graphing Health Maintenance Organizations' Membership Data

Medical costs have risen dramatically over the last 10 to 15 years. Health maintenance organizations (HMOs) were created as an alternative to traditional health insurance to help decrease medical costs. HMOs provide a range of comprehensive health care services to people who pay an enrollment fee and become members. By joining an HMO, a member gains access to a team of doctors 365 days a year. Employers, labor unions, government agencies, and consumer groups often provide this type of medical coverage for their employees.

Figure 5-44 shows a table of the enrollment in HMO programs by major insurer.

Enrollment in HMOs

Insurer	Millions of members
Blue Cross	15.5
Cigna	3.6
Aetna	2.5
Metropolitan	2.4
Prudential	2.2
Travelers	1.6

Figure 5-44

Use the data in Figure 5-44 to do the following:

1. Construct a pie chart.

2. Explode the Aetna segment.

3. Add appropriate titles and labels.

4. Create the named graph PIE_HMO.

5. Save your worksheet as S5HMO.

6. Save the pie chart as a .PIC file. Use the name PPIE_HMO.

7. Print the pie chart.

2. Graphing Data on Cellular Telephone Subscribers and Revenues

Many people are using cellular telephones more and more in their business and personal lives. Figure 5-45 shows the changes in the number of cellular telephone subscribers in the U.S. and the revenue they generated from 1985 through 1990.

Figure 5-45

U.S. Cellular Telephones						
	1985	**1986**	**1987**	**1988**	**1989**	**1990**
Subscribers	200	500	1000	1600	2700	4300
Revenue	1500	4500	5000	8000	13500	21000

Create a worksheet file from the table above and do the following:

1. Create a line chart that shows the growth in number of subscribers and revenues from 1985 through 1990.

2. Enter appropriate titles and legends.

3. Create the named graph LINE_TELE for the line chart.

4. Graph this same data using a bar graph. Create the named graph BAR_TELE for the bar graph.

5. Save your worksheet as S5TELE.

6. Save each graph setting as a .PIC file. Save the line chart as PLNE_TEL and the bar graph as PBAR_TEL.

7. Print the line chart and the bar graph.

3. Using Line Charts to Analyze Stock Prices

Levon Smith, a stock analyst for the firm of Morris-Sorensen, specializes in recommending what computer industry stock investors should buy. Levon wants to analyze indexes and stock prices at the end of each month for 1990 to identify any trends. He has collected month-end data (Figure 5-46) on the following indexes and companies: Standard & Poor's 500 stock index, computer industry stock index, IBM, Digital Equipment Corporation, Cray Research, and Apple Corporation.

	S&P 500	Computer Index	Digital Equipment	IBM	Apple	Cray Research
Jan	297	205	118	130	44	64
Feb	289	213	120	130	37	61
Mar	295	195	104	121	34	60
Apr	310	189	97	116	40	59
May	321	191	90	114	49	59
Jun	318	190	86	115	50	58
Jul	346	195	90	116	40	56
Aug	351	193	105	120	45	55
Sep	349	181	104	119	46	54
Oct	340	170	84	110	50	45
Nov	346	164	84	101	47	42
Dec	353	190	80	102	45	40

Figure 5-46
Selected month-end index and stock prices

Retrieve the worksheet P5STOCK.WK1 and do the following:

1. Create a line chart of the month-end Standard & Poor's 500 and computer industry indexes. Remember to include a title and a legend. Name this graph LINE_MARKET.

2. Create a second line chart that includes the month-end stock prices for IBM, Digital, Cray Research, and Apple so Levon can observe the trend in stock prices for these companies. Remember to include a title and a legend. Name this graph LINE_COMPANY.

3. Save your worksheet as S5STOCK.

4. Save each line chart as a .PIC file. Save the first line graph as PLNE_MRK and the second graph as PLNE_CMP.

5. Print the graphs.

4. The U.S. Airline Industry

During the 1980s, U.S. airline companies consolidated into eight major carriers. With growth of international travel expected to exceed domestic U.S. travel in the 1990s, these eight major carriers are scrambling to increase their number of international routes. Figure 5-47 shows passenger revenues generated by international routes from 1985 through 1989 for each carrier. These numbers are rounded to the nearest million.

Figure 5-47
Passenger
revenues

Passenger Revenues International Routes					
Carrier	1985	1986	1987	1988	1989
American	400	472	672	884	1858
Continental	249	319	526	743	843
Delta	216	227	410	634	742
Northwest	936	1094	1362	1767	2051
Pan Am	2197	1806	2088	2353	2154
TWA	1369	872	1123	1294	1321
UAL	114	802	1112	1514	1780

Figure 5-48 shows the amount of net income these eight carriers earned from their international routes from 1985 through 1989. These numbers are rounded to the nearest thousand.

Figure 5-48

Net Income International Routes					
Carrier	1985	1986	1987	1988	1989
American	7438	6650	-10911	-866	8723
Continental	13196	31238	46247	125272	83013
Delta	11722	8386	32028	58686	18104
Northwest	36862	49313	77146	114318	167207
Pan Am	302913	-157149	13142	-70600	-165392
TWA	-18021	-24852	49210	133499	-6051
UAL	-23662	-36840	11715	163313	100507

Retrieve the worksheet P5AIRLN.WK1. The worksheet contains Figures 5-47 and 5-48. Use the data to do the following:

1. Prepare a bar graph that illustrates passenger revenue for American, TWA, and UAL from 1985 through 1989. Remember to include appropriate titles and legends. Name this graph BAR_REV.

2. Prepare a stacked bar graph showing the same data as Problem 1. Name this graph STK_REV.

3. Prepare a bar graph comparing net income for these three companies. Name this graph BAR_INC.

4. Prepare a pie chart of passenger revenues for each carrier during 1985. Name this graph PIE_85. Remember to include appropriate titles.

5. Prepare a second pie chart with similar data for 1989. Name this graph PIE_89. Remember to include appropriate titles.

6. Save your worksheet as S5AIRLN.

7. Save the named graphs as separate .PIC files.

8. Print your graphs.

Tutorial 6

Using a Database

A Customer/Accounts Receivable Database

Case: Medi-Source Inc.

Medi-Source Inc. distributes supplies to hospitals, medical laboratories, and pharmacies throughout the United States. Files of all Medi-Source customers and accounts receivable data are available to department managers on the company's mainframe computer.

Joan Glazer, the manager of the credit and collection department, was recently reviewing these data and noticed that the outstanding balance of several Massachusetts and Rhode Island customers appeared to be higher than that of the average Medi-Source customer, which is approximately $6,000. She wants to study the accounts in these two states more carefully.

Joan asks Bert Spivak, the manager of the information systems department, to prepare several reports to help her analyze the data. Bert tells her that he and his programming staff are backed up on projects and will not be able to help her for four to six weeks. He suggests instead that he retrieve the Rhode Island and Massachusetts data from the mainframe database and provide her with a Lotus 1-2-3 file. Then she can analyze the data herself. Joan thinks this is a great idea. Bert says he'll have the data to her in two days.

While waiting for the data, Joan thinks about the analysis she will do. She decides to plan her project and makes a list of her goals, output, input and calculations (Figure 6-1a). Joan realizes the worksheet will be large and will include several sections. As a part of her planning, she develops a sketch to help organize the overall structure of the worksheet (Figure 6-1b).

Objectives

In this tutorial you will learn to:

- Define the terms *field, record, file,* and *database*

- Sort a database

- Use statistical functions: @AVG, @MAX, @MIN

- Find records that match specified criteria

- Extract records that match specified criteria

- Use database statistical functions

My Goals
    Review the Rhode Island and Massachusetts customer database to
    determine whether balances owed by customers in those states are higher
    than average Medi-Source customers.

What results do I want to see?
    List records in database by:
        customer name
        outstanding balance
        state and within state by outstanding balance
    List customers with outstanding balances above Medi-Source average.
    Report showing summary statistics for RI and MA customers.
    Report of outstanding balance by state.

What information do I need?
    Subset of Medi-Source database – all RI and MA customer records.

What calculations will I perform?
    Total outstanding balance
    Average outstanding balance
    Maximum outstanding balance
    Minimum outstanding balance
    Count number of customers

Figure 6-1a
Joan's planning
sheet

RI & MA Database   Summary Report
~~~~ ~~~~~~ ~~   RI and MA Customers
~~~ ~~~~ ~~~~~   Medi-Source
~~~ ~~~~ ~~~~~.
                                                        Outstanding Balance
  .
  .   Total   xxxx
                                        Average   xxxx
  .   Maximum   xxxx
                                        Minimum   xxxx
                                        Count   xxxx

Criteria Range

Output Range   Outstanding Balance
                                        by State
                                        Medi-Source

                                                        RI   MA
                                        Total   xx   xx
                                        Average   xx   xx

Figure 6-1b
Joan's worksheet
sketch

In this tutorial, you will learn some new database terms, learn how to arrange data into
a meaningful order through sorting, search a database to locate and extract records that meet

specific criteria, and use database statistical functions to perform statistical analysis on selected records within the database.

Introduction to File Concepts

Before you retrieve the Medi-Source file, you need to understand important terms that are critical to understanding and using computerized databases. These terms are field, record, file, and database.

A **field** is an attribute (characteristic) of some object, person, or place. For example, each item of data that Medi-Source tracks is referred to as a field or a data element. Customer #, customer name, balance customer owes, and year-to-date sales represent attributes about a customer (Figure 6-2).

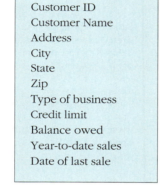

Figure 6-2
Fields in Medi-Source's customer database

Customer ID
Customer Name
Address
City
State
Zip
Type of business
Credit limit
Balance owed
Year-to-date sales
Date of last sale

Related fields are grouped together to form a **record**, a collection of attributes describing a person, place, or thing. All the data about a customer, such as Bristol Pharmacy, are referred to as a record. The Bristol Pharmacy record consists of data fields such as customer #, customer name, and balance customer owes (Figure 6-3). If Medi-Source has 1,500 customers, then the company will have 1,500 records.

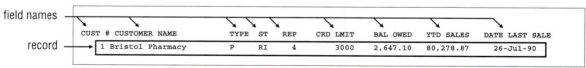

field names

record

CUST #	CUSTOMER NAME	TYPE	ST	REP	CRD LMIT	BAL OWED	YTD SALES	DATE LAST SALE
1	Bristol Pharmacy	P	RI	4	3000	2,647.10	80,278.87	26-Jul-90

Figure 6-3
Bristol Pharmacy's record

A collection of related records is called a **data file**. The 1,500 customer records at Medi-Source, viewed in their entirety, represent the customer data file. Figure 6-4 shows a few of the records from the data file.

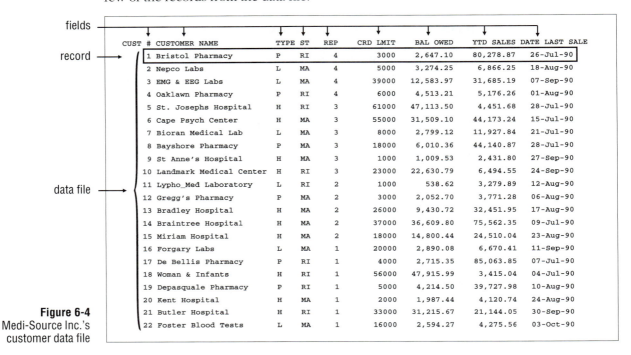

fields

record

data file

CUST #	CUSTOMER NAME	TYPE	ST	REP	CRD LMIT	BAL OWED	YTD SALES	DATE LAST SALE
1	Bristol Pharmacy	P	RI	4	3000	2,647.10	80,278.87	26-Jul-90
2	Nepco Labs	L	MA	4	5000	3,274.25	6,866.25	18-Aug-90
3	EMG & EEG Labs	L	MA	4	39000	12,583.97	31,685.19	07-Sep-90
4	Oaklawn Pharmacy	P	RI	4	6000	4,513.21	5,176.26	01-Aug-90
5	St. Josephs Hospital	H	RI	3	61000	47,113.50	4,451.68	28-Jul-90
6	Cape Psych Center	H	MA	3	55000	31,509.10	44,173.24	15-Jul-90
7	Bioran Medical Lab	L	MA	3	8000	2,799.12	11,927.84	21-Jul-90
8	Bayshore Pharmacy	P	MA	3	18000	6,010.36	44,140.87	28-Jul-90
9	St Anne's Hospital	H	MA	3	1000	1,009.53	2,431.80	27-Sep-90
10	Landmark Medical Center	H	RI	3	23000	22,630.79	6,494.55	24-Sep-90
11	Lypho_Med Laboratory	L	RI	2	1000	538.62	3,279.89	12-Aug-90
12	Gregg's Pharmacy	P	MA	2	3000	2,052.70	3,771.28	06-Aug-90
13	Bradley Hospital	H	MA	2	26000	9,430.72	32,451.95	17-Aug-90
14	Braintree Hospital	H	MA	2	37000	36,609.80	75,562.35	09-Jul-90
15	Miriam Hospital	H	MA	2	18000	14,800.44	24,510.04	23-Aug-90
16	Forgary Labs	L	MA	1	20000	2,890.08	6,670.41	11-Sep-90
17	De Bellis Pharmacy	P	RI	1	4000	2,715.35	85,063.85	07-Jul-90
18	Woman & Infants	H	RI	1	56000	47,915.99	3,415.04	04-Jul-90
19	Depasquale Pharmacy	P	RI	1	5000	4,214.50	39,727.98	10-Aug-90
20	Kent Hospital	H	MA	1	2000	1,987.44	4,120.74	24-Aug-90
21	Butler Hospital	H	RI	1	33000	31,215.67	21,144.05	30-Sep-90
22	Foster Blood Tests	L	MA	1	16000	2,594.27	4,275.56	03-Oct-90

Figure 6-4
Medi-Source Inc.'s
customer data file

Typically, companies maintain many different files to store related customer data. One file stores the basic customer data; a second file stores data on each outstanding invoice; a third file tracks each payment made by a customer; a fourth file tracks customer orders that have not yet been shipped. These four files may be thought of as the customer database. Thus, a **database** is a collection of logically related files.

At Medi-Source, the credit and collection department is working with only one data file. Thus, our database in this tutorial consists of just one data file. Spreadsheet software works well when you are processing records from a single file such as this one. But when you must process data from multiple files, other software packages process the data more effectively than spreadsheets. These other software packages are referred to as **database packages.**

Retrieving the Worksheet

To retrieve the Medi-Source database:
❶ Retrieve the file C6FILE1.WK1 from your Lotus 1-2-3 data diskette. See Figure 6-5.

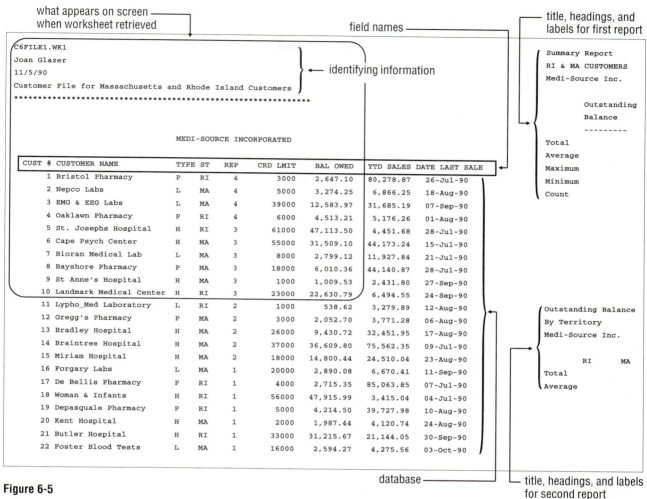

what appears on screen when worksheet retrieved

field names

title, headings, and labels for first report

identifying information

```
C6FILE1.WK1
Joan Glazer
11/5/90
Customer File for Massachusetts and Rhode Island Customers
*************************************************************
```

```
                    MEDI-SOURCE INCORPORATED


CUST #  CUSTOMER NAME         TYPE ST  REP    CRD LMIT    BAL OWED    YTD SALES DATE LAST SALE
     1  Bristol Pharmacy       P   RI   4        3000     2,647.10   80,278.87   26-Jul-90
     2  Nepco Labs             L   MA   4        5000     3,274.25    6,866.25   18-Aug-90
     3  EMG & EEG Labs         L   MA   4       39000    12,583.97   31,685.19   07-Sep-90
     4  Oaklawn Pharmacy       P   RI   4        6000     4,513.21    5,176.26   01-Aug-90
     5  St. Josephs Hospital   H   RI   3       61000    47,113.50    4,451.68   28-Jul-90
     6  Cape Psych Center      H   MA   3       55000    31,509.10   44,173.24   15-Jul-90
     7  Bioran Medical Lab     L   MA   3        8000     2,799.12   11,927.84   21-Jul-90
     8  Bayshore Pharmacy      P   MA   3       18000     6,010.36   44,140.87   28-Jul-90
     9  St Anne's Hospital     H   MA   3        1000     1,009.53    2,431.80   27-Sep-90
    10  Landmark Medical Center H  RI   3       23000    22,630.79    6,494.55   24-Sep-90
    11  Lypho_Med Laboratory   L   RI   2        1000       538.62    3,279.89   12-Aug-90
    12  Gregg's Pharmacy       P   MA   2        3000     2,052.70    3,771.28   06-Aug-90
    13  Bradley Hospital       H   MA   2       26000     9,430.72   32,451.95   17-Aug-90
    14  Braintree Hospital     H   MA   2       37000    36,609.80   75,562.35   09-Jul-90
    15  Miriam Hospital        H   MA   2       18000    14,800.44   24,510.04   23-Aug-90
    16  Forgary Labs           L   MA   1       20000     2,890.08    6,670.41   11-Sep-90
    17  De Bellis Pharmacy     P   RI   1        4000     2,715.35   85,063.85   07-Jul-90
    18  Woman & Infants        H   RI   1       56000    47,915.99    3,415.04   04-Jul-90
    19  Depasquale Pharmacy    P   RI   1        5000     4,214.50   39,727.98   10-Aug-90
    20  Kent Hospital          H   MA   1        2000     1,987.44    4,120.74   24-Aug-90
    21  Butler Hospital        H   RI   1       33000    31,215.67   21,144.05   30-Sep-90
    22  Foster Blood Tests     L   MA   1       16000     2,594.27    4,275.56   03-Oct-90
```

Summary Report
RI & MA CUSTOMERS
Medi-Source Inc.

Outstanding
Balance

Total
Average
Maximum
Minimum
Count

Outstanding Balance
By Territory
Medi-Source Inc.

RI   MA
Total
Average

database

title, headings, and labels for second report

Figure 6-5
Joan's initial worksheet

Notice that each *row* in the database represents a customer record. The first row of the database, row 10, contains the **field names**. Field names are labels that identify the fields in a database as needed, and they *must* be in the first row of any database you use in 1-2-3.

❷ Press **[PgDn]** and **[Tab]** as needed to view the entire file.

❸ Press **[Home]** to return to cell A1.

The field names in the customer database are:

Field	Description
CUST #	Unique identification number assigned to each customer
CUSTOMER NAME	Name of each customer
TYPE	Code indicating the type of business, for example, P = Pharmacy, L = Laboratory, and H = hospital
ST	State abbreviation: RI = Rhode Island; MA = Massachusetts
REP	ID of the sales representative assigned to make sales calls on this customer
CRD LMIT	Maximum amount of credit the customer is allowed
BAL OWED	Amount of money customer currently owes Medi-Source
YTD SALES	Total sales to customer since the beginning of the year
DATE LAST SALE	Date of the last sales transaction with this customer

Now that you are familiar with the Medi-Source customer file, you are ready to manipulate the file.

Sorting Data

The Data Sort command lets you arrange the file in an order that you specify. For instance, you could arrange your data alphabetically by customer name or numerically by the amount of money the customer owes to Medi-Source.

Before performing the data sort, you need to understand three terms related to sorting data in 1-2-3: data range, primary key, and secondary key.

Data-Range

The **data range** represents the records in the database you want to sort. This range usually includes all the records in the database. The data range does *not* include the field names of the columns, because the field names are merely labels and not part of the data you want to sort. You *must* be sure to include *all* the fields (columns) for the records you specify in the data-range; otherwise, you will alter the relationships among data fields in the database.

Primary Key

A field that determines the order in which you sort the database is called a **sort key**. The **primary key** (primary sort key) represents the field (column) you want 1-2-3 to use to determine the new order for the database records. For example, if you want 1-2-3 to arrange the data by the amount customers' owe Medi-Source, the primary key is the field balance owed (BAL OWED).

Secondary Key

The **secondary key** (secondary sort key) represents a second field (column) to determine the sort order within the primary sort key field. For example, you might select type of customer as the primary sort key, and customer name as the secondary sort key. Thus, you could sort the data by customer type (such as hospital, lab, pharmacy) and within each customer type alphabetically by customer name. To explain this example further, all the hospital customers appear first in alphabetical order, followed by an alphabetized list of laboratory customers, and finally the pharmacy customers appear arranged in alphabetical order.

Sorting Using the Primary Key

Joan wants to sort the data alphabetically by customer name. Ordering the data by customer name will make it easier for her to locate a customer than will the current order of the database, which is by customer number.

To sort a data file by customer name:

❶ Select /Data Sort (**/DS**), and the sort settings sheet appears. See Figure 6-6.

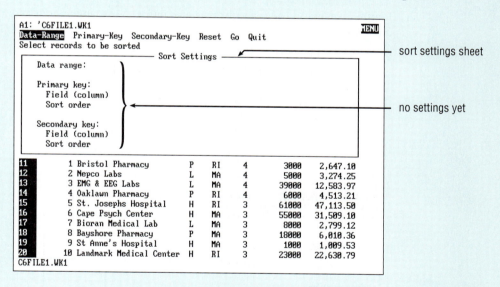

Figure 6-6

The settings sheet indicates the settings for the data range, the primary key, and the secondary key. Currently there are no settings.

Now identify the area of the worksheet to be sorted, which 1-2-3 refers to as the data range.

❷ Select Data Range (**D**). The worksheet appears on your screen.

❸ Move the cell pointer to the first cell in the data range, A11, and press [**.**] to anchor the cell. Highlight A11..I32 and press [**Enter**]. See Figure 6-7 on the next page.

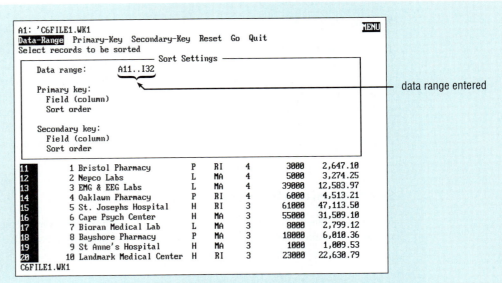

Figure 6-7

1-2-3 enters A11..I32 as the data range on the settings sheet. Remember that field names are not part of the data range and that every column in your database should be included in the data range.

Joan wants to sort the data by customer name. Next, specify customer name as the primary sort key.

❹ Select Primary-Key (**P**). Move the cell pointer to the first record in the customer field, cell B11, the customer name field, and press **[Enter]**.

Actually you can move the cell pointer to any cell in column B to indicate that the primary sort key is customer name.

Next you specify the sort order.

❺ Type **A** to specify ascending sort order and press **[Enter]**. See Figure 6-8.

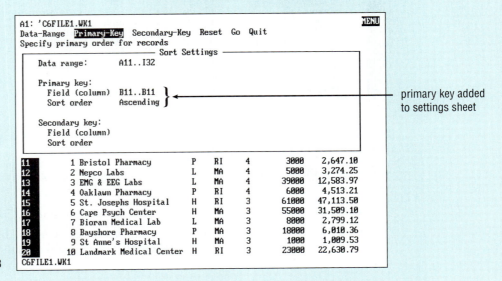

Figure 6-8

Ascending order for labels means arranging the data alphabetically from A to Z and numerically from lowest to highest number. Descending order for labels means arranging the data alphabetized backward from Z to A and numerically from highest to lowest number.

6 Select Go (**G**) to sort the data file. When sorting is completed, your screen should show the records alphabetized by customer name. See Figure 6-9.

what appears on screen →

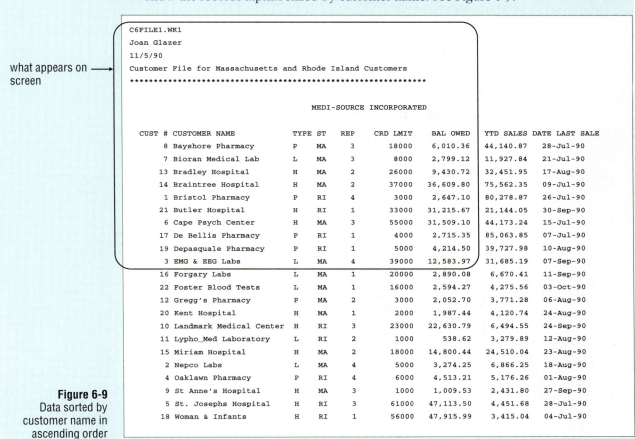

```
C6FILE1.WK1
Joan Glazer
11/5/90
Customer File for Massachusetts and Rhode Island Customers
****************************************************************

                        MEDI-SOURCE INCORPORATED

CUST # CUSTOMER NAME        TYPE ST   REP   CRD LMIT    BAL OWED   YTD SALES DATE LAST SALE
     8 Bayshore Pharmacy      P   MA    3     18000     6,010.36   44,140.87   28-Jul-90
     7 Bioran Medical Lab     L   MA    3      8000     2,799.12   11,927.84   21-Jul-90
    13 Bradley Hospital       H   MA    2     26000     9,430.72   32,451.95   17-Aug-90
    14 Braintree Hospital     H   MA    2     37000    36,609.80   75,562.35   09-Jul-90
     1 Bristol Pharmacy       P   RI    4      3000     2,647.10   80,278.87   26-Jul-90
    21 Butler Hospital        H   RI    1     33000    31,215.67   21,144.05   30-Sep-90
     6 Cape Psych Center      H   MA    3     55000    31,509.10   44,173.24   15-Jul-90
    17 De Bellis Pharmacy     P   RI    1      4000     2,715.35   85,063.85   07-Jul-90
    19 Depasquale Pharmacy    P   RI    1      5000     4,214.50   39,727.98   10-Aug-90
     3 EMG & EEG Labs         L   MA    4     39000    12,583.97   31,685.19   07-Sep-90
    16 Forgary Labs           L   MA    1     20000     2,890.08    6,670.41   11-Sep-90
    22 Foster Blood Tests     L   MA    1     16000     2,594.27    4,275.56   03-Oct-90
    12 Gregg's Pharmacy       P   MA    2      3000     2,052.70    3,771.28   06-Aug-90
    20 Kent Hospital          H   MA    1      2000     1,987.44    4,120.74   24-Aug-90
    10 Landmark Medical Center H  RI    3     23000    22,630.79    6,494.55   24-Sep-90
    11 Lypho_Med Laboratory   L   RI    2      1000       538.62    3,279.89   12-Aug-90
    15 Miriam Hospital        H   MA    2     18000    14,800.44   24,510.04   23-Aug-90
     2 Nepco Labs             L   MA    4      5000     3,274.25    6,866.25   18-Aug-90
     4 Oaklawn Pharmacy       P   RI    4      6000     4,513.21    5,176.26   01-Aug-90
     9 St Anne's Hospital     H   MA    3      1000     1,009.53    2,431.80   27-Sep-90
     5 St. Josephs Hospital   H   RI    3     61000    47,113.50    4,451.68   28-Jul-90
    18 Woman & Infants        H   RI    1     56000    47,915.99    3,415.04   04-Jul-90
```

Figure 6-9
Data sorted by customer name in ascending order

7 Press **[PgDn]** to view all the customer records. Press **[Home]** to return to cell A1.

Joan also planned to sort the customer data by balance owed, with customers having the largest outstanding balance appearing first, that is, in descending order. That way Joan can quickly identify the customers that have the highest outstanding balance.

To sort a data file in descending order by balance owed:

❶ Select /Data Sort (**/DS**) 1-2-3 displays the sort settings sheet.

Since the range of cells to be sorted was previously entered and still appears in the sort settings sheet, you do not have to select the data range again.

The next step is to change the primary sort key from customer name to balance owed (BAL OWED).

❷ Select Primary-Key (**P**). Move the cell pointer to cell G11, or any cell in the BAL OWED column, and press **[Enter]**.

❸ Type **D** to specify descending sort order and press **[Enter]**. See Figure 6-10.

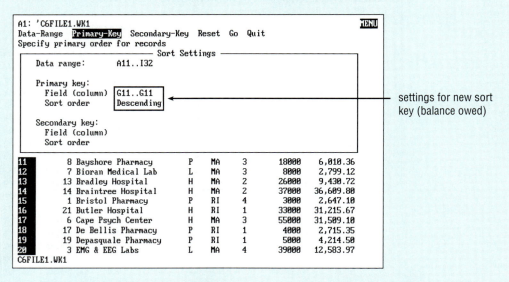

Figure 6-10

❹ Select Go (**G**) to sort the database. When sorting is completed, your screen should look like Figure 6-11. Notice that the customer having the highest balance owed appears first. The customer with the lowest balanced owed is last.

```
C6FILE1.WK1
Joan Glazer
11/5/90
Customer File for Massachusetts and Rhode Island Customers
************************************************************
```

		MEDI-SOURCE INCORPORATED						
CUST #	CUSTOMER NAME	TYPE	ST	REP	CRD LMIT	BAL OWED	YTD SALES	DATE LAST SALE
18	Woman & Infants	H	RI	1	56000	47,915.99	3,415.04	04-Jul-90
5	St. Josephs Hospital	H	RI	3	61000	47,113.50	4,451.68	28-Jul-90
14	Braintree Hospital	H	MA	2	37000	36,609.80	75,562.35	09-Jul-90
6	Cape Psych Center	H	MA	3	55000	31,509.10	44,173.24	15-Jul-90
21	Butler Hospital	H	RI	1	33000	31,215.67	21,144.05	30-Sep-90
10	Landmark Medical Center	H	RI	3	23000	22,630.79	6,494.55	24-Sep-90
15	Miriam Hospital	H	MA	2	18000	14,800.44	24,510.04	23-Aug-90
3	EMG & EEG Labs	L	MA	4	39000	12,583.97	31,685.19	07-Sep-90
13	Bradley Hospital	H	MA	2	26000	9,430.72	32,451.95	17-Aug-90
8	Bayshore Pharmacy	P	MA	3	18000	6,010.36	44,140.87	28-Jul-90
4	Oaklawn Pharmacy	P	RI	4	6000	4,513.21	5,176.26	01-Aug-90
19	Depasquale Pharmacy	P	RI	1	5000	4,214.50	39,727.98	10-Aug-90
2	Nepco Labs	L	MA	4	5000	3,274.25	6,866.25	18-Aug-90
16	Forgary Labs	L	MA	1	20000	2,890.08	6,670.41	11-Sep-90
7	Bioran Medical Lab	L	MA	3	8000	2,799.12	11,927.84	21-Jul-90
17	De Bellis Pharmacy	P	RI	1	4000	2,715.35	85,063.85	07-Jul-90
1	Bristol Pharmacy	P	RI	4	3000	2,647.10	80,278.87	26-Jul-90
22	Foster Blood Tests	L	MA	1	16000	2,594.27	4,275.56	03-Oct-90
12	Gregg's Pharmacy	P	MA	2	3000	2,052.70	3,771.28	06-Aug-90
20	Kent Hospital	H	MA	1	2000	1,987.44	4,120.74	24-Aug-90
9	St Anne's Hospital	H	MA	3	1000	1,009.53	2,431.80	27-Sep-90
11	Lypho_Med Laboratory	L	RI	2	1000	538.62	3,279.89	12-Aug-90

sort of balance owed in descending order

Figure 6-11

⑤ Press **[PgDn]** to view all the customer records. When you are finished viewing the records, press **[Home]** to return to cell A1.

Sorting Using a Secondary Key

You can organize data on more than one sort key. For example, Joan wants to organize the customers by state, and within each state, she wants to arrange the customers from highest balance owed to lowest balance owed. This will allow Joan to see which customers in each state owe the most to Medi-Source.

To sort a file on two sort keys:

❶ Select /Data Sort (**/DS**), and the sort settings sheet appears.

Since the range of cells to be sorted was previously entered and still appears in the sort settings sheet, you do not have to select the data range again.

Next specify state as the primary sort key.

❷   Select Primary-Key (**P**). Move the cell pointer to cell D11, the ST field, and press **[Enter]**.

❸   Type **A** to specify ascending sort order and press **[Enter]**.

Now specify balance owed as the secondary sort key.

❹   Select Secondary-Key (**S**). Move the cell pointer to cell G11, the BAL OWED field, and press **[ENTER]**.

❺   Press **[Enter]** if D (descending) already appears as the sort order for BAL OWED. If A appears, type D and press **[Enter]**.

❻   Select Go (**G**) to sort the data file. See Figure 6-12.

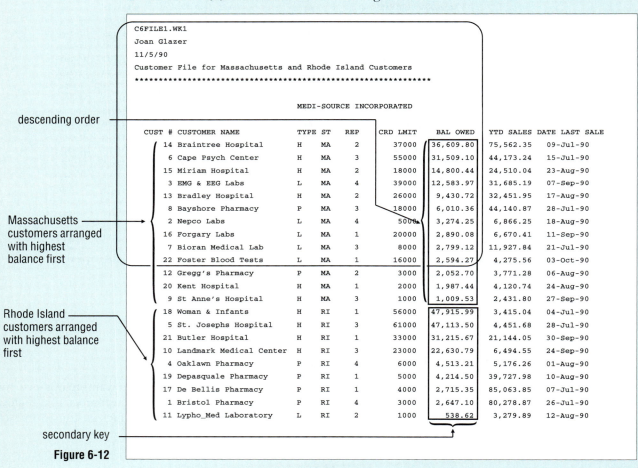

descending order

Massachusetts customers arranged with highest balance first

Rhode Island customers arranged with highest balance first

secondary key

Figure 6-12

Notice that all Massachusetts customers are grouped together, followed by all customers from Rhode Island. Within each state, the customer records are arranged by balance owed, with customers having the highest balance appearing first. Joan observes that the hospital customers from both states have large outstanding balances.

Data Query Command — Finding Records

Now that Joan has sorted the data, she wants to examine specific customer accounts. While sorting the data, she noticed that customers in the hospital category have outstanding balances that are high compared to customers in the lab and pharmacy categories. So, she decides to examine these accounts first.

The Data Query command lets 1-2-3 select records that match certain criteria and finds (highlights) or extracts (copies) these records without examining every record in the database. Before 1-2-3 can find a record in the database, you must specify an input range and set up a criteria range. Let's discuss what we mean by these two ranges.

Input Range

An **input range** is the range of data, *including field names*, to be searched as part of the query. When you specify an input range to use with any Data Query command, you must include the field names as part of the range. This is unlike the data range in the Data Sort command, which does *not* include the field names.

You can assign a range name to represent the input range, although 1-2-3 does not require that you do this to execute the Data Query command. This will allow you to specify the database without having to remember the exact cell locations of your database.

To assign a range name to the database:

❶ Move the cell pointer to cell A10, the upper left corner of the database. Remember when you use the Data Query command, you must include the field names in the input range.

❷ Select /Range Name Create (**/RNC**).

❸ Type the name **DATABASE** and press **[Enter]**.

❹ Highlight the database cells A10..I32. Press **[Enter]**. The range name DATABASE has been assigned to this range of cells.

Again, note that the range includes the field names and the data records.

Criteria Range

The **criteria range** is a small area in your worksheet where you describe the records for which you are searching. This range must be at least two rows. The first row of the criteria range contains some or all of the field names from the database. The field names in the criteria range must be identical to the database field names. The rows below the field names in the criteria range include the search criteria.

The criteria range is often established below the database. Let's use cells A35 to I36. In the first row of the criteria range, you must enter the criteria field names. Since these names must be *identical* to the database field names, it is best to copy the database field names to the criteria range, so no difference can occur between the database field names and the criteria field names.

To copy the database fields names to the criteria range:

❶ Make sure the cell pointer is in cell A10, the location of the first database field name to be copied.

❷ Select /Copy (**/C**).

❸ Highlight A10..I10 Press **[Enter]**.

❹ Now move the cell pointer to cell A35, the location where you will place the field names for the criteria range. Then press **[Enter]**.

❺ Move the cell pointer to cell A35, so you can see that the database field names have been copied to the criteria range. See Figure 6-13.

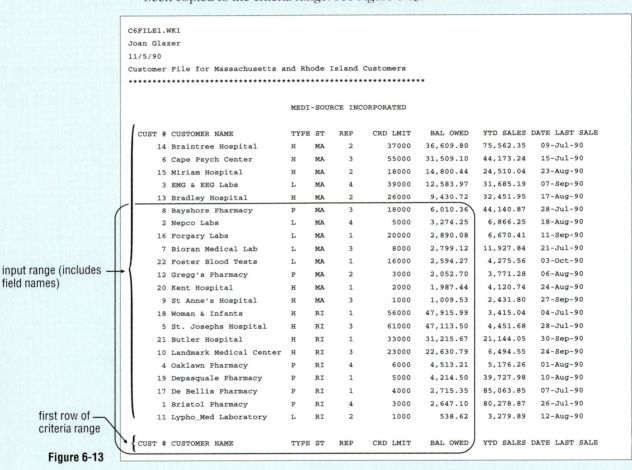

```
C6FILE1.WK1
Joan Glazer
11/5/90
Customer File for Massachusetts and Rhode Island Customers
******************************************************************

                            MEDI-SOURCE INCORPORATED

CUST # CUSTOMER NAME           TYPE ST  REP   CRD LMIT    BAL OWED   YTD SALES DATE LAST SALE
    14 Braintree Hospital        H   MA   2      37000   36,609.80   75,562.35   09-Jul-90
     6 Cape Psych Center         H   MA   3      55000   31,509.10   44,173.24   15-Jul-90
    15 Miriam Hospital           H   MA   2      18000   14,800.44   24,510.04   23-Aug-90
     3 EMG & EEG Labs            L   MA   4      39000   12,583.97   31,685.19   07-Sep-90
    13 Bradley Hospital          H   MA   2      26000    9,430.72   32,451.95   17-Aug-90
     8 Bayshore Pharmacy         P   MA   3      18000    6,010.36   44,140.87   28-Jul-90
     2 Nepco Labs                L   MA   4       5000    3,274.25    6,866.25   18-Aug-90
    16 Forgary Labs              L   MA   1      20000    2,890.08    6,670.41   11-Sep-90
     7 Bioran Medical Lab        L   MA   3       8000    2,799.12   11,927.84   21-Jul-90
    22 Foster Blood Tests        L   MA   1      16000    2,594.27    4,275.56   03-Oct-90
    12 Gregg's Pharmacy          P   MA   2       3000    2,052.70    3,771.28   06-Aug-90
    20 Kent Hospital             H   MA   1       2000    1,987.44    4,120.74   24-Aug-90
     9 St Anne's Hospital        H   MA   3       1000    1,009.53    2,431.80   27-Sep-90
    18 Woman & Infants           H   RI   1      56000   47,915.99    3,415.04   04-Jul-90
     5 St. Josephs Hospital      H   RI   3      61000   47,113.50    4,451.68   28-Jul-90
    21 Butler Hospital           H   RI   1      33000   31,215.67   21,144.05   30-Sep-90
    10 Landmark Medical Center   H   RI   3      23000   22,630.79    6,494.55   24-Sep-90
     4 Oaklawn Pharmacy          P   RI   4       6000    4,513.21    5,176.26   01-Aug-90
    19 Depasquale Pharmacy       P   RI   1       5000    4,214.50   39,727.98   10-Aug-90
    17 De Bellis Pharmacy        P   RI   1       4000    2,715.35   85,063.85   07-Jul-90
     1 Bristol Pharmacy          P   RI   4       3000    2,647.10   80,278.87   26-Jul-90
    11 Lypho_Med Laboratory      L   RI   2       1000      538.62    3,279.89   12-Aug-90

CUST # CUSTOMER NAME           TYPE ST  REP   CRD LMIT    BAL OWED   YTD SALES DATE LAST SALE
```

input range (includes field names) →

first row of criteria range →

Figure 6-13

Now enter the search criteria into the second row of the criteria range. Joan is searching for all hospital customers. To search for an exact match, enter the value you are searching for exactly as it appears in the database. Enter the value below the appropriate field name in the criteria range.

To enter the search criteria to find hospital customers:

❶ Move the cell pointer to cell C36, the location in the criteria range that stores the search criteria for the type of customer.

❷ Type **H** and press **[Enter]**. See Figure 6-14.

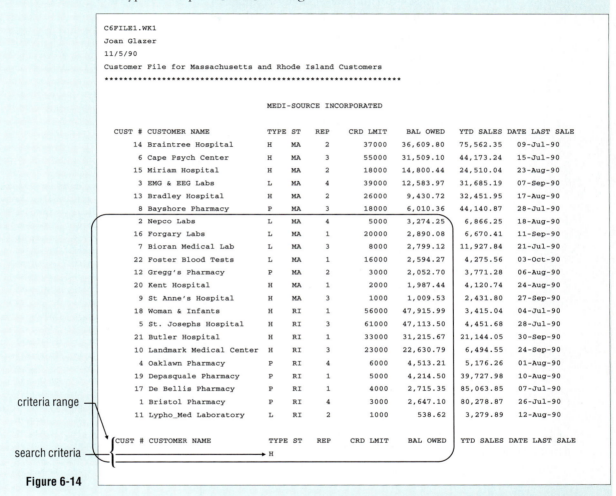

```
C6FILE1.WK1

Joan Glazer

11/5/90

Customer File for Massachusetts and Rhode Island Customers
****************************************************************

                          MEDI-SOURCE INCORPORATED


  CUST #  CUSTOMER NAME          TYPE ST   REP    CRD LMIT    BAL OWED    YTD SALES DATE LAST SALE
      14  Braintree Hospital      H   MA    2       37000    36,609.80    75,562.35   09-Jul-90
       6  Cape Psych Center       H   MA    3       55000    31,509.10    44,173.24   15-Jul-90
      15  Miriam Hospital         H   MA    2       18000    14,800.44    24,510.04   23-Aug-90
       3  EMG & EEG Labs          L   MA    4       39000    12,583.97    31,685.19   07-Sep-90
      13  Bradley Hospital        H   MA    2       26000     9,430.72    32,451.95   17-Aug-90
       8  Bayshore Pharmacy       P   MA    3       18000     6,010.36    44,140.87   28-Jul-90
       2  Nepco Labs              L   MA    4        5000     3,274.25     6,866.25   18-Aug-90
      16  Forgary Labs            L   MA    1       20000     2,890.08     6,670.41   11-Sep-90
       7  Bioran Medical Lab      L   MA    3        8000     2,799.12    11,927.84   21-Jul-90
      22  Foster Blood Tests      L   MA    1       16000     2,594.27     4,275.56   03-Oct-90
      12  Gregg's Pharmacy        P   MA    2        3000     2,052.70     3,771.28   06-Aug-90
      20  Kent Hospital           H   MA    1        2000     1,987.44     4,120.74   24-Aug-90
       9  St Anne's Hospital      H   MA    3        1000     1,009.53     2,431.80   27-Sep-90
      18  Woman & Infants         H   RI    1       56000    47,915.99     3,415.04   04-Jul-90
       5  St. Josephs Hospital    H   RI    3       61000    47,113.50     4,451.68   28-Jul-90
      21  Butler Hospital         H   RI    1       33000    31,215.67    21,144.05   30-Sep-90
      10  Landmark Medical Center H   RI    3       23000    22,630.79     6,494.55   24-Sep-90
       4  Oaklawn Pharmacy        P   RI    4        6000     4,513.21     5,176.26   01-Aug-90
      19  Depasquale Pharmacy     P   RI    1        5000     4,214.50    39,727.98   10-Aug-90
      17  De Bellis Pharmacy      P   RI    1        4000     2,715.35    85,063.85   07-Jul-90
       1  Bristol Pharmacy        P   RI    4        3000     2,647.10    80,278.87   26-Jul-90
      11  Lypho_Med Laboratory    L   RI    2        1000       538.62     3,279.89   12-Aug-90


  CUST #  CUSTOMER NAME          TYPE ST   REP    CRD LMIT    BAL OWED    YTD SALES DATE LAST SALE
                                  H
```

criteria range

search criteria

Figure 6-14

1-2-3 considers lowercase and uppercase characters the same in the criteria range.

You can also assign a range name to the criteria range, although you do not have to do so to use the Data Query command. This allows you to specify the location of the criteria range without remembering the cell locations of this range.

To assign the range name SEARCH to the criteria range:

❶ Move the cell pointer to A35, the upper left corner of the criteria range.

❷ Select /Range Name Create (**/RNC**).

❸ Type **SEARCH** and press **[Enter]**. Highlight the criteria range A35..I36. Press **[Enter]**. Now the criteria range A35..I36 has the name SEARCH.

❹ To document that this range of cells is the criteria range, move the cell pointer to cell A34, type **Criteria Range**, and press **[Enter]**. See Figure 6-15.

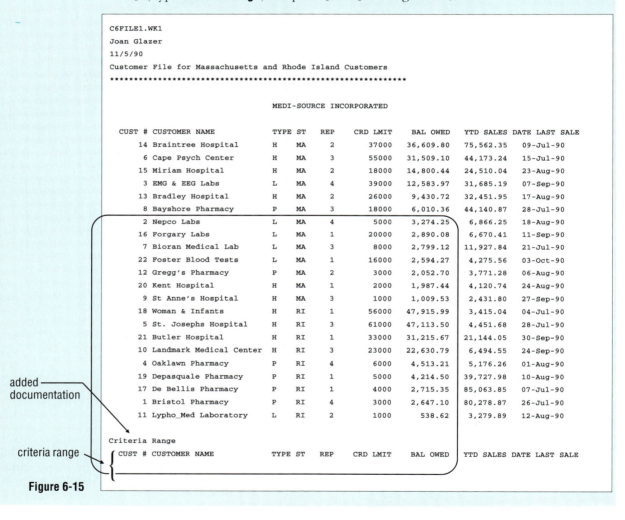

```
C6FILE1.WK1
Joan Glazer
11/5/90
Customer File for Massachusetts and Rhode Island Customers
****************************************************************

                          MEDI-SOURCE INCORPORATED

  CUST # CUSTOMER NAME          TYPE ST    REP    CRD LMIT    BAL OWED    YTD SALES DATE LAST SALE
      14 Braintree Hospital      H    MA     2      37000    36,609.80    75,562.35  09-Jul-90
       6 Cape Psych Center       H    MA     3      55000    31,509.10    44,173.24  15-Jul-90
      15 Miriam Hospital         H    MA     2      18000    14,800.44    24,510.04  23-Aug-90
       3 EMG & EEG Labs          L    MA     4      39000    12,583.97    31,685.19  07-Sep-90
      13 Bradley Hospital        H    MA     2      26000     9,430.72    32,451.95  17-Aug-90
       8 Bayshore Pharmacy       P    MA     3      18000     6,010.36    44,140.87  28-Jul-90
       2 Nepco Labs              L    MA     4       5000     3,274.25     6,866.25  18-Aug-90
      16 Forgary Labs            L    MA     1      20000     2,890.08     6,670.41  11-Sep-90
       7 Bioran Medical Lab      L    MA     3       8000     2,799.12    11,927.84  21-Jul-90
      22 Foster Blood Tests      L    MA     1      16000     2,594.27     4,275.56  03-Oct-90
      12 Gregg's Pharmacy        P    MA     2       3000     2,052.70     3,771.28  06-Aug-90
      20 Kent Hospital           H    MA     1       2000     1,987.44     4,120.74  24-Aug-90
       9 St Anne's Hospital      H    MA     3       1000     1,009.53     2,431.80  27-Sep-90
      18 Woman & Infants         H    RI     1      56000    47,915.99     3,415.04  04-Jul-90
       5 St. Josephs Hospital    H    RI     3      61000    47,113.50     4,451.68  28-Jul-90
      21 Butler Hospital         H    RI     1      33000    31,215.67    21,144.05  30-Sep-90
      10 Landmark Medical Center H    RI     3      23000    22,630.79     6,494.55  24-Sep-90
       4 Oaklawn Pharmacy        P    RI     4       6000     4,513.21     5,176.26  01-Aug-90
      19 Depasquale Pharmacy     P    RI     1       5000     4,214.50    39,727.98  10-Aug-90
      17 De Bellis Pharmacy      P    RI     1       4000     2,715.35    85,063.85  07-Jul-90
       1 Bristol Pharmacy        P    RI     4       3000     2,647.10    80,278.87  26-Jul-90
      11 Lypho_Med Laboratory    L    RI     2       1000       538.62     3,279.89  12-Aug-90

Criteria Range
  CUST # CUSTOMER NAME          TYPE ST    REP    CRD LMIT    BAL OWED    YTD SALES DATE LAST SALE
```

added documentation

criteria range

Figure 6-15

Finding Records Using a Constant

Now that you have set up the input and criteria ranges, you can use the Data Query command to find (highlight) all hospital customers. The Find command is used to activate the search of the database records, finding each record that satisfies the criteria you specified in the criteria range.

To find hospital customers in the database:

❶ Select /Data Query (**/DQ**). The query settings sheet appears. See Figure 6-16.

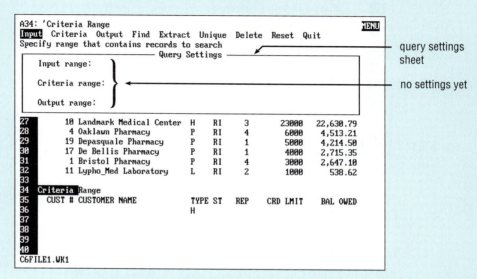

Figure 6-16

This sheet describes the ranges 1-2-3 will use to perform the data query operations. Currently, none of the query settings are defined.

To use the Find command, you must specify the locations of the input and criteria ranges. First, let's specify the input range.

❷ Select INPUT (**I**), to indicate the range of cells you want to search.

Enter the name of the input range.

❸ Type **DATABASE** and press **[Enter]**.

DATABASE, the range name you assigned to cells A10..I32, appears in the query settings sheet.

Next, specify the criteria range.

❹ Select Criteria (**C**) to indicate the range of cells that contains the search criteria.

Enter the name of the criteria range.

⑤ Type **SEARCH** and press **[Enter]**.

SEARCH, the range name you assigned to your criteria range, that is, cells A35..I36, appears in the query settings sheet. See Figure 6-17.

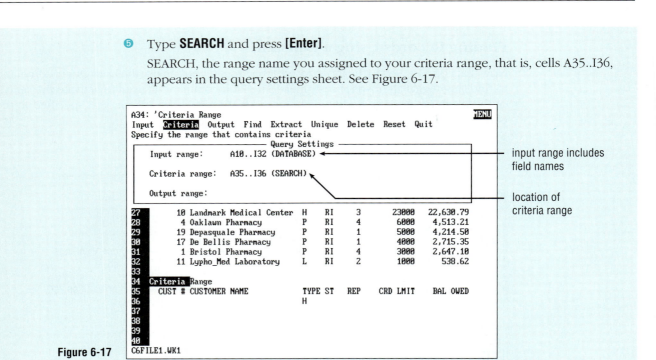

Figure 6-17

Now use the Find command to highlight the records that meet the search criteria.

To find all hospital customers:

❶ Select Find **(F)**.

1-2-3 highlights the first record that matches the criteria of TYPE equal to H. See Figure 6-18.

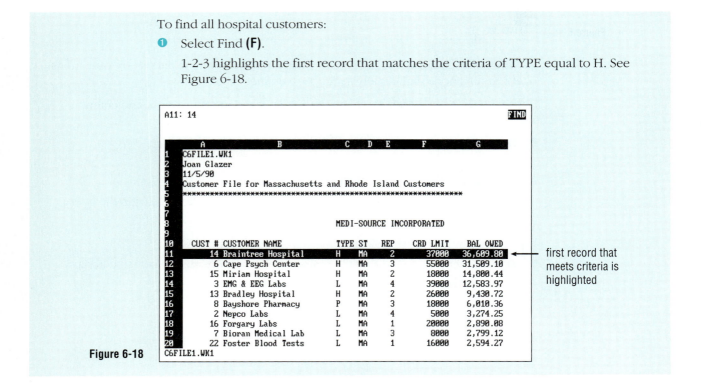

Figure 6-18

❷ Press [↓] to find the next hospital customer. Continue to press [↓] to find all hospital customers.

You can also press [↑] to search the database in the other direction. 1-2-3 will beep when you try to move beyond the first or the last matching record.

❸ Press **[Esc]** or **[Enter]** to return to QUERY mode.

❹ Quit **(Q)** to return to READY mode.

Finding Records Using a Search Formula

Remember that the average customer's outstanding balance is $6,000. This average was based on customers from all states in which Medi-Source does business. Now Joan wants to identify Rhode Island and Massachusetts customers who owe more than the average Medi-Source customer.

This query requires a search formula be included beneath the BAL OWED field name in the criteria range. When entering a formula as a criterion, begin the formula with a plus sign (+). Follow the plus sign with the cell address of the *first record* that appears immediately under the field name in the input range. Next in the formula is a comparison operator and a value to compare against the cell address.

In the following steps, you will enter the search formula, +G11>6000. This is the search criteria to find all customers who owe more than $6,000.

First, erase the search criteria from the previous query that still appears in the criteria range.

To erase the search criteria from row 36:

❶ Move the cell pointer to the second line of the criteria range, cell A36.

❷ Select /Range Erase (**/RE**).

❸ Highlight A36..I36 and press **[Enter]**. The row that stores the search criteria is now erased.

Now enter the new search criteria:

❹ Move the cell pointer to cell G36.

❺ Type **+G11>6000** and press **[Enter]**. See Figure 6-19.

search formula

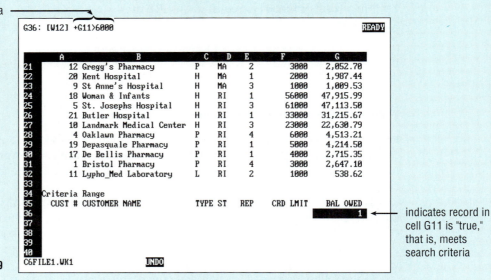

Figure 6-19

indicates record in cell G11 is "true," that is, meets search criteria

Remember, you must place the + sign in front of the cell address; otherwise, 1-2-3 will treat the condition as a label. Also remember that you *must reference the first database cell* following the field name in the column you are searching.

Notice that a 1 appears in cell G36. When a condition containing a search formula is assigned to a cell in the criteria range, a 0 or a 1 will appear. The value in G36, the cell with the formula +G11>6000, depends on the value in cell G11. If the value in cell G11 is greater than 6000, then the condition is true, and a 1 appears. If the condition is false, a 0 appears.

You can choose to have the formula appear in the criteria range instead of the value 0 or 1. This is often done because the formula is more meaningful than a 1 or a 0. To display the formula in the cell, you use the Range Format Text command.

To display the formula in the cell:

❶ Make sure the cell pointer is at G36.

❷ Select /Range Format Text (/**RFT**).

❸ Highlight G36..G36 and press **[Enter]**. The formula for the search criteria now appears
in cell G36. See Figure 6-20.

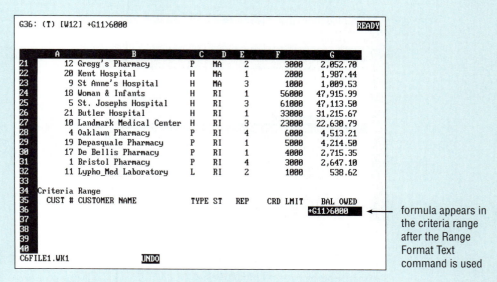

Figure 6-20

formula appears in
the criteria range
after the Range
Format Text
command is used

Now Joan uses the Data Query Find command to highlight all customers with a balance
above $6,000.

To use the Data Query Find command:

❶ Select /Data Query (/**DQ**).

The same input and criteria ranges appear on the query settings sheet that were
used earlier in the tutorial. Since you defined the input and criteria ranges when
you searched for hospital customers, you do not need to define these ranges again.

Once the input and criteria ranges are defined, you can search the database records by
choosing the Find command.

❷   Select Find (**F**).

1-2-3 highlights the first record with an outstanding balance greater than 6,000. See Figure 6-21.

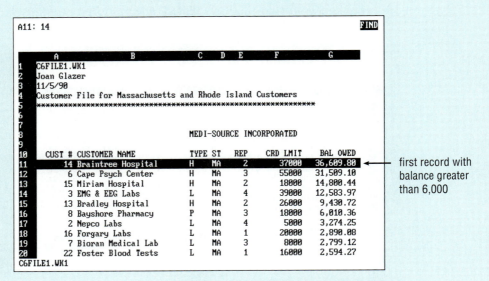

A11: 14   FIND

	A	B	C	D	E	F	G
1	C6FILE1.WK1						
2	Joan Glazer						
3	11/5/90						
4	Customer File for Massachusetts and Rhode Island Customers						
5	**						
6							
7							
8					MEDI-SOURCE INCORPORATED		
9							
10	CUST #	CUSTOMER NAME	TYPE	ST	REP	CRD LMIT	BAL OWED
11	14	Braintree Hospital	H	MA	2	37000	36,609.80
12	6	Cape Psych Center	H	MA	3	55000	31,509.10
13	15	Miriam Hospital	H	MA	2	18000	14,800.44
14	3	EMG & EEG Labs	L	MA	4	39000	12,583.97
15	13	Bradley Hospital	H	MA	2	26000	9,430.72
16	8	Bayshore Pharmacy	P	MA	3	18000	6,010.36
17	2	Nepco Labs	L	MA	4	5000	3,274.25
18	16	Forgary Labs	L	MA	1	20000	2,890.08
19	7	Bioran Medical Lab	L	MA	3	8000	2,799.12
20	22	Foster Blood Tests	L	MA	1	16000	2,594.27

C6FILE1.WK1

← first record with balance greater than 6,000

Figure 6-21

❸   Press [↓] to find the next matching record in the database.

Continue to press [↓] to find all customers with a balance above $6,000. 1-2-3 will beep when you try to move beyond the last matching record.

❹   Press [**Esc**] and then Quit (**Q**) to return to READY mode.

Data Query Command — Extracting Records

Joan has been using the Data Query Find command to highlight (locate) all records that meet the search criteria. Now she wants to copy customer records with balances greater than $6,000 to a different part of the worksheet. In this separate area of the worksheet, she wants to list only those records that have balances above $6,000. This will make it easier for Joan to print or perform calculations on these records.

The Data Query Extract command lets you copy all records from the input range that match specific criteria in the criteria range to a location in the worksheet called the output range.

Before you use the Data Query Extract command, you must define the input range, the criteria range, and the output range.

Input Range

The input range identifies the database 1-2-3 will search. This range includes the field names in addition to the records of the database. You specify this range by using the Input option of the Data Query command. The input range was defined when the Find command was used earlier in the tutorial, so you do not need to enter it again.

Criteria Range

The criteria range specifies the criteria you want to use to extract records from the database. You specify the criteria range by using the Criterion option of the Data Query command. Joan wants to extract records of customers with balances above $6,000. Since the search criteria are the same as those used earlier in this tutorial, you do not have to enter the search criteria again.

Output Range

The **output range** is an area of the worksheet where records from the input range that meet the search criteria are copied. The first row of the output range must contain field names that are identical to field names in the input range. The Extract command copies all matching records into the output range beginning in the row below the field names of the output range. Since the Extract command erases all data values that were previously in these cells, it's best to choose an area of your worksheet that contains no data for the placement of the output range. Let's begin the output range in row 40.

When you define an output range, you usually specify the row with the field names as the range of the output range. 1-2-3 uses as many rows below the output range as it needs to copy the records to this area.

To copy the field names to row 40, the first row of the output range:

❶ Move the cell pointer to cell A10.

❷ Select /Copy (**/C**).

❸ Highlight cells A10..I10, then press **[Enter]**.

❹ Move the cell pointer to A40 and press **[Enter]**. The database field names appear in row 40.

❺ Move the cell pointer to A40 to see the copied field names.

❻ Move the cell pointer to A39, type **Output Range**, and then press **[Enter]**. This label helps identify this area of the worksheet. See Figure 6-22 on the next page.

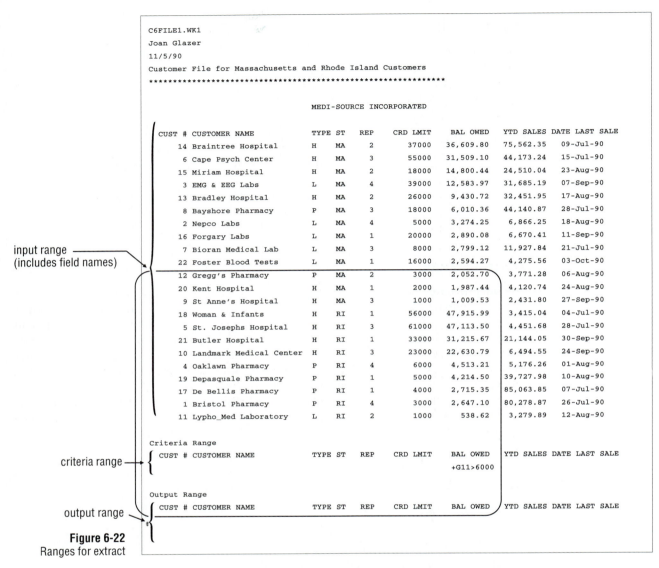

```
C6FILE1.WK1
Joan Glazer
11/5/90
Customer File for Massachusetts and Rhode Island Customers
**************************************************************

                        MEDI-SOURCE INCORPORATED


CUST # CUSTOMER NAME        TYPE ST   REP   CRD LMIT   BAL OWED   YTD SALES DATE LAST SALE
    14 Braintree Hospital    H   MA    2      37000   36,609.80   75,562.35  09-Jul-90
     6 Cape Psych Center     H   MA    3      55000   31,509.10   44,173.24  15-Jul-90
    15 Miriam Hospital       H   MA    2      18000   14,800.44   24,510.04  23-Aug-90
     3 EMG & EEG Labs        L   MA    4      39000   12,583.97   31,685.19  07-Sep-90
    13 Bradley Hospital      H   MA    2      26000    9,430.72   32,451.95  17-Aug-90
     8 Bayshore Pharmacy     P   MA    3      18000    6,010.36   44,140.87  28-Jul-90
     2 Nepco Labs            L   MA    4       5000    3,274.25    6,866.25  18-Aug-90
    16 Forgary Labs          L   MA    1      20000    2,890.08    6,670.41  11-Sep-90
     7 Bioran Medical Lab    L   MA    3       8000    2,799.12   11,927.84  21-Jul-90
    22 Foster Blood Tests    L   MA    1      16000    2,594.27    4,275.56  03-Oct-90
    12 Gregg's Pharmacy      P   MA    2       3000    2,052.70    3,771.28  06-Aug-90
    20 Kent Hospital         H   MA    1       2000    1,987.44    4,120.74  24-Aug-90
     9 St Anne's Hospital    H   MA    3       1000    1,009.53    2,431.80  27-Sep-90
    18 Woman & Infants       H   RI    1      56000   47,915.99    3,415.04  04-Jul-90
     5 St. Josephs Hospital  H   RI    3      61000   47,113.50    4,451.68  28-Jul-90
    21 Butler Hospital       H   RI    1      33000   31,215.67   21,144.05  30-Sep-90
    10 Landmark Medical Center H RI    3      23000   22,630.79    6,494.55  24-Aug-90
     4 Oaklawn Pharmacy      P   RI    4       6000    4,513.21    5,176.26  01-Aug-90
    19 Depasquale Pharmacy   P   RI    1       5000    4,214.50   39,727.98  10-Aug-90
    17 De Bellis Pharmacy    P   RI    1       4000    2,715.35   85,063.85  07-Jul-90
     1 Bristol Pharmacy      P   RI    4       3000    2,647.10   80,278.87  26-Jul-90
    11 Lypho_Med Laboratory  L   RI    2       1000      538.62    3,279.89  12-Aug-90

Criteria Range
 CUST # CUSTOMER NAME        TYPE ST   REP   CRD LMIT   BAL OWED   YTD SALES DATE LAST SALE
                                                       +G11>6000

Output Range
 CUST # CUSTOMER NAME        TYPE ST   REP   CRD LMIT   BAL OWED   YTD SALES DATE LAST SALE
```

input range
(includes field names)

criteria range

output range

Figure 6-22
Ranges for extract

Although it is not required to extract records, you can assign a range name to the output range A40..I40. This allows you to specify the output range without remembering the cell locations.

To assign the range name HIGH_BALANCE to the output range:

❶ Move the cell pointer to the first field name in the output range, cell A40.

❷ Select /Range Name Create (**/RNC**).

❸ Type **HIGH_BALANCE** and press **[Enter]**.

❹ Highlight the field names of the output range, A40..I40, then press **[Enter]**.
   The output range has the name HIGH_BALANCE.

Before you can use the Data Query Extract command, you must specify the input, criteria, and output ranges.

Since the input and criteria ranges were specified earlier in this tutorial, you do not need to enter them again. However, the output range has not been specified.

To specify the output range for the Data Query command:

❶ Select /Data Query (**/DQ**).

❷ Select Output (**O**), press **[F3]** (NAME), and highlight the range name **HIGH_BALANCE**, which is the output range. Press **[Enter]**. See Figure 6-23. The cell locations of the output range now appear in the query settings sheet.

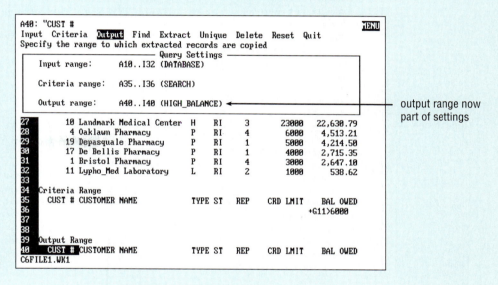

output range now part of settings

Figure 6-23

Extracting Records

Now that the input, criteria, and output ranges are specified, you can use Extract command. Joan wants to extract customer records with an outstanding balance above $6,000.

To extract records with a balance above $6,000:

❶ Select Extract (**E**).

1-2-3 copies to the output range all records from the database that meet the search formula you entered, in this case, customers whose balance is greater than $6,000.

❷ Select Quit (**Q**) to return to READY mode.

❸ Move the cell pointer to A53 and view all the extracted records. See Figure 6-24. Notice that 1-2-3 has extracted only the records that meet the criteria, that is, only those customers whose outstanding balance is greater than 6000.

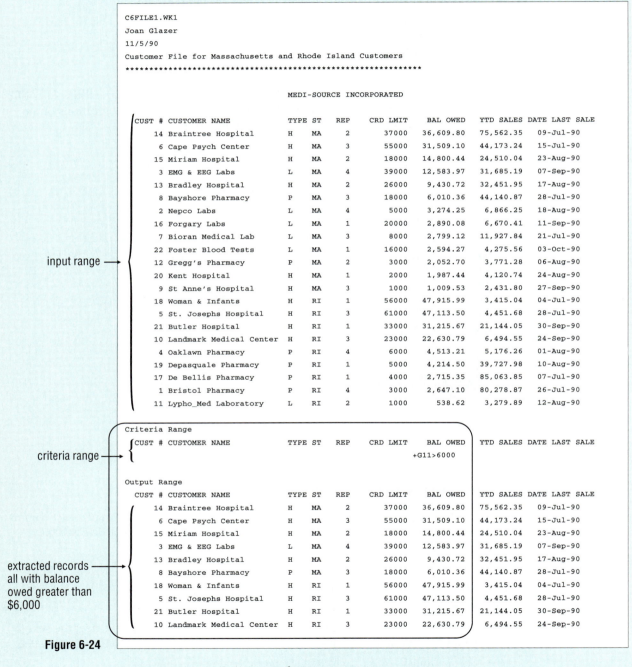

```
C6FILE1.WK1
Joan Glazer
11/5/90
Customer File for Massachusetts and Rhode Island Customers
**************************************************************

                          MEDI-SOURCE INCORPORATED

CUST # CUSTOMER NAME          TYPE ST   REP   CRD LMIT    BAL OWED   YTD SALES DATE LAST SALE
    14 Braintree Hospital      H   MA    2     37000     36,609.80   75,562.35  09-Jul-90
     6 Cape Psych Center       H   MA    3     55000     31,509.10   44,173.24  15-Jul-90
    15 Miriam Hospital         H   MA    2     18000     14,800.44   24,510.04  23-Aug-90
     3 EMG & EEG Labs          L   MA    4     39000     12,583.97   31,685.19  07-Sep-90
    13 Bradley Hospital        H   MA    2     26000      9,430.72   32,451.95  17-Aug-90
     8 Bayshore Pharmacy       P   MA    3     18000      6,010.36   44,140.87  28-Jul-90
     2 Nepco Labs              L   MA    4      5000      3,274.25    6,866.25  18-Aug-90
    16 Forgary Labs            L   MA    1     20000      2,890.08    6,670.41  11-Sep-90
     7 Bioran Medical Lab      L   MA    3      8000      2,799.12   11,927.84  21-Jul-90
    22 Foster Blood Tests      L   MA    1     16000      2,594.27    4,275.56  03-Oct-90
    12 Gregg's Pharmacy        P   MA    2      3000      2,052.70    3,771.28  06-Aug-90
    20 Kent Hospital           H   MA    1      2000      1,987.44    4,120.74  24-Aug-90
     9 St Anne's Hospital      H   MA    3      1000      1,009.53    2,431.80  27-Sep-90
    18 Woman & Infants         H   RI    1     56000     47,915.99    3,415.04  04-Jul-90
     5 St. Josephs Hospital    H   RI    3     61000     47,113.50    4,451.68  28-Jul-90
    21 Butler Hospital         H   RI    1     33000     31,215.67   21,144.05  30-Sep-90
    10 Landmark Medical Center H   RI    3     23000     22,630.79    6,494.55  24-Sep-90
     4 Oaklawn Pharmacy        P   RI    4      6000      4,513.21    5,176.26  01-Aug-90
    19 Depasquale Pharmacy     P   RI    1      5000      4,214.50   39,727.98  10-Aug-90
    17 De Bellis Pharmacy      P   RI    1      4000      2,715.35   85,063.85  07-Jul-90
     1 Bristol Pharmacy        P   RI    4      3000      2,647.10   80,278.87  26-Jul-90
    11 Lypho_Med Laboratory    L   RI    2      1000        538.62    3,279.89  12-Aug-90

Criteria Range
CUST # CUSTOMER NAME          TYPE ST   REP   CRD LMIT    BAL OWED   YTD SALES DATE LAST SALE
                                                         +G11>6000

Output Range
CUST # CUSTOMER NAME          TYPE ST   REP   CRD LMIT    BAL OWED   YTD SALES DATE LAST SALE
    14 Braintree Hospital      H   MA    2     37000     36,609.80   75,562.35  09-Jul-90
     6 Cape Psych Center       H   MA    3     55000     31,509.10   44,173.24  15-Jul-90
    15 Miriam Hospital         H   MA    2     18000     14,800.44   24,510.04  23-Aug-90
     3 EMG & EEG Labs          L   MA    4     39000     12,583.97   31,685.19  07-Sep-90
    13 Bradley Hospital        H   MA    2     26000      9,430.72   32,451.95  17-Aug-90
     8 Bayshore Pharmacy       P   MA    3     18000      6,010.36   44,140.87  28-Jul-90
    18 Woman & Infants         H   RI    1     56000     47,915.99    3,415.04  04-Jul-90
     5 St. Josephs Hospital    H   RI    3     61000     47,113.50    4,451.68  28-Jul-90
    21 Butler Hospital         H   RI    1     33000     31,215.67   21,144.05  30-Sep-90
    10 Landmark Medical Center H   RI    3     23000     22,630.79    6,494.55  24-Sep-90
```

input range →

criteria range →

extracted records all with balance owed greater than $6,000 →

Figure 6-24

❹ Save your worksheet as S6FILE1.

Using @AVG, @MIN, @MAX, @COUNT Statistical Functions

According to her plan, Joan also wants to create two reports. The first report will show summary statistics for all Rhode Island and Massachusetts customers. She wants this report to include a count of the number of customers, the total and the average balance owed, and the highest and lowest balances owed for all customers. She wants the second report to show the total and the average balances owed separately for Rhode Island and Massachusetts customers.

To prepare the first report, you will use several statistical functions that perform calculations on a range of numbers. The statistical functions used in this report are summarized in Figure 6-25.

Function	Description	Example
@AVG(range)	Calculates the average of the range	@AVG(G11..G20)
@COUNT(range)	Calculates the number of nonblank cells in the range	@COUNT(G11..G20)
@MAX(range)	Determines the largest value in the range	@MAX(G11..G20)
@MIN(range)	Determines the smallest value in the range	@MIN(G11..G20)
@SUM(range)	Calculates the sum of the range	@SUM(G11..G20)

Figure 6-25
Statistical
functions

To work more easily with the statistical functions, let's first assign a range name, OWED, to the group of cells representing the balance owed.

To assign the range name OWED:
1. Move the cell pointer to G11, the first cell containing a balance owed value.
2. Select /Range Name Create (**/RNC**).
3. Type **OWED** and press **[Enter]**. Highlight G11..G32 and press **[Enter]**.

   The range name, OWED, has been assigned to the cells G11..G32.

Let's now prepare Joan's first report, which calculates the sum, the average, the minimum, and the maximum balance owed for all customers in the database. Place this report in the range N1 to P10. The headings and labels for the report have already been entered in the worksheet.

Now calculate the statistics for the report.

To enter the @functions:

First, to calculate the total amount owed by all RI and MA customers:

❶ Move the cell pointer to cell O8, type **@SUM(OWED)**, and press **[Enter]**. The total owed is 291056.50.

To calculate the average owed by all RI and MA customers:

❷ Move the cell pointer to cell O9, type **@AVG(OWED)**, and press **[Enter]**. The average owed is 13229.84.

To calculate the maximum amount owed by RI and MA customers:

❸ Move the cell pointer to cell O10, type **@MAX(OWED)**, and press **[Enter]**. The maximum owed is 47915.99.

To calculate the minimum amount owed by RI and MA customers:

❹ Move the cell pointer to cell O11, type **@MIN(OWED)**, and press **[Enter]**. The lowest balance is 538.62.

Finally, to count the number of customers in the database:

❺ Move the cell pointer to O12, type **@COUNT(OWED)**, and press **[Enter]**. There are 22 customers. See Figure 6-26.

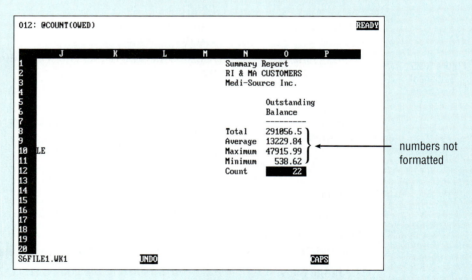

Figure 6-26
Joan's first report

The statistics for the report are completed. The appearance of the report, however, can be improved. Specifically, the values in O8..O11 can be formatted using currency format.

To improve the appearance of the report using Currency format:

❶ Move the cell pointer to O8.

❷ Select /Range Format Currency (**/RFC**).

❸   Type **0** for the number of decimal places and press **[Enter]**.

With balances this large, Joan believes numbers rounded to the nearest whole number are appropriate.

❹   Highlight O8..O11. Press **[Enter]**.

Your worksheet should look like Figure 6-27. Notice the cell O12 is not included in the range because count does not represent a dollar quantity.

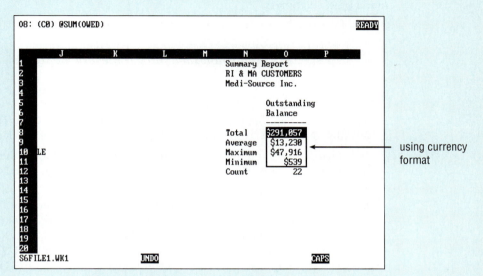

```
O8: (C0) @SUM(OWED)                                                  READY

        J         K         L         M         N         O         P
 1                                              Summary Report
 2                                              RI & MA CUSTOMERS
 3                                              Medi-Source Inc.
 4
 5                                                        Outstanding
 6                                                        Balance
 7                                                        ───────────
 8                                              Total     $291,057
 9                                              Average    $13,230              ◀── using currency
10  LE                                          Maximum    $47,916                  format
11                                              Minimum       $539
12                                              Count          22
13
14
15
16
17
18
19
20
S6FILE1.WK1                      UNDO                               CAPS
```

Figure 6-27

Joan is satisfied with the first report. She notices that the average outstanding balance for Rhode Island and Massachusetts customers is $13,230, more than twice the Medi-Source company average.

Before she begins her next task, Joan saves the worksheet.

❺   Save your worksheet as S6FILE1.WK1.

Understanding Database @Functions

In addition to the report already developed, Joan wants a report that shows the total and average outstanding balances by state. One approach to calculate these statistics is to use the database functions available in 1-2-3.

Lotus 1-2-3 has seven database @functions: @DAVG, @DSUM, @DMAX, @DMIN, @DCOUNT, @DSTD, and @DVAR. Each function calculates a value based on records in the database that match criteria in the criteria range. The database @functions differ from the corresponding statistical @functions, because the database @functions calculate statistics *only* for the records in a database that match the criteria you specify. For example, you used @AVG to calculate the average balance owed for all the records in the database. You will use @DAVG to calculate the average balance owed for only those records that meet the criteria of RI customers.

All of the database @functions have the same format, which is:

@function(input range,offset,criteria range)

---

where:

@function is one of the following: @DAVG, @DSUM, @DCOUNT, @DMAX, @DMIN, @DSTD, @DVAR and each database function consists of three arguments:

Input range — the range that contains the database, including the field names in the range definition. The range can be specified as a range name or as cell addresses.

Offset — the position number of the column in the database that is to be summed, averaged, counted, etc. 1-2-3 assigns the first field in the database the offset number 0, the second field the offset number 1, and so on. For example, CUTS # is the first column in the database and has the offset number 0; CUSTOMER NAME is the second column, so it has the offset number 1; and BAL OWED is the seventh column in the database, so it has the offset number 6.

Criteria range — an area of your worksheet where you specify the search criteria to determine which records you will use in the calculations.

Figure 6-28 summarizes the 1-2-3 database functions.

Function Name	Description	Example
@DAVG	Averages the values in the offset column that meet specified criteria	@DAVG(A11..G32,6,T25..T26)
@DSUM	Sums the values in the offset column that meet specified criteria	@DSUM(A11..G32,6,T25..T26)
@DMAX	Determines the largest value in the offset column that meets specified criteria	@DMAX(A11..G32,6,T25..T26)
@DMIN	Determines the smallest value in the offset column that meets specified criteria	@DMIN(A11..G32,6,T25..T26)
@DCOUNT	Counts the number of records in which values in the offset column meet specified criteria	@DCOUNT(A11..G32,6,T25..T26)
@DSTD	Calculates the standard deviation of the values in the offset column that meet specified criteria	@DSTD(A11..G32,6,T25..T26)
@DVAR	Calculates the variance of the values in the offset column that meet the specified criteria	@DVAR(A11..G32,6,T25..T26)

Figure 6-28
Database functions

Using Database @Functions

Joan wants to calculate separate statistics for Rhode Island and Massachusetts customers. She wants to know if there is a difference between the total and the average amount owed by customers in each state.

To calculate these statistics, you will use the database @functions @DSUM and @DAVG. Each function requires an input range, an offset range, and a criteria range.

The input range identifies the records to use in calculations. You already defined this range earlier in the tutorial. The input range includes cells A10..I32 and has been assigned the name DATABASE.

You set up separate criteria ranges for each group of records on which you are performing calculations.

Let's first set up a criteria range at S25..S26 to use when you search for Rhode Island customers:

❶ Move the cell pointer to cell D10, the field name that is to be copied to the criteria range.

❷ Select /Copy (**/C**) and press **[Enter]**.

③ Type **S25** and press **[Enter]**. The label ST is copied to cell S25.

④ Move the cell pointer to S26, the second row of the criteria range.

⑤ Type **RI** and press **[Enter]**. The criteria range for RI customers is complete.

Notice that the criteria range includes only one database field name. The criteria range does not have to include all field names in the database. It needs to include only the field names you intend to search.

Next, set up a separate criteria range at T25..T26 to search for customers in Massachusetts:

① Move the cell pointer to S25 to copy the field name to the second criteria range.

Now copy the label ST to cell T25.

② Select /Copy (**/C**) and press **[Enter]**.

③ Type **T25** and press **[Enter]**. The label ST appears in cell T25.

④ Move the cell pointer to T26, the second row of the criteria range.

⑤ Type **MA** and press **[Enter]**. The criteria range for specifying MA customers is complete. See Figure 6-29.

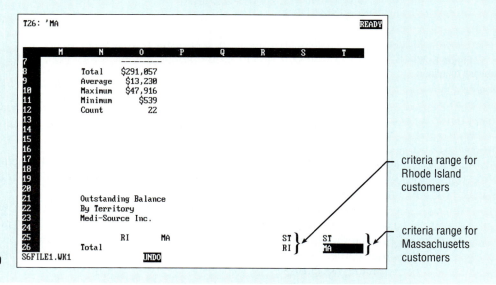

Figure 6-29

criteria range for Rhode Island customers

criteria range for Massachusetts customers

Now that you have defined the input and criteria ranges, let's determine the offset number for the balance owed field.

To determine the offset number for balance owed:

❶ Move the cell pointer to cell A10, the first field in the database.

❷ Starting with 0 for the CUST # field, count the columns to determine the offset number for column G, BAL OWED. Your answer should be 6. See Figure 6-30.

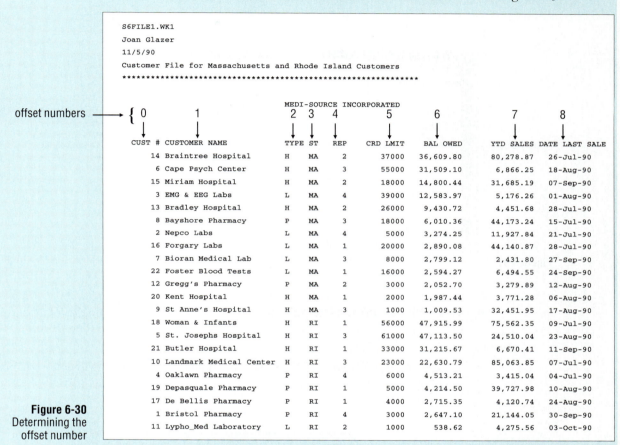

offset numbers

```
S6FILE1.WK1
Joan Glazer
11/5/90
Customer File for Massachusetts and Rhode Island Customers
****************************************************************
```

	MEDI-SOURCE INCORPORATED							
0	1	2	3	4	5	6	7	8
CUST #	CUSTOMER NAME	TYPE	ST	REP	CRD LMIT	BAL OWED	YTD SALES	DATE LAST SALE
14	Braintree Hospital	H	MA	2	37000	36,609.80	80,278.87	26-Jul-90
6	Cape Psych Center	H	MA	3	55000	31,509.10	6,866.25	18-Aug-90
15	Miriam Hospital	H	MA	2	18000	14,800.44	31,685.19	07-Sep-90
3	EMG & EEG Labs	L	MA	4	39000	12,583.97	5,176.26	01-Aug-90
13	Bradley Hospital	H	MA	2	26000	9,430.72	4,451.68	28-Jul-90
8	Bayshore Pharmacy	P	MA	3	18000	6,010.36	44,173.24	15-Jul-90
2	Nepco Labs	L	MA	4	5000	3,274.25	11,927.84	21-Jul-90
16	Forgary Labs	L	MA	1	20000	2,890.08	44,140.87	28-Jul-90
7	Bioran Medical Lab	L	MA	3	8000	2,799.12	2,431.80	27-Sep-90
22	Foster Blood Tests	L	MA	1	16000	2,594.27	6,494.55	24-Sep-90
12	Gregg's Pharmacy	P	MA	2	3000	2,052.70	3,279.89	12-Aug-90
20	Kent Hospital	H	MA	1	2000	1,987.44	3,771.28	06-Aug-90
9	St Anne's Hospital	H	MA	3	1000	1,009.53	32,451.95	17-Aug-90
18	Woman & Infants	H	RI	1	56000	47,915.99	75,562.35	09-Jul-90
5	St. Josephs Hospital	H	RI	3	61000	47,113.50	24,510.04	23-Aug-90
21	Butler Hospital	H	RI	1	33000	31,215.67	6,670.41	11-Sep-90
10	Landmark Medical Center	H	RI	3	23000	22,630.79	85,063.85	07-Jul-90
4	Oaklawn Pharmacy	P	RI	4	6000	4,513.21	3,415.04	04-Jul-90
19	Depasquale Pharmacy	P	RI	1	5000	4,214.50	39,727.98	10-Aug-90
17	De Bellis Pharmacy	P	RI	1	4000	2,715.35	4,120.74	24-Aug-90
1	Bristol Pharmacy	P	RI	4	3000	2,647.10	21,144.05	30-Sep-90
11	Lypho_Med Laboratory	L	RI	2	1000	538.62	4,275.56	03-Oct-90

Figure 6-30
Determining the offset number

Let's put this second report in cells N21 to O25. The headings and descriptive labels for the report have already been entered in the worksheet. Now let's use the database @functions to complete the report.

To use database @functions to calculate the statistics:

❶   Press **[F5]** (GOTO), type **N21**, and press **[Enter]**. The cell pointer is now in the section of the worksheet where you will calculate the Outstanding Balance by State Report. See Figure 6-31.

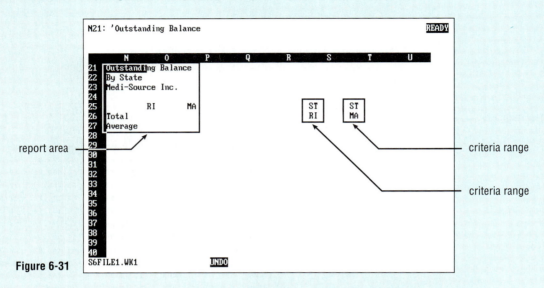

Figure 6-31

❷   Move the cell pointer to cell O26, under the cell labelled RI.

❸   Type **@DSUM(DATABASE,6,S25..S26)** and press **[Enter]** to calculate the total balance owed for Rhode Island customers. The total 163504.7 appears on the screen.

❹   Move the cell pointer to cell O27.

❺   Type **@DAVG(DATABASE,6,S25..S26).** Press **[Enter]** to calculate the average balance owed by Rhode Island customers. The average balance owed is $18,167.19. See Figure 6-32.

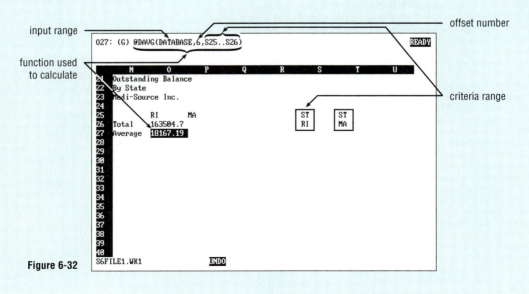

Figure 6-32

⑥ Move the cell pointer to cell P26, under the cell labelled MA.

⑦ Type **@DSUM(DATABASE,6,T25..T26)**. Press **[Enter]** to calculate the total balance owed by all Massachusetts customers. Massachusetts customers owe 127551.70.

⑧ Move the cell pointer to cell P27.

⑨ Type **@DAVG(DATABASE,6,T25..T26)**. Press **[Enter]** to calculate the average balance owed by Massachusetts customers. On average, Massachusetts customers owe 9811.25.

The statistics for the report are complete. The appearance of the report, however, can be improved. Specifically, the values in O26..P27 can be formatted using Currency format.

To improve the appearance of the report, using Currency format:

❶ Move the cell pointer to O26.

❷ Select /Range Format Currency (**/RFC**).

❸ Type **0** and press **[Enter]**.

❹ Highlight O26..P27. Press **[Enter]**.

Your worksheet should look like Figure 6-33.

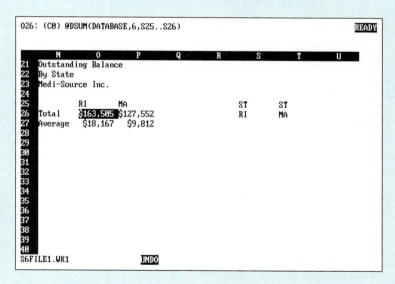

Figure 6-33
Joan's calculated information about Rhode Island and Massachusetts customers

Joan notices that the average outstanding balance for Rhode Island customers is $18,167, more than three times the Medi-Source company average.

❺ Save your worksheet as S6FILE1.WK1.

Summary

In this tutorial, you sorted a database, prepared two reports using statistical functions, searched the database to locate specific records, and summarized the data using database statistical functions.

Exercises

1. The customer database that you used in this tutorial, C6FILE1.WK1, contains how many fields? How many records?

2. To sort the customer names in Z to A order, you would use which sorting option?

3. List the steps you would follow to locate Kent Hospital in the customer database using the Find command.

4. List the steps you would follow to extract all Rhode Island customers using the Extract command.

5. What @function would you use to calculate the following statistics:
   a. the average sales for the year for sales representative #4
   b. the highest balance owed by all customers in the database
   c. the number of pharmacies in the database

6. If you had used the database statistical function @DAVG(DATABASE,7,T25..T26) in this tutorial, what statistic would you be calculating?

Tutorial Assignments

Before you begin these Tutorial Assignments, check your working copy of the Data Disk. Be sure you have space to save the additional worksheet files you'll create in these assignments (at least 85,000 bytes). If not, save your files as appropriate to another formatted diskette.

Retrieve the worksheet T6FILE1.WK1 and do the following:

1. Sort the database by year-to-date (YTD) sales with the customer having the lowest YTD sales appearing first. Save the file as S6FILE2.

2. Sort the database in descending order using the field TYPE (type of customer) as the primary sort key. Save the file as S6FILE3.

3. Arrange the customer database by type of customer (ascending order) and, within type of customer, arrange the accounts in alphabetical order by customer name. Print the sorted records.

Use the Data Query command for Assignments 4 through 7.

4. Copy the database field names to the first row of criteria range, row 40.

5. Query the database to find all customers located in Rhode Island (code = RI). Save the worksheet as S6FILE4.

6. Query the database to find all customers with average YTD sales above $50,000. Save the worksheet as S6FILE5.

7. Query the database to extract and print all customers assigned to sales representative #4. Set up an output range beginning at row 50. Save the worksheet as S6FILE6.

Use statistical functions for Assignments 8 and 9:

8. Calculate the average YTD sales for all records in the database. Place the result in cell O8.

9. Calculate the maximum YTD sales using all the records in the database. Place the result in cell O9. Save your current worksheet as S6FILE7.

Complete Assignments 10 through 12 using the database statistical function @DAVG. Three criteria ranges have been partially set up in cells R25, S25, and T25.

10. Calculate the average outstanding balance for hospitals. Complete the criteria range in R25..R26. Place your result in cell O27.

11. Calculate the average outstanding balance for labs. Complete the criteria range in S25..S26. Place your result in cell O28.

12. Calculate the average outstanding balance for pharmacies. Complete the criteria range in T25..T26. Place your result in cell O29.

13. Print this Outstanding Balance Report by Type of Customer.

14. Save your worksheet as S6FILE8.

Use the Reference section of *Lotus 1-2-3 for Business* and do the following:

15. You can combine conditional expressions to specify more complex search criteria. For example, suppose you want to identify pharmacy customers who had $50,000 or more in sales during the year. Two conditional expressions are needed here:

    CUSTOMER TYPE = P and YTD SALES > 50000

    Two common ways to combine search criteria are to:

    • select records that match all the criteria specified — the AND case
    • select records that match at least one of the criteria specified — the OR case

    Read in the Reference section about such topics as Data Query — Entering Multiple Field Criteria or Data Query Criteria. Then, using the worksheet T6FILE1, extract the pharmacy customers with $50,000 or more in sales. Print the records you extract. Save your worksheet as S6FILE9.

Case Problems

1. Human Resource Database

The human resource department of a small furniture manufacturer has developed a human resource database. The field names in this database are:

Field	Description
EMP#	Employee number
LNAME	Last name
FNAME	First name
BIRTH	Date of birth (yyyymmdd)
SEX	Code for sex (M = male; F = female)
MAR	Code for marital status (Y = married; N = not married)
DEP	Number of dependents
ANNSAL	Annual salary
HIREDT	Date employee hired (yyyymmdd)
XMPT	Exempt employee (X = exempt; N = nonexempt)
MED	Code for medical plan (F = family plan; I = individual plan; N = not on medical plan)
401K	401K retirement plan (Y = making contributions to plan; N = not making contributions to plan)
DIV	Division where employee works
JOBTITLE	Job title
PER	Payment method (H = hourly; M = monthly)

Retrieve the worksheet P6PERSNL and do the following:

1. Sort and print the database alphabetically by last name.

2. Sort and print the database by hire date.

3. Sort and print the database by division and, within division, by salary in descending order.

4. Find all employees that have the family medical plan. The code is F.

5. Find all employees with one or more dependents.

6. Extract and print the records of all married employees.

7. Print a summary report showing salaries categorized by sex. Format the report as sketched below:

Salaries — By Sex		
	Females	Males
Average	$ xxxx	$ xxxx
Maximum	$ xxxx	$ xxxx
Minimum	$ xxxx	$ xxxx
Count	xxxx	xxxx

8. Save your worksheet as S6PERSNL.

2. The Top 50 U.S. Companies

Every year, a leading business magazine publishes a list of the 50 largest U.S. companies and presents financial data about them.

Retrieve the worksheet P6TOP50. The field names in the file containing these data are:

Field	Description
COMPANY	Name of company
INDUSTRY	Industry code
SALES	Sales revenue for the year
PROFITS	Net income
ASSETS	Total assets
EQUITY	Portion of assets owned by stockholders
MKT VAL	Market value of company

Do the following:

1. Sort and print the database alphabetically by company.

2. Sort and print the database arranged by sales, with the company with the highest sales appearing first.

3. Calculate rate of return (ROR) for each company. The formula is:

$$ROR = \frac{Profit}{Equity}$$

Place this new field in column H and label the column ROR. Format using the Percent format with one decimal place.

4. Sort the database by ROR, with the company having the highest rate of return appearing first. *Hint*: Think about your data range.

5. Print the database, which now includes the rate of return field.

6. Extract and print all companies in the computer industry (industry code = 6).

7. Prepare and print a summary report comparing the average, maximum, and minimum sales for companies in the oil industry (code = 17) versus companies in the aerospace industry (code = 1). Format the report as sketched below:

	Top 50 U.S. Companies Industry Comparison	
	Oil	Aerospace
Average sales	$ xxx	$ xxx
Minimum sales	xxx	xxx
Maximum sales	xxx	xxx

8. Save your worksheet as S6TOP50.

3.   Inventory of Microcomputer Software

A company that sells microcomputer software just completed its annual physical inventory prior to preparing its financial statement. The data from this inventory was entered into a 1-2-3 worksheet.

Retrieve the worksheet P6SFTWRE. The field names for this inventory database include:

Field	Description
ITEM #	Unique number to identify each product
TITLE	Name of product
CAT	Category of software
COST	Cost to company per unit
QOH	Number of packages on hand (in inventory)
QOO	Number of package on order
PRICE	Retail price of software package
YTD SALES	Year-to-date sales

The codes for the category of software (CAT) are:

CO	=	Communications
DP	=	Desktop publishing
DB	=	Database
GR	=	Graphics
SP	=	Spreadsheet
WP	=	Word processing
UT	=	Utility

Do the following:

1.   Print a list of current software products arranged by category and, within category, alphabetized by title.

2.   Find the software products that have one or more units on order.

3.   Extract and print the database (DB) software products.

4.   Add two columns to the worksheet, Inventory Value — Cost (column I) and Inventory Value — Retail (column J). Calculate and print the total cost value and the total retail value of all inventory items. (*Hint*: You can use the following formulas: Inventory Value — Cost = QOH × COST and Inventory — Retail = QOH × PRICE.)

5.   Calculate and print the total retail value of the inventory by software category. Be sure your report has a separate total for each of the seven category codes listed above. Format this report as sketched below:

Inventory - Retail Value
By Software Category

	Total Value
Communication	xxxx
Desktop Publishing	xxxx
Database	xxxx
Graphics	xxxx
Spreadsheet	xxxx
Word Processing	xxxx
Utility	xxxx
Total	$

6. Prepare a pie chart illustrating the same data that were calculated in Assignment 5. Create a PIC file named PIESOFT.

7. Save your worksheet as S6SFTWRE.

8. Print the pie chart PIESOFT.

Tutorial 7

Creating and Using Macros

Case: Krier Marine Services Revisited

Remember Vince Diorio from Tutorial 1? He is the part-time employee at Krier Marine Services who helped Mrs. Krier create a worksheet for her employee payroll. Vince, in his senior year at the University of Rhode Island, will graduate next month and begin working as a programmer for a nearby major insurance company. He knows that Mrs. Krier will continue to use the worksheet he created and that she is nervous about using it without him around to help her.

Vince has recently been using macros to become a more productive user of 1-2-3. To him, macros are stored keystrokes. For example, he created a macro to print a worksheet. With this macro, he saves himself the time and the trouble of making 15 keystrokes every time he wants to print a worksheet. He presses only two keys, and Lotus 1-2-3 automatically prints the payroll worksheet. Vince knows that Mrs. Krier, in addition to printing the worksheet, will need to save the payroll worksheet at the end of each payroll period. He decides, therefore, that creating a macro to save the worksheet will be useful. Vince also plans to create a macro to create range names, because he frequently assigns range names to use with macros as well as for other 1-2-3 functions.

Vince decides to show Mrs. Krier his macro for printing and plans to create additional macros to make it easier for her to use the payroll worksheet. He prepares his planning sheet (Figure 7-1) before beginning the revision of the worksheet.

Objectives

In this tutorial you will learn how to:

- Plan a macro
- Create a macro
- Execute a macro
- Edit and debug a macro
- Use LEARN mode

My Goal:
    To simplify the use of the payroll worksheet to Mrs. Krier by
    creating macros.

What results do I want to see?
    Weekly payroll report

What information do I need?
    Payroll data
    Macro data

What macros do I want?
    Print worksheet
    Save worksheet
    Name Ranges
    Format columns using Currency

Figure 7-1
Vince's planning
sheet

In this tutorial, you will first run a macro from the payroll worksheet. Then you will add several macros to this worksheet. This involves planning, placing, entering, naming, and documenting each macro. Next, you will execute each macro. You will also use an alternative approach to create macros, the LEARN mode. Finally, you will learn how to find errors in macros using the STEP mode and how to correct them.

What Are Macros?

A **macro** is a series of keystrokes and special commands stored in a worksheet as cell entries. You can run a macro whenever you want to use it. Macros are most often created to automate frequently used Lotus 1-2-3 tasks, such as printing a worksheet, naming a range, saving a worksheet, or formatting cells. Thus, macros save time. They also help less sophisticated users of 1-2-3 by making the worksheet easier to use.

A macro can be used to carry out a simple task and save a few keystrokes, such as a macro to print a worksheet, or it can be used to help prevent typing or keystroke errors. For example, you can avoid errors by creating a macro that automatically moves the cell pointer to specified cells in a worksheet and automatically enters the date and time. Otherwise, you would have to move the cell pointer to the cells where you want to enter the date and time and then enter this information. A macro can also be designed to accomplish a series of more complex and repetitive tasks, such as preparing a weekly report that (1) lists all receivables over 30 days old, (2) sorts the list alphabetically by account, and then (3) prints three copies using compressed print — all in one macro — all automatically!

Retrieving the Worksheet

Vince has been using macros to make his work at Krier Marine Services more productive. For instance, he developed a print macro to simplify the printing of the Krier Marine Services payroll. Let's retrieve the payroll worksheet and run Vince's print macro.

To retrieve the worksheet and run the macro:

❶ Select /File Retrieve (**/FR**).

❷ Move the menu pointer to C7FILE1.WK1 and press **[Enter]**. See Figure 7-2.

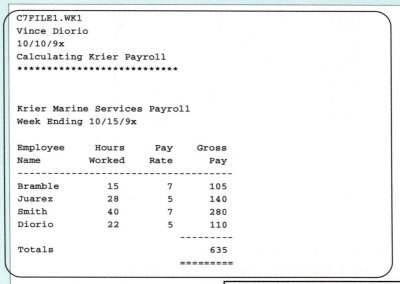

```
C7FILE1.WK1
Vince Diorio
10/10/9x
Calculating Krier Payroll
****************************


Krier Marine Services Payroll
Week Ending 10/15/9x

Employee        Hours      Pay    Gross
Name            Worked    Rate     Pay
------------------------------------
Bramble           15        7      105
Juarez            28        5      140
Smith             40        7      280
Diorio            22        5      110
                                ---------
Totals                             635
                                =========
```

area of worksheet
reserved for macros

```
MACRO AREA

Name     Macro        Description
-----------------------------
\P       /pp          print the payroll worksheet
         ra8.d20~     specifies print range
         agpq         align, go, page, quit
```

Figure 7-2
Vince's initial
worksheet

Vince named his printing macro \P and saved it with this worksheet. The \P macro automates printing of the payroll worksheet.

❸ Turn your printer on and make sure it's ready to print.

❹ Press **[Alt][P]** to run the macro named \P.

To run a macro that begins with a \ (Backslash), you press the [Alt] key in place of the \ (Backslash).

⑤   The macro automatically prints the payroll worksheet. See Figure 7-3.

```
Krier Marine Services Payroll
Week Ending 10/15/9x

Employee      Hours      Pay     Gross
Name          Worked     Rate     Pay
-------------------------------------
Bramble         15         7       105
Juarez          28         5       140
Smith           40         7       280
Diorio          22         5       110
                                 ---------
Totals                             635
                                 =========
```

Figure 7-3
Printout of Vince's
worksheet using
his print macro

Now let's look at the section of the worksheet where the print macro, \P, is located.

To examine the \P macro:

❶   Press **[F5]** (GOTO), type **I21**, and press **[Enter]** to move the cell pointer to the area of the worksheet where Vince plans to store the macros. See Figure 7-4. Vince has labelled cell I21 MACRO AREA to identify this section of the worksheet.

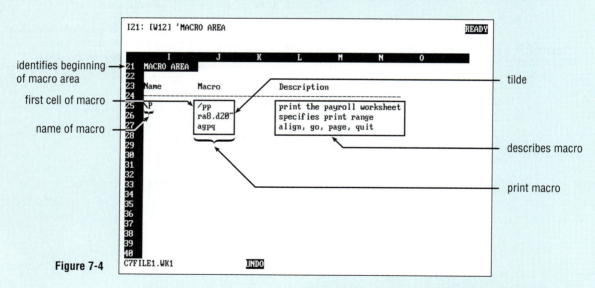

identifies beginning of macro area

first cell of macro

name of macro

tilde

describes macro

print macro

Figure 7-4

❷   Move the cell pointer to cell J25. Here you find the first cell of the actual macro, that is, the stored keystrokes. The complete macro is found in cells J25, J26, and J27. The print macro is a series of keystrokes stored as a label. This macro contains the following stored keystrokes:

/pp	(cell J25)	/print printer
ra8.d20~	(cell J26)	Range A8..D20 press [Enter]
agpq	(cell J27)	Align Go Page Quit

To run a macro, you must assign a range name to it. Vince has assigned the name \P to his print macro.

The keystroke [Enter] is represented in a macro by the ~ (Tilde). On many keyboards, this key is found in the upper left corner of the keyboard, to the left of the "1" key.

❸ Move the cell pointer to cell I25. In this cell, Vince has entered the name of the print macro. By including the name of the macro next to the stored keystrokes, he can easily identify the name assigned to the macro.

❹ Move the cell pointer to cell L25, the first line of the description of the macro. The entire description is found in cells L25, L26, and L27. Like cell I25, these cells serve to document the macro.

As you have seen, the print macro automatically prints the payroll worksheet. This saves Vince some time and allows others who may be less familiar with 1-2-3 commands to print the worksheet.

Special Keys

Before you create your own macros, you need to know one more thing about them. Some keys require a special entry to represent the actual keystroke in the macro. As we've just seen, for example, the ~ (Tilde) represents the [Enter] key in Vince's print macro.

Function keys, cursor-movement keys, and other special keys are represented by the name of the key enclosed in braces. For instance, to represent pressing the right arrow key in a macro, you would type {right}. To represent pressing the [Home] key, you would type {home}. Figure 7-5 on the next page shows what you should enter in a macro to represent function keys, cursor-movement keys, and other special keys.

Action	Macro entry
	Cursor-movement keys
Move cursor up one row	{up} or {u}
Move cursor down one row	{down} or {d}
Move cursor left one column	{left} or {l}
Move cursor right one column	{right} or {r}
Jump to cell A1	{home}
Jump to intersection of first blank and non-blank cell	{end} + (Arrow macro key)
Jump up 20 rows	{pgup}
Jump down 20 rows	{pgdn}
Move left one screen	{bigleft}
Move right one screen	{bigright}
	Function keys
F2; edit current cell	{edit}
F3; list range names in POINT mode	{name}
F4; relative, absolute	{abs}
F5; move cursor to specified cell	{goto}
F6; switch between windows	{window}
F7; repeat last /Data Query command	{query}
F8; repeat last /Data Table command	{table}
F9; recalculate the worksheet	{calc}
F10; display current graph	{graph}
	Other special keys
Press the [Enter] key	~
Press the [Esc] key	{esc}
Press the [Backspace] key	{bs}
Press the [Delete] key	{del}
Cause a pause in running of macro	{?}

Figure 7-5
Special keys used
for macro
keystrokes

Creating the Macro

It takes time to plan and develop macros, but they can save you a great deal of time and effort.

The process of developing a macro involves several steps:

- Planning the macro
- Placing the macro
- Entering the macro
- Naming the macro

- Documenting the macro
- Running and testing the macro
- Debugging or correcting any problems
- Saving the worksheet that includes the macro

Planning the Macro

One way to plan a macro is to write down on paper the keystrokes as you type them. For example, whenever Vince saves the Krier Payroll worksheet, he presses the following keys:

Keystrokes	Action
/	To call the command menu
F	To select the File command
S	To select the Save command Prompt appears "Enter name of file to save: filename"
[Enter]	Prompt appears "Cancel Replace Backup"
R	To select Replace to update file

Thus, Vince writes these keystrokes on a piece of paper:

/FS[Enter]R

This is the macro Vince wants to develop.

Placing the Macro

After planning the macro, you are ready to enter it. First, however, you must decide where to place it in the worksheet. The location of a macro should be in a part of the worksheet that will not be affected by changes made in the rest of the worksheet. One recommendation for the placement of macros is in an unused section of your worksheet, below and to the right of the current worksheet entries. Thus, your macros are not stored in an area that is likely to have data copied to it, nor in an area in which you might insert or delete rows (Figure 7-6).

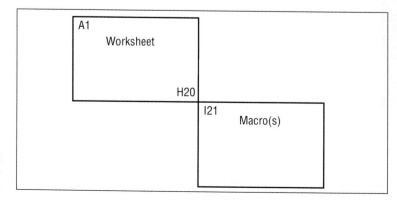

Figure 7-6
Where to place
macros

Vince has decided to enter the macros in an area beginning at cell I21. He has placed the label, MACRO AREA, in this cell to identify this area of the worksheet.

Entering the Macro

You can enter a macro in two different ways:

- By typing the keystrokes that represent the task (macro) as a series of labels directly into the worksheet cells
- By having 1-2-3 automatically record your keystrokes as you perform the task. You use the LEARN mode, explained later in this tutorial, to do this.

A macro is stored in a cell just like a number, a letter, or a formula. However, a macro *must* be entered as a label. Thus, you begin a macro with a label prefix, usually the ['] (Apostrophe), and enter the macro in a column of one or more cells. Although a cell can hold up to 240 keystrokes (all 240 keystrokes won't appear in the cell unless the column width is increased, but they are stored in the cell), it is easier to understand a macro if only a small number of related keystrokes are entered in a cell.

Vince has planned his macro. He knows what keystrokes he needs to enter and where to place them. He is now ready to enter the save macro by typing it in cell J29.

To enter the macro worksheet:

❶ Move the cell pointer to cell J29, the location of the keystrokes for this macro.

❷ Type **'/fs~r** then press **[Enter]**. The keystrokes for this macro appear in cell J29. See Figure 7-7.

first character in
macro is apostrophe

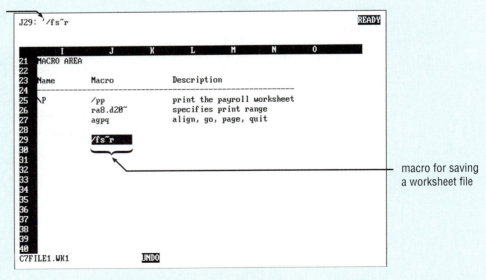

macro for saving
a worksheet file

Figure 7-7

Since macros are entered as labels, the first entry for a macro is a label prefix. If you do not begin the macro with a label prefix, the 1-2-3 command menu will appear on the screen. If this happens, press [Esc] and retype the macro with an apostrophe as the first character.

If you type the macro keystrokes incorrectly, just reenter the keystrokes.

Leave a blank cell below the last macro instruction to indicate the end of the macro.

Naming the Macro

Before you execute a macro, you must assign a range name to it. You can assign two types of range names to a macro:

- A \ (Backslash) and a single letter, such as \P
- A range name consisting of up to 15 characters

With either approach, you give the macro its name by using the Range Name Create (/RNC) command.

When you name a macro, you assign the range name to only the *first* cell of the macro. This is because 1-2-3 reads down the column of macro instructions until it reaches an empty cell; thus, you need name only the first cell.

Vince used the first type of name mentioned (Backslash plus a letter) to name his print macro (\P). For the macros you create in this tutorial, you will use the second approach, a range name with up to 15 characters. Although names such as \P are somewhat simpler to use, they can also be more difficult to remember. If you have several macros in a worksheet, you might forget which letter executes a particular task. By using a more descriptive name, you will be able to remember more about what your macro does.

Vince decides to name this macro SAVEPAY; he feels this name should make the macro easy to remember.

To name the save macro SAVEPAY:

❶ Be sure the cell pointer is in cell J29, the first cell containing the macro. Select /Range Name Create (**/RNC**).

❷ Type the range name **SAVEPAY** and press **[Enter]**.

❸ Press **[Enter]** to indicate you want to assign the name SAVEPAY to cell J29.

There is no need to assign every cell in the macro to the range name. 1-2-3 will automatically move to the next cell below the current cell in the macro until it finds a blank cell, which indicates the end of the macro.

Documenting the Macro

Whenever you create a macro, a good habit is to include a label containing the macro's name in a cell to the *left* of the macro so you can easily see the name when you examine the macro. It is also a good idea to enter a short description of the macro's function to the *right* of the macro. In this way, you can see at a glance what the macro does. Documenting a macro is not required to make it work, but it is a good habit to develop because some macros can be quite complex and difficult to read. Good macro documentation will save you time and help you avoid confusion.

Let's document Vince's save macro:

❶ Move the cell pointer to cell I29 and type the label **SAVEPAY**. Press **[Enter]**.

❷ Move the cell pointer to cell L29 and type **saves a worksheet file**, then press **[Enter]**. See Figure 7-8.

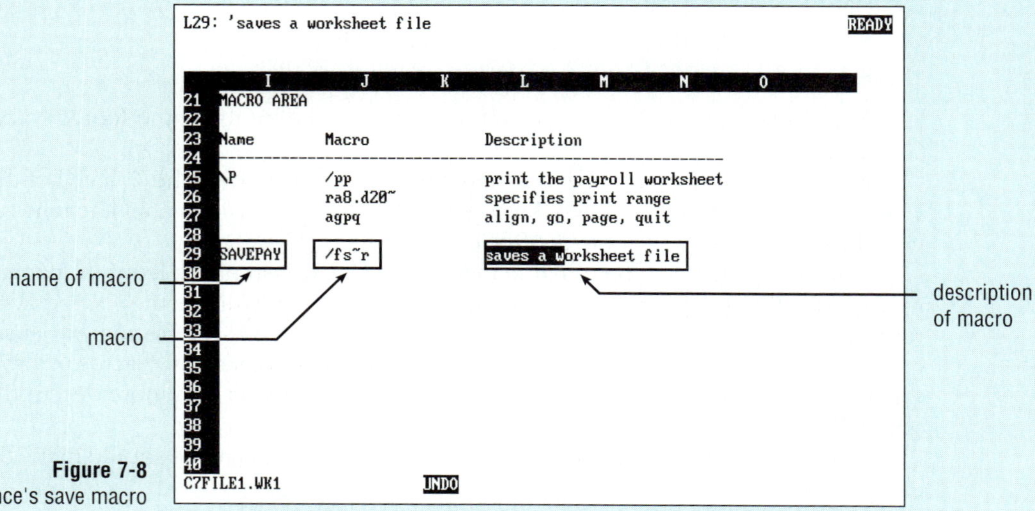

name of macro

macro

description of macro

Figure 7-8
Vince's save macro

Running and Testing the Macro

Once you have entered and named your macro, you can run it. How you issue the command to run a macro depends on the type of name you assigned to the macro.

- If you named the macro with a backslash and a letter, you press the [Alt] key while pressing the letter of the macro name. You used this approach to run the print macro.

- If you named the macro with a range name of up to 15 characters, you use [Alt][F3] (RUN) and select the name of the macro you want to execute from a list of names that appears on the control panel.

When you run a macro, 1-2-3 reads the macro keystrokes starting with the first cell of the macro. When all the keystrokes in the first cell have been run, 1-2-3 continues reading down the column of cells, executing all keystrokes in each cell. It continues this process until it encounters an empty cell, which 1-2-3 interprets as the end of the macro.

As a general rule, you should save your worksheet prior to running your macro for the first time. This is a good habit to develop because *running a macro with an error could damage a worksheet.*

Now let's save the current version of the worksheet before you test the macro you just entered.

To save your worksheet as S7FILE1:

❶ Press **[Home]** to move the cell pointer to cell A1.

❷ Type **S7FILE1.WK1** and press **[Enter]**, to change the identifying information in the worksheet.

❸ Select /File Save (**/FS**).

❹ Type **S7FILE1** and press **[Enter]**. The worksheet is saved.

Now you can test the macro to see if it is working correctly.

To run the SAVEPAY macro :

❶ Press **[Alt][F3]** (RUN). See Figure 7-9. A list of range names appears in the control panel.

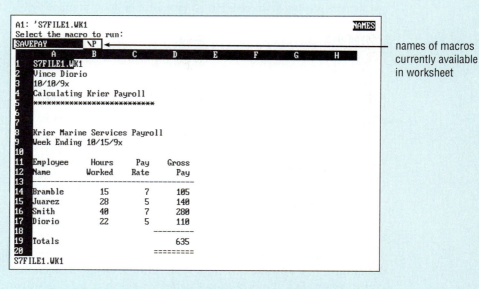

names of macros currently available in worksheet

Figure 7-9

❷ Make sure the menu pointer highlights the SAVEPAY macro.

❸ Press **[Enter]** to run the macro.

The macro runs and saves the current worksheet.

Interrupting a Macro

If you need to interrupt a macro during execution, press [Ctrl][Break]. 1-2-3 returns you immediately to READY mode. If the ERROR mode indicator flashes in the upper right corner of your screen when you press [Ctrl][Break], press [Esc]. This clears the error and returns you to READY mode.

Editing a Macro

Don't be surprised if your macro doesn't work the first time you execute it. When you typed the macro, you may have forgotten a tilde, included spaces, or entered the wrong command. The process of eliminating such errors is called **debugging**. If an error message appears when you run a macro, press [Esc] to return to READY mode. Then correct the macro by moving the cell pointer to the cell that contains the macro and do one of the following:

- Type over the current macro.
- Edit the cell of the macro that contains the error by pressing [F2] (EDIT) and changing the necessary keystrokes.

Creating Interactive Macros

Vince also planned to create a macro to create range names, because he frequently assigns range names to use with macros as well as for other 1-2-3 functions. He writes down the keystrokes required for assigning a range name to a range of cells:

Keystrokes	Action
/	To call the command menu
R	To select the Range command
N	To select the Name command
C	To select the Create command Prompt appears "Enter name"
Type range name	
[Enter]	1-2-3 prompts for range
Highlight range	
[Enter]	Indicates end of Range Name command

In looking over his notes, Vince realizes that the macro must pause to allow him to type the range name and the cells that represent the range. You can create macros that prompt you to enter data, enter a range name, or select a 1-2-3 command, and then the macro continues to run. A macro that pauses during its run is called an **interactive macro**.

To create an interactive macro, you use the Pause command, which is represented by {?}. You can enter {?} anywhere in your macro instruction. When 1-2-3 reads the {?} command, it temporarily stops the macro from running so you can manually enter a range name, move the cell or menu pointer, complete part of a command, or enter data for the macro to process. The macro continues to run when you press [Enter].

When you use {?} in a macro, you must complete the cell entry with a ~ (Tilde). This instructs 1-2-3 to continue running the macro after you press [Enter].

Vince writes down the keystrokes required for the range name macro:

/RNC{?}~{?}~

This interactive macro selects /Range Name Create. At the first {?} command, the macro pauses so you can specify the name of the range. When you press [Enter], the macro continues to run. The macro encounters another {?} command and pauses again. This time, you highlight the range of cells included in the range name. Press [Enter] again, to indicate that you want to end the pause. 1-2-3 then encounters the tilde and executes [Enter] to store the range. The macro is then complete.

To enter an interactive macro:

❶ Move the cell pointer to the macro area, cell J31, the location where you will enter the interactive macro.

❷ To enter the macro, type **'/rnc{?}~{?}~** and press **[Enter]**. See Figure 7-10.

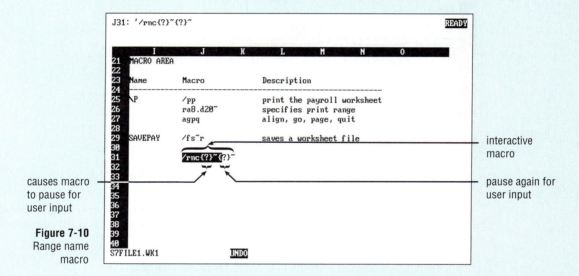

Figure 7-10
Range name macro

causes macro to pause for user input

interactive macro

pause again for user input

Now name the macro NAMEARANGE. You will select the Range Name Create command instead of using the NAMEARANGE macro, because you are still in the process of creating the NAMEARANGE macro.

❸ With the cell pointer at cell J31, Select /Range Name Create (**/RNC**). Type **NAMEARANGE** and press **[Enter]**.

❹ Press **[Enter]** to assign the range name to cell J31.

Let's document the macro with a name and a description of what it does.

❺ Move the cell pointer to cell I31, type **NAMEARANGE**, and press **[Enter]**.

⑥   Move the cell pointer to cell L31, type **assign range name to a range of cells** and press
    [Enter]. See Figure 7-11.

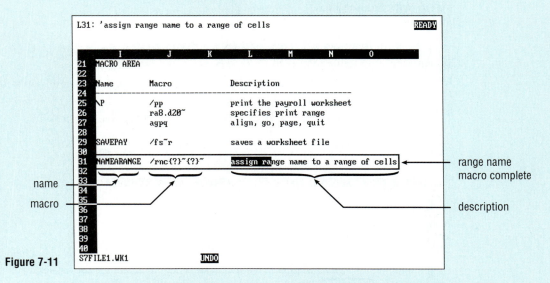

Figure 7-11

The NAMEARANGE macro is now complete.

Let's determine if the macro works properly. Again you need to save the current version
of the worksheet before you run the new macro for the first time. Use the SAVEPAY macro
you created earlier in the tutorial to save your worksheet.

To save your worksheet using the SAVEPAY macro:
❶   Press **[Alt][F3]** and highlight **SAVEPAY** from the list of range names listed on the con-
    trol panel. Press **[Enter]**. The current version of the worksheet has been saved.

You are now ready to test the NAMEARANGE macro, but first let's do something that
will save us time as we work through this tutorial. Since this is a tutorial on macros, we'll be
going to the macro area frequently. Let's assign the name MACROS to cell I21, so you can
use this name with the GOTO key [F5] to move directly to the macro area from any point in
the worksheet.

To run the NAMEARANGE macro:
❶   Move the cell pointer to cell I21.
❷   Press **[Alt][F3]** and highlight **NAMEARANGE** from the list of range names listed in the
    control panel. Press **[Enter]**. See Figure 7-12.

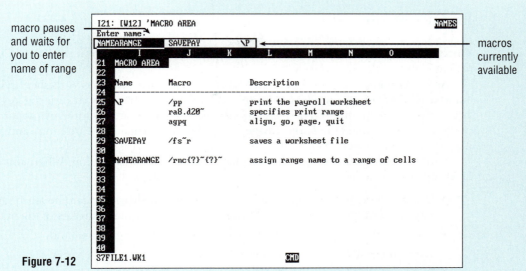

macro pauses
and waits for
you to enter
name of range

macros
currently
available

Figure 7-12

The macro begins to run. When 1-2-3 encounters the {?} command, the macro stops running, and the prompt "Enter name" appears in the control panel.

Notice that the status indicator CMD appears at the bottom of the screen whenever a macro is interrupted.

Now enter the range name.

❸ Type **MACROS**. Press **[Enter]**.

The macro pauses, waiting for you to highlight the range of cells for the range name.

❹ Press **[Enter]** since the range of the macro is a single cell, I21.

The macro continues to run until 1-2-3 encounters a blank cell, at which point it stops.

Let's verify that the NAMEARANGE macro worked properly.

To test the NAMEARANGE macro:

❶ Press **[Home]** to move the cell pointer to cell A1.

❷ Press **[F5]** (GOTO), type **MACROS**, and press **[Enter]**.

The cell pointer should now be at cell I21.

LEARN Mode

Vince wants to create a macro that he can use to format any column of data to Currency format with two decimal places.

As we mentioned earlier, Vince could type this macro directly into worksheet cells or he could use 1-2-3's LEARN mode. In LEARN mode, 1-2-3 automatically records the keystrokes as it performs a sequence of 1-2-3 operations. The keystrokes are captured in a separate area of the worksheet called the **learn range**. Vince can then name the learn range and execute it as a macro whenever he chooses.

Let's use LEARN mode to create Vince's macro to format a column. When you use the LEARN mode to create a macro, you must follow these steps:

- Decide where in the worksheet you want to put the learn range. The learn range must be a single column, long enough to contain all the keystrokes of the macro.
- Specify the learn range, using the Worksheet Learn Range command.
- Turn on LEARN mode to start recording all keystrokes.
- Perform the task you want 1-2-3 to record.
- Turn off LEARN mode to stop recording keystrokes.
- Assign a range name to the first cell in the learn range.
- Run the macro.

Now let's follow these steps and use the LEARN mode to create a macro that will format a column of numbers in Vince's worksheet.

First, Vince decides to place the learn range in cells J33 to J38.

To specify the learn range and record the macro:

❶ Move the cell pointer to cell J33 and select /Worksheet Learn Range (**/WLR**).

❷ Press **[.]** to anchor the cell. Highlight the range J33..J38, and press **[Enter]**. The learn range is now defined.

❸ Move the cell pointer to cell C14, the point where you want to begin formatting the values.

Follow the next steps carefully because once you turn on LEARN mode every keystroke you make will be recorded. For example, if you press [Backspace] several times to correct typing errors, 1-2-3 will record the [Backspace] keystrokes.

Now turn LEARN Mode on:

❹ Press **[Alt][F5]** (LEARN) to turn on LEARN mode. Notice that the status indicator LEARN appears at the bottom of your screen. See Figure 7-13.

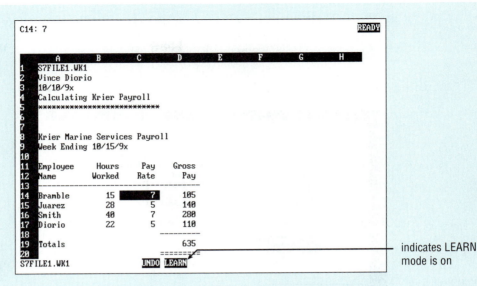

Figure 7-13

indicates LEARN
mode is on

The next step is to perform the tasks you want to record.

❺ Select /Range Format Currency (**/RFC**) and press **[Enter]**. Press **[End]** [↓] and press
[Enter]. The column is now formatted using the currency format. See Figure 7-14.

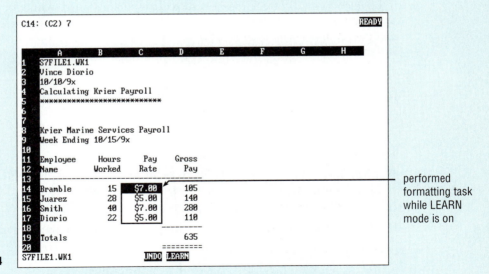

Figure 7-14

performed
formatting task
while LEARN
mode is on

Now you should turn off LEARN mode to stop recording the keystrokes.

❻ Press **[Alt][F5]** (LEARN) to turn off LEARN mode. Notice that the status indicator
LEARN no longer appears on the screen.

⦿ Press **[Enter]** so the recorded keystrokes appear in the learn range. Move the cell pointer to cell J33, the first cell in the learn range, to view the keystrokes that 1-2-3 has recorded. See Figure 7-15.

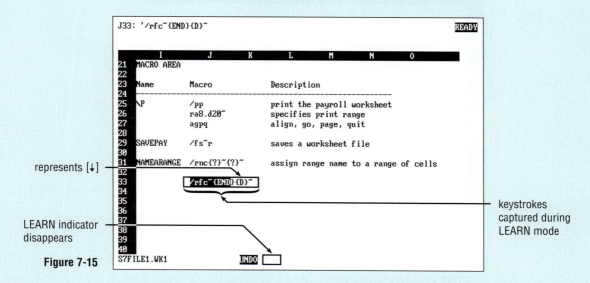

represents [↓]

LEARN indicator disappears

keystrokes captured during LEARN mode

Figure 7-15

If the macro looks correct, the next step is to specify a range name for it. On the other hand, if the macro needs corrections, you can edit it as you would any other cell. Note that the {End} {D} symbol moves the cell pointer down the column to the intersection of a blank and not-blank cell.

Let's name the macro CURRENCY2 using the NAMEARANGE macro.

To name and document the macro:

❶ With the cell pointer in cell J33. Press **[Alt][F3]** and highlight **NAMEARANGE** from the list of range names on the control panel. Press **[Enter]**.

❷ Type **CURRENCY2** and press **[Enter]** to enter the range name.

❸ Press **[Enter]** to assign the range name to the first cell of the learn range.

Now let's document the macro.

❹ Move the cell pointer to cell I33. Type **CURRENCY2**, then press **[Enter]**. Move the cell pointer to cell L33. Type **format range of cells to currency** and press **[Enter]**. See Figure 7-16.

If you now wanted to create another macro using LEARN mode, you would have to reset the learn range to another range of cells (/Worksheet Learn Range); otherwise, the new macro would be added to the end of the existing macro.

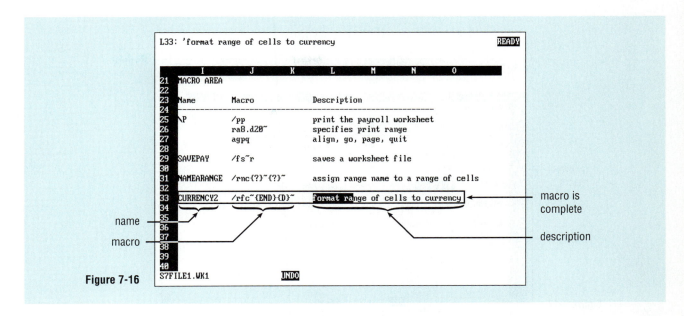

L33: 'format range of cells to currency   READY

	I	J	K	L	M	N	O
21	MACRO AREA
22
23	Name	Macro		Description
24	--------
25	\P	/pp		print the payroll worksheet
26		ra8.d20~		specifies print range
27		agpq		align, go, page, quit
28
29	SAVEPAY	/fs~r		saves a worksheet file
30
31	NAMEARANGE	/rnc{?}~{?}~		assign range name to a range of cells
32
33	CURRENCY2	/rfc~{END}{D}~		format range of cells to currency
34
35
36
37
38
39
40

name →

macro →

macro is complete

description

S7FILE1.WK1   UNDO

Figure 7-16

Finally, let's run the CURRENCY2 macro to see if it works.

To run the macro:

❶ Move the cell pointer to cell D14.

❷ Press **[Alt][F3]** and highlight **CURRENCY2** from the list of range names on the control panel. Press **[Enter]**.

The gross pay values appear in the Currency format.

❸ Save your worksheet as S7FILE1 using the SAVEPAY macro.

Using STEP Mode to Debug a Macro

The first time you run a macro, it may not work as you intended. In a simple macro, you can easily identify errors by comparing the keystrokes in the worksheet with the keystroke entries you planned. In large macros, however, it is more difficult to identify errors, so Lotus 1-2-3 has a special feature to help you in debugging macros. This feature, called **STEP mode**, allows you to run a macro one keystroke at a time.

To demonstrate the use of STEP mode, let's run the SAVEPAY macro in STEP mode. First, we'll modify the SAVEPAY macro so it is intentionally incorrect; then we'll see how STEP mode can help us find the error.

To modify the SAVEPAY macro and intentionally enter an error:

❶ Move the cell pointer to cell J29, the location of the SAVEPAY macro.

❷   Type **'/f~s~r** and press **[Enter]**. See Figure 7-17.

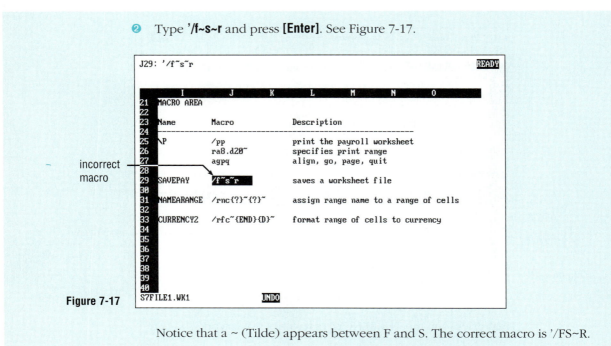

incorrect
macro

Figure 7-17

Notice that a ~ (Tilde) appears between F and S. The correct macro is '/FS~R.

Let's try to use this modified SAVEPAY macro.

To run the incorrect SAVEPAY macro:

❶   Press **[Alt][F3]** (Run) and highlight **SAVEPAY** from the list of range names on the control panel. Press **[Enter]**. See Figure 7-18.

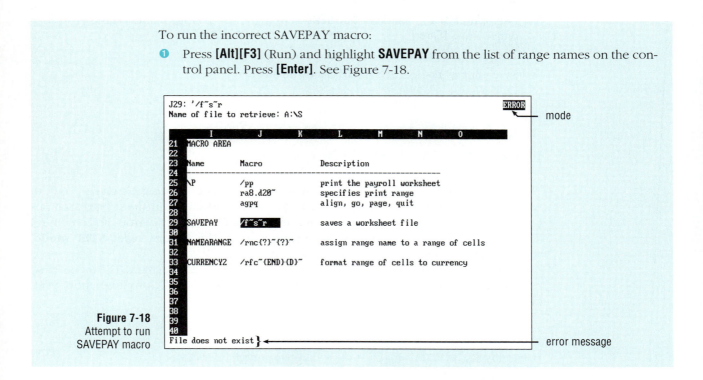

Figure 7-18
Attempt to run
SAVEPAY macro

mode

error message

Notice that the mode indicator in the upper right corner has changed to ERROR and is blinking. This indicates something is wrong with your macro. In addition, the message appearing in the status line says that the "File does not exist."

❷ Press **[Esc]** to clear the error condition and return to READY mode.

What happened? Why did the macro stop running? If the reason is not obvious to you from looking at the macro keystrokes, you can use STEP mode to help debug the macro.

To use STEP mode:

❶ Press **[Alt][F2]** (Step). This turns STEP mode on. See Figure 7-19. Notice that the STEP indicator appears in the status line at the bottom of the screen.

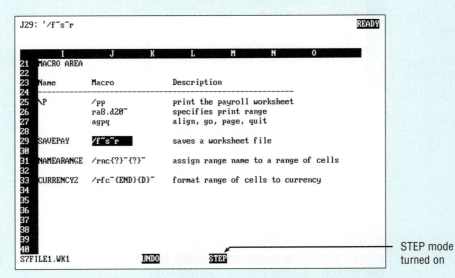

Figure 7-19

To run a macro in STEP mode, you press any key to run the macro one keystroke at a time. This way, you can see each step the macro takes and perhaps determine the problem with the macro.

Now rerun the macro:

❷ Press **[Alt][F3]** (Run) and highlight **SAVEPAY** from the list of range names on the control panel. Press **[Enter]**. See Figure 7-20.

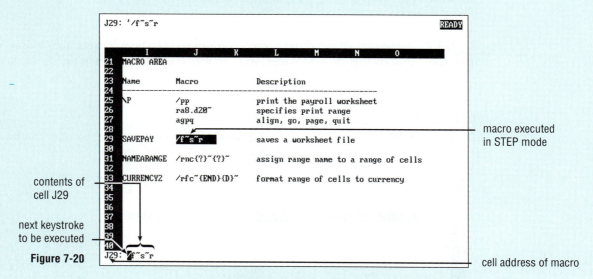

contents of
cell J29

next keystroke
to be executed

Figure 7-20

macro executed
in STEP mode

cell address of macro

The cell address that contains the macro appears on the status line, along with the contents of that cell. The keystroke to be executed the next time you press a key is highlighted.

❸ Press **[Space]**. This executes the first keystroke of the macro, the / (Slash). See Figure 7-21.

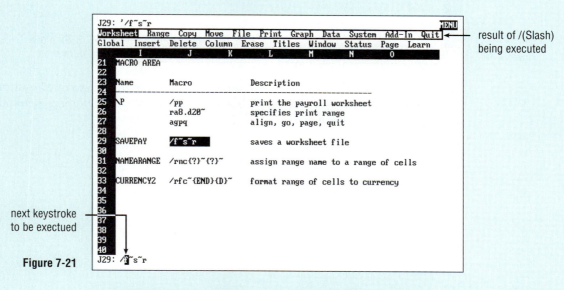

next keystroke
to be exectued

Figure 7-21

result of /(Slash)
being executed

Notice that the Command menu appears in the control panel. In addition, in the status line, the keystroke that will be executed next, F, is highlighted.

❹ Press **[Space]** once more. This executes the next keystroke in the macro. See Figure 7-22.

highlighted →

next keystroke
to be executed

Figure 7-22

← result of F command
being executed

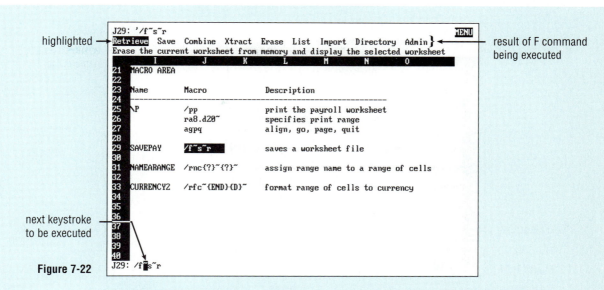

The File command from the Command menu is selected, and the File command
options appear on the control panel. The Retrieve command is highlighted. Also
notice that the ~ (Tilde) in the status line is highlighted. This is the next keystroke
to be executed.

❺ Press **[Space]** once again. This runs the ~, that is, the [Enter] keystroke. See Figure 7-23.
Since the Retrieve command was highlighted in the control panel, pressing [Enter] executes Retrieve rather than Save. The prompt "Name of the file to retrieve" appears in
the control panel. Notice that the next keystroke to be executed, S, is highlighted in
the status line.

next keystroke →

Figure 7-23

Retrieve command
executed as a result
of erroneous ~ (Tilde)

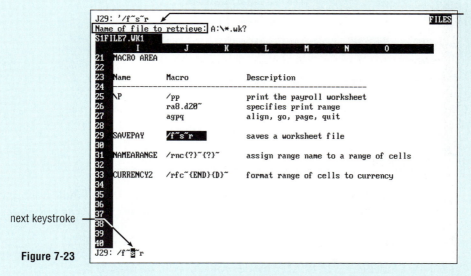

❻ Press **[Space]** again. S is entered as the name of the file to retrieve. See Figure 7-24 on
the next page.

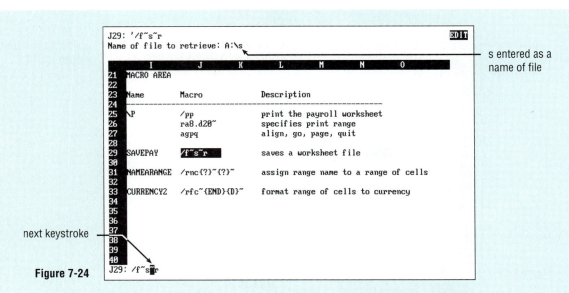

Figure 7-24

The status line indicates the ~ (Tilde) will be the next keystroke to be executed.

❼ Press **[Space]**. 1-2-3 interprets the ~ as the [Enter] keystroke and attempts to retrieve a file named S. See Figure 7-25.

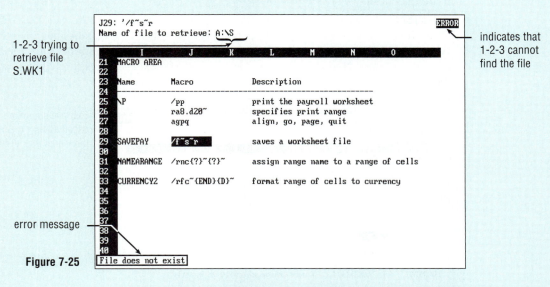

Figure 7-25

1-2-3 doesn't find the file S.WK1 on your Data Disk. The ERROR indicator appears in the upper right corner of your screen, and the error message "File does not exist" appears in the status line.

❽ Press **[Esc]** to clear the error message and return to READY mode.

Once your worksheet is in READY mode, you can edit the macro.

❾ Be sure the cell pointer is in cell J29. Type **'/FS~R** and press **[Enter]** to correct the macro.

You are still in STEP mode, which means if you attempt to run another macro, 1-2-3 will continue to run the macro one keystroke at a time.

⓾ Press **[Alt][F2]** (Step). This turns STEP mode off. Now the macros will run normally. The status indicator STEP disappears from the status line.

The Final Worksheet

As a final step in preparing the worksheet for Mrs. Krier, Vince decides to create a section of the worksheet that will guide Mrs. Krier and other users through the various options of the worksheet. This section will also provide instructions that walk a user through the various steps to run these options. Figure 7-26a shows Vince's sketch of the instruction section he plans to enter into his worksheet.

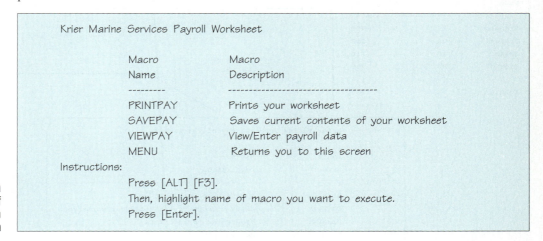

Figure 7-26a
Vince's sketch of the instruction section

Figure 7-26b shows his revised worksheet map.

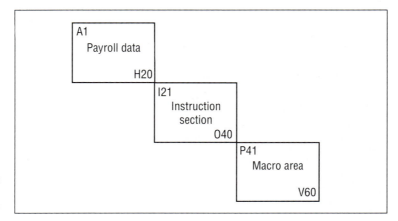

Figure 7-26b
Vince's revised worksheet map

To retrieve Vince's revised worksheet:

❶ Select /File Retrieve (**/FR**).

❷ Highlight C7FILE2 and press **[Enter]**. See Figure 7-27. The instruction screen appears immediately upon retrieval of the worksheet. This way, the first thing a user sees when retrieving the worksheet will be instructions on how to use the worksheet.

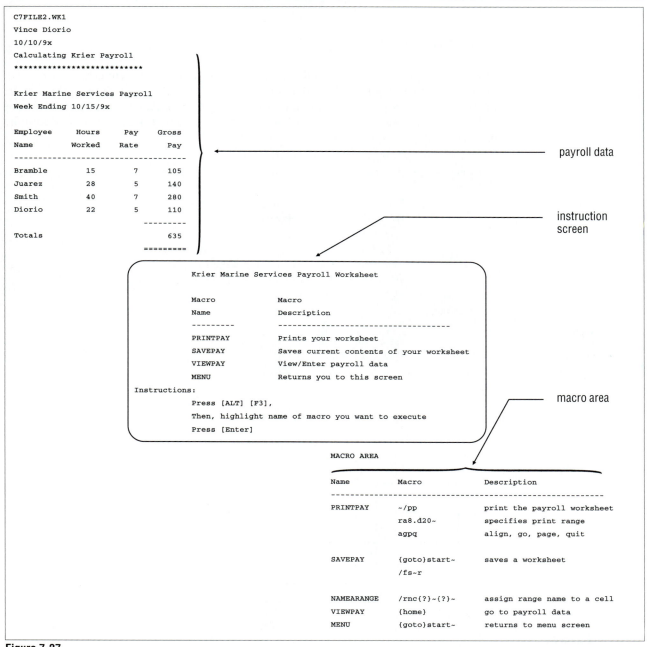

Figure 7-27
Vince's final worksheet

Vince has made some modifications to the worksheet. For instance, the print macro is named PRINTPAY instead of /P. He also has added a macro named MENU that returns the user to the instruction screen from any location in the worksheet.

Let's try out the revised worksheet.

To view the payroll data:

❶ Press **[Alt][F3]** (Run), highlight VIEWPAY, and press **[Enter]**. The payroll worksheet appears on the screen.

To return to the instruction screen:

❷ Press **[Alt][F3]** (Run), highlight MENU, and press **[Enter]**. The instruction screen reappears.

Vince is satisfied with the worksheet and is ready to show Mrs. Krier how to use the macros he's created.

Summary

In this tutorial, you learned to create and invoke macros to automate repetitive tasks. You also used 1-2-3's LEARN mode to record the keystrokes in a macro. Then you named and documented the macro for easy reference.

Once you had begun using macros, you learned to find and edit problems using STEP mode.

Exercises

1. What keystrokes are used to do the following?
   a. Run a macro
   b. Turn STEP mode on and off
   c. Turn LEARN mode on and off

2. What do you use in a macro to represent the following?
   a. Pressing the [Enter] key
   b. A pause in the running of a macro
   c. Pressing [F5] (GOTO) key
   d. The [↑] key

3. What do the following macros do?
   a. {goto}MACROS~ (Note: MACROS is a range name)
   b. /rff{?}~{?}~
   c. /rfc2~{end}{down}~
   d. /c~{down}~
   e. /ppoocqq

Tutorial Assignments

Before you begin these Tutorial Assignments, check your working copy of the Data Disk. Be sure you have space to save the additional worksheet files you'll create in these assignments (at least 30,000 bytes). If not, save your files as appropriate to another formatted diskette.

Retrieve the worksheet T7FILE1.WK1. This worksheet contains the four macros created in this tutorial. Make the following additions or modifications to the macro area.

1. First, save this worksheet as S7FILE2.

2. Modify the SAVEPAY macro so the cell pointer moves to cell A1 before the worksheet is saved. Save the worksheet using the revised SAVEPAY macro. What is the purpose of moving the cell pointer to cell A1 before saving the worksheet?

3. Whenever you run the macro SAVEPAY, it replaces the previously saved payroll worksheet with the current worksheet, thereby erasing any record of the earlier pay period.
    a. Modify the SAVEPAY macro again so that you can enter the filename during execution of the SAVEPAY macro. Be sure that this macro pauses to allow you to assign a new worksheet name to the current worksheet before saving the worksheet.
    b. Use the SAVEPAY macro and save the worksheet as S7FILE3.

4. Each week, Vince retrieves the payroll worksheet and before entering the new hours worked for each employee, he erases the Hours Worked column from the previous pay period.
    a. Use the typing method to create a macro that erases a range of cells.
    b. Name this macro ERASECELLS.
    c. Document the macro.
    d. Save your worksheet as S7FILE3.
    e. Run the ERASECELLS macro and then enter the following hours for Bramble, Juarez, Smith, and Diorio, respectively: 20, 35, 35, and 10.

5. Create a macro as follows:
    a. Use LEARN mode to develop a macro to format a range of cells using Currency format with zero decimal places.
    b. Name this macro CURRENCY0.
    c. Document the macro.
    d. Save the worksheet as S7FILE3.
    e. Format the Gross Pay and Pay Rate columns using this macro.

6. Create a macro as follows:
    a. Use LEARN mode to create a macro to set print settings to compressed print. (Remember to change the learn range before you create this macro). This macro will set the right margin to 132 and the setup string to the code for compressed print used by your printer. For many printers, the setup string for compressed print is \015.
    b. Name this macro COMPRSPRINT.
    c. Document the macro.
    d. Save the worksheet as S7FILE3.
    e. Run the COMPRSPRINT macro. Check the print settings sheet to determine if your macro worked properly.

7. Create a macro as follows:
   a. Use the typing method to create a macro that sets the print settings to normal print. This macro will set the right margin to 76 and the setup string to the code for normal print used by your printer. For many printers, the setup string for normal print is \018.
   b. Name this macro NORMPRINT.
   c. Document the macro.
   d. Save the worksheet as S7FILE3.
   e. Run the NORMPRINT macro. Check your print settings sheet to determine if your macro worked properly.

8. Print the payroll worksheet using compressed type. First, run the COMPRSPRINT macro and then the print (\P) macro.

9. Print the payroll worksheet using normal type. First, run the NORMPRINT macro and then the print (\P) macro.

Retrieve worksheet file T7FILE2. This worksheet has two new macros in addition to the four that were originally in the T7FILE1 worksheet.

10. The first new macro, COLWIDTH, located in cell J35, is supposed to change the column width. It doesn't work properly.
    a. Run the macro.
    b. Correct the macro.
    c. Run the corrected macro to increase the column width in column I from 12 to 15 characters.

11. The second macro, DELARANGE, located in cell J37, is supposed to allow you to select a range name to delete. When it runs, an error occurs.
    a. Run the macro.
    b. Correct the macro so it deletes a range name.
    c. Run the corrected macro and delete the range name /P.
    d. Use the NAMEARANGE macro in the worksheet to assign the macro in cell J25 the name PRINTPAY.
    e. Print the worksheet using the PRINTPAY macro.
    f. Make the appropriate changes to the documentation in the macro documentation.
    g. Print the worksheet using the macro PRINTPAY.

12. Save your worksheet as S7FILE4. Do not use the SAVE macro to save this file.

Use the Reference section of *Lotus 1-2-3 for Business* to do the following:

13. Vince recalls from his Lotus 1-2-3 course that a "Lotus-like" menu can be created as an aid in selecting other macros. These menus go by many names; macro menus, user-defined menus, and customized menus are some of the more common names.

    When the macro menu is activated, the menu items appear in the second line of the control panel. A menu description of the highlighted menu item appears in the third line of the control panel (Figure 7-28a to Figure 7-28d).

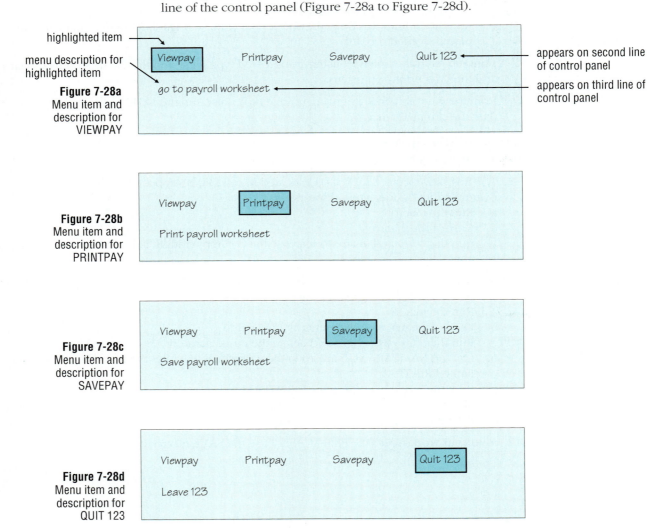

highlighted item

menu description for highlighted item

appears on second line of control panel

appears on third line of control panel

Figure 7-28a
Menu item and description for VIEWPAY

Viewpay   Printpay   Savepay   Quit 123

go to payroll worksheet

Figure 7-28b
Menu item and description for PRINTPAY

Viewpay   Printpay   Savepay   Quit 123

Print payroll worksheet

Figure 7-28c
Menu item and description for SAVEPAY

Viewpay   Printpay   Savepay   Quit 123

Save payroll worksheet

Figure 7-28d
Menu item and description for QUIT 123

Viewpay   Printpay   Savepay   Quit 123

Leave 123

    a.   Read the Reference section of the text, looking up topics such as Macro menu, MENUBRANCH, MENUCALL, and BRANCH to learn how to create a macro menu. Then use Figure 7-29 to help you complete this assignment.

    b.   Retrieve file T7FILE3 and create and debug the macro menu shown in Figure 7-29.

To execute the Macro menu, run the macro BEGIN. When BEGIN is run, the command {MENUBRANCH PAYMENU} branches to the PAYMENU macro, which results in the menu in Figure 7-28b appearing in the control panel.

Setup for Macro menu:

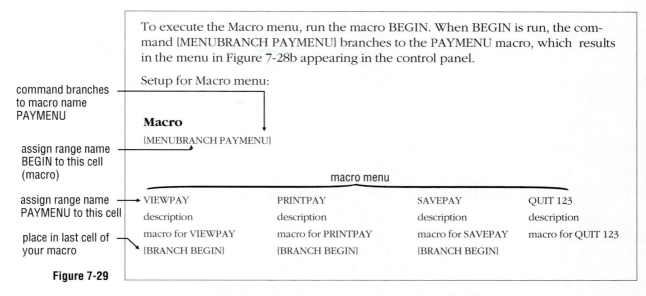

command branches
to macro name
PAYMENU

Macro

{MENUBRANCH PAYMENU}

assign range name
BEGIN to this cell
(macro)

macro menu

assign range name
PAYMENU to this cell

VIEWPAY	PRINTPAY	SAVEPAY	QUIT 123
description	description	description	description
macro for VIEWPAY	macro for PRINTPAY	macro for SAVEPAY	macro for QUIT 123
{BRANCH BEGIN}	{BRANCH BEGIN}	{BRANCH BEGIN}	

place in last cell of
your macro

Figure 7-29

c. Place the macro menu in the macro area, beginning in cell I21.
d. Save your worksheet as S7FILE5.
e. Test your macro menu.

Case Problems

1. Reporting on Word Processing Software

A marketing research firm has compiled data on the number of units the top six word processing software packages have shipped worldwide during 1989 (Figure 7-30).

Product	Units Shipped
WordPerfect	1,400,000
Microsoft Word	500,000
WordStar	345,000
Display Write	300,000
Professional Write	250,000
Multimate	200,000

Figure 7-30

1. Create a worksheet using the data from Figure 7-30.

2. Prepare a report that includes all the products and has the following format:

	Add title	
Product	Units shipped	Market share
XXXXXXXXXXX	XXXXX	XX.X%
XXXXXXXXXXX	XXXXX	XX.X%
.	.	.
.	.	.
.	.	.
Total Units	XXXXX	

3. Create a pie chart of shipments by product. Name the graph PIE_SHIP.

4. Create a bar graph of shipments by product. Name the graph BAR_SHIP.

5. Create a macro to print the report. Name the macro PRINT.

6. Create a macro to view the pie chart. Name the macro PIEWP.

7. Create a macro to view the bar graph. Name the macro BARWP.

8. Include within your worksheet an instruction section that will help anyone who uses the macros in this worksheet. This section should be the first screen that appears when a user retrieves the worksheet.

9. Save your worksheet as S7WORD.

10. Use the macro PRINT to print the report from number 2 above.

2. Tutorial 2 Revisited

Retrieve the worksheet P2FUND, the final version of the Balboa Mutual Fund worksheet from Tutorial 2, and do the following:

1. Modify the worksheet so that the first screen includes the following:

Macro name	Description
ERASERANGE	Erase a column
PRINTFUND	Print fund report
SAVEFUND	Save the worksheet
RETURN	Return to this screen
[Place instructions on how to run a macro here]	

2. Create a macro to erase the prices from the Current Prices column. You should be able to select (highlight) the range of cells to erase. Name the macro ERASERANGE.

3. Create a macro to print the Mutual Fund Report. Name the macro PRINTFUND.

4. Create a macro to save the worksheet. You should be able to name the worksheet that you are saving. Name the macro SAVEFUND.

5. Create a macro to return the instruction screen.

6. Enter the Current Prices for November 12, 1990. The current prices for that day were:

IBM	127
Coca-Cola	44
AT&T	35
Boeing	45

    First, use your macro to erase the Current Price column. Then enter the new prices. Remember to also change the date.

7. Print the Net Asset Value report for November 12, 1990, using your print macro.

8. Save your file as S2FUND using your save macro.

3. Tutorial 6 Revisited

Retrieve the worksheet P6CUST, the final version of the Customer database of Rhode Island and Massachusetts customers from Tutorial 6. Let's modify this worksheet to include macros to do the following:

- View the statistical summary report for Rhode Island and Massachusetts customers
- View the outstanding balance report by state
- Sort the database
- Print the database

Do the following:

1. Modify the worksheet so that the first screen includes the following:

Macro name	Description
REPORT1	Go to Summary Report
REPORT2	Go to Outstanding Balances by state
SORT	Sort database by field you select
PRINT	Print all records in database
RETURN	Return to this screen
[Place instructions on how to run a macro here]	

2. Create a macro to go to the first report in this worksheet. This is the summary report that shows total, average, maximum, and minimum outstanding balances for all Rhode Island and Massachusetts customers (cells N1..O12).

3. Create a macro to go to the second report in this worksheet. This report shows the outstanding balances by state (cells N21..P27).

4. Create a macro that sorts the data file on any primary sort key that you choose and also lets you select the sort order (ascending or descending). Be sure that all other steps in the sort macro are done automatically.

5. Create a macro to print the database. Run this macro.

6. Create a macro to return to the instruction screen. Run this macro.

7. Save your worksheet as S6CUST.

8. Use the SORT macro to sort the worksheet by YTD Sales in descending order.

9. Print the database.

10. Remember to document all your macros.

11. Prepare a worksheet map.

Part Three . . .

Additional Cases

Case 1

Preparing an Invoice for Island Influences

Natalie Ryad moved to Barbados a few years ago and opened Island Influences, a gift gallery featuring the works of Caribbean artists. Their works evoke the flavor of the islands through paintings on plates, mugs, glasses, coasters, and other giftware.

Natalie's business has done quite well, but customers continue to ask her if she has a mail order catalog from which they could order gifts. After studying the catalog business concept, Natalie decides to develop a mail order business to supplement her retail business. She believes sales will come from people who have visited Barbados and her shop and who want to purchase additional giftware without returning to the island.

As the catalog orders begin to come in, Natalie manually processes the mail orders (customers use forms included in the catalogs). She calculates the amount of each item ordered, adds the island tax and shipping costs, and then totals the final amount owed. But after 13 months, the catalog business represents 23 percent of Natalie's total sales. She decides it is time to computerize.

Natalie will use Lotus 1-2-3 to help her prepare invoices. Actually, she will create an invoice **template,** a preformatted worksheet that contains the labels and formulas needed to process an invoice but that does not include any values. Natalie will enter the values when she prepares an invoice for each customer. She will enter formulas into the template so that as she enters the customer's order, 1-2-3 will automatically perform calculations for the

In this case you will do the following:

- Format a worksheet to improve its appearance

- Create a template

- Protect worksheet cells

- Use the @IF function

- Develop a print macro

- Consult the Reference section to use:
  Manual Recalculation
  @NOW function
  Date formatting
  Setting cells to blank when zero

invoice. These calculations will include the dollar amount of each item ordered, the total amount of all items ordered, tax, shipping charges, and the total amount owed.

Figure 1-1a shows the invoice template that Natalie sketched and Figure 1-1b shows the calculations she plans to perform for each order. The boxed numbers are guides to help you relate Natalie's sketch to the calculations.

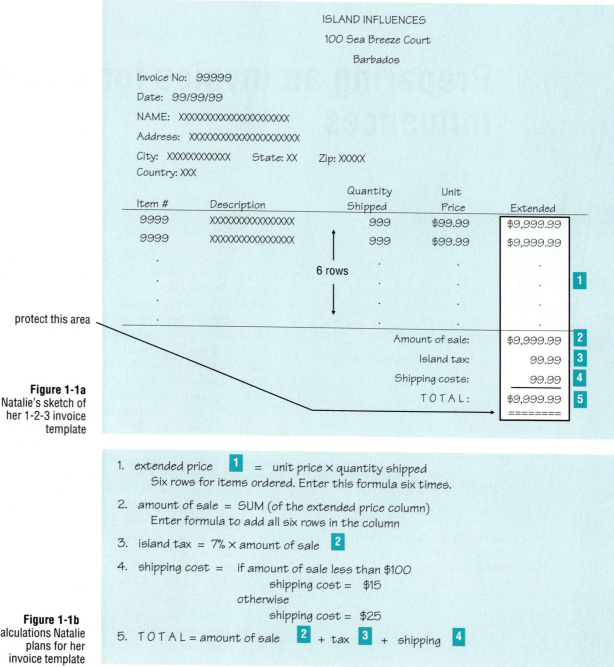

Figure 1-1a
Natalie's sketch of her 1-2-3 invoice template

Figure 1-1b
Calculations Natalie plans for her invoice template

Do the following:

1. Begin your worksheet by entering the labels for the invoice template. Adjust column widths if necessary. The placement of the labels and their corresponding values do not have to match Natalie's sketch exactly.

2. Enter the formulas in Figure 1-1b into your worksheet.

3. Format the following columns or cells as Currency with two decimal places:
   a. unit price
   b. extended price
   c. Island tax
   d. shipping charges
   e. total sales

4. Protect the worksheet so that the cell pointer cannot enter any cell whose value is determined by a formula.

5. Develop a macro to print the invoice. Name the macro PRINT_INVOICE.

6. Save the worksheet template as S1INVC1.

7. Process the sales order shown in Figure 1-2.

ISLAND INFLUENCES
Catalog Order Form

Ordered by:
  Martin Felsap
  123 Archway St
  Atlanta, Ga 97812

Item#	Description	Qty	Unit Price
64	Island Scene Mug 12 oz	6	12.00
93	Mini Tray	2	7.00
47	Pitcher	1	28.00

Figure 1-2
Sales order received by Island Influences

a. Retrieve the preformatted worksheet file S1INVC1 from Assignment 6 above.
b. Enter the data from Mr. Felsap's order form into the invoice template. This will be invoice number 1078 and use today's date. Note how the calculations are automatically calculated as you enter the data.
c. Print the invoice using the macro you created in Assignment 5, above.

Use the Reference section of *Lotus 1-2-3 for Business* to do the following:

8. Improve the appearance of the worksheet by formatting it. Use the Blank when Zero (Worksheet Global Zero) command to convert cells that contain zero to blank cells.

9. Improve the efficiency of using the invoice template by doing the following:
    a. Use the @NOW function and date formatting to automatically enter today's date on your worksheet.
    b. Set CALCULATION mode to manual. This command stops any calculations of formulas until you press the F9 key.

10. Save the revised template S1INVC2.

11. Repeat Assignment 7 above using the revised template, which is now in S1INVC2. Note that you must reissue the Blank when Zero command each time you retrieve the template if you want zeroes to appear in blank cells.

Case 2

Bidding for a Contract with the U.S. Navy

Quidnesset Shipyard has completed a prototype of a new submarine. The Navy, impressed with the prototype, asks Quidnesset to bid on a contract to build 10 additional submarines.

As a member of the cost accounting group at Quidnesset Shipyard, you have accumulated the following information about what it will cost to build the new submarines (Figure 2-1).

In this case you will do the following:

- Use exponents in a formula

- Create a one-way data table

- Prepare and print a report

- Create a named graph

- Print a graph

- Ask *what-if* questions about the completed worksheet

Direct materials (per sub)	$1,000,000
Direct labor and overhead	
(100,000 hours @ $50/hour)	$5,000,000
Total Cost	$6,000,000

Figure 2-1

Since labor represents such a large portion of the cost, Quidnesset management wants an accurate estimate of labor hours so they can submit a realistic and competitive bid to the Navy. They believe that they should allow for the learning process as workers and management build each submarine. The amount of time required to build the second submarine will probably be less than the first, the third submarine will require less time than the second, and in general the time to build each additional sub will decrease. As workers continue to gain experience, their dexterity on repetitive tasks should improve. Also, as the managers become more familiar with building the submarines, they should be able to schedule work more efficiently.

One approach to how you can estimate the reduced time needed to build each submarine is to use what is called the *learning curve*. This is a mathematical formula to calculate how labor hours per unit manufactured decline as the units of output increase. A popular learning curve formula is:

$$m = ax^b$$

where

m = time to produce the last single unit

x = number of units produced (x is 1, or x is 2, x is 3, . . . x is 11)

a = time required to produce the prototype unit

b = rate of learning

Quidnesset Shipyards uses an 80-percent learning curve to estimate the number of direct labor hours to complete each submarine. For example, as the quantity of units produced is *doubled*, from say the second submarine to the fourth submarine, the time needed to produce the fourth submarine is 80 percent of the time needed to produce the second submarine. The parameters Quidnesset Shipyard uses in the learning curve formula are:

x = 1, 2, 3, 4, 5, 6, 7, 8, 9, 10, 11

b = –.3219 (where b is the precalculated number for an 80% learning curve)

a = 100000

Do the following:

1. Use the Data Table command to develop a table that displays the number of hours required to produce the first submarine (the prototype), the second submarine, the third, and so on, until you reach the eleventh. In this table, have the first column list x, the number of units produced (x = 1, x = 2, x = 3, etc.). Have the second column list the hours required to build each corresponding submarine in the first column.

Hint: When $x = 1$, the formula calculates that it will take 100000 hours to build the prototype. Thus, when you create this data table, what you are really interested in is the time it would take to build the second to the eleventh submarines.

When $x = 2$, the formula calculates that it will takes approximately 80000 hours to build the second submarine.

In 1-2-3, the characters you use to represent an exponent is ^. For example, you would enter 4^2 as 4^2.

2. Use the results from Assignment 1, above, to calculate the cost of assembling each submarine. Use Figure 2-1 to construct a formula for cost estimation.

3. Prepare and print the report as sketched in Figure 2-2.

Figure 2-2

```
              Quidnesset Shipyards
                 Cost Estimate


  Submarine              Hours   Cost
      2                   xxx    $xxxx
      3                   xxx     xxxx
     . . .               . . .   . . .
     11                   xxx     xxxx

  Totals                  xxx    $xxxx
```

4. Create a line graph of the number of hours it takes to build each submarine. Name the graph LINEHOUR.

5. Save your worksheet as S2SUBS.

6. Create a PIC file for your line graph named LNHRS.PIC. Print your graph.

7. What if, due to a union renegotiation of wages, the direct labor and overhead costs increase to $52 per hour? Rerun your model and print out a second report using the format in Assignment 3, above.

Case 3

Auto Financing: One Great Rate

This month's *CorporateWorld Magazine* includes an advertisement for financing cars and trucks at 7.9-percent annual interest. The ad says that borrowers can have loans for 24-, 36-, or 48-month terms, and it encourages readers to "Choose the term that fits your budget."

The ad includes the three tables in Figure 3-1.

In this case you will do the following:

- Create a one-way data table

- Use the @PMT function

- Use the Table function key to answer *what-if* questions

- Consult the Reference section to use:
    Two-way data table

24 Months		36 Months		48 Months	
Amount Financed	Monthly Payment	Amount Financed	Monthly Payment	Amount Financed	Monthly Payment
$10,000	$452	$10,000	$313	$10,000	$244
$12,000	$542	$12,000	$375	$12,000	$292
$15,000	$678	$15,000	$469	$15,000	$365

Figure 3-1

You have recently decided to buy a car, and this ad attracts your attention. You know that Lotus 1-2-3 provides various financial functions that make loan calculations much simpler, so you decide to use 1-2-3 to help you decide if you should apply for the advertised loan.

The @PMT function of 1-2-3 calculates the periodic payment of a loan based on the amount of the loan. It can also help you calculate the interest rate and the number of periods to pay back the loan. The format of this function is:

@PMT(amount of loan, interest rate, total number of payments)

The arguments of the @function can be cell addresses or range names. For example, a $100,000 loan payable in annual payments over 25 years at 10-percent interest would be entered as:

@PMT(100000,0.10,25)

If the $100,000 loan required monthly payments, you would enter the information as follows:

@PMT(100000,0.10/12,25*12)

Do the following:

1. Create a worksheet that verifies the accuracy of the monthly payments in Figure 3-1. Use a one-way data table to calculate monthly payments. Your data table should have one column for amount financed and a second column for the monthly loan payment. Are the numbers in Figure 3-1 accurate?

2. Print your results.

3. Save your worksheet as S3RATES1.

4. What if you don't qualify for this financing and have to borrow from a bank at 12 percent interest? How would this affect the monthly payments for each of the three terms? Print your results. Save your worksheet as S3RATES2.

5. Use the Reference section of *Lotus 1-2-3 for Business* and do the following:
   a. Read about two-way data tables (/Data Table 2).
   b. Develop a two-way data table using *amount of loan* and *number of periods* as the two variables. Assume that the interest rate is 7.9%.
   c. Print your results.
   d. Save your worksheet as S3RATES3.

Case 4

Budgeting for Employee Benefits at BranCo International

Salaries and other forms of employee compensation, such as benefits, are one of a company's major human resource expenditures. The cost of employee benefits often represents 30 percent to 35 percent of an employee's total compensation; thus, company managers must carefully budget to pay for employee benefits.

Manula Abba, vice president of administration for BranCo International, has asked you to help her calculate the annual human resources budget. You agree to help and begin by retrieving the employee worksheet, P4PERSL.WK1. This file contains BranCo employee data as a 1-2-3 database.

In this case you will do the following:

- Work with a 1-2-3 database

- Use @IF function

- Add new variables to a worksheet

- Sort records

- Create and print one detail and one summary report

- Create several macros

- Create one graph

- Consult the Reference section to:
  Hide columns

- Ask *what-if* questions about the completed worksheet

The field names in the employee database are as follows:

Field	Description
EMP#	employee number
LNAME	last name
FNAME	first name
BIRTH	date of birth (yyyymmdd)
SEX	code for sex (M = male; F = female)
MAR	code for marital status (Y = married; N = not married)
DEP	number of dependents
ANNSAL	annual salary
HIREDT	date employee hired (yyyymmdd)
XMPT	exempt employee (X = exempt; N = nonexempt)
MED	code for medical plan (F = family plan; I = individual plan; N = no medical plan)
401K	401K retirement plan (Y = contributing to plan; N = not contributing to plan)
DIV	division in which employee works
JOBTITLE	job title
PER	payment method (H = hourly; M = monthly)

BranCo's Benefits Program

Manula wants you to first study carefully the BranCo benefits package. It includes:

- A medical plan for employees and their dependents
- A group life insurance plan
- A 401K retirement plan
- Worker's compensation
- Contributions to social security
- Federal unemployment insurance
- State unemployment insurance

Medical Plan

BranCo provides medical insurance for its employees through an insurance company. This insurance company charges two premiums, one for individual employees and one for employees with families (dependents). The company pays 80 percent of the cost of this medical insurance and the employee pays 20 percent. The total monthly premiums are:

Individual	$195 per month
Family	$250 per month
No coverage	$ 0

Employees who have other medical insurance, such as with their spouses' employers, can choose no coverage at BranCo.

Hint: This calculation requires an @IF function embedded or nested within an @IF function. Use the Reference section of *Lotus 1-2-3 for Business* to read more about @IF functions.

Group Life Insurance

BranCo pays entirely for group life insurance. The annual fee is $1.70 per $1000 of coverage. The benefit for employees varies, depending on whether the employee is exempt (not eligible for overtime pay) or nonexempt (eligible for overtime pay). An exempt employee's benefit is two times his or her annual salary; a nonexempt employee's benefit is one and one-half times his or her annual salary excluding overtime. For example, if an exempt employee's annual salary is $34,200, then the insurance coverage is $68,400 (2 × $34,200); the premium paid by the company to cover this employee is $116.28 ($1.70 × 68.4).

401K Retirement Plan

To help employees save for their retirement, the company provides a 401K plan. Employees can contribute up to 5 percent of their pretax salaries to the savings plan, and the money they contribute is not taxable until they withdraw it at retirement. In addition, the company matches what an employee contributes dollar for dollar up to the first 3 percent of the participating employee's salary. The code Y in the 401K field in the employee database indicates employees who participate in the plan. For the purposes of this budget, Manula wants you to assume all participating employees will contribute the maximum allowed.

Worker's Compensation

BranCo is required by law to provide this benefit. It is an insurance that pays the medical bills of workers injured on the job. The workers compensation premium is based on a fee of $4.68 per $1,000 of annual salary. For example, if an employee earns $40,400, then the firm pays a premium of $189.07 per year for this employee ($4.68 × 40.4).

FICA Taxes (Social Security)

FICA taxes, also called Social Security, are paid equally by the employee and the employer. The employee's share is withheld from his or her paycheck, and BranCo pays an equal share to each employee's FICA account. For 1990, Social Security tax for each employee was 7.65% of the first $50,400 the employee earned. For example, if an employee earns $30,000, then the FICA tax is $2,295 (.0765 × 30000). BranCo also must pay $2,295 to this employee's account. As another example, if an employee earns $60,000, then the FICA tax is $3,855.60 (.0765 × 50400). No FICA tax is applied to the amount an employee earns over $50,400. The employee and BranCo each must pay $3,855.60 toward the employee's FICA account.

Federal Unemployment Tax (FUTA)

BranCo, like other employers, must pay an unemployment tax equal to 6.2 percent of the first $7,000 of each employee's annual salary. FUTA tax is paid only by the employer.

State Unemployment Tax (SUTA)

Employers pay an unemployment tax to the state equal to 3 percent of the first $7,000 of each employee's annual salary. SUTA is paid only by the employer.

Creating the Worksheet

After studying the details of the benefits program at BranCo, you begin by sketching the final employee benefits budget for 1990 (Figure 4-1).

```
                    BranCo Corporation
                  Employee Benefits Budget

                            1990
           Programs         Amount
           ─────────────────────────

           Medical plan        $xxxx
           Life insurance       xxxx
           401K plan            xxxx
           Worker's comp        xxxx
           FICA taxes           xxxx
           FUTA                 xxxx
           SUTA                 xxxx


           Total benefits      $xxxxx


           Note: The budget for employee benefits rep-
           resents expenditures made only by the com-
           pany, not by the employees.
```

Figure 4-1

You realize that before you can develop a final budget showing the company's costs per benefit, you must add additional columns to the employee database to calculate each employee's individual benefits.

Do the following:

1. Retrieve the worksheet, P4PERSL.WK1 and expand the employee database to include seven additional columns, one for each benefit. Calculate the cost of each benefit for each employee by incorporating the appropriate formulas described for each benefit.

Hint: Consider setting up an input section in your worksheet that references the variables in the benefits formulas. Then, if the formulas change, you won't have to reenter the formulas for each employee.

2. Set up an output area in your worksheet for the Benefits Summary Report; then create the Benefits Summary Report.

3. Create a macro to print the Benefits Summary Report. Name the macro PRINT_BENEFIT.

4. Use the data from the Benefits Summary Report to create a graph comparing the cost of each benefit. Choose a graph that you feel will most appropriately show the comparison of the costs. Name your graph BENEFITS.

5. Create a macro that will allow Manula to view this graph easily and quickly. Name the macro VIEWGRAPH.

6. Create a second report, entitled Detailed Employee Benefits Report. This report should show the total compensation (salaries plus benefits) for each employee. Include the following columns: employee last name, salary, each benefit (seven columns), total benefits (sum of previous seven columns), and total compensation (salary plus total benefits). Include totals for the columns when appropriate. Arrange the employee records by division and, within division, alphabetically by last name.

   Hint: Use the Data Query Extract command to retrieve the columns you need for the Detailed Employee Benefits Report. Or use the Reference section of *Lotus 1-2-3 for Business* to learn about hiding columns without erasing cell formulas.

7. Create a macro to print the Detailed Employee Benefits Report. Name the macro PRINT_DETAIL.

8. Print the Detailed Employee Benefits Report using the macro PRINT_DETAIL.

9. Print the Benefits Summary Report using the macro PRINT_BENEFIT.

10. Save your worksheet as S4PERSL1.

11. What if, due to rising costs for medical insurance, BranCo management increases employees' share of medical insurance payments from 20 percent to 30 percent?
    a. What cost savings are achieved by increasing the employees' share of medical insurance payments?
    b. Print this Benefits Summary Report.
    c. Save your worksheet as S4PERSL2.

12. What if Congress revises the tax laws for 1991, and the new law affects the payments employees and employers make to FICA taxes? Suppose the new law calculates FICA taxes as follows:

If salary is	Then FICA is
less than or equal to $53,400	$7.45\% \times$ annual salary
greater than $53,400 but less than or equal to $125,000	$\$3,821.85 + (\text{annual salary} - 53,400) \times 1.45\%$
greater than $125,000	$5,016.50

Remember that 7.45% and 1.45% can also be entered as .0745 and .0145, respectively.

    a. Revise the FICA calculation in your worksheet based on this new Federal tax law.

b. How much more will BranCo have to pay in FICA taxes as a result of the new law?
c. Print the Benefits Summary Reports.
d. Save your worksheet as S4PERSL3.

Case 5

Financial Planning at Urbano Pharmaceutical

Urbano Pharmaceutical, a manufacturer of prescription drugs, makes and markets a number of pain reliever products. Urbano's pain reliever products division is responsible for all of its own marketing, production, accounting, distribution, and planning. It markets its products through pharmaceutical drug distributors.

Urbano Pharmaceutical is planning for next year. The planning department, responsible for compiling data for budgets, asks you to use your knowlege of 1-2-3 to help in the planning process. They want you to create a worksheet to assist the department in preparing the budget.

You begin by gathering information from several departments. From marketing you receive forecasts of expected unit sales of each product and the expected selling price to distributors. Figure 5-1 shows the data you receive from marketing. The boxed numbers in Figures 5-1 and 5-2 are guides to help you through the following discussion.

In this case you will do the following:

- Use a worksheet map

- Create and print a report

- Create and use several macros

- Create and print several graphs

- Use the input area of a worksheet to answer *what-if* questions

Product	Forecasted unit sales [1]	Price per packaged product [2]
Cedrin, 50 coated 500-mg caplets	41,700	$5.26
Covil, 100 coated 200-mg caplets	62,315	4.97
Criskan, 24 coated 500-mg caplets	37,820	3.10
Koprin, 100 coated 200-mg caplets	50,780	5.28

Figure 5-1

The production and cost accounting departments provide data about each drug and the ingredients used to produce it. These data appear on what is called a cost sheet. A cost sheet lists the ingredients, the quantity of each ingredient needed to produce a single caplet, the unit cost of the ingredient, and the cost of each ingredient in the caplet. Figure 5-2 shows the cost sheet for Cedrin, one of Urbano's leading products.

Cost Sheet
Cedrin, 500-mg caplets

Ingredients	Qty/ caplet [3]	Measure	Ingredient cost/unit [4]	Cost per caplet [5]
Acetaminophen	500	mg	0.000120	0.060000
Diphenhydramine citrate	38	mg	0.000028	0.001064
Benzoic acid	5	ml	0.000073	0.000365
Carnauba wax	10	mg	0.000031	0.000310
Cornstarch	12	mg	0.000090	0.001080

Total cost per caplet [6]		0.062819
Number of caplets in retail package [7]		50
Cost of caplets in retail package [8]		$3.140950

Figure 5-2

The cost per caplet is calculated as follows:

1. Determine the cost of each ingredient in one caplet [5]. You multiply the ingredient cost per unit [4] by the quantity needed to produce one caplet [3].

2. Determine the cost of one caplet of this product [6]. To do this you sum the cost of each ingredient per caplet [5].

3. Determine the total cost of each retail packaged product [8]. To determine this you multiply the cost of one caplet [6] by the number of caplets in a retail package [7].

After all the cost sheets have been completed, the revenue and cost data are summarized in the Financial Projections Report, the format for which is presented in Figure 5-3.

Urbano Pharmaceutical
Projected Revenues, Costs, and Profits
For Year Ending December 31, 199x

Product	Revenue [9]	Cost [10]	Profit [11]	Profit/ [12] Revenue	Profit [13] Contribution
xxxxx	xxxxxxx	xxxx	xxxxx	xxxxx	xxxxx
xxxxx	xxxxxxx	xxxx	xxxxx	xxxxx	xxxxx
. . .					
--------	----------	----------	----------	----------	----------
Total	xxxxxxx [14]	xxxx [15]	xxxxx [16]		
	=======	====	=====		

Notes regarding projected revenues, costs, and profits:

Calculate 1–3, 5, and 6 below for *each product.*

1. Revenue [9] = Price/package [2] × Forecasted units sold [1]
2. Cost [10] = Cost per package [8] × Forecasted units sold [1]
3. Profit [11] = Revenue [9] less cost [10]
4. Total first three columns: revenue [14], cost [15], and profits [16]
5. Profit/Revenue [12] = Profit [11] divided by revenue [9]
6. Profit Contribution [13] = Profit [11] divided by Total profit [16]

Figure 5-3

Reviewing the worksheet map will help you locate the different sections in this worksheet (Figure 5-4). The marketing data shown in Figure 5-1 are found in an input section of this worksheet (cells A21..E40), so that management can see what happens to profits when marketing assumptions are changed.

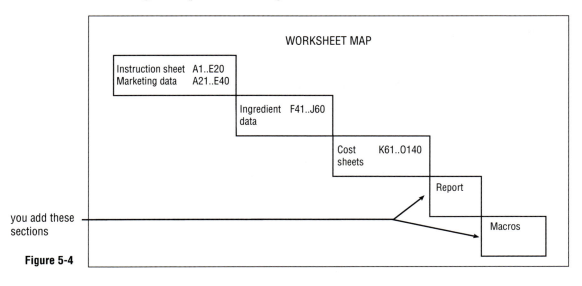

WORKSHEET MAP

Instruction sheet A1..E20
Marketing data   A21..E40

Ingredient F41..J60
data

Cost   K61..O140
sheets

Report

Macros

you add these
sections

Figure 5-4

Management would like to predict the effect that rising ingredient costs have on the cost of the packaged product. If ingredient costs rise, management might decide to raise the price of the product to distributors. Management would also like to see what happens to profits as costs of materials change. As you can see from the worksheet map, the ingredients used in manufacturing the drugs and their unit cost are also included as inputs in the worksheet (cells F41..J60).

Do the following:

1. Retrieve the worksheet file, P5DRUGS.WK1. In addition to the marketing and ingredient data in this worksheet, you will also find a cost sheet for each product (cells K61..O140). The cost sheets are incomplete. Use Figure 5-2 to help you complete the cost calculations for each product.

2. Create the Financial Projections Report as sketched in Figure 5-3.

3. Create a pie chart of revenues (in dollars) by product. Name the chart PIEREV.

4. Create a pie chart of profits by product. Name the chart PIEPROFIT.

5. Create a macro to print the Financial Projections Report.

6. Create a macro to print all the cost sheets.

7. Create a macro to print all marketing data and another macro to print all ingredient data.

8. Create a macro to view the Financial Projections Report .

9. Create a macro to view all the cost sheets.

10. Create a macro to view all marketing data and another macro to view all ingredient data.

11. Create a macro to view the PIEREV pie chart.

12. Create a macro to view the PIEPROFIT pie chart.

13. Develop an instruction screen to help other people who will use the worksheet. This input screen should be the first screen they see when they load the worksheet.

14. Print the Financial Projections Report, cost sheets, and marketing and ingredient data.

15. Save your worksheet as S5DRUG1.

16. Create a PIC file for each pie chart. Print each pie chart.

17. What if management increases the retail price of each product by 3 percent (assume no change in forecasted unit sales)? How does this affect profits?

    Print the new Financial Projections Report, cost sheets, and marketing data that reflect this change in retail price. Save your worksheet as S5DRUG2.

18. What if the supplier of Ibuprofen tells Urbano pharmaceutical that the price of Ibuprofen will increase from .00011 per unit to .000132 per unit as of the first of the year. How will this cost increase affect the total cost of each product? How will the cost increase affect profits?

    Print the new Financial Projections Report, cost sheets, and marketing and ingredient data that reflect this change in Ibuprofen's price. Save your worksheet as S5DRUG3.

Part Four . . .

Reference

Reference 1

Using 1-2-3

This chapter explains the basic concepts you need to know to use Lotus 1-2-3 Release 2.2 efficiently and effectively. These concepts provide a foundation for entering data and using the commands, special functions, and other 1-2-3 capabilities discussed in the other chapters in this *Reference*.

Contents

This chapter contains the following sections:

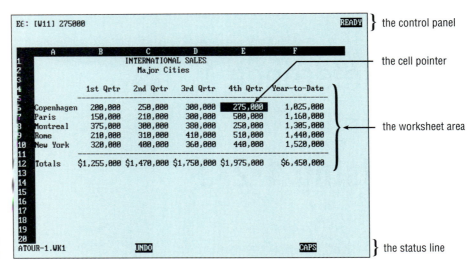

the control panel

the cell pointer

the worksheet area

the status line

Figure 1-1
The 1-2-3 screen

1-2-3 Screen

The 1-2-3 screen is made up of three main areas: the **worksheet area,** the **control panel**, and the **status line**. See Figure 1-1.

The worksheet area, which occupies the largest section of the screen, is where you enter and calculate data. It displays a section of the worksheet you are currently working on. The **worksheet** is a grid made up of rows and columns. The worksheet contains 8,192 rows and 256 columns. Each intersection of a row and column forms a cell, in which you can store data (a value or a label).

A **row number** in the left border of the worksheet identifies a row. Rows are numbered consecutively from 1 to 8192. A **column letter** in the top border of the worksheet identifies a column. Columns are lettered A-Z, then AA-AZ, then BA-BZ, and so on to column IV. A **cell** is a unit of the worksheet that stores data. It is formed by the intersection of a column and a row and has a unique address that consists of its column letter and row number.

The **cell pointer** is a rectangular highlight that appears on one cell in the worksheet and identifies it as the current cell. You can move the cell pointer to any cell in the worksheet. The **current cell** contains the cell

pointer, which indicates that your next entry or procedure affects this cell.

The **control panel** displays information about what 1-2-3 is doing and about your work. See Figure 1-2.

The **first line** of the control panel displays information about the current cell and the mode, or state, of 1-2-3.

At the far left of the first line, 1-2-3 displays the current cell's **address.** After the cell address, 1-2-3 displays the cell format, protection status, and column width. After this information, 1-2-3 displays the entry in the current cell, if the cell contains an entry.

The **cell format** controls the way 1-2-3 displays values in the cell if you used /Range Format to change the default cell format.

The cell's **protection status** determines whether you can make changes to the cell when worksheet protection is on. 1-2-3 displays U if you used /Range Unprotect to unprotect the cell or PR if you used /Worksheet Global Protection Enable to turn worksheet protection on and you have not unprotected the cell.

The cell's **column width** determines the number of characters 1-2-3 displays in the cell, if you used /Worksheet Column to change the default column width.

Figure 1-2
The control panel

```
F12: (C0) [W14] @SUM(F6..F10)                                          MENU
Worksheet  Range  Copy  Move  File  Print  Graph  Data  System  Add-In  Quit
Format  Label  Erase  Name  Justify  Prot  Unprot  Input  Value  Trans  Search
```

At the far right of the first line of the control panel, 1-2-3 displays the **mode indicator**, which tells you what **mode**, or state, 1-2-3 is currently in. For example, when it is waiting for you to type or select a command, 1-2-3 is in READY mode.

The **second line** of the control panel displays the current entry when you are creating or editing the entry. It displays the **main menu,** a list of commands that appears when you press / (Slash) or the < (Less-than symbol) in READY mode, as well as the submenus that appear after you make a selection from the main menu. The rectangular highlight that appears on one of the commands in the menu is called the **menu pointer**. The second line of the control panel also displays **prompts**, or requests for information that 1-2-3 needs to complete a command you have selected.

The **third line** of the control panel displays information about the command highlighted by the menu pointer. 1-2-3 lists either the submenu commands for the highlighted command or a description of the highlighted command.

The **status line** (see Figure 1-1) is the last line of the screen, which 1-2-3 uses to display the date-and-time indicator, the status indicators, and error messages.

The **date-and-time indicator** appears in the left corner of the status line. The default setting is for 1-2-3 to display the current date and time in the indicator. You can, however, use /Worksheet Global Default Other Clock to change the display to show the current file name or suppress this indicator.

An **error message** appears in place of the date-and-time indicator when 1-2-3 detects a mistake or cannot perform a task. If an error message appears, press [HELP] (F1) for a description of the error message and why it occurs; or press [Esc] or [Enter] to clear the error and continue work.

A **status indicator** appears when you use certain 1-2-3 keys and when a particular program condition exists. For example, UNDO indicates you can press [UNDO] (Alt-F4) to undo your last action and NUM indicates the [Num Lock] key is on.

1-2-3 Indicators

An indicator is a highlighted word that 1-2-3 displays to provide you with information about the program or special keys. 1-2-3 has two types of indicators: mode and status.

During a 1-2-3 work session, a **mode indicator** is always visible at the far right of the first line of the control panel to tell you what mode, or state, 1-2-3 is currently in.

Status indicators appear in the status line at the bottom of your screen. They appear when you use certain 1-2-3 keys and when a particular program condition exists.

The following tables describe the various 1-2-3 mode and status indicators.

Mode indicator	Meaning
EDIT	You pressed [EDIT] (F2) to edit an entry or entered a formula incorrectly.
ERROR	1-2-3 is displaying an error message. Press [HELP] (F1) to display a Help screen that describes the error; or press [Esc] or [Enter] to clear the error message.
FILES	1-2-3 is displaying a menu of file names in the control panel. Press [NAME] (F3) to display a full-screen menu of file names.
FIND	You selected /Data Query Find or pressed [QUERY] (F7) to repeat the last /Data Query Find you specified, and 1-2-3 is highlighting a database record that matches your criteria.
FRMT	You selected /Data Parse Format-Line Edit to edit a format line.
HELP	You pressed [HELP] (F1) and 1-2-3 is displaying a Help screen.
LABEL	You are entering a label.
MENU	You pressed / (Slash) or < (Less-than symbol), and 1-2-3 is displaying a menu of commands.
NAMES	1-2-3 is displaying a menu of range names, graph names, or attached add-in names.
POINT	1-2-3 is prompting you to specify a range or you are creating a formula by highlighting a range.
READY	1-2-3 is ready for you to enter data or select a command.
STAT	You selected /Worksheet Status or /Worksheet Global Default Status, and 1-2-3 is displaying the corresponding status screen.
VALUE	You are entering a value (a number or formula).
WAIT	1-2-3 is completing a command or process.

Status indicator	Meaning
CALC	Formulas in the worksheet need to be recalculated; press [CALC] (F9).
CAPS	The [Caps Lock] key is on.
CIRC	The worksheet contains a formula that refers to itself (occurs only when the recalculation order is Natural, which is the default setting). You can use /Worksheet Status to get information about the circular reference.
CMD	1-2-3 is pausing during a macro.
END	The [End] key is on.
LEARN	You pressed [LEARN] (Alt-F5) to turn on the Learn feature and 1-2-3 is recording your keystrokes in the Learn range.
MEM	The amount of computer memory available for entering new data has fallen below 4096 bytes. If you continue to enter data without first increasing the amount of available memory, you may get a "Memory full" error.
NUM	The [Num Lock] key is on.
OVR	The [Ins] key is on. Instead of inserting the character you type to the left of the cursor, 1-2-3 replaces the character at the cursor with the character you type.
RO	The worksheet has read-only status. The RO indicator appears when you are using 1-2-3 on a network and do not have the reservation for the current shared worksheet file.
SCROLL	The [Scroll Lock] key is on. Using the pointer-movement keys scrolls the worksheet in the direction indicated, instead of moving the cell pointer.
SST	A macro being executed in single-step mode is waiting for user input.
STEP	Single-step mode has been turned on; once invoked, macros are processed one step at a time.
UNDO	You can press [UNDO] (Alt-F4) to cancel any changes made to your worksheet since 1-2-3 was last in READY mode.

1-2-3 Keys

The following sections contain tables describing all the keys you can use in 1-2-3: keys for moving around (pointer-movement keys), function keys, and special keys.

Keys for Moving the Pointer

The **pointer-movement keys** allow you to move around in 1-2-3. These keys have different effects depending on what mode 1-2-3 is in.

READY and POINT Modes The following table lists the pointer-movement keys and the effect on the cell or menu pointer of pressing each key in READY and POINT Modes.

Key	Effect (READY and POINT modes)
[←]	Moves left one column.
[→]	Moves right one column.
[↑]	Moves up one row.
[↓]	Moves down one row.
[Tab]	Moves right one screen (READY).
[Shift][Tab]	Back Tab: Moves left one screen (READY).
[Ctrl][←]	Big Left: Moves left one screen.
[Ctrl][→]	Big Right: Moves right one screen.
[End]	(Must be used in combination with another pointer-movement key.)
[End] then [←]	Moves left to intersection of a blank and a nonblank cell. (A nonblank cell is a cell that contains data, a label prefix, and/or formatting.)
[End] then [→]	Moves right to intersection of a blank and a nonblank cell.
[End] then [↑]	Moves up to intersection of a blank and a nonblank cell.
[End] then [↓]	Moves down to intersection of a blank and a nonblank cell.
[Home]	Moves to cell A1 or upper left if /Worksheet Titles has been used.
[End] then [Home]	Moves to lower right corner of active area (the rectangular area between cell A1 and the lowest and rightmost nonblank cell).
[PgDn]	Moves down one screen.
[PgUp]	Moves up one screen.

MENU and HELP Modes The following table lists the pointer-movement keys and the effect on the cell or menu pointer of pressing each key in MENU and HELP Modes.

Key	Effect (MENU and HELP modes)
[←]	Moves left one item. If pointer is highlighting first item in a menu or Help screen, pressing [←] moves it to last item.
[→]	Moves right one item. If pointer is highlighting last item in a menu or Help screen, pressing [→] moves it to first item.
[↑]	Moves up one topic (HELP).
[↓]	Moves down one topic (HELP).
[End]	Moves to last item or topic.
[Home]	Moves to first item or topic.

Function Keys

You use the function keys on your keyboard to perform special operations. Each function key, except [F6], performs two operations: one when you press only the function key and another when you hold down [Alt] (or [Shift]) and then press the function key.

Regular Function Keys The table below describes the action of each of the function keys.

Key and name	Description
[F1] [HELP]	Displays a 1-2-3 Help screen related to task you are performing. HELP mode: Displays first Help screen you viewed. ERROR mode: Displays a Help screen that explains error message 1-2-3 is displaying.
[F2] [EDIT]	READY mode: Puts 1-2-3 in EDIT mode and displays contents of the current cell in control panel, so you can edit entry. EDIT mode: Switches between EDIT mode and LABEL or VALUE mode (EDIT mode if entry displayed in control panel is a label, or VALUE mode if entry displayed in control panel is a value).
[F3] [NAME]	POINT mode: Displays a menu of named ranges. FILES and NAMES modes: Switches between displaying a menu of names in third line of control panel and displaying a full-screen menu of names. VALUE mode: Displays a menu of named ranges when pressed after typing + − / ^ (or * in a formula.
[F4] [ABS]	POINT and EDIT modes: Cycles a cell or range address between relative, absolute, and mixed.
[F5] [GOTO]	READY mode: Moves cell pointer directly to cell or named range you specify.
[F6] [WINDOW]	READY mode: Moves cell pointer between two windows created with /Worksheet Window. MENU mode: Turns off display of settings sheets. Press [WINDOW] (F6) again to redisplay settings sheets.
[F7] [QUERY]	READY mode: Repeats last /Data Query you specified. FIND mode: Switches 1-2-3 between FIND mode and READY mode.
[F8] [TABLE]	READY mode: Repeats last /Data Table you specified.
[F9] [CALC]	READY mode: Recalculates all formulas in worksheet. VALUE and EDIT modes: Converts a formula to its current value.
[F10] [GRAPH]	READY mode: Displays current graph.

[Alt] Function Keys The table below describes the action of each of the function keys with the [Alt] key depressed.

Key and name	Description
[Alt][F1] [COMPOSE]	READY, EDIT, and LABEL modes: When used in combination with alphanumeric keys, creates international characters and other characters you cannot enter directly from keyboard.
[Alt][F2] [STEP]	Turns on STEP mode, which executes macros one step at a time for debugging. Press [STEP] (Alt-F2) again to turn off STEP mode.
[Alt][F3] [RUN]	READY mode: Displays a list of range names so you can select a macro to run. If you press [Esc] after pressing [RUN] (Alt-F3), 1-2-3 switches to POINT mode so you can highlight the first cell of the macro you want to run.
[Alt][F4] [UNDO]	READY mode: Cancels any changes made to worksheet since 1-2-3 was last in READY mode. Press [UNDO] (Alt-F4) again to restore changes.
[Alt][F5] [LEARN]	Turns on Learn feature and records subsequent keystrokes in learn range. Pressing [LEARN] (Alt-F5) again turns off Learn feature.
[Alt][F7] [APP1]	READY mode: Activates add-in program assigned to key, if any.
[Alt][F8] [APP2]	READY mode: Activates add-in program assigned to key, if any.
[Alt][F9] [APP3]	READY mode: Activates add-in program assigned to key, if any.
[Alt][F10] [APP4]	READY mode: If no add-in program is assigned to key, displays the Add-In menu. Otherwise, activates add-in assigned to key.

Special Keys

There are a number of other keys on your keyboard that have important uses in 1-2-3 as described in the following table.

Name	Description
[Alt]	READY mode: Runs a macro when used in combination with a single-letter macro name.
[Backspace]	EDIT mode: Erases character to left of cursor. HELP mode: Displays previous Help screen. POINT mode: If cell is not anchored, returns cell to wherever it was before 1-2-3 entered POINT mode (the current cell). If cell is anchored, removes highlighting, if any, unanchors cell, and returns cell to wherever it was before 1-2-3 entered POINT mode. FILES mode: Displays a menu of subdirectories within displayed directory.
[Caps Lock]	Makes letter keys produce only uppercase letters; number and punctuation keys are not affected.
[Ctrl]	When used in combination with certain keys, changes their functions.
[Ctrl][Break]	Cancels current procedure.
[Del]	EDIT mode: Erases current character.
[Enter]	Completes an entry, a command, or part of a command. ERROR mode: Clears error message from screen.
[Esc]	MENU mode: Returns 1-2-3 to previous menu or command step. EDIT, VALUE, and LABEL modes: Cancels current entry. HELP mode: Leaves Help system and returns you to point in 1-2-3 where you were. POINT mode: If cell is anchored, removes highlighting, if any, and unanchors cell. FILES mode: Erases default extension 1-2-3 displays. Pressing [Esc] a second time erases default drive and directory 1-2-3 displays. Pressing [Esc] a third time returns you to previous menu. ERROR mode: Clears error message from screen.

Special Keys (continued)

Name	Description
[Ins]	EDIT mode: Switches between inserting new text by moving existing text to right and writing over existing text.
[<] (Less-than)	READY mode: Displays 1-2-3 main menu.
[Num Lock]	Switches between number keys and pointer-movement keys on numeric keypad.
[.] (Period)	POINT mode: If cell pointer is unanchored, pressing [.] (Period) anchors cell pointer. If cell pointer is already anchored, pressing [.] (Period) changes position of free cell in highlighted range to next corner clockwise.
[Scroll Lock]	Switches pointer-movement keys between moving cell pointer and scrolling entire worksheet.
[Shift]	When used in combination with another key on typewriter section of keyboard, produces upper symbol on key.
[/] (Slash)	READY mode: Displays 1-2-3 main menu.
[Space]	LABEL, VALUE, and EDIT modes: Inserts a space in an entry. MENU mode: Moves right one item. If menu pointer is highlighting last item in a menu, moves pointer to first item.

Using 1-2-3 Menus

To tell 1-2-3 what to do, you select a series of commands from menus either by highlighting or by typing. When you press / (Slash) or < (Less-than symbol) to display the 1-2-3 main menu, a rectangular highlight, called the **menu pointer**, appears in the second line of the control panel.

To select a command by highlighting, move the menu pointer with the [←], [→], [Home], or [End] key to the command you want and then press [Enter]. This method is useful while you are becoming familiar with

1-2-3 because you can see the description or submenu 1-2-3 displays for each command.

To select a command by typing, type the first letter (uppercase or lowercase) or character of the command you want to select. Because this method is faster, you will find it useful once you are familiar with the commands in each 1-2-3 menu.

To complete many commands, 1-2-3 requires you to supply more information either through more menu choices or in answer to a prompt, a message asking you to enter specific information in the second line of the control panel.

When selecting commands, if you change your mind or realize that you have made a mistake, press [Esc] to back up one menu level or command step at a time. If you want to completely stop a procedure and return to READY mode, press [Ctrl][Break].

A **settings sheet** is a special status screen that helps you keep track of the choices you are making. It shows you the current settings for all the options associated with a task. You change settings in the settings sheet for certain 1-2-3 commands such as /Graph or /Print Printer by selecting the appropriate commands from the menu.

Entering and Editing Data

When you enter data in a cell, 1-2-3 classifies every entry as one of two types: labels or values. Labels are text entries. Values are number and formula entries.

When you start typing an entry, 1-2-3 determines whether the entry is a label or value based on the first character you type and changes the mode indicator to LABEL or VALUE accordingly. For example, if the first character you type is a letter or one of the label prefixes ' " ^ \ or |, 1-2-3 displays LABEL in the mode indicator. If the first character is a number (0 through 9) or one of the numeric symbols + − @ . (# or $, 1-2-3 changes the mode indicator to VALUE. If the entry is not valid, 1-2-3 switches to EDIT mode and displays the data in the second line of the control panel for editing.

Labels

A label is a text entry. It can include letters, special characters, numbers, and numeric symbols. For example, Caroline Wilson, 1620 Hill Road, 606–999–0001, and $19,803 can all be entered as labels.

Use the following guidelines when entering labels:

• The entry cannot be longer than 240 characters.

• To create a label that begins with a number (0 through 9) or one of the numeric symbols + − @ . (# or $, precede the entry with one of the label prefixes described later in this section. (1-2-3 displays the label prefix in the control panel when you highlight the cell.)

• To change the way 1-2-3 positions the label in the cell or to control whether 1-2-3 prints the label, precede the entry with the appropriate label prefix.

Label Prefixes   Besides allowing you to enter labels that 1-2-3 would usually recognize as values, **label prefixes** also allow you to control the way 1-2-3 aligns labels in cells and to control whether 1-2-3 prints a label.

Prefix	Effect
,	Aligns the label with the left edge of the cell (default alignment for labels).
"	Aligns the label with the right edge of the cell.
^	Centers the label in the cell.
\	Repeats the characters in the label to fill the cell.
|	When at the beginning of a row of data, tells 1-2-3 not to print the row.

Long Labels   When a label is longer than the cell's column width, it is called a **long label** and 1-2-3 displays as much of the label as it can. If cells to the right of the label are blank, 1-2-3 displays the part of the label that overlaps those cells. Otherwise, it does not display the overlapping part of the label. The long label displays fully in the control panel.

Values

A **value** is an entry that begins with a number or one of the numeric symbols + − @ . (# or $. The entry can be a number or a formula. 1-2-3 always right-aligns numeric values in cells. Unlike labels, you cannot change their alignment. You can, however, control the way 1-2-3 displays values by setting the cell format with /Range Format or /Worksheet Global Format. For example, 1-2-3 can display the value 2.47 as $2, $2.47, 247%, or 2.47E+00, depending on the cell format you specify.

Numbers   You can enter any number from 10^{-99} to 10^{99}. The number of significant digits 1-2-3 displays in a cell depends on the cell format, column width, and the magnitude of the number. If you enter a number with more digits than 1-2-3 can display, 1-2-3 rounds the number.

Use the following guidelines when entering numbers:

• Begin the entry with a number (0 through 9) or one of the numeric symbols + − @ . (# or $. If you begin a number with a $ (Dollar sign), 1-2-3 will enter the number but will not display the $. You must change the format of the cell to include a currency symbol.

• Do not include spaces, commas, or more than one decimal point in the entry. You can change the format of the cell to include commas.

• The entry cannot be longer than 240 characters.

• To enter numbers in scientific notation, type a positive or negative number followed by an e or E, and an exponent from −99 to 99.

Formulas   A **formula** is an entry that performs a calculation. You can enter several types of formulas in 1-2-3: numeric formulas, string formulas, and logical formulas. These types of formulas and methods for entering formulas are described in detail in "Working with Formulas," later in this chapter.

The number of decimal places 1-2-3 displays for a calculated value depends on the cell format in which the formula is entered. Regardless of how many decimal places 1-2-3 displays, however, it calculates the value to a precision of 15 decimal places unless you use @ROUND to specify a different precision.

Note: *For details on formatting values, see "/Range Format" and "/Worksheet Global Format." in Reference 2, Commands.*

Long Values   A **long value** is a value wider than the cell's column width minus 1. 1-2-3 handles long values as follows:

- If the cell is formatted as anything other than General or is not wide enough to display the value in scientific notation, 1-2-3 displays asterisks across the cell instead of the value. To display the value, widen the column with /Worksheet Column Set-Width or /Worksheet Global Column-Width.

- If the cell in which you enter a long value is formatted as General and the integer part of the value exceeds the cell's column width, 1-2-3 displays the value in scientific notation. For example, in a nine-character-wide cell, the value 123456789.99 appears as 1.2E+08.

Dates and Times   Entering a date or time requires that you enter a date or time number (a value that corresponds to the date or time) and assign the cell a date or time format.

1-2-3 assigns an *integer* to each of the 73,050 days from January 1, 1900 to December 31, 2099, inclusive. These integers are called **date numbers**. For example, the integer 5 corresponds to January 5, 1900; the integer 32774 to September 23, 1989. To display the date rather than the date number, use /Range Format to change the cell's format to one of the five date formats.

1-2-3 assigns a *decimal number* to each second from midnight to 11:59:59 PM, inclusive. These decimal numbers are called **time numbers**. For example, the decimal number .5 corresponds to 12:00:00 PM (noon); the decimal number .999988 corresponds to 11:59:59. To display the time rather than the time number, use /Range Format to change the cell's format to one of the four time formats. You can enter a date (or time) number using a date @function, which calculates the date (or time number) for the date (or time) you specify as the argument for the @function. For example, to enter the date number for September 23, 1989, you could enter @DATE(89,9,23) in the worksheet and 1-2-3 would calculate the date number as 32774. Or, to enter the time number for 11:59 PM, you could enter

@TIME(23,59,0) and 1-2-3 would calculate the time number as .999305.

Note: *For more information on entering Dates and Times, see "/Range Format" in Reference 2, Commands and "Date and Time Functions" in Reference 3, 1-2-3 @Functions.*

Editing an Entry

Editing an entry means altering existing data rather than replacing it with entirely new data. You can edit an entry either as you type it or after you have entered it in a cell. You can edit an entry in three ways as you type it:

- To erase characters to the left of the cursor, press [Backspace].

- To erase everything you typed and start again, press [Esc].

- To change part of what you typed, press [EDIT] (F2) to enter EDIT mode and use the editing keys in the table that follows.

To edit a completed entry, move the cell pointer to the cell and press [EDIT] (F2) to put 1-2-3 in EDIT mode. Use the editing keys to change the entry, and then press [Enter] or a pointer-movement key to enter the edited data in the worksheet.

Name	Description
[→]	Moves cursor right one character.
[←]	Moves cursor left one character.
[↑]	Completes editing and moves cell pointer up one row.
[↓]	Completes editing and moves cell pointer down one row.
[Backspace]	Erases character to left of cursor.
[Ctrl][→] or [Tab]	Moves cursor right five characters.
[Ctrl][←] or [Shift][Tab]	Moves cursor left five characters.
[Del]	Erases current character.
[End]	Moves to last character in entry.
[Enter]	Completes editing.
[Esc]	Erases all characters in entry.
[Home]	Moves to first character in entry.
[Ins]	Switches between inserting text by moving existing text to right (INS mode) and writing over existing text (OVR mode).
[PgUp]	Completes editing and moves cell pointer up a screen.
[PgDn]	Completes editing and moves cell pointer down a screen.

Name	Description
[↑]	Moves pointer up one topic.
[↓]	Moves pointer down one topic.
[←]	Moves pointer left one topic.
[→]	Moves pointer right one topic.
[Backspace]	Displays previous Help screen.
[End]	Moves pointer to last topic.
[Enter]	Displays Help screen for highlighted topic.
[Backspace]	Returns to 1-2-3.
[HELP]	Displays Help screen.
[Home]	Moves pointer to first topic.

Using the Help System

1-2-3 provides Help screens that you can view any time during a 1-2-3 session by pressing [HELP] (F1). The 1-2-3 Help system is context-sensitive, that is, the screen that 1-2-3 displays describes what you are currently doing. Help also provides other types of information, including explanations of the status indicators and a task reference. Each Help screen includes additional Help topics that are displayed in a brighter intensity or in color.

The following table lists the keys you use with the Help system.

Working with Ranges

A **range** is a rectangular block of adjacent cells. It can be a single cell, a row, a column, or several rows and columns, as long as all the cells are adjacent to one another. You use ranges in commands and formulas to perform operations on more than one cell at the same time. To use a range in a command or formula, you need to identify, or **specify** the range. You can specify a range in three ways: type the range address, use a range name, or highlight the range.

With some commands, such as /Print [Printer or File] Range, 1-2-3 "remembers" the most recent range you specified. The next time you select the same command, 1-2-3 automatically highlights the range you last specified and displays its address in the control panel. Press [Enter] to accept that range or press [Esc] or [Backspace] to clear the remembered range and specify a different range.

Typing a Range Address

You can specify a range by typing its range address, which consists of the cell addresses of the two most distant cells in the range, separated by one or two periods. This address follows these guidelines:

- If a range is a group of adjoining cells in a single column or row, the range address consists of the cell addresses of the two opposite ends of the range.

- If a range is a group of adjoining cells that spans several columns or rows, the range address consists of the cell addresses of any two diagonally opposite corners of the range.

- If a range is a single cell, the range address consists of that cell address as both the starting and ending point of the range, for example, B3..B3. To specify a single cell range, however, you need to type the cell address only once.

You can use either uppercase or lowercase letters when typing the range address. Once you enter the range address, however, 1-2-3 always displays it in uppercase letters. Also, regardless of which set of corner cells you use and whether you type one or two periods, 1-2-3 displays the range address as the range's upper left and lower right corner cells (except in a formula), separated by two periods.

Using Range Names

/Range Name Create and /Range Name Labels assign a name to a specified range, creating a range name. You can use range names in place of range addresses in commands and formulas. For example, if you want to move the data in A54..B98 and you have assigned the name SALES to that range, you can specify SALES instead of A54..B98 as the range to move. You can also use SALES in any @function that takes a range name or address as an argument, for example, @SUM(SALES).

Whenever a command prompts you for a range, you can specify a range name by typing the range name and pressing [Enter]. Alternatively, you can press [NAME] (F3) to display a menu of range names in the current worksheet and then select a name from the menu. You can also use press [NAME] (F3) when entering a formula.

Highlighting a Range

When 1-2-3 is in POINT mode, you can specify a range by highlighting it. To highlight a range, you must first **anchor** the cell pointer by moving it to a corner cell in the range and pressing [.] (Period). This cell is now the **anchor cell**.

Some commands that prompt you for ranges (such as /Copy, /Move, and /Range Format) automatically anchor the cell pointer in the current cell. When 1-2-3 asks you to specify a range, you can tell if the cell pointer is anchored by examining the prompt in the control panel. A single cell address (such as B3) means the cell pointer is not anchored, while a range address (B3..B3) means it is anchored.

If 1-2-3 automatically anchors the cell pointer and you want to highlight a range that starts somewhere else, press [Esc] to unanchor the cell pointer, move the cell pointer to the appropriate cell, and press [.] (Period) to anchor the cell pointer there.

Once a corner of the range you want to highlight is anchored, use the pointer-movement keys to expand the highlight until it covers the range. As you expand the highlight, 1-2-3 displays the address of the highlighted area in the control panel. When you have highlighted the entire range, press [Enter] to complete the range specification.

Working with Formulas

A formula is an entry that performs a calculation using numbers, other formulas, or strings. The calculation can be a simple mathematical operation, such as subtracting one number from another, or a more complicated operation, such as determining the net present value of a series of future cash flows. When you enter a formula, 1-2-3 displays the value that results from the calculation in the cell. When the cell pointer is in the cell, however, 1-2-3 displays the formula itself in the first line of the control panel.

You can use range addresses and range names in formulas to include worksheet data in your calculations. When you create a formula this way, 1-2-3 automatically changes the value of the formula if you change any value in the referenced cells. For example, suppose you enter the formula +B2+C2 in cell C4. When B2 and C2 contain the values 25 and 5, the formula results in the value 30. If you change the entry in either B2 or C2, 1-2-3 automatically changes the result of the formula.

1-2-3 lets you enter three types of formulas: numeric, string, and logical, in addition to **@functions**, which are built-in formulas in 1-2-3 that perform numeric, string, or logical calculations.

Type and description	Example and explanation
Numeric Calculates numeric values using arithmetic operators + – * / and ∧ and/or @functions.	**2 * H16** Multiplies value in H16 by 2. **@SUM(H16..H32)2.** Divides the sum of values in H16..H32 by 2.
String Calculates string values using the string operator & (Ampersand) and/or @functions.	**+"Dear Mr. and Mrs. "&D4** (D4 contains the label Robinson). Joins (concatenates) the text in quotation marks, called a literal string, with D4's contents: Dear Mr. and Mrs. Robinson.
Logical Returns either 1 (true) or 0 (false). Uses logical operators =, <, >, <=, >=, <>, #AND#, #OR#, #NOT#, and/or @functions.	**+A12>=500** Returns 1 (true) if A12 contains a value greater than or equal to 500; otherwise, returns 0 (false).

Note: *To display formulas in cells instead of their results, use /Range Format Text or /Worksheet Global Format Text.*

Entering Formulas

Note the following guidelines for formulas:

- A formula can begin with a number or one of the numeric symbols + – @ . (or $. In addition, the # symbol can be used to begin a logical formula.

- 1-2-3 can calculate any numeric formula whose value is between 10^{-308} and 10^{308}, but the value must be between 10^{-99} and 10^{99} for 1-2-3 to display it in the worksheet. When a formula's value is outside this range, 1-2-3 displays asterisks in the cell containing the formula.

- When the first element in a formula is a cell address, range name, or file reference, begin the formula with + – (or $. For example, +B7/B8, –B7*B8, $SALES/12, (SALES–EXPENSES), and +<<BUDGET.WK1>> B7 are all valid formulas.

- When a string formula starts with a literal string, begin the formula with + or (. For example, +"Ms.•"&LAST and ("Ms.•"&LAST) are both valid formulas. (Each • represents one space.)

- A formula can contain up to 240 characters, but no spaces, except within literal strings in string formulas.

Note: *If the specified cell or range in a formula has a range name, 1-2-3 automatically substitutes the name for the address in the formula. If the specified cell or range has more than one range name, 1-2-3 displays the range name that is alphabetically first.*

You can use the following types of data in a formula:

- Numbers (for example 450, –92, 7.1E12, date numbers, and time numbers)

- Literal strings enclosed in double quotes (for example, "Budget for" or "TOTAL")

- @Functions (for example, @SUM(A4..A8))

- Cell and range addresses (for example, B12, FF23..FH35)

- Range names (for example, JANSALES, BUDGET_90)

Order of Precedence

The following table shows the arithmetic, string, and logical operators you can use in formulas and their order of precedence. Precedence numbers represent the order in which 1-2-3 performs operations in a formula. The lower the precedence number, the earlier 1-2-3 performs the operation. Operations with the same precedence number are performed sequentially from left to right.

Operator	Precedence
^ (Exponentiation)	1
− or + (Identifies value as negative or positive)	2
* or / (Multiplication or division)	3
+ or − (Addition or subtraction)	4
= or < > (Equal-to or not- equal-to tests)	5
< or > (Less-than or greater-than tests)	5
<= (Less-than-or- equal-to test)	5
>= (Greater-than-or- equal-to test)	5
#NOT# (Logical-NOT test)	6
#AND# or #OR# (Logical-AND or logical-OR tests)	7
& (String concatenation)	7

You can override the order of precedence by enclosing an operation in parentheses. 1-2-3 performs operations inside parentheses first. Within each set of parentheses, precedence numbers apply. You can nest one set of parentheses inside another set and create as many nesting levels as you want.

Figure 1-3 shows the order in which 1-2-3 performs the operations in a formula that contains nested parentheses.

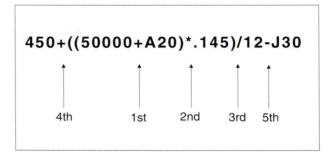

450+((50000+A20)*.145)/12-J30

4th   1st   2nd   3rd   5th

Figure 1-3 Order in which 1-2-3 performs operations

Using Cell and Range References in Formulas

To include a cell or range reference in a formula, you can use any of the three methods — typing, highlighting, or selecting a range name — as described earlier in this chapter in "Working with Ranges." You can use three types of cell and range references in a formula: **relative**, **absolute**, and **mixed**. The type of reference you use determines what happens when you copy the formula with /Copy.

Relative Reference A relative reference is a cell or range reference that 1-2-3 interprets as a location relative to the cell containing the formula cell. For example, when you enter the formula +B1+B2 in cell B4, 1-2-3 interprets the formula as "add the contents of the cell three rows above to the contents of the cell two rows above." If you later copy the formula, 1-2-3 adjusts the relative cell references. To create a relative reference in a formula, you simply type the address or range name, such as B1, D25..D30, or PROFITS.

Absolute References Sometimes when you copy a formula, you want 1-2-3 to keep the original cell or range reference in the copied formula. To keep the original cell or range reference in a formula, regardless of where that formula is copied, you use an **absolute reference**. To create an absolute address, type a $ (Dollar sign) in front of both the column letter and row number of the address (for example, $F$2 or $A$5..$B$10). To create an absolute range name, type a $ in front of the range name ($RATE).

Mixed References Sometimes when you copy a formula that references a cell, you want part of the cell address to stay the same in the copied formula and part of the address to change. For example, you may want the column letter to stay the same and the row number to change. You do this by using a **mixed cell address** in the formula. Mixed references can be created only with addresses, not with range names. To create a mixed reference, precede the column letter or the row number with a $ (Dollar sign) — for example, $C4 or C$4.

Using [ABS] (F4) to Change Reference Types

When entering or editing a formula, press [ABS] (F4) when the cursor is on or immediately to the right of a cell address or range address. 1-2-3 cycles the address through the different reference types. 1-2-3 always cycles through the types of cell address in the same order, regardless of whether the original address type is relative, absolute, or mixed.

For example, the following table shows how pressing [ABS] (F4) changes the address C5 after you type +C5.

When Control Panel displays	Press [ABS] (F4) to display
+C5	$C$5 (absolute address)
+$C$5	C$5 (mixed address with absolute row reference)
+C$5	$C5 (mixed address with absolute column reference)
+$C5	C5 (relative address)

A range name is a relative reference unless you include a $ (Dollar sign) in front of the name. For example, if you are using the range name SALES in a formula and you want it to be an absolute reference, type $SALES. You cannot create a mixed reference with a range name.

Linking Files

1-2-3's file-linking feature allows you to use values from cells in other worksheets in the **current worksheet** (the worksheet file currently in memory). You create a link between two files by entering a linking formula in one file that refers to a cell in the other file. The file in which you enter the formula is called the **target file** because it receives the data. The file that the formula refers to is called the **source file** because it supplies the data.

Once the two files are linked, 1-2-3 copies the value of the cell in the source file (the **source cell**) to the cell in the target file (the **target cell**). The value of the target cell is automatically updated whenever you retrieve the target file or, if using 1-2-3 on a network, select /File Admin Link-Refresh while you are working on the target file.

File linking saves you the effort of manually updating every worksheet affected by a change in another worksheet. One of the most useful applications of file linking is the consolidation of data from a number of worksheets in a summary worksheet. You can also use the linking feature to create links to cells that depend on other linked cells.

If the data you are linking to depends on other linked cells, you can get incorrect results unless you update the files in an "upward" order within the hierarchy of links. Always start updating at the lower level — retrieving the file, making changes, and saving the file — and work to the top level — retrieve the file and then resave it to update its values.

Note: *When you use /File Directory, 1-2-3 updates any linking formula in which the source file reference does not include a path. For example, if a file named SOURCE.WK1 exists in C:\1990 and a file named SOURCE.WK1 also exists in C:\1991, then changing the current file directory from C:\1990 to C:\1991 will update the target file to use SOURCE.WK1 in the 1991 directory.*

Creating a Link

To create a **linking formula**, a formula that refers to a cell in another file, you must use the following format:

+ << *file reference* >> *cell reference*

The file and cell references can be entered in uppercase or lowercase letters. 1-2-3 will always display the references in uppercase letters.

When entering a file reference, you may need to enter additional information.

- If the source file does not have the default file extension .WK1, you must include the appropriate file extension.

- If the source file is not in the default directory (the directory specified with /File Directory), you must include a directory name to tell 1-2-3 where to look for the file.

- If the source file is not on the disk in the default drive (the drive specified with /File Directory), you must include a drive name to tell 1-2-3 where to look for the file.

If any of the following conditions exist, 1-2-3 displays an error message when you try to enter the formula:

- The source file does not exist.

- The specified directory does not exist so 1-2-3 cannot find the source file.

- The specified drive is not ready (for example, you have not closed the door on a diskette drive).

- The specified range name does not exist in the source file.

- The source file is a password-protected worksheet.

- You are sharing files on a network and the source file is being retrieved or saved by another user.

- The data in the file cannot be read by 1-2-3.

Tips and Restrictions for Linking Files

The following discussion provides additional information to help you link files:

- You can use absolute, relative, and mixed reference cell references in a linking formula. If you copy the linking formula to another location in the target file, 1-2-3 will adjust cell references in the copied formulas properly.

- If you are sharing files on a network and you have entered linking formulas in the current worksheet, you should periodically use /File Admin Link-Refresh to update the linking formulas, because other network users may be making changes to the source files referenced by the linking formulas. It is also recommended that you always select /File Admin Link-Refresh before saving the worksheet.

You should be aware of the following restrictions before you try to link files:

- If you did not include a path as part of the file reference and the source file is no longer in the default directory (for example, if you used /File Directory or /Worksheet Global Default Directory to change the default directory), 1-2-3 displays ERR in the target cell.

- If you erase or rename the source file referenced in a linking formula, 1-2-3 displays ERR in the target cell the next time you retrieve the target file.

- If you delete or reset a range name referenced in a linking formula, 1-2-3 displays ERR in the target cell the next time you retrieve the target file.

- You cannot include a linking formula in another formula. For example, +<<USSALES>>C15 *<<UKSALES>>D30 and @ROUND(<<UKSALES>>A12 ,2) are not valid formulas.

- If you reference a cell address in a linking formula, and you subsequently move the source cell to a different location in the source file, 1-2-3 does not adjust the linking formula. For this reason, it is good practice to use /Range Name Create to name the source cell and then use that range name as the cell reference in the linking formula. This will maintain the correct link if you move the source cell.

Using the Undo Feature

The Undo feature is an important safeguard against time-consuming mistakes. You can use it whenever the UNDO indicator is displayed on the status line at the bottom of the screen. If the UNDO indicator is not displayed, pressing [UNDO] (Alt-F4) will have no effect.

When the Undo feature is on, you can press [UNDO] (Alt-F4) when 1-2-3 is in READY mode to cancel the most recent operation that changed worksheet data and/or settings. When you use [UNDO] (Alt-F4), 1-2-3 automatically restores whatever worksheet data and settings existed the last time 1-2-3 was in READY mode. In addition, if you change your mind about what you just undid, you can press [UNDO] (Alt-F4) again and 1-2-3 will undo the effect of the Undo operation.

You can use Undo to reverse the effects of both simple data entry errors and much more complex operations. For example, suppose you accidentally write over a complicated formula by entering a number in the same cell as the formula. If the Undo feature is on, you can cancel the mistake by pressing [UNDO] (Alt-F4) immediately after entering the number; 1-2-3 erases the new entry and restores the formula in the cell.

What You Need to Know to Use Undo

Undo is a valuable tool. However, before you use it, you should be aware of these important specifics to guard against unexpected results when you use [UNDO] (Alt-F4).

- Initially, the Undo feature is on, but you can turn it off with /Worksheet Global Default Other Undo Disable. If you then use /Worksheet Global Default Update to modify the 1-2-3 configuration file, Undo will automatically be turned off whenever you start 1-2-3. In order to undo your last operation, 1-2-3 must reserve a portion of memory to keep a copy of the worksheet. This reduces the amount of available memory.

- Any series of 1-2-3 commands performed after you press / (Slash) to display the main menu and before 1-2-3 returns to READY mode is a single undoable operation. For example, if you select /Graph, complete a series of Graph commands without leaving the /Graph menu, and then return 1-2-3 to READY mode, pressing [UNDO] (Alt-F4) cancels the entire series of Graph commands you completed.

- If you press [UNDO] (Alt-F4) after running a macro, 1-2-3 returns your worksheet data and settings to the state they were in prior to running the macro, regardless of how many individual changes the macro made. If you did not run the macro from READY mode, 1-2-3 returns the worksheet to the state it was in when you last left READY mode. If you use Undo immediately after 1-2-3 finishes running an autoexecute macro, 1-2-3 undoes the effects of the macro and the /File Retrieve operation.

- If you turn off the Undo feature, then retrieve a worksheet or attach an add-in, and then try to turn on Undo, you will not be able to do so if any part of the Undo buffer is in conventional memory. This is because 1-2-3 cannot reserve the memory it needs for the Undo buffer once you have retrieved a worksheet or attached an add-in. To turn on Undo in these situations, save the worksheet with /File Save, erase it with /Worksheet Erase, or detach the add-in with /Add-In Detach. Then turn on Undo with /Worksheet Global Default Other Undo Enable, and retrieve the worksheet or attach the add-in again.

When Does 1-2-3 Back Up the Worksheet?

1-2-3 creates a temporary backup copy of the worksheet, including data, range names, and settings, when you press any key that might lead to a worksheet change. For example, 1-2-3 backs up the worksheet when you press / (Slash) to display the main menu, press a character that begins a label or value, or press the [TABLE] (F8) or [QUERY] (F9) keys. This allows 1-2-3 to restore your work to its previous state if you press [UNDO] (Alt-F4).

Note that 1-2-3 does not wait for you to complete a command or cell entry before backing up the worksheet. Therefore, if you press / (Slash) to select a new command but then press [Esc] because you decide you want to undo your previous operation, you will not be able to undo the previous operation because 1-2-3 backed up the worksheet as soon as you pressed /, (Slash).

What Operations Can't You Undo?

Some 1-2-3 commands (such as /File Save and /File Erase) create, modify, or delete files on disk. When you press [UNDO] (Alt-F4) to undo one of these commands, 1-2-3 undoes any changes to the state of the worksheet, including worksheet data, range names, and settings. 1-2-3 cannot, however, undo the changes the command made to files on disk.

If you press [UNDO] (Alt-F4) after using /Print Printer Go, 1-2-3 undoes any changes you made to 1-2-3 print settings with the Print [Printer or File] commands, but it cannot undo any changes the command made to your printer's internal settings.

Although you can press [UNDO] (Alt-F4) to undo the changes you make to most 1-2-3 settings, there are a few exceptions: the default directory setting (/File Directory and /Worksheet Global Default Directory); the Help access method (/Worksheet Global Default Other Help); and, with networks, the current file's reservation status, if you use /File Admin Reservation Get or Release to change it.

Reference 2

Commands

This chapter describes each command in detail. The commands are listed in alphabetical order.

Contents

This chapter contains the following sections:

The Add-In Commands

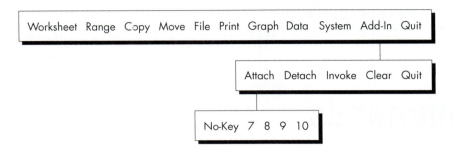

The Add-In commands let you use 1-2-3 add-in applications. **Add-ins** are programs created by Lotus and other software developers that you can run while you are using 1-2-3 and that provide 1-2-3 with additional capabilities. Your 1-2-3 package includes one add-in — the Macro Library Manager add-in — which lets you store macros, formulas, and ranges of data in a library that you can use with any worksheet. For information on using the Macro Library Manager, see *Reference 4*.

You can use the Add-In commands by selecting /Add-In from the 1-2-3 main menu or by pressing [APP4] (Alt-F10) if you have not assigned that key to an add-in program. The Add-In commands perform the following tasks:

/Add-In Attach Loads an add-in program into memory (see below).

/Add-In Clear Removes all attached add-in programs from memory (except add-in @functions).

/Add-In Detach Removes an attached add-in program from memory (except add-in @functions). You must specify the filename of the add-in to remove.

/Add-In Invoke Activates an attached add-in program (see below).

/Add-In Attach

/Add-In Attach lets you load an add-in program into memory. Add-ins remain in memory until you detach them or until you end the current 1-2-3 session. An attached add-in is not activated until you select /Add-In Invoke or press the key you have assigned to the add-in.

❶ If you have a two-diskette system, make sure the disk that contains the add-in is in one of the diskette drives. ❷ Select /Add-In Attach to display a menu of files with the .ADN extension in the directory from which you started 1-2-3. ❸ Edit the drive and/or directory name, if necessary, to display .ADN files in another directory and then press [Enter]. ❹ Specify the filename of the add-in you want to attach and press [Enter]. ❺ Select the key, if any, you want to use to invoke the add-in:

Key	Description
No-Key	Does not assign the add-in to any key (invoke using /Add-In Invoke).
7	Assigns the add-in to [APP1] (Alt-F7).
8	Assigns the add-in to [APP2] (Alt-F8).
9	Assigns the add-in to [APP3] (Alt-F9).
10	Assigns the add-in to [APP4] (Alt-F10).

Note: *The amount of conventional memory in your computer determines the maximum number of add-ins you can attach at one time.*

/Add-In Invoke

/Add-In Invoke lets you activate an add-in program that you have attached with /Add-In Attach. If you assigned the add-in to a key, you can use that key to invoke the add-in.

❶ Select /Add-In Invoke to display the names of all attached add-ins. ❷ Specify the name of the add-in you want to invoke and press [Enter] to pass control to the add-in program.

The Copy Command

/Copy copies a range of data and the cell formats to another range in the same worksheet. Use /Copy to make one copy or multiple copies of a range of data.

When you copy formulas, 1-2-3 may adjust cell references in the formulas, depending on the kind of cell references you use. Before you use /Copy to copy formulas, be sure that the cell reference in the formula corresponds to the type of copy you intend: relative, absolute, or mixed. This applies to all copied formulas, including formulas using range names.

- If a formula contains relative cell references, 1-2-3 adjusts the references in the copied formula to refer to the new worksheet location. The copied formula now refers to different cells, but cells that are in the same position relative to the cell that contains the formula.

- If a formula contains absolute cell references, 1-2-3 retains the specific cell or range address.

- If a formula contains mixed cell references, 1-2-3 adjusts the relative part of the cell reference in the copied formula and retains the absolute part of the cell reference.

/Copy

❶ Select /Copy. ❷ Specify the range you want to copy FROM and press [Enter]. ❸ Specify the range you want to copy TO and press [Enter].

If you are copying a range from one location to another, you need to specify only the upper left cell in the TO range. If the FROM range is one cell and the TO range is larger than one cell, 1-2-3 makes multiple copies of the same data. If your TO and FROM ranges overlap, you may get unexpected results.

Caution: *The TO range can be any unprotected area of the worksheet. Make sure, however, that the worksheet location is blank or contains unimportant data; 1-2-3 writes over existing data when it copies data to the range you specify. To avoid possible data loss , save the worksheet before using /Copy. If you make a mistake when copying data and the Undo feature is on, press [UNDO] (Alt-F4) to restore the worksheet to its original state.*

The Data Commands

The Data commands let you analyze and manipulate data in ranges and in 1-2-3 databases. Use the Data commands to perform the following tasks:

/Data Distribution Calculates the frequency of values in a range that fall within specified numeric intervals.

/Data Fill Enters a sequence of values in a specified range.

/Data Matrix Inverts or multiplies matrices formed by rows and columns of entries.

/Data Parse Converts a column of long labels into a range of labels or numbers.

/Data Query Locates and edits selected records in a database.

/Data Regression Performs a regression analysis (determines the relationships among up to 16 independent variables) on data.

/Data Sort Arranges data in a range or records in a database in the order you specify.

/Data Table Calculates values based on what-if scenarios.

1-2-3 Databases

A 1-2-3 **database** is a range of related data organized in rows and columns in a worksheet. A worksheet can contain many different databases, each of which contains **records** and **fields**. A record is a collection of information about one item in a database, and a field is a category that each record in the database has in common.

In a 1-2-3 database, each row is a record and each column is a field. The top row of a database contains the field names, one per column. The **field names** are the labels that identify the fields in the database. Any collection of data that you organize in records and fields can be a database in 1-2-3.

When you create a 1-2-3 database, follow these guidelines:

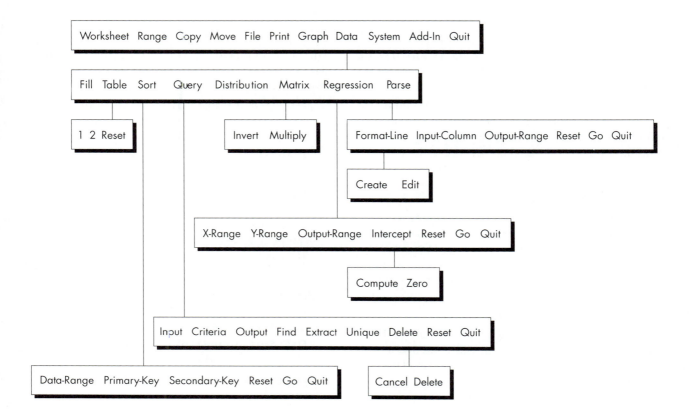

- The first row of the database must contain the field names. Subsequent rows must contain the records. Do not insert any blank rows or divider lines between the field names (the first row) and the records.
- The entries in a field must be either all labels or all values. Do not enter values in some records and labels in other records for the same field.
- Field names must be unique within a database.
- A database can contain up to 256 fields and 8,191 records.

Caution: *Many Data commands create output ranges in the same worksheet where you have entered data. Always save your worksheet before using Data commands for which you specify output ranges to avoid losing data by writing over existing data by mistake. If you make a mistake and the commands Undo feature is on, press [UNDO] (Alt-F4) to restore the worksheet.*

/Data Distribution

/Data Distribution lets you calculate the frequency distribution of a value within a range by counting the number of values in a range (**the values range**) that fall within specified numeric intervals (**the bin range**). Before you use Data Distribution, you must specify a values range and create a bin range in the worksheet. The values range can be any range of values in the worksheet. Be sure that the values are together in a range and that there are no blank cells or cells that contain either labels, ERR, or NA within the range.

For the bin range, find two empty adjacent columns and enter the values, or intervals, you want 1-2-3 to use to distribute the data in the first column as the bin range. 1-2-3 automatically uses the empty adjacent column to the right as an output range for entering the frequency distribution when you select the command. You can use any values (including formulas) in the bin range, as long as each value within the range is unique, and the values are in ascending order (smallest value at the top).

❶ Enter values in a bin range. ❷ Select /Data Distribution. ❸ Specify the values range and press [Enter]. ❹ Specify a single column as the bin range and press [Enter].

1-2-3 places the frequency values in the column to the right of the bin range. The last frequency value in the column appears in the row below the last row of the bin range. These numbers represent how many values in the values range are less than or equal to the adjacent value in the bin range, but greater than the preceding value. The last number in the column is the number of values in the values range that are greater than the last value in the bin range.

/Data Fill

/Data Fill lets you enter a sequence of values in a specified range called the **fill range**. The range is automatically filled with values according to the information you enter at the prompts. 1-2-3 prompts you for a start value, a step value, and a stop value. The **start value** (default value 0) is the first value 1-2-3 enters in the fill range, the **step value** (default value 1) is the increment between each of the values in the sequence, and the **stop value** (default value 8191) is the value 1-2-3 uses as a limit (or stopping place) for the sequence.

The start, step, and stop values can be any value (including a formula, a cell, or a range name that evaluates to a value). If you specify a negative step value, you must specify a stop value that is less than the start value. 1-2-3 fills cells column by column, from left to right.

❶ Select /Data Fill. ❷ Specify the fill range and press [Enter]. ❸ Specify the start value and press [Enter]. ❹ Specify the step value and press [Enter]. ❺ Specify the stop value and press [Enter].

/Data Matrix

/Data Matrix lets you perform two of the most common matrix algebra operations — matrix inversion and matrix multiplication. You can also use it to solve simultaneous equations.

/Data Matrix Invert

/Data Matrix Invert lets you create the inverse of a matrix. Note that only square matrices have inverses, but not all square matrices have inverses. If you try to use /Data Matrix Invert on a matrix that has no inverse, 1-2-3 displays an error message.

❶ Select /Data Matrix Invert. ❷ Specify the matrix range you want to invert and press [Enter].The matrix range must have the same number of columns and rows, and can contain up to 80 columns and 80 rows. ❸ Specify the output range (where 1-2-3 enters the results of the inversion) and press [Enter].

/Data Matrix Multiply

/Data Matrix Multiply lets you multiply the columns of one matrix by the rows of a second matrix and creates a third matrix that contains the results of the multiplication. When you multiply matrices, there must be the same number of columns in the first matrix as there are rows in the second matrix. 1-2-3 can multiply any matrix of values up to a maximum of 256 rows by 256 columns. The resulting matrix will have the same number of rows as the first matrix and the same number of columns as the second matrix.

❶ Select /Data Matrix Multiply. ❷ Specify the first range you want to multiply and press [Enter]. ❸ Specify the second range you want to multiply and press [Enter]. ❹ Specify the output range (where 1-2-3 enters the results of the multiplication) and press [Enter].

/Data Parse

1-2-3 treats data you import with /File Import Text as long labels. /Data Parse lets you convert a column of long labels into a range of numbers or labels. Long labels are contained in one column, even though the data may appear to extend across several columns. You can view or print long labels, but you cannot perform calculations on numbers in long labels, nor can you break apart or move a long label easily. /Data Parse let you convert an imported text file into separate columns of data by using the following commands:

Format-Line Creates or edits a format line to control how 1-2-3 divides a long label into individual cell entries.

Go Parses the labels in the input column and places them in the output range.

Input-Column Specifies the single column range that contains the format line and data you want to parse. The first cell in the input column must be a format line.

Output-Range Specifies the range where 1-2-3 places the parsed data. If you specify one cell, 1-2-3 uses that cell as the upper left corner of the output range.

Quit Returns 1-2-3 to READY mode without parsing the data.

Reset Clears the input column and output range settings.

A **format line** determines the way 1-2-3 parses the label below the format line into individual entries, separating the label wherever there are one or more spaces. When you use /Data Parse Format-Line Create, 1-2-3 analyzes the label in the current cell, inserts a row, creates a format line in that cell, and moves the range of data down one row. 1-2-3 treats each group of characters separated by one or more blank spaces as a single **data block** and identifies each of these data blocks as one of the following data types: a value, date, time, or label. The characters in the format line represent the data type and width of each of the data blocks. 1-2-3 uses the format line to guess how it should parse the label.

Format lines can contain the following symbols:

Symbol	Description
D	Represents the first character of a date block.
L	Represents the first character of a label block.
S	Skips the data block immediately below the symbol when parsing. You enter the skip symbol (S) when you edit a format line. Use this symbol when your labels include a data block you do not want 1-2-3 to parse.
T	Represents the first character of a time block.
V	Represents the first character of a value block.
>	Represents characters in a data block. For example, 1-2-3 displays a value block that is four characters wide as V>>>.
*	Represents blank space that can become part of a data block if that block in any label requires extra characters.

Caution: *You must include as many character symbols or asterisks in the format line as the longest label in any one block, or you may lose data.*

How to Use /Data Parse

❶ Position the cell pointer in the cell that contains the first long label you want to parse. ❷ Select /Data Parse Format-Line Create. 1-2-3 creates a format line and returns to the Parse submenu. If necessary, use /Data Parse Format-Line Edit to edit the format line. ❸ Select Input-Column and specify the column range that contains the format lines and labels you want to parse. (The first cell in the input column range must contain a format line.) ❹ Select Output-Range and specify the address or range name of the first cell in a blank range large enough to hold the parsed data. ❺ Select Go.

1-2-3 produces a parsed copy of the imported data. In some cases, you may need to create additional format lines or edit the current format line to better suit your imported data.

Create an additional format line if any label contains a block whose data type or width does not match the format line. Or, if your imported data contains titles, column headings, other descriptive labels, or a row of characters separating different parts of the worksheet, create a format line to parse this data correctly.

Edit the format line if the data block (including adjacent * characters) is not wide enough to accommodate the data to be parsed, if any block width or data type character is incorrect, or if any single block contains a space.

Note: *If a data block contains an ambiguous entry — that is, data that could be assigned more than one data type — 1-2-3 determines the data type using the following order of precedence: value, date, time, and label.*

Several keys have special functions when you use them to edit a format line.

Key	Description
[↑]	Scrolls the unparsed labels below the format line up one row at a time so you can compare each label with the format line.
[↓]	Scrolls the unparsed labels below the format line down one row at a time so you can compare each label with the format line.
[Ctrl][Break]	Cancels edits you made to the format line and returns 1-2-3 to READY mode.
[Esc]	Erases the format line, but does not delete the row.
[Home]	Returns the cursor to its initial position in the format line and, if you scrolled the unparsed labels below the format line, displays the unparsed labels that were visible before you began scrolling.
[PgDn]	Scrolls the unparsed labels below the format line down by the number of rows on the screen so you can compare each label with the format line.
[PgUp]	Scrolls the unparsed labels below the format line up by the number of rows on the screen so you can compare each label with the format line.

/Data Query

The Data Query commands let you locate and edit selected records in a database. Use the Data Query commands to perform the following tasks:

Criteria Specifies the criteria range, which contains the selection criteria for records in the database.

Delete Deletes the records in the input range that match the criteria you specified in the criteria range.

Extract Copies the records in the input range that match the criteria you specified in the criteria range to the output range.

Find Highlights the records in the input range that match the criteria you specified in the criteria range.

Input Specifies the range that contains the records you want to search.

Output Specifies the range in which you want 1-2-3 to place the results of /Data Query Extract or /Data Query Unique.

Quit Returns 1-2-3 to READY mode.

Reset Clears the input, criteria, and output ranges.

Unique Copies the records in the input range that match the criteria you specified in the criteria range to the output range. Unlike /Data Query Extract, /Data Query Unique eliminates any duplicate records in the output range.

You can use [QUERY] (F7) to repeat the last query operation you performed. You can change values in the database or the criteria range and then repeat the query without using the menu.

Before you can use /Data Query to locate or work with records in a database, you need to create three ranges: an input range, a criteria range, and an output range. When you select /Data Query, 1-2-3 displays a settings sheet and you enter the locations of the ranges by selecting one of the /Data Query commands. 1-2-3 uses these ranges when you use the /Data Query commands to find, copy, or delete records.

The **input range** specifies the location of the database you are using. The **criteria range** provides information (the criteria) 1-2-3 uses to evaluate the database records. The **output range** is where 1-2-3 places copies of the data that matches the criteria when you use /Data Query Extract or /Data Query Unique. (An output range is not required if you only want to highlight or delete matching records with /Data Query Find or /Data Query Delete.)

When you set up a criteria range, you must enter criteria to tell 1-2-3 which records to search for in a database. **Criteria** are cell entries that 1-2-3 uses to test and evaluate records in a database. The criteria determine whether or not a /Data Query command selects or affects a particular record. You can write criteria that match either label or value entries in the database and you can use more than one criteria.

Follow these guidelines for entering label criteria:

- To search for exact matches, enter labels exactly as they appear in the input range.

- Use the symbols ? and * to search for similar labels in the input range: ? matches any single character; * matches all characters to the end of a label.

- Precede a label with a ~ (tilde) to search for all labels except that one. For example, ~Smith matches all records with an entry in that field other than Smith.

- Combine the label-matching symbols to create label criteria. For example, ~S* matches all records with an entry in that field that do not begin with S.

- 1-2-3 never matches a label criterion with blank cells in the input range.

Follow these guidelines for entering value criteria:

- To search for exact value matches, enter the value as the criterion. The format does not need to match the format of the value in the database.

- You can enter one or more formulas linked by logical operators to search for values that meet a condition you set, such as all entries greater than 1500. Enter the condition as a logical expression in the criteria range, using the cell address of the corresponding field of the first record in the database. You can use any of the logical operators listed in "Working with Formulas" in *Reference 1* in your formula to compare a cell entry to a given value.

- Use relative cell addresses in formulas that refer to database fields in the input range. Use absolute cell addresses to refer to values outside the input range. For example, use the criterion +B2<>C2 to search for records whose entry in the B field is not equal to its entry in the C field. Use +B2<>$J$2 to search for records whose entry in the B field is not equal to the value in J2 outside the database.

- You can enter formulas that contain database @functions. Make sure the database @function does not refer to that criteria range that results in a circular reference, causing 1-2-3 to display an error message when you perform the query.

Follow these guidelines for entering multiple field criteria:

- Enter criteria for different fields in a single-row of the criteria range to search for only those records that match all the criteria at once. 1-2-3 treats criteria in the same row as if they were linked by the logical operator #AND#.

- A blank cell in the criteria range tells 1-2-3 to include any records in the input range, as long as the records match the other criteria.

- Enter criteria for different fields in separate rows of the criteria range to search for records that match any of the criteria. 1-2-3 treats criteria in separate rows as if they were linked by the logical operator #OR#.

- If a multiple-row criteria range contains a blank row, 1-2-3 ignores the blank row and selects all the records that match any criteria in the remaining row(s) of the criteria range.

- Use the logical operators #AND#, #NOT#, or #OR# in formulas to create criteria that match more than one condition in the same field.

/Data Query Criteria

/Data Query Criteria lets you specify the criteria range, which contains the selection criteria for records in the database. The criteria range must include a top row containing the field names of the fields you want to query and one or more rows below containing the criteria. You must use /Data Query Criteria before you can complete any data query operation.

❶ Select /Data Query Criteria. ❷ Specify the criteria range and press [Enter].

/Data Query Delete

/Data Query Delete lets you delete the records in the input range that match the criteria you specified in the criteria range and shrink the input range to remove the blank rows. As a safety precaution, 1-2-3 prompts you for confirmation before it deletes the records. Use /Data Query Find to preview the records that 1-2-3 will delete before 1-2-3 deletes the records. /Data Query Delete does *not* highlight the records before deleting them.

❶ Before you use /Data Query Delete, you must specify an input range and a criteria range. ❷ Select /Data Query Delete. ❸ Select Cancel to return to the /Data Query menu without deleting any records, or Delete to delete all records in the input range that match the criteria in the criteria range.

/Data Query Extract

/Data Query Extract lets you copy to the output range the records in the input range that match the criteria you specified in the criteria range.

❶ Specify an input range, a criteria range, and an output range. ❷ Select /Data Query Extract.

1-2-3 copies to the output range the records from the input range(s) that match your criteria. The records are in the same order they were in the database. 1-2-3 copies only data for the fields you explicitly included in the output range.

/Data Query Find

/Data Query Find lets you locate the records in the input range that match the criteria you specified in the criteria range. Use /Data Query Find to locate records that you want to edit.

❶ Specify an input range and a criteria range. ❷ Select /Data Query Find. 1-2-3 highlights the first record in the input range that matches the criteria. If there are no matching records, 1-2-3 returns to the /Data Query menu. ❸ Use the keys in the following table to move among the matching records in the input range. ❹ Press [Enter] and select Quit to return 1-2-3 to READY mode.

Key	Description
[↑]	Moves the cell pointer up to other records in the input range that match the criteria. If there are no more matching records in that direction, 1-2-3 beeps.
[↓]	Moves the cell pointer down to other records in the input range that match the criteria. If there are no more matching records in that direction, 1-2-3 beeps.
[←]	Moves the cursor left one field within a highlighted record.
[→]	Moves the cursor right one field within a highlighted record.
[EDIT] (F2)	Lets you edit the field displayed in the current record. Press [Enter] to save the changes and continue using /Data Query Find; press [Esc] to cancel the changes and continue using /Data Query Find.
[Esc]	Moves the cell pointer to the last record in the input range.
[Esc] or [Enter]	Ends /Data Query Find and returns you to the /Data Query menu.
[Home]	Moves the cell pointer to the first record in the input range that matches the criteria.
[QUERY] (F7)	Ends /Data Query Find, leaves the cell pointer in the current cell, and returns 1-2-3 to READY mode.

/Data Query Input

/Data Query Input lets you specify the range that contains the records you want 1-2-3 to search. You must use /Data Query Input before you can complete any data query operation. Be sure to include the field names in the first row.

❶ Select /Data Query Input. ❷ Specify an input range containing all the data you want to query and press [Enter].

/Data Query Output

/Data Query Output lets you specify the range in which you want 1-2-3 to place the results of /Data Query Extract or /Data Query Unique. You must use /Data Query Output before you can use either of these commands. Be sure to include the field names as the first row.

❶ Select /Data Query Output. ❷ Specify the output range as either a single-row or multiple-row range and press [Enter].

Specify a single-row output range containing just the field names if you have a lot of empty space below the field names and are not concerned about any existing entries being written over. 1-2-3 uses as many rows below the field names as it needs.

Specify a multiple-row output range with the field names as the first row if you want to be certain that 1-2-3 does not write over existing entries. 1-2-3 writes only to the multiple-row range you specify. If the range is not large enough to accommodate all the records that match your selection criteria, 1-2-3 displays an error message.

/Data Query Quit

/Data Query Quit lets you return 1-2-3 to READY mode.

/Data Query Reset

/Data Query Reset lets you clear the range address settings for the input, criteria, and output ranges you specified.

/Data Query Unique

/Data Query Unique lets you perform the same operation as /Data Query Extract except you can eliminate any duplicate records in the output range. /Data Query Unique uses the fields in the output range to match duplicates. For example, even though two records in the input range are not exactly alike, if the output range contains only fields that are the same for those two records, 1-2-3 does not copy the second record.

❶ Specify an input range, a criteria range, and an output range. ❷ Select /Data Query Unique.

1-2-3 copies to the output range the records in the input range that match your criteria, eliminating any duplicate records in the output range. Like /Data Query Extract, 1-2-3 keeps the records in the same order they were in in the database.

/Data Regression

/Data Regression lets you perform a regression analysis on existing data. A **regression analysis** is a statistical procedure used to predict future data based on current data or to show the relationship between one variable and others.

> **Go**   Calculates a data regression for the selected X range, Y range, and output range.
>
> **Intercept**   Determines whether 1-2-3 calculates the y axis intercept automatically (default) or uses zero as the intercept. The y axis intercept appears in the results as the constant.
>
> **Output-Range**   Specifies the range where 1-2-3 enters the results of the regression analysis.
>
> **Quit**   Returns 1-2-3 to READY mode.
>
> **Reset**   Clears the X range, Y range, and output range; resets the intercept to Compute.
>
> **X-Range**   Specifies the independent variables.
>
> **Y-Range**   Specifies the dependent variable.

Use /Data Regression to predict a value for a dependent variable based on the values for one or more independent variables. /Data Regression also indicates the statistical accuracy of these values. You can also use /Data Regression when you have several sets of values and you want to see how and whether one set is dependent on the others, as well as to fit a straight line through a series of points.

Before you can use /Data Regression to perform a regression analysis, you need to create three data regression ranges: an X range, a Y range, and an output range. The X range contains the independent variables in the database. The Y range contains the dependent variable in the database. The output range is where 1-2-3 will place the results of the regression analysis.

❶ Select /Data Regression. ❷ Select X-Range, specify the independent variables and press [Enter]. ❸ Select Y-Range, specify the Y range and press [Enter]. ❹ If you select Intercept, select either Compute to calculate the y axis intercept automatically; or Zero to use zero as the y axis intercept. (Do not select Zero unless your data is such that when all of the independent variables equal zero, the dependent variable must equal zero.) ❺ Select Output-Range, specify the output range in a blank area of the worksheet, and press [Enter]. ❻ Select Go to calculate the regression or select Quit to return 1-2-3 to READY mode without calculating the regression.

When you perform a data regression, 1-2-3 enters the following information in the output range:

Item	Description
Constant	The y axis intercept.
Degrees of freedom	The number of observations minus the number of independent variables minus 1. If you use a zero intercept, the degrees of freedom equal the number of observations minus the number of independent variables.
No. of observations	The number of rows of data in the X and Y ranges.
R squared	A measure of the reliability of the regression (a value from 0 to 1, inclusive).
Std Err of Coef	The standard error of each of the x coefficients.
Std Err of Y Est	The standard error of the estimated y values.
X coefficient(s)	The slope for each independent variable.

Note: *If 1-2-3 displays an R squared value less than zero, you may have specified a zero intercept when it was not appropriate to do so. Use /Data Regression Intercept Compute and then /Data Regression Go to recalculate the regression and adjust the R^2 value accordingly.*

/Data Sort

/Data Sort lets you arrange the data in a range in the order you specify. The range can be records in a database or rows in the worksheet. Use the following commands to perform a data sort:

Data-Range Selects the range you want to sort.

Go Sorts the data according to the current selections and returns 1-2-3 to READY mode.

Primary-Key Determines the primary field for sorting records or rows. The data can be in either ascending or descending order.

Quit Returns 1-2-3 to READY mode and does not sort the records or rows.

Reset Clears range address settings and sort keys.

Secondary-Key Determines the order for records or rows that have the same primary sort key entries. The data can be in either ascending or descending order.

Make sure that the data you want to sort is in a range, and that you have similar data in the columns of the range. You must specify a data range and a primary sort key before you select /Data Sort Go. A secondary sort key is optional. When you select /Data Sort, 1-2-3 displays a settings sheet where you enter the location of the data range, primary sort key, and secondary sort key. These are the settings 1-2-3 uses to perform a sort.

Note: *The data range must contain all the fields for all the records or rows you want to sort. If you are sorting a database, do not include the field names (the first row of the database).*

❶ Select /Data Sort Data-Range. ❷ Specify the range you want to sort and press [Enter]. ❸ Select Primary-Key. ❹ Specify the primary sort key by entering the cell address of any cell in the field you want 1-2-3 to use to determine the new order for your records. ❺ Enter the primary sort order (A for ascending or D for descending). ❻ If some records have the same entries in the primary sort key field and you want these records arranged in a specific order, then select Secondary-Key. ❼ Specify the secondary sort key by entering the cell address of any cell in the field you want 1-2-3 to use to break ties in the primary sort key field and press [Enter]. ❽ Enter the secondary sort order (A for ascending or D for descending). ❾ Select Go to sort the database or range.

Caution: *Be careful when you sort ranges that contain formulas. If a cell that contains a formula moves when you select /Data Sort Go, 1-2-3 adjusts relative cell addresses in the formulas to reflect the new position of the cell.*

Note: *You may want to use /Data Fill to enter a field of record numbers in a database before you use /Data Sort, and include the record numbers in the data range. You can then use the field that contains these numbers as the primary sort key if you want to resort the records back to their original order.*

/Data Table

The Data Table commands produce tables that show the results of a formula that calculates each time you change a value in the formula. You can use the Data Table commands to perform "what-if" or "sensitivity" analyses and cross-tabulate the information in a 1-2-3 database.

How to Use /Data Table

Before using /Data Table you must have a formula containing a variable, plus the input values you want 1-2-3 to substitute for the variable. For example, suppose you have a formula that multiplies an hourly wage by a changing number of hours to calculate the payment due. The variable is the number of hours; the input values are the range of hours you specify. 1-2-3 will then calculate the range of payments due.

1-2-3 can create two types of data tables: one-way and two-way. The type of data table you create depends on the number of variables you want to use in your formulas. Use /Data Table 1 if you have a formula with one variable for which you want to substitute a range of numbers; use /Data Table 2 if you have a formula with two variables for which you want to substitute a range of numbers. Formulas in data tables can contain values, strings, or cell addresses. You can use [TABLE] (F8) to repeat the last Data Table command you selected. This key lets you change values and then instantly repeat the command without using the menu.

/Data Table 1

/Data Table 1 produces a table that shows the effect of changing one variable in one or more formulas. 1-2-3 places the results of each formula in the column below the formula. Before using /Data Table 1, you must set up the data table range.

To create a one-way data table, use the following structure:

* The left column contains the variables.
* The upper left cell is empty.
* The formula is located in the top cell of the second column.
* Additional formulas are located in adjacent cells to the right of the first formula.

❶ Choose a location for the data table range in the worksheet. ❷ Decide on the location for the input cell. ❸ Enter the formula in the first row at the top of the second column of the data table range. Make sure the formula refers to the input cell. ❹ In the first column of the data table range, starting with the second cell, enter the input values you want to use in each of the formulas. ❺ Select /Data Table 1. ❻ Specify the data table range and press [Enter]. ❼ Specify the input cell and press [Enter].

The resulting values are calculated by substituting each of the input values for the input cell in the formula.

/Data Table 2

/Data Table 2 produces a table that shows the effect of changing two variables in one formula. 1-2-3 places the results of each formula in the column below. Before using /Data Table 2, you must set up the data table range.

To create a two-way data table, use the following structure:

* The upper left cell contains the formula.
* The left column contains the first set of variables.
* The first row contains the second set of variables.

❶ Choose a location for the data table range in the worksheet. ❷ Decide on the location for the two input cells. ❸ Enter the formula in the upper left cell of the table range, above the first column of data. Make sure the formula refers to both input cells. ❹ Enter the input values for the variable associated with input cell 2. ❺ Select /Data Table 2. ❻ Specify the data table range and press [Enter]. ❼ Specify the input cell 1 and press [Enter]. ❽ Specify the input cell 2 and press [Enter].

1-2-3 pairs each input value in the top row of the data table range with each input value in the first column of the data table range and calculates the formula using each pair of values. The result of each calculation appears in the cell at the intersection of the row and column containing the two input values. The values are calculated by substituting each of the input values for the corresponding input cell in the formula.

The File Commands

You use the File commands to save worksheets in files on disk and to read the files into 1-2-3. In addition, the File commands help you consolidate data from different files and organize and maintain the information you store in files. Use the File commands to perform the following tasks:

/File Admin   Creates a table of information about files, updates file links in the current worksheet, and controls access to a worksheet file's reservation.

/File Combine   Incorporates data from a worksheet file on disk into the current worksheet.

/File Directory   Changes the directory for the current 1-2-3 session.

/File Erase   Erases a file on disk.

/File Import   Reads data from a text file on disk into current worksheet.

/File List   Displays a temporary list of information about files.

/File Retrieve   Reads a worksheet file into memory. The retrieved file replaces the current worksheet.

/File Save   Saves the current worksheet to a worksheet file on disk.

/File Xtract   Copies a range of data from the current worksheet and saves it in a worksheet file on disk.

Working with Files

To keep a permanent record of the work you do during a 1-2-3 session, you must **save** your worksheet (copy it from memory to a file on disk). Unless you save a worksheet in a file, your work is preserved only as long as the worksheet remains in memory. Once you create a worksheet file, you can **read** the file (copy the file from disk into memory with /File Retrieve) at any time. When you do, 1-2-3 displays the file exactly as it was when you last saved it.

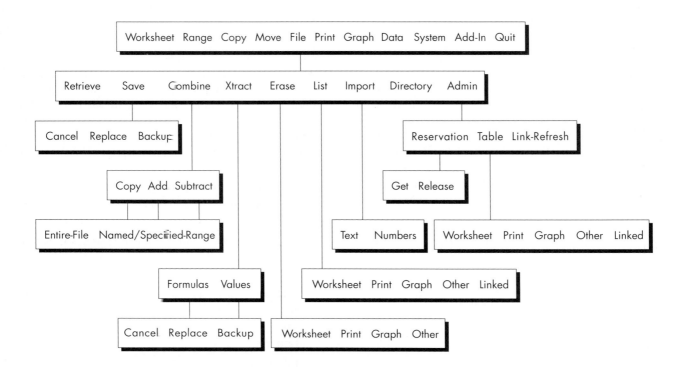

Specifying a File

When you use a 1-2-3 command that prompts you for a filename, 1-2-3 displays a list of files in the current directory (the directory specified with /File Directory or /Worksheet Global Default Directory) that are of the appropriate type. (The only exceptions to this rule are /Add-In Attach and /Worksheet Global Default Other Add-In Set. When you select one of these commands, 1-2-3 displays a menu of files in the directory from which you started 1-2-3.)

You can specify a file to use by selecting a filename from the menu. To see a full-screen menu of filenames, press [NAME] (F3). Highlight the appropriate filename and then press [Enter] to select it. Alternatively, you can type a filename.

If, however, you want to use a file in another directory, you also need to specify a path. The following figure shows one way of specify a worksheet filename BOSTON that is stored on a disk in drive C in the subdirectory name 1991 in the directory budgets.

Path

The **path** supplies two pieces of information: the drive name and the directory name where the file is located.

- The **drive name** tells 1-2-3 where the disk that stores the file is located. A drive name always consists of a letter followed by a colon, for example, B: or C:. If the file is located on a disk in the current drive, you do not need to specify a drive name.

- The **directory name** tells 1-2-3 in which directory on the specified drive the file is located. If the file you are specifying is in a subdirectory (a directory included in another directory), the path will include more than one directory name. You must use a backslash to separate each directory name from the next and to separate the last directory name from the filename. If the file is located in the current directory, you do not need to specify a directory name.

Filename

Every file in a directory has a unique name, which you assign when you first create the file. It is a good idea to use descriptive filenames so you can easily remember them.

Use the following general guidelines for assigning filenames:

- Use any combination of letters, numbers, _ (underscores), and – (hyphens) in filenames.

- Do not use more than eight characters to name a file. If you enter more than eight characters, 1-2-3 ignores the extra characters.

- Do not use the name AUX, CON, COM1, COM2, LPT1, NUL, or PRN.

- Do not include spaces in a filename.

- Use either uppercase or lowercase letters when typing filenames.

Types of Files

In addition to creating worksheet files in 1-2-3, you can create graph, backup worksheet, print, and macro library files.

- **Graph files**, which you create with /Graph Save, store 1-2-3 graphs in a picture format for use with PrintGraph.

- **Backup files** store previous versions of worksheets. When you select /File Save or /File Xtract, specify the name of an existing worksheet file, and then select Backup from the menu 1-2-3 displays, 1-2-3 creates a backup file of the version of the worksheet stored on disk before writing over the existing worksheet (.WK1) file with your changes.

- **Text or print files**, which you create with /Print File, store worksheet data in text or ASCII format.

- **Macro Library files**, which you create with the Macro Library Manager add-in.

A **file extension** is an optional suffix you can add to a filename. It consists of a . (Period) followed by one to three characters. File extensions let you group files into categories by giving more information about what is in a file. If you do not provide your own extension, 1-2-3 automatically adds an extension to the filename depending on the file type.

File type	Extension
Backup worksheet file	.BAK
Graph file	.PIC
Print or text file	.PRN
Worksheet file	.WK1

Using Wild Card Characters in Filenames and Extensions

When 1-2-3 prompts you for a filename, you can display a menu of files with similar names or extensions by including wild card characters (* and ?) in your response to the prompt.

The * (Asterisk) wild card character represents any number of consecutive characters in a filename or extension. For example, to have 1-2-3 list all files that begin with B and have the extension .WK1, you would type b*.wk1 at the filename prompt and press [Enter].

The ? (Question mark) wild card character represents any single character in a filename or extension. For example, to have 1-2-3 list all worksheet files with names that begin with LOT, have any single character in the next position, end with DEPT, and have the default extension .WK1, you would type lot?dept at the filename prompt and press [Enter]. Some possible files listed could be LOT1DEPT.WK1, LOTXDEPT.WK1, and LOT8DEPT.WK1.

Figure 2-1 Sample file specification

Displaying and Using Filenames

Whenever 1-2-3 prompts you for a filename and you want to display files in a different drive and/or a different directory or with a different extension from that shown, do one of the following:

- To display files with a different extension, type *. followed by another extension and then press [Enter].

- To display all files in the current directory, type *.* and then press [Enter].

- To display files in a different drive and/or directory, press [Esc] to clear the filenames, edit the drive and/or directory, and then press [Enter].

If you have a two-diskette system, make sure the disk that contains the file you want is in one of the diskette drives.

/File Admin

Use /File Admin to perform the following tasks:

Link-Refresh Recalculates formulas in the current worksheet that include references to files on disk by retrieving the current contents of the linked cells.

Reservation Lets you get and release a file's reservation, or lock. Use this command when you share worksheet files on a network and want to save files or allow other people to save files (see below).

Table Creates a table of information about files on disk (see below).

/File Admin Reservation

/File Admin Reservation lets you get and release the current file's reservation when you are working with shared files on a network. A reservation prevents a file from being worked on and saved by several people at the same time. Files shared on a network can be read by several people at one time, but only the person who has the file's one reservation can save changes to the file.

When you retrieve a shared file from a network, you will automatically get its reservation unless someone else has already retrieved the file with its reservation.

If you try to retrieve a file and someone else has the reservation, 1-2-3 will ask you if you want to retrieve the file without its reservation.

If you retrieve the file without its reservation, you will see at the bottom of the screen an RO, or read-only, indicator, which means you cannot save changes to the same filename. If you want to save a file whose reservation you do not have, wait a while, and then use /File Admin Reservation Get to try to get the reservation if the previous user is finished with it.

❶ Select /File Admin Reservation. ❷ Select Get to retrieve the file reservation for a file if it is available and no one has saved the file since you read it into memory, or Release to give up the reservation for a file.

If you are going to release a file's reservation, be sure to save any changes you have made first with /File Save. If you retrieve a file and plan to use, but not save it, use /File Admin Reservation Release to release the reservation so that someone else can save the file.

Note: *It is possible for a shared file to have been assigned a read-only status. If you try to get the reservation for this type of file, 1-2-3 displays a message indicating that it is a read-only file.*

/File Admin Table

/File Admin lets you create a table of information about files and directories on disk.

❶ If you have a two-diskette system, make sure the disk that contains the files you want to work with is in one of the diskette drives. ❷ Decide on a worksheet location for the file table. ❸ Select /File Admin Table. ❹ Select Worksheet, Print, Graph, Other, or Linked. ❺ If you selected Linked, go directly to step 6; otherwise, to list files, press [Enter], or edit the displayed drive and/or directory, and then press [Enter]. ❻ Specify the range you decided on in Step 2 and press [Enter].

1-2-3 creates a table listing the names of all relevant files in the specified directory (or, for Linked, files linked to the current worksheet), the date and time each file was last saved (as date and time serial numbers), and the size of the file on disk in bytes. Format the second and third columns in the table with /Range Format Date and /Range Format Time.

Caution: *The table can be placed in any unprotected area of the worksheet. Make sure, however, that the* *worksheet location is blank or contains unimportant data; 1-2-3 writes over existing data when it creates the table. The table will occupy four columns and as many rows as the number of files you are listing plus one blank row.*

/File Combine

Use /File Combine to perform the following tasks:

Add Adds incoming numeric data to numbers or blank cells in the current worksheet.

Copy Copies all incoming data to the current worksheet.

Subtract Subtracts incoming numeric data from numbers or blank cells in the current worksheet.

Caution: *To avoid possible data loss from combining files incorrectly, save the worksheet before using /File Combine Add. If you make a mistake when combining data and the Undo feature is on, press [UNDO] (Alt-F4) immediately to restore the worksheet to its original state.*

When you use /File Combine, 1-2-3 incorporates data from another worksheet file into the current worksheet beginning at the cell pointer location. Therefore, before you use /File Combine, verify that the worksheet is large enough to hold all incoming data and that the cell pointer is positioned correctly for the desired results.

1-2-3 changes cell formats in the current worksheet to reflect those of the incoming data. It does not, however, change column widths or other worksheet settings in the current worksheet and does not add to or change any of the current worksheet's range names.

You can incorporate data from any 1-2-3 Release 1A, Release 2, or Release 2.01 worksheet file or from a 1-2-3 Release 3 worksheet file that has been saved in the .WK1 worksheet file format.

Combining Files — General Procedure

The following steps describe the general procedure for combining files. For details on a particular File Combine command — Add, Copy, or Subtract — read the command-specific discussion that follows.

❶ Move the cell pointer to wherever you want 1-2-3 to start combining data from the file on disk. ❷ Select /File Combine Add, Copy, or Subtract. ❸ Select Entire-File to combine all data in a file on disk with the current worksheet or Named/Specified-Range to combine data in a range in a file on disk with the current worksheet. ❹ If you selected Named/Specified-Range, specify the range of numeric data that you want to add to the current worksheet and press [Enter]. ❺ Specify the file whose data you want to combine with the current worksheet and press [Enter].

/File Combine Add

/File Combine Add works with numeric data only. 1-2-3 adds numbers and the results of numeric formulas in a worksheet file on disk to numbers and blank cells in the current worksheet. The incoming data has no effect on labels or formulas in the current worksheet.

Use /File Combine Add to summarize and consolidate numeric data in several different files. For example, you can use /File Combine Add to create year-to-date totals by consolidating sales data from several monthly files into the current worksheet.

/File Combine Copy

/File Combine Copy copies both labels and values from a worksheet file on disk to the current worksheet, beginning at the cell pointer location. Use /File Combine Copy to combine data from several smaller files into one file. For example, you can combine database records from several files into one database.

/File Combine Subtract

/File Combine Subtract works with numeric data only and works the same way as /File Combine Add, except it subtracts instead of adds. 1-2-3 subtracts numbers and the results of numeric formulas in a file on disk from numbers or blank cells in the current worksheet. The incoming data has no effect on labels or formulas in the current worksheet.

/File Directory

/File Directory lets you change the directory for the current 1-2-3 session, which is the path (drive and directory names) 1-2-3 uses if you do not specify a path along with a filename when you save, read, or list files.

Note: *If you have a two-diskette system, the directory consists of a drive name (such as B:) followed by a \ (Backslash).*

Use /File Directory to override the default directory for the current session. For example, suppose your default directory is C:\123, but the data files you want to use during the current session are on a diskette in drive B. You can use /File Directory to make B:\ the current directory.

❶ Select /File Directory. ❷ Press [Enter] to accept the displayed directory, or type a new directory and press [Enter].

1-2-3 uses the specified directory until you use /File Directory again, use /Worksheet Global Default Directory, or end the 1-2-3 session.

/File Erase

/File Erase lets you erase a file on disk.

Note the differences between /File Erase and /Worksheet Erase. /File Erase erases a file without affecting the current worksheet in memory, while /Worksheet Erase removes the current worksheet from memory but has no effect on the files on the disk.

❶ Select /File Erase. ❷ Select Worksheet, Print, Graph, or Other to display the appropriate files in the current directory. ❸ If 1-2-3 cannot find any files of the specified type, it displays a prompt and enters EDIT mode, at which point you can display other files by typing *. followed by another extension, or *.* and pressing [Enter]. ❹ Specify the name of the file you want to erase and press [Enter]. ❺ Select No to cancel the command without erasing the file or Yes to erase the file on disk.

Caution: *Once you erase a file on disk, you cannot retrieve the data in that file or use [UNDO] (Alt-F4) to recover the file. Therefore, before using /File Erase, make certain that you no longer need the data in the file you are erasing.*

/File Import

/File Import lets you copy data from a **print** or **text file**, a file on disk in ASCII format that was created with 1-2-3 or another program, into the current worksheet beginning at the cell pointer location.

Caution: *To avoid possible data loss from incorrectly importing files, save the current worksheet before using /File Import. If you make a mistake when importing data and the Undo feature is on, press [UNDO] (Alt-F4) immediately to restore the worksheet to its original state.*

Before you use this command, you need to know about the two types of text files from which you can import data — delimited and nondelimited text files.

- A **delimited text file** contains characters, called delimiters (typically, commas, spaces, colons, or semicolons), that separate data. In order for 1-2-3 to import this type of text file correctly, labels must be enclosed in quotation marks, and all labels and numbers must be separated by a delimiter. Numbers must not be formatted with commas because the commas will act as delimiters.

  To import data from a delimited text file into the current worksheet, use /File Import Numbers to import both labels and numbers and enter them in separate cells. You should not use /File Import Text to import a delimited text file.

- A **nondelimited text file** does not separate data. In order for 1-2-3 to import this type of text file correctly, each line in the file must end with a carriage return or line-feed and must not exceed 240 characters.

  To import only numbers from a nondelimited text file, use /File Import Numbers. 1-2-3 enters each number in a separate cell. To import both labels and numbers, use /File Import Text. 1-2-3 treats each line of data in the text file as a long label, entering it in a separate cell. You can view or print data imported with /File Import Text, but you cannot use the numbers in calculations unless you use /Data Parse to place the labels and numbers in separate cells in the worksheet.

❶ Move the cell pointer to an area of the worksheet that is large enough to include all the imported data. ❷ Select /File Import. ❸ Select Text or Numbers. ❹ Specify the name of the text file you want to import and press [Enter].

Note: *Some word processing programs produce files that contain special non-ASCII characters. 1-2-3 cannot import these characters properly with /File Import.*

/File List

/File List lets you display a temporary list of files that overlays the current worksheet. When you highlight a filename in the list, 1-2-3 displays specific information about that file.

❶ Select /File List. ❷ Select Worksheet, Print, Graph, Other, or Linked to list appropriate files in the current directory or files linked to the current Worksheet. ❸ If 1-2-3 cannot find any files of the specified type, it displays a prompt and enters EDIT mode, at which point you can display other files by typing *. followed by another extension or *.* and pressing [Enter]. ❹ Use the pointer-movement keys to highlight different filenames and display specific information about each file. ❺ Press [Enter] to return 1-2-3 to READY mode and redisplay the current worksheet.

Note: *To create a table of file-related information in the worksheet rather than displaying a temporary list, use /File Admin Table.*

/File Retrieve

/File Retrieve lets you read a file from disk into memory. The retrieved worksheet file replaces the worksheet that was current when you selected /File Retrieve. When you use /File Retrieve, 1-2-3 uses the recalculation and worksheet window settings in the newly retrieved file. These settings may be different from the recalculation and worksheet window settings you were using.

Caution: *If you want to save the current worksheet, use /File Save before you select /File Retrieve. /File Retrieve replaces the current worksheet without saving it. If the Undo feature is on, however, you can press [UNDO] (Alt-F4) immediately to restore the worksheet that was in memory when you selected /File Retrieve.*

❶ Select /File Retrieve to display files with .WK1, .WKS, and .WK3 extensions in the current directory. (You cannot retrieve files saved in the .WK3 worksheet file format.) ❷ Specify the name of the file you want to retrieve and press [Enter]. ❸ If you are trying to retrieve a file shared on a network and someone else is using the file and has the file reservation, select Yes to retrieve the file without the reservation or No to cancel the command without retrieving the file.

Note: *If you are sharing files on a network, 1-2-3 automatically gets the reservation for a file when you retrieve the file. The reservation of the previous worksheet file is released. If you do not have the reservation for the file, 1-2-3 displays the RO indicator at the bottom of the screen. Do not change or add data to the worksheet because 1-2-3 will not let you save the file to the same filename without the reservation. Use /File Admin Reservation Get to try to get the reservation if it is available.*

Retrieving a File Automatically

You can cause 1-2-3 to read a particular worksheet into memory automatically every time you start the program. To specify a worksheet for automatic file retrieval, use /File Save to save the worksheet in a file named AUTO123.WK1 in the default directory (the directory specified with /Worksheet Global Default Directory).

You can also retrieve a file when you start 1-2-3 by including a –w and the name of the file on the operating system command line. For example, to retrieve a file called JANUARY.WK1 in the current directory, type "123 –wjanuary" .

/File Save

/File Save lets you save worksheet data and settings in a file on disk. You use /File Save both to create new files on disk and to update existing files. You can change the filename or extension when you save it. 1-2-3 assigns a .WK1 extension to files you create with /File Save unless you enter a different extension when you name the file.

You must use /File Save to make a permanent copy of your work on disk before you erase the worksheet, end the 1-2-3 session, or turn off the computer. Save your files frequently so you do not lose work in the case of a power failure or a problem with your computer system.

❶ Select /File Save to display the current directory, default file extension and if the file has been saved before, current filename. ❷ Based on the worksheet's present status and intended result, proceed according to the following table:

Worksheet status and intended result	Action
Unnamed Save in current directory	Type filename and press [Enter].
Unnamed Save in different path	Press [Esc], edit drive and/or directory, type filename, and press [Enter].
Previously saved Save with same name	Press [Enter].
Previously saved Save with new name, same path	Type new filename and press [Enter].
Previously saved Save in different path	Press [Esc] twice, edit drive and/or directory, specify filename, and press [Enter].

❸ Select Cancel to return 1-2-3 to READY mode without saving the worksheet; Replace to write over the worksheet file on disk with a copy of the current worksheet; or Backup to copy the worksheet file on disk to a backup file with the same filename but the extension .BAK, and save the current worksheet with the existing filename.

Note: *If the file exists on disk and it is a file shared on a network, you need a reservation to save it to the same filename. If the RO, or read-only, indicator appears at the bottom of the screen, use /File Admin Reservation Get to see if the reservation is available. If it is not and you want to save changes you have made to the file, you must save it under a different filename.*

Saving a File with a Password

You can limit access to a worksheet file by saving it with a password. When you save a file with a password, no one can read the file without the password. A password can include any combination of up to 15 characters. 1-2-3 displays blanks as you type the password.

Caution: *Remember your password. When you save a file with a password, you can read the file into memory again only if you enter the exact password, including the exact combination of uppercase and lowercase letters you typed.*

❶ Select /File Save. ❷ If you are updating the file, press [SPACE] once to enter a space after the current filename or edit the filename and then press [SPACE] once. Do not press [Enter]. If the file is new, enter the filename and press the space bar once. Do not press [Enter]. ❸ Type p and then press [Enter]. ❹ At the prompt, type a password and press [Enter]. ❺ Type the same password again at the "Verify password" prompt and press [Enter]. ❻ If you are updating the file, select Replace to save the file with the password.

Changing a Password

❶ Select /File Save. ❷ Press [Backspace] once to clear the [PASSWORD PROTECTED] prompt. ❸ Press [SPACE] once. ❹ Follow Steps 3 through 6 in the preceding procedure.

Deleting a Password

❶ Select /File Save. ❷ Press [Backspace] once to clear the [PASSWORD PROTECTED] prompt and press [Enter]. ❸ Select Replace to update the file without a password.

/File Xtract

/File Xtract lets you extract a range of data by copying the data from the current worksheet and saving it in a worksheet file on disk. /File Xtract also saves in the extracted file all settings associated with the worksheet. Use /File Xtract to create a smaller file from one large file. This command does not change the current worksheet.

1-2-3 assigns a .WK1 extension to files you create with /File Xtract unless you enter a different extension when you name the file. If the CALC indicator appears at the bottom of the screen, press [CALC] (F9) to update formulas before you use /File Xtract Values.

If you extract a formula, be certain that you extract all the data that is referred to by the formula. If all the data is not in the extracted file, then the formula will not produce the results you intended. If you extract data in a named range, be certain that you extract the entire named range. If you extract only part of a named range, the range name will appear in the extracted file but it will no longer refer to the correct range of data.

Note: *Do not use /File Xtract if you are working with shared files on a network.*

❶ Select /File Xtract. ❷ Select Formulas to copy a range of data in the current worksheet to a file on disk, including labels, numbers, formulas, and all worksheet settings; or Values to copy a range of data in the current worksheet to a file on disk, including labels, numbers, the values of formulas, and all worksheet settings. ❸ Specify a filename for the extracted range and press [Enter]. ❹ Specify the range of data you want to extract and press [Enter]. ❺ If you specified a filename that already exists, select Cancel to return 1-2-3 to READY mode without extracting the range; Replace to write over the file on disk with the extracted range; or Backup to rename the file on disk with the extension .BAK and save the extracted range with the existing filename.

1-2-3 enters the extracted range in the file, beginning in cell A1. If you extracted formulas, 1-2-3 adjusts the cell references in formulas to reflect their new locations in the extracted file.

Extracting a File with a Password

You can limit access to a current worksheet by extracting it with a password. When you extract a file with a password, no one can read the file without knowing and specifying the password. During the /File Xtract procedure, you can create a password-protected current worksheet when you name the file. Follow the same password procedures described under "Saving a File with a Password."

The Graph Commands

Graphs are tools for illustrating the relationships between numbers. Because of their visual nature, graphs often convey messages about numbers more quickly and dramatically than the numbers themselves.

Use the Graph commands to perform the following tasks:

/Graph A-F Specifies the ranges that contain the numeric data you want to graph.

/Graph Group Specifies multiple graph data ranges at once when the ranges are located in consecutive columns or rows.

/Graph Name Creates, modifies, and deletes named graphs in the current worksheet and creates tables of named graphs.

/Graph Options Adds enhancements such as titles, legends, colors, and grid lines to a graph and determines the scaling method for the graph's axes.

/Graph Quit Returns 1-2-3 to READY mode.

/Graph Reset Resets some or all of the current graph settings to the default graph settings.

/Graph Save Saves the current graph in a graph (.PIC) file for use with PrintGraph.

/Graph Type Specifies the kind of graph to create: line graph, bar graph, XY graph, stacked bar graph, or pie chart.

/Graph View Displays the current graph on your screen.

/Graph X Specifies the range that contains the x-axis labels, the x-axis values for an XY graph, or the pie slice labels.

Graph Basics

When you select /Graph, 1-2-3 displays a special screen called the graph settings sheet. The graph settings sheet allows you to see all the settings for the current graph at a glance. 1-2-3 will use the settings the next time you display a graph with /Graph View or [GRAPH] (F10). You can change any of the settings with the Graph commands displayed in the menu above the settings sheet.

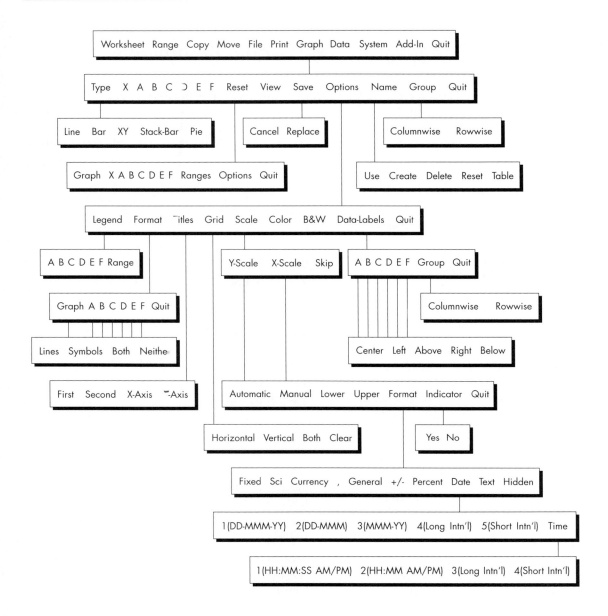

1-2-3 Graph Types

With 1-2-3, you can create five basic graph types: bar, line, pie, stacked bar, and XY (scatter). For additional information on creating these graphs, see "/Graph A-F" and "/Graph X," later in this section.

Bar graphs consist of a series of bars, each bar representing a value. You can use bar graphs to compare related data at a given point in time.

- For a single-range bar graph, use /Graph A to indicate the range of values you want each bar to represent.

- For a multiple-range bar graph, use /Graph A-F to indicate the ranges of values you want to represent simultaneously.

- Use /Graph X to indicate labels for the x axis.

Line graphs are generally used to plot changes in one or more data values over time. Each line represents a category of data, and each point along the line represents the data's value at a particular time. Because line graphs stress continuity of data over time, they are particularly useful for identifying trends and making projections.

- Use /Graph A to indicate the set of values you want to represent with your first line or with one single line.

- Use /Graph B-F to indicate the sets of values you want to represent with each additional line.

- Use /Graph X to indicate labels for the x axis.

Pie charts are used to relate two or more values to one another by representing the values as slices of a pie. They are useful for comparing parts to the whole. You can emphasize one or more values in a pie chart by **exploding** (separating slightly from the pie) the slices that represent those values.

- Use /Graph A to indicate the set of values you want to represent as slices of pie.

- Use /Graph B (optional) to indicate the range where you entered values for controlling the hatch patterns or colors for slices of pie or for exploding slices of pie.

- Use /Graph X to indicate labels for the slices of pie.

Stacked bar graphs compare values by stacking them one on top of the next in a single bar and using different colors or hatch patterns to differentiate the parts of the bar.

- Use /Graph A-F to indicate each set of values you want to represent as portions of bars. Positive values are stacked by range in ascending alphabetical order: the portion that represents the A data range appears below the portion that represents the B data range, and so on. Negative values are stacked by range in descending alphabetical order.

- Use /Graph X to indicate labels for the x axis.

XY graphs, also called scatter charts, are used to show correlations between two types of numeric data. XY graphs resemble line graphs in the sense that values are plotted as points in the graph. Unlike line graphs, however, XY graphs use a numeric scale along the x axis.

- Use /Graph X to indicate the set of values you want to plot on the x axis.

- Use /Graph A to indicate the set of values you want to plot on the y axis in your first line or in one single line.

- Use /Graph B-F to indicate the sets of values you want to plot in each additional line.

Creating a Graph — General Procedure

You create 1-2-3 graphs using worksheet data. After reading this general description, see "/Graph X" and "/Graph A-F" for detailed information.

❶ Select /Graph Type. ❷ Select Line, Bar, XY, Stacked-Bar, or Pie. ❸ Use /Graph X to specify the graph's X data range. ❹ Use /Graph A-F to specify the graph's numeric data ranges (the worksheet ranges that contain the numbers to be graphed). If the X and A-F data ranges are in consecutive columns or rows of a range, you can use /Graph Group instead of /Graph X and A-F to specify the graph data ranges. ❺ To view the graph, select View from the /Graph menu or press [GRAPH] (F10). ❻ To redisplay the worksheet, press any key. ❼ If you want to add explanatory text, colors, grid lines, and other enhancements to the basic graph, use /Graph Options. ❽ To save the graph so you can view it at another time, name the graph with /Graph Name Create. ❾ To print the graph with PrintGraph, save the graph in a graph or picture (.PIC) file with /Graph Save. ❿ To return 1-2-3 to READY mode, select /Graph Quit.

Note: *If your monitor cannot display graphs, or if the screen display driver you selected in the Install program cannot display graphs, the screen goes blank when you try to show the graph. The screen also goes blank if 1-2-3 cannot display the graph for any other reason (for example, you have not specified enough data for 1-2-3 to draw the graph). To get back to the worksheet, press any key.*

Saving and Printing Graphs

Whenever you select /Graph View or press [GRAPH] (F10), 1-2-3 displays a graph based on whatever graph settings are currently specified; this graph is called the **current graph**. As you use the Graph commands to specify new graph settings, the current graph changes. The current graph can be preserved in its present form for worksheet use, printing, or both.

Saving a Graph for Worksheet Use Use /Graph Name Create to store the current graph as a **named graph**, so you can display it at another time. You can continue to change the graph settings and create and store new graphs. If you want to display a named graph, select /Graph Name Use and specify the graph you want to be current. Use /File Save to save the worksheet that contains the named graphs. This saves all the named graphs you created for use in future 1-2-3 sessions.

Saving a Graph for Printing Use /Graph Save to save the current graph so you can print it with Print-Graph. /Graph Save creates a graph (.PIC) file on disk. (PIC files cannot be printed or modified in 1-2-3.) To print the saved graphs use the PrintGraph program. For information on Print-Graph, see *Reference 5, Print-Graph.*

/Graph A-F

/Graph A, B, C, D, E, and F (/Graph A-F) specify the A-F data ranges, the ranges that contain the numeric data you want to graph. The way 1-2-3 uses the A-F data ranges depends on the type of graph you create:

- In a bar graph, 1-2-3 uses the A-F data ranges as the sets of bars in the graph. 1-2-3 creates one set of bars for each data range, with each bar representing one value in the range.

- In a line graph, 1-2-3 uses the A-F data ranges as the lines in the graph. 1-2-3 creates one line for each data range, with each point along the line representing one value in the range.

- In a pie chart, 1-2-3 uses the A data range as the set of pie slices, the B data range to determine the color or hatch pattern of each pie slice (depending on whether graph display is set to color or black and white) and whether the slice explodes (separates slightly) from the rest of the pie, and the X data range as labels for each pie slice.

  To assign either colors or hatch patterns to the slices in a pie chart, create a B data range the same size as the A data range and enter a value from 1 to 8 in each cell in the B data range. When graph display is set to color, the B data range values determine the

colors of the pie slices; the color each value represents depends on your monitor. When graph display is set to black and white, the B data range values determine the hatch patterns, which are the same for all monitors.

To explode one or more slices in a pie chart, add 100 to the B data range values that correspond to the slices you want to explode. For example, to explode the slice with color or hatch pattern 6, enter 106 in the corresponding B data range cell.

- In a stacked bar graph, 1-2-3 uses the A-F data ranges as portions of the bars. Positive values are stacked by range in ascending alphabetical order: the portion that represents the A data range appears below the portion that represents the B data range, the portion that represents the B data range appears below the portion that represents the C data range, and so on. Negative values are stacked by range in descending alphabetical order.

- In an XY graph, 1-2-3 uses the A-F data ranges as points plotted against the X data range. 1-2-3 creates one set of points for each data range you set.

❶ Select /Graph A, B, C, D, E, or F. ❷ Specify the range you want to use as the data range and press [Enter].

The range you specify for this command should include only numeric data (numbers and/or numeric formulas). Cells containing labels or blanks will be interpreted by 1-2-3 as zero. The range can include any number of columns and rows.

/Graph Group

/Graph Group specifies all graph data ranges (X and A-F) at once, when the X and A-F data ranges are in consecutive columns or rows of a range.

❶ Select /Graph Group. ❷ Specify the group range you want to divide into graph data ranges and press [Enter]. ❸ Select Columnwise to divide the group range into data ranges by columns; or Rowwise to divide the group range into data ranges by rows.

1-2-3 uses the first column or row of the group range as the X data range and subsequent columns or rows as the A-F data ranges. If the range includes more than seven columns or rows, 1-2-3 stops assigning data ranges after the seventh column or row.

/Graph Name

/Graph Name lets you perform the following tasks:

Create Creates or modifies named graphs (see below).

Delete Deletes a named graph.

Reset Deletes all named graphs in the worksheet.

Table Creates a table of named graphs in the worksheet (see below).

Use Retrieves a named graph, making it the current graph (see below).

/Graph Name Create

/Graph Name Create creates or redefines a named graph by storing the current graph settings with the name you specify. Once you name a graph, you can retrieve it at any time with /Graph Name Use. The number of named graphs you can create is limited only by available memory. If you want to use any named graphs in another 1-2-3 session, use /File Save to save the worksheet.

❶ Display the current graph using /Graph View or [GRAPH] (F10) to verify that the graph looks the way you want it to look. ❷ Select /Graph Name Create. ❸ Specify an existing graph name or a new graph name of up to 15 characters and press [Enter]. 1-2-3 does not distinguish between uppercase and lowercase letters in graph names.

Follow these guidelines when you create graph names:

- Do not include spaces, commas, semicolons, or the characters + * − / & > < { @ and # in graph names.

- Do not use a name that already exists; if you do, you will write over the graph that was previously stored with that name.

- Do not use names that look like cell addresses, such as P10 or EX100.

- Do not use @function names, advanced macro command keywords, or 1-2-3 key names as graph names.

/Graph Name Table

/Graph Name Table creates a three-column table that alphabetically lists all named graphs in the worksheet, as well as graph types and titles.

❶ Decide on a location for the graph name table. ❷ Select /Graph Name Table. ❸ Specify the location you decided on in Step 1 and press [Enter]. You need to specify only the first cell of the table's location.

Caution: *Graph Name Table will create a table that occupies three columns and as many rows as there are named graphs plus one blank row. To avoid possible data loss from writing over existing data, save the worksheet before using /Graph Name Table. If you make a mistake when placing the table and the Undo feature is on, press [UNDO] (Alt-F4) immediately to restore the worksheet to its original state.*

/Graph Name Use

/Graph Name Use retrieves a named graph, making it the current graph.

Caution: *When you retrieve a named graph, you lose all of the previous graph settings. To preserve those settings for future use, assign them a name with /Graph Name Create before you use /Graph Name Use. If you modify a named graph after you retrieve it and want to save the changed settings, use /Graph Name Create, select the previous name, and then use /File Save.*

❶ Select /Graph Name Use. ❷ Specify a named graph and press [Enter]. 1-2-3 displays the specified graph and makes it the current graph. ❸ Press any key to redisplay the worksheet.

/Graph Options

/Graph Options lets you perform the following tasks:

B&W Causes 1-2-3 to display graphs in black and white, using hatch patterns instead of color.

Color Causes 1-2-3 to display graphs in colors (assuming you have a color monitor).

Data-Labels Uses the contents of a range as labels for the points or bars in a graph (see below).

Format In line and XY graphs, sets whether 1-2-3 connects the data points with lines, uses symbols to mark the points, uses symbols and lines, or uses neither symbols nor lines (see below).

Grid Adds or removes grid lines in a graph (see below).

Legend Creates legends for the A-F data ranges (see below).

Quit Returns you to the Graph menu.

Scale Determines axis scaling and sets the format of the numbers along an axis (see below).

Titles Adds graph titles to a graph (see below).

Note: *If you have a color printer or plotter, you can use /Graph Options Color with /Graph Save even if your monitor cannot display colors. When you save the graph, 1-2-3 assigns a different color to each data range so that PrintGraph can draw each data range with a different color.*

/Graph Options Data-Labels

/Graph Options Data-Labels uses the contents of a range as labels for the points or bars in a graph. The labels come from the ranges you specify as the A-F **data label ranges.** The data label range can contain any combination of numbers, labels, or formulas. 1-2-3 uses the current value of a formula as the data label. (To label the slices in a pie chart, use /Graph X, not /Graph Options Data-Labels.)

❶ Select /Graph Options Data-Labels. ❷ Select A-F to assign the data label range you specify in Step 3 to the selected data range; Group to assign the data label range you specify in Step 3 to all data ranges at once and to clear any settings you previously established with /Graph Options Data-Labels; or Quit to return to the /Graph Options menu. ❸ If you selected A, B, C, D, E, or F, specify a data label range of the same size as the selected data range and press [Enter]; if you selected Group, specify a data label range of the same size as all the data ranges combined and press [Enter]. ❹ If you are creating data labels for a line or XY graph, select Center to place data labels on top of the points in a line; Left to place data labels to the left of the points in a line; Above to place data labels above the points in a line; Right to place data labels to the right of the points in a line; Below to place data labels below the

points in a line. ❺ Select Quit to return to the Graph Options menu.

If you are creating data labels for a bar or stacked bar graph, 1-2-3 places data labels above the corresponding bars if the values are positive and below if the values are negative, regardless of the placement you specify.

Note: *If you clear one or more data ranges with /Graph Reset A-F or /Graph Reset Ranges, 1-2-3 automatically clears the corresponding data label ranges.*

/Graph Options Format

/Graph Options Format sets the way 1-2-3 displays each line in a line or XY graph. 1-2-3 can use symbols to mark the points along a line, connect the points with lines, use both symbols and lines, or use neither symbols nor lines.

❶ Select /Graph Options Format. ❷ Select Graph to format all lines in the graph at once; A-F to format the line defined by the specified data range; or Quit to return to the Graph Options menu. ❸ Select Lines to connect the points along the line with lines; Symbols to display a symbol at each data point (different symbol for each data range); Both to display a symbol at each point along the line and connect the points with lines (the default); or Neither to display neither symbols nor connecting lines, effectively hiding the data on the graph unless you use /Graph Options Data-Labels to label the specified line. ❹ Select Quit to return to the /Graph Options menu.

/Graph Options Grid

/Graph Options Grid adds or removes grid lines in all graph types except pie charts.

❶ Select /Graph Options Grid. ❷ Select Horizontal to draw grid lines across the graph, originating from the left border; Vertical to draw grid lines up the graph, originating from the bottom border; Both to draw horizontal and vertical grid lines; or Clear to clear all grid lines, returning the graph to the 1-2-3 default display.

/Graph Options Legend

/Graph Options Legend creates legends for the graph's data ranges. The legends, located below the graph, identify the data range represented by each symbol, color, or hatch pattern in the graph. To assign legends to the slices of a pie chart, use the X data range.

To ensure that your legends will be displayed fully and will print out completely, keep them each under 19 characters. Legends will wrap to a second line if necessary. 1-2-3 truncates legends that extend beyond the graph frame and does not display legends that, because of their specified placement, would appear outside of the graph frame.

❶ Select /Graph Options Legend. ❷ Select A-F to assign a legend to an individual data range; or Range to assign legends to all data ranges at once. ❸ If you selected Range, specify the legend range and press [Enter]. The **legend range** is the range that contains the legend for each graph data range. ❹ If you selected A, B, C, D, E, or F, specify the legend for the data range.

When specifying the legend you can type the actual legend (up to 19 characters) and press [Enter]. Alternatively you can press \ (backslash), specify the cell that contains the legend, and then press [Enter] to display a longer legend than 19 characters.

/Graph Options Scale

/Graph Options Scale determines the scaling method for the y axis and (for XY graphs) x axis scaling and the format of the numbers that appear along each axis. /Graph Options Scale also sets which entries in the X data range appear along the x axis in line, bar, and stacked bar graphs.

❶ Select /Graph Options Scale. ❷ Select Y-Scale to set the scaling for the y axis; X-Scale to set the scaling for the x axis; or Skip to set a skip factor for the x-axis labels. ❸ If you selected Skip, specify a skip factor and press [Enter]. The **skip factor** determines which entries in the X data range 1-2-3 displays along the x axis. For example, if you set a skip factor of 3, 1-2-3 displays along the x axis only the first, fourth, seventh, tenth (and so on) entries in the X data range. The skip factor setting does not affect pie charts or XY graphs. ❹ If you selected Y-Scale or X-Scale, select one of the following options:

Automatic Sets the scaling method for the selected axis to automatic (the default), so 1-2-3 automatically creates a scale that shows all the graph data.

Manual Sets the scaling method for the selected axis to manual, so 1-2-3 creates a scale using the upper and lower limits you specify. When 1-2-3 draws the graph, it displays only the data that falls within those limits.

Lower Used only when you select /Graph Options [Y-Scale or X-Scale] Manual. Sets the lower scale limit (the default is 0) for the selected axis. In some instances, 1-2-3 rounds down the limit you specify. You cannot set a lower limit with bar graphs. The lower limit for bar graphs is always 0.

Upper Used only when you select /Graph Options [Y-Scale or X-Scale] Manual. Sets the upper scale limit (the default is 0) for the selected axis. In some instances, 1-2-3 rounds up the limit you specify.

Format Sets the format in which 1-2-3 displays the numbers along a scale. You can select Comma, Currency, Date, Fixed, General (the default), Hidden, Percent, +/−, Sci (Scientific), Text, or Time format. See the table in /Range Format for a description of each format.

Indicator Determines whether the scale indicator is displayed. When 1-2-3 uses an order of magnitude other than 0 for the numbers along a scale, it creates a **scale indicator**, such as "(thousands)," to identify the order of magnitude. The scale indicator appears between the scale and the axis title. When you select Indicator, 1-2-3 displays a Yes/No menu. Select Yes (the default) to display the scale indicator as described above. Select No to suppress display of the scale indicator entirely.

Quit Returns you to the Graph Options menu.

/Graph Options Titles

/Graph Options Titles adds graph titles and axis titles to a graph.

❶ Select /Graph Options Titles. ❷ Select First to set the first line of the graph title; Second to set the second line of the graph title; X-axis to set the title for the x axis; or Y-axis to set the title for the y axis. ❸ Specify a title by typing up to 39 characters and pressing [Enter], or pressing \ (Backslash), specifying the cell that contains the title, and then pressing [Enter]. ❹ Repeat Steps 2 and 3 to specify another title. ❺ Select Quit to return to the Graph Options menu.

/Graph Quit

/Graph Quit removes the Graph menu and returns 1-2-3 to READY mode. To save the current settings for use later in the current worksheet session, use /Graph Name Create before you use /Graph Quit. To save the current graph for future worksheet sessions, use /Graph Name Create and /File Save before you use /Graph Quit. To print the current graph, save it in a graph (.PIC) file by using /Graph Save before you use /Graph Quit.

❶ Select /Graph Quit.

/Graph Reset

/Graph Reset resets some or all of the current graph settings, returning them to the default settings.

❶ Select /Graph Reset. ❷ Select Graph to reset all graph settings and return to the /Graph menu; X to reset the X data range setting; A-F to reset the A-F data range settings and corresponding data label settings, if any; Ranges to reset all data range settings (X, A-F, and Group) and data label settings; Options to reset all current /Graph Options settings; or Quit to return to the Graph menu. ❸ Select Quit to return to the Graph menu.

Note: *Selecting /Graph Reset Options or /Graph Reset Ranges is equivalent to selecting /Graph Reset Graph except that the /Graph Type settings are not reset.*

/Graph Save

/Graph Save saves the current graph in a graph (.PIC) file so you can use the graph with other programs, such as PrintGraph. You cannot retrieve a graph file with 1-2-3 itself. To save the current graph for future work-

sheet use within 1-2-3, use /Graph Name Create and /File Save.

❶ Select /Graph Save. ❷ Specify a graph filename and press [Enter]; or press [Esc], edit the directory, type a filename, and press [Enter]. ❸ If you enter an existing graph filename, select Cancel to end the command without saving the current graph; or Replace to complete the command, replacing the graph file on disk with the current graph.

/Graph Type

/Graph Type sets the basic type of graph you are creating: bar, line, pie, stacked bar, or XY.

❶ Select /Graph Type. ❷ To set a basic graph type, select an options from the menu.

/Graph View

/Graph View temporarily removes the worksheet from the screen and displays the current graph.

❶ Select /Graph View or press [GRAPH] (F10). ❷ When you finish viewing the graph, press any key to redisplay the worksheet.

1-2-3 will display a blank screen when your monitor cannot display graphs, when you selected a screen display driver with the Install program that is not the correct one for your computer system, when none of the A-F data ranges are specified, when the A data range is not specified in a pie chart or in an XY graph, or when the X data range and/or one of the A-F data ranges are not specified. If 1-2-3 displays a blank screen, press any key to return to the worksheet.

/Graph X

/Graph X specifies the X data range for a graph. The way 1-2-3 uses the contents of this range depends on the type of graph you create:

- In line, bar, or stacked bar graphs, 1-2-3 uses the contents of the X data range as the x-axis labels. The X data range can contain either values or labels.

- In pie charts, 1-2-3 uses the contents of the X data range as the pie slice labels. These labels appear with the percentage labels 1-2-3 automatically creates. The X data range can contain either values or labels. 1-2-3 pairs the text in the first cell of the X data range with the value in the first cell of the A data range, and so on.

- In XY graphs, 1-2-3 uses the contents of the X data range to determine the x-axis scale and where along the x-axis scale to plot the data in the A-F data ranges. The X data range must contain numeric values.

❶ Select /Graph X. ❷ Specify the range that contains the entries you want to use as the graph's X data range and press [Enter].

When 1-2-3 uses the contents of the X data range as the x-axis labels (in line, bar, and stacked bar graphs) and the labels are long enough to overlap one another, 1-2-3 automatically staggers the labels. To suppress display of some of the X data range contents in a graph, use /Graph Options Scale Skip.

The Move Command

/Move transfers a range of data and cell formats to another range in the same file. Read the following information before you use the Move command:

- If you move data that a formula refers to, the cell references in the formula automatically change to reflect the data's new location. For example, the formula @SUM(A1..A3) adds the numbers entered in the range A1..A3. If you move the data to C1..C3, the formula will change to @SUM(C1..C3).

- If you move data out of the specified cells of a range in a formula, 1-2-3 changes the range definition. For example, if you refer to the range A3..D8 in the formula @SUM(A3..D8) and then move the contents of cell D8 to F6, 1-2-3 changes the formula to @SUM(A3..F6) and includes any data in the expanded range.

- If you move data into the cells that define a range in a formula, the range changes to ERR and formulas that refer to that range evaluate to ERR. For example, if you have the formula @SUM(A1..C3) and move data into A1 or C3, 1-2-3 changes the formula to @SUM(ERR) and evaluates to ERR.

- If you move data into the upper left or lower right cells of a named range, the range loses its definition and formulas that refer to that range evaluate to ERR. For example, the range A1..C3 is named TOTALS and you have the formula @SUM(TOTALS). If you move data into A1 or C3, the range name loses its definition and the formula evaluates to ERR.

/Move

❶ Select /Move. ❷ Specify the range you want to move FROM and press [Enter]. ❸ Specify the range you want to move TO and press [Enter]. You need to specify only the upper left cell in the TO range.

Caution: *The TO range can be any unprotected area of the worksheet. Make sure the worksheet location is blank or contains unimportant data; 1-2-3 writes over existing data when it moves data to the range you specify. Save the worksheet before using /Move. If you make a mistake when moving data and the Undo feature is on, press [UNDO] (Alt-F4) immediately to restore the worksheet.*

The Print Commands

The Print commands create printed copies of your worksheet. You can use the Print commands to print directly on a printer or to print to a standard ASCII **text file** (a file with a .PRN extension) on disk. You can print the text file later with an operating system command or use the text file in another program.

Use the Print commands to perform the following tasks:

/Print [Printer or File] Align Tells 1-2-3 that the paper in the printer is correctly positioned at the top of a page and ready for printing and resets the page number to 1.

/Print [Printer or File] Clear Erases some or all of the current print settings and returns them to the default settings.

/Print [Printer or File] Go Starts the print job.

/Print [Printer or File] Line Advances the paper in the printer one line.

/Print [Printer or File] Options Establishes printing settings, including the header, footer, margins, borders, setup string, page length, and range format.

/Print [Printer or File] Page Advances the paper in the printer to the top of next page.

/Print [Printer or File] Quit Returns 1-2-3 to READY mode.

/Print [Printer or File] Range Specifies the range to print.

Printing Basics

The following sections describe the general procedure for printing to a printer and printing to a file. After reading this overview, see the specific command descriptions later in this chapter for more detailed information.

When you select /Print Printer or select /Print File and specify a filename, 1-2-3 displays a special screen called the /Print settings sheet. The /Print settings sheet allows you to see all the settings for the current print job at a glance. 1-2-3 will use these settings the next time you print your work. You can change any of the settings with the Print [Printer or File] commands displayed in the menu above the settings sheet. As you select commands to change settings, the settings sheet changes to reflect your choices.

Printing to a Printer — General Procedure

If you are going to print your work on a printer, be sure you used the Install program to install that printer for use with 1-2-3. If you are not sure if you installed a text printer, select /Worksheet Global Default and check the printer name setting in the settings sheet. If there is no printer name listed, refer to the installation instructions at the beginning of this book.

If you selected more than one text printer when you installed 1-2-3, use /Worksheet Global Default Printer Name to select the printer you want to use to print the current job.

Make sure that the printer you want to use is turned on, properly connected, and ready to print (on-line) and that the paper in the printer is aligned at the top of a new page.

The following steps describe the general procedure for printing a worksheet range to a printer.

❶ Select /Print Printer to display the commands and /Print settings sheet. ❷ Select Range. ❸ Specify the range you want to print and press [Enter]. ❹ If you want to change any of the current print settings, select Options and make the changes you require. ❺ When you are done specifying print options, select Quit as many times as necessary to return 1-2-3 to the Print menu. ❻ Select Align to tell 1-2-3 the paper in the printer is correctly positioned at the top of a page and ready for printing. ❼ Select Go to print the range on the printer. ❽ Select Page to advance the paper to the top of the next page and include the footer (if you have specified one) on the last line of the page. ❾ Select Quit to complete the print job and return 1-2-3 to READY mode.

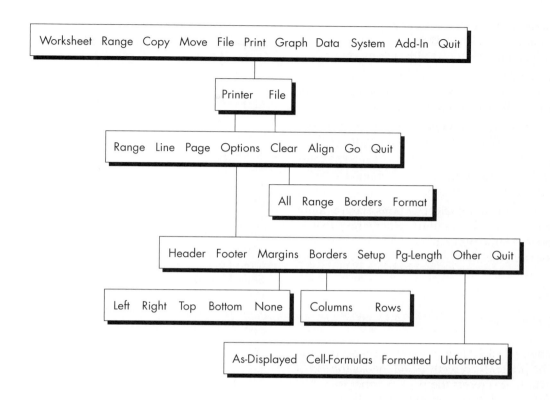

If you do not change the margins or page length, 1-2-3 uses the following default settings when it prints the range:

Left margin	4 characters from left edge of the paper
Right margin	76 characters from left edge of the paper
Top margin	2 lines from the top of the paper
Bottom margin	2 lines from the bottom of the paper
Page length	66 lines

Printing to a Text File — General Procedure

The following steps describe the general procedure for printing a worksheet range to a text file (a file with a .PRN extension) on disk.

❶ If you are using a two-diskette system, make sure there is a data disk in one of the drives. ❷ Select /Print File to display a list of files with a .PRN extension in the current directory. ❸ If you want to display files in a different drive and/or directory or with a different extension, use wild card characters or edit the path as described in "File Commands, Working with Files." ❹ Specify the name of the text file you want 1-2-3 to create and press [Enter]. ❺ If you specify the name of a text file that already exists, select Cancel to return 1-2-3 to READY mode without specifying a text file as the print destination, or Replace to write over the existing text file on disk when you select /Print File Go.

Then continue as follows:

❶ Select Range. ❷ Specify the range you want to print and press [Enter]. ❸ If you want to change any of the current print settings, select Options and make the changes you require. (See discussion following these steps.) ❹ When you are done specifying print options, select Quit as many times as necessary to return 1-2-3 to the Print menu. ❺ Select Align. ❻ Select Go to print the range to a text file. ❼ If you want to include other worksheet ranges in the same text file at the end of the previous range, repeat Steps 1, 2, and 6. ❽ If you specified a footer and you want it to appear on the last line of the page, select Page. ❾ Select Quit to complete the print job and return 1-2-3 to READY mode.

If you are creating a text file on disk so you can use 1-2-3 data with another program, you probably want to change the following print options:

- To eliminate headers, footers, and page breaks from the text file 1-2-3 creates, select Options Other Unformatted.

- To set the left margin to 0, select Options Margins Left and enter 0.

- To set the right margin, select Options Margins Right and enter a number for the right margin that is appropriate for the program in which you are going to use the text file.

/Print [Printer or File] Align

/Print [Printer or File] Align lets you tell 1-2-3 that the paper in the printer is correctly positioned at the top of a new page. It also resets the page number to 1. Use this command each time you reposition the paper in the printer at the top of a new page.

Use /Print [Printer or File] Align even when the print destination is a text file on disk. Use /Print [Printer or File] Align just before /Print [Printer or File] Go.

❶ If you are printing on a printer, position the paper in the printer at the top of a page, with the perforation just above the print head. ❷ Select /Print [Printer or File] Align.

/Print [Printer or File] Clear

/Print [Printer or File] Clear lets you reset some or all of your current print settings and returns them to the default settings.

❶ Select /Print [Printer or File] Clear. ❷ Select All to clear the current print range (clear all borders, headers, and footers; reset all formats and options to their default settings); Range to clear the current print range; Borders to clear all borders (column and row ranges); or Format to reset margins, page length, and setup strings to their default settings. ❸ Select other settings

from the Print menu or select Quit to return 1-2-3 to READY mode.

/Print [Printer or File] Go

/Print [Printer or File] Go lets you start the print job, sending your worksheet data to a printer or to a file on disk.

❶ Make sure you specified a print range using /Print [Printer or File] Range. ❷ If you are printing on a printer, make sure the printer you want to use is turned on, properly connected, and ready to print (on-line) and that the paper in the printer is aligned at the top of a new page. ❸ Select /Print [Printer or File] Align. ❹ Select Go. ❺ If you want to print additional ranges with different options as part of the same print job, change your options, select the new ranges, and select Go again. ❻ Select Quit.

Quit closes the print job and returns 1-2-3 to READY mode. If you do not select Quit, when printing to a text file on disk, using a print spooler, or using a network, the process will not be finished. 1-2-3 also closes your print job when you press [Ctrl][Break] or press [Esc] enough times to return 1-2-3 to the Print menu.

/Print [Printer or File] Line

/Print [Printer or File] Line lets you force a line feed on a printer or in a file. It also adds one line to the internal line count 1-2-3 maintains to ensure that headers, footers, and page breaks will be in the correct spot when you print and that pages will be completely filled. Use /Print [Printer or File] Line to insert blank lines between print ranges if you are printing several different ranges in the same print job.

❶ Select /Print [Printer or File] Line to advance the paper in the printer one line or insert a new line in a text file.

/Print [Printer or File] Options

Use /Print [Printer or File] Options to perform the following tasks:

Borders Prints descriptive information from specified columns and rows in your worksheet, to the left and top edges of every page of print output.

Footers Prints a line of text just above the bottom margin of every page.

Headers Prints a line of text just below the top margin of every page.

Margins Sets left, right, top, and bottom margins for the print output or clears all margins.

Other Determines whether 1-2-3 prints the worksheet data or the formulas underlying the data, and whether 1-2-3 prints headers and footers and inserts page breaks.

Pg-Length Sets the number of lines to be printed on a page.

Quit Returns you to the /Print menu.

Setup Lets you specify additional printer attributes available on your printer.

/Print [Printer or File] Options Borders

/Print [Printer or File] Options Borders lets you print descriptive information on every page from specified columns and rows in your worksheet above or to the left of the range you are printing. For instance, if you specify D3..D15 as your print range and column A as your border, 1-2-3 prints the entries in cells A3 through A15 as the border.

❶ Select /Print [Printer or File] Options Borders. ❷ Select Columns to create vertical headings that are repeated on the left side of each page of print output; or Rows to create horizontal headings that are repeated on the top of each page of print output. If you have previously specified borders, 1-2-3 highlights this range. ❸ Specify the range you want to print as borders and press [Enter].

Select columns when the print range contains more columns of data than will fit across one page and you have labels or other information in a column or columns that will help identify data printed on subsequent pages. Select rows when the print range contains more

rows of data than will fit down one page and you have labels or other information in a row or rows that will help identify data printed on subsequent pages.

/Print [Printer or File] Options Footer/Header

/Print [Printer or File] Options Footer lets you create a page **footer**, which is a line of text printed just above the bottom margin of every page of print output. 1-2-3 prints the footer on the line above the bottom margin and leaves two blank lines between printed data and the footer. For example, if you have a bottom margin of 2, 1-2-3 uses five lines at the bottom of each page — two between the data and the footer, one for the footer, and two for the bottom margin.

/Print [Printer or File] Options Header lets you create a page **header**, which is a line of text printed just below the top margin of every page of print output. 1-2-3 prints the header on the line below the top margin and leaves two blank lines between printed data and the header. For example, if you have a top margin of 2, 1-2-3 uses five lines at the top of each page — two between the data and the header, one for the header, and two for the top margin.

Use the following guidelines when creating footers and headers:

- A footer or header can contain up to 240 characters, depending on your print margin and setup string settings.

- Although footers and headers are limited to a single line each, 1-2-3 allows you to divide the line into separate segments for the right, left, and center portions of each line. Use the | (Split Vertical Bar) to separate the information segments. 1-2-3 left-aligns text you type before a | (Split Vertical Bar), centers text you type after a | (Split Vertical Bar), and right-aligns text you type after a second | (Split Vertical Bar). If you do not use any split vertical bars, 1-2-3 left-aligns the entire footer or header.

- Use the # symbol to include a page number on every page of print output. It can be combined with text for additional description, such as "Page #."

- Use @ (At sign) to include the current date on every page of print output. 1-2-3 uses the date supplied by your computer's internal clock. The @ (At sign) can be combined with text for additional description, such as "Today's Date: @."

- Use \ (Backslash) followed by a cell address or range name to use the contents of a cell as the footer or header. For example, entering \B1 uses the contents of cell B1. The contents of the cell will be the only text in the footer or header, but can include any of the standard conventions, such as the use of the split vertical bar. If the | (Split Vertical Bar) is the first character in the cell, you must precede it with another | (Split Vertical Bar) as a label prefix for the footer to work.

The following table shows some examples of footers:

Enter	Resulting footer		
GOODWIN	GOODWIN		
I GOODWIN		GOODWIN	
GOODWIN I I Page #	GOODWIN		Page 15
@I GOODWIN I Page # 4/1/89	GOODWIN		Page 15

❶ Select /Print [Printer or File] Options Footer or Header. 1-2-3 displays the current footer or header, if any. ❷ If 1-2-3 displays a footer or header, edit the displayed text and press [Enter] when you are done. Otherwise, specify the footer or header by typing the text or typing a backslash followed by the address or range name of the cell that contains the text and then pressing [Enter].

Note: *1-2-3 will not print the footer on the last page of the print job unless you select /Print [Printer or File] Page after printing the print job.*

/Print [Printer or File] Options Margins

The Print [Printer or File] Options Margins commands let you override the default print margins set with /Worksheet Global Default Printer. Use the Options Margins commands to perform the following tasks:

Bottom Sets the bottom margin for printed pages.

Left Sets the left margin for printed pages.

None Clears the current margins and resets the top, left, and bottom margins to 0 and the right margin to 240.

Right Sets the right margin for printed pages.

Top Sets the top margin for printed pages.

These commands are described below.

/Print [Printer or File] Options Margins Bottom /Top This command lets you set the bottom or top margin for printed pages, in number of standard lines from the edge of the paper. You can specify any number from 0 to 32. Use this command only if you need to set a bottom or top margin that is different from the default margin setting.

❶ Select /Print [Printer or File] Options Margins Bottom or Top. 1-2-3 displays the current margin setting. ❷ Press [Enter] to accept the current margin setting or change the setting by typing the number of standard characters (0 to 240) for the margin and pressing [Enter].

/Print [Printer or File] Options Margins Left/Right

This command lets you set the margins for printed pages, in number of standard characters from the edge of the paper. You can specify any number from 0 to 240, but the left margin setting must be smaller than the right margin setting. Use /Print [Printer or File] Options Margins Left or Right only if you need to set margins that are different from the default margins set with /Worksheet Global Default Printer Left or Right.

❶ Select /Print [Printer or File] Options Margins Left or Right. 1-2-3 displays the current left margin setting. ❷ Press [Enter] to accept the current setting or change the setting by typing the number of standard characters (0 to 240) for the margin and pressing [Enter].

1-2-3 measures the left and right margin in standard-size characters. For instance, if your left margin is 2, 1-2-3 leaves space in the left margin for two standard-size characters. If, however, you use a setup string to specify pitch, 1-2-3 does not measure margins in standard-size characters. You will have to change your left and right margin settings to accommodate the new number of characters per line.

/Print [Printer or File] Options Margins None

This command lets you clear the current margins and reset the top, left, and bottom margins to 0 and the right margin to 240.

/Print [Printer or File] Options Other

/Print [Printer or File] Options Other lets you specify whether 1-2-3 prints the data in the worksheet or the formulas underlying the data, and whether 1-2-3 prints headers and footers and inserts page breaks.

The choices under /Print [Printer or File] Options Other are as follows:

As-Displayed Prints the data as it appears on your screen (the default setting). This means that results of formulas are printed as they are displayed on the screen, as are cell formats and column widths. Use the As-Displayed option to restore standard printing after you have selected Cell-Formulas.

Cell-Formulas Prints the contents of each non-blank cell in the print range, one cell per line. Each line contains exactly what appears in the first line of the control panel when the cell pointer is on the cell: the cell address, the cell format, the protection status (P or U), and the cell contents (number, formula, or label). 1-2-3 does not print borders, even if you specify them.

Formatted Prints with all specified formatting options (the default setting), including page breaks, headers, and footers. Use this option to restore standard printing after you have selected Unformatted.

Unformatted Prints without page breaks, headers, footers, and top and bottom margins. Use this option if you are printing to a text file and do not want to leave space in the file for page breaks.

If you want to select a combination of options, such as Cell-Formulas and Unformatted, select Other again and then select another option.

/Print [Printer or File] Options Pg-Length

/Print [Printer or File] Options Pg-Length lets you override the default page length set with /Worksheet Global Default Printer Pg-Length.

Page length is measured in standard lines. The default page length is 66 lines, which is appropriate for printers that print 6 lines per inch on 11-inch paper. When you print with the default page length, 1-2-3 uses the 66 lines as follows:

Lines 1 and 2	Default top margin
Line 3	Header (or blank line if you did not enter text for header)
Lines 4 and 5	Blank lines
LInes 6 through 61	Worksheet data (total of 56 lines)
Lines 62 and 63	Blank lines
Lines 64	Footer (or blank line if you did not enter text for footer)
Lines 65 and 66	Default bottom margin

❶ Select /Print [Printer or File] Options Pg-Length to display the current page length setting. ❷ Press [Enter] to accept the current setting or change the setting by typing the number of standard lines (1 to 100) for the page length and pressing [Enter].

/Print [Printer or File] Options Quit

/Print [Printer or File] Options Quit lets you return to the /Print menu.

/Print [Printer or File] Options Setup

/Print [Printer or File] Options Setup lets you override the default setup string specified with /Worksheet Global Default Printer Setup.

A **setup string** is a series of characters preceded by a \ (backslash) that 1-2-3 uses to tell your printer to print a certain way. For example, you can send a setup string that causes the printer to compress or underline type. You create setup strings by translating the printer control codes for your printer into setup string format. 1-2-3 sends the setup string to your printer before printing begins. 1-2-3 ignores setup strings when you are printing to a text file on disk.

Caution: *To avoid complications when printing, do not use setup strings to control print settings, such as page length and margins, that you can control through 1-2-3 commands.*

❶ Select /Print [Printer or File] Options Setup to display the current setup string, if any. ❷ If 1-2-3 displays a setup string, edit the displayed string and press [Enter] when you are done or specify a setup string (up to 39 characters) and press [Enter].

Note: *Some printers have a setup string buffer that can be used only once. If this is the case, you need to turn your printer off and then back on to start another print job using the same setup string. With some printers, you may need to turn your printer off and then back on if you change the setup string during a 1-2-3 session. This cancels the effect of the previous setup string. On some printers, however, changing the setup string cancels the effect of the previous setup string. For more details, see your printer manual.*

/Print [Printer or File] Page

/Print [Printer or File] Page lets you advance the paper in the printer to the top of the next page or insert blank lines in a text file on disk. If you specified a footer with /Print [Printer or File] Options Footer, 1-2-3 prints the footer at the bottom of the current page before advancing to the next page.

/Print [Printer or File] Quit

/Print [Printer or File] Quit lets you close the current print job and return 1-2-3 to READY mode.

/Print [Printer or File] Range

/Print [Printer or File] Range lets you specify the **print range**, the data 1-2-3 prints when you select /Print [Printer or File] Go. Whether you are printing on a printer or to a file on disk, you must specify the cells you want 1-2-3 to print. You can print every nonblank cell in the worksheet or just a few cells. If the data in the print range is wider than the paper you are printing on, 1-2-3 automatically prints the data that extends beyond the right margin on a separate page.

❶ Select /Print [Printer or File] Range. If you have previously specified a print range, 1-2-3 highlights this range. ❷ Specify the range you want to print and press [Enter].

If the print range includes long labels, the print range must include the cells the long label overlaps as well as the cell in which you entered the long label. For example, to print a long label entered in A1 that overlaps B1 and C1, be sure cells A1, B1, and C1 are included in the print range.

Note: *When you print long labels on a printer that supports proportionally spaced fonts, the number of characters your printer prints may differ from the number of characters you specified in your 1-2-3 print range. This discrepancy occurs because your printer changes the size of the characters, making them wider or narrower than regular characters. Because the characters are a different size, more characters or fewer characters may fit in the space you specified to print.*

The Quit Command

/Quit lets you end the 1-2-3 session and return to either the operating system or to the Access system menu, depending on how you started 1-2-3.

/Quit

❶ Select /Quit. ❷ Select No to return 1-2-3 to READY mode or Yes to end 1-2-3 session. ❸ If you selected Yes and you have changed the worksheet but not saved it, 1-2-3 displays another No/Yes menu. Select No to return to READY mode so you can use /File Save to save the worksheet; Yes to end 1-2-3 session without saving changes to the worksheet, that is, losing all changes to the current worksheet.

Note: *To suspend 1-2-3 temporarily without ending the session so you can use operating system commands, use /System. Save your work before using /System.*

The Range Commands

The Range commands let you work with ranges. A **range** is any rectangular block of cells — a single cell, a row or column, parts of several rows and columns, or an entire worksheet.

Use the Range commands to perform the following tasks:

/Range Erase Erases data in a range.

/Range Format Changes the display of data in a range.

/Range Input Restricts cell pointer movement to unprotected cells in a range. (Used with /Range Unprot.)

/Range Justify Rearranges a column of labels so the labels fit within a specified width.

/Range Label Left-aligns, right-aligns, or centers labels in a range.

/Range Name Creates, modifies, and deletes range names; generates tables of range names.

/Range Prot Reprotects cells in a range (that have been unprotected with /Range Unprot) when global worksheet protection is on.

/Range Search Finds or replaces a specified string in a range.

/Range Trans Copies a range of data, transposing the layout of the copied data and replacing any copied formulas with their current values.

/Range Unprot Unprotects and allows changes to cells in a range when global worksheet protection is on. Allows changes to cells in a range that will be used with /Range Input.

/Range Value Copies a range of data, replacing any copied formulas with their current values.

/Range Erase

/Range Erase lets you erase the data in a range but does not change the format(s) or protection status of cells in the range. Make sure you have selected the correct range whose contents you want to delete before you select erase.

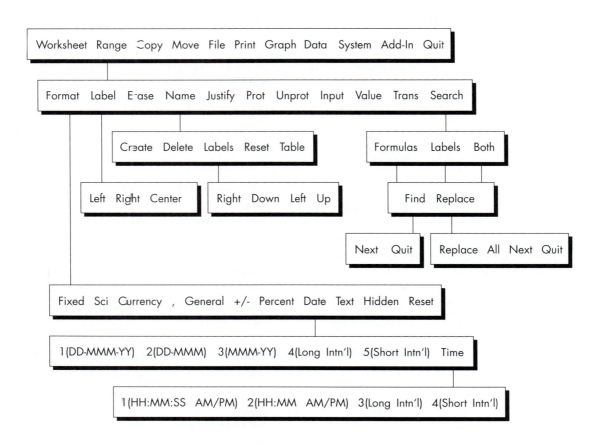

❶ Select /Range Erase. ❷ Specify the range you want to erase and press [Enter].

Note: *To erase data in protected cells, you must turn off worksheet protection using /Worksheet Global Protection Disable or unprotect the cells whose contents you want to erase with /Range Unprot.*

/Range Format

/Range Format lets you set the **cell format** or the way 1-2-3 displays data for a specific range of cells. It overrides the global cell format set with /Worksheet Global Format. You can change the format of a range either before or after entering data in the range. 1-2-3 initially displays data in the General format, which displays numbers with a minus sign for negatives, no

thousands separators, and no trailing zeros to the right of the decimal point.

Changing a cell's format changes the way 1-2-3 displays a value in the cell, but it does not change the value itself. You can, for example, choose a cell format to display 45.123 as $45; 1-2-3 still stores the cell's value as 45.123 and uses the entire number in all calculations.

1-2-3 displays a format indicator in the edit panel to describe the format of a selected cell as described in the following table:

Indicator	Format
C0 to C15	Currency, 0 to 15 decimal places
F0 to F15	Fixed, 0 to 15 decimal places
G	General, a label or a blank cell
P0 to P15	Percent, 0 to 15 decimal places
S0 to S15	Scientific, 0 to 15 places
,0 to ,15	, (Comma), 0 to 15 decimal places
+/−	+ for positive values, − for negative values
D1	DD-MMM-YY
D2	DD-MMM
D3	MMM-YY
D4	MM/DD/YY, DD/MM/YY, DD.MM.YY, or YY-MM-DD
D5	MM/DD, DD/MM, DD.MM, or MM-DD
D6	HH:MM:SS AM/PM
D7	HH:MM AM/PM
D8	HH:MM:SS (24 hour), HH.MM.SS (24 hour), or HH,MM,SS (24 hour), or HHhMMmSSs (display varies according to the Worksheet Global Default Other International setting)
D9	HH:MM (24 hour), HH.MM (24 hour), HH,MM, or HHhMMm (display varies according to the Worksheet Global Default Other International setting)
T	Text format
H	Hidden format

When changing the format of a cell or range containing numbers, keep these guidelines in mind:

- If a cell is too narrow to display a cell's formatted value, 1-2-3 either displays the value in scientific notation, rounds the value, or fills the cell with asterisks, depending on the cell format. The column must be one character wider than the width of the formatted value to display fully.

- Regardless of how the number is displayed, 1-2-3 always stores the full value of the cell and uses the full value in all relevant calculations.

- When you move data from a formatted range, 1-2-3 moves the format with the data. The original range reverts to the default cell format. When you copy data in a formatted range, 1-2-3 copies the cell format with the data.

❶ Select /Range Format. ❷ Select a cell format, as described below under "Format Options," and, if requested, enter the number of decimal places required. ❸ Specify the range you want to format and press [Enter].

The Decimal Places field becomes available when you select Fixed, Scientific, Currency, , (Comma), or Percent. When you select any one of these formats, you can specify the number of decimal places you want. The default setting is 0, except for Currency, which has a default decimal setting of 2.

To format a Time, select Data, then Time, from the menu.

Format Options

Fixed Displays numbers with up to 15 decimal places, a minus sign for negatives, and a leading zero for decimal values. For example, 12.389 displays as 12 in Fixed format when you specify 0 decimal places.

Scientific Displays numbers in scientific (exponential) notation, with up to 15 decimal places in the mantissa and an exponent from −99 to +99. For example, 12.245 displays as 1.2E+01 in Scientific format with 1 decimal place. The value 124500000000 displays as 1.25E+11 when you specify 2 decimal places.

Currency Displays numbers with a currency symbol, thousands separators, up to 15 decimal places, parentheses or a minus sign for negatives, and a leading zero for decimal values. The currency symbol, thousands separators, and negative symbol 1-2-3 uses depend on the settings specified with /Worksheet Global Default Other International. The initial Currency Symbol setting is $. For example, −.256 displays as ($0.3) when you specify 1 decimal place. The value 12 displays as $12.00 when you specify 2 decimal places.

, (Comma) Displays numbers with thousands separators, up to 15 decimal places, parentheses or a minus sign for negatives, and a leading zero for decimal values. For example, 8999 displays as 8,999.00 when you specify 2 decimal places and use a comma (the default) for the thousands separator.

General Displays numbers with a minus sign for negatives, no thousands separators, and no trailing zeros to the right of the decimal point. For example, 1650.00 displays as 1650, and −12.42700 displays as −12.427. When the number of digits to the left of the decimal point exceeds the column width minus one, the number displays in scientific notation. For example, 130000000 displays as 1.3E+11 (when the column width is 12). When the number of digits to the right of the decimal point exceeds the column width, the decimal number is truncated. For example, 123.456789 displays as 123.4567 (when the column width is 9). General is the initial global cell format for 1-2-3 worksheets.

+/− Displays a series of plus or minus signs or a period. The number of plus or minus signs equals the integer value of the entry. Plus signs indicate a positive value, minus signs indicate a negative value, and a period indicates a number between −1 and 1. (If the integer value of the entry exceeds the column width, 1-2-3 displays asterisks.) For example, 5.9 displays as +++++.

Percent Displays numbers as percentages (that is, multiplied by 100 and shown with a percent sign), with up to 15 decimal places. For example, 12.42738 displays as 1242.7% and −.0425 displays as −4.25%.

Date Displays numbers in the Date format you select. 1-2-3 assigns a number for each date from January 1, 1990 (1) to December 31, 2099 (73050). 1-2-3 looks only at integers and ignores decimals. The date displays according to one of the five Date formats (D1 through D5): DD-MMM-YY, DD-MMM, MMM-YY, International long, and International short. The International Date options depend on the setting specified in /Worksheet Global Default Other International.

Date format	Cell display
(D1) DD-MMM-YY	14-Aug-89
(D2) DD-MMM	14-Aug
(D3) MMM-YY	Aug-89
(D4) Intn'l long	08/14/89 *(if today is 8/14/89)*
(D5) Intn'l short	08/14 *(if today is 8/14)*

Time Displays numbers in the Time format you select. 1-2-3 represents the time of day in decimal format: .000 = midnight, .5 = noon, .99988 = 11:59 PM. You can also enter a time in fraction format based on a 24-hour clock. For example, 15/24 = 03:00 PM, and so on

For positive numbers, 1-2-3 calculates the time number by adding the decimal part of the number to zero. For negative numbers, 1-2-3 calculates the time number by subtracting the decimal part of the number from one. The four Time formats (D6 through D9) are: HH:MM:SS (AM/PM), HH:MM (AM/PM), International long (24 hour), and International short (24 hour). The International Time options depend on the setting specified in /Worksheet Global Default Other International.

Time format	Cell display
(D6) HH:MM:SS	02:03:07 PM
(D7) HH:MM	09:56 AM
(D8) Intn'l long	14:03:07
(D9) Intn'l short	14:03 *(if it is 2:03 PM)*

Text Displays formulas as you enter them, rather than as their result. Numbers in formulas display in General format. For example, 165.00 displays as 165 and @SUM(A1..A5) displays as @SUM(A1..A5), not as the computed value.

Hidden Makes worksheet data invisible, though the data still exists. The data appears in the control panel unless the cells are protected. When you select Hidden, you can avoid accidentally writing over hidden data by protecting the worksheet. You can then unprotect specific cells with /Range Unprot.

Reset Restores the default format specified with /Worksheet Global Format to a specified range. Reset redisplays all or part of a Hidden range of cells.

/Range Input

/Range Input lets you limit cell pointer movement and data entry to unprotected cells in a range so you can enter or edit data in those cells but not in others. This command works with /Range Unprot. In most cases, /Range Input is used for data entry in a fill-in-the-blanks entry form, with the unprotected cells acting as the blanks in the form. /Range Input is commonly used in interactive macros.

❶ If you want a fill-in-the-blanks entry form, set up the form. The entry form should include text that will prompt for the information you want entered in the blanks; for example, Name:, Job Title:, Salary:. ❷ Select /Range Unprot. ❸ Specify the cell or cells in which you want to enter or edit data during /Range Input and press [Enter]. ❹ Select /Range Input. ❺ Specify the data input range. The **data input range** is any range that includes the cells you unprotected in Step 3. If you set up an entry form, be sure to include the entire entry form, not just the blank cells, in the data input range. Then press [Enter]. 1-2-3 moves the data input range to the upper left corner of the screen, with the cell pointer in the first unprotected cell in the range. ❻ Enter or edit data in the unprotected cells. You can move the cell pointer only to the unprotected cells in the data input range. ❼ To end /Range Input, press [Enter] or [Esc] when 1-2-3 is in READY mode. 1-2-3 returns the cell pointer to the cell it was in before you selected /Range Input and restores unrestricted cell pointer movement.

/Range Justify

/Range Justify lets you treat a column of labels as a paragraph and rearranges (justifies) the labels to fit within a width you specify. To use this command, global worksheet protection must be off. Use /Range Justify to equalize the length of a series of long labels, to fit text into a specific width for viewing or printing, to create a paragraph in a worksheet, or to rejustify an

edited paragraph. /Range Justify justifies only one column of labels at a time. (A blank cell or numeric value marks the end of a column of labels.)

❶ Move the cell pointer to the first cell in the column of labels you want to justify. ❷ Select /Range Justify. ❸ Specify the justify range and press [Enter].

The total width of the columns in the justify range determines the maximum width of the justified labels (to a limit of 240 characters).

If you specify a single-row justify range, 1-2-3 justifies the entire column of labels to fill the width of the justify range using as many rows as necessary. If the justified labels occupy more rows than the original labels, 1-2-3 moves down any subsequent data in the column. If the justified labels occupy fewer rows than the original labels, 1-2-3 moves up any subsequent data. Use a single-row justify range only if all cells below the labels you are justifying are blank or if movement of data below the labels is acceptable.

If you specify a multiple-row justify range, 1-2-3 limits the justification to the specified range and does not move data below the justify range. If you use a multiple-row justify range, be sure the range is wide and deep enough to hold the entire series of justified labels.

Note: *1-2-3 has some text editing capabilities, such as search and replace, but it is not a word processing program. To process text that you generate in 1-2-3, use /Print File to store the text in a text file, then use a word processing program to edit the text file. Conversely, to bring text stored in text files into a worksheet, use /File Import Text.*

/Range Label

/Range Label lets you change the alignment of labels in a range by changing their label prefix: ' (left-aligned), " (right-aligned), or ^ (centered).

❶ Select /Range Label. ❷ Select Left to align labels with left edge of cells, Right to align labels with right edge of cells, or Center to center label in cells. ❸ Specify the range of labels whose alignment you want to change and press [Enter].

Labels that exceed the width of a column appear left-aligned no matter what label prefix they have. Right-aligned labels leave a blank space to the right if there is enough room.

/Range Name

Range names are names of up to 15 characters that you use instead of cell or range addresses in commands and formulas. For example, if you assign the name SALES to A5..A9, you can total the numbers in A5..A9 with the formula @SUM(SALES). Range names are generally easier to remember and can be typed more quickly than the addresses to which they correspond.

Use the /Range Name commands to perform the following tasks:

Create Creates or modifies a range name.

Delete Deletes a range name.

Labels Creates range names for single cell ranges, using labels in adjacent cells as the range names.

Reset Deletes all range names in the worksheet.

Table Creates a table in the worksheet of range names and their corresponding range addresses.

When you copy formulas that contain range names, 1-2-3 treats the range names as relative references and replaces the old addresses in the copied formulas with the new addresses. For example, suppose you enter the formula @SUM(TOTALS) in A10, where TOTALS is the name for A1..A5, and then copy the formula to C10. The copied formula in C10 reads @SUM(C1..C5). To have 1-2-3 treat a range name in a formula as an absolute reference, precede the range name with a $ (Dollar Sign). For example, if you enter @SUM($TOTALS) in A10 and then copy it to C10, the formula in C10 reads @SUM($TOTALS), where TOTALS still refers to A1..A5.

1-2-3 automatically replaces a range address in a formula that refers to a range you named with /Range Name Create or /Range Name Labels. For example, suppose the formula @SUM(A1..A5) exists when you assign the name TOTALS to A1..A5. 1-2-3 automatically changes @SUM(A1..A5) to @SUM(TOTALS).

If, when using /Move, you move data into the upper left or lower right cell of a named range, the range name becomes undefined. Formulas that used that range evaluate to ERR.

/Range Name Create

/Range Name Create lets you assign a name to a range or redefine which cells an existing range refers to. You can also use /Range Name Create to edit a range name by selecting an existing name, pressing [EDIT] (F2), and editing it. The number of range names you can create is limited only by available memory. 1-2-3 does not distinguish between uppercase and lowercase letters in range names and converts lowercase to uppercase when you press [Enter].

Follow these guidelines when you create range names:

* Do not include spaces, commas, semicolons, or the characters + * – / & @ or # in range names.

* Do not create names that look like cell addresses, such as Q2 or EX100.

* Do not use @function names, advanced macro command keywords, or 1-2-3 key names as range names.

* Do not create range names that begin with a number, such as 20DEC, or consist entirely of numbers, such as 1989. You cannot include such range names in a formula.

❶ Select /Range Name Create. ❷ Specify a range name of up to 15 characters and press [Enter]. ❸ Specify the range to name and press [Enter].

Use /Range Name Create to edit a range name by selecting an existing name, pressing [EDIT] (F2), and editing it.

When /Move, /Worksheet Delete, /Worksheet Insert, or /Worksheet Page moves the upper left or lower right cell of a named range, 1-2-3 adjusts the range name's definition.

Note: *Use [NAME] (F3) to list named ranges when completing a command or writing a formula.*

/Range Name Delete

/Range Name Delete lets you delete a range name but leave the data in the range unchanged. In any formulas that use the deleted range name, 1-2-3 replaces the range name with the corresponding range address.

❶ Select /Range Name Delete. ❷ Specify the range name you want to delete and press [Enter].

/Range Name Labels

/Range Name Labels lets you assign range names to single cell ranges, using existing adjacent labels as the range names. To prevent confusion when using range names in formulas and advanced macro commands, make sure that the labels you are going to use to create range names meet the guidelines described under /Range Name Create. Because labels typically describe the contents of a range, this command lets you use this label as a range name as well.

Caution: *If a label you use as a range name duplicates an existing range name, 1-2-3 reassigns the range name to the new range. Formulas that refer to the named range as it was previously defined now refer to the new range.*

❶ Select /Range Name Labels. ❷ Select Right if cell to name is to the right of the label; Down if cell to name is below the label; Left if cell to name is to the left of the label; Up if cell to name is above the label. ❸ Specify the range that contains the labels you want to use as range names and press [Enter].

Note: *1-2-3 uses only the labels in the range as range names; it ignores any numbers or formulas in the range. If any of the labels exceed 15 characters, 1-2-3 uses only the first 15 characters.*

/Range Name Reset

/Range Name Reset lets you delete all range names in the current worksheet but leave the data in the ranges unchanged. In formulas that use any of the deleted range names, 1-2-3 replaces the range names with the corresponding range addresses. To delete individual range names, use /Range Name Delete.

Caution: *Named macros are disabled with /Range Name Reset.*

/Range Name Table

/Range Name Table lets you create a two-column table that alphabetically lists range names in the worksheet and their corresponding addresses. The table will occupy two columns and as many rows as there are range names plus one blank row.

❶ Decide on a location for the range name table. ❷ Select /Range Name Table. ❸ Specify the location you decided on in Step 1 and press [Enter]. You need to specify only the first cell of the table's location.

Note: *If you use /Range Name Table frequently, assign a range name to a worksheet area you designate as the table location. Whenever you select /Range Name Table, specify the table location's range name. This technique saves time and helps avoid the possibility of writing over data when you create a range name table.*

/Range Prot

/Range Prot lets you reprotect cells in a range (that have been unprotected with /Range Unprot) when global worksheet protection is on. (When global worksheet protection is on, 1-2-3 displays a PR in the control panel to indicate protected cells.)

❶ Select /Range Prot. ❷ Specify the range containing the unprotected cells you want to protect again and press [Enter].

/Range Search

/Range Search lets you locate character strings consisting of letters or numbers in labels and/or formulas within a specified range. Use /Range Search to find range names in formulas. /Range Search does not locate numbers that are not in formulas. 1-2-3 searches rightwards by column, starting with column A, then B, and so on. /Range Search does not search hidden columns, but does search cells formatted with /Range Format Hidden. /Range Search ends with an error message if you attempt a replacement that would cause a formula to become invalid.

The search string is not case sensitive. If you specify "A" as the search string, 1-2-3 will search for both uppercase and lowercase A's. The replacement string is, however, case sensitive. If you specify "HiLo" as the replacement string, 1-2-3 will use that exact combination of uppercase and lowercase letters.

/Range Search Find

Use /Range Search Find to locate a specified string.

❶ Select /Range Search. ❷ Specify the range you want 1-2-3 to search and press [Enter]. ❸ Type the string you want 1-2-3 to search for and press [Enter]. Or, if 1-2-3 displays a default string, press [Enter] to accept that string or press [Backspace] to edit it. ❹ Select Formulas to look only in formulas for the search string; Labels to look only in labels for the search string; or Both to look in both formulas and labels for the search string. ❺ Select Find to highlight the first occurrence of the search string. ❻ Select Next to highlight the next occurrence of the search string or Quit to stop the search and return 1-2-3 to READY mode. ❼ When 1-2-3 cannot find any more occurrences of the search string in the search range, it displays an error message. Press [Esc] or [Enter] to return to 1-2-3 to READY mode.

/Range Search Replace

Use /Range Search Replace to locate the specified string and replace it with another string. Using the contents of the cell as displayed in the control panel, 1-2-3 will replace numeric strings in formulas, but will not replace numbers entered directly in cells.

Caution: *1-2-3 searches and replaces rightwards by column, starting with column A, then B, and so on. When you replace range names in formulas, you may get unexpected results depending on the location of the range name references.*

❶ Select /Range Search. ❷ Follow Steps 2, 3 and 4 as in the prior procedure. ❸ Select Replace to replace occurrences of the search string with a different (replacement) string. ❹ Type the replacement string and press [Enter]. Or, if 1-2-3 displays a default string, press [Enter] to accept that string or press [Backspace] to edit it. ❺ When 1-2-3 highlights the cell containing the first occurrence of the search string, select Replace to replace the current string with the replacement string and highlight the next cell containing the search string; All to replace all remaining occurrences of the search string with the replacement string; Next to find the next occurrence of the search string without replacing the current string; or Quit to stop the search and return 1-2-3 to READY mode without replacing the current string.

/Range Trans

/Range Trans lets you copy a range of data rearranging the range from columns to rows, or from rows to columns. It replaces any copied formulas with their current values. The data in the worksheet changes from a horizontal arrangement to a vertical one or vice versa.

Note: *If the CALC indicator appears at the bottom of the screen, press [CALC] (F9) to update formulas before you use /Range Trans. If any of the formulas whose values you will be transposing refer to cells in files on disk, you also need to use /File Admin Link-Refresh to make sure those formulas' values are up to date.*

❶ Select /Range Trans. ❷ Specify the FROM range (the range whose data you want to transpose) and press [Enter]. ❸ Specify the TO range (the location for the transposed data) and press [Enter]. You need to specify only the first cell of the TO range. Each cell in the TO range inherits the cell format and protection status of the corresponding cell in the FROM range.

Caution: *If the FROM and TO ranges overlap, you may get unexpected results.*

/Range Unprot

/Range Unprot lets you unprotect cells. This allows changes to cells in a range when global worksheet protection is on. When the cell pointer is on an unprotected cell, 1-2-3 displays a U in the control panel. When you are through working with the range of cells you have unprotected, reprotect the cells with /Range Prot.

❶ Select /Range Unprot. ❷ Specify the range you want to unprotect and allow changes to and press [Enter].

Note: *Unprotected cells are displayed in color or in a brighter intensity.*

/Range Value

/Range Value lets you copy a range of data, replacing any copied formulas with their current values.

Note: *If the CALC indicator appears at the bottom of the screen, press [CALC] (F9) to update formulas before* *you use /Range Value. If any of the formulas whose values you will be transposing refer to cells in files on disk, use /File Admin Link-Refresh to make sure those formulas' values are up to date.*

❶ Select /Range Value. ❷ Specify the FROM range (the range whose current values you want to copy) and press [Enter]. ❸ Specify the TO range (the location for the copied values) and press [Enter]. You need to specify only the first cell of the TO range. Each cell in the TO range takes on the cell format and protection status of the corresponding FROM range cell.

Note: *To convert a formula to its current value without using /Range Value, move the cell pointer to the cell containing the formula, press [EDIT] (F2), press [CALC] (F9), then press [Enter].*

The System Command

/System lets you temporarily suspend 1-2-3 and return to the operating system without clearing the current worksheet from memory. Use /System when you want to use operating system commands without ending the current 1-2-3 session. You can perform many operating system tasks after selecting /System, including copying files or creating a new directory. In general, however, do not load memory-resident programs or use the operating system PRINT command or you may not be able to resume the 1-2-3 session.

Caution: *Before you use the System command, it is recommended that you use /File Save to save your work.*

/System

❶ Select /System to replace the worksheet temporarily with the operating system prompt. ❷ Type any operating system commands desired at the operating system prompt. ❸ To return to the 1-2-3 session and the current worksheet, type "exit" and press [Enter] at the operating system prompt.

The Worksheet Commands

The Worksheet commands let you control the display and organization of your work. They also let you control **global settings**, which are 1-2-3 settings that affect the entire worksheet and 1-2-3 as a whole. Use the Worksheet commands to perform the following tasks:

/Worksheet Column Sets the width of one or more columns, resets columns to the global column width, and hides and redisplays columns.

/Worksheet Delete Removes entire columns and rows from the worksheet.

/Worksheet Erase Removes the worksheet from memory.

/Worksheet Global Sets the global cell format, label alignment, column width, protection status, recalculation method, and zero-display setting for the worksheet. Also sets 1-2-3 default settings, which are used every time you begin a 1-2-3 session.

/Worksheet Insert Inserts blank columns or rows.

/Worksheet Learn Specifies a range in which to record keystrokes to run as a macro.

/Worksheet Page Creates a page break in a worksheet, which causes 1-2-3 to begin a new page when printing the worksheet.

/Worksheet Status Displays the current global settings, including information about memory use, recalculation, circular references, cell display, and global protection.

/Worksheet Titles Freezes rows and/or columns along the top and left edges of a worksheet so they remain in view as you scroll through the worksheet.

/Worksheet Window Splits the screen into two horizontal or vertical windows, turns synchronized scrolling on or off, and restores single window display.

/Worksheet Column

/Worksheet Column lets you change the display of one or more columns. Use /Worksheet Column to perform the following tasks:

Column-Range Changes the column width of a range of columns (overriding the global default column width) or resets a range of columns to the global default column width (9 characters).

Display Redisplays one or more hidden columns.

Hide Hides one or more columns.

Reset-Width Resets the current column to the global default column width (9 characters).

Set-Width Changes the width of the current column (overriding the global default column width).

/Worksheet Column Column-Range

/Worksheet Column Column-Range lets you change the width of a range of adjacent columns. After you set the width of a column with /Worksheet Column Column-Range Set-Width, the column's width appears in brackets in the control panel when the cell pointer is anywhere in that column.

❶ Select /Worksheet Column Column-Range. ❷ Select Set-Width to change the width of a range of columns; or Reset-Width to reset a range of columns to the global default column width (9 characters). ❸ Specify the range of columns whose widths you want to set or reset and press [Enter]. ❹ If you selected Set-Width, in Step 2, specify the new width by typing a number from 1 to 240 or pressing [←] or [→].

/Worksheet Column Display

/Worksheet Column Display lets you redisplay hidden columns.

❶ Select /Worksheet Column Display to redisplay temporarily all hidden columns with asterisks next to their column letters. ❷ Specify the range of columns you want to redisplay and press [Enter].

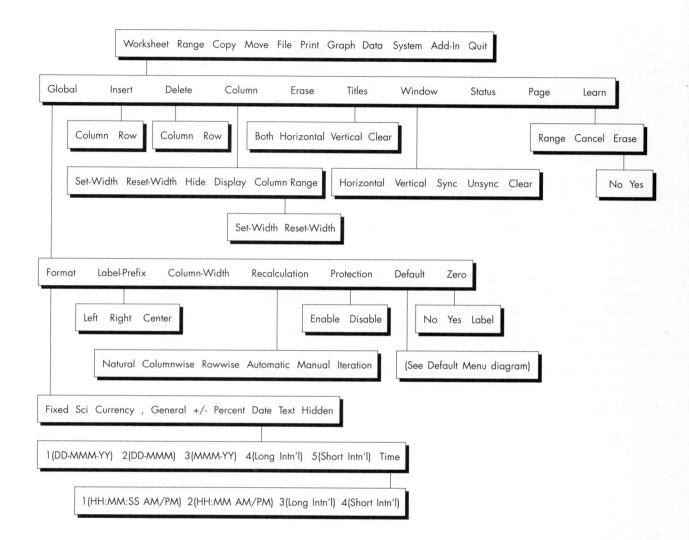

/Worksheet Column Hide

/Worksheet Column Hide lets you hide one or more columns without permanently erasing the data in those columns. Formulas in hidden columns and formulas that refer to cells in hidden columns continue to work correctly.

❶ Select /Worksheet Column Hide. ❷ Specify the range of columns you want to hide and press [Enter].

1-2-3 temporarily redisplays hidden columns whenever it changes to POINT mode, using asterisks next to the column letters to identify them as hidden columns.

/Worksheet Column Reset-Width

/Worksheet Column Reset-Width lets you restore the global default column width (9 characters) for the column that contains the cell pointer.

❶ Select /Worksheet Column Reset-Width.

/Worksheet Column Set-Width

/Worksheet Column Set-Width lets you change the width of the column that contains the cell pointer. After you set the width of a column with /Worksheet Column Set-Width, the column's width appears in brackets in the control panel when the cell pointer is in that column.

❶ Select /Worksheet Column Set-Width. ❷ Specify a width for the current column by typing a number from 1 to 240 or pressing [←] or [→] to decrease or increase the width and press [Enter].

/Worksheet Delete

/Worksheet Delete lets you remove one or more columns or rows from the worksheet. 1-2-3 closes up the space left by the deletion.

Caution: *Worksheet Delete permanently deletes columns and rows from the worksheet. Check the entire column or row to make sure it does not contain data you want to save. To avoid possible data loss from deleting columns or rows, save the worksheet before using /Worksheet Delete. If, however, you make a mistake when deleting columns or rows and the Undo feature is on, press [UNDO] (ALT-F4) immediately to restore the worksheet to its original state.*

❶ Select /Worksheet Delete. ❷ Select Column to delete one or more columns or Row to delete one or more rows. ❸ Specify the range of columns or rows you want to delete and press [Enter].

When a column or row deletion moves a cell used in a formula, 1-2-3 adjusts the cell address in the formula. When a column or row deletion moves the upper left or lower right cell of a named range, 1-2-3 redefines the named range accordingly. Formulas that refer to a deleted cell or to a range with a deleted upper left or lower right corner are replaced by ERR.

To erase a range without deleting rows or columns, use /Range Erase.

/Worksheet Erase

/Worksheet Erase lets you remove the worksheet from memory and replace it with a blank worksheet.

Caution: *Worksheet Erase removes the current worksheet from memory. To avoid data loss, use /File Save to save the worksheet before using /Worksheet Erase. If you make a mistake when erasing a worksheet and the Undo feature is on, press [UNDO] (ALT-F4) immediately to restore the worksheet to its original state.*

❶ Select /Worksheet Erase. ❷ Select No to return 1-2-3 to READY mode without erasing the worksheet; or Yes to erase the worksheet.

/Worksheet Global

The /Worksheet Global commands let you change settings that affect the current worksheet as well as configuration settings that 1-2-3 uses every time you start a 1-2-3 session. Use /Worksheet Global to perform the following tasks:

Column-Width Sets the global column width.

Default Changes the 1-2-3 configuration settings.

Format Sets the global cell format.

Label-Prefix Sets the global label alignment.

Protection Turns global protection on and off.

Recalculation Sets the recalculation method.

Zero Sets the display for cells whose value is zero.

Global and Default Settings Sheets

When you select /Worksheet Global or /Worksheet Global Default, 1-2-3 displays a special status screen called a **settings sheet**.

You may want to vary the settings you use with different worksheets. For example, you might want to set the recalculation method to Manual, for a particular worksheet. The next time you retrieve the worksheet, recalculation will still be set to Manual, even if you started the 1-2-3 session with recalculation set to Automatic.

Global and default settings in 1-2-3 are affected by some commands, but not by others. The following table lists which commands affect either global or default settings.

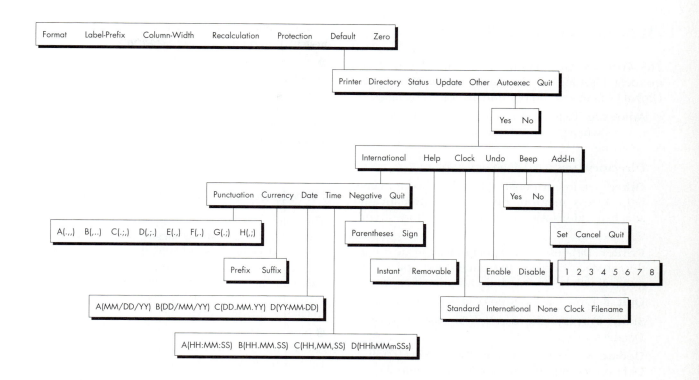

Command	Settings affected
/File Save	Global settings — except zero suppression — are saved with worksheet. Whenever worksheet is retrieved, those settings become current. Default settings are not saved with worksheet.
/Worksheet Erase	Global settings are erased along with worksheet. Default settings remain in effect.
/Worksheet Global Default Update	Default settings are saved in 1-2-3 configuration file. Those settings are in effect for every 1-2-3 session until you change them. Global settings are not saved.

For further information on how 1-2-3 saves default settings, see "/Worksheet Global Default" later in this section.

/Worksheet Global Column-Width

/Worksheet Global Column-Width lets you change the width of all columns in the worksheet except those columns whose widths you set individually with /Worksheet Column Set-Width or /Worksheet Column Column-Range Set-Width.

The minimum column width is 1; the maximum is 240. The default global column width setting is 9 characters.

❶ Select /Worksheet Global Column-Width. ❷ Specify a column width by typing a number from 1 to 240 or pressing [←] or [→] to decrease or increase the width and press [Enter].

To see the column width setting for the entire worksheet, select /Worksheet Status and check the status screen, or select /Worksheet Global and check the settings sheet.

/Worksheet Global Default

The Worksheet Global Default commands let you control default settings for the 1-2-3 session. /Worksheet Global Default lets you perform the following tasks:

Autoexec Tells 1-2-3 whether to run autoexecute macros when it retrieves a worksheet file that contains one.

Directory Sets the default directory.

Other Sets international and clock display formats, help access method, beep, and automatically attached add-ins. Also turns the Undo feature on and off.

Printer Defines the brand of printer you are using, the interface between the printer and your computer, and the default settings for printed pages.

Quit Returns 1-2-3 to READY mode.

Status Displays the current /Worksheet Global Default settings.

Update Saves the current /Worksheet Global Default settings in the 1-2-3 configuration file (123.CNF) for use in future sessions.

Although the settings you establish with /Worksheet Global Default apply globally during the current 1-2-3 session, you can override some of them with other commands. For example, you can override print margins set with /Worksheet Global Default Printer by using /Print Printer Option Margins.

The settings you specify with /Worksheet Global Default are stored in a file called 123.CNF. This file is read by 1-2-3 each time you start a session, and the settings take effect automatically. If you have changed some settings and want to save them for future sessions, you must select /Worksheet Global Default Update, which will save the changes in the 123.CNF file. To view your current settings, select /Worksheet Global Default Status and check the status screen; or select /Worksheet Global Default and check the settings sheet.

/Worksheet Global Default Autoexec

This command lets you tell 1-2-3 whether to run autoexecute macros — macros named \0 (Zero) —

when it retrieves a file that contains one. For more information on macros, see *Reference 4*.

❶ Select /Worksheet Global Default Autoexec. ❷ Select Yes to automatically execute macros named \0 (Zero), or No to not automatically execute macros named \0 (Zero). ❸ Select Update from the Worksheet Global Default menu to update the 123.CNF file so 1-2-3 uses the new setting in future sessions.

/Worksheet Global Default Directory

This command lets you set the path (drive and directory names) that 1-2-3 automatically searches when you save, read, or list files. Initially, the default directory is the directory that contains the 1-2-3 program files. If the files you most frequently work with are in another directory, you will probably want to use this command to change the directory.

❶ Select /Worksheet Global Default Directory. ❷ Specify the new directory and press [Enter]. ❸ Select Update from the Worksheet Global Default menu to update the 123.CNF file so 1-2-3 uses the new setting in future sessions.

Note: *To override the default directory and change the current directory for the current session only, use /File Directory rather than /Worksheet Global Default Directory.*

/Worksheet Global Default Other

This command lets you specify a number of functional settings for 1-2-3. /Worksheet Global Default Other lets you perform the following tasks:

Add-In Sets and cancels auto-attach add-ins.

Beep Turns your computer's bell on or off during 1-2-3 sessions.

Clock Sets the display for the date-and-time indicator.

Help Specifies the Help access method.

International Sets the punctuation for numbers, the argument separators for @functions and advanced macro commands, the currency symbol, the international date and time formats, and the way

1-2-3 displays negative numbers in Comma and Currency formats.

Undo Turns the Undo feature on and off.

/Worksheet Global Default Other Add-In

Lets you configure 1-2-3 so it automatically attaches an add-in program whenever you start 1-2-3. You can specify up to eight auto-attach add-ins. You can also specify whether you want 1-2-3 to automatically invoke an add-in as well. Only one add-in can be auto-invoked.

❶ Select /Worksheet Global Default Other Add-In. ❷ Select Set to set an auto-attach add-in, and attach the add-in; Cancel to cancel an auto-attach add-in and detach the add-in; or Quit to return to the Worksheet Global Default menu. ❸ Select the number (1 through 8) of the auto-attach add-in to set or cancel. ❹ Specify the filename of the add-in you want to attach automatically and press [Enter]. ❺ Select No-Key not to assign the add-in to a key, 7 to assign the add-in to [APP1] (ALT-F7), 8 to [APP2] (ALT-F8), 9 to [APP3] (ALT-F9), or 10 to [APP4] (ALT-F10). ❻ Select Yes to invoke the auto-attach add-in whenever you start 1-2-3, or No to attach add-in but not automatically invoke it. ❼ Select Update from the Worksheet Global Default menu to update the 123.CNF file so 1-2-3 uses the new setting in future sessions.

/Worksheet Global Default Other Beep

Lets you control whether 1-2-3 sounds the computer bell when errors occur and when executing {BEEP} commands in a macro.

❶ Select /Worksheet Global Default Other Beep. ❷ Select Yes to sound the bell; or No not to sound the bell. ❸ Select Update from the Worksheet Global Default menu to update the 123.CNF file so 1-2-3 uses the new setting in future sessions.

/Worksheet Global Default Other Clock

Sets the display for date-and-time indicator in the lower left corner of the screen.

❶ Select /Worksheet Global Default Other Clock. ❷ Select one of the following menu options:

Standard Sets the date and time format for the date-and-time indicator as DD-MMM-YY and HH:MM (AM/PM), respectively.

International Sets the date and time formats for the date-and-time indicator as D4 (Intn'l long) and D5 (Intn'l short), respectively. You customize the D4 and D9 formats with /Worksheet Global Default Other International Date and Time.

None Displays nothing in the lower left-hand corner.

Clock Displays the date and time in the lower left corner, using the most recently selected format.

Filename Displays the filename in the lower left corner, if the current worksheet has been retrieved from or saved in a file.

❸ Select Update from the Worksheet Global Default menu to update the 123.CNF file so 1-2-3 uses the new setting in the future sessions.

/Worksheet Global Default Other Help

Lets you specify the method 1-2-3 uses to access the Help system.

❶ Select /Worksheet Global Default Other Help. ❷ Select Instant to open the Help file the first time you press [HELP] (F1) in a 1-2-3 session and keep the file open for the rest of the session; or Removable to open the Help file each time you press [HELP] (F1) and close the file again when you press [Esc] to leave Help. ❸ Select Update from the Worksheet Global Default menu to update the 123.CNF file so 1-2-3 uses the new setting in future sessions.

Instant Help works best if you use a hard disk system; Removable if using a two-diskette system.

Caution: *If you select Instant when running 1-2-3 on a two-diskette system, do not remove the Help disk from the drive. If you do, you may cause a system failure.*

/Worksheet Global Default Other International

Lets you set a variety of display formats, including the punctuation for numbers, the argument separators for @functions and advanced macro commands, the currency symbol, the international date and time formats, and the negative number display in Comma and Currency formats.

❶ Select /Worksheet Global Default Other International. ❷ Select a menu option according to the following list:

Punctuation Sets the characters 1-2-3 uses as the decimal point, argument separator for @functions and advanced macro commands, and thousands separator for numbers. You can choose from eight combinations of three, listed in order of decimal point, argument separator, and thousands separator: A (.,,), B (,..), C (.;,), D (,;.), E (.,), F (,.), G (.;), and H (,;). **Note:** *If you select B or F, which sets the period as the argument separator, you must always use two periods when you type range addresses. You can always use a semicolon as an argument separator.*

Currency Sets the currency symbol 1-2-3 uses in cells formatted as Currency and whether the currency symbol precedes or follows numbers. (The default is $ Prefix.)

Date Sets the International Date format 1-2-3 uses for cells formatted as D4 (Intn'l long) or D5 (Intn'l short) and the International Date display for the date-and-time indicator. The options are A (MM/DD/YY), B (DD/MM/YY), C (DD,MM,YY), and D (YY-MM-DD).

Time Sets the International Time format 1-2-3 uses for cells formatted as D8 (Intn'l long) or D9 (Intn'l short) and the International Time Display for the date-and-time indicator. The four options are A (HH:MM:SS), B (HH.MM.SS), C (HH,MM,SS), and D (HHhMMmSSs).

Negative Sets whether 1-2-3 uses parentheses (the default setting) or a minus sign for negative values in cells formatted as Comma or Currency.

Quit Returns you to the Worksheet Global Default menu.

❸ Follow the prompts to select or specify a new setting. ❹ Select Update from the Worksheet Global Default menu to update the 123.CNF file so 1-2-3 uses the new setting in future sessions.

Note: *To use a character that is not on the keyboard as part of the default currency symbol, use COMPOSE (ALT-F1). For example, to specify the British pound as the default currency symbol, press COMPOSE (ALT-F1), type L= and press [Enter].*

/Worksheet Global Default Other Undo Lets you turn the Undo feature on and off. When the Undo feature is on, you can press [UNDO] (ALT-F4) to cancel any changes made to the worksheet since 1-2-3 was last in READY mode. For further information on Undo, see "Using the Undo Feature" in *Reference 1*.

❶ Select /Worksheet Global Default Other Undo. ❷ Select Enable to turn on the Undo feature, or Disable to turn off the Undo feature. ❸ Select Update from the Worksheet Global Default menu to update the 123.CNF file so 1-2-3 uses the new settings in future sessions.

When Undo is on, 1-2-3 reserves a portion of memory for the Undo buffer, which is used to make a backup copy of the worksheet. 1-2-3 uses expanded memory for the Undo buffer if possible, but uses conventional memory if there is not enough (or any) expanded memory available. Using conventional memory for the Undo buffer significantly reduces the amount of memory for worksheet data and add-ins. If necessary, use /Worksheet Global Default Other Undo Disable to turn off the Undo feature and increase your available memory.

When Undo is off, you will not be able to turn on Undo if the conventional memory needed for the Undo buffer already contains worksheet data or add-ins. To turn on Undo in this situation, save the worksheet to a file (/File Save), detach all add-ins (/Add-In Clear), erase the worksheet from memory (/Worksheet Erase), and turn on Undo (/Worksheet Global Default Other Undo Enable). You can then retrieve the worksheet (/File Retrieve) and attach any add-ins (/Add-In Attach). To avoid this situation, Undo should be enabled whenever you start a 1-2-3 session. Set this with /Worksheet Global Default Other Undo Enable, followed by Update.

/Worksheet Global Default Printer

The /Worksheet Global Default Printer commands let you provide 1-2-3 with information about your printer at the start of each 1-2-3 session. Use /Worksheet Global Default Printer to perform the following tasks:

AutoLF Controls the signal 1-2-3 sends to your printer at the end of each line of output.

Bot Sets the default bottom margin for printed pages.

Interface Identifies the interface, or port, through which your printer and computer are connected.

Left Sets the default left margin for printed pages.

Name Selects the printer to use if you specified more than one printer when you installed 1-2-3.

Pg-Length Sets the length of each printed page.

Quit Returns you to the Worksheet Global Default menu.

Right Sets the default right margin for printed pages.

Setup Specifies the default setup string to send to your printer before printing begins.

Top Sets the default top margin for printed pages.

Wait Tells 1-2-3 whether to pause after it prints each page.

Note: *Printer settings you select with /Print Printer Options override corresponding /Worksheet Global Default Printer settings. Use /Print Printer Options rather than /Worksheet Global Default Printer to specify settings for individual print jobs.*

/Worksheet Global Default Printer AutoLF
Lets you control the signal 1-2-3 sends to your printer at the end of each line of output.

To determine the correct AutoLF setting for your printer, print a range of two or more rows. If the printing is double-spaced, set AutoLF to Yes. If the paper in the printer does not advance, set AutoLF to No (the default setting).

❶ Select /Worksheet Global Default Printer AutoLF. ❷ Select Yes not to send line feeds to your printer (because your printer automatically advances at the end of each line of output); or No to send line feeds to your printer at the end of each line of output (because your printer does not automatically advance). ❸ Select Update from the Worksheet Global Default menu to update the 123.CNF file so 1-2-3 uses the new setting in future sessions.

/Worksheet Global Default Printer Bot/Top
Lets you set the default bottom or top margin for printed pages, in number of standard lines. The default setting is 2.

❶ Select /Worksheet Global Default Printer Bot or Top. ❷ Specify the number of standard lines (0 to 32) for the default bottom margin and press [Enter]. ❸ Select Update from the Worksheet Global Default menu.

/Worksheet Global Default Printer Interface
Lets you specify the interface for your printer. The interface, or port, refers to the way your printer is connected to the computer. The interface may be parallel or serial, and your computer may have more than one interface of either type. If you are unsure of the kind of interface you have, check your printer manual or ask your technical resource person.

The default is 1 (Parallel 1), which is the most common configuration. Settings 1 through 4 are for printers physically linked to your computer; settings 5 through 8 are generally used to connect printers over a network.

Note: *If you have a serial interface, you will also need to indicate the baud rate for which your printer is set. The **baud rate** is the speed at which 1-2-3 sends data to the printer. The baud rate setting must match your printer's baud rate.*

❶ Select /Worksheet Global Default Printer Interface.
❷ Select a menu option from the following list:

1	Parallel 1	5	LPT1
2	Serial 1	6	LPT2
3	Parallel 2	7	LPT3
4	Serial 2	8	LPT4

❸ If you select a serial interface (setting 2 or 4), select a menu option from the following list:

1	110 baud	6	2400 baud
2	150 baud	7	4800 baud
3	300 baud	8	9600 baud
4	600 baud	9	19200 baud
5	1200 baud		

❹ Select Update from the Worksheet Global Default menu to update the 123.CNF file so 1-2-3 uses the new setting in future sessions.

If you are using a serial printer, change the following settings on your printer — these are not settings you can change in 1-2-3. For instructions on changing these settings, see your printer manual.

Data bits: 8

Stop bits: 2 if 110 baud; otherwise 1

Parity: None

Handshaking (XON/XOFF): Enabled

/Worksheet Global Default Printer Left/Right

Lets you set the default left or right margin for printed pages, in number of standard characters from the respective edge of the paper. For the left margin, specify a number that is smaller than the right margin setting. For the right margin, specify a number that is greater than the left margin setting. The default left margin setting is 4, the default right margin 76.

❶ Select /Worksheet Global Default Printer Left or Right. ❷ Specify the number of standard characters (0 to 240) for the default margin and press [Enter]. ❸ Select Update from the Worksheet Global Default menu to update the 123.CNF file so 1-2-3 uses the new setting in future sessions.

/Worksheet Global Default Printer Name

Lets you specify which printer you want to use if you selected more than one text printer when you installed 1-2-3. The default setting is the first printer you selected in the Install program.

❶ Select /Worksheet Global Default Printer Name. 1-2-3 displays a menu of one or more numbers, corresponding to the text printer(s) you selected with the Install program. ❷ Select the printer you want to use. ❸ Select Update from the Worksheet Global Default menu to update the 123.CNF file so 1-2-3 uses the new setting in future sessions.

Note: *When you change the Printer Name setting, you may also have to change the Interface setting because the specified printer may be connected to your computer through a different printer port.*

/Worksheet Global Default Printer Pg-Length

Lets you set the length of each printed page. Page length is measured in standard lines. This setting determines the number of printed lines per page and where 1-2-3 creates page breaks when printing. The default setting is 66. Generally, the Pg-Length setting should equal the number of standard lines per inch for your printer times the length of your paper in inches.

❶ Select /Worksheet Global Default Printer Pg-Length. ❷ Specify the number of standard lines (1 to 100) for the page length and press [Enter]. ❸ Select Update from the Worksheet Global Default menu to update the 123.CNF file so 1-2-3 uses the new setting in future sessions.

/Worksheet Global Default Printer Quit
Returns you to the Worksheet Global Default menu.

/Worksheet Global Default Printer Setup

Lets you enter a default setup string, which is a series of characters preceded by a \ (Backslash) that 1-2-3 sends to your printer to tell it to print a certain way. For example, you can send a setup string that causes the printer to compress type or underline text. You create setup strings by translating the printer control codes for your printer into the appropriate format.

Caution: *To avoid problems when printing, do not use setup strings to control print settings that you can control through 1-2-3 commands, such as page length or margins.*

❶ Select /Worksheet Global Default Printer Setup. ❷ Specify the default setup string and press [Enter]. ❸ Select Update from the Worksheet Global Default menu to update the 123.CNF file so 1-2-3 uses the new setting in future sessions.

/Worksheet Global Default Printer Wait

Lets you tell 1-2-3 to pause after it prints each page so you can insert a new piece of paper. The default setting is No. Use No if you are using a print spooler.

❶ Select /Worksheet Global Default Printer Wait. ❷ Select Yes to pause after printing each page, or No not to pause after printing a page. ❸ Select Update from the Worksheet Global Default menu.

/Worksheet Global Default Quit

This command lets you return 1-2-3 to READY mode.
❶ Select /Worksheet Global Default Quit.

/Worksheet Global Default Status

This command lets you display current worksheet settings, such as the default printer settings. The status screen temporarily overlays the worksheet. The status screen is similar to the Worksheet Global Default settings sheet except that it does not have a menu.

❶ Select /Worksheet Global Default Status. ❷ Press any key to redisplay the worksheet.

Note: *To see information about available memory, recalculation settings, circular references, the math coprocessor you are using, the global cell format, label prefix, column width and zero display settings, and the protection status of the current worksheet, select either /Worksheet Status or /Worksheet Global to display the settings sheet.*

/Worksheet Global Default Update

This command lets you save the current /Worksheet Global Default settings in the 1-2-3 configuration file (123.CNF). 1-2-3 reads the new Worksheet Global Default settings each time you start the program until you change the settings and again select /Worksheet Global Default Update.

❶ Select /Worksheet Global Default Update to save the current settings in the 123.CNF file and return to the Worksheet Global Default menu.

/Worksheet Global Format

/Worksheet Global Format lets you set the global cell format for the worksheet. The **cell format** setting determines the way 1-2-3 displays data in the worksheet.

❶ Select /Worksheet Global Format. ❷ Choose the cell format you want from the series of menus and prompts 1-2-3 displays. For a complete discussion of cell formats, see "/Range Format."

Note: *Cells you format with /Range Format override the global format set with /Worksheet Global Format.*

/Worksheet Global Label-Prefix

/Worksheet Global Label-Prefix lets you set the global label alignment for the worksheet. The command affects future entries only; it does not change the alignment of labels already entered in the worksheet. Labels that exceed the width of a column always appear left-aligned regardless of the global label alignment setting.

❶ Select /Worksheet Global Label-Prefix. ❷ Select Left to align labels at the left edge of cells; Right to align

labels at the right edge of cells; or Center to center labels in cells.

You can override the global label alignment setting either by using /Range Label after you enter a label, or by typing a label prefix as the first character in a label you are entering: ' = left align; " = right align; and ^ = center.

/Worksheet Global Protection

/Worksheet Global Protection lets you turn global protection on or off for the worksheet. When global protection is on, you can make changes only to cells that you explicitly unprotect with /Range Unprot. 1-2-3 displays PR in the control panel when the cell pointer is on a protected cell.

❶ Select /Worksheet Global Protection. ❷ Select Enable to turn on worksheet protection or Disable to turn off worksheet protection.

/Worksheet Global Recalculation

/Worksheet Global Recalculation lets you control when and in what order 1-2-3 recalculates worksheet formulas and how many recalculation passes 1-2-3 performs each time it recalculates the formulas.

The settings you specify remain in effect until you end the 1-2-3 session or read into memory another worksheet file with different recalculation settings. The default setting is Automatic (recalculation method) and Natural (recalculation order).

❶ Select /Worksheet Global Recalculation. ❷ Select from the following options to specify a new recalculation order (Natural, Columnwise, or Rowwise), recalculation method (Automatic or Manual), or number of recalculation passes (Iteration):

Natural Before recalculating a particular formula, 1-2-3 recalculates any other formulas on which that formula depends.

Columnwise Starting in A1, 1-2-3 moves column by column through the worksheet, recalculating all formulas.

Rowwise Starting in A1, 1-2-3 moves row by row through the worksheet, recalculating all formulas.

Automatic Each time you change the contents of a cell, 1-2-3 recalculates any formulas affected by the change.

Manual Recalculates formulas only when you press CALC (F9), which appears in the lower right whenever any entries have changed since the last recalculation.

Iteration Sets the number of recalculation passes (from 1 to 50) 1-2-3 makes for a complete recalculation. The default setting is 1. 1-2-3 uses the Iteration setting only when the recalculation order is Columnwise or Rowwise, or when the recalculation order is Natural and a circular reference exists.

❸ If you selected Iteration, specify the number of recalculation passes (1 to 50) and press [Enter].

Note: *Whenever the recalculation order specified with /Worksheet Global Recalculation is Natural, 1-2-3 recalculates only those cells that have changed since the worksheet was last recalculated and the cells that depend on them. Known as* **minimal recalculation**, *this feature decreases recalculation time. If you change the recalculation order to Columnwise or Rowwise, 1-2-3 recalculates all the formulas in the worksheet when you make a change. However, if the recalculation order is Natural and the worksheet contains a circular reference, 1-2-3 does not use minimal recalculation but instead does a full recalculation.*

/Worksheet Global Zero

/Worksheet Global Zero lets you specify whether 1-2-3 displays a zero, a label, or nothing in cells that contain either the number zero or a formula that evaluates to zero. Regardless of the options you choose, 1-2-3 continues to display the contents of these cells in the control panel. Any remaining zeros represent nonzero values whose format makes them look like zero.

❶ Select /Worksheet Global Zero. ❷ Select No to display zero in cells whose value is zero (the default setting); Yes to cause cells whose value is zero to appear blank; or Label to display a label in cells whose value is zero. ❸ If you selected Label, type the label to display in cells whose value is zero and then press [Enter]. The label can be any combination of up to 240 characters.

To cancel a label being displayed in cells whose value is zero, select /Worksheet Global Zero No.

Note: *Zero suppression is not saved with /File Save or /Worksheet Global Default Update.*

/Worksheet Insert

/Worksheet Insert lets you insert one or more blank columns or rows in the worksheet.

❶ Select /Worksheet Insert. ❷ Select Column to insert one or more blank columns to the left of the first column of the insert range, or Row to insert one or more blank rows above the first row of the insert range. ❸ Specify a range that includes at least one cell in each of the columns or rows you are inserting and press [Enter].

When an insertion moves a cell used in a formula, 1-2-3 adjusts the cell address in the formula. When an insertion moves the upper left or lower right cell of a range used in a formula, 1-2-3 adjusts the range address in the formula. When an insertion moves the upper left or lower right cell of a named range, 1-2-3 redefines the named range accordingly.

/Worksheet Learn

/Worksheet Learn provides an alternative method of entering macro instructions. Instead of typing the macro instructions, you perform the task that you want to automate.

Once you specify a Learn range and turn on the Learn feature with [LEARN] (ALT-F5), 1-2-3 translates your keystrokes into macro instructions and records them in the Learn range. 1-2-3 continues recording the keystrokes you make until you turn off the Learn feature by pressing [LEARN](ALT-F5) again or until you fill the Learn range. You then name the macro as you would any other macro. When you run the macro, 1-2-3 automatically executes the instructions recorded in the Learn range.

For more information on how to use /Worksheet Learn to write macros, see *Reference 4.*

Use /Worksheet Learn to perform the following tasks:

Cancel Cancels the currently specified Learn range. If you want 1-2-3 to record keystrokes when you turn on the Learn feature, you must specify another Learn range.

Erase Clears the contents of all cells in the currently specified Learn range without canceling the Learn range. The range is still defined and if you turn on the Learn feature by pressing [LEARN] (ALT-F5), 1-2-3 will record new keystrokes in the range.

Range Specifies the Learn range where 1-2-3 will store macro instructions (see below).

/Worksheet Learn Range

/Worksheet Learn Range lets you specify the range where 1-2-3 will record keystrokes as labels.

❶ Select /Worksheet Learn Range. ❷ Specify a long, single column range in an empty (no date, no range format) part of the worksheet and press [Enter].

Note: *If 1-2-3 displays a "Learn range is full" error message, you can increase the size of the Learn range (without losing keystrokes) and then continue saving keystrokes in the Learn range. Press [Esc] to clear the error message, select /Worksheet Learn Range, specify a new Learn range that is large enough to accommodate your macro, and then press [Enter].*

/Worksheet Page

/Worksheet Page lets you insert a row in the worksheet that contains the symbol :: (two colons). When you print the worksheet range, this symbol forces a page advance and resets the line counter in 1-2-3. Do not enter data to be printed in the same row as the page break symbol. Except for the page break symbol, 1-2-3 ignores this row when printing.

❶ Position the cell pointer in the leftmost column of the range you are printing and the row where you want a new page to start. ❷ Select /Worksheet Page to insert a row that contains :: (page break symbol) in the current cell. 1-2-3 moves the remaining rows down, adjusting cell and range addresses in formulas and redefining named ranges.

To remove a page break symbol, you can either use /Range Erase or /Worksheet Delete Row, edit the cell containing the symbol, or write over the symbol with another entry.

/Worksheet Status

/Worksheet Status lets you display information about available memory, recalculation, cell display format, circular references, and global protections in a status screen that overlays the worksheet.

Use /Worksheet Status to check the current worksheet's global settings, to track down circular references, and to check available memory before using /File Combine or when the MEM indicator is flashing.

❶ Select /Worksheet Status. ❷ Press any key to remove the status screen and redisplay the worksheet.

Note: *The status screen displays only one circular reference at a time. If you eliminate the displayed circular reference, select /Worksheet Status again to see whether another circular reference exists.*

/Worksheet Titles

/Worksheet Titles lets you freeze rows and/or columns along the top and left edges of the worksheet so they remain in view as you scroll through the worksheet.

❶ To freeze worksheet titles, position the cell pointer one row below and/or one column to the right of where you want the titles to be frozen. ❷ Select /Worksheet Titles. ❸ Select Both to freeze rows above cell pointer and columns to the left of the pointer; Horizontal to freeze rows above cell pointer; Vertical to freeze columns to the left of cell pointer; or Clear to unfreeze all title rows and columns.

To edit a frozen title, press [GOTO] (F5) and specify the address or range name of the cell you want to go to. 1-2-3 displays a second set of the frozen rows or columns immediately below or to the right of the first set and moves the cell pointer to the specified cell there. To clear the second set of frozen rows or columns, press [PgDn] and then [PgUp] (for rows) or [BIG RIGHT]

([Ctrl][→]) and then [BIG LEFT] ([Ctrl][←]) (for columns).

Note: *If you use /Worksheet Titles after splitting the screen into two windows with /Worksheet Window Horizontal or Vertical, /Worksheet Titles affects only the current window. When you clear the second window with /Worksheet Window Clear, 1-2-3 uses the top or left window's Worksheet Title settings.*

/Worksheet Window

/Worksheet Window lets you view your work in several ways: it lets you split the screen horizontally or vertically into two windows, and synchronize scrolling in the windows or scroll them independently. Use /Worksheet Window Vertical or Horizontal to view two parts of the same or different worksheets simultaneously. To move the cell pointer from one window to the other, use [WINDOW] (F6).

❶ To create windows, move the cell pointer to the row you want as the top edge of the second window or to the column you want as the left edge of the second window. ❷ Select /Worksheet Window. ❸ Select Horizontal to create two windows with the screen split horizontally; Vertical to create two windows with the screen split vertically; Sync to synchronize window scrolling (the default setting); Unsync to unsynchronize window scrolling, allowing windows to scroll independently in all directions; or Clear to restore a single window that occupies the whole screen and uses the contents and settings of the top or left window.

For horizontal windows, Sync keeps the same columns on the screen in both windows when you scroll through columns in one window. For vertical windows, Sync keeps the same rows on the screen in both windows when you scroll through rows in one window.

Note: *With horizontal or vertical windows, all commands that change the worksheet display affect both windows, except for /Worksheet Column, /Worksheet Global Column-Width, and /Worksheet Titles, which affect only the window in which the cell pointer resides.*

Reference 3

1-2-3 @Functions

The 1-2-3 **@functions** are built-in formulas that perform a variety of calculations. You can use @functions for financial, mathematical, statistical, string, or date-and-time calculations. You can also use @functions to create conditional formulas or perform such tasks as looking up a value in a table.

This chapter includes a discussion of syntax, a short list of functions organized by type, and a complete alphabetical list of all @functions with examples.

Contents

This chapter contains the following sections:

Syntax of @Functions

Each @function has a specific structure, or **syntax**. Unless you follow this syntax exactly, 1-2-3 cannot interpret the @function.

@FUNCTION(*argument1,argument2, . . .,argumentn*)

@FUNCTION represents the name of the @function. It tells 1-2-3 which calculation to perform. *Argument1,argument2,...,argumentn* represent the data 1-2-3 uses in the @function calculations. Arguments must be enclosed in parentheses.

Arguments

Arguments supply the information 1-2-3 needs to complete the @function calculation. For example, when 1-2-3 encounters the function @SUM(B4..B25), the argument B4..B25 tells 1-2-3 to add the values in the range B4..B25. The arguments in an @function can be any length, providing the total number of characters in the cell that contains the @function does not exceed 240.

@Functions use four types of information as arguments: values, strings, locations (cells or ranges), and conditions (usually logical formulas).

- For value arguments, you can use a number, a numeric formula, or the range name or address of a cell that contains a number or numeric formula.

- For string arguments, you can use a **literal string** (any sequence of letters, numbers, and symbols enclosed in quotation marks), a string formula, or the range name or address of a cell that contains a label or string formula.

Note: *Every literal string used as a string argument should be enclosed in quotation marks. This prevents 1-2-3 from interpreting the literal string as a number, formula, address, or range name. It also prevents 1-2-3 from interpreting commas, semicolons, or periods within the literal string as argument separators.*

- For location arguments, you can use a range name or address.

- For condition arguments, you typically use a **logical formula** (a formula that uses one of the logical operators < > = <> >= <= #NOT# #AND# #OR#) or the range name or address of a cell that contains a logical formula. However, you can also use any numeric or string formula, number, literal string, or cell reference as a condition argument.

Basic Rules of Syntax

Use these general guidelines when you enter @functions:

- Begin every @function with the @ (At sign) symbol.

- You can type @functions in either uppercase or lowercase letters; 1-2-3 displays them in uppercase letters.

- Do not include spaces between the @function name and its arguments.

- Always enclose an @function's arguments in parentheses.

- When you use an @function as an argument, enclose the arguments for each @function in parentheses.

- Separate multiple arguments with a , (Comma) or a ; (Semicolon).

- You can use an @function by itself as a formula, combine it with other @functions and formulas, or use it in a macro.

- 1-2-3 assigns the value zero to blank cells whose addresses are used as arguments in financial, logical, and mathematical @functions.

Types of @Functions

1-2-3 @functions can be grouped into nine categories.

- Database @functions perform statistical calculations and queries in 1-2-3 databases.

- Date and time @functions calculate values that represent dates and times.

- Financial @functions calculate loans, annuities, and cash flows.

- Logical @functions calculate the results of conditional (logical) formulas.

- Mathematical @functions perform a variety of calculations with values.

- Special @functions perform a variety of tasks, such as looking up a value in a table or providing information about a specific cell.

- Statistical @functions perform calculations on lists of values.

- String @functions calculate with **strings** — labels, string formulas, or **literal strings** (any sequence of letters, numbers, and symbols enclosed in quotation marks).

- Add-in @functions that perform a variety of tasks are available from third-party software developers.

The following tables list the @functions by category and briefly describe each @function. For a complete description of a specific @function and an example of how it works, see "@Function Descriptions," later in this chapter.

Database @Functions

@DAVG Averages the values in a database field based on certain criteria.

@DCOUNT Counts the nonblank cells in a database field based on certain criteria.

@DMAX Finds the largest value in a database field based on certain criteria.

@DMIN Finds the smallest value in a database field based on certain criteria.

@DSTD Calculates the population standard deviation of the values in a database field based on certain criteria.

@DSUM Sums the values in a database field based on certain criteria.

@DVAR Calculates the population variance of the values in a database field based on certain criteria.

Guidelines for Using Database @Functions

- All database @functions have three arguments: *input*, *field*, and *criteria*.

- *Input* is the range that contains the database. *Input* can be the address or name of a range that contains a database.

- *Field* is the field's offset number. A field's **offset number** corresponds to the position of the column the field occupies in the *input* range. The first field of the *input* range has an offset number of 0, the second field has an offset number of 1, and so on. If the field's offset number is a value larger than the number of columns minus 1, database @functions return the value ERR.

- *Criteria* is a range you create to specify selection requirements. Each *criteria* range must include field names from the *input* range and the criteria you want 1-2-3 to use. You must enter the criteria directly below their corresponding field names. *Criteria* can be a range address or a range name.

Date and Time @Functions

Date Calculations

@DATE Calculates the date-number for a set of year, month, and day values. For example, @DATE(89,1,7) returns 32515, the date-number for January 7, 1989.

@DATEVALUE Converts a string that looks like a date into its equivalent date-number. For example, @DATEVALUE("7-Jan-89") returns the date-number 32515.

@DAY Calculates the day of the month in a date-number. For example, @DAY(32515) returns the value 7 because 32515 is the date-number for January 7, 1989.

@MONTH Calculates the number of the month in a date-number. For example, @MONTH(32515) returns the value 1 because 32515 is the date-number for January 7, 1989.

@YEAR Calculates a two- or three-digit value for the year in a date-number. For example, @YEAR(32515) returns the value 89 because 32515 is the date-number for January 7, 1989.

Time Calculations

@HOUR Calculates the hour in a time-number (based on a 24-hour format). For example, @HOUR(0.604745) returns the value 14 because 0.604745 is the time-number for 2:30:50 PM.

@MINUTE Calculates the minutes in a time-number. For example, @MINUTE(0.604745) returns the value 30 because 0.604745 is the time-number for 2:30:50 PM.

@SECOND Calculates the seconds in a time-number. For example, @SECOND(0.604745) returns the value 50 because 0.604745 is the time-number for 2:30:50 PM.

@TIME Calculates the time-number for a set of hour, minutes, and seconds values. For example, @TIME(14,30,50) returns 0.604745, the time-number for 2:30:50 PM.

@TIMEVALUE Converts a string that looks like a time into its equivalent time-number. For example, @TIMEVALUE("02:30:50 PM") returns the time-number 0.604745.

Current Date and Time Calculations

@NOW Calculates the value that corresponds to the current date and time on the computer's clock. For example, @NOW returns the value 32515.604745 at 2:30:50 PM (the time-number 0.604745) on January 7, 1989 (the date-number 32515).

Guidelines for Using Date and Time @Functions.

- Date @functions use **date-numbers**, consecutive integers that correspond to dates from January 1, 1900 (the date-number 1) through December 31, 2099 (the date-number 73050).

- Time @functions use **time-numbers**, consecutive decimal values that correspond to times from midnight (the time-number 0.000000) through 11:59:59 PM (the time-number 0.999988).

- To format date- and time-numbers so 1-2-3 displays them as actual dates and times, use /Range Format Date or /Worksheet Global Format Date.

Financial @Functions

Capital Budgeting Tools

@IRR Calculates the internal rate of return for a series of cash flows.

@NPV Calculates the net present value of a series of cash flows.

Depreciation

@DDB Calculates the double-declining balance depreciation allowance of an asset for one period.

@SLN Calculates the straight-line depreciation allowance of an asset for one period.

@SYD Calculates the sum-of-the-years'-digits depreciation allowance of an asset for one period.

Ordinary Annuities

@FV Calculates the future value of a series of equal payments.

@PMT Calculates the amount of the periodic payment needed to pay off a loan.

@PV Calculates the present value of a series of equal payments.

@TERM   Calculates the number of payment periods of an investment.

Single-Sum Compounding

@CTERM   Calculates the number of compounding periods necessary for an investment to grow to a future value.

@RATE   Calculates the periodic interest rate necessary for an investment to grow to a future value.

Guidelines for Using Financial @Functions

- Within an @function, express the term and the interest rate in the same unit of time. For example, in @PMT(1000, .05/12, 36) the term is 36 months, so the annual interest rate is divided by 12 to produce a monthly interest rate.

- 1-2-3 accepts interest rates as either percentages or decimal values. For example, you can enter 15.5% either as .155 or as 15.5%. 1-2-3 automatically converts all percentages to decimal values.

- The financial @functions assume that annuities are ordinary annuities. An annuity is a series of equal payments made at regular intervals. An ordinary annuity is an annuity in which the payments are made at the end of each time interval.

Logical @Functions

@FALSE   Returns the logical value 0 (false).

@IF   Takes one action if a condition is true; another if the condition is false.

@ISAFF   Returns 1 (true) for a defined add-in @function; 0 (false) for any other entry.

@ISAPP   Returns 1 (true) for a currently attached add-in; 0 (false) for any other entry.

@ISERR   Returns 1 (true) for the value ERR; 0 (false) for any other value.

@ISNA   Returns 1 (true) for the value NA; 0 (false) for any other value.

@ISNUMBER   Returns 1 (true) for a numeric value, NA, ERR, or a blank cell; 0 (false) for a string.

@ISSTRING   Returns 1 (true) for a string; 0 (false) for a numeric value, NA, ERR, or a blank cell.

@TRUE   Returns the logical value 1 (true).

Guidelines for Using Logical @Functions

- You use @ISERR and @ISNA to test for the values ERR (error) and NA (not available). These values cause a **ripple-through effect**. A ripple-through effect exists when a formula evaluates to ERR or NA and other formulas refer to the cell that contains the formula. A formula that refers to a cell that contains the values ERR or NA also evaluates to ERR or NA. For example, if a formula in G12 evaluates to ERR, +E12+F12+G12 also evaluates to ERR.

  You can use @ISERR and @ISNA in @IF formulas to stop the ripple-through effect. For example, you want to divide the value in G12 by the value in K12. The value in G12 is the result of a complex formula and you want to be sure the formula has not evaluated to ERR before you use G12 in other calculations. @IF(@ISERR–(G12),0,G12/K12) returns 0 if G12 contains the value ERR; this prevents 1-2-3 from evaluating the G12/K12 formula if G12 contains the value ERR. If G12 does not contain the value ERR, the @IF formula returns the result of G12/K12.

- You can use @ISNUMBER and @ISSTRING to prevent errors that would occur if a cell used in a formula contained the wrong type of data. For example, @IF(@ISNUMBER(G12),@AVG (A12..K12),"Label") returns @AVG(A12..K12) if G12 contains a value. If G12 contains a label, the @IF formula returns the word Label.

Mathematical @Functions

General

@ABS   Calculates the absolute (positive) value of a value.

@EXP Calculates the number *e* raised to a specified power.

@INT Returns the integer portion of a value.

@LN Calculates the natural logarithm (base *e*) of a value.

@LOG Calculates the common logarithm (base 10) of a value.

@MOD Calculates the remainder (modulus) of two values.

@RAND Generates a random value between 0 and 1.

@ROUND Rounds a value to a specified number of decimal places.

@SQRT Calculates the positive square root of a value.

Trigonometric

@ACOS Calculates the arc cosine of a value.

@ASIN Calculates the arc sine of a value.

@ATAN Calculates the arc tangent of a value.

@ATAN2 Calculates the four-quadrant arc tangent of two values.

@COS Calculates the cosine of an angle.

@PI Returns the value π (calculated at 3.1415926536).

@SIN Calculates the sine of an angle.

@TAN Calculates the tangent of an angle.

Guidelines for Using Mathematical @Functions

- You must express angles you enter as arguments for @COS, @SIN, and @TAN in radians. To convert degrees to radians, multiply the number of degrees by @PI/180.

- @ACOS, @ASIN, @ATAN, and @ATAN2 produce angle values in radians. To convert radians to degrees, multiply the number of radians by 180/@PI.

Special @Functions

Cell and Range Information

@@ Returns the contents of the cell whose cell address another cell contains.

@CELL Returns information about a cell. For example, @CELL("type",B5) returns v if B5 contains a value, b if B5 is blank, and l if B5 contains a label.

@CELLPOINTER Returns information about the current cell. (See @CELL.)

@COLS Counts the columns in a range.

@ROWS Counts the rows in a range.

Error Trapping

@ERR Returns the value ERR (error).

@NA Returns the value NA (not available).

Lookup Calculations

@CHOOSE Finds a specified value or string in a list of values and/or strings.

@HLOOKUP Finds the contents of a cell in a specified row in a range.

@INDEX Finds the value of the cell in a specified row and column in a range.

@VLOOKUP Finds the contents of the cell in a specified column in a range.

Guidelines for Using Special @Functions

- @ERR and @NA mark cells that contain formulas with errors (@ERR) or unavailable values (@NA). They assign the same value to every cell that depends on formulas that contain ERR or NA, creating a ripple-through effect.

  For example, you want to use the formula @SUM(Q_1,Q_2,Q_3,Q_4) to calculate annual travel expenses but do not have figures for the fourth quarter. Enter @NA in the cell named Q_4 to show that the value is not yet available. The @SUM formula will also evaluate to NA until you replace @NA with a value for fourth-quarter expenses.

Statistical @Functions

@AVG Averages a list of values.

@COUNT Counts the nonblank cells in a list of values.

@MAX Finds the maximum value in a list of values.

@MIN Finds the minimum value in a list of values.

@STD Calculates the population standard deviation of a list of values.

@SUM Sums a list of values.

@VAR Calculates the population variance of a list of values.

Guidelines for Using Statistical @Functions

- All statistical @functions perform calculations on lists of values, which are represented by the argument named *list*. The values in *list* can be entered as one or more numbers, numeric formulas, references to ranges that contain values, or any combination of numbers, formulas, and references to ranges.

- 1-2-3 assigns the value 0 to any strings used as arguments in statistical @functions. Therefore, labels within ranges in *list* will not cause statistical @functions to evaluate to ERR. 1-2-3 assigns the value 0 to all labels in a range and includes them in calculations. For example, if you use @AVG to calculate the average of the values in a range and the range contains a label, 1-2-3 considers the label to have the value 0 when it calculates the average.

Caution. *Always check for labels in the ranges you use in list to guard against unexpected results.*

- The statistical @functions ignore blank cells in ranges in *list*. For example, if you use @AVG to average the values in a range that spans eight cells, and the range contains a blank cell, 1-2-3 divides the sum by seven to find the correct average.

- Each of the statistical @functions has an equivalent database @function. For example, you use @AVG to average values in a range; you use @DAVG to average the values in a field of a database that meet certain criteria.

String @Functions

@CHAR Returns the character that a Lotus International Character Set (LICS) code produces.

@CLEAN Removes control characters from a string.

@CODE Returns the LICS code that corresponds to the first character in a string.

@EXACT Returns 1 (true) if two strings are the same; 0 (false) if the strings are different.

@FIND Calculates the position of the first character of one string within another string.

@LEFT Returns the first n characters in a string.

@LENGTH Counts the characters in a string.

@LOWER Converts all the letters in a string to lowercase.

@MID Returns a number of characters in a string, starting at a specified character.

@N Returns the value in the first cell in a range or 0 if the cell contains a label.

@PROPER Converts the first letter in each word in a string to uppercase and the rest of the letters in each word to lowercase.

@REPEAT Duplicates a string a specified number of times.

@REPLACE Replaces characters in one string with characters from a different string.

@RIGHT Returns the last n characters in a string.

@S Returns the label in the first cell in a range or a blank cell if the cell contains a value.

@STRING Converts a value into a label with a specified number of decimal places. For example, @STRING(34.567,1) returns the label (not the value) 34.5.

@TRIM Removes leading, trailing, and consecutive spaces from a string.

@UPPER Converts all the letters in a string to uppercase.

@VALUE Converts a string that looks like a number into a value. For example, @VALUE("34.5") returns the value 34.5.

Guidelines for Using String @Functions

- Always enclose literal strings used as arguments in quotation marks. 1-2-3 treats strings not enclosed in quotation marks as range names.

  For example, @LENGTH("EXPENSES") returns the number of characters in the string "EXPENSES" while @LENGTH(EXPENSES) returns the number of characters in the label located in single cell range named EXPENSES.

- Some string @functions use **offset numbers**, which locate the position of a character in a string. The first offset number is always 0.

  For example, the string "Red Shoes" contains nine characters. The R is at position 0, the first e is at position 1, and so on. The last offset number is always one less than the length of the string.

- Uppercase and lowercase letters have different LICS codes. For example, @CODE("A") returns the code 65, but @CODE("a") returns the code 97.

- If you use blank cells as arguments in string @functions, 1-2-3 returns the value ERR. For example, @LENGTH(D9) returns the value ERR if D9 is a blank cell.

- If a cell contains one of the label prefixes " ' ^ or | but contains no text, 1-2-3 treats it as an **empty string**, a string with a length of zero. The cell looks blank, but 1-2-3 will not return the value ERR when you use it as an argument in a string @function.

@Function Descriptions

This section contains descriptions and examples of the 1-2-3 @functions listed alphabetically. @Functions, advanced macro command keywords, cell addresses, and range names appear in uppercase letters, but they can be entered in either uppercase or lowercase letters.

@@

@@(*location*) returns the contents of the cell to which *location* refers.

The *location* acts as a pointer to another cell, whose contents @ returns. *Location* must be the name or address of a single cell range that contains a valid cell reference. If you specify a multiple cell range for *location*, @ evaluates to ERR.

Examples

@@(D4) = 37, when cell D4 contains the label F5, and cell F5 contains the value 37.

@@(D4) = Balance, when D4 contains the label INPUT, INPUT is the name of cell F6, and cell F6 contains the string Balance.

@ABS

@ABS(*x*) calculates the absolute (positive) value of *x*. *X* can be any value.

Use @ABS when printing certain negative numbers in a report, such as percentage differences between actual and budgeted values, or when you want to find the absolute difference between values in a list of positive and negative values.

Examples

@ABS(1.258) = 1.258

@ABS(–6.2) = 6.2

@ABS("Jones") = 0, because *x* is a string value and a string has a value of 0.

@ACOS

@ACOS(*x*) calculates the arc cosine of a value. The arc (or inverse) cosine is the angle, measured in radians, whose cosine is *x*. The result of @ACOS is a value from 0 to π. *X* can be any value from –1 to 1.

Examples

@ACOS(.3) = 1.266103 (radians)

@ACOS(.5)*180/@PI = 60 (degrees)

@ASIN

@ASIN(x) calculates the arc sine of a value. The arc (or inverse) sine is the angle, measured in radians, whose sine is x. The result of @ASIN is a value from $\pi/2$ to $-\pi/2$. X can be any value from -1 to 1.

Examples

@ASIN(−.246) = −0.248551 (radians)

@ASIN(1)*180/@PI = 90 (degrees)

@ATAN

@ATAN(x) calculates the arc tangent of a value. The arc (or inverse) tangent is the angle, measured in radians, whose tangent is x. The result of @ATAN is a value from $\pi/2$ to $-\pi/2$. X can be any value.

Examples

@ATAN(1) = 0.785398 (radians)

@ATAN(@SQRT(3))*180/@PI = 60 (degrees)

@ATAN2

@ATAN2(x,y) calculates the four-quadrant arc tangent of y/x. The four-quadrant arc (or inverse) tangent is the angle, measured in radians, whose tangent is y/x. X and y can be any values. If y is 0, @ATAN2 returns 0; if both x and y are 0, @ATAN2 returns the value ERR.

Note: *@ATAN2 differs from @ATAN in that the result of @ATAN2 is a value from $-\pi$ to π.*

The table below lists the value ranges for @ATAN2.

x,y	@ATAN2(x,y) results
Positive, Positive	from 0 to $\pi/2$
Negative, Positive	from $\pi/2$ to π
Negative, Negative	from $-\pi$ to $-\pi/2$
Positive, Negative	from $-\pi/2$ to 0

Examples

@ATAN2(1.5,2) = 0.927295 (radians)

@ATAN2(−1.5,2)*180/@PI = 126.8698 (degrees)

@AVG

@AVG(*list*) averages the values in *list*. *List* can be any combination of values and ranges.

Example

If C5 = 80, D5 = 130, and E5 = 50, then @AVG(C5..E5) = 86.66666

@CELL

@CELL(*attribute,range*) returns information about an *attribute* for the first cell in *range*. *Attribute* can be any of the 10 strings in the following list. *Attribute* can be entered as a literal string, a string formula, or a reference to a cell that contains a label. *Range* can be any range name or address.

Note: *@CELL evaluates the first cell in range at the point when that cell was last recalculated; be sure you recalculate your work before you use @CELL.*

address The absolute cell address for the first cell in *range* (for example, $A$1).

col The column letter, as a value from 1 to 256 (1 for column A, 5 for column E, etc.).

contents The contents of the first cell in *range*.

filename The name of the current file including the path.

format The format for the first cell in *range*, from the following table:

Result	Meaning
C0 to C15	Currency, 0 to 15 decimal places
F0 to F15	Fixed, 0 to 15 decimal places
G	General, a label, or a blank cell
P0 to P15	Percent, 0 to 15 decimal places
S0 to S15	Sci (Scientific), 0 to 15 decimal places
,0 to ,15	, (Comma), 0 to 15 decimal places
+	+/– format
D1	DD-MMM-YY
D2	DD-MMM
D3	MMM-YY
D4	MM/DD/YY, DD/MM/YY, DD.MM.YY, or YY-MM-DD
D5	MM/DD, DD/MM, DD.MM, or MM-DD
D6	HH:MM:SS AM/PM
D7	HH:MM AM/PM
D8	HH:MM:SS (24 hour), HH.MM.SS (24 hour), HH,MM,SS (24 hour), or HHhMMmSSs
D9	HH:MM (24 hour), HH.MM (24 hour), HH,MM, or HHhMMm
T	Text format
H	Hidden format

prefix The label prefix for the first cell in *range*, from the following table:

Result	Meaning
'	the cell contains a left-aligned label
"	the cell contains a right-aligned label
^	the cell contains a centered label
\	the cell contains a repeating label
|	the cell contains a nonprinting label
Blank (no symbol)	the cell is empty or contains a value

protect The protection status for the first cell in *range*, from the following table:

Result	Meaning
1	protected
0	not protected

row The row number for the first cell in *range*, from 1 to 8192.

type The type of data for the first cell in *range*, from the following table:

Result	Meaning
b	it is blank (that is, has no entry)
v	it contains a numeric value or a formula
l	it contains a label

width The column width for the first cell in *range*.

Example

You can use @CELL to check input during a macro to guard against certain types of entries; you can also use it to check whether a particular cell contains data, with the result directing a macro subroutine. For example, consider the macro instructions:

{IF @CELL("type",C5)="b"}{BEEP}{INDICATE "Do Not Leave Blank!"}

If C5 is blank, @CELL("type",C5) returns B; 1-2-3 then beeps and the mode indicator changes to "Do Not Leave Blank!"

@CELLPOINTER

@CELLPOINTER(*attribute*) returns information about an *attribute* for the current cell. *Attribute* can be any of the ten valid *attribute* arguments for @CELL. See the descriptions under @CELL (above) for a list of attributes. *Attribute* can be entered as a literal string, a string formula, or a reference to a cell that contains a label.

Note: *1-2-3 automatically updates @CELLPOINTER only when you make an entry. To make @CELL-POINTER return information about the current cell if you have simply moved the cell pointer to it, you must recalculate the worksheet.*

Example

@CELLPOINTER is useful in macros when you need to test the cell pointer's current location or when you need to evaluate a formula based on the contents of the current cell. For example, consider the macro instructions:

    {IF @CELLPOINTER("type")="b"}{BEEP 2}{QUIT}

@CELLPOINTER is used to evaluate the contents of the current cell. If the current cell is blank, 1-2-3 beeps and ends the macro.

@CHAR

@CHAR(x) returns the character that the Lotus International Character Set (LICS) code x produces. X can be any integer from 1 to 255. Values outside this range yield ERR. @CHAR is useful for entering foreign language characters and mathematical symbols. Whether a character prints depends on the capabilities of your printer.

If your computer monitor cannot display the character that corresponds to x, 1-2-3 displays a character that resembles the desired character when possible. If no displayable character approximates the character, 1-2-3 displays nothing.

Examples

@CHAR(244) = ô

The formula

    +"Champs-"&@CHAR(201)&"lys"&@CHAR(233)&"es"

returns Champs-Élysées.

@CHOOSE

@CHOOSE(*offset,list*) finds the value or string in *list* that is specified by *offset*. *Offset* represents an offset number. An offset number corresponds to the position an item occupies in *list*. The first item has an offset number of 0, the second item has an offset number of 1, and so on. *Offset* can be zero or any positive integer that is less than or equal to the number of items in *list* minus 1. For example, if *list* contains 50 items, the largest number you can use for *offset* is 49. *List* can contain one or more values, strings, references to ranges that contain values or strings, or any combination of values, strings, and range references.

Use @CHOOSE to enter a list of lookup values without setting up a lookup table.

Examples

@CHOOSE(1,"Profit","Loss","Bankruptcy") = Loss
@CHOOSE(H5,B1,B2,B3) = the value in cell B2 if H5 contains the value 1.

@CLEAN

@CLEAN(*string*) removes certain control characters from *string*. @CLEAN removes the following characters: control characters with ASCII codes below 32; the begin and end attribute characters, as well as the attribute character itself; the merge character (LICS 155) and the character following.

Example

You imported data into 1-2-3 from a word processing program. Cell A45 contains the label → Second, we must act soon.←

@CLEAN(A45) = Second, we must act soon.

@CODE

@CODE(*string*) returns the Lotus International Character Set (LICS) code that corresponds to the first character in *string*. *String* can be a literal string, the range name or address of a cell that contains a label, or a formula or @function that evaluates to a string. If *string* is a cell address or range name that refers to a blank cell or a value, @CODE returns the value ERR.

Examples

@CODE("A") = 65
@CODE(C5) = 77 if C5 contains the label Ms. Jones, because 77 is the LICS code for M.

@COLS

@COLS(*range*) counts the number of columns in *range*. *Range* can be any range name or address.

Examples

@COLS(EMPLOYEES) = 20 if EMPLOYEES is the range name for B3..U75.

Use @COLS to determine the width of a range in order to set appropriate margins when printing a report. For example, if you set the global column width to 10, the formula @COLS(COST) * 10 tells you the width of the range *cost* (including blanks and spaces).

@COS

@COS(x) calculates the cosine of an angle (x) measured in radians. The result of @COS is a value from −1 to 1. X can be any value.

Examples

@COS(.523598) = 0.866025
@COS(@PI/180) = 0.707106

@COUNT

@COUNT(list) counts the nonblank cells in a list of ranges. List can be any combination of ranges. If list contains only blank ranges, @COUNT evaluates to 0. If you enter a single cell address in list it will increase the count by one, even if the cell is blank. For example, if A2 is blank, @COUNT(A2) = 1.

@COUNT considers cells that contain labels, as well as those that contain values, to be nonblank. If you want to keep an accurate count of values in a range, make sure the range does not contain any labels, such as column headings. @COUNT does not ignore cells that evaluate to ERR or NA.

Examples

@COUNT(B5..B11) = 7 if none of the cells are blank.
@COUNT(C5..C10,D5,E5..E10) = 1 if all the cells are blank because D5 is not entered as a range.

Use @COUNT to stop a macro when the cell pointer reaches a blank row. For example, {IF @COUNT(WORK)=0}{QUIT} stops the macro because the range WORK is a blank row.

@CTERM

@CTERM(interest,future-value,present-value) calculates the number of compounding periods it takes for an investment (present-value) to grow to a future-value, earning a fixed interest rate per compounding period.

Interest can be any value greater than −1. Future-value and present-value can be any values, but both must be positive or negative.

@CTERM uses the following formula to calculate the compounding period:

$$\frac{ln(fv/pv)}{ln(1+int)}$$

In this formula, fv = the future value, pv = the present value, int = the interest rate, and ln represents the natural logarithm.

Example

You just deposited $10,000 in an account that pays an annual interest rate of 10% (.10), compounded monthly. You want to determine how many years it will take to double your investment.

@CTERM(.10/12,20000,10000)/12 = 6.9603; in other words, it will take about seven years to double the original investment of $10,000.

Note: *Because @CTERM calculates the total number of compounding periods, you may need to include the number of periods the* interest *rate is compounded in order to express the term and interest rate in the same unit of time. In the example above, the annual interest rate of 10%, compounded monthly, is entered as .10/12 (interest divided by the number of compounding periods per year).*

@DATE

@DATE(year,month,day) calculates the date-number for the specified year, month, and day. Year can be any integer from 0 (the year 1900) to 199 (the year 2099). Month can be any integer from 1 (January) to 12 (December). Day can be any integer from 1 to 31. The value you use for day must be a valid day for month. For example, you cannot use 31 for day if you use 4 (April) for month. If year, month, or day is not a value, @DATE returns the value ERR.

Use @DATE to sort by date or to set up search criteria using dates. See also "Date and Time @Functions" earlier in this chapter.

Examples

@DATE(89,9,27) = 32778 (or 27-Sep-89 in D1 format)
@DATE(82,9,27) = 30221 (or 9/27/82 in D4 format)
@DATE(88,9,31) = ERR, because September has only 30 days.

Note: *Even though February 29, 1900 did not exist (it was not a leap year), 1-2-3 assigns a date-number to this "day." This does not invalidate any of your date calculations, unless you use dates between January 1, 1900 and March 1, 1900. If you are using dates within that period, subtract 1 from any results within the period.*

@DATEVALUE

@DATEVALUE(string) calculates the date-number for a string that looks like a date. String can be a literal string, the range name or address of a cell that contains a label, or a formula or @function that evaluates to a string. String must be in one of the 1-2-3 Date formats.

For a description of the 1-2-3 Date formats, see /Range Format.

Use @DATEVALUE when you want to convert dates entered as labels to date-numbers so that you can use the dates in calculations. @DATEVALUE is also useful with data that has been imported from another program, such as a word processing program. See also "Date and Time @Functions" earlier in this chapter.

Examples

@DATEVALUE("23-Aug-89") = 32743

@DATEVALUE("23-Aug") = 32743 if 1989 is the current year.

@DATEVALUE("Aug-89") = 32721

@DATEVALUE(B3) = date-number of the date string in B3, if it is a correct Date format.

@DAVG

@DAVG(*input,field,criteria*) averages values in a *field* of the *input* range that meet criteria in the *criteria* range. See also "Database @Functions" earlier in this chapter.

Example

You created a database of your expenses for a recent trip in Canada. You want to determine the average amount you spent on gas in Toronto. In Figure 3-1, @DAVG(EXPENSES, 2,CRIT_RANGE) searches the *input* range EXPENSES for records that match the criteria in the *criteria* range CRIT_RANGE, and then averages the selected values in the *field* whose offset number is 2 (GAS).

```
D15: (C2) @DAVG(EXPENSES,2,CRIT_RANGE)

        A                    B          C          D          E
1  TRIP EXPENSES
2
3  CITY                   DATE        GAS      HOTEL       FOOD
4  Winnipeg             17-Nov     $27.85      $0.00      $4.50
5  Toronto              18-Nov      18.25      58.65      32.65
6  Toronto              19-Nov       6.85      58.65      28.00
7  Ottawa               20-Nov      23.45      60.50      33.74
8  Montreal             21-Nov      24.38      55.00      29.83
9  Montreal             22-Nov       6.33      55.00      35.70
10 Ottawa               23-Nov      22.97      60.50      42.00
11
12 CITY
13 Toronto
14
15 Average spent on gas in Toronto:           $12.55
16
17
18
19
20
3-1.WK1                 UNDO
```

Figure 3-1

@DAY

@DAY(*date-number*) calculates the day of the month (an integer from 1 to 31) in *date-number. Date-number* can be any integer from 1 (January 1, 1900) to 73050 (December 31, 2099). Usually, another date @function supplies *date-number.* See also "Date and Time @Functions" earlier in this chapter.

Example

@DAY(@NOW) = the current day of the month.

@DCOUNT

@DCOUNT(*input,field,criteria*) counts nonblank cells in a *field* of the *input* range that meet criteria in the *criteria* range. See also "Database @Functions" earlier in this chapter.

Example

You created a database of your expenses during a recent trip in Canada. You want to determine how many days you spent more than $20.00 on gas. In Figure 3-2, @DCOUNT(EXPENSES,2,CRIT_RANGE) searches the *input* range EXPENSES for records that match the criteria in the *criteria* range CRIT_RANGE, and then counts the selected values in the *field* whose offset number is 2 (GAS).

```
E15: @DCOUNT(EXPENSES,2,CRIT_RANGE)

        A                    B          C          D          E
1  TRIP EXPENSES
2
3  CITY                   DATE        GAS      HOTEL       FOOD
4  Winnipeg             17-Nov     $27.85      $0.00      $4.50
5  Toronto              18-Nov      18.25      58.65      32.65
6  Toronto              19-Nov       6.85      58.65      28.00
7  Ottawa               20-Nov      23.45      60.50      33.74
8  Montreal             21-Nov      24.38      55.00      29.83
9  Montreal             22-Nov       6.33      55.00      35.70
10 Ottawa               23-Nov      22.97      60.50      42.00
11
12 GAS
13 +C4>20
14
15 Number of days gas cost more than $20.00:               4
16
17
18
19
20
3-2.WK1                 UNDO
```

Figure 3-2

@DDB

@DDB(*cost,salvage,life,period*) calculates the depreciation allowance of an asset for a specified *period*, using the double-declining balance method.

Cost represents the amount paid for the asset. *Cost* can be any value greater than or equal to *salvage*. *Salvage* represents the estimated value of the asset at the end of its useful life. *Salvage* can be any value. *Life* represents the number of periods it will take to depreciate the asset to its salvage value. *Life* can be any value greater than 2. *Period* represents the time period for which you want to find the depreciation allowance. *Period* can be any value greater than or equal to 1.

The double-declining balance method accelerates the rate of depreciation so that more depreciation expense occurs (and can be written off) in earlier periods than in later ones. Depreciation stops when the book value of the asset — that is, the total cost of the asset minus its total depreciation over all prior periods — reaches the salvage value.

@DDB uses the following formula to calculate the double-declining balance depreciation for any period:

$$\frac{(bv*2)}{n}$$

In this formula, bv = the book value in the period being computed and n = life of the asset.

Example

You just purchased an office machine for $10,000. The useful life of this machine is eight years, and the salvage value after eight years is $1200. You want to calculate the depreciation expense for the fifth year, using the double-declining balance method.

@DDB(10000,1200,8,5) returns $791.02, the depreciation expense for the fifth year of the asset's life.

@DMAX

@DMAX(*input,field,criteria*) finds the largest value in a *field* of the *input* range that meets the criteria in the *criteria* range. See also "Database @Functions" earlier in this chapter.

Example

You created a database of your expenses for a trip in Canada. You want to determine the last day you spent in Montreal. In Figure 3-3, @DMAX(EXPENSES,1,CRIT_RANGE) searches the *input* range EXPENSES for records that match the criteria in the *criteria* range CRIT_RANGE, and then selects the largest value in the *field* whose offset number is 1 (DATE).

@DMIN

@DMIN(*input,field,criteria*) finds the smallest value in a *field* of the *input* range that meets the criteria in the *criteria* range. See also "Database @Functions" earlier in this chapter.

Example

You want to determine the first day you spent in Ottawa. See Figure 3-3. If you enter @DMIN(EXPENSES,1, CRIT_RANGE), 1-2-3 searches the *input* range EXPENSES for records that match the criteria in the *criteria* range CRIT_RANGE, and then selects the smallest value in the *field* whose offset number is 1 (DATE).

Figure 3-3

@DSTD

@DSTD(*input,field,criteria*) calculates the population standard deviation of the values in a *field* of an *input* range that meet the criteria in the *criteria* range. See also "Database @Functions" earlier in this chapter.

Standard deviation measures the degree to which individual values in a list vary from the mean (average) of all values in the list. The lower the standard deviation, the less individual values vary from the mean, and the more reliable the mean. A standard deviation of zero indicates that all values in the list are equal. The standard deviation is the square root of variance.

@DSTD produces most accurate results when the number of observations is large. @DSTD uses the n method (biased) to calculate the standard deviation of population data. The n method uses the following formula:

$$\sqrt{\frac{\sum(v_i - avg)^2}{n}}$$

In this formula, n = the number of items in the list, v_i = the ith item in list, and avg = the average of the values in list.

Example

The database in Figure 3-4 contains test scores for students in several cities. You want to determine the standard deviation of test scores for 16-year-olds. @DSTD(REGION,2, CRIT_RANGE) searches the *input* range for records that match the criteria in the *criteria* range CRIT_RANGE, and then calculates the standard deviation of the selected values from the *field* whose offset is 2 (SCORE).

```
E63: @DSTD(REGION,2,CRIT_RANGE)

        A         B         C         D         E         F
1  SCORES FOR STUDENTS IN REGION THREE
2
3  CITY         AGE       SCORE
49 Haberland     16        645
50 Haberland     17        640
51 Haberland     16        635
52 Haberland     17        630
53 Haberland     16        625
54 Mayfair       16        610
55 Haberland     17        600
56 Haberland     16        600
57 Haberland     16        595
58 Haberland     17        590
59 Haberland     16        590
60 Haberland     16        500
61
62 Population standard deviation
63 of 16-year-olds' test scores:        28.72779
64
65
05-Feb-91  12:12 PM              UNDO
```

Figure 3-4

@DSUM

@DSUM(*input,field,criteria*) sums the values in a *field* of an *input* range that meet the criteria in the *criteria* range. See also "Database @Functions" earlier in this chapter.

Example

You want to determine the total amount you spent on hotels in Montreal. See Figure 3-3. If you enter @DSUM(EXPENSES,3,CRIT_RANGE), 1-2-3 searches the *input* range EXPENSES for records that match the criteria in the *criteria* range CRIT_RANGE, and then adds the selected values from the *field* whose offset number is 3 (HOTEL).

@DVAR

@DVAR(*input,field,criteria*) calculates the population variance of the values in a *field* of an *input* range that meet the criteria in the *criteria* range. See also "Database @Functions" earlier in this chapter.

Variance is a measure of the degree to which individual values in a list vary from the mean (average) of all the values in the list. The lower the variance, the less individual values vary from the mean and the more reliable the mean. A variance of 0 indicates that all values in the list are equal. Variance is the square of standard deviation.

@DVAR produces most accurate results when the number of observations is large. @DVAR uses the n (biased) method to calculate variance with the following formula:

$$\frac{\sum(v_i - avg)^2}{n}$$

In this formula, n = the number of items in the list, v_i = the ith item in list, and avg = the average of values in list.

Example

The database in Figure 3-4 contains test scores for students in several cities. You want to determine the standard deviation of test scores for students from the city of Haberland. If you enter @DVAR(REGION,"SCORE",CRIT_RANGE), 1-2-3 searches the *input* range for records that match the criteria in the *criteria* range CRIT_RANGE, and then calculates the standard deviation of the selected values from the *field* whose offset number is 2 (SCORE).

@ERR

@ERR returns the value ERR (error). ERR is a special value in 1-2-3 that indicates an error in a formula. ERR has a ripple-through effect on formulas. @ERR is seldom used by itself, but is often used with @IF to indicate an ERR value only under certain conditions.

Note that you cannot substitute the label ERR for the value ERR in formulas. For example, the formula +A2+34 = ERR if A2 contains @ERR, but equals 34 if A2 contains the label ERR.

Example

@IF(B14>3,@ERR,B14) = ERR when the value in B14 is greater than 3.

@EXACT

@EXACT(*string1,string2*) tests whether *string1* and *string2* are the same. If the two strings match exactly, @EXACT returns 1 (true); if the two strings are not the same, @EXACT returns 0 (false). *String1* and *string2* can be literal strings, range names or addresses of cells that contain labels, or formulas or @functions that evaluate to strings.

@EXACT provides a more precise alternative to the equal operator (=) in a string formula because it distinguishes between uppercase and lowercase letters, between letters with and without accent marks, and between strings that contain leading or trailing spaces and those that do not. You can use @EXACT in a macro to check user input against a required entry before the macro continues processing.

Examples

@EXACT("Debit",B2) = 0 (false) when B2 contains the label DEBIT or debit.

@IF(@EXACT(A6,"Posted"),A25,@NA) = the value in A25 if A6 contains the label Posted. If A6 contains any other label, the formula returns the value NA.

@EXP

@EXP(*x*) calculates the value of *e* (approximately 2.718282) raised to the power *x*.

e is the constant used as the base in natural logarithms. *X* can be any value less than or equal to 709. If *x* is greater than 230 or smaller than −227, 1-2-3 can calculate and store the result of @EXP but cannot display it. If *x* is larger than 709, the calculation is too large for 1-2-3 to store, and @EXP returns the value ERR. If *x* is smaller than −709, @EXP returns the value 0.

Examples

@EXP(1.25) = 3.490342
@EXP(−1.25) = 0.286504

@FALSE

@FALSE returns the logical value 0 (false). Use @FALSE with macros or @functions such as @IF that require a logical value of 0 (false). You can use either @FALSE or the value 0 in formulas that evaluate logical conditions, but @FALSE makes the formula easier to read.

Example

@IF(A6=500,@TRUE,@FALSE) = 0 when A6 contains a value less than 500.

@FIND

@FIND(*search-string,string,start-number*) calculates the position in *string* at which 1-2-3 finds the first occurrence of *search-string*. @FIND begins searching *string* at the position indicated by *start-number*. If 1-2-3 does not find *search-string* in *string*, @FIND returns the value ERR.

Search-string and *string* can be literal strings, range names or addresses of cells that contain labels, or formulas or @functions that evaluate to strings. *Start-number* represents an offset number of a character in *string*. The first character has an offset number of 0; and the second, 1; and so on. @FIND is case sensitive; for example, @FIND will not find *search-string* pay in *string* PAYMENT.

Example

@FIND("P","Accounts Payable",0) = 9 because *search-string* P is at position 9 in *string* Accounts Payable.

@FV

@FV(*payments,interest,term*) calculates the future value of an investment, based on a series of equal *payments*, earning a periodic *interest* rate, over the number of payment periods in *term*. *Payments* and *term* can be any values. *Interest* can be any value greater than -1.

1-2-3 assumes that calculations made with @FV use an investment that is an ordinary annuity (one in which payments are made at the end of each period).

@FV uses the following formula to calculate future value:

$$pmt * \frac{(1 + int)^n - 1}{int}$$

In this formula, *pmt* = the periodic payment, *int* = the periodic interest rate, and *n* = the number of periods.

Examples

You plan to deposit $2,000 each year for the next 20 years into an Individual Retirement Account. The account pays 7.5% interest, compounded annually; interest is paid on the last day of each year. You want to calculate the value of your account in 20 years. You make each year's contribution on the last day of the year.

@FV(2000,0.075,20) returns $86,609, the value of your account at the end of 20 years.

Note: *If you make each year's contribution on the first day of the year, you would calculate the amount for an annuity due. To calculate the future value of an annuity due, use the formula @FV(payments,interest, term)*(1+interest). For example, @FV(2000,0.075,20)*(1+0.075) = $93,105, the value of your account in 20 years if you make each deposit on the first day of each year.*

@HLOOKUP

@HLOOKUP(*x, range, row-offset*) finds the contents of a cell in the specified row of a horizontal lookup table. A **horizontal lookup table** is a range whose values are in ascending order in the top row.

@HLOOKUP compares the value *x* to each cell in the top row of the table. When 1-2-3 locates a cell in the top row that contains the value *x* (or the value closest to, but not larger than, *x*) it moves down that column the number of rows specified by *row-offset* and returns the contents of the cell as the answer.

X can be any value greater than or equal to the first value in *range*. If *x* is smaller than the first value in *range*, @HLOOKUP returns the value ERR. If *x* is larger than the last value in *range*, @HLOOKUP stops at the last cell in the row and returns the contents of that cell.

Range represents the location of the horizontal lookup table. *Range* can be any range name or address. *Row-offset* represents an offset number. An offset number corresponds to the position the row occupies in *range*. The top row has an offset number of 0, the second row has an offset number of 1, and so on.

Use @HLOOKUP to locate entries in a table, such as a tax table or a sales commissions table.

Example

The table in Figure 3-5 contains the number of employees in various departments of a company during a 20-year period.

@HLOOKUP(1975,B3..F7,3) entered in D9 returns 12, the number of employees in the Documentation department in 1975.

Figure 3-5

@HLOOKUP(1981,B3..F7,1) entered in D11 returns 24. 1981 does not appear in the top row of the table, so @HLOOKUP stops at column D, because 1980 is the value closest to, but not larger than, 1981.

@HOUR

@HOUR(*time-number*) calculates the hour, an integer from 0 (midnight) to 23 (11:00 PM), in a *time-number*.

Time-number is a decimal value from .000000 (midnight) to .999988 (11:59:59 PM). Usually, another time @function supplies *time-number*. See also "Date and Time @Functions" earlier in this chapter.

Examples

@HOUR(.51565) = 12 (noon), because .51565 is the time-number for 12:22:32 PM.

@HOUR(@TIME(13,45,18)) = 13 (1:00 PM), because 13 is the *hour* argument for @TIME(13,45,18).

@IF

@IF(*condition*,*x*,*y*) evaluates *condition* and takes one of two actions, depending on the result of the evaluation. If *condition* is true, @IF returns *x*; if *condition* is false, @IF returns *y*. See the flowchart below.

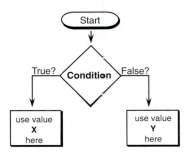

Condition is usually a logical formula or a reference to a cell that contains a logical formula. However, you can use any formula, number, literal string, or cell reference as *condition*. 1-2-3 evaluates any *condition* that does not equal zero as true and any *condition* that does equal zero as false. Blank cells and strings equal zero when used as *condition*. *X* and *y* can be values or strings.

The following relational and logical operators are often used in the *condition* argument of @IF:

Operator and meaning	Type of operator
= Equals	Relational
> Greater than	Relational
>= Greater than or equal to	Relational
< Less than	Relational
<= Less than or equal to	Relational
<> Not equal to	Relational
#AND# True only if both conditions are true	Logical
#OR# True if either or both conditions are true	Logical
#NOT# True if expression is false	Logical

Example

The worksheet in Figure 3-6 contains @IF statements in the range G3..K6. The worksheet also contains an explanation of each @IF statement (in row 3).

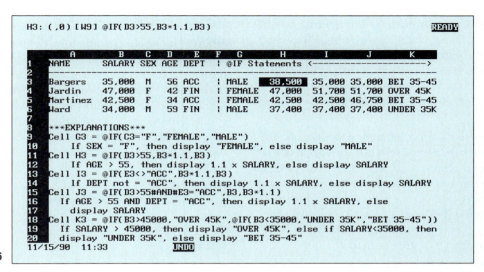

```
H3: (,0) [W9] @IF(D3>55,B3*1.1,B3)                                    READY

          A       B     C   D   E    F    G      H       I       J       K
1     NAME     SALARY SEX AGE DEPT : @IF Statements <----------------------->
2     -----------------------------------------------------------------------
3     Bargers  35,000  M   56  ACC  : MALE   38,500  35,000 35,000 BET 35-45
4     Jardin   47,000  F   42  FIN  : FEMALE 47,000  51,700 51,700 OVER 45K
5     Martinez 42,500  F   34  ACC  : FEMALE 42,500  42,500 46,750 BET 35-45
6     Ward     34,000  M   59  FIN  : MALE   37,400  37,400 37,400 UNDER 35K
7
8     ***EXPLANATIONS***
9     Cell G3 = @IF(C3="F","FEMALE","MALE")
10        If SEX = "F", then display "FEMALE", else display "MALE"
11    Cell H3 = @IF(D3>55,B3*1.1,B3)
12        If AGE > 55, then display 1.1 x SALARY, else display SALARY
13    Cell I3 = @IF(E3<>"ACC",B3*1.1,B3)
14        If DEPT not = "ACC", then display 1.1 x SALARY, else display SALARY
15    Cell J3 = @IF(D3>55#AND#E3="ACC",B3,B3*1.1)
16      If AGE > 55 AND DEPT = "ACC", then display 1.1 x SALARY, else
17        display SALARY
18    Cell K3 = @IF(B3>45000,"OVER 45K",@IF(B3<35000,"UNDER 35K","BET 35-45"))
19      If SALARY > 45000, then display "OVER 45K", else if SALARY<35000, then
20        display "UNDER 35K", else display "BET 35-45"
11/15/90  11:33        UNDO
```

Figure 3-6

@INDEX

@INDEX(*range,column-offset,row-offset*) finds the value in the cell located at a specified *column-offset* and *row-offset* of *range*.

Range can be any range name or address. *Column-offset* and *row-offset* represent offset numbers. An offset number corresponds to the position the column or row occupies in *range*. The first column or row has an offset number of 0, the second column or row has an offset number of 1, and so on.

Use @INDEX instead of @HLOOKUP or @VLOOKUP when you want to use a lookup table but need to use the relative positions of the rows or columns, instead of specified values, to find an entry.

Example

Figure 3-7 shows the number of children enrolled in kindergarten through third grade at an elementary school. @INDEX(SCHOOL,3,4) entered in D11 returns 114, the number of students in the third grade (*row-offset* number 4) in 1986 (*column-offset* number 3).

@INT

@INT(*x*) returns the integer portion of *x*, without rounding the value. *X* can be any value.

Note that if you want to display values as integers in the worksheet but want 1-2-3 to calculate the values to their full precision, use /Range Format Fixed 0 or /Worksheet Global Format Fixed 0. Do not use @INT in this situation.

Examples

@INT(35.67) = 35

@INT(@NOW) = the date-number for the current date without the time, because the time portion is a decimal value.

@IRR

@IRR(*guess,range*) calculates the internal rate of return expected from a series of cash flows generated by an investment. The internal rate of return is the percentage rate at which the present value of an expected series of cash flows is equal to the present value of the initial investment. 1-2-3 assumes the cash flows are received at regular, equal intervals.

```
D11: @INDEX(SCHOOL,3,4)

          A              B         C         D         E
1                              SCHOOL POPULATION
2     ===================================================
3     GRADE          1984      1985      1986      1987
4     Kindergarten     83        98        90        94
5     First            85       106        98        90
6     Second           79       114       105       100
7     Third            88        78       114       103
8
9     @INDEX(SCHOOL,0,2) ======>          First
10
11    @INDEX(SCHOOL,3,4) ======>                    114
12
13
```

Figure 3-7

Guess represents your estimate of the internal rate of return. *Guess* can be any value. *Range* can be the name or address of the range that contains the cash flows. 1-2-3 considers negative numbers as cash outflows and positive numbers as cash inflows. Normally, the first cash flow in *range* is a negative number representing the investment.

@IRR uses a series of approximations to calculate the internal rate of return. Because @IRR uses approximations, you enter a guess as the first argument. Enter a guess that you think is reasonable for the internal rate of return. In most cases, your guess should be a percentage between 0 (0%) and 1 (100%). Because more than one solution may be possible, try another guess if the result is less than 0 or greater than 1.

If @IRR cannot approximate the result to within 0.0000001 after 30 calculation iterations, the formula evaluates to ERR. If your guesses continue to return ERR, use @NPV to determine a better guess. If @NPV returns a positive value, your guess is too low. If @NPV returns a negative value, your guess is too high. @NPV returns 0 if your guess is accurate.

Note that @IRR assigns the value 0 to all blank cells in *range* and includes them in the calculation.

Example

In Figure 3-8, @IRR(A2,B2..B14) entered in B16 returns 6.11% over a 12-month term; the initial investment is $1000 (in B2) and the 12 cash flows are each $120 (in B3..B14). @IRR(D2,E2..E14) entered in E16 returns 7.09% over a 12-month term; the initial investment is $1000 (in E2) and the 12 cash flows are those shown in E3..E14.

```
E16: (P2) @IRR(D2,E2..E14)

        A         B          C       D         E
1             Guess  Cash flows          Guess  Cash flows
2              5%    ($1,000)            5%     ($1,000)
3                     $120                       $120
4                      120                        124
5                      120                        128
6                      120                        132
7                      120                        136
8                      120                        130
9                      120                        120
10                     120                        124
11                     120                        128
12                     120                        132
13                     120                        120
14                     120                        124
15
16                   6.11%                               7.09%
17
18
```

Figure 3-8

@ISAFF

@ISAFF(*name*) tests name for a defined add-in @function. If *name* is a defined add-in @function, @ISAFF returns 1 (true); if *name* is not a defined add-in @function, @ISAFF returns 0 (false). *Name* represents the name of the add-in @function you want to test. *Name* can be entered as a literal string, a string formula, or a reference to a cell that contains a label. Do not include the initial @ (at sign) in *name*.

Example

@ISAFF("dsum") = 0 because @DSUM is a built-in 1-2-3 @function, not an add-in @function.

@ISAPP

@ISAPP(*name*) tests name for an attached add-in. If *name* is an attached add-in, @ISAPP returns 1 (true); if *name* is not an attached add-in, @ISAPP returns 0 (false).

Name represents the name of the add-in you want to test. *Name* can be entered as a literal string, a string formula, or a reference to a cell that contains a label. Do not include the .ADN extension in *name*.

Note: *@ISAPP returns 1 (true) only for any add-ins you invoke using /Add-In Invoke. For add-ins that only define add-in @functions, or for any add-in installed in your driver set, @ISAPP returns 0 (false). Use @ISAFF to test for add-in @functions.*

Example

@ISAPP("finance") = 1 if an add-in called FINANCE is currently attached.

@ISERR

@ISERR(*x*) tests *x* for the value ERR. If *x* is the value ERR, @ISERR returns 1 (true); if *x* is not the value ERR, @ISERR returns 0 (false). *X* can be any string, value, location, or condition. Use @ISERR to stop the ripple-through effect of the value ERR. For an explanation of the ripple-through effect, see "Logical @Functions" earlier in this chapter.

Example

@ISERR is frequently used to block errors that arise from division by 0. For example, @IF(@ISERR(A1/A2),0,A1/A2) tests the result of the division A1/A2. If the result is the value ERR, the formula returns 0. If the result is any other value, the formula returns that result.

@ISNA

@ISNA(x) tests x for the value NA. If x is the value NA, @ISNA returns 1 (true); if x is not the value NA, @ISNA returns 0 (false). X can be any string, value, location, or condition.

Use @ISNA to stop the ripple-through effect of the value NA. For an explanation of the ripple-through effect, see "Logical @Functions" earlier in this chapter.

Example

@ISNA(B1) = 1 if B1 contains the value NA; @ISNA(B1) = 0 if B1 contains any other entry.

@ISNUMBER

@ISNUMBER(x) tests x for a value. If x is a value or a blank cell, @ISNUMBER returns 1 (true); if x is a string, @ISNUMBER returns 0 (false). X can be any string, value, location, or condition. Use @ISNUMBER to prevent errors that would occur if a cell used in a formula contained the wrong type of data.

Example

@ISNUMBER is often used in macros to make sure a user enters the correct type of information (values or labels). In the macro instructions

{IF @ISNUMBER(C6)=0}{BEEP}{QUIT}

@ISNUMBER returns 0 if C6 contains a label; 1-2-3 then beeps and ends the macro.

@ISSTRING

@ISSTRING(x) tests x for a string. If x is a literal string or cell that contains a label or string formula, @ISSTRING returns 1 (true); if x is a value or blank cell, @ISSTRING returns 0 (false). X can be any string, value, location, or condition.

Use @ISSTRING to prevent errors that would occur if a cell used in a formula contained the wrong type of data. Note that @ISSTRING returns 1 even if a cell contains only a label prefix or space.

Example

@ISSTRING is often used in macros to make sure a user enters the correct type of information (values or labels). In the macro instructions

{IF @ISSTRING(C6)=0}{BEEP}{QUIT}

@ISSTRING returns 0 if C6 contains a value or is blank; 1-2-3 then beeps and ends the macro.

@LEFT

@LEFT($string, n$) returns the first n characters in *string*. *String* can be a literal string, the range name or address of a cell that contains a label, or a formula or @function that evaluates to a string. N can be any positive integer or zero. If n is zero, the result of @LEFT is an empty string. If n is greater than or equal to the length of *string*, @LEFT returns the entire *string*.

1-2-3 counts punctuation and spaces as characters in @LEFT. @LEFT is useful for copying only part of a label into another cell.

Example

The formula @LEFT(A4,3)&D4 generates an account number by combining the first three letters of a customer's last name (in A4) with her zip code (in D4).

@LENGTH

@LENGTH($string$) counts the number of characters in *string*. *String* can be a literal string, the range name or address of a cell that contains a label, or a formula or @function that evaluates to a string. 1-2-3 counts punctuation and spaces as characters in @LENGTH.

Examples

In these examples, each • represents one space.
@LENGTH("Mr.• Jones") = 9
@LENGTH(B1) = 16 when B1 contains the label Accounts Payable.

@LN

@LN(x) calculates the natural logarithm of x. Natural logarithms use the number e (approximately 2.718281) as a base. X can be any value greater than 0.

Examples

@LN(2) = 0.693147
@LN(@EXP(1)) = 1, because @EXP(1) = 2.718281.

@LOG

@LOG(x) calculates the common logarithm (base 10) of x. X can be any value greater than 0.

Examples

@LOG(4) = 0.60206
@LOG(1.0E+14) = 14

@LOWER

@LOWER(*string*) converts all uppercase letters in *string* to lowercase. *String* can be a literal string, the range name or address of a cell that contains a label, or a formula or @function that evaluates to a string.

Examples

@LOWER("EXPENSES") = expenses

@LOWER(B2) = e.e. cummings if B2 contains the label E.E. Cummings.

@MAX

@MAX(*list*) finds the largest value in *list*. *List* can contain one or more numbers, numeric formulas, references to ranges that contain numbers or numeric formulas, or any combination of numbers, formulas, and references to ranges.

Examples

@MAX(55,39,50,28,67,43) = 67

@MAX(A1..C10) returns the largest value in A1..C10.

@MID

@MID(*string,start-number,n*) returns *n* characters from *string*, beginning with the character at *start-number*. *String* can be a literal string, the range name or address of a cell that contains a label, or a formula or @function that evaluates to a string. The first character has an offset number of 0; the second, 1; and so on. *Start-number* represents the offset number of a character in *string*. If *start-number* is greater than the length of *string* minus 1, the result of @MID is an empty string. *N* can be any positive integer or 0. If *n* is 0, the result of @MID is an empty string.

1-2-3 counts punctuation and spaces as characters in @MID. Use @MID when you need to extract a part of a label that is not located at the beginning or end of the label. If you need to extract part of a label but you don't know its *start-number*, use @MID with @FIND.

Note: *Use a large number for n if you don't know the length of string; 1-2-3 will return the remainder of string.*

Example

@MID("Daily Account Balance",6,7) = Account

@MIN

@MIN(*list*) finds the smallest value in *list*. *List* can contain one or more numbers, numeric formulas, references to ranges that contain numbers or numeric formulas, or any combination of numbers, formulas, and references to ranges.

Examples

@MIN(55,39,50,28,67,43) = 28

@MIN(A1..C10) returns the smallest value in A1..C10.

@MINUTE

@MINUTE(*time-number*) calculates the minutes, an integer from 0 to 59, in *time-number*. *Time-number* can be any decimal value from .000000 (midnight) to .999988 (11:59:59 PM). Usually, another time @function supplies *time-number*. See also "Date and Time @Functions" earlier in this chapter.

Examples

@MINUTE(0.333) = 59 because 0.333 is the time-number for 7:59:31.

@MINUTE(@TIME(11,15,45)) = 15 because 15 is the *minutes* argument for @TIME(11,15,45).

@MOD

@MOD(*x,y*) calculates the remainder (modulus) of x/y. X can be any value. If x is 0, @MOD returns 0. The sign (+ or −) of x determines the sign of the result. Y can be any value except 0. @MOD uses the following formula to calculate the modulus:

$$x–(y*@INT(x/y))$$

Example

@MOD(9,4) = 1

You can use @MOD to calculate the day of the week by entering a date-number as x and 7 (the number of days in a week) as y. The remainder of the date-number, divided by 7, will be the day of the week: 0 for Saturday, 1 for Sunday, up to 6 for Friday. For example, @MOD(@DATE(85, 11,18),7) = 2; November 18, 1985 was a Monday.

@MONTH

@MONTH(*date-number*) calculates the month in *date-number* as an integer from 1 (January) to 12 (December). *Date-number* can be any integer from 1 (January 1, 1900) to 73050 (December 31, 2099). Usually, another date @function supplies *date-number*.

See also "Date and Time @Functions" earlier in this chapter.

Examples

@MONTH(20181) = 4 because 20181 is the date-number for April 2, 1955.

@MONTH(@NOW) = the current month.

@N

@N(*range*) returns the entry in the first cell in *range* as a value: if the cell contains a value, @N returns that value; if the cell contains a label, @N returns the value 0. *Range* can be any range name or address.

Example

Use @N in error-trapping routines in macros to prevent errors that would result if a cell used in formulas contained the wrong type of data. In the macro instructions

{IF @N(B6)=0}{BEEP}{INDICATE "ENTRY MUST BE NUMERIC"}

@N returns 0 if B6 contains a label; 1-2-3 then beeps and changes the mode indicator to ENTRY MUST BE NUMERIC.

@NA

@NA returns the value NA (not available). NA is a special value in 1-2-3 that indicates that a value needed to complete a formula is not available. NA has a ripple-through effect on formulas.

Use @NA when you are building a worksheet that will contain data that you have not yet determined. You can use @NA in cells where you will enter that data; formulas that refer to those cells will have the value NA until you supply the data.

Note: *You cannot substitute the label NA for the value NA in formulas. For example, the formula +A2+34 = NA when A2 contains @NA, but equals 34 when A2 contains the label NA.*

Example

@IF(B14=" ",@NA,B14) = the value NA because B14 is blank.

@NOW

@NOW calculates the value that corresponds to the current date and time on the computer's clock. This includes both a date-number (integer portion) and a time-number (decimal portion). See also "Date and Time @Functions" earlier in this chapter.

You can format the value of @NOW in any of the 1-2-3 Date or Time formats. If you format @NOW as a date, 1-2-3 displays only the date (integer) portion of the date- and time-number; if you format @NOW as a time, 1-2-3 displays only the time (decimal) portion of the date- and time-number. In both cases, 1-2-3 continues to calculate with the entire date-and-time-number.

@NOW recalculates each time you recalculate your work. If you set recalculation to Automatic, 1-2-3 recalculates @NOW whenever it recalculates another value.

Examples

@NOW = 31048.5 at noon on January 25, 1985.

@NOW = 32688.395 at 9:45 AM, June 29, 1989.

@NPV

@NPV(*interest,range*) calculates the net present value of a series of future cash flows discounted at a fixed, periodic *interest* rate. 1-2-3 assumes that the cash flows occur at equal time intervals, that the first cash flow occurs at the end of the first period, and subsequent cash flows occur at the end of subsequent periods. *Interest* can be any value greater than −1. *Range* can be the name or address of the range that contains the cash flows. @NPV is similar to @PV, except that with @PV all cash flows are equal amounts.

@NPV calculates the net present value using the following formula:

$$\sum_{i=1}^{n} \frac{v_i}{(1+int)^i}$$

In this formula, $v_i...v_n$ = the series of cash flows in range, int = the interest rate, n = the number of cash flows, and i = the current iteration (1 through n).

Example

In Figure 3-9, @NPV(B2,D2..D6) entered in B5 returns $6,707.90, the net present value of the cash flows in D2..D6.

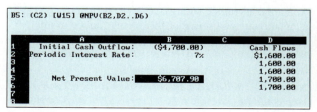

Figure 3-9

Note: *To determine the net present value of an investment where you make an initial cash outflow immediately, followed by a series of future inflows, you must factor the initial outflow separately, because it is not affected by the interest. For example, +INITIAL+@NPV(RATE,SERIES) = $904.07 when INITIAL is the initial cash outflow, RATE is the interest rate, and SERIES is the series of future cash inflows.*

@PI

@PI returns the value π (calculated at 3.1415926536). π is the ratio of the circumference of a circle to its diameter.

Example

@PI*4^2 = 50.26548, the area of a circle with a radius of 4.

@PMT

@PMT(*principal,interest,term*) calculates the amount of the periodic payment needed to pay off a loan, given a specified periodic *interest* rate and number of payment periods. 1-2-3 assumes your calculations are for payments you make at the end of each payment period (an ordinary annuity).

Principal represents the value of the loan. *Principal* can be any value. *Interest* represents the periodic interest rate. *Interest* can be any value greater than −1. *Term* represents the number of payment periods. *Term* can be any value except 0. Enter *interest* and *term* in the same units of time. For example, if you are calculating a monthly payment, enter the interest and term in monthly increments. (See the example below.)

@PMT uses the following formula to calculate periodic payment:

$$prin * \frac{int}{1 - (int + 1)^{-n}}$$

In this formula, *prin* = the principal, *int* = the periodic interest rate, and *n* = the term of the loan.

Examples

You are considering taking out an $8,000 loan for 3 years at an annual interest rate of 14%, compounded monthly. You want to determine your monthly payment.
@PMT(8000,0.14/12,36) returns $273.42, the monthly payment.

Note: *If you make payments at the beginning of each month, you would instead calculate the amount for an annuity due. To calculate the amount of the periodic payment on an annuity due, use the formula @PMT(principal, interest,*

term)/(1+interest). Therefore, @PMT(8000, 0.14/12,36)/ (1+0.14/12) = $270.27, the monthly payment.

@PROPER

@PROPER(*string*) converts the letters in *string* to proper capitalization: the first letter of each word uppercase, and the remaining letters in each word lowercase. *String* can be a literal string, the range name or address of a cell that contains a label, or a formula or @function that evaluates to a string. Use @PROPER when you combine data from several sources and want labels to be consistent throughout your worksheet.

Examples

In these examples, each • represents one space.
@PROPER("354-a•babcock") = 354-A Babcock
@PROPER(A7&";•"&G7) returns Morton Smith; Athens, Georgia if A7 contains the label "MORTON SMITH" and G7 contains the label "Athens, georgia". (Note that the ; (Semicolon) is in quotation marks and is therefore treated as a literal string instead of an argument separator.)

@PV

@PV(*payments,interest,term*) determines the present value of an investment. @PV calculates the present value based on a series of equal investments (*payments*), discounted at a periodic *interest* rate over the number of periods in *term*. *Payments* and *term* can be any values. *Interest* can be any value greater than −1.

@PV calculates present value with the following formula:

$$pmt * \frac{1 - (1 + int)^{-n}}{int}$$

In this formula, *pmt* = the periodic payment, *int* = the periodic interest rate, and *n* = the term, or number of payments.

Examples

You won $1,000,000. You can receive either 20 annual payments of $50,000 at the end of each year or a single payment of $400,000 instead of the $1,000,000 annuity. You want to find out which option is worth more in today's dollars. If you were to accept the annual payments of $50,000, you assume that you would invest the money at a rate of 8%, compounded annually.

If you enter @PV(50,0.08,20) 1-2-3 returns $490,907. The $1,000,000 paid over 20 years is worth $490,907 in present dollars.

Note: *If you received the annual payments at the beginning of each year, you would calculate the amount for an annuity due. To calculate the present value of an annuity due, use the formula @PV(payments,interest,term)*(1+interest). Therefore, @PV(50000, 0.08,20)*(1+0.08) = $530,180, the value of $1,000,000 paid over 20 years as an annuity due in present dollars.*

@RAND

@RAND generates a random value between 0 and 1. Each time 1-2-3 recalculates your work, @RAND generates a new random value. @RAND is useful for generating test data for simulations. To generate random values in different numeric intervals, multiply @RAND by the size of the interval. (See the second and third examples below.)

Examples

@RAND = 0.419501 or any value between 0 and 1.
@RAND*10 = 6.933674 or any value between 0 and 10.
@INT(@RAND*50)+1 = 49 or any integer from 1 to 50.

@RATE

@RATE(*future-value,present-value,term*) calculates the periodic interest rate necessary for an investment (*present-value*) to grow to a *future-value* over the number of compounding periods in *term*. *Future-value* can be any value. *Present-value* and *term* can be any values except 0.

@RATE uses the following formula to calculate the periodic interest rate:

$$\left(\frac{fv}{pv}\right)^{\frac{1}{n}} - 1$$

In this formula, fv = the future value, pv = the present value, and n = the term, or number of payments.

Example

You invested $10,000 in a bond. The bond matures in five years and has a maturity value of $18,000. Interest is compounded monthly. You want to determine the periodic interest rate for this investment.
If D2 = $10,000, D3 = 60(months), and D4 = $18,000, then @RATE(D4,D2,D3) returns .984%, the periodic (monthly) interest rate. To determine the annual rate, multiply the above formula by 12. This yields a result of 11.8% annually.

@REPEAT

@REPEAT(*string,n*) duplicates *string* n times. *String* can be a literal string, the range name or address of a cell that contains a label, or a formula or @function that evaluates to a string. *N* can be any positive integer. @REPEAT is not limited by the current column width as is the repeating label prefix \ (Backslash).

Examples

In these examples, each • represents one space.
@REPEAT("Hello•",3) returns Hello Hello Hello.
@REPEAT("x",3) returns xxx.

@REPLACE

@REPLACE(*original-string,start-number,n,new-string*) replaces *n* characters in *original-string*, beginning at *start-number*, with *new-string*. *Original-string* and *new-string* can be literal strings, the range name or address of cells that contain labels, or formulas or @functions that evaluate to strings. *Start-number* represents the offset number of a character in *original-string*. The first character has an offset number of 0; the second, 1; and so on. *N* can be any positive integer or zero.

By making *n* equal the number of characters in *original-string*, you can replace the entire *original-string* with *new-string*. By specifying a position immediately beyond the end of *original-string* as *start-number*, you can append *new-string* to *original-string*. By making *n* equal 0, you can insert a new string. By making *new-string* an empty string, you can delete a string.

1-2-3 counts punctuation and spaces as characters in @REPLACE. If you use @REPLACE to append or insert strings, remember to include the necessary spaces.

Examples

In these examples, each • represents one space.
@REPLACE("January",0,3,"Febr") = February
@REPLACE("January",10,0,"•February") = January February

@RIGHT

@RIGHT(*string,n*) returns the last *n* characters in *string*. *String* can be a literal string, the range name or address of a cell that contains a label, or a formula or @function that evaluates to a string. *N* can be any positive integer or 0. If *n* is 0, the result of @RIGHT is an empty string. If *n* is greater than or equal to the length of *string*, @RIGHT returns the entire *string*.

1-2-3 counts punctuation and spaces as characters in @RIGHT. @RIGHT is useful for copying only part of a label to another cell.

Examples

@RIGHT("Average Daily Balance",7) = Balance

@RIGHT(B3,5) = Sales when B3 contains the label January Sales.

@ROUND

@ROUND(*x,n*) rounds the value *x* to *n* places. *X* can be any value. *N* can be any integer from –15 to 15. If *n* is positive, 1-2-3 rounds *x* to *n* digits to the right of the decimal point. If *n* is negative, 1-2-3 rounds *x* to the positive *n*th power of 10. For example, if *n* is –2, 1-2-3 rounds *x* to the nearest hundred. If *n* is 0, 1-2-3 rounds *x* to an integer.

Note: *If you want to display values with a specific number of decimal places but want 1-2-3 to calculate those values to their full precision, use /Range Format Fixed or /Worksheet Global Format Fixed. Do not use @ROUND.*

Examples

@ROUND(134.578,2) = 134.58

@ROUND(134.578,0) = 135

@ROUND(134.578,–2) = 100

@ROWS

@ROWS(*range*) counts the number of rows in *range*. *Range* can be any range name or address. You can use @ROWS to find the length of a range you want to print.

Example

@ROWS(SCORES) = 43 if SCORES is the range B3..B45.

@S

@S(*range*) returns the entry in the first cell in *range* as a label: if the cell contains a label, @S returns that label; if the cell contains a value, @S returns an empty string. *Range* can be any range name or address.

Example

Use @S in error-trapping routines in macros to prevent errors that would result if a cell used in formulas contained the wrong type of data. In the macro instructions

{IF @S(B6)=""}{BEEP}{INDICATE "ENTRY MUST BE A LABEL"}

@S returns an empty string if B6 contains a value; 1-2-3 then beeps and changes the mode indicator to ENTRY MUST BE A LABEL.

@SECOND

@SECOND(*time-number*) calculates the seconds, an integer from 0 and 59, in *time-number*. See also "Date and Time @Functions" earlier in this chapter.

Time-number can be any decimal value from .000000 (midnight) to .999988 (11:59:59 PM). Usually, another time @function supplies *time-number*.

Examples

@SECOND(0.333) = 31 because 0.333 is the time-number for 7:59:31.

@SECOND(@TIME(11,15,45)) = 45 because 45 is the *seconds* argument for @TIME(11,15,45).

@SIN

@SIN(*x*) calculates the sine of an angle (*x*) measured in radians. *X* can be any value.

Examples

@SIN(.883) = 0.772646

@SIN(35*@PI/180) = 0.573576

@SLN

@SLN(*cost,salvage,life*) calculates the straight-line depreciation allowance of an asset for one period. *Cost* represents the amount paid for the asset. *Cost* can be any value. *Salvage* represents the estimated value of the asset at the end of its life. *Salvage* can be any value. *Life* represents the number of periods it will take to depreciate the asset to its salvage value. *Life* can be any value except 0.

Straight-line depreciation divides the depreciable cost (the actual cost minus the salvage value) evenly over the useful life of an asset. The useful life is the number of periods (typically years) over which an asset is depreciated.

@SLN uses the following formula to calculate straight-line depreciation:

$$\frac{(c-s)}{n}$$

In this formula, c = cost of the asset, s = salvage value of the asset, and n = useful life of the asset.

Example

You have an office machine worth $10,000. The useful life of this machine is 10 years, and the salvage value in 10 years will be $1200. You want to calculate yearly depreciation expense, using the straight-line method.

@SLN(10000,1200,10) returns $880, the yearly depreciation allowance.

@SQRT

@SQRT(x) calculates the positive square root of x. X can be any positive value or 0.

Examples

@SQRT(@INT(25.768)) = 5 because @INT(25.768) = 25.
@SQRT(–2) = ERR because x is negative.

@STD

@STD(*list*) calculates the population standard deviation of the values in *list*. *List* can contain one or more values, strings, references to ranges that contain values or strings, or any combination of values, strings, and range references.

Standard deviation measures the degree to which individual values in a list vary from the mean (average) of all values in the list. The lower the standard deviation, the less individual values vary from the mean and the more reliable the mean. A standard deviation of 0 indicates that all values in the list are equal. Standard deviation is the square root of variance (@VAR).

Population standard deviation is most accurate when the number of observations is large. @STD uses the n (biased) method to calculate standard deviation of population data, with the following formula:

$$\sqrt{\frac{\sum (v_i - avg)^2}{n}}$$

In this formula, n = the number of items in list, v_i = the ith item in list, and avg = average of values in list.

Example

In Figure 3-10, @STD(C3..C43) = 40.05, the population standard deviation of the test scores in C3..C43.

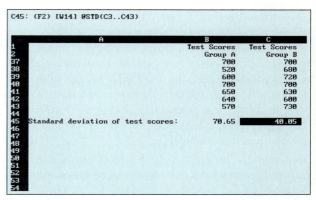

Figure 3-10

@STRING

@STRING(x, n) converts the value x into a string with n decimal places. X can be any value. N can be any integer from 0 to 15.

Note: *@STRING ignores any formatting characters included in x. For example, if A7 contains the formatted value $45.23, @STRING(A7,2) returns the string 45.23.*

Examples

In these examples, each • represents one space.
@STRING(1.23587,0) = the string 1
@STRING(20%,1) = the string 0.2
@STRING(B3,0)&"•"&B4 returns the string 100 Kilsyth Road if B3 contains the value 100 and B4 contains the label Kilsyth Road.

@SUM

@SUM(*list*) adds the values in list.

List can contain one or more numbers, strings, references to ranges that contain numbers or strings, or any combination of numbers, strings, and range references.

Example

If B2 = 5, B3 = 7, B4 = 10, then @SUM (B2..B4) = 22.

@SYD

@SYD(*cost,salvage,life,period*) calculates the sum-of-the-years'-digits depreciation allowance of an asset for a specified *period*.

Cost represents the amount paid for the asset. *Cost* can be any value. *Salvage* represents the value of the asset at the end of its life. *Salvage* can be any value. *Life* represents the number of periods (typically years) it will take to depreciate the asset to its salvage value. *Life* can be any value greater than or equal to 1. *Period* represents the time period for which you want to find the depreciation allowance. *Period* can be any value greater than or equal to 1.

The sum-of-the-years'-digits method accelerates the rate of depreciation so that more depreciation expense occurs in earlier periods than in later ones. The depreciable cost is the actual cost minus the salvage value.

@SYD uses the following formula to calculate depreciation using the sum-of-the-years'-digits method:

$$\frac{(c-s)*(n-p+1)}{(n*(n+1)/2)}$$

In this formala, c = cost of the asset, s = salvage value of the asset, n = calculated useful life of the asset, and p = the period for which depreciation is being calculated.

Example

You have an office machine worth $10,000. The useful life of the machine is 10 years, and the salvage value in 10 years will be $1200. You want to calculate depreciation expense for the fifth year, using the sum-of-the-years'-digits method.

@SYD(10000,1200,10,5) returns $960, the depreciation allowance for the fifth year.

@TAN

@TAN(*x*) calculates the tangent of an angle (x) measured in radians. *X* can be any value.

Examples

@TAN(.52) = 0.572561

@TAN(35*@PI/180) = 0.700207

@TERM

@TERM(*payments,interest, future-value*) calculates the number of payment periods in the term of an investment necessary to accumulate a *future-value*, assuming *payments* of equal value, when the investment earns a periodic *interest* rate.

Payments can be any value except 0. *Interest* can be any value greater than −1. *Future-value* can be any value.

1-2-3 assumes that calculations made with @TERM use an investment that is an ordinary annuity (payments at the end of each period).

@TERM uses the following formula to calculate the payment term:

$$\frac{\ln(1+fv*int/pmt)}{\ln(1+int)}$$

In this formula, *pmt* = the periodic payment, *fv* = the future value, *int* = the periodic interest rate, and ln is the natural logarithm.

Examples

You deposit $2,000 at the end of each year into a bank account. Your account earns 7.5% a year, compounded annually. You want to determine how long it will take to accumulate $100,000.

@TERM(2000,0.075,100000) returns 21.5, the number of years it will take to accumulate $100,000 in your account.

If you made payments at the beginning of each year, you would calculate the amount for an annuity due. To calculate the number of payment periods in an annuity due, use the formula @TERM(*payment,interest,future value/* (1+*interest*)). Therefore, @TERM(2000, 0.075,100000/ (1+0.075)) = 20.8, the number of years it would take to accumulate $100,000 if you made deposits at the beginning of each year.

Note: *You can calculate the term necessary to pay back a loan by using @TERM with a negative future value. For example, you want to know how long it will take to pay back a $10,000 loan at 10% yearly interest, making payments of $1,174.60 per year. @ABS (@TERM (1174.6,0.1,−10000)) = 20 years to pay back the loan.*

@TIME

@TIME(*hour,minutes,seconds*) calculates the time-number for the specified *hour, minutes*, and *seconds*. Use @TIME to enter times as time-numbers that 1-2-3 can use in time-arithmetic calculations — for example, to keep track of elapsed times. See also "Date and Time @Functions" earlier in this chapter.

Hour can be any integer from 0 (midnight) to 23 (11:00 PM). *Minutes* and *seconds* can be any integers from 0 to 59.

Example

You want to determine a consultant's payment. The following formula calculates the amount due on a given day:

(@TIME(13,0,0)–@TIME(9,15,0))*95*24

This formula subtracts the start time (9:15 AM) from the stop time (1:00 PM) and multiplies the result by an hourly rate of $95.00. The result is $356.25.

@TIMEVALUE

@TIMEVALUE(*string*) calculates the time-number for a *string* that looks like a time. *String* can be a literal string, the range name or address of a cell that contains a label, or a formula or @function that evaluates to a string. *String* must be in one of the 1-2-3 Time formats. For a description of the 1-2-3 Time formats, see /Range Format.

Use @TIMEVALUE when you want to convert times entered as labels to time-numbers so that you can use the times in calculations. @TIMEVALUE is useful with data that has been imported from another program, such as a word processing program. See also "Date and Time @Functions" earlier in this chapter.

Examples

@TIMEVALUE("3:12:00 PM") = 0.6333 (D6 format)
@TIMEVALUE("3:12 PM") = 0.6333 (D7 format)

@TRIM

@TRIM(*string*) removes leading, trailing, and consecutive spaces from *string*. *String* can be a literal string, the range name or address of a cell that contains a label, or a formula or @function that evaluates to a string. Use @TRIM to control spacing during data entry or to combine strings that have unknown spacing.

Examples

In these examples, each • represents one space.
@TRIM("•45••3/8") = 45 3/8
@TRIM("•500•••South••St.") = 500 South St.

@TRUE

@TRUE returns the logical value 1 (true).

Use @TRUE with macros or @functions such as @IF and @CHOOSE that require a logical value of 1 (true). You can use either @TRUE or any nonzero value in formulas that evaluate logical conditions, but @TRUE makes the formula easier to read.

Example

@IF(A6>500,@TRUE,@FALSE) = 1 when A6 contains a value greater than 500.

@UPPER

@UPPER(*string*) converts all lowercase letters in *string* to uppercase. *String* can be a literal string, the range name or address of a cell that contains a label, or a formula or @function that evaluates to a string.

Examples

@UPPER("Account Number") = ACCOUNT NUMBER
@UPPER(B2) = WARNING if B2 contains the label warning.

@VALUE

@VALUE(*string*) converts a number entered as a *string* to its corresponding value. *String* can be a literal string, the range name or address of a cell that contains a label, or a formula or @function that evaluates to a string. *String* must contain only numbers or numeric symbols. If *string* is a blank cell or empty string, @VALUE returns 0. If *string* contains nonnumeric characters, @VALUE returns the value ERR.

@VALUE ignores leading and trailing spaces in *string*; however, if *string* contains spaces separating symbols from the numbers (such as $ 32.85 or £   56.20), @VALUE returns the value ERR. Use @VALUE when you want to convert a string that contains numbers into values that can be used in mathematical calculations.

Note: *You cannot do calculations within a string argument in @VALUE; however, you can create a formula with several @VALUE functions. (See the third example below.)*

Examples

@VALUE(B3) = 49.75, if B3 contains the label 49 3/4.
@VALUE("85%") = .85
@VALUE("22"+"20") = 0, but @VALUE("22")+@VALUE("20") = 42

@VAR

@VAR(*list*) calculates the population variance of the values in *list*. *List* can contain one or more numbers, numeric formulas, references to ranges that contain numbers or numeric formulas, or any combination of numbers, formulas, and references to ranges.

Variance is a measure of the degree to which individual values in a list vary from the mean (average) of all the values in the list. The lower the variance, the less individual values vary from the mean and the more reliable the mean. A variance of 0 indicates that all values in the list are equal. Variance is the square of standard deviation (@STD).

The results of @VAR are most accurate when the number of observations is large. @VAR uses the n (biased) method to calculate variance with the following formula:

$$\frac{\sum (v_i - avg)^2}{n}$$

In this formula, n = the number of items in the list, v_i = the ith item in list, and avg = the average of values in list

Example

In the example in Figure 3-10 (see @STD), if you entered @VAR(B3..B43) in B46, 1-2-3 would return 963.44, the population variance of the test scores in B3..B43.

@VLOOKUP

@VLOOKUP(*x,range,column-offset*) finds the contents of the cell in a specified column of a vertical lookup table. A **vertical lookup table** is a range with value information in ascending order in the first column.

@VLOOKUP compares the value x to each cell in the first column of the table. When 1-2-3 locates a cell in the first column that contains the value x (or the value closest to, but not larger than, x), it moves across that row the number of columns specified by *column-offset* and returns the contents of the cell as the answer.

X can be any value greater than or equal to the first value in *range*. If x is smaller than the first value in *range*, @VLOOKUP returns the value ERR. If x is larger than the last value in *range*, @VLOOKUP stops at the last cell in the column and returns the contents of the cell as the answer.

Range represents the location of the vertical lookup table. *Range* can be any range name or address. *Column-offset* represents an offset number. An offset number corresponds to the position the column occupies in *range*. The first column has an offset number of 0, the second column has an offset number of 1, and so on.

Use @VLOOKUP to locate entries in a table, such as a tax table or a sales commissions table.

Examples

Figure 3-11 shows a tax table.

@VLOOKUP(A8,$A$17,$E$19,B8) entered in C8 returns $9,241, the amount of tax you would pay if your income was $35,050 and you were a Status 1 taxpayer.

@VLOOKUP(A9,$A$17,$E$19,B9) entered in C9 returns $11,364, the amount of tax you would pay if your income was $35,150 and you were a Status 3 taxpayer. $35,150 does not appear in the first column of the table, so @VLOOKUP stops at row 19, because $35,100 is the value closest to, but not larger than, $35,150.

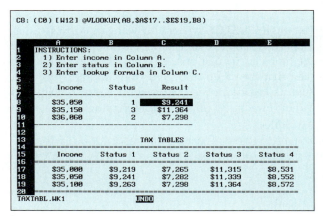

Figure 3-11

@YEAR

@YEAR(*date-number*) calculates the year, an integer from 0 (1900) to 199 (2099), in *date-number*. *Date-number* can be any integer from 1 (January 1, 1900) to 73050 (December 31, 2099). See also "Date and Time @Functions" earlier in this chapter.

Examples

@YEAR(20181) = 55 because 20181 is the date-number for April 2, 1955.

@YEAR(@DATE(91,14,2)) = 91 because 91 is the *year* argument in @DATE(91,14,2).

@YEAR(@NOW) = the current year.

Note: *Add 1900 to the result of an @YEAR calculation to convert it into a four-digit year. For example, @YEAR(20181)+1900 returns 1955.*

Reference 4

Macros

A **macro** is a set of commands and keystroke instructions that you create to perform a 1-2-3 task. You enter the macro in a worksheet (as one or more labels in a column) and assign it a range name. Whenever you run the macro with [Alt] or [RUN] (Alt-F3) (depending on the macro's range name), 1-2-3 reads through the commands and keystroke instructions in the macro and performs them automatically. They save time that would otherwise be spent performing simple but repetitive tasks, and they streamline complex procedures.

Macro instructions are like a programming language that tells 1-2-3 what actions to perform. They can be made up of keystroke instructions or advanced macro commands.

C o n t e n t s

This chapter contains the following sections:

Keystroke instructions are representations of keys on the typewriter section of the keyboard; using them in a macro instructs 1-2-3 to do what it does when you press those keys. **Advanced macro commands** instruct 1-2-3 to perform built-in, programming functions or special commands not available in the 1-2-3 menus. (See "Using Advanced Macro Commands" later in this chapter.)

Keystroke instructions can be divided into two groups: instructions that consist of a single character, such as / (Slash), w, and ~ (Tilde), and instructions that consist of a key name within { } (Braces), such as {RIGHT}.

The single-character keystroke instruction duplicates the action of a key on the typewriter keyboard. For example, the keystroke instruction to display the 1-2-3 main menu is / (Slash); the keystroke instruction to select Worksheet from the main menu is w. The only single-character keystroke instruction not identical to a key is the ~ (Tilde). The tilde is the keystroke instruction that corresponds to pressing [Enter].

Keystroke instructions, consisting of a key name within { } (Braces), represent the pointer-movement keys, function keys, and a few other keys, and are listed in the following table.

1-2-3 key	Macro keystroke instruction
[↓]	{DOWN} or {D}
[↑]	{UP} or {U}
[←]	{LEFT} or {L}
[→]	{RIGHT} or {R}
[Ctrl][←] or [Shift][Tab]	{BIGLEFT}
[Ctrl][→] or [Tab]	{BIGRIGHT}
[PgUp]	{PGUP}
[PgDn]	{PGDN}
[End]	{END}
[Home]	{HOME}
[Del]	{DELETE} or {DEL}
[Ins]	{INSERT} or {INS}
[Esc]	{ESCAPE} or {ESC}
[Backspace]	{BACKSPACE} or {BS}
/ (Slash) or < (Less-than)	/, <, or {MENU}
~ (Tilde)	{ ~ }
{ (Open Brace)	{ { }
} (Close Brace)	{ } }
[HELP] (F1)	{HELP}
[EDIT] (F2)	{EDIT}
[NAME] (F3)	{NAME}
[ABS]] (F4)	{ABS}
[GOTO] (F5)	{GOTO}
[WINDOW] (F6)	{WINDOW}
[QUERY] (F7)	{QUERY}
[TABLE] (F8)	{TABLE}
[CALC] (F9)	{CALC}
[GRAPH] (F10)	{GRAPH}
[APP1] (Alt-F7)	{APP1}
[APP2] (Alt-F8)	{APP2}
[APP3] (Alt-F9)	{APP3}
[APP4] (Alt-F10)	{APP4}

Note: *1-2-3 does not have macro key names for the following keys: [Caps Lock], [COMPOSE] (Alt-F1), [LEARN] (Alt-F5), [Num Lock], [Print Screen], [RUN] (Alt-F3), [Scroll Lock], [Shift], [STEP] (Alt-F2), and [UNDO] (Alt-F4). Therefore, you cannot use these keystrokes in a macro.*

Creating and Working with Macros

To create and work with a macro, you follow these steps:

1. Plan the macro.

2. Enter the macro in a worksheet.

3. Name the macro.

4. Document the macro.

5. Run the macro.

6. If necessary, debug, or correct problems, in the macro.

7. Save the macro by saving the worksheet.

Planning a Macro

To create a macro, you must first identify the steps of the 1-2-3 task to automate. In some cases, identifying the steps means performing the task once manually and noting each key that you press. In other cases, mapping out the procedure with a flow chart can help you work through each step.

Entering a Macro

You can enter a macro by typing it directly in a worksheet or by using the Learn feature. See "/Worksheet Learn" in *Reference 2, Commands* for more information.

You can enter macros in a worksheet that contains other data or you can save them in a special file that contains only macros (a **macro library**).

If you plan to use a macro with only one worksheet, enter the macro in that worksheet. If you plan to use the macro with a number of worksheets, enter it in a

macro library that you read into memory along with the worksheet. For more information on macro libraries, see the section "Using the Macro Library Manager" later in this chapter.

Follow these guidelines when entering a macro:

- Unless a macro is very short, divide the macro intructions among a series of labels, making the macro easier to read and debug.

- Enter labels in consecutive rows within a column. 1-2-3 reads a macro by starting at the first cell and moving down the column until it reaches a blank cell, a cell that contains a numeric value, or the advanced command {QUIT}.

- Type a label prefix (' " ^ or |) before typing a macro instruction that begins with a / (Slash), \ (Backslash), < (Less-than), a number, or one of the numeric symbols + − @ . (# or $.

- Begin and end any instruction in { } (Braces) in the same cell. Splitting these instructions between two or more cells produces an error.

- You can type any instruction in braces in uppercase or lowercase letters, or a combination of both.

Naming a Macro

Assign the macro a range name to use when you run the macro. To assign a range name to a macro, use /Range Name Create. If you plan to move the macro to another location in the worksheet, specify the entire macro as the range, not just the first cell. You can then use the range name when moving the macro.

When creating a macro range name, be aware of the following:

Macro range names can consist of any combination of up to 15 characters. Like any other range name, however, they should not duplicate cell addresses; they should not include spaces, commas, semicolons, or periods; and they should not duplicate @function names, advanced macro command key words, or 1-2-3 key names.

If you use a macro range name that consists of a backslash and a single letter, such as \N, you can use the [Alt] key to run the macro. Pressing [Alt] and typing the letter is the simplest way to run a macro.

If you use a macro range name that consists of any other combination of characters, such as NEW_ROW, you must use [RUN] (Alt-F3) to execute the macro.

If you use branching and subroutine calls in a macro (see {*subroutine*}, {BRANCH}, and {FOR} in "Advanced Macro Command Descriptions"), it is a good idea to assign range names to the branch locations and subroutines as well as to the main macro.

Note: *Pressing [RUN] (Alt-F3) displays a list of all range names in the worksheet (both macro range names and other range names) and any current macro library ranges. You may want to start all the macro range names with the same character to distinguish them from other range names.*

Documenting a Macro

Document both the macro's range name and the macro instructions. By doing this, you can quickly identify the macro range name, understand the purpose of the macro, and review the macro procedure. Documentation can be extremely helpful when you or someone else needs to revise the macro or when you are trying to figure out what a macro does if you haven't used it for a while.

Document the macro's range name by entering the name as a label to the left of the first cell of macro instructions. Document the macro instructions by entering comments to the right of the macro.

Running a Macro

You run a macro in one of two ways: with [Alt] or with [RUN] (Alt-F3). The method you use depends on the macro's name.

Caution: *Before you run a macro, use /File Save to save your work. If the macro produces unexpected results, you can easily retrieve the original version of the worksheet. Also, if the Undo feature is on, you can press [UNDO] (Alt-F4) immediately after the macro is done executing to restore the worksheet.*

If the macro's name consists of a backslash and a single letter (for example, \N), you can use [Alt] and the letter to run the macro:

❶ Hold down [Alt] and then press the letter in the macro range name.

If the macro's name consists of any other combination of characters (for example, NEW_ROW), use [RUN] (Alt-F3) to run the macro:

❶ Press [RUN] (Alt-F3). 1-2-3 displays a list of range names in the worksheet and in any macro libraries currently in memory. If there are many range names, press [NAME] (F3) to see a full-screen list. ❷ To specify the macro to run, type the macro range name or address and press [Enter]; highlight the macro range name in the list of range names and press [Enter]; or press [Esc] to switch 1-2-3 to POINT mode, move the cell pointer to the first cell of the macro, and press [Enter].

Note: *You can interrupt a macro by pressing [Ctrl] [Break] and then [Esc]. 1-2-3 returns to READY mode and you can continue working in the worksheet.*

Debugging a Macro

If the macro does not do what you expected it to do, or if 1-2-3 displays an error message, you need to **debug**, or find the macro instructions that are causing the problem and edit them.

The instructions that cause an error in a lengthy or complicated macro may not be easy to find. To help you diagnose problems in a macro, 1-2-3 lets you run a macro one instruction at a time, until you locate the error in STEP mode.

❶ With 1-2-3 in READY mode, press [STEP] (Alt-F2) to turn on STEP mode. The STEP indicator appears at the bottom of the screen. ❷ Start the macro using one of the methods described earlier. ❸ Press a key (the space bar is recommended) to execute the first macro instruction. ❹ Repeat Step 3 as many times as necessary to find the part of the macro that contains the error. ❺ Once you find the error, end the macro by pressing [Ctrl] [Break] followed by [Esc] or [Enter] ❻ Edit the macro to correct the problem. You do not need to turn off STEP mode before you edit the macro. ❼ Run the macro in STEP mode again if you need to locate any other problems. ❽ To turn off STEP mode in order to run the macro normally, press [STEP] (Alt-F2) again.

Each time you press a key while in STEP mode, 1-2-3 executes another instruction in the macro and replaces the STEP indicator with two pieces of information: the address of the cell that contains the macro instructions being executed and the contents of that cell. The current macro instruction (the one to be executed next) appears in reverse video. If the instruction includes an @function or label, each keystroke on your part steps through one character of the @function or label. If the macro is getting input because of an advanced macro command such as {GETLABEL} or {?}, key indicators such as NUM or CAPS may appear in place of an instruction to show you what kind of input the macro is expecting.

If you're using STEP mode with a macro in a library, you see the macro library name instead of a range address. If the library is protected with a password, however, all you see is the library name; the contents of the macro do not appear on the screen.

Saving a Macro

Once the macro runs correctly, save it for future use by saving the worksheet with /File Save. You can run the macro any time you retrieve the worksheet.

Troubleshooting Checklist

Here are some common mistakes made when entering macro instructions:

- Spelling errors in a macro key name, advanced macro command keyword, or range name, such as {DLETE} instead of {DELETE}, {WINDOWOFF} instead of {WINDOWSOFF}, or PROFT instead of PROFIT.

- Spaces where there shouldn't be any, for example, between arguments in an @function or advanced macro command.

- Missing tildes in a command sequence, for example, /rfp0~ instead of /rfp0~~.

- Missing steps in a command sequence, for example, /rf0~~ instead of /rfp0~~.

- Square brackets or parentheses instead of braces around a key name or advanced macro command, for example, [up] or (up) instead of {up}.

- Incorrect cell or range references, for example, A1..VV3 (a nonexistent range) or RANGES when RANGES is a nonexistent range name.

- Range names that duplicate macro key names or advanced macro command keywords, for example NAME, END, HELP, or QUIT.

- Misspelled keywords, missing arguments, arguments of the wrong type, or misplaced or missing argument separators in macros that include advanced macro commands.

Note: *Macro error messages include the location where 1-2-3 encountered the error. Check the cell items listed in the troubleshooting checklist. If you don't find the problem in the referenced cell, check the macro instruction in a cell above. When you find the error, move the cell pointer to the appropriate cell, press [EDIT] (F2), correct the error, and press [Enter].*

Tips for Creating a Macro

- When you enter keystroke instructions in { } (Braces), such as {PGUP} and {DOWN}, you can specify two or more consecutive uses with a number following the key name, separated by a space, within the braces. For example, {PGUP 5} tells 1-2-3 to scroll the worksheet up five times. Or, you can include a cell reference (address or range name) that contains a value after the key name. For example, the instruction {DOWN SOME} moves the cell pointer down the number of rows specified by the value in the cell named SOME.

- It's better to use range names in a macro than cell addresses when specifying worksheet locations. If you move a range (for example, by inserting some rows above the range), a macro that refers to the range by name continues to work correctly, but a macro that refers to the range by address does not.

- If you create a number of macros at the same time, you can name them all at once. Enter the macros in the same column (with at least one blank cell between them) and enter the name of each macro to the left of the macro's starting cell. Position the cell pointer in the column that contains the names. Then use /Range Name Labels Right and specify this column of names to assign them to all the macros at once.

- Create an autoexecute macro for a worksheet file by naming the macro \0 (Backslash zero). If the /Worksheet Global Default Autoexec setting is Yes (the default setting), 1-2-3 runs the autoexecute macro automatically when you read that file into memory.

- You can run a macro with [Alt] either when 1-2-3 is in READY mode or during a command. [RUN] (Alt-F3) works only in READY mode.

- To interrupt, or stop, a macro before 1-2-3 completes all the macro instructions, press [Ctrl][Break]. Then press [Esc] to clear the error message and return 1-2-3 to READY mode. In some cases you may need to press [Ctrl][Break] more than once.

Using the Advanced Macro Commands

An **advanced macro command** is a macro instruction that tells 1-2-3 to perform a built-in programming function. For example, the advanced macro command {LET} tells 1-2-3 to enter a label or number in a cell. The advanced macro command {BRANCH} tells 1-2-3 to continue processing macro instructions in another location. The advanced macro command {BEEP} tells 1-2-3 to sound your computer's bell. 1-2-3 has 50 advanced macro commands.

Advanced Macro Commands

The 50 advanced macro commands can be grouped in five command categories: data manipulation, file manipulation, flow-of-control, interactive, and screen control.

Data manipulation commands These commands enter data, edit existing entries, erase entries, and clear control panel prompts. The data manipulation commands are {BLANK}, {CONTENTS}, {LET}, {PUT}, {RECALC}, and {RECALCCOL}.

File manipulation commands These commands work with **text files**. Text files, also called **print files**, are files on disk in ASCII format. You can use the file manipulation commands to create a new text file, copy data from a text file to a worksheet, or copy data from a worksheet to a text file. The file manipulation commands are {CLOSE}, {FILESIZE},

{GETPOS} {OPEN}, {READ}, {READLN}, {SETPOS}, {WRITE}, and {WRITELN}.

Flow-of-control commands These commands direct the path of macro execution so you can create a macro that includes for loops, branches, subroutine calls, and conditional processing. The flow-of-control commands are {subroutine}, {BRANCH}, {DEFINE}, {DISPATCH}, {FOR}, {FORBREAK}, {IF}, {ONERROR}, {QUIT}, {RESTART}, {RETURN}, and {SYSTEM}.

Interactive commands These commands suspend macro execution for keyboard input, control the timing of macro execution, and prevent undesired changes to a worksheet while a macro is running. The interactive commands are {?}, {BREAK}, {BREAKOFF}, {BREAKON}, {GET}, {GETLABEL}, {GETNUMBER}, {LOOK}, {MENUBRANCH}, {MENUCALL}, and {WAIT}.

Screen control commands These commands control different parts of the screen display, change the contents of the mode indicator, and sound your computer's bell. The screen control commands are {BEEP}, {BORDERSOFF}, {BORDERSON}, {FRAMEOFF}, {FRAMEON}, {GRAPHOFF}, {GRAPHON}, {INDICATE}, {PANELOFF}, {PANELON}, {WINDOWSOFF}, and {WINDOWSON}.

Syntax of Advanced Macro Commands

Each advanced macro command has a specific structure, or **syntax.** Unless you follow this syntax exactly, 1-2-3 cannot interpret the command.

The first word in an advanced macro command is the keyword. The **keyword** is often the verb in the command — it tells 1-2-3 what action to perform. The words shown in braces in the preceding section are the advanced macro command keywords. Most advanced macro commands also include one or more arguments. **Arguments** supply the information 1-2-3 needs to complete the command.

Arguments can be numbers, strings, locations (cells or ranges), and conditions (usually logical formulas). For number arguments, you can use a number, a numeric formula, or the range name or address of a cell that contains a number or numeric formula. For string arguments, you can use a **literal string** (any sequence of letters, numbers, and symbols enclosed in quotation marks), a string formula, or the range name or address of a cell that contains a label or string formula.

Note: *Every literal string used as a string argument should be enclosed in quotation marks. This prevents 1-2-3 from interpreting the string as a number, formula, address, or range and prevents 1-2-3 from interpreting commas, semicolons, or periods within the literal string as argument separators, or colons within the literal string as argument-type specifiers.*

For location arguments, you can use a range name, address, or any formula that evaluates to a range name or address. You can use a link to data in another file as an argument to a macro. For condition arguments, you typically use a **logical formula** (a formula that uses one of the logical operators <, >, =, <>, >=, <=, #NOT#, #AND#, and #OR#) or the range name or address of a cell that contains a logical formula. You can also use any numeric or string formula, number, literal string, or cell reference as a condition argument.

Basic Rules of Syntax

To include an advanced macro command in a macro, follow these guidelines:

- Start and end the advanced macro command in the same cell.

- Start the command with { (Open brace) and end it with } (Close brace).

- Immediately after the open brace, type the keyword. You can type it in uppercase or lowercase letters.

- If the command includes arguments, separate the keyword from the first argument with one space.

- If the command includes two or more arguments, separate the arguments from one another with argument separators. Semicolons and commas are the default argument separators for advanced macro commands.

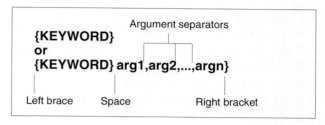

Figure 4-1 Syntax of advanced macro commands

- The only space in the command syntax occurs between the keyword and the first argument. Do not include any other spaces in the command, unless they are part of an argument (for example, the prompt in a {GETLABEL} command can include spaces between the words in the prompt). If the command takes no arguments, the command should include no spaces.

- You can include any combination of advanced macro commands and keystroke instructions in the same cell, as long as the total number of characters does not exceed 240.

Advanced Macro Command Descriptions

This section lists the advanced macro commands alphabetically by keyword. You will be able to use the information in this section most effectively if you have some programming experience or at least some familiarity with programming concepts (conditional processing, subroutines, and for loops, for example).

Command Description Conventions

As you read through the advanced macro command descriptions, keep in mind the following conventions:

- Advanced macro command keywords, @functions, cell addresses, and range names appear in uppercase letters, but you can enter them in uppercase or lowercase letters.

- [ ] (Brackets) around an argument mean the argument is optional. For example, {BEEP [*tone-number*]} means the {BEEP} command works even if you don't specify a tone-number.

- When an argument is italicized, it means you must substitute something else when you write the command. For example, {BRANCH *location*} means you must include a location in the command. When an argument is not italicized, you must include that exact word as the argument in the command.

- Some examples use ... (Ellipses) to indicate omission of macro instructions preceding or following the instruction(s) in the example and/or a •(Bullet) to indicate spaces in advanced macro command arguments and/or results.

List of Command Descriptions

{?}

{?} suspends macro execution to let you move the cell or menu pointer, complete part of a command, or enter data for the macro to process. When you press [Enter], the macro continues. To have 1-2-3 enter what you typed while macro execution was suspended, follow the {?} command with a ~ (Tilde).

{BEEP}

{BEEP [*tone-number*]} sounds your computer's bell. The optional *tone-number* argument (1, 2, 3, or 4) specifies the tone of the bell. {BEEP} without an argument is equivalent to {BEEP 1}.

Use {BEEP} to signal the end of a macro or waiting period within a macro (see {WAIT}), to alert a user to an on-screen message, or to signal the beginning of an interactive command.

{BLANK}

{BLANK *location*} erases the contents of *location*, which can be a cell or a range. {BLANK} does not change the cell format of the cells in *location*. You can precede location with a + (Plus) if you want to indicate that it contains a reference to another cell or range that you want to erase.

{BORDERSOFF}

{BORDERSOFF} suppresses display of the worksheet frame (column letters and row numbers). The worksheet frame remains hidden until 1-2-3 reaches a {BORDERSON} command or the macro ends. When the macro ends, the borders return to their default state of being displayed. {BORDERSOFF} and {BORDERSON} are identical in functionality to {FRAMEOFF} and {FRAMEON}.

{BORDERSON}

{BORDERSON} restores the display of the worksheet format.

{BRANCH}

{BRANCH *location*} transfers macro control from the current macro cell to *location* for further macro instructions. Use {BRANCH} in conjunction with {IF} to implement "if-then-else" processing — that is, to have a macro do different things depending on the current data. You can also use {BRANCH} to create an **infinite loop** (a series of macro instructions that repeats indefinitely, which only [Ctrl][Break] can interrupt).

You can specify a cell or a range as *location*. If you specify a range, 1-2-3 branches to the first cell in the range. You can also precede *location* with a + (plus) to indicate that it contains the address of a cell where macro control is being transferred.

Note: *{BRANCH} produces different results from {subroutine}. {subroutine} (a subroutine call) executes the specified subroutine and then returns control to the original macro instructions while {BRANCH} transfers macro control to the new location permanently. Control does not return to the original macro instructions when 1-2-3 completes the instructions in the branch location.*

{BREAK}

{BREAK} produces the effect of pressing [Ctrl][Break] in MENU mode, so you can return 1-2-3 to READY mode. {BREAK} simulates pressing [Esc] one or more times; it will not interrupt a macro.

{BREAKOFF}

{BREAKOFF} and {BREAKON} have no connection to the {BREAK} macro key name, which works only in MENU mode to return you to READY mode. {BREAKOFF} disables [Ctrl][Break] while a macro is running. Normally, you can stop a macro at any time by pressing [Ctrl][Break]. While {BREAKOFF} is in effect, however, you cannot use [Ctrl][Break] to stop the macro.

You can use {BREAKOFF} to prevent users from stopping a macro to alter data or look at restricted data. {BREAKOFF} stays in effect until canceled with {BREAKON} or until the macro ends.

Caution: *Add {BREAKOFF} commands to a macro only after you have thoroughly tested the macro. If {BREAKOFF} is in effect and the macro goes into an infinite loop, the only way to stop the macro is to restart the computer.*

Example

In the following excerpt from a macro, assume subroutine PAYROLL_INPUT extracts payroll information to a master file. The macro disables [Ctrl][Break] before starting the PAYROLL_INPUT subroutine to make sure information is copied without any interruption. When the PAYROLL_INPUT subroutine ends, it restores use of [Ctrl][Break].

```
{BREAKOFF}
{PAYROLL_INPUT}
{BREAKON}
...
```

{BREAKON}

{BREAKON} restores use of [Ctrl][Break] while a macro is running, undoing a {BREAKOFF} command.

{CLOSE}

{CLOSE} closes the open text file, if one is open. After executing a {CLOSE} command, 1-2-3 goes directly to the next cell in the macro. You should, therefore, keep {CLOSE} on a separate line.

If a text file is already open when 1-2-3 executes an {OPEN} command, 1-2-3 automatically closes the currently open file before opening the new one — you don't need a {CLOSE} command before the {OPEN} command. 1-2-3 does not, however, automatically close a text file that is open when a macro ends. To close the last-opened text file in a macro, you must use a {CLOSE} command.

{CONTENTS}

{CONTENTS *target-location,source-location,[width],[cell-format]*} copies the contents of *source-location* to *target-location* as a label. Use {CONTENTS} to store a numeric value as a string so you can use it in a string formula.

For both *source-location* and *target-location,* you can specify either a cell or a range. If you specify a range, 1-2-3 uses the first cell of the range. You can also precede *source-location* and *target-location* with a + (Plus) to indicate they contain a reference to another location.

If you include the optional *width* argument, 1-2-3 creates a label of the specified width. If you include the optional *cell-format* argument, 1-2-3 creates a label whose contents look like a numeric cell in the specified format. The *target-location* does not have its format changed. *Width* can be a number, numeric formula, or reference to a cell that contains a number or numeric formula whose value is from 1 to 240.

Cell-format must be one of the code numbers from the following list, a formula that evaluates to a code number, or a reference to a cell that contains a code number. For a description of each cell format, see "/Worksheet Global Format" in *Reference 2, Commands.*

Code number	Corresponding cell format
0 to 15	Fixed, 0 to 15 decimal places
16 to 31	Scientific, 0 to 15 decimal places
32 to 47	Currency, 0 to 15 decimal places
48 to 63	Percent, 0 to 15 decimal places
64 to 79	Comma, 0 to 15 decimal places
112	+/−
113	General
114	D1 (DD-MMM-YY)
115	D2 (DD-MMM)
116	D3 (MMM-YY)
117	Text
118	Hidden
119	D6 (HH:MM:SS AM/PM)
120	D7 (HH:MM AM/PM)
121	D4 (Long Intn'l)
122	D5 (Short Intn'l)
123	D8 (Long Intn'l)
124	D9 (Short Intn'l)
127	Worksheet's global cell format (specified with /Worksheet Global Format)

You can include a *cell-format* argument without a *width* argument. To do so, use this syntax, which tells 1-2-3 you skipped the *width* argument:

{CONTENTS *target-location,source-location,,cell-format*}

{DEFINE}

{DEFINE *location1,location2,...locationn*} stores arguments passed to a subroutine in a {*subroutine*} command so those arguments can be used later in the subroutine. You must include a {DEFINE} command in any subroutine to which you pass arguments, and the {DEFINE} command must come before the point in the subroutine where the arguments are used.

Each *location* argument in a {DEFINE} command specifies the storage location for one argument in a {*subroutine*} command. Therefore, the {DEFINE} command must have the same number of arguments as the {*sub-*}

routine} command or 1-2-3 will terminate the macro with an error at the {DEFINE} command.

For each *location* argument, you can specify either a cell or a range. If you specify a range, 1-2-3 uses the first cell of the range as the storage location.

You can add one of two suffixes — :string or :value (or an abbreviation of string or value, as long as the first letter is s or v, respectively) — to each *location* argument in a {DEFINE} command. The suffix tells 1-2-3 how to process the corresponding argument in the {*subroutine*} command. Omitting the suffix is equivalent to specifying :string.

The :string suffix tells 1-2-3 to store the argument as a left-aligned label, even if the argument looks like a number, formula, or cell or range reference.

The :value suffix tells 1-2-3 to evaluate the argument before storing it. If the argument is a number, 1-2-3 stores it as a number. If the argument is a formula, 1-2-3 evaluates the formula and stores the result either as a left-aligned label (for a string formula) or a number (for a numeric formula). If the argument is a cell address or range name, 1-2-3 evaluates the contents of the referenced cell and stores the result as a label or number.

When you use suffixes with {DEFINE}, 1-2-3 treats the suffix as an additional argument. This means that you can have a maximum of 15 arguments (rather than the usual 31) passed by a subroutine.

Example

In the following excerpt from a macro, the {*subroutine*} command in macro \A passes three arguments to SUBR1. The {DEFINE} command at the beginning of SUBR1 evaluates all three arguments before storing them. Thus, it stores the value of the first argument, today's date, as a number in cell ONE; the value of the second argument, the string Closing Price:, as a label in cell TWO; and the value of the third argument, the contents of cell CLOSING (presumably, the closing stock price), as a number in cell THREE.

The macro then formats the current cell as Date 2 and enters in that cell the number stored in cell ONE; moves right one cell and enters in that cell the label stored in cell TWO; and again moves right one cell, formats the cell as Currency, 2 decimal places, and enters in the cell the number stored in cell THREE. The result of this macro might therefore be

```
09-Mar Closing Price: $123.35
\A      {SUBR1 @NOW,+"Closing"&"•Price:",CLOSING}
...
SUBR1        {DEFINE ONE:V,TWO:V,THREE:V}
        /rfd2~{LET @CELLPOINTER("address"),ONE}{R}
        {LET @CELLPOINTER("address"),TWO}{R}
        /rfc2~~{LET @CELLPOINTER("address"),THREE}
```

{DISPATCH}

{DISPATCH *location*} performs an indirect branch by transferring macro control to the cell whose name or address is entered in *location*. Use {DISPATCH} to have 1-2-3 branch to one of several possible macro routines, depending on the contents of *location* when 1-2-3 executes the {DISPATCH} command. *Location* must be a single cell.

Example

The following excerpt from a macro includes a series of {IF} commands. These determine which range name (YOU_OWE, I_OWE, or NEITHER_OWES) 1-2-3 enters in cell SWITCH. When 1-2-3 gets to the {DISPATCH} command, it transfers macro control to the routine whose range name is in SWITCH.

```
...
{LET  SWITCH,"NEITHER_OWES"}
{IF YOURS>MINE}{LET  SWITCH,"YOU_OWE"}
{IF YOURS<MINE}{LET  SWITCH,"I_OWE"}
{DISPATCH SWITCH}
```

{FILESIZE}

{FILESIZE *location*} enters a number in *location*. This number reports the number of bytes in the open text file. You must open a text file with {OPEN} before using {FILESIZE}.

You can specify a cell or a range as *location*. If you specify a range, 1-2-3 enters the number in the first cell of the range. You can also precede *location* with a + (Plus) sign to indicate it contains the address of a cell where you want to enter the file size.

If 1-2-3 succeeds in executing a {FILESIZE} command, it goes directly to the next cell in the macro. If 1-2-3 cannot report on the number of bytes because a file is not open, it continues to the next macro instruction in the same cell as {FILESIZE}.

{FOR}

{FOR *counter,start-number,stop-number,step-number, subroutine*} creates a **for loop** — it repeatedly performs a subroutine call to *subroutine*. The *start, stop,* and *step* numbers determine the total number of repetitions, and *counter* keeps a running count of the repetitions. 1-2-3 stores the start, stop, and step values internally. You can precede both *counter* and *subroutine* with a + (plus) to indicate they contain an address of another cell.

When 1-2-3 encounters a {FOR} command, it does the following: 1. Enters *start-number* in *counter* (*counter* is a cell in the worksheet). 2. Compares the number in *counter* with *stop-number*. If the number in *counter* is less than or equal to *stop-number*, 1-2-3 performs a subroutine call to *subroutine* and goes to Step 3. If the number in *counter* is greater than *stop-number*, 1-2-3 does not perform a subroutine call to *subroutine,* but returns to the location of the {FOR} command and continues the macro at the instruction following {FOR}. 3. Increases the number in *counter* by *step-number* and returns to Step 2.

1-2-3 stores the start, stop, and stop values internally. You cannot have the subroutine modify these values once it starts. You can, however, have other parts of the macro rely on them.

Example

This macro repeats subroutine FORMAT 10 times, keeping track of the repetitions in a cell named REP_NUM:

```
{FOR REP_NUM,1,10,1,FORMAT}
```

{FORBREAK}

{FORBREAK} ends a for loop created by a {FOR} command. Macro execution continues at the instruction immediately following the {FOR} command. You must use {FORBREAK} only within a for loop. Using {FORBREAK} anywhere else causes the macro to terminate with an error.

{FRAMEOFF}

{FRAMEOFF} is identical to {BORDERSOFF}.

{FRAMEON}

{FRAMEON} is identical to {BORDERSON}.

{GET}

{GET location} suspends macro execution until you press a key, then records your keystroke as a left-aligned label in location. You can press any typewriter key or any of the keys listed in the table in "Entering a Macro" earlier in this chapter, except for [Ctrl][Break].

You can specify a cell or a range as location. If you specify a range, 1-2-3 records the keystroke in the first cell in the range. You can also precede location with a + (Plus) to indicate it contains a reference to another cell where you want to store the keystroke.

{GETLABEL}

{GETLABEL prompt,location} displays prompt in the control panel and suspends macro execution while you type a response. When you press [Enter], 1-2-3 stores whatever you typed as a left-aligned label in location and continues the macro. (The {GETLABEL} prompt and your response appear in the control panel even after a {PANELOFF} command.)

You can use any literal string, with as many characters as fit within the control panel edit line, as prompt. (The maximum number of characters 1-2-3 displays is a few characters less than the full screen width.) Prompt can also be the range name or address of a cell that contains the prompt string, or a string formula that evaluates to the prompt string.

You can specify a cell or a range as location. If you specify a range, 1-2-3 stores your response in the first cell of the range. You can also precede location with a + (Plus) to indicate it contains a reference to another cell where you want to store the keystroke.

The response to the prompt can include up to 240 characters. If you press [Enter] without typing anything, 1-2-3 enters an apostrophe label prefix in location. If you enter a numeric value, it is converted to a label in location.

{GETNUMBER}

{GETNUMBER prompt,location} displays prompt in the control panel and suspends macro execution while you type a response. When you press [Enter], 1-2-3 evaluates your response, stores the resulting number in location, and continues the macro. (The {GETNUMBER} prompt and your response appear in the control panel even after a {PANELOFF} command.) See {GETLABEL} for discussion of prompt and location arguments.

The response to the prompt must be a number, a numeric formula, or a reference to a cell containing a number or numeric formula. The response can include up to 240 characters. If you enter a label, string formula, or reference to a cell containing a label or string formula as the response, 1-2-3 enters ERR in location. 1-2-3 also enters ERR if you press [Enter] without typing anything.

{GETPOS}

{GETPOS location} enters a number in location. This number reports the current byte pointer position (the position at which data is read from or written to) in the open text file. You must open a text file with {OPEN} before using {GETPOS}.

You can specify a cell or a range as location. If you specify a range, 1-2-3 enters the number in the first cell in the range. You can also precede location with a + (Plus) to indicate it contains the address of a cell where you want to store the byte pointer position.

If 1-2-3 succeeds in executing the {GETPOS} command, it continues to the next cell in the macro. If no file is open, 1-2-3 ignores a {GETPOS} command and continues to the next macro instruction in the same cell as {GETPOS}.

Note: *The first position in a text file is reported as 0, not 1. Thus, if the byte pointer is on the first byte in the file, {GETPOS} enters 0 in location; if the byte pointer is on the tenth byte, {GETPOS} enters 9, and so on.*

{GRAPHOFF}

{GRAPHOFF} removes a graph displayed by a {GRAPHON} command and redisplays the worksheet.

{GRAPHON}

{GRAPHON [named-graph],[nodisplay]} has three possible results, depending on the syntax you use.

{GRAPHON} with no arguments displays a full-screen view of the current graph while the macro continues to run. {GRAPHON *named-graph*} makes the *named-graph* settings the current graph settings and displays a full-screen view of *named-graph* while the macro continues to run. {GRAPHON *named-graph*,nodisplay} makes the *named-graph* settings the current graph settings without displaying the graph.

When 1-2-3 reaches a {GRAPHOFF} command, another {GRAPHON} command, an {INDICATE} or {?} command, a command that displays a prompt or menu in the control panel ({GETLABEL}, {GETNUMBER}, {MENUCALL}, {MENUBRANCH}), or the end of the macro, 1-2-3 removes the graph from the screen.

{IF}

{IF *condition*} evaluates *condition* as true or false. If *condition* is true, 1-2-3 continues to the macro instruction immediately following the {IF} command in the same cell. If *condition* is false, 1-2-3 goes immediately to the next cell in the column, skipping any further instructions in the same cell as the {IF} command.

Typically, *condition* is a logical formula or a reference to a cell that contains a logical formula. However, you can use any formula, number, literal string, or cell reference as *condition*. 1-2-3 evaluates any *condition* that does not equal zero as true and any *condition* that does equal zero as false. Blank cells, strings, and ERR and NA values all equal zero when used as *condition*.

Note: *If you use {IF} to implement if-then-else processing in a macro, be sure to include a {BRANCH} or {QUIT} command at the end of the "then" instructions (the instructions that follow the {IF} command in the same cell). This keeps 1-2-3 from continuing to the "else" instructions (the instructions that start in the cell below the {IF} command), as shown in the example below.*

Example

The following macro creates mailing labels from the records in a database table. The macro first checks to see whether the current cell is blank. (A blank cell indicates the end of the database table). If it is blank, the macro branches to the printing routine. If the cell is not blank, the macro calls subroutine MAKE_A_LABEL, which contains the macro instructions for creating a mailing label. 1-2-3 then moves the cell pointer down one cell and repeats macro \A from the beginning.

```
\A    {IF @CELLPOINTER("type")="b"}{BRANCH PRINT}
      {MAKE_A_LABEL}
      {DOWN}{BRANCH \A}
```

{INDICATE}

{INDICATE [*string*]} displays *string* as the mode indicator. The indicator continues to display *string* until 1-2-3 reaches another {INDICATE} command or until you retrieve another file, select /Worksheet Erase Yes, or end the 1-2-3 session.

For *string* you can use any literal string, with as many characters as fit within the first line of the control panel. (If your screen is wider than 240 characters, 1-2-3 will cut off any characters after 240.) You can also use a reference to a cell that contains the indicator string, or a string formula that evaluates to the indicator string.

Using an empty string as *string* ({INDICATE ""}) removes the mode indicator from the control panel entirely. {INDICATE} with no argument restores standard operation of the mode indicator in the control panel. The indicator displays READY, EDIT, WAIT, LABEL, VALUE, and so on, depending on the current operation.

{LET}

{LET *location,entry*} enters a number or left-aligned label in *location*.

You can specify a cell or a range as *location*. If you specify a range, 1-2-3 enters the number or label in the first cell of the range. You can also precede *location* with a + (Plus) to indicate it contains the address of a cell where you want to store the entry. *Entry* can be a number, literal string, formula, or reference to a cell that contains a number, label, or formula. If you use a formula for *entry*, 1-2-3 evaluates the formula and enters the result in *location*. {LET} does not enter formulas.

Example

In the following macro, if cell QTR_1 exists, the macro enters the result of 1.5 times the value of cell QTR_1 in cell QTR_2. Otherwise the macro enters 1.5*QTR_1 as a label in cell QTR_2.

```
{LET QTR_2,1.5*QTR_1}
```

You can add a :string or :value suffix to *entry* to tell 1-2-3 explicitly whether to treat the argument as a literal string (enter the argument verbatim) or evaluate the argument before entering it. See {DEFINE} for details.

{LOOK}

{LOOK *location*} checks the keyboard buffer for key-strokes and records the first keystroke (if any) in *location* as a left-aligned label. If the buffer is empty, 1-2-3 enters an apostrophe label prefix in *location*.

The **keyboard buffer** is the place 1-2-3 stores key-strokes you make during noninteractive parts of a macro. It contains all the keystrokes you made since the last interactive command (if there was one) or since the macro began. 1-2-3 uses the contents of the key-board buffer in the next {?}, {GET}, {GETLABEL}, or {GETNUMBER} command.

You can specify a cell or a range as *location*. If you specify a range, 1-2-3 records the keystroke in the first cell of the range. You can also precede *location* with a + (Plus) to indicate it contains the address of a cell where you want to store the keystroke.

{MENUBRANCH} and {MENUCALL}

{MENUBRANCH *location*} displays in the control panel the macro menu that starts in the first cell of *location*, waits for you to select an item from the menu, and then branches to the macro instructions associated with the menu item you select.

{MENUCALL *location*} displays in the control panel the macro menu found at *location,* waits for you to select an item from the menu, and then performs a subroutine call to the macro instructions associated with the menu item you select. You can precede *location* with a + (Plus) to indicate it contains the address of the range that contains the macro menu for both {MENUBRANCH} and MENUCALL}.

A **macro menu** is a menu you set up for use during a macro. Macro menus work just like 1-2-3 menus — when the menu is activated, the menu items appear in the second line of the control panel and the description of the highlighted menu item appears in the third line of the control panel. You select a menu item either by moving the menu pointer to the item and pressing [Enter] or by pressing the first character of the item's name. A macro menu can include up to eight items. (A macro menu appears in the control panel even after a {PANELOFF} command.)

Follow these guidelines when entering menu items and item descriptions:

- Make sure each menu item starts with a different letter or number so you can select an item by pressing the first character. If two or more menu items have the same first character, 1-2-3 selects the first item (reading from left to right) when you press that character.

- Try to make each menu item a single word. If you use multiple-word items, connect the words with a – (Hyphen), for example, First-Quarter. Otherwise, a user might think the words are separate menu items.

- The combined menu items and delimiting spaces are restricted to the width of the screen. If you exceed the width of the screen, an error will occur.

- You can enter labels or string formulas as menu item descriptions, but the description of each menu item cannot exceed the width of the screen, or an error will occur.

To create a macro menu, follow these steps:

❶ Decide on a location for the macro menu. ❷ Enter up to eight menu items in consecutive cells in the first row of the menu location. Leave the cell after the final menu item blank. ❸ Enter the description for each menu item in the cell directly below the menu item. ❹ Immediately below the menu item descriptions (that is, starting in the third row of the macro menu range), enter the macro instructions that 1-2-3 performs if you select that menu item. Or, enter a {BRANCH} or {*sub-routine*} command that directs 1-2-3 to a set of macro instructions. ❺ Use /Range Name Create to assign a range name to the first menu item in your macro menu.

After you select an item from a macro menu that {MENUBRANCH} activated, macro control branches to the associated macro instructions in the third line of the macro menu. Because this is a branch, macro control does not return to the original macro location when 1-2-3 completes the macro menu instructions.

After you select an item from a macro menu that {MENUCALL} activated, 1-2-3 performs the associated macro instructions as a subroutine. When 1-2-3 completes the instructions, macro control returns to the statement in the original macro that follows {MENUCALL}.

Note: *Pressing [Esc] when a macro menu appears in the control panel cancels the {MENUBRANCH} or {MENUCALL} command that activated the menu. Macro control returns to the location from which {MENUBRANCH} or {MENUCALL} command was* *issued, and the macro continues at the instruction following the {MENUBRANCH} or {MENUCALL} command. Once you choose a menu item, you must either complete the macro or press [Ctrl][Break] to exit the macro.*

{ONERROR}

{ONERROR *branch-location,[message-location]*} traps and handles errors that occur while a macro is running.

Note: *{ONERROR} does not trap macro syntax errors (typing errors in macro instructions that prevent 1-2-3 from interpreting the instructions). When 1-2-3 encounters a syntax error, it ends the macro and displays an error message that describes the error.*

Normally, if an error occurs while a macro is running, 1-2-3 displays an error message, changes the mode indicator to ERROR, and ends the macro. However, if an {ONERROR} command is in effect when the error occurs, 1-2-3 returns to READY mode and branches to *branch-location* for further macro instructions instead of ending the macro. If you include the optional *message-location* argument, 1-2-3 records the error message in *message-location*.

For both *branch-location* and *message-location* you can specify either a cell or a range. If you specify a range, 1-2-3 goes to the first cell in the range. You can also precede the location arguments with a + (Plus) to indicate they contain the address of another cell.

An {ONERROR} command remains in effect until (1) an error occurs (each {ONERROR} command can handle only one error), (2) it is superseded by a subsequent {ONERROR} command, or (3) the macro ends. Use {ONERROR} at any point in which there is a possibility of an error. In addition, {ONERROR} clears the subroutine stack. If the error occurs in a subroutine, 1-2-3 does not return to the location from which the subroutine call was issued after completing the instructions at the {ONERROR} *branch-location*.

Caution: *Pressing [Ctrl][Break] causes a 1-2-3 error. Therefore, if you press [Ctrl][Break] while an {ONERROR} command is in effect, the command will trap that error rather than the one you want it to trap. You may want to disable [Ctrl][Break] with {BREAKOFF} if you are using {ONERROR} to trap a specific error.*

{OPEN}

{OPEN *file-name,access-type*} opens a text file for read-only processing or for read-and-write processing, depending on the type of access you specify. You must open a file with {OPEN} before you can use any of the other file-manipulation commands. Only one text file can be open at a time. If a text file is open when 1-2-3 performs an {OPEN} command, 1-2-3 automatically closes that text file before opening the new one.

If 1-2-3 succeeds in opening the specified file, it goes directly to the next cell in the macro, skipping any further instructions in the same cell as the {OPEN} command. If 1-2-3 does not succeed in opening the file (that is, the {OPEN} command fails), it continues to the next macro instruction in the same cell as {OPEN}.

File-name is the full name (including the extension) of a text file or a reference to a cell that contains a text file name. Unless the text file is in the current directory, you must specify the path as part of *file-name* and enclose the argument in quotation marks.

Access-type is one of the four characters r, w, m, or a (in uppercase or lowercase letters) or a reference to a cell that contains one of those characters. The character specifies the type of access you have to the file once it is opened:

r (read access) Opens an existing file for reading only, placing the byte pointer at the beginning of the file. You can use {READ}, {READLN}, {GETPOS}, and {SETPOS} but not {WRITE} and {WRITELN} with a file opened with read access.

w (write access) Opens a new file for reading and writing. You can use {READ}, {READLN}, {GETPOS}, {SETPOS}, {WRITE}, and {WRITELN} with a file opened with write access. **Caution:** *If you open an existing file with write access, 1-2-3 erases the current contents of the file when it opens the file. To open an existing file for writing and retain the existing file contents, use modify or append access.*

m (modify access) Opens an existing file for reading and writing, placing the byte pointer at the beginning of the file. You can use {READ}, {READLN}, {GETPOS}, {SETPOS}, {WRITE}, and {WRITELN} with a file opened with modify access.

a (append access) Opens an existing file for reading and writing, placing the byte pointer at the end of the file. You can use {READ}, {READLN},

{GETPOS}, {SETPOS}, {WRITE}, and {WRITELN} with a file opened with append access.

Note: *When opening a new file (a file that does not yet exist in the specified directory), you can use write access only. If you try to open a new file with read, modify, or append access, the {OPEN} command will fail. If a text file is open when a macro ends, 1-2-3 does not automatically close the text file. You must include a {CLOSE} command in the macro to close the file.*

{PANELOFF}

{PANELOFF [clear]} freezes the control panel and status line until 1-2-3 encounters a {PANELON} command or the macro ends. If you include the optional clear argument, 1-2-3 clears the control panel and status line before freezing them. Use {PANELOFF} in interactive macros to suppress activity in the control panel and status line that might be distracting to users.

Note that {PANELOFF} suppresses control-panel activity that results only from keystroke instructions. The advanced macro commands that cause changes in the control panel — {MENUBRANCH}, {MENUCALL}, {GETLABEL}, {GETNUMBER}, {WAIT}, and {INDICATE} — override a {PANELOFF} condition.

{PANELON}

{PANELON} unfreezes the control panel and status line.

{PUT}

{PUT *location,column-offset,row-offset,entry*} enters a number or left-aligned label in a cell within *location*. {PUT} is a variant of {LET}. In a {LET} command, you specify the target cell by its name or address. In a {PUT} command, you identify the target cell by its row-and-column position within a range.

Location can be a two-dimensional range of any size, as long as it contains the cell in which you are entering data. *Location* can also be preceded by a + (Plus) to indicate it contains a reference to another range where you want the entry placed.

Column-offset and *row-offset* are numbers that identify the column and row position of the data-entry cell within *location*. The first column and row of the range have the offset number 0, the second column and row

have the offset number 1, the third column and row have the offset number 2, and so on.

Entry can be a number, literal string, formula, or reference to a cell that contains a number, label, or formula. If *entry* is a string formula, precede it with a + (Plus).

Example

In the following example, assume range COSTS occupies the range A1..D5.
This macro places the number 45 in cell D3:

    {PUT COSTS,3,2,45}

{QUIT}

{QUIT} ends a macro immediately, returning keyboard control to the user. Any instructions that follow a {QUIT} command in a macro are never completed. Even if you use {QUIT} in a subroutine, the command ends the entire macro, not just the subroutine. If a macro encounters a blank cell as the next command, it ends the macro. A {QUIT} command in this case is optional.

Example

In the following excerpt from a macro, if cell YEAR has the value 1999, the macro ends. Otherwise, 1-2-3 continues to the next cell for further macro instructions.

    {IF YEAR=1999}{QUIT}
    ...

{READ}

{READ *byte-count,location*} starts at the current byte pointer position in the open text file, copies the specified number of bytes (*byte-count*) to *location*, and advances the byte pointer *byte-count* bytes. You must open a text file with {OPEN} before you use {READ}.

Byte-count can be a number, numeric formula, or reference to a cell that contains a number or numeric formula whose value is from 0 to 240. If the value of *byte-count* is greater than the number of bytes remaining in the file, 1-2-3 copies all of the remaining bytes to *location*. Using a negative number or a number greater than 240 as *byte-count* is equivalent to using 240.

You can specify a cell or range as *location*. If you specify a range, 1-2-3 enters the data in the first cell of the range.

{READ} copies the carriage-return and line-feed characters at the end of text lines. If you don't want to copy the carriage-return and line-feed characters, use {READLN}.

If 1-2-3 succeeds in reading the specified file, it goes directly to the next cell in the macro, skipping any further instructions in the same cell as the {READ} command. If the text file is not open, 1-2-3 ignores the {READ} command and continues to the next instruction in the same cell as the {READ} command.

Example

In the following example, assume the open text file contains these two lines:

    Total Sales
    for the Year Ending 1988

Assume that the byte pointer is on the T in Total (position 0). The following macro enters the left-aligned label Total Sa (the first eight bytes in the file) in cell CHARS and advances the byte pointer to the position eight (the l in Sales).

    {READ 8,CHARS}

{READLN}

{READLN location} starts at the current byte pointer position in the open text file, copies the remainder of the current line to location, and advances the byte pointer to the beginning of the next line in the file. You must open a text file with {OPEN} before you use {READLN}.

You can specify a single cell or a range as location. If you specify a range, 1-2-3 enters the data in the first cell of the range. You can also precede location with a + (Plus) to indicate it contains the address of a cell where you want the rest of the line copied.

With {READLN}, 1-2-3 does not copy the end-of-line sequence (carriage-return and line-feed characters) to the worksheet. To copy those characters to the worksheet, use {READ}.

If 1-2-3 succeeds in reading the specified file, it goes directly to the next cell in the macro, skipping any further instructions in the same cell as the {READLN} command. If the text file is not open, 1-2-3 ignores the {READLN} command and continues to the next instruction in the same cell as the {READLN} command.

{RECALC} and {RECALCCOL}

{RECALC location,[condition],[iterations]} recalculates the values in location, proceeding row by row. Use {RECALC} to recalculate formulas located below and to the left of cells on which they depend.

{RECALCCOL location,[condition],[iterations]} recalculates the values in location, proceeding column by column. Use {RECALCCOL} to recalculate formulas located above and to the right of cells on which they depend.

The optional condition argument tells 1-2-3 to repeat the recalculation until condition is true. The optional iterations argument tells 1-2-3 to perform the specified number of recalculation passes. When you include both optional arguments, 1-2-3 repeats the recalculation until condition is true or until it has performed the specified number of recalculation passes, whichever happens first.

Location can be any cell or range. You can also precede location with a + (Plus) to indicate it contains the address of a cell or range where you want recalculation to take place. Condition is typically a logical formula or reference to a cell containing a logical formula, but it can be any formula, number, literal string, or cell reference. 1-2-3 evaluates any condition that does not equal zero as true and any condition that does equal zero as false. Blank cells, strings, and ERR and NA values all equal zero when used as condition. Iterations can be a number, numeric formula, or reference to a cell that contains a number or numeric formula. You cannot use the iterations argument without the condition argument.

Note: *If condition is a reference to a cell that contains a formula, and the formula needs to be recalculated for the {RECALC} or {RECALCCOL} command to work correctly, be sure the referenced cell is inside location.*

Caution: *When 1-2-3 recalculates a range with {RECALC} or {RECALCCOL}, it does not update formulas outside the range. To ensure that all formulas are up-to-date at the end of a macro that uses {RECALC} or {RECALCCOL}, include a {CALC} instruction in the macro, change worksheet recalculation to Automatic, or press [CALC] (F9) when the macro ends.*

{RESTART}

{RESTART} is used in subroutines to clear the subroutine stack. When 1-2-3 encounters a {RESTART} command, it continues to the end of the current subroutine, but instead of returning to the original macro location after it completes the subroutine, the macro ends.

Example

In the example, the {subroutine} command {CHECKS} called the subroutine. In the following excerpt, if cell CHKSTAT contains the label "not ok" or a string formula that evaluates to "not ok", the macro ends after 1-2-3 completes the remainder of subroutine CHECKS. If cell CHKSTAT contains any other label or is blank, macro control returns to the location from which the subroutine call {CHECKS} was issued after 1-2-3 completes the remainder of the subroutine.

```
CHECKS        ...
       {IF CHKSTAT="not ok"}{RESTART}
       ...
       {RETURN}
```

{RETURN}

{RETURN} affects flow of control in subroutines. In a subroutine called by {subroutine} or {MENUCALL}, {RETURN} immediately returns macro control from the subroutine to the location from which the {subroutine} or {MENUCALL} command was issued. In a subroutine called by a {FOR} command, {RETURN} ends the current iteration of the subroutine and immediately starts the next iteration. {RETURN} is optional in a subroutine. If a macro encounters a blank cell at the end of a subroutine, it interprets this as a {RETURN}.

When used in the main body of macro instructions rather than in a subroutine, {RETURN} is equivalent to {QUIT}; it ends the macro immediately.

{SETPOS}

{SETPOS offset-number} positions the byte pointer in the open text file offset-number bytes from the first byte in the file. After executing a {SETPOS} command, 1-2-3 goes directly to the next cell in the macro, skipping any further instructions in the same cell as the {SETPOS} command. You must open a text file with {OPEN} before you use {SETPOS}.

Offset-number can be a number, numeric formula, or reference to a cell that contains a number or numeric

formula. The argument specifies the position of the byte pointer relative to the first byte in the file, which is at position 0. Using a negative offset-number is the same as using 0.

If 1-2-3 succeeds with the {SETPOS} command, it goes to the instructions in the next cell, skipping any further instructions in the same cell as {SETPOS}. If no text file is open, however, 1-2-3 ignores the {SETPOS} command and continues to the next macro instruction in the same cell as {SETPOS}.

Note: *1-2-3 does not prevent you from placing the byte pointer past the end of a file. If necessary, use {FILESIZE} to determine the size of a file before using {SETPOS}. If you do place the byte pointer beyond the end of the file and use a {READ} or {READLN} command, you may read in data from another file on a disk.*

{SUBROUTINE}

{subroutine [arg1],[arg2],...[argn]} performs a subroutine call. A **subroutine** is a discrete unit of macro instructions. A **subroutine call** causes 1-2-3 to complete the instructions in the specified subroutine before continuing the current macro instructions.

When 1-2-3 encounters a {subroutine} command, it does the following: 1. Shifts macro control from the current column of macro instructions to the specified subroutine. (subroutine is the range name or address of the subroutine's starting cell.) 2. Passes any included arguments to the {DEFINE} command in the subroutine for evaluation and storage (see {DEFINE}). 3. Executes the instructions in the subroutine. 4. When it reaches a {RETURN} command or a blank or numeric cell in the subroutine, returns to the original macro location and continues the macro at the instruction immediately following the {subroutine} command.

Note: *Although you can use a cell address as the subroutine argument, you should use a range name. That way, if you move the subroutine, the {subroutine} command will still work correctly.*

You can include up to 31 optional arguments (arg1, arg2,...argn) in the {subroutine} command as information for the subroutine to use. These arguments can be numbers, labels, formulas, or cell references. If you do include optional arguments, you must include a {DEFINE} command in the subroutine you are calling.

{DEFINE} evaluates and stores the arguments so they can be used in the subroutine.

Note, however, that depending on how you use {DEFINE} you may be limited to 15 arguments. For example, in a statement such as {DEFINE a1:v, B1:v,C1:v}, each V suffix counts as a separate argument resulting in a total of six arguments. See {DEFINE} for further information on {subroutine} command arguments.

In general, avoid having a subroutine call itself. If you do this repeatedly, you will get an error message telling you that you have too many nesting levels in the macro.

If 1-2-3 encounters a subroutine call while executing a subroutine, it immediately performs the second subroutine before completing the rest of the instructions in the first subroutine. Putting subroutine calls within other subroutines is called **nesting** subroutines, or creating a **subroutine stack**. The number of subroutines you can include in a stack is limited to 32. To clear a subroutine stack, use {RESTART}. In general, avoid using a {BRANCH} command to leave a subroutine. Doing so can cause stack nesting problems and result in an error.

{SYSTEM}

{SYSTEM *command*} temporarily suspends the 1-2-3 session and executes the specified operating system command. When the command is completed, the 1-2-3 session automatically resumes and the macro continues. *Command* can be any operating system command, including batch commands or commands to run another program such as an editor, to a maximum of 125 characters. It's advisable to always enclose *command* in double quotes.

If you want to temporarily suspend the 1-2-3 session without specifying an operating system command, use the System command (/S) in the macro.

Caution: *Do not use {SYSTEM} to load memory-resident programs such as terminate-and-stay-resident programs. If you do so, you may not be able to resume 1-2-3.*

{WAIT}

{WAIT *time-number*} suspends macro execution and displays WAIT as the mode indicator until the time specified by *time-number*. When the specified time arrives, 1-2-3 removes the WAIT indicator and continues the macro. During a {WAIT} command, the only keystroke 1-2-3 responds to is [Ctrl][Break] (unless you used {BREAKOFF} earlier in the macro to disable use of [Ctrl][Break]).

Time-number can be a number, numeric formula, or reference to a cell that contains a number or numeric formula. The number must represent a future moment in time.

{WINDOWSOFF}

{WINDOWSOFF} freezes the worksheet area of the screen, including worksheet borders, during macro execution. It also suppresses the display of settings sheets if you previously used a {WINDOWSON} command to turn on settings sheets during macro execution. The area remains frozen until 1-2-3 encounters a {WINDOWSON} command or the macro ends. Use {WINDOWSOFF} in noninteractive parts of a macro to suppress the flashing in the worksheet area and to speed up macro execution significantly (updating the screen display takes time).

{WINDOWSON}

{WINDOWSON} restores normal updating of the worksheet area, undoing a {WINDOWSOFF} command. By default, settings sheets do not appear while a macro is running. To display settings sheets in a macro, use {WINDOWSON}. If you've used {WINDOWOFF} to turn off the display of the worksheet area, use {WINDOWSON} *twice*: once to redisplay the worksheet and the second time to redisplay settings sheets.

Unless you've used {WINDOWSOFF} to turn off the display of the worksheet area, you can also use {WINDOW} (which simulates [WINDOW] (F6)) to turn settings sheets on or off, but only while in MENU mode. If you have used {WINDOWSOFF}, you must use {WINDOWSON} to redisplay the worksheet area before you can redisplay the settings sheets.

Note: *{WINDOWSOFF} and {WINDOWSON} are often used in conjunction with {PANELOFF} and {PANELON}. {PANELOFF} freezes the control panel and status line, and {PANELON} unfreezes the control panel and status line.*

{WRITE}

{WRITE *string*} copies *string* to the open text file, starting at the current byte pointer position. {WRITE} works only if a text file was opened with write, append, or modify access (see {OPEN}). *String* can be a literal string, string formula, or reference to a cell that contains a label or string formula.

1-2-3 evaluates *string* and converts the result from LICS codes (the codes 1-2-3 Release 2.2 uses to represent characters) to the codes the operating system uses to represent characters. It then copies the converted result to the file, starting at the current position of the byte pointer, and advances the byte pointer to the position just beyond the last character written. If necessary, 1-2-3 extends the length of the file to accommodate the incoming string. A subsequent {WRITE} or {WRITELN} command begins writing where this command stopped, unless you change the position of the byte pointer with a {SETPOS} command.

Note: *To use {WRITE} to write values or formulas that evaluate to values, use @STRING to convert the value to a string; for example,*
{WRITE @STRING(NUMBER,0)}.

If 1-2-3 succeeds in writing to a file, it goes to the instructions in the next cell, skipping any further instructions in the same cell as {WRITE}. If, however, no text file is open, or if the open file was opened with read access, 1-2-3 ignores the {WRITE} command and goes to the next macro instruction in the same cell as {WRITE}.

{WRITELN}

{WRITELN *string*} works the same way {WRITE} does, except that it adds an end-of-line sequence (a carriage return and line feed) to the string it writes to the file. {WRITELN} works only if a text file was opened with write, append, or modify access (see {OPEN}). As with {WRITE}, *string* can be a literal string, string formula, or reference to a cell that contains a label or string formula. If you use an empty string ("") as *string*, 1-2-3 simply writes a carriage return and line feed to the text file.

See {WRITE} for detailed information.

Using the Macro Library Manager

The Macro Library Manager is a 1-2-3 **add-in** program that lets you create macro libraries and use them in your work with 1-2-3. A **macro library** is a range taken from a 1-2-3 worksheet by Macro Library Manager and stored both in memory (in an area that is separate from the worksheet) and in a file on disk called a **library file** (with a .MLB file extension). The range can contain a single macro, a number of macros, a combination of macros and data (including formulas), or just data.

Like all add-ins, before you start working with Macro Library Manager, you must attach it and then invoke it. Macro Library Manager is in a file called MACROMGR.ADN on the Install Disk that came in your 1-2-3 package. If you have a hard-disk system, this file should be in the directory that contains your 1-2-3 program files. If you have a two-diskette system, you must insert the Utilities Disk in one of the diskette drives before you can attach Macro Library Manager.

❶ Select /Add-In Attach. 1-2-3 displays a menu of add-ins (*.ADN) in the current directory. ❷ Specify MACROMGR.ADN as the add-in to attach and press [Enter]. ❸ Select the key you want to use to invoke Macro Library Manager (see table below). ❹ Select Quit to return 1-2-3 to READY mode. Macro Library Manager is now attached, or in memory. To use it, you must invoke it. ❺ Press the key you selected when you attached Macro Library Manager or select /Add-In Invoke, and select MACROMGR.ADN from the menu of attached add-ins. The Macro Library Manager menu appears.

/Add-In Attach menu selection	Result
No-Key	Does not assign Macro Library Manager to any key.
7	Assigns Macro Library Manager to [APP1] (Alt-F7).
8	Assigns Macro Library Manager to [APP2] (Alt-F8).
9	Assigns Macro Library Manager to [APP3] (Alt-F9).
10	Assigns Macro Library Manager to [APP4] (Alt-F10).

Note: *If you want 1-2-3 to attach Macro Library Manager automatically whenever you start 1-2-3, use /Worksheet Global Default Other Add-In to specify MACROMGR.ADN. Use /Worksheet Global Default Update to update the 1-2-3 configuration file with this information.*

Basic Rules

Follow these basic rules for using the Macro Library Manager:

- You must attach Macro Library Manager before you save data in a library or load a library file into memory. If you detach Macro Library Manager, the macro libraries you have saved or loaded disappear from memory. The library files saved on disk are not affected.

- A macro library is stored in an area of memory separate from the worksheet so there are different rules for accessing the information. To use the data from a macro library in a macro, the data in the library must be in a named range and you must use the range name in the macro. Note that /Worksheet Erase and /File Retrieve do not erase macro libraries from memory.

- You use the same techniques to run a macro stored in a library as you would use with a macro in a worksheet.

- You can specify a password of up to 80 characters when you save data in a macro library. Passwords protect libraries from editing or from viewing in STEP mode. You must use the exact combination of uppercase or lowercase letters for the password.

- You cannot have two or more libraries in memory with the same name.

- Try to assign unique names to each range you save in the library. When you edit a library, you copy its contents, including range names, into the worksheet. If there are range names in the library that match range names in the worksheet, a prompt appears asking whether you want to ignore or write over range names. Avoid using the same range name in more than one library. If you have two ranges with the same name, 1-2-3 uses the first one it finds, so you may not get the macro you wanted.

- Macro Library Manager will not let you save a range in a library if the range includes a reference, or **link**, to data in another file.

The Macro Library Manager Commands

The Macro Library Manager commands let you create and manage the macro libraries that you use with 1-2-3.

The Macro Library Manager menu appears when you invoke the add-in.

Use the Macro Library Manager commands to perform the following tasks:

Edit Copies the contents of a macro library in memory to a range in the worksheet so you can make changes to the library. Edit lets you copy a macro library from memory into the worksheet so you can make changes to the contents of the library or use its contents in the worksheet. Macro Library Manager leaves a copy of the library in memory and in the library (.MLB) file on disk. You can use the Edit command to include the same information in each worksheet without retyping it.

Load Copies the contents of the library (.MLB) file on disk into memory so you can use the library. Load lets you copy data from a library file (a file with a .MLB extension) on disk into a library in memory. The library is stored separately from the worksheet.

Name-List Enters a list in the worksheet of the range names contained in a macro library. Name-List lets you create a list in the worksheet of the range names contained in a library. The list consists of a column of labels.

Quit Leaves the Macro Library Manager menu and returns you to 1-2-3. Quit lets you leave the Macro Library Manager menu, but keeps Macro Library Manager attached. The data in macro libraries that you have loaded or saved is still available.

Remove Erases a macro library from memory. Remove lets you erase a macro library from memory, but Macro Library Manager leaves a copy of the library intact on disk. To use the library again, use the Load command.

Save Moves the contents of a range and its range names into a macro library in memory as well as to a library (.MLB) file on disk. Save lets you move a worksheet range to both a macro library in memory (independent of the worksheet) and a library file (a file with a .MLB extension) on disk. The contents of the range are removed from the worksheet. Range names associated with the cells no longer refer to the worksheet; they now refer to library locations.

Note: *You can keep libraries on a network file server for shared use if you are careful. Loading a library into memory and using its contents is not a problem. If both you and another user are editing the same library at the same time, one set of changes will be lost. If you save your changes first, the other user's changes will replace yours.*

A macro library can contain up to 16,376 cells. This is equivalent to a range that is two columns wide and 8,188 rows long. Macro Library Manager places a library in memory when you select either the Load or the Save command from the Macro Library Manager menu. You can have up to ten libraries in memory simultaneously.

When you specify the range you want to save in a library, Macro Library Manager allocates a cell in conventional memory for each cell in the range, even if it is empty. To save memory, try to make your macros as compact as possible and specify ranges with as few empty cells as possible.

When you save a large amount of information in libraries, you may find that the available memory for creating a worksheet is less than normal. In general, you should load only the libraries you need into memory and remove them when you are finished.

Reference 5

PrintGraph

The PrintGraph program is a 1-2-3 utility program that lets you print graphs from files you create in 1-2-3 with the Graph Save command. /Graph Save stores an image of the current graph in a graph file (a file with a .PIC extension). Graph files are the only type of files PrintGraph can print.

To use PrintGraph, you must have a printer or plotter that is capable of printing graphs. If you are not sure whether your printer can print graphs, check your 1-2-3 Hardware Chart or your printer manual or ask your technical resource person. In addition, you need to have selected an appropriate driver for printing graphs when you installed 1-2-3.

Contents

This chapter contains the following sections:

- PrintGraph Basics

- The PrintGraph Commands

- Common Problems and Solutions

PrintGraph Basics

Follow the instructions in this section to start Print-Graph from either the operating system prompt or from the Access system.

If you have a two-diskette system, these instructions assume that your diskette drives are drive A and drive B. If you have a hard-disk system, these instructions assume that your hard disk is drive C and that the PrintGraph files are stored in your Release 2.2 program directory, which is named 123. If this is not so, substitute the correct drive letter and/or directory name wherever appropriate in the steps that follow. If you are not sure, ask your technical resource person for assistance.

Starting PrintGraph from the Operating System

Starting PrintGraph directly from your computer's operating system prompt gives you more of your computer's memory for work and saves the step of going through the Access System. When you start Print-Graph from the operating system, you return to the operating system when you end the PrintGraph session.

❶ Make sure your computer is turned on and the operating system prompt is displayed, and remove any disks from the diskette drives. ❷ If you have a two-diskette system, insert the PrintGraph Disk in drive A. Then type "a:" and press [Enter] to make drive A the current drive. If you have a hard-disk system, type "cd\123" and press [Enter] to make the Release 2.2 program directory the current directory. ❸ Type "pgraph" and press [Enter] to display the PrintGraph main menu and settings sheet.

Note: *If using a two-diskette system, do not remove the PrintGraph Disk from the drive until after you end the session.*

Note: *To use a named driver set with PrintGraph, type "pgraph" followed by a space and the name of the driver set at the operating system prompt. Include a path in front of the driver set name if it is stored on a separate disk or in a different directory. For example,* **pgraph b:\portable** *.*

Starting PrintGraph from Access

The Access system lets you start PrintGraph by choosing the program's name from a menu. Access makes it easy to switch back and forth between 1-2-3 and PrintGraph and Install. When you start PrintGraph from the Access system, you return to the Access system when you end the PrintGraph session.

❶ Follow Steps 1 and 2 as described in the prior section. ❷ Type "lotus" and press [Enter] to display the Access menu. ❸ Highlight the PrintGraph menu item and then press [Enter], or just type "p" to select PrintGraph and display the PrintGraph main menu and settings sheet.

Note: *To use a named driver set when starting Print-Graph from Access, type "lotus" followed by a space and the name of the driver set at the operating system prompt. Include a path in front of the driver set name if it is stored on a separate disk or in a different directory.*

Printing a Graph — General Procedure

After you start PrintGraph, the PrintGraph settings sheet appears on the screen and remains on the screen throughout the session. The PrintGraph main menu also appears at the top of the screen when you start PrintGraph. You do not need to press / (Slash) to display the menu. Otherwise, select commands from PrintGraph menus just as you do in 1-2-3.

❶ Save the graph in a graph (.PIC) file using /Graph Save in 1-2-3. ❷ Start PrintGraph from DOS or Access. ❸ Select Settings from the PrintGraph main menu to make any necessary changes to the current settings, so PrintGraph can work with your hardware setup. ❹ Select Image-Select and follow the on-screen instructions. ❺ Make sure the printer is properly connected to your computer, turned on, and on-line (ready to print), and that the paper is at the top of a new sheet. ❻ Select Align to tell PrintGraph that you have positioned the paper at the top of a page. ❼ Select Go to begin printing. ❽ When printing is complete, select Page to advance the paper to the top of the next page. ❾ When finished, select Exit to leave PrintGraph.

Note: *If you want to save the graph so you can view or modify it at another time, you must also name the graph using /Graph Name Create in 1-2-3 and then save the worksheet with /File Save. You cannot make changes to a graph (.PIC) file in PrintGraph or 1-2-3.*

To modify a graph, you must return to 1-2-3, retrieve the worksheet containing the graph, change the graph's settings, and save it again in a graph file (/Graph Save) before returning to PrintGraph.

Note: *To stop printing, press [Ctrl][Break]; do not turn off the printer. If the WAIT indicator comes on for a while but nothing prints, your printer port is not specified correctly. Select Settings Hardware Interface and make a new selection.*

The PrintGraph Commands

The PrintGraph commands allow you to select the graphs you want to print and to enhance the appearance of the printed graphs by specifying the layout, proportions, angle, typeface styles, and colors of the printed graph. These commands also allow you to configure PrintGraph to work with your hardware setup. Use the PrintGraph commands to perform the following tasks:

Align Tells PrintGraph that the paper in the printer is correctly positioned at the top of a page.

Exit Ends the PrintGraph session.

Go Starts printing the selected graph(s).

Image-Select Lets you select one or more graph files (files with a .PIC extension) to print.

Page Advances the paper in the printer to the top of the next page.

Settings Controls all PrintGraph settings, including the size and proportion of the graph, the fonts and colors (if any) used in the graph, and the hardware you are using.

Align

Align lets you tell PrintGraph that the paper in the printer is correctly positioned at the top of a page. PrintGraph automatically assumes that the paper is aligned at the top of the print page only at the beginning of a PrintGraph session. If you adjust the paper's position manually during the session, use Align before you select Go to tell PrintGraph the paper is at the beginning of a page.

❶ Turn off the printer and adjust the paper so that the top of the page is correctly positioned for printing; then turn on the printer. ❷ Select Align (there is no paper movement). ❸ If you are using a plotter, PrintGraph prompts you to set up the plotter and press [Space].

Note: *With some printers, you must also set the printer's Top of Page or Home position. For more information, see your printer manual.*

Exit

Exit lets you end the PrintGraph session and return to either the operating system or to the Access system, depending on how you started PrintGraph. Note that PrintGraph does not automatically save the current image and hardware settings. If you want to use the current settings in future sessions, save them with Settings Save before you select Exit.

❶ Select Exit. ❷ Select No to stay in PrintGraph; or Yes to end PrintGraph.

Go

Go lets you send the graph(s) you selected with Image-Select to the printer. Before you select Go, make sure that you have specified the right settings and selected all the graphs you want to print.

❶ Select Go to print the graph(s). ❷ If you are using a plotter, PrintGraph prompts you to load the pens in the order of the list displayed. After you finish loading the pens, press [Space].

There may be a brief pause before printing begins. During printing, the control panel will display messages about what PrintGraph is doing and your printer may pause for several seconds. When PrintGraph finishes printing, the main menu reappears in the control panel.

To stop printing a graph, press [Ctrl][Break]; do not turn off the printer. The printer may not, however, stop printing immediately if the printer's buffer still contains information.

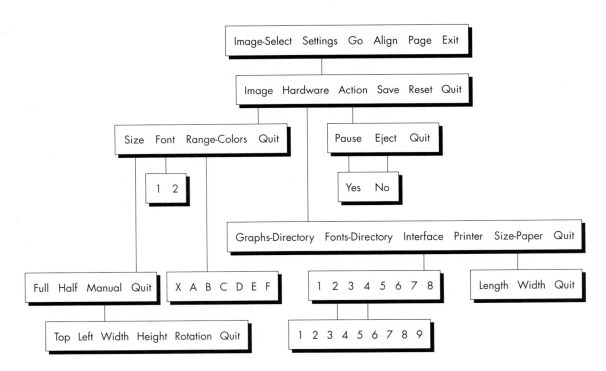

Image-Select

Image-Select lets you specify which graph (.PIC) files you want to print. When you select Go, the selected graphs print in the order in which you chose them.

❶ Use Settings Hardware Graphs-Directory to specify the drive and directory where the graph file(s) you want to print are located, if you have not already done so. ❷ Select Image-Select to display an alphabetical menu of graph files in the specified directory. ❸ Highlight the graph file you want to print and mark your selection by pressing [Space]. (You can select more than one file.) To remove the # symbol from a selection, highlight the selection and press [Space] again. ❹ Press [Enter] to confirm your selection(s) and return to the PrintGraph main menu. The names of the graph files you selected appear in the PrintGraph settings sheet.

If you selected a graphics display driver when you used the Install program, you can preview a graph before you print it. Just highlight one of the graph files in the menu and press [GRAPH] (F10). Press any key to remove the graph from the screen.

Note: *The graph that appears may not reflect all of the PrintGraph settings you have chosen. For example, PrintGraph uses the Block 1 font for titles, legends, or* *scale numbers when you preview a graph — even if you have selected a different font.*

Page

Page lets you advance the paper in the printer to the top of the next page. If you have not manually adjusted the printer paper since the beginning of the session or since you last selected Align, you do not need to use Align.

❶ Select Page to advance the paper to the top of the next page.

If you are printing on a network, you need to select Page to close the graph file you send to the printer queue. Otherwise PrintGraph will not print the graph. If you are printing several files on a network, select Page to close the last file.

Since graph files may be very large, be sure your network server's hard-disk has enough room to hold the queued graph files — about .5 megabyte of disk space if you are using a high-density printer driver.

Some printers may not print until you release the print spooler. Consult your technical resource person.

```
Copyright 1986, 1989 Lotus Development Corp.  All Rights Reserved. V2.2  MENU

Select graphs to print or preview
Image-Select  Settings  Go  Align  Page  Exit

        GRAPHS    IMAGE SETTINGS                  HARDWARE SETTINGS
        TO PRINT  Size              Range colors  Graphs directory
                  Top       .395    X                A:\
                  Left      .750    A             Fonts directory
                  Width    6.500    B                A:\
                  Height   4.691    C             Interface
                  Rotation  .000    D                Parallel 1
                                    E             Printer
                  Font              F
                  1  BLOCK1                        Paper size
                  2  BLOCK1                          Width      8.500
                                                     Length    11.000

                                                 ACTION SETTINGS
                                                 Pause  No   Eject  No
```

Figure 5-1
Default PrintGraph
settings

Settings

The PrintGraph settings let you specify what printer and interface you are using, how you want your graph to look, when PrintGraph should do certain things such as eject paper, and whether PrintGraph should save or reset the current settings. Figure 5-1 shows the Print-Graph settings sheet with the default settings that 1-2-3 supplies.

When you change a setting, PrintGraph updates the current settings on the screen. When you select Go, PrintGraph uses the settings you see to print graphs previously selected with the Image-Select commands. These settings remain current until you change them again or end the PrintGraph session. To save the settings for a future session, select Settings Save. For more information, see "Settings Reset" later in this chapter.

Action Controls whether PrintGraph pauses or advances the page between printing graphs.

Hardware Specifies printer and printer interface, page size, and location of graph and font files.

Image Controls graph size, fonts, colors, angle of rotation, and top and left margins.

Quit Returns you to the PrintGraph main menu.

Reset Replaces the current settings with the settings stored in the PrintGraph configuration file (PGRAPH.CNF).

Save Saves the current settings in the PrintGraph configuration file (PGRAPH.CNF).

Settings Action

Use the Settings Action command to control how Print-Graph and your printer interact when printing.

Settings Action Eject Controls whether PrintGraph automatically advances the paper in the printer to the next page after printing a graph. When it advances the paper automatically, PrintGraph prints one graph per page. If you are using continuous-form paper, the paper advances to the top of a new page before printing resumes. If you are using single sheets, Print-Graph prompts you to insert a new sheet of paper before resuming printing.

❶ Select Settings Action Eject. ❷ Select Yes to advance the paper in the printer automatically after each graph is printed, or No to continue printing on the same page. If you selected No and PrintGraph determines that the next graph is too long for the current page, PrintGraph advances the paper to the top of the next page.

Settings Action Pause Controls whether PrintGraph pauses before printing each graph. Pausing is useful if you need to change paper or switch settings on a printer between graphs. When printing on a network printer, Settings Action Pause has no effect.

❶ Select Settings Action Pause. ❷ Select Yes to pause the printer between graphs (PrintGraph signals the pause by beeping continuously until you press [Space] to continue printing), or No to print continuously.

Settings Action Quit   Lets you return to the Settings menu.

❶ Select Settings Action Quit.

Settings Hardware

The Settings Hardware commands let you tell Print-Graph what kind of printer you are using, where your graph and font files are located, which interface your printer uses, and what paper size you are using. Unless you change printers, you usually have to change these settings only once.

Settings Hardware Fonts-Directory   Specifies the drive and directory that PrintGraph searches for font files (files with a .FNT extension) before it prints or displays a graph. The default Fonts-Directory setting is A:\.

If you have a two-diskette system, the font files are on the PrintGraph Disk. You must insert this disk in the drive you specify. If you have a hard-disk system, the font files should be in your Release 2.2 program directory.

❶ Select Settings Hardware Fonts-Directory. ❷ Type the drive and directory that contains the PrintGraph font files and press [Enter].

Settings Hardware Graphs-Directory   Specifies the drive and directory that PrintGraph searches for graph (.PIC) files. The default Graphs-Directory setting is A:\.

❶ Select Settings Hardware Graphs-Directory. ❷ Type the drive and directory that contain the graph files you want to print and press [Enter].

For example, if the graph files are in a directory called QTR1, which is a subdirectory of FINANCE on drive D, enter d:\finance\qtr1 as the directory. Or, if the graph files are on a data disk in drive B, enter b:\.

Settings Hardware Interface   Specifies the interface for your printer. The **interface**, or port, refers to the way your printer is connected to the computer. Your interface may be parallel or serial, and your computer may have more than one interface of either type. If you are unsure of the kind of interface you have, check your printer manual or ask your technical resource person. The default interface setting is Parallel 1, which is the most common configuration.

Note: *If you have a serial interface, you will also need to indicate the baud rate for which your printer is set. The baud rate is the speed at which PrintGraph sends data to the printer. Select the fastest baud rate that will correctly send data to your printer without losing it. Check your printer manual for details.*

❶ Select one of the following options to specify the printer interface (Settings 1 to 4 are for printers linked physically to your computer; settings 5 to 8 are for logical devices and are generally used to connect printers over a network):

1	Parallel 1	5	LPT1
2	Serial 1	6	LPT2
3	Parallel 2	7	LPT3
4	Serial 2	8	LPT4

❷ If you selected a serial interface, select one of the following options to specify the baud rate at which to send data to the printer:

1	110 baud	6	2400 baud
2	150 baud	7	4800 baud
3	300 baud	8	9600 baud
4	600 baud	9	19200 baud
5	1200 baud		

Note: *If you are using a serial printer, change the following settings on your printer. These are not settings you can change in PrintGraph.*

Data bits: 8

Stop bits: 2 if 110 baud; otherwise 1

Parity: one

Settings Hardware Printer   Lets you specify which printer you want to use. In some cases, it also lets you specify the print density — high or low — indicating the relative **density**, or resolution, of the printing. Denser printing means finer detail in your graphs, but it also means much slower printing. If you are using a dot-matrix printer, some fonts will print only if you are using high density. See "Settings Image Font" later in this chapter for more information.

❶ Select Settings Hardware Printer to display a menu of the graphics printers you selected with the Install program. ❷ Highlight the printer you want to use and mark your selection by pressing [Space]. (To remove the # symbol from a selection, highlight the selection and press [Space] again.) ❸ Press [Enter] to confirm your selection and return to the Hardware menu.

Settings Hardware Quit   Lets you return to the Settings menu.

Settings Hardware Size-Paper   Lets you specify the size of paper your printer uses. The default setting is 8.5 by 11 inches.

❶ Select Settings Hardware Size-Paper. ❷ Select Length. ❸ Type the length in inches and press [Enter]. ❹ Select Width. ❺ Type the width in inches and press [Enter]. ❻ Select Quit to return to the Settings menu.

If you change this setting, you must also manually adjust the settings for paper length (sometimes called form length) on your printer. See your printer manual for information. If you cannot adjust the paper length setting on your printer manually, use the default setting of 11 inches.

Settings Image

Settings Image lets you control the appearance of a graph by letting you specify the graph's size, fonts (typefaces), color, angle of rotation, and top and left margins.

Settings Image Font   Lets you specify which font PrintGraph uses in printing the graph's text portions. A **font**, or typeface, refers to the overall design of the printed characters. Each font has a distinct appearance, and all the characters within the font share common design characteristics.

You can use two different fonts for the text in graphs. PrintGraph uses the font you select as Font 1 for the first line of the graph's title, and the font you select as Font 2 for all other alphanumeric characters in the graph, including the other titles, legends, and scale numbers. If you do not choose a second font, Print-Graph uses Font 1 to print all the text in the graph. PrintGraph uses only its own fonts; you cannot use your printer's fonts.

❶ Select Settings Image Font. ❷ Select 1 to specify the font for the first line of the graph's title; or 2 to specify the font for all other graph text. PrintGraph displays a menu of available fonts. ❸ Highlight the font you want to use and mark your selection by pressing [Space]. (To remove the # symbol from a selection, highlight the selection and press [Space] again.) ❹ Press [Enter] to confirm your selection and return to the Image menu.

The numbers at the end of similar font names indicate how heavy (dark) each font is; for example, Block 2 is heavier than Block 1. The heavier font produces high-quality graphs only with high-resolution printers. Plotters, on the other hand, reproduce all the fonts in high quality.

Note: *If you are using a two-diskette system, the fonts PrintGraph uses are stored on the PrintGraph Disk. Do not remove the disk from the drive during the Print-Graph session.*

Note: *Some PrintGraph fonts are designed for plotters, not raster graphics printers such as dot-matrix and ink jet printers. In particular, the Italic and Script fonts will probably be unsatisfactory with a dot-matrix printer. The Bold, Forum, and Roman fonts work well on dot-matrix printers if you choose a high enough density. Generally, the Block fonts provide the best results with a dot-matrix printer.*

Settings Image Quit   Lets you return to the Settings menu.

Settings Image Range-Colors   Lets you assign colors to graph data ranges. In the PrintGraph settings sheet, you can see the default color that will be used to print each graph data range. If you have a color printer and want to assign colors to data ranges, first specify the printer with Settings Hardware Printer.

The color you assign to the X data range determines the color of the box that contains the graphed data and everything — except legends — outside the box. This includes scale numbers, titles, and exponents. Print-Graph uses the colors you assign to the A to F data ranges to print the graphed data and the legends. These colors are independent of the colors that appear when you view the graph in 1-2-3 or preview it with [GRAPH] (F10).

❶ Select Settings Image Range-Colors. ❷ Specify one of the graph ranges (X, A through F). ❸ Select a color for the range. Depending on the type of printer you are using, this menu may offer several colors or only black.

When you print a pie chart, the colors of the slices are determined by the values that were entered in the pie chart's B data range when you saved the graph in 1-2-3 with /Graph Save, and by the colors you assigned to ranges in PrintGraph with Settings Image Range-Colors.

Each value in the B data range you specified in 1-2-3 corresponds to a specific data range in PrintGraph as follows: 1 = X; 2 = A; 3 = B; 4 = C; 5 = D; 6 = E; 7 = F.

PrintGraph uses the color you assign to a data range with Settings Image Range-Colors to print each slice that has the corresponding B data range value. For example, if one of the values in the pie chart's B data range is 4 (or 104, if the slice is exploded), PrintGraph prints the slice in the color you assign to the C data range using Settings Image Range-Colors; if two of the values in the B data range are 6, PrintGraph prints those two slices in the color you assign to the E data range; and so on.

PrintGraph uses the color you assign to the X data range for printing labels and titles. It uses the color assigned to the A data range to print the pie chart's border.

If you are using a plotter, 1-2-3 prompts you to load the pens in a specific order when you select Go. Depending on the plotter, PrintGraph beeps and prompts you when it is time to change the color of a pen. Refer to your plotter documentation for information on using different pens.

When you print a graph on a plotter on a network, the number of pens in the plotter limits the number of colors you can use because you are not present to change pens. To match your printer settings, you need to have previously loaded the pens in the correct order. In addition, the number of colors you specify when you are using a remote plotter cannot exceed the number of pen stalls in the plotter.

Settings Image Size   Lets you specify the size and proportions of the printed graph. This command controls the values (in inches) for margins, height, and width, and the value (in degrees) for rotation. The height always refers to the graph's size vertically (from top to bottom, as the paper feeds into the printer). The

width always refers to the graph horizontally (across the page, as it feeds into the printer).

❶ Select Settings Image Size. ❷ Select one of the following options:

Full   Sets rotation to 90 to print the graph sideways on the page. (The x axis is drawn along the height of the page.) Proportions are close to those displayed on the screen. With 8.5 by 11-inch paper, this setting prints one graph per page. (PrintGraph sets the height and width automatically; these settings do not change when you specify a different paper size.)

Half   Sets rotation to 0. (The x axis spans the width of the page.) With 8.5 by 11-inch paper, this setting lets you print two graphs per page. (PrintGraph sets the height and width automatically; these settings do not change when you specify a different paper size.)

Manual   You set the height and width, the margins, and the rotation.

Quit   Returns to the Image menu.

❸ If you selected Manual in Step 2, select one or more of the following options:

Top   Sets the size of the top margin in inches.

Left   Sets the size of the left margin in inches.

Width   Sets the width of the graph (horizontal distance) in inches.

Height   Sets the height of the graph (vertical distance) in inches.

Rotation   Sets the number of degrees the graph is turned counterclockwise (90 produces a quarter turn to the left).

Quit   Returns to the Size menu.

PrintGraph has a default top margin of .5 inch that it adds to what you specify. Even if you set the top margin to 0 (zero), the top margin will be .5 inch.

The Width, Height, and Rotation settings affect the proportions of your graph. If you set these manually and want to retain the standard proportions of the graph, you must consider the following:

- When PrintGraph sets a graph's size automatically, it preserves the **aspect ratio**, or the ratio of the graph's width to its height: approximately 1.385 (x axis) to 1 (y axis). If you want to maintain these proportions, you must calculate this ratio. For instance, if X = 3.0, then Y = 2.166 (because Y = X/1.385). If Y = 4.5, then X = 6.233 (because X = Y*1.385).

- If, however, you change the Rotation to anything except 0, you must calculate the aspect ratio again to retain the standard proportions. Height and Width are always measured in relation to the page, not in relation to the graph's axes. Thus, if rotation is set to 0, the Height setting refers to the y axis. If rotation is set to 90, the Height setting refers to the x axis. To maintain the same proportions when setting rotation from 0 to 90, you must invert the Width and Height settings.

- Rotation settings that turn rectangular graphs along vertical or horizontal axes (0, 90, 180, or 270) always create right-angled corners. If you select other rotations, you must make another calculation to preserve the right-angled corners. Without this calculation, your graphs will be drawn as rhombuses (parallelograms without right angles), and your pie charts as ellipses (ovals).

- Pie charts must always retain the standard aspect ratio of 1 (y axis) to 1.385 (x axis) to preserve their circular shape. The first radial line drawn always runs from the center of the pie towards the title line at the top of the graph. PrintGraph interprets this line as the y axis when rotating the pie chart.

Settings Quit

Settings Quit returns you to the PrintGraph main menu after changing any settings.

Settings Reset

Settings Reset lets you replace the current PrintGraph settings with those in the PrintGraph configuration file PGRAPH.CNF. Use Settings Reset if you have changed, but not saved, the settings during the current session and want to set up another graph to print by restoring the settings you had the last time you used Settings Save.

Do not use Settings Reset if you have finished using PrintGraph and you don't want to save the current settings.

Settings Save

Settings Save lets you store the current PrintGraph settings (except for selected graphs) in the PrintGraph configuration file, PGRAPH.CNF. Each time you start a session or select Settings Reset, PrintGraph reads settings from PGRAPH.CNF. You can change these settings any time during the current session, but you must use Settings Save to copy your changes to PGRAPH.CNF if you want them to be the standard settings for your PrintGraph sessions.

Note: *If you have a two-diskette system, make sure the PrintGraph Disk is in the disk drive and that there is no write-protect tab on the disk before you select Settings Save.*

Common Problems and Solutions

This section offers solutions to some of the most common problems people have when using the PrintGraph program.

Problem

When I try to run PrintGraph, I get a message saying that there is no driver for the graphics printer I selected.

Solution

The printer setting you saved in PrintGraph does not match any of the graphics printers you selected in the Install program. Press [Esc] to clear the error message and select Settings Hardware Printer. If the correct printer is in the list that appears, select it. Then select Settings Save to save the information for future PrintGraph sessions. If the correct printer is not in the list, end PrintGraph and run the Install program to select a driver for the graphics printer you want to use.

Problem

If I start 1-2-3 from the Access menu, then quit 1-2-3 and try to start PrintGraph, I get a DOS error message instead.

Solution

This problem occurs only for floppy-disk based systems running DOS 2.0 or 2.1. Upgrade your system to a later version of DOS.

Problem

When I try to start PrintGraph from the Access system, I get the message "Cannot find COMMAND.COM."

Solution

This problem is often caused by memory-resident programs you may be running, such as Metro, Express, or local area network software. Unload any such programs and try running PrintGraph again.

Problem

Sometimes my printed graphs look different from the way they looked on the screen.

Solution

This problem occurs because the capabilities of your printer are different from those of your screen display. For instance, your printer may use a different font from the one your screen uses or your printer may size characters differently from the way your screen displays them.

Problem

When I try to print a graph, I get a message saying that there is no graphics printer active.

Solution

You did not select a graphics printer during installation. Leave PrintGraph and run the Install program to select a graphics printer.

Problem

I tried to print, but I got the message "No graph files found in this disk/directory."

Solution

PrintGraph needs to know where to look for the graph (.PIC) files that you are trying to print. Select Settings Hardware Graphs-Directory and type the full path of the directory that contains the graph files, for example, C:\GRAPHS or B:\. Then save the setting with Settings Save so you do not have to specify it again unless you move the graph files to another directory.

Problem

I tried to print, but got a message about a font not being found.

Solution

PrintGraph needs to know where to look for the font (.FNT) files it uses to print graphs. If you have a hard-disk system, these fonts should be in your Release 2.2 program directory. If you have a two-diskette system, these fonts should be on the PrintGraph Disk. Select Settings Hardware Fonts-Directory and type the full path of the directory that contains the font files, for example, C:\123 or A:\. Then save the setting with Settings Save so you do not have to specify it again unless you move the fonts files to another directory.

Problem

I am using an HP LaserJet printer and have had trouble printing a graph in landscape orientation.

Solution

If you try to print a graph with the LaserJet set to landscape orientation (sideways printing), you will get either a blank page or a printout of indecipherable characters. The printer will be set for landscape orientation if the previous document was printed that way or, on the Series II, if you used the control panel to specify a font in landscape orientation.

You need to reset the printer to portrait orientation. To do so, press the Hold to Reset key on the LaserJet Plus, press the Enter/Reset Menu key on the Series II, or turn the printer off and then back on. If you were using a soft font, be aware that turning off the printer removes the font from memory. If you want to change the orientation of the graph you can do so by changing its rotation with Settings Image Size Manual Rotation.

Problem

I cannot print a full-page graph on my HP LaserJet printer.

Solution

If you have more than 512 kilobytes of internal printer memory, you may have some soft fonts loaded from another application. Reset the printer to clear out the soft fonts. If you have only 512 kilobytes of internal printer memory, you cannot print out a full-page high-density (300 dots per inch) graph on a LaserJet printer. You must either purchase additional printer memory or decrease the size or resolution of the graph.

Use the Install program to select drivers both for a LaserJet printer and a LaserJet Plus printer. The LaserJet driver allows you to print graphs at 75 dots per inch (dpi), while the LaserJet plus driver allows you to print graphs at either low density (100 dpi) or high density (300 dpi). By specifying both drivers during installation, you can then choose from three graphic densities when you use PrintGraph. Just select Settings Hardware Printer, and the three options will appear for you to choose from.

Problem

I am having trouble printing two half-size graphs on the same page with my HP LaserJet printer.

Solution

LaserJet printers cannot print in the bottom half inch of the page, so define the following settings with Settings Image Size Half for your half-size graphs: Top equal to .395, Left equal to 1.102, Height equal to 4.191, and Width equal to 5.805.

Glossary

absolute cell address See *absolute reference*.

absolute range name See *absolute reference*.

absolute reference In a formula, a cell address that always refers to the same cell, or a range name or address that always refers to the same range, even if you copy or move the formula. In an absolute cell address, a $ (dollar sign) precedes the column letter and row number (e.g., $A$4). In an absolute range name, a $ precedes the range name (e.g., $INTEREST). For example, to calculate the effects of a constant interest rate on varying principal amounts, you can create a formula that uses an absolute cell address to refer to the cell that contains the interest rate. See also *mixed cell reference* and *relative reference*.

Access system The menu that allows you to move among 1-2-3 and the utility programs that come with 1-2-3 (Install and PrintGraph). You display the Access menu by typing "lotus" at the operating system prompt.

active area The area bounded by A1 and the lowest and rightmost nonblank cell in the active area. Use [End] [Home] to find this cell. See also *nonblank cell*.

add-ins Special programs, such as Macro Library Manager, created by Lotus or other software developers, that you can use with 1-2-3 to extend its capabilities. Using Add-In commands, you can attach an add-in when you need to use it and detach it when you need more memory for other tasks.

address See *cell address* and *range address*.

advanced macro command An instruction in a macro that tells 1-2-3 to perform a built-in programming function.

Each advanced macro command consists of a keyword and its arguments (if any), enclosed in braces. {READLN G22} is an example of an advanced macro command.

alignment The position of a label in a cell. A label can be aligned with the left or right side of the cell, or centered in the cell. To control alignment, use the label prefixes ' " \ and ^.

anchor The action of setting the cell pointer so it remains fixed in one cell while 1-2-3 is in POINT mode.

You can expand the highlight in any direction from the anchor cell. The anchor cell, however, always stays in the same position. When you select some commands, 1-2-3 automatically anchors the cell pointer. In other cases, you type a . (Period) in POINT mode to anchor the cell pointer.

anchor cell The cell in which you begin to highlight a range in POINT mode. See also *anchor*.

argument A string, value, location (range name, range address, or cell address), or condition that provides information to an @function or an advanced macro command. Arguments are what @functions act on. The arguments follow the @function name in parentheses and are separated by argument separators. For example, @SUM(B3..B25,D3..D25) has two arguments. Macro arguments follow the macro keyword and are separated by commas or semicolons as in {GETLABEL "Monthly Totals", B2}.

argument separator A punctuation mark that sets off one argument from another in an @function or advanced macro command.

arithmetic formula A mathematical expression that uses arithmetic operators and/or @functions and results in a value.

arithmetic operator See *operator*.

ASCII (American Standard Code for Information Interchange) Standard character set many computers and communications devices use.

ASCII file A file that contains only ASCII characters. See also *text file*.

aspect ratio The ratio of the width to the height of a 1-2-3 graph. The standard Lotus aspect ratio of a graph's x axis to the y axis is approximately 1.385 to 1.

attach The action of loading an add-in program into your computer's memory.

autoexecute macro A macro named \0 (Zero) that 1-2-3 executes automatically if the /Worksheet Global Default Autoexec setting is Yes when you retrieve the worksheet that contains the macro.

@function A built-in formula that performs a specific calculation. For example, the formula @SUM(B2..B15) uses the @SUM @function to add the numbers in cells B2 through B15. @Function is pronounced "at function." See also *argument.*

backup file A worksheet file with a .BAK extension that 1-2-3 creates when you select /File Save or /File Xtract, specify the name of an existing file, and then select Backup. The backup file contains the contents of the original worksheet before you made any changes. When you select Backup, 1-2-3 also saves the current worksheet with your changes by updating the existing worksheet (.WK1) file on disk.

bar graph A graph that compares related data at a given point in time by representing the data as bars along the x-axis. Each bar represents one value in the y-axis range.

baud rate The speed at which a program sends data to a printer with a serial interface.

blank cell A cell that contains no visible data, but may include range formats and label prefixes. See also *nonblank cell.*

border See *print border.*

branch The transfer of macro control from the current column of macro instructions to another column through the use of the advanced macro command {BRANCH}.

byte pointer The starting location of a group of contiguous bytes in a file.

cell The intersection of a column and a row in a worksheet where you can enter information. See also *cell address.*

cell address The location of a particular cell in a worksheet, identified by a column letter and row number (e.g., A25 or B36). See also *absolute reference, mixed cell reference, range address,* and *relative reference.*

cell format The way 1-2-3 displays values on the screen. A number's cell format may differ from its value as entered; for example, the entry 25.451 may appear as $25.45, 2545%, or 25.4, depending on its cell format.

cell pointer The highlight that indicates the current cell in the worksheet. You can move the cell pointer to any cell in the worksheet. In POINT mode, you can press [.] (Period) to anchor the cell pointer to highlight a range. When referring to the use of expanded memory, a cell pointer is information stored in conventional memory that allows 1-2-3 to locate an entry stored in expanded memory. Each cell pointer uses 4 bytes of conventional memory.

cell reference The address or the range name of a cell used in a formula. Cell references can be absolute, relative, or mixed. See also *absolute reference, mixed cell reference,* and *relative reference.*

circular reference The result of a formula that refers to itself, either directly or indirectly. For example, a circular reference occurs if you enter the formula +B1+1 in cell B1. When you are using Natural recalculation, 1-2-3 displays the CIRC indicator on the status line at the bottom of the screen whenever it detects a circular reference. You can select /Worksheet Status to see what cell is causing the circular reference.

collating sequence See *sort order.*

column A vertical block of cells in a worksheet that is one cell wide and runs the entire length of the worksheet. For example, column B contains cells B1 through B8192. A worksheet contains 256 columns. In a database table, a column is called a field. See also *field.*

column letters The letters A through IV in the horizontal worksheet border. Each letter or pair of letters identifies one column (e.g., column A or column BC).

column width The number of characters that 1-2-3 displays in a column. The default column width is 9 characters, but you can assign a column any width from 1 to 240 characters. A cell can store up to 240 characters, even if its column width is too small to display them all. See *long label* and *long value.*

command An instruction you give 1-2-3. To select a command in 1-2-3, press / (Slash) or < (Less-than symbol) to display the main menu and then choose items from the menu.

command menu See *menu.*

compose sequence A series of keystrokes beginning with COMPOSE (Alt-F1) that you use to produce a character that is not on your keyboard. See also *ASCII* and *LICS*.

concatenate To join strings with a string formula. The string formula +"Sales "&"Totals" concatenates the text inside the quotation marks to produce the label Sales Totals.

configuration settings The settings that 1-2-3 uses when it loads its program files. These settings control how 1-2-3 communicates with printers and disk drives and how it performs standard procedures. Select /Worksheet Global Default to see the current configuration settings.

control panel The top three lines of the 1-2-3 screen. The control panel displays information about the current cell and the current mode. It also displays entries while you type or edit them. If you press / (Slash) or < (Less-than symbol) while 1-2-3 is in READY mode, the control panel displays a menu, prompts, and your responses to those prompts.

criteria Cell entries you enter in a criteria range that 1-2-3 uses as tests for the records in a database. When you use many of the Data commands, the current criteria determine whether the command affects a particular record.

criteria range The range you set up in a worksheet to contain criteria.

current cell The cell that contains the cell pointer, which indicates that your next entry or procedure affects this cell. The current cell address always appears in the first line of the control panel unless you are running a macro with {PANELOFF} or {BORDERSOFF}.

current directory The directory that 1-2-3 automatically uses during the current session to save, read, or list files. The current directory can be the default directory or a directory that you specify through File Directory.

current graph The graph that appears when you select Graph View. The current graph uses the specified graph settings. See also *graph settings*.

current worksheet The 1-2-3 worksheet that is loaded in your computer's memory and that appears on your screen.

cursor The blinking underscore that shows the position of the next character you type when you are entering data or editing an entry. The cursor also appears in the current cell when you are highlighting a range. See also *cell pointer*.

data Information you enter in a worksheet. You can enter two types of data in 1-2-3: labels and values (numbers and formulas).

database An organized collection of related information. A 1-2-3 database consists of fields, which contain one kind of information, and records, which contain entries in each field for one item.

1-2-3 stores fields in columns and records in rows; each cell in the database contains one field entry. For example, an employee database contains fields such as Last Name, First Name, and so on. Each record, or row in the database, contains information about one employee. You use the Data commands and database @functions to manage the database.

database data table A data table created using database @functions with a database as the input range, allowing you to perform calculations using data from only those records that meet your criteria.

data labels The labels you assign to bars or points within a graph.

data range The range of values you use to create a graph.

data table A table that records the effects of changing one or two values in one or more formulas. Used to perform "what-if" analyses.

date-and-time indicator The indicator that appears in the bottom left corner of your screen. The default setting is for 1-2-3 to display the current date and time in this indicator. You can, however, use /Worksheet Global Default Other Clock to change the contents of the display or to suppress the indicator display.

date format The way in which 1-2-3 displays date numbers in cells.

Date Format		Example
D1	DD-MMM-YY	18-Nov-89
D2	DD-MMM	18-Nov
D3	MMM-YY	Nov-89
D4	Long International	11/18/89
D5	Short International	11/18

date-number A number from 1 to 73050 that corresponds to each date from January 1, 1900 (date number 1) to December 31, 2099 (date number 73050).

debug To make corrections in a macro or subroutine so it performs correctly.

default directory The directory 1-2-3 automatically uses when you start. To change the default directory, use Worksheet Global Default Directory, followed by Worksheet Global Default Update. See also *current directory.*

default setting A setting 1-2-3 or PrintGraph automatically uses until you change it. For example, the default column width (9) remains the same until you change it with Worksheet Column. Some default settings are saved with the worksheet; others are saved in the 1-2-3 configuration file and are automatically used for all future worksheets. See also *configuration settings.*

delimited text file An ASCII file that contains delimiters, which are characters that separate the data within a row. A delimiter is a , (Comma), : (Colon), ; (Semicolon), or space. You can import a delimited text file into 1-2-3.

detach The action of removing an attached add-in program from your computer's memory.

directory A subdivision of a disk. You can create and name a directory and store related files in it when you save the files on a disk; this makes the files easier to find.

directory name The name of a directory. A \ (Backslash) separates the directory names in a path from each other and from the filename. For example, in C:\1-2-3\FEBRUARY\BUDGET.WK1, the drive is C:, the directory names are 1-2-3 and FEBRUARY, and the filename is BUDGET.WK1.

disk A magnetic storage medium for your files, such as a 5¼-inch or 3½-inch disk or a hard disk.

DOS Disk Operating System. Pronounced "doss." See also *operating system.*

drive A piece of computer hardware that holds a disk, reads data stored on a disk into memory, and saves new data from memory on a disk.

drive name The two characters (a letter and a colon) that identify the disk drive. For example, C: is the name of drive C, the hard disk drive on a computer.

driver A program that enables 1-2-3 to communicate with your equipment, such as a printer or monitor. You select 1-2-3 drivers with the Install program.

driver set The collection of 1-2-3 drivers you create when you use the Install program. Driver sets are stored in files on disk with a .SET extension.

dual mode Using 1-2-3 with both a monochrome monitor and a graphics monitor connected to your computer. 1-2-3 displays text on the monochrome monitor and graphs on the graphics monitor.

entry Data entered in a cell. Every entry is a label or a value.

error message A message that appears in the lower left corner of the screen when a program detects a mistake or cannot perform a task. You can press [HELP] (F1) to get more information about what caused the error, or press [Esc] to clear the error. If the error message appears somewhere other than in the lower left corner of the screen, it is an operating system error message. See your operating system manual.

extension A . (Period) followed by up to three characters, at the end of a filename. When 1-2-3 creates a file, it automatically adds the extension .WK1 to worksheet files, .PIC to graph files, and .PRN to text files. You can override these extensions by entering your own extension when you save a file.

field In a database table, a labeled column that contains the same kind of information for each record. For example, the Last Name field contains all the last names in a database table. A database table can contain up to 256 fields. Fields can contain either labels or values.

field names Labels in the first row of a database table that identify the kind of information appearing in the column below. The field names must be unique for each field within a database table.

file A named collection of data saved on disk. With 1-2-3, you save a worksheet in a worksheet file, graphs in a graph file, and text in ASCII format in a text file.

filename The name you give to a file when you use File Save. In general, 1-2-3 filenames can contain up to eight characters including letters, numbers, and the – (hyphen) and _ (underscore) characters. See also *extension*.

file reference The name of a worksheet file enclosed in << >> (double angle brackets), such as <<INCOME89.WK1>>. A file reference is used in linking formulas to specify a file on disk that contains a cell whose contents you want to use in the current worksheet. A file reference may also include a path, for example, <<C:\NEWDATA\INCOME89.WK1>>.

flow of control The way in which control passes from one location to another during a macro. You use a flow-of-control advanced macro command to direct the transfer of control of a macro.

font A typeface of a particular size that the PrintGraph program uses for text when printing or plotting graphs. A font's size is normally measured as the height of the font in points.

footer A line of text 1-2-3 prints above the bottom margin of each page.

format See *cell format*.

formula An expression that performs a calculation in a worksheet. A 1-2-3 formula can include @functions, and can be a numeric formula, a string formula, or a logical formula. See also *@function*.

formula criteria Formula criteria use logical formulas to determine whether a record is selected when you are using the Data Query commands. For example, if there is a field called AGE in column B of your database, you can use the formula criterion +B2<59 to select the records that contain values greater than 59 in the AGE field.

@function A built-in formula that performs a specific calculation. For example, the formula @SUM(B2..B15) uses the @SUM @function to add the numbers in cells B2 through B15. @Function is pronounced "at function." See also *argument*.

function keys Keys [F1] through [F10] on your keyboard. The function keys perform special functions when used individually or in combination with [Alt].

global setting A setting that affects the entire worksheet (such as /Worksheet Global Column-Width, which sets the width of all columns in the worksheet) or 1-2-3 as a whole (such as /Worksheet Global Recalculation, which sets the way 1-2-3 reevaluates formulas).

graph file A file that stores a 1-2-3 graph for use with PrintGraph and other programs. Graph files have the .PIC file extension. You must save a graph in a graph file with /Graph Save before you can print it.

graph settings The options you specify when creating a graph, such as graph type, titles, scaling, and ranges. You can save graph settings to use again with new data.

hard disk A permanent magnetic storage medium that has a much greater storage capacity than a 5¼-inch disk or 3½-inch disk and is usually built into a computer.

hatch pattern The pattern of lines that distinguishes one bar from another in bar graphs and one slice from another in pie charts.

header A line of text that 1-2-3 prints above the top margin of each page.

Help The 1-2-3, PrintGraph, and Install on-line reference manual. To get Help about the procedure you are currently doing, press [HELP] (F1).

highlight A distinctly colored rectangle on the screen. In POINT mode, you expand the highlight with the pointer-movement keys and press [Enter] to specify a range. The cell pointer, menu pointer, and indicators are also highlights.

indicator A highlighted word that provides information about the program or special key status. Status indicators appear at the bottom of the screen. Mode indicators appear in the upper right corner of the screen.

Install program The program you use to create a driver set so that 1-2-3 can work with your equipment.

interface Also known as a port, the interface refers to the way in which a printer is connected to your computer. The interface may be parallel or serial, and your computer may have more than one interface of either type.

invoke The action of activating an attached add-in program.

keystroke instruction An instruction in a macro that represents a key on the keyboard, such as {bs} for [Backspace], and duplicates its effect. When 1-2-3 reads a keystroke instruction, it performs as it would if you had pressed the corresponding key.

keyword The first word in an advanced macro command, such as {LET} or {QUIT}.

label Any entry that begins with a letter or a label prefix.

label alignment The way a label appears in a cell: left-aligned, right-aligned, centered, or repeating across the cell. Label prefixes control label alignment. See also *label prefix*.

label prefix One of the four characters that control the alignment of a label in a cell. You use label prefixes to indicate that you are entering a label and to specify its alignment. You must use a label prefix with entries that begin with a number or with + - (# . @ or $ (or the default currency symbol) if you want 1-2-3 to treat them as labels.

Label Prefix	Alignment	Placement in Cell
'	Left-aligned	LABEL
^	Centered	LABEL
"	Right-aligned	LABEL
\	Repeating	LABELLABELLABELLA

The | (split vertical bar) is also a label prefix, but it has a special use. If used as the label prefix for a label that is located at the beginning of a row of data, it tells 1-2-3 not to print the row.

Learn feature A 1-2-3 feature you can use to create macros. When the Learn feature is on, 1-2-3 automatically records your keystrokes as you perform the task you want to automate. To use the Learn feature, you must specify a learn range with /Worksheet Learn Range and then turn on the Learn feature by pressing [LEARN] (Alt-F5).

legend A guide to the symbols, lines, hatch patterns, or colors in a graph. The legend appears beneath the graph.

LICS (Lotus International Character Set) The 256 codes (0 to 255) 1-2-3 uses to display, store, and print characters that are not on your keyboard. You can use LICS codes to produce characters. Codes 32 through 127 represent ASCII characters 32 through 127. Codes 128 through 255 represent various international characters and special symbols, such as £ (British pound).

line graph A graph that plots changes in one or more values over time. Each range of values appears as a line.

linked cell A cell in the current worksheet whose value depends on the value of a cell in another file. Cells are linked using a linking formula.

linking formula A formula in a worksheet in memory that refers to a cell in a worksheet file on disk. A linking formula must start with a + (plus) and include a file reference and cell reference (for example, +<<C:\123DATA\UKSALES.WK1>>B16) .

literal string Text (letters, numbers, punctuation marks, spaces, and special characters) enclosed in quotation marks. Literal strings are used in string formulas and @functions.

logical formula A formula that evaluates a condition by using a logical operator or a logical @function. A logical formula results in a value that you can use in other calculations (1 for true, 0 for false). For example, the formula +A>28 returns 1 (true) when the value in A2 is greater than 8; it returns 0 (false) when the value in A2 is 8 or less.

logical function An @function that tests a statement to see if it is true or false. A logical function results in a value of 1 (true) or 0 (false). For example, the result of @ISNUMBER(B27) is 1 if cell B27 contains a number or a formula that evaluates to a numeric value; 0 if it contains a label.

logical operator An operator you use in a logical formula to evaluate equality or inequality.

Logical Operator	Meaning
=	Equal to
<	Less than
>	Greater than
<=	Less than or equal to
>=	Greater than or equal to
<>	Not equal to
#AND#	Logical AND
#NOT#	Logical NOT
#OR#	Logical OR

long label   A label that is longer than a cell's column width. If the cell to the right is blank, the long label appears to extend into the next column. If the cell to the right is not blank, 1-2-3 displays only as many characters as fit within the column width. Even if it cannot display or print the entire label, 1-2-3 stores the entire label.

long value   A value that when displayed in a particular format is wider than the cell's column width minus 1. For example, in a cell with a column width of 9 that has been formatted as Currency with 2 decimal places, 1500 is a long value because $1,500.00 contains nine characters, which is one more than the cell's column width minus 1. Depending on the cell format, 1-2-3 either displays a long value in scientific notation or displays asterisks. To display the value, make the column wider.

lookup table   A range of values organized as a matrix, or table, in which the first row and/or column contain values or labels in ascending order. This layout lets you use the row and/or column as an index to the information in the table.

macro   A set of instructions for automating a 1-2-3 task. Macros include keystroke instructions and advanced macro commands. You can use a macro to enter data or to perform a series of 1-2-3 commands that will format a worksheet, guide users through specific applications, calculate complex formulas with variable data, and so on.

macro library   A collection of macros, data, or formulas in memory that you can use with any worksheet. The library is also stored in a file on disk, identified with a .MLB extension. You create macro libraries with the Macro Library Manager add-in.

macro menu   A menu that you can set up for use during a macro that works just like a 1-2-3 menu.

matching criteria   Criteria that a label or a value in a record must match exactly. For example, to select only records of employees who are 65, you use a matching criterion of 65 in the Age field. You can use both values and labels as matching criteria.

memory   The temporary storage area in which a computer holds both programs and data. For example, the 1-2-3 worksheet you see on the screen is in memory.

menu   The series of choices that appear in the control panel after you press / (Slash) or < (Less-than symbol) when 1-2-3 is in READY mode.

menu pointer   The rectangular highlight that appears in the second line of the control panel when the 1-2-3 menu is being displayed. You can select a command by moving the menu pointer to the command to highlight it and then pressing [Enter].

merge character   A character that is not in the Lotus International Character Set, which 1-2-3 creates by overstriking one character over another. The compose sequence for a merge character is [COMPOSE] (Alt-F1) mg. To print an o with an acute accent (ó), for example, type o, press [COMPOSE] (Alt-F1), and type mg'.

mixed address   See *mixed cell reference*.

mixed cell reference   In a formula, a cell address that is part relative and part absolute. A $ (Dollar sign) precedes the absolute part of the address. For example, if a formula in cell B2 contains the cell address A$1 and you copy the formula to cell G8, the cell address becomes F$1. See also *absolute reference* and *relative reference*.

mode   A 1-2-3 state in which you can perform a particular process. For example, when 1-2-3 is in READY mode the program is ready to accept cell entries or commands. When 1-2-3 is in POINT mode you can specify a range by expanding the highlight.

mode indicator   The indicator, located in the upper right corner of the screen, that tells you the program's current mode of operation. For example, when you are editing an entry in 1-2-3, the mode indicator displays EDIT.

named graph A graph and its settings that you have named. When you retrieve a named graph, its settings become the current graph settings.

named range A single cell or range of cells that you named using /Range Name Create.

nonblank cell A cell that contains data, range formats, or label prefixes. To find the nonblank cell in a worksheet, press [END] then [HOME]. See also *blank cell*.

numeric formula A mathematical expression that uses arithmetic operators and/or @functions and that results in a number.

offset number The number, in some @functions, that corresponds to the position of a specified row, column, or character. The first row, column, or character always has an offset number of zero.

operating system A collection of routines that perform various tasks, such as allocating memory and managing other programs, like 1-2-3, that run on your computer. The most common operating system is the Disk Operating System (DOS).

operator A symbol you use in a formula to indicate the operation to be performed or the relationship between two values. 1-2-3 uses logical operators, the string operator (&), and the standard arithmetic operators: + (addition), - (subtraction), * (multiplication), / (division), and ^ (exponentiation).

order of precedence The order in which 1-2-3 performs arithmetic operations in a formula. See also *precedence number*.

output range The area of the worksheet to which 1-2-3 copies the results of a /Data Parse, /Data Query Extract, /Data Query Unique, or a /Data Regression operation.

overwrite Write over existing data with new data. You can overwrite data in a cell or a range by typing over it or by copying data to the cell or the range. A file can also overwrite another file if you save both files with the same filename and extension.

password-protected file A worksheet file that was saved or extracted with a password. You cannot use /File Retrieve or /File Combine to read a password-protected file into 1-2-3 unless you know the password. You also cannot create linking formulas that reference a password-protected file.

path The drive, directory, and subdirectory (if there is one) where a file is stored. For example, C:\BUDGETS\QTR1\ means the file is located in drive C, in the directory named BUDGETS, in the subdirectory named QTR1.

picture file (.PIC) See *graph file*.

pie chart A graph that compares parts to the whole. In a pie chart, each value in the A data range is a slice of the pie. The size of each slice corresponds to the percentage of the total each value represents.

pointer See *cell pointer, byte pointer, menu pointer*.

pointer-movement keys Keys that control the movement of the cell pointer in the worksheet area.

precedence number A number that represents the order in which 1-2-3 performs operations in a formula. The lower the precedence number, the earlier 1-2-3 performs the operation. You can use parentheses to override precedence. Operations with the same precedence number are performed sequentially from left to right.

preheader The header that prints your name and a Course Technology message at the top of every printed page.

printer control code A sequence of nonprinting characters that tells your printer to use certain settings or to switch to a particular print mode, such as printing in italics, underlining, double spacing lines, or compressing print. Each printer recognizes only its own set of printer control codes. In 1-2-3, you send printer control codes by creating setup strings. For more information, see your printer manual.

print file See *text file*.

PrintGraph The program that prints graph files you create with /Graph Save in 1-2-3.

print queue An assortment of files sent from different computers to a shared printer. The files are lined up and printed in the order you specify.

print settings The options you specify for printing a worksheet, range, or graph. Special margins, headers, and footers might be included in the print settings. See also *graph settings*.

program disk One of the disks containing the Release 2.2 program files, such as the System disk, Install Library Disk, or Help Disk.

prompt Any message a program displays in the control panel when you are selecting a command.

protect To prevent changes to a range or worksheet.

RAM (Random Access Memory) The temporary storage area, also called conventional or main memory, in which your computer holds both programs and data. Your operating system, 1-2-3, and the current worksheet are all stored in RAM.

range Any rectangular block of cells — a single cell, a row or a column, parts of several rows and columns, or an entire worksheet.

range address The location of a range in a file. A range address consists of the cell addresses of any two diagonally opposite corner cells of the range, separated by one or two periods (e.g., A12..C20).

range name A name you specify that identifies a range in the worksheet. A range name can have up to 15 characters. You can use range names instead of range addresses in formulas and commands.

read To copy a file from disk into memory with a command such as /File Retrieve. See also *memory*.

recalculation Calculation of formulas in the current worksheet using the latest cell values.

recalculation method One of two ways 1-2-3 recalculates formulas in the current worksheet. Automatic recalculates affected formulas every time you enter data in a cell; Manual recalculates formulas only when you press [CALC] (F9).

recalculation order One of three orders 1-2-3 uses to recalculate formulas in the current worksheet. Natural recalculates any values on which a particular formula depends before recalculating that formula, Columnwise recalculates column by column, and Rowwise recalculates row by row.

record A one-row collection of information about one item in a database table. The first row of a database table contains field names; all other rows contain records. Each record contains information about one particular item in the database table. A database table can contain up to 8191 records. See also *field names*.

relative cell address See *relative reference*.

relative reference In a formula, a reference to a cell or a range that changes when you copy the formula. The reference can be an address or range name. A relative cell address, for example, refers to the relative position of the original cell to the original formula. For example, when you enter the formula +B1+B2 in cell B4, 1-2-3 interprets the formula as "add the contents of the cell three rows above to the contents of the cell two rows above." If you copy a formula that contains a relative reference, 1-2-3 adjusts the reference in the copied formula. Therefore, if you copy the formula +B1+B2 from cell B4 to C4, the formula becomes +C1+C2. If you don't want a cell or range reference to change when you copy it, you must use an absolute reference or a mixed reference. See also *absolute reference* and *mixed cell reference*.

repeating label A label that repeats across the entire width of a cell. You create a repeating label with the \ (Backslash) label prefix. For example, entering \- in a cell prints a succession of hyphens across the cell.

reservation A guarantee that a network user who has changed a shared 1-2-3 data file can save the changes to the file on disk.

reset To clear a setting or group of settings or to restore default settings.

retrieve To bring a worksheet file from a disk into your computer's memory, making it the current worksheet.

root directory The directory your operating system creates when you format a disk. You can make the root directory the current directory by typing cd\ and pressing [Enter].

row A horizontal block of 256 cells in a worksheet. A row is one cell high and runs across the entire width of the worksheet. For example, row 4 contains cells A4..IV4.

There are 8192 rows in a worksheet. In a database table, a row is called a record. See also *record*.

row numbers The numbers 1 through 8192 in the vertical worksheet border. Each number identifies one row.

save To copy a worksheet from memory to a file on disk.

scrolling Moving the screen as well as the cell pointer when you use the pointer-movement keys. To scroll through the worksheet, press [Scroll Lock] and then use the pointer-movement keys.

select To choose a command or option using one of the following methods:

- Highlight the item and press [Enter].
- Type the first letter of the item and press [Enter].

Also, to specify a range by highlighting cells in the worksheet.

settings sheet A status screen that shows you the current settings for all the options associated with a particular task, such as creating a graph. Settings sheets help you keep track of the choices you are making as you select commands to change settings.

setup string A series of characters preceded by a \ (Backslash) that 1-2-3 uses to tell your printer to print a certain way. For example, you can send a setup string that causes the printer to compress type by choosing /Print Printer Options Setup and entering the appropriate setup string at the prompt. You create setup strings by translating the printer control codes for your printer into the setup string format.

sort To arrange the records in a database table in a particular order, determined by the contents of one or more fields. For example, you can sort records in an employee database table alphabetically by last name or chronologically by date of hire. See also *sort order*.

sort order The order 1-2-3 uses for letters, blank cells, symbols, and numbers when you use Data Sort. 1-2-3 sorts data in ascending (A through Z, 0 through 9) or descending (Z through A, 9 through 0) order. To change the method 1-2-3 uses, you must use the Install program.

source cell When you are linking files, the cell in the source file that contains the value you want to use in the target file. Each linking formula you create must contain a source cell reference. See also *target cell*.

source file The worksheet file that supplies the data when you are linking files.

specify To identify a range of cells or provide data in response to menu options and prompts.

spreadsheet A tool used in financial analysis and modeling that establishes mathematical and logical relationships among numbers and formulas that appear in rows and columns. The 1-2-3 worksheet is an electronic spreadsheet. See also *worksheet*.

stacked bar graph A graph that compares values by stacking sections of bars one on top of the other. A stacked bar graph displays a bar for each item on the x axis. Each bar comprises differently hatched or colored sections, each of which represents a value in one of the data ranges.

status indicator A highlighted word that appears on the bottom line of the screen. A status indicator describes a program or special key condition. For example, the [UNDO] indicator tells you that you can press [UNDO] (Alt-F4) to reverse the effects of the last operation you performed.

status line The bottom line of the 1-2-3 screen, which displays the date-and-time indicator or the current file name, information about the status of the program and special keys, error messages, and macro instructions being executed in STEP mode.

STEP mode The 1-2-3 mode in which you can run a macro one instruction at a time, to help you debug the macro when it is not working correctly. In STEP mode, each time you press a key, 1-2-3 executes another instruction in the macro and replaces the status line with the cell address of the current macro instruction cell and the contents of that cell.

string One or more characters treated as a label. A literal string contains text-letters, numbers, punctuation marks, or other characters — enclosed in quotation marks.

string formula A formula that manipulates strings. The string formula +"Yearly "&"Sales" combines the text inside the quotation marks to produce the label Yearly

Sales. String formulas use the string operator (&) and/or @functions.

string operator The & (Ampersand) is the only operator used in string formulas. The ampersand joins, or concatenates, two strings.

string value A label used in or produced by a formula or @function. You must enclose string values in quotation marks when you use them in formulas, for example, @PROPER("TESSA LANE").

subdirectory A subdivision of a directory.

subroutine A macro that is executed within another macro. When the original macro calls the subroutine (referred to as a subroutine call), control passes to the subroutine. After the subroutine is executed, control returns to the original macro. Putting subroutine calls within other subroutines is called nesting subroutines.

target cell The cell in the target file in which you enter a linking formula. 1-2-3 copies the value of the source cell to the target cell.

target file The worksheet file that receives the data when you are linking files.

text collation See *sort order.*

text file Also known as a print file, a standard ASCII file that you can read into memory with /File Import. You can create a print file in 1-2-3 using /Print File. The default extension in 1-2-3 for print files is .PRN.

time format The way 1-2-3 displays time numbers in cells. The time format sets the display of time numbers.

Time Format	Example
1 HH:MM:SS AM/PM	8:45:23 PM
2 HH:MM AM/PM	8:45 PM
3 Long International	20:45:23
4 Short International	20:45

time-number Decimal values that correspond to times from midnight (time number 0.000000) through 11:59:59 PM (time number 0.999988).

title Rows or columns that are frozen in place on the top and left of the worksheet area when you use /Worksheet Titles. These frozen titles remain on the screen when you move the cell pointer down or across the worksheet. Refers also to titles you place on a graph using /Graph Options Titles.

value A number or a formula that evaluates to a number, or a range name, range address, or cell address that contains a number or a formula that evaluates to a number.

variable A part of a formula for which differing values can be substituted.

what-if analysis Calculations that test the effect of using a number of differing values in formulas to determine potential outcomes of different situations.

wild card character The * (Asterisk) or the ? (Question mark) in a filename, used to represent any single character (?) or any number of sequential characters (*) when listing files or searching for similar labels in a /Data Query operation.

worksheet The 1-2-3 electronic spreadsheet. A worksheet contains 256 columns and 8192 rows. You use the worksheet to enter and manipulate data, create graphs, and manage database tables. See also *spreadsheet.*

worksheet area The currently displayed portion of the worksheet. The worksheet area is the largest section of the screen.

worksheet file A file that stores a 1-2-3 worksheet. Unless you provide a different extension, 1-2-3 assigns the .WK1 extension to the filename when you save the file.

x axis The bottom line of a graph frame.

XY (scatter) graph A graph that shows correlations between two types of numeric data. An XY graph is the only 1-2-3 graph that uses a scaled x axis.

y axis The left line of a graph frame.

Index

Note: @Functions are listed first, then special keys and symbols, then the alphabetical listing. Keys and symbols are alphabetized by their common names.

Keys

A

D

XYZ